Jimmy Swaggart Bible Commentary

Job

JIMMY SWAGGART BIBLE COMMENTARY

- » Genesis [639 PAGES 11-201]
- » Exodus [639 PAGES 11-202]
- » Leviticus [435 PAGES 11-203]
- » Numbers
  Deuteronomy [493 PAGES 11-204]
- » Joshua
  Judges
  Ruth [329 PAGES 11-205]
- » I Samuel
  II Samuel [528 PAGES 11-206]
- » I Kings
  II Kings [560 PAGES 11-207]
- » I Chronicles
  II Chronicles [505 PAGES 11-226]
- » Ezra
  Nehemiah
  Esther [288 PAGES 11-208]
- » Job [320 PAGES 11-225]
- » Psalms [688 PAGES 11-216]
- » Proverbs [320 PAGES 11-227]
- » Ecclesiastes
  Song Of Solomon [245 PAGES 11-228]
- » Isaiah [688 PAGES 11-220]
- » Jeremiah
  Lamentations [688 PAGES 11-070]
- » Ezekiel [520 PAGES 11-223]
- » Daniel [403 PAGES 11-224]
- » Hosea
  Joel
  Amos [496 PAGES 11-229]
- » Obadiah
  Jonah
  Micah
  Nahum
  Habakkuk
  Zephaniah [530 PAGES 11-230]
- » Haggai
  Zechariah
  Malachi [448 PAGES 11-231]
- » Matthew [625 PAGES 11-073]
- » Mark [606 PAGES 11-074]
- » Luke [626 PAGES 11-075]
- » John [717 PAGES 11-076]
- » Acts [832 PAGES 11-077]
- » Romans [536 PAGES 11-078]
- » I Corinthians [632 PAGES 11-079]
- » II Corinthians [589 PAGES 11-080]
- » Galatians [478 PAGES 11-081]
- » Ephesians [550 PAGES 11-082]
- » Philippians [476 PAGES 11-083]
- » Colossians [374 PAGES 11-084]
- » I Thessalonians
  II Thessalonians [498 PAGES 11-085]
- » I Timothy
  II Timothy
  Titus
  Philemon [687 PAGES 11-086]
- » Hebrews [831 PAGES 11-087]
- » James
  I Peter
  II Peter [730 PAGES 11-088]
- » I John
  II John
  III John
  Jude [377 PAGES 11-089]
- » Revelation [602 PAGES 11-090]

For prices and information please call: 1-800-288-8350
Baton Rouge residents please call: (225) 768-7000
Website: www.jsm.org • E-mail: info@jsm.org

Jimmy Swaggart Bible Commentary

Job

**WORLD
EVANGELISM
PRESS**

ISBN 978-1-934655-56-6

11-225 • COPYRIGHT © 2010 World Evangelism Press®
P.O. Box 262550 • Baton Rouge, Louisiana 70826-2550
Website: www.jsm.org • Email: info@jsm.org
(225) 768-8300
16 17 18 19 20 21 22 23 24 25 / EBM / 12 11 10 9 8 7 6 5 4 3

All rights reserved. Printed and bound in U.S.A.
No part of this publication may be reproduced in any form or by any means
without the publisher's prior written permission.

TABLE OF CONTENTS

1. Job Introduction......................... 1
2. Job... 3
3. Index 299

THE BOOK OF JOB

INTRODUCTION

Job was one of the sons of Issachar (Gen. 46:13), and the grandson of Jacob.

When his father went down into Egypt, along with Jacob and, in fact, all of Jacob's sons, actually, the entire clan, Job went as well. It is believed that he was about 20 years of age at the time. Sometime later he left Egypt to go into the land of Uz (Gen. 22:20; Jer. 25:20).

It is not known exactly as to where Uz was located. There have been numerous suggestions. One of those suggestions has been the area of modern Kuwait. But again, that's only speculation; however, one can be certain that there was an area called *"Uz"* at the time of Job. The Bible says so.

THE AUTHOR OF THE BOOK OF JOB

It is believed that Moses wrote the Book of Job, actually in collaboration with Job himself. If Moses wrote the Book, he did so while in the wilderness, possibly at about the time he was some 50-60 years of age. Job would have been possibly about 80 years of age at that time. At any rate, the Book of Job is without a doubt, the oldest Book in the world.

It is for certain that the Book was written before the Law was given, because no mention is made of the Law in any shape or form.

THE REASON FOR THE BOOK

Concerning this Book, Williams says, *"Job presents to us the discovery of the worthlessness of self, which should be the first step in the Christian experience.*

"Job does not symbolize an unconverted,

NOTES

but rather a converted man. It was necessary that one of God's children should be chosen for this trial; for the subject of the Book is not the conversion of the sinner, but rather the consecration of the Saint. It is evident that an unconverted man needs to be brought to the end of himself; but that a man who feared God, who was perfect, and who hated evil, should also need this, is not so clear; nevertheless, it is a Scriptural fact."

Williams went on to say, *"The effect of the Divine action was that Job abhorred himself (Job. 42:5-6). The terminology used by Job shows that he had previously thought well of himself. But the sharp trials through which Job went, and especially the anger which the unjust accusations of his friends stirred up in his heart, revealed to himself unknown depths of moral ugliness; and, finally, his being challenged to measure himself up beside the Lord, made him conscious that in him, that is, in his 'flesh,' there dwelt no good thing."*[1]

A MOVING OF THE HOLY SPIRIT

The Book of Job is very special to me personally, even as it is for many Believers. It is special for many reasons, but primarily because of the Moving and Operation of the Holy Spirit on my heart personally, as it regards this trial and test of so long, long ago. I debated whether to relate it or not, but about an hour ago while in prayer, I felt like the Holy Spirit instructed me to include that which He showed me years ago.

If I remember correctly, the year was 1953. Frances and I were married in 1952, and Donnie was born in October of 1954. So the time at hand must have been the summer of 1953.

THE CRUSADE IN BATON ROUGE

Frances and I, along with my Mother and Dad, had gone to Baton Rouge, Louisiana, to hear David Nunn. At the time, my Mother and Dad were pastoring a Church in North East Louisiana, a Church incidentally which he planted a short time before. Brother Nunn's meeting was being conducted under a giant tent. I really don't remember the size of the crowd that night, but if I remember correctly, Frances and I were seated in the second row.

At any rate, at a given point in the Service, Brother Nunn stepped up to the podium and began to sing a song I had not previously heard. The following are the words.

"I can feel the hand of Satan,
"As the tempter pressed me sore,
"And he's been before the Father,
"Asking leave to tempt me more."

"Though God slay me, yet I'll trust Him,
"For I'll then come forth as gold,
"For I know my Redeemer liveth,
"For I feel Him in my soul."

As he began to sing, with the accompaniment of only a piano, instantly the Presence of God came mightily over me. I began to weep greatly, even to the place that I thought I wouldn't be able to stand it. It was one of the most powerful Movings of the Spirit I had ever experienced, but yet, at the same time, there was something negative about it.

At a given point in time, when I had gathered my composure, at least somewhat, I looked out over the crowd, and they did not seem to be moved.

At the time I did not know nor understand as to why the Lord moved on me as He did. I was not to understand it until many years later.

AN EARLY MORNING PRAYER MEETING

I think it was some time in 2002. Once again, if I remember correctly, we were in the middle of a Radiothon. I had come somewhat early to the office to spend a little time in prayer before I went on the air.

As I began to pray that morning, the Spirit of God came over me, and brought to my mind the happening I've just related to you, which had occurred about 50 years earlier.

The Lord took me back to that tent, and I saw it as plainly in my spirit as when I was there those many, many years before. I heard the song all over again, I felt the impact of the Spirit of God, actually, in the same manner. I sat on the floor there in the office seeking the Lord, sobbing as I had those many years before. And then the Lord spoke the following to my heart.

"I moved upon you that night in Brother Nunn's meeting, and through the song, 'Job's God Is True,' in effect, to tell you that you would have to go through a trial that would be in some cases, nearly as severe as that which Job had to endure." I remember sobbing before the Lord, and saying, *"But Lord, I failed You, and Job didn't."* The Lord quickly answered, saying:

"All have failed Me, even Job."

And then without premeditation at all, the Lord instantly brought to my mind what happened to Job at the end of this terrible ordeal. The Lord spoke to my heart again and said, *"I restored to Job twice as much as he had lost."*

That's all that the Lord said to me as it regards that; however, He was letting me know, I believe, that as He gave Job twice over again what he had lost, that He would do the same for me. And that He has already begun to do. Among so many other things He has done, and will do, the privilege He has given me to write the notes for THE EXPOSITOR'S STUDY BIBLE, is the greatest honor that the Lord could ever provide for anyone. There is nothing greater than the Word of God, it being the only revealed Truth in the world today and, in fact, ever has been. That means that anything that pertains to the Word, is of great worth indeed. In other words, anything that the Lord would allow one to do to help make the Word of God more understandable for the Body of Christ, is an honor indeed! But I believe that as wonderful as that is, that the Lord is going to do even greater things. I anticipate that! I believe that!

I pray that this Commentary on Job, the oldest Book in the world, will be of great blessing to you. If the Lord helps us it will,

I believe, be a Blessing.

"Saved! Saved! Saved! My sins are all forgiven;
"Christ is mine! I'm on my way to Heaven;
"Once a guilty sinner, lost, undone,
"Now a Child of God, Saved through His Son."

"Saved! Saved! Saved! By Grace and Grace alone;
"Oh, what wondrous love to me was shown,
"In my stead Christ Jesus bled and died,
"Bore my sins, for me was crucified."

"Saved! Saved! Saved! Oh joy beyond compare!
"Christ my life, and I His constant Care;
"Yielding all and trusting Him Alone,
"Living now each moment as His Own."

"Saved! I'm Saved through Christ, my all in all;
"Saved! I'm Saved, whatever may befall,
"He died upon the Cross for me,
"He bore the awful penalty;
"And now I'm Saved eternally,
"I'm Saved! Saved! Saved! Saved!"

CHAPTER 1

(1) "THERE WAS A MAN IN THE LAND OF UZ, WHOSE NAME WAS JOB; AND THAT MAN WAS PERFECT AND UPRIGHT, AND ONE WHO FEARED GOD, AND ESCHEWED EVIL.

(2) "AND THERE WERE BORN UNTO HIM SEVEN SONS AND THREE DAUGHTERS.

(3) "HIS SUBSTANCE ALSO WAS SEVEN THOUSAND SHEEP, AND THREE THOUSAND CAMELS, AND FIVE HUNDRED YOKE OF OXEN, AND FIVE HUNDRED SHE ASSES, AND A VERY GREAT HOUSEHOLD; SO THAT THIS MAN WAS THE GREATEST OF ALL THE MEN OF THE EAST.

(4) "AND HIS SONS WENT AND FEASTED IN THEIR HOUSES, EVERY ONE HIS DAY; AND SENT AND CALLED FOR THEIR THREE SISTERS TO EAT AND TO DRINK WITH THEM.

(5) "AND IT WAS SO, WHEN THE DAYS OF THEIR FEASTING WERE GONE ABOUT, THAT JOB SENT AND SANCTIFIED THEM, AND ROSE UP EARLY IN THE MORNING, AND OFFERED BURNT OFFERINGS ACCORDING TO THE NUMBER OF THEM ALL: FOR JOB SAID, IT MAY BE THAT MY SONS HAVE SINNED, AND CURSED GOD IN THEIR HEARTS. THUS DID JOB CONTINUALLY."

The construction is:

1. (Vs. 1) Although no one knows for sure, some believe that the *"land of Uz"* was probably located between Edom and Saudi Arabia.

2. (Vs. 1) Job, as previously stated, was the son of Issachar, which means that Jacob was his grandfather.

3. The word *"perfect"* as used in Verse 1 doesn't mean sinless perfection, but rather perfect in his efforts in doing all he could to please the Lord.

4. (Vs. 1) The Book of Job is believed to be the oldest Book in the world. It was probably written by Moses (Lk. 24:27, 44). It explains the problem of why good men are afflicted. It is in order to effect their Sanctification. It is interesting that this difficult question should be the first taken up and answered in the Bible.

5. (Vs. 3) Job was one of the richest men in the world; in other words, God had blessed him greatly.

6. (Vs. 5) Before the giving of the Law, the father of the family was the Priest of the family. It was his responsibility to bless, purify, and offer sacrifice.

The offering up of these sacrifices, a ram for each Burnt Offering, and one for each son and daughter, proclaimed the fact that Job had placed his Faith and trust in the Sacrifice of Christ; however, the offering up of these sacrifices, although a great blessing to him, could not atone for the sins of his sons and daughters, unless they personally placed their faith in such. There is no evidence they did!

THE MAN IN THE LAND OF UZ WHOSE NAME WAS JOB

As previously stated, Job was the son of Issachar, who was the son of Jacob, which made Jacob the grandfather of Job. While the location of the land of Uz is uncertain, it is believed by some to have been in the region of northeastern Arabia. Job was a man of great wealth and high social position and, as well, the greatest man of God in the world of his day, of which there were only a few and, in fact, of all time.

The Lord would use this man to explain the effect of Sanctification, as he would few, if any. And when we consider that this subject of Sanctification is the first taken up in the Bible, considering that the Book of Job is the oldest Book in the Bible and, thereby, the world, we now begin to understand just how important this great subject actually is.

Justification is an instant affair, all brought about by simple Faith in Christ. Justification is the act of God declaring one not guilty, and on the basis of satisfaction rendered by our Lord and Saviour Jesus Christ, Who paid the price we could not pay. Upon simple Faith in Him and what He did for us at the Cross of Calvary, a perfect Righteousness, the Righteousness of Christ, is instantly imputed to the believing sinner. As such, the individual is perfectly justified in the Eyes of God and, in fact, this is the only manner in which one can be justified (Rom. 5:1-2).

Sanctification is a little different, in fact, a great deal different. At the moment of conversion, the believing sinner is instantly, totally, completely, and perfectly sanctified. Notice what Paul said:

"But you are washed (refers to the Blood of Jesus cleansing from all sin), *but you are sanctified* (one's position in Christ), *but you are justified* (declared not guilty) *in the Name of the Lord Jesus* (refers to Christ and what He did at the Cross, in order that we might be Saved), *and by the Spirit of our God* (proclaims the Third Person of the Triune Godhead as the Mechanic in this great Work of Grace)" (I Cor. 6:11.)

NOTES

Notice the progression as Paul gave it. We are first of all *"washed,"* and then *"sanctified,"* and then *"justified,"* all in the *"Name of the Lord Jesus."*

As someone has said, Sanctification is making one clean, while Justification is declaring one clean. One cannot be declared clean, until one has been made clean. So, washing and Sanctification come before Justification, as should be obvious. As stated, that is our *"position"* in Christ, a position, incidentally, which never changes; however, our *"condition"* is something else altogether. In fact, our condition changes almost by the hour, all according to our conduct, our attitude, our motivation, our consecration or the lack thereof.

It is the business of the Holy Spirit, Who lives within our hearts and lives, and does so constantly (I Cor. 3:16), to bring our *"condition"* up to our *"position."* In fact, it is a lifelong project. It's not something that we as Believers can do, no matter how hard we try. The Holy Spirit Alone can accomplish this task (Rom. 8:2, 11; Gal. 2:20).

CAN THE BELIEVER EVER REACH A STATE OF PERFECTION?

No!

The Bible does not teach sinless perfection, at least not until the Trump of God sounds. At that time the Scripture says: *"For the trumpet shall sound* (it is the 'Trump of God') *. . . and we shall be changed* (put on the Glorified Body). *For this corruptible* (sin nature) *must put on incorruption* (a Glorified Body with no sin nature), *and this mortal* (subject to death) *must put on immortality* (will never die)" (I Cor. 15:52-53).

Even Paul did not claim sinless perfection. He also said:

"Not as though I had already attained, either were already perfect (the Apostle is saying he doesn't claim sinless perfection)*: but I follow after* (to pursue), *if that I may apprehend* (Paul is pursuing absolute Christlikeness) *that for which also I am apprehended of Christ Jesus.* (He was Saved by Christ for the purpose of becoming Christlike, and so are we!)

"Brethren, I count not myself to have apprehended (in effect, repeats what he said

in the previous Verse): *but this one thing I do, forgetting those things which are behind* (refers to things the Apostle had depended upon to find favor with God, and the failure that type of effort brought about [Phil. 3:5-6]), *reaching forth unto those things which are before* (all our attention must be on that which is ahead, and not on what is past; *'those things'* consist of all the victories of the Cross),

"*I press toward the mark* (this represents a moral and Spiritual target) *for the prize of the high calling of God* (Christlikeness) *in Christ Jesus* (proclaims the manner and means in which all of this is done, which is the Cross [I Cor. 1:17-18; 2:2]).

"*Let us therefore, as many as be perfect* (mature), *be thus minded* (have our minds on what Christ has done at the Cross, and was done for us): *and if in anything you be otherwise minded, God shall reveal even this unto you.* (This means some were actually otherwise minded. But through the words of Paul, the Holy Spirit was going to show them the right way, which is to pull them back to the Cross)" (Phil. 3:12-15).

SANCTIFICATION AND THE CROSS

As we have already stated, the Holy Spirit Alone, can bring about our Sanctification, which means to be set apart exclusively from the world to God. We are set apart from something to something, and that exclusively. The Holy Spirit Who works exclusively within the parameters of the Cross of Christ, and He will work no other way, which means that our Faith must be exclusively in the Cross and nothing else. In other words, the Cross of Christ must ever be the Object of our Faith, through which the Holy Spirit works (Rom. 6:1-14; 8:1-2, 11; I Cor. 1:17-18, 23; 2:2; Gal., Chpt. 5; 6:14; Eph. 2:13-18; Col. 2:14-15).

Christians have ever tried to sanctify themselves. In fact, I think I can say without fear of exaggeration or contradiction, that every one of us has fallen in this trap, none excluded. But no matter what the Believer does, one cannot sanctify oneself. It is impossible. The only thing that will tend to be done, with such an effort, is that self-righteousness will be produced within our lives, which is the bane of the Believer.

SELF-RIGHTEOUSNESS AND THE CROSS

This is so important that we need to deal with it a little more.

Everything the Believer receives from the Lord is brought about by what Jesus did at the Cross, and our Faith in that Finished Work. Our Lord is the Source of all things that we receive from God, and the Cross is the Means by which these things are received, all superintended by the Holy Spirit (Rom. 8:1-2, 11). If the Believer attempts to bring about Righteousness, to bring about Holiness by any method other than Faith in Christ and the Cross, and that exclusively, the only thing that will be developed in the life of such a person is self-righteousness. We must remember the following:

Self-righteousness is at least one of the vilest sins which can attach itself to a person. It is self-righteousness which nailed Christ to the Cross. We must never forget that!

What I'm about to say I do not say with joy, but I do feel it needs to be said.

The modern church, due to the fact of ignoring the Cross, or registering unbelief toward the Cross, is eaten up with self-righteousness. I realize that is a strong statement, but I know it to be true. Righteousness and Holiness, and I speak of that which the Lord Alone can give, can only be brought about in one's life by one registering simple Faith in Christ and what Christ has done at the Cross. That being done and maintained, the Holy Spirit Who Alone can accomplish this task, will begin to work within our lives (Rom. 8:1-2, 11; Gal. 2:20-21; Chpt. 5; 6:14).

If the Christian doesn't have the Cross of Christ as the Object of his Faith, and the Object of his Faith exclusively, then automatically he will turn to law, i.e., "*works.*" The law, i.e., "*works,*" is very appealing to the flesh, because it appeals to our pride. Faith is never appealing to the flesh, and I speak of Biblical Faith, because it appeals totally and solely to the Cross of Christ. Law and works can only produce pride while Faith in the Cross of Christ produces what the Holy Spirit can give, which is everything.

HOW IS IT THAT THE CROSS OF CHRIST IS THE ANSWER?

First of all, the Cross of Christ holds no magical properties. There is a reason, and obviously evident once it is understood, as to how the Cross is the answer and, in fact, the only answer.

Paul said: *"For the preaching of the Cross is to them who perish foolishness; but to we who are Saved, it is the Power of God"* (I Cor. 1:18).

The Cross is the answer for the following reasons:

• When Jesus died on the Cross, He atoned for all sin, past, present and future, at least for all who will believe (Jn. 3:16). When the believing sinner accepts Christ as his personal Saviour, due to the fact that all sin has been atoned at the Cross, the sins of that particular person are totally and completely forgiven, and washed clean by the Precious Blood of Jesus Christ. In fact, it has already been done, it was done at the Cross, and it remains only for us to believe.

• With all sin atoned, the Holy Spirit now has the legal right to come into the heart and life of the Believer and to function as He Alone can function. The Holy Spirit is God and, as such, there is nothing He cannot do. The Believer must understand that whatever we need as a Christian, and I speak of Righteousness, Holiness, the Fruit of the Spirit, in effect, all the things that the Lord does, the Holy Spirit Alone can carry out these great works within our hearts and lives. We cannot do it ourselves, in fact, such according to our own strength and ability is impossible.

• For the Holy Spirit to carry out His Work and, as stated, He can do anything, He requires only one thing of us, and that is that our Faith ever be in the Cross of Christ. In other words, that the Cross of Christ ever be the Object of our Faith (Lk. 9:23; Rom. 6:1-14; 8:1-2, 11). This means that the Believer must understand that everything we receive from God, Jesus Christ is the Source of that Blessing, but the Cross, we must ever understand, is the Means, all superintended by the Holy Spirit (Rom. 8:2; Gal., Chpt. 5; 6:14; Col. 2:14-15).

That which we have given is how the Cross makes possible all that the Holy Spirit does, which tells us that the Cross of Christ is the only answer for the perversions, sins, aberrations, and iniquities of humanity. As the song says, *"All else is sinking sand."*

THE PERFECTION OF JOB

The Scripture that says Job was perfect and upright does not mean that he was sinlessly perfect. No one has ever been sinlessly perfect, and no one ever will be, other than the Lord Jesus Christ. It simply means that he was doing all that was within his power to obey the Lord as the High Priest of his family.

Before the Law, and Job lived before the Law, the man of the house was to be the Priest of the family. He was to offer up sacrifices, which Job did. He was to be the guiding light, even as Job was. As stated, he did his very best to carry out this function as he should have done so, and the Holy Spirit is quick to bring out this fact. The Truth is Job was the godliest man in the world of his time. Actually, precious few individuals in the world of that day were acquainted with Jehovah. Most were idol worshippers, but Job knew the True and the Living God.

JOB'S WEALTH

The record is that Job had been immensely blessed by the Lord. He was blessed so much, in fact, that the Scripture says that he *"was the greatest of all the men of the east."* He was noted, as we shall see, not only for his material wealth, but also for his wisdom. He had been truly blessed by God.

Will the Lord bless others accordingly at this present time?

Most definitely He shall!

In fact, Believers presently have a greater opportunity for blessing than even did those in Job's time. We now have a much better Covenant built on much better Promises (Heb. 8:6-7).

If a modern Believer does his very best to hold to the Word of God, which means that he is doing his very best to live for God as he should, and he lives a life of Faith, meaning that he lives a life of expectancy, he can expect the Lord to bless him accordingly.

All too often we have not because we ask not, and then again, many times we ask only to satisfy our lusts, whatever that might be. Such refers to the fact, if it actually is the case, that we are not seeking the Will of God but actually our own personal will (James 4:3).

A PERSONAL SALVATION

The Scripture plainly tells us that Job offered up sacrifices for his sons and daughters, but the record seems to be that they were not too very much interested in the Ways of the Lord. And, as well, despite Job's good intentions, his consecration to the Lord did not include his sons and daughters. Let it ever be understood, Salvation is personal. In other words, one individual cannot by proxy get Salvation for someone else. It doesn't work that way.

No matter how many sacrifices that Job offered up on behalf of his sons and daughters, if they, in fact, had no personal acquaintance with the Lord, which seems to be the case, his good intentions afforded no great help.

What he did, he should have done; however, what he did did not save these young men and young women. And the evidence is, despite Job's efforts and intentions, his sons and daughters seemingly were lost.

Did Job fail in this?

About 700 years later Solomon would say, *"Train up a child in the way he should go, and when he is old, he will not depart from it"* (Prov. 22:6).

The words, *"Train up,"* mean to *"hedge up"* or *"hedge in."* It is like building a fence around a child; however, what ought to be fenced in must be two things, *"the child and the Bible."* This is the *"way he should go."*

So we might assume from that, and to be sure we shouldn't assume too much, that quite possibly Job did not raise his children as he should have.

In our Church, Family Worship Center in Baton Rouge, Louisiana, when dedicating babies, I always tell the parents as they hold the little child in their arms, that they, as well, hold the eternal destiny of that child in their hands. If they bring it up as they ought to, which means in the fear of God, and in the Ways of the Lord, they have the Promise of God that when that child is old it will not depart from what it has been taught. That is a Promise of the Lord, one to which parents in this jaded age, must hold to with determination.

(6) "NOW THERE WAS A DAY WHEN THE SONS OF GOD CAME TO PRESENT THEMSELVES BEFORE THE LORD, AND SATAN CAME ALSO AMONG THEM.

(7) "AND THE LORD SAID UNTO SATAN, WHERE HAVE YOU BEEN? THEN SATAN ANSWERED THE LORD, AND SAID, FROM GOING TO AND FRO IN THE EARTH, AND FROM WALKING UP AND DOWN IN IT.

(8) "AND THE LORD SAID UNTO SATAN, HAVE YOU CONSIDERED MY SERVANT JOB, THAT THERE IS NONE LIKE HIM IN THE EARTH, A PERFECT AND AN UPRIGHT MAN, ONE WHO FEARS GOD, AND HATES EVIL?

(9) "THEN SATAN ANSWERED THE LORD, AND SAID, DOES JOB FEAR GOD FOR NOUGHT?

(10) "HAVE YOU NOT MADE AN HEDGE ABOUT HIM, AND ABOUT HIS HOUSE, AND ABOUT ALL THAT HE HAS ON EVERY SIDE? YOU HAVE BLESSED THE WORK OF HIS HANDS, AND HIS SUBSTANCE IS INCREASED IN THE LAND.

(11) "BUT PUT FORTH YOUR HAND NOW, AND TOUCH ALL THAT HE HAS, AND HE WILL CURSE YOU TO YOUR FACE.

(12) "AND THE LORD SAID UNTO SATAN, BEHOLD, ALL THAT HE HAS IS IN YOUR POWER; ONLY UPON HIMSELF PUT NOT FORTH YOUR HAND. SO SATAN WENT FORTH FROM THE PRESENCE OF THE LORD."

The exegesis is:

1. The phrase, *"Sons of God"* of Verse 6, when used in this sense, always speaks of Angels, whether righteous or fallen (Gen. 6:2). This meeting took place in Heaven, at the Throne of God.

2. (Vs. 6) In the Hebrew, the definite article is before Satan, meaning that it reads *"the Satan,"* specifying the leader of evil. This tells us that these angelic ministers appear at appointed seasons to give account of their actions to God. This is the first instance in the Bible of this mighty angel

being named *"Satan,"* or *"the Adversary."* Some time in eternity past, he led a revolution against God, with one-third of the Angels throwing in their lot with him (Rev. 12:4, 7-11). From the time of that revolution unto the present, this war between good and evil, between righteousness and unrighteousness, has raged; however, it is not long before this battle will end (Rev. 20:1-3, 7-10).

3. (Vs. 7) When the Lord said unto Satan, *"Where have you been?"* of course, the Lord already knew the answer to that.

4. (Vs. 7) Pulpit says, *"Satan searches the whole Earth continually, never pausing, never resting, but 'going about,' as Peter said (I Pet. 5:8), 'like a roaring lion . . . seeking whom he may devour.'"* As stated, the end of his darkness and destruction is very soon (Rev. 20:1-2).

5. (Vs. 8) While it doesn't say that Job at this particular time is the only one on Earth living for God, it does say that he is closer to God than anyone else. We learn from this of the minute attention given by the Lord of all those who love and follow Him.

It is a sobering thought to realize that conversations may be conducted in Heaven, even by the Lord Himself, as it regards some of His Children. What is He saying about me? about you?

6. (Vs. 9) Satan insinuates that Job's motive is purely selfish. He intimates that Job is serving God, not out of love for God, but for what he gets out of it. Regrettably, that just might be true concerning some, hence, Satan asking this question.

7. Verse 10, proves how absolutely secure from Satanic malignity are the Children of God, that is, unless the Lord purposely allows certain things. In other words, Satan can only do, whatever it might be, whatever the Lord allows him to do.

8. We find in the Eleventh Verse that the Lord gave Satan permission to do certain things as it regards Job. This tells us that Satan has to have permission from the Lord to do whatever he might want to do or try to do, as it regards any Saint of God.

9. (Vs. 12) There were limitations placed on what Satan could do, as there are with all Believers. Concerning this, Williams says: *"Job does not symbolize an unconverted, but a converted man. It was necessary that one of God's children should be chosen for this trial; for the subject of the Book is not the conversion of the sinner, but the consecration of the Saint. It is evident that an unconverted man needs to be brought to the end of himself; but that a man who feared God, who was perfect, and who hated evil should also need this is not so clear."*

10. (Vs. 12) *"We find in this Book that God uses Satan, calamity, and sickness to be His instruments in creating character and making men partakers of His Holiness. Such were the instruments; but the Hand that used them was God's; and the facts of this Book explain to Christian people, who, like Job, are conscious of personal integrity, why calamities, sorrows, and diseases are permitted to afflict them."*

SATAN

The name *"Satan"* means *"adversary,"* or *"slanderer."*

Satan is an Angel, albeit fallen. He was created by God along with all the other angels sometime in the distant past. According to Ezekiel, it says that he *"sealed up the sum, full of wisdom, and perfect in beauty"* (Ezek. 28:12).

The phrase, *"You seal up the sum,"* means that Lucifer, for this was his name, when originally created by God, was the perfection of wisdom and beauty. In fact, the phrase intimates that Lucifer was the wisest and most beautiful Angel created by God, and that he served the Lord in Holiness and Righteousness for a given period in time.

"Perfect in beauty," means that he was the most beautiful of God's Angelic Creation. The Holy Spirit even labeled his beauty as *"perfect."*

The Prophet Ezekiel went on to say, *"You were perfect in your ways from the day that you were created, till iniquity was found in you"* (Ezek. 28:15).

Pride was the form of this iniquity (Lk. 10:17-18). The rebellion of Lucifer against God probably caused the catastrophe which occurred between the First and Second Verses of Genesis, Chapter 1.

We have no way of knowing how long he faithfully served the Lord, but ever how long it was, the Scripture says, *"You were perfect in your ways...."*

The Prophet Isaiah gives us a little more information concerning this created being. He said: *"How are you fallen from Heaven, O Lucifer, son of the morning! how are you cut down to the ground, which did weaken the nations!* ('*Lucifer'* is the name of Satan. Actually, he is an Angel, and as stated, originally created by God, who served the Lord in righteousness for an undetermined period of time.

"When he fell, he led a revolution against God, with about one third of the Angels, it seems, throwing in their lot with him [Rev. 12:4]. Therefore, all the pain, suffering, misery, heartache, death, and deception which have ruled the nations from the very beginning can be laid at the doorstep of this revolution headed up by Satan.)"

Isaiah continues: *"For you have said in your heart, I will ascend into Heaven, I will exalt my throne above the stars of God: I will sit also upon the mount of the congregation, in the sides of the north:*

"I will ascend above the heights of the clouds; I will be like the Most High. (In these two Verses, we see the foment of Satan's rebellion and revolution against God. It seems that Lucifer, while true to the Lord, was given dominion of the Earth, which was before Adam. After his fall, he worked deceitfully to get other Angelic rulers to follow him in his war against God)" (Isa. 14:12-14).

WHY HAS THE LORD ALLOWED SATAN TO CONTINUE?

That's a good question!

The Holy Spirit refers to this as a *"mystery."* He says: *"But in the days of the voice of the seventh Angel, when he shall begin to sound* (proclaims the beginning of the last half of the Great Tribulation, which will be worse than ever), *the mystery of God should be finished* (this *'mystery'* pertains to the reason God has allowed Satan to continue his reign over this Earth for these thousands of years [II Cor. 4:4]), *as He has declared to His servants the Prophets"* (Rev. 10:7).

We are not given the meaning of the *"mystery"* as to why Satan has been allowed to continue, but only that his days are numbered.

We know that God, being Almighty, could have stopped Satan at any time. But He has allowed him to continue for a reason. Had He wanted us to know more than we presently know, He would have told us in His Word. One thing we do know, the Lord does all things perfectly. As well, He has a reason for all that He does. Sometimes He tells us what that reason is, and sometimes He doesn't. We are to trust Him, knowing that He knows best, and always does best.

SATAN CAN DO ONLY WHAT THE LORD ALLOWS HIM TO DO

We learn from the first two Chapters of Job, some things about Satan that we would do well to remember.

First of all and foremost, Satan can only do what the Lord allows him to do, no more, no less! As well, he has to ask permission of God for whatever he does, and then the Lord draws the boundaries, not Satan.

Satan is constantly telling Believers, as he has told all of us, terrible things that he is going to do to us. He tells us that he is going to kill us, that he is going to take our family, that he is going to steal our health, that he's going to steal our children, that he's going to drive us into bankruptcy, in fact, anything, any lie that he can get us to believe. But have you ever stopped to think the following:

Despite all the blow and bluster of the Evil One, you are still here, serving God, and many of you are doing better than ever, and all of us could do better than ever if we would only trust the Lord evermore. Satan hasn't done all of these things, he had threatened, and actually not any of them, simply because he can't do it. If he could do it, he would have done it a long time ago. He is a liar and the father of it. As stated, he can only do what the Lord allows him to do, and the Lord allows him certain latitude, not to hurt us, but that our faith may be tested, and that we may grow in Grace and the knowledge of the Lord.

Yes, the Lord uses Satan as He uses everything.

THE CONVERSATION WITH SATAN ABOUT JOB

I think it is obvious from this First Chapter of Job, that the Lord has trophies on this Earth. I speak of Believers, whomever they might be, and wherever they might be, who love the Lord supremely, and are doing their very best to serve God to the very best of their ability. I may not know these people, and you may not know these people, but God knows them, and of that we can be certain.

So, *"The Lord said unto Satan, have you considered My servant Job, that there is none like him in the Earth, a perfect and an upright man, one who fears God, and hates evil?"*

I think it is obvious here from the terminology, that the Lord was very proud of Job, if we would be allowed to use such terminology about the Lord. As we said in the headings, what is the Lord saying about you? What is the Lord saying about me?

The Lord labels Job as being such *"that there is none like him in the Earth."* This tells us that he was the greatest man of God on the face of the Earth of that particular time. It is almost certain that his grandfather Jacob had now passed away. Quite possibly his Uncle Joseph had also passed away.

So, the Lord will use the godliest man on Earth to teach all of us certain lessons. At least some of those lessons are:

• God desired a man whom He could use as an object lesson to teach certain things. That man had to be one who was *"perfect and upright, who feared God, and hated evil."*

• In this lesson men will be taught as to why godly people suffer.

• The lesson will show us that for all of man's efforts of Righteousness, still, in comparison to God he is *"vile."*

• This example will show God's supremacy and Satan's limitations.

THE ACCUSATION THAT SATAN MADE AGAINST GOD AND AGAINST JOB

When the Lord posed the consecration of Job, Satan answered the Lord, and said, *"Does Job fear God for naught?"*

In this question posed by Satan we find the bedrock of God's demands on the human race. Satan's contention was that no man actually loved God, that if, in fact, they did serve Him, it was only because of God's Blessings on them. Satan's name not only means *"adversary,"* but *"slanderer"* as well. He constantly slanders God. He contends that the whole world serves him (Satan) and those who pretend to serve God do so out of selfish motives.

Job will be used as an example to prove the fallacy of this contention. Satan's argument is powerful insomuch that even many godly people believe at least a part of it.

Elijah claimed that he was the only one in Israel who loved God. The Lord informed him that there were 7,000 others who did as well. Satan slanders God by telling God that men only serve Him for what they can get out of it. Sadly, this is true in some cases.

A part of the *"Western Gospel,"* which is, in reality, no gospel at all, contends that the way to riches, happiness, and prosperity is to follow the Lord. It is a heady gospel and, in fact, has much truth in it.

Nevertheless, it falls perfectly into Satan's charge — *"What's in it for me?"* This prominent *"other gospel,"* in effect, denies the problem of man, which is sin, and the need of man, which is a Saviour. In effect, this *"other gospel"* says that man's problem is poverty, and man's need, therefore, is money.

While the Lord most definitely does bless people, even with Job being the perfect example; still, the real need of man is a Saviour, and that Saviour Alone is the Lord Jesus Christ. To say it another way, man's problem is sin, and man's solution is a Saviour, in fact, the Saviour, the Lord Jesus Christ.

The greatest Blessing of all is the Eternal Life afforded us by what Jesus did on our behalf at the Cross of Calvary.

THE HEDGE

We learn from the Tenth Verse of this First Chapter, that the Lord had a hedge about Job, and we learn from that, that He also has a hedge about every Child of God. This means that Satan cannot touch one of God's Children, meaning that he cannot break through the hedge, unless the Lord allows such, even as He did with Job.

The *"hedge"* means that the Lord *"made a sort of invisible fence around him, through which no evil could creep."*

Within this hedge, the Lord poured out Blessings upon Job, and delighted in doing so! In fact, I believe we can say without fear of contradiction, that the Lord delights in blessing all of His Children. This means that we can have Blessings, I think, in every capacity. We should ask for these Blessings, we should expect the Lord to hear us, and to answer us in a positive sense.

Of course, all of this is predicated on the Believer desiring to please God, desiring the Will of God for his or her life, etc. Unfortunately, many modern Christians have been taught that if they can raise their faith level to a certain degree, they can get all type of things from God.

Please understand, while the degree of faith, of course, is extremely important, as should be obvious, still, in the final alternative, it's not Faith alone that moves God necessarily, but rather His Will. The Disciples themselves thought that if they could raise their faith level, that they could do all type of things for the Lord, and receive all type of things from the Lord. So they said to Christ:

"Increase our Faith" (Lk. 17:5). The Lord answered them in the following manner:

"If you had faith as a grain of mustard seed (a very small seed, telling us, in effect, that it's not really the amount of faith, but rather the correct object of Faith; the correct Object is the Cross [I Cor. 1:18]), *you might say unto this sycamine tree, Be thou plucked up by the root, and be thou planted in the sea; and it should obey you* (the removal of trees and mountains were proverbial figures of speech among the Jews at that time, expressing the overcoming of great difficulties)" (Lk. 17:6).

It's not actually the quantity of faith, but rather the quality of Faith. And the *"quality of Faith,"* pertains to the proper Object of Faith, which is always the Cross of Christ (Rom. 6:3-6; 8:11).

THE PERMISSION OF THE LORD

Satan made his accusations that Job was serving the Lord because of what he was getting out of it, and not because he truly loved the Lord. So, the Lord takes Satan up on his challenge.

He *"said unto Satan, Behold, all that he has is in your power; only upon himself put not forth your hand."*

So, the Lord lets down the hedge, but only to a certain degree. Satan could destroy the material goods of Job, and even his children, but could not touch Job personally.

To be sure, this within itself was a gargantuan blow. To lose all of his material goods was one thing, even as we shall see, but to lose all ten of his children was something else altogether. As well, he was to lose all of his servants.

In other words, all the things that made Job big and great in the eyes of his fellowman, were to be stripped away from him, and instantly!

Satan has contended that Job is serving the Lord because of these material things. If they are taken away, or so the adversary says, *"he will curse You to Your face."*

Of course, the Lord knew exactly what Job would do. He knew the beginning from the end and the end from the beginning. But He would use this to prove a point, to teach Job some lessons that he needed to learn and, as well, to bless Job even to a greater degree than ever.

(13) "AND THERE WAS A DAY WHEN HIS SONS AND HIS DAUGHTERS WERE EATING AND DRINKING WINE IN THEIR ELDEST BROTHER'S HOUSE:

(14) "AND THERE CAME A MESSENGER UNTO JOB, AND SAID, THE OXEN WERE PLOWING, AND THE ASSES FEEDING BESIDE THEM:

(15) "AND THE SABEANS FELL UPON THEM, AND TOOK THEM AWAY; YES, THEY HAVE KILLED THE SERVANTS WITH THE EDGE OF THE SWORD; AND I ONLY AM ESCAPED ALONE TO TELL YOU.

(16) "WHILE HE WAS YET SPEAKING, THERE CAME ALSO ANOTHER, AND SAID, THE FIRE OF GOD IS FALLEN FROM HEAVEN, AND HAS BURNED UP THE SHEEP, AND THE SERVANTS, AND CONSUMED THEM; AND I ONLY AM ESCAPED ALONE TO TELL YOU.

(17) "WHILE HE WAS YET SPEAKING,

THERE CAME ALSO ANOTHER, AND SAID, THE CHALDEANS MADE OUT THREE BANDS, AND FELL UPON THE CAMELS, AND HAVE CARRIED THEM AWAY, YES, AND KILLED THE SERVANTS WITH THE EDGE OF THE SWORD; AND I ONLY AM ESCAPED ALONE TO TELL YOU.

(18) "WHILE HE WAS YET SPEAKING, THERE CAME ALSO ANOTHER, AND SAID, YOUR SONS AND YOUR DAUGHTERS WERE EATING AND DRINKING WINE IN THEIR ELDEST BROTHER'S HOUSE:

(19) "AND, BEHOLD, THERE CAME A GREAT WIND FROM THE WILDERNESS, AND SMOTE THE FOUR CORNERS OF THE HOUSE, AND IT FELL UPON THE YOUNG MEN, AND THEY ARE DEAD; AND I ONLY AM ESCAPED ALONE TO TELL YOU.

(20) "THEN JOB AROSE, AND RENT HIS MANTLE, AND SHAVED HIS HEAD, AND FELL DOWN UPON THE GROUND, AND WORSHIPPED,

(21) "AND SAID, NAKED CAME I OUT OF MY MOTHER'S WOMB, AND NAKED SHALL I RETURN THITHER: THE LORD GAVE, AND THE LORD HAS TAKEN AWAY; BLESSED BE THE NAME OF THE LORD.

(22) "IN ALL THIS JOB SINNED NOT, NOR CHARGED GOD FOOLISHLY."

The synopsis is:

1. (Vs. 17) All these evil things that happened to Job show us that this is exactly what would happen to every Believer if the Lord allowed such. Satan's hatred would demand this. But, as stated, the Evil One can only do what the Lord allows him to do.

2. (Vs. 19) The loss of property is one thing; however, the loss of one's family is something else altogether. Why did the Lord allow the latter?

3. (Vs. 19) The Lord did not choose to directly tell us. However, if it is to be noted, the only thing that was said about those sons and daughters was that they were *"eating and drinking."* I think it is clear that the consecration of Job definitely was not their consecration. Having little, if any, desire for the Lord, they were taken away. This we do know:

Whatever the Lord does is right. It's not right just because He does it, but because, in fact, it is right.

4. (Vs. 20) While blow after blow fell upon Job, almost enough to kill a man, still, we see here the depths of his consecration by his worship of the Lord, even at this terrible time. In times like these, only a few worship, while most blame God! What a testimony on the part of Job.

5. (Vs. 21) Satan said that Job would curse God to His Face, if such calamity fell upon him. However, before the entirety of the spirit world, the Lord proved that this would not be the case. In fact, all of us are *"compassed about with so great a cloud of witnesses"* (Heb. 12:1). What type of testimony are we giving to the spirit world?

6. (Vs. 22) Some foolishly claim that Job was not showing faith regarding his words of Verse 21; however, the Holy Spirit says the very opposite!

THE TERRIBLE CALAMITIES OF JOB

Someone has said that all men have a breaking point. But it didn't actually seem that Job did.

He suffered calamity after calamity, any one which was enough to kill a man, the loss of all his property and wealth, the loss of his servants, and above all the loss of his ten children. And all of this happened suddenly!

One day Job was a multimillionaire, and the next day he was nothing. And we must understand, while we know what was happening in Heaven as we read the Book of Job, at the time of its happening, Job had no idea as to what was taking place, or why it was taking place. The indication is that the Lord gave him no warning whatsoever. It all just suddenly happened, one calamity right after the other.

WORSHIP

Praise is what we do, while worship is what we are. The idea is, every single action by the Believer, everything that happens, we are to respond to it, irrespective as to what it might be, with worship, meaning that we worship the Lord, meaning that we do not blame Him, meaning that we trust Him and do so explicitly.

THE LORD GIVES AND
THE LORD TAKES AWAY

Many have chastised Job for the statement,

"The LORD gave, and the LORD has taken away; blessed be the Name of the LORD." But we find that the Holy Spirit did not fault Job for this statement.

In fact, we must ever understand that everything we have is a gift from the Lord. He has a right to give it, if He chooses to do so, and He has the right to take it away, if He chooses to do so. That is what Job is saying, and rightly so!

Job did not blame the Lord at all! In effect, he did the very opposite as to what Satan claimed that he would do. Instead of cursing God for these terrible calamities which had come his way, which he did not at all understand, and which the Lord in no way explained to him, instead, he blessed the Lord.

How galling this must have been to the Evil One! How it must have angered him to see what he had done to Job, and that it had had no ill effect on the great patriarch, at least as it regards blaming God.

When the Lord said to Satan as it regards Job, *"that there is none like him in the Earth, a perfect and an upright man, one who fears God and hates evil,"* he said it exactly as it was.

We should learn from this, as we should already know, that the Lord knows us. He knows who we are, what we are, and how we are! We may not know ourselves, but to be sure, God knows us. And the great question looms, *"What is He saying about us?"*

"Oh Jesus, I have promised,
"To serve You to the end;
"Be Thou forever near me,
"My Master and my Friend;
"I shall not fear the battle,
"If You are by my side,
"Nor wander from the pathway,
"If You will be my Guide."

"Oh, let me feel You near me:
"The world is ever near;
"I see the sights that dazzled,
"The tempting sounds I hear;
"My foes are ever near me,
"Around me and within;
"But, Jesus, draw Thou nearer,
"And shield my soul from sin."

"Oh, let me hear You speaking,

NOTES

"In accents clear and still,
"Above the storms of passion,
"The murmurs of self-will;
"Oh, speak to reassure me,
"To hasten, or control;
"Oh, speak, and make me listen,
"Thou Guardian of my soul."

"Oh, Jesus, You have promised,
"To all who follow Thee,
"That where you are in Glory,
"There shall Your servant be;
"And, Jesus, I have promised,
"To serve You to the end;
"Oh, give me Grace to follow,
"My Master and my Friend."

"Oh, let me see Your Foot Marks,
"And in them plant my own:
"My hope to follow duly,
"Is in Your Strength alone.
"Oh, guide me, call me, draw me,
"Uphold me to the end;
"And then in Heaven receive me,
"My Saviour and my Friend."

CHAPTER 2

(1) "AGAIN THERE WAS A DAY WHEN THE SONS OF GOD CAME TO PRESENT THEMSELVES BEFORE THE LORD, AND SATAN CAME ALSO AMONG THEM TO PRESENT HIMSELF BEFORE THE LORD.

(2) "AND THE LORD SAID UNTO SATAN, FROM WHERE DO YOU COME? AND SATAN ANSWERED THE LORD, AND SAID, FROM GOING TO AND FRO IN THE EARTH, AND FROM WALKING UP AND DOWN IN IT.

(3) "AND THE LORD SAID UNTO SATAN, HAVE YOU CONSIDERED MY SERVANT JOB, THAT THERE IS NONE LIKE HIM IN THE EARTH, A PERFECT AND AN UPRIGHT MAN, ONE WHO FEARS GOD, AND HATES EVIL? AND STILL HE HOLDS FAST HIS INTEGRITY, ALTHOUGH YOU MOVED ME AGAINST HIM, TO DESTROY HIM WITHOUT CAUSE.

(4) "AND SATAN ANSWERED THE LORD, AND SAID, SKIN FOR SKIN, YES, ALL THAT A MAN HAS WILL HE GIVE

FOR HIS LIFE.

(5) "BUT PUT FORTH YOUR HAND NOW, AND TOUCH HIS BONE AND HIS FLESH, AND HE WILL CURSE YOU TO YOUR FACE.

(6) "AND THE LORD SAID UNTO SATAN, BEHOLD, HE IS IN YOUR HAND; BUT SAVE HIS LIFE.

(7) "SO WENT SATAN FORTH FROM THE PRESENCE OF THE LORD, AND SMOTE JOB WITH SORE BOILS FROM THE SOLE OF HIS FOOT UNTO HIS CROWN.

(8) "AND HE TOOK HIM A POTSHERD TO SCRAPE HIMSELF WITHAL; AND HE SAT DOWN AMONG THE ASHES."

The exegesis is:

1. (Vs. 1) Regrettably, Satan always comes *"again."*

2. The Lord reminds Satan that Job did not do what Satan said he would do, which was to curse God (1:11).

3. (Vs. 6) Once again, the Lord sets the limits; Job's health can be affected, and severely so, but Satan cannot take his life. Again we state, all of this shows that Satan can only do what the Lord allows him to do.

4. (Vs. 7) It is believed that the disease which Satan put upon Job was *"elephantiasis,"* which is a strongly developed form of leprosy. While it is a non-contagious disease, it is extremely painful, coming from a burning and ulcerous swelling. Generally, it attacks only a certain part of the body, however, Job was afflicted over the entirety of his body, which was not only notoriously painful, but, as well, terribly humiliating, as would be obvious.

5. (Vs. 8) The sores, it is said, emit a fluid with an offensive odor. Job used the potsherd to scrape it away.

AGAIN

The word, *"again,"* denotes the fact that Satan had failed in his first effort. Job had lost all his possessions as well as the lives of his sons and daughters. He had come from being *"the greatest of all the men of the east,"* to a position of poverty. But, still, he did not blame God. Satan now asks permission for greater latitude.

The word *"again"* is interesting! It should be understood, that there is nothing the Saint of God can do that will stop Satan from coming again, in whatever capacity that the Lord allows him to come. To which we have already alluded, the Lord uses Satan, as difficult as it may seem at times, for the betterment of God's Children. Of course, it is Satan's desire to steal, kill, and destroy, in other words, to destroy the Faith of the Child of God. In fact, every single attack by Satan, whether it be physical, domestical, financial, or spiritual, is for but one purpose, and that is to destroy our Faith, or at least to seriously weaken it. Faith is the key! It is the means by which God works, and when we say *"faith,"* of course, we are speaking of Faith in Christ and what Christ did at the Cross. That being accomplished in the life of the Believer, means that such a Believer has Faith unalterably in the Word of God. In fact, proper Faith cannot be registered in the Word, until it is anchored in Christ and the Cross (Jn. 1:1, 14, 29).

The Lord allows Satan certain latitude, even as we see here with Job, in order that the Believer may use his Faith, and that it be strengthened, in other words, that our trust in God would increase. Of course, it is Satan's effort to destroy us, and it is God's effort to build us up. Unfortunately, there are some Christians who give in, who allow Satan to have his way, who do not use their Faith as they should and, thereby, lose their way. The Believer should always understand the following:

Whatever type of attack that Satan levels against us, the Lord has given him permission to do such, and for our good. Thereby, we should seek to learn the lesson that desires to be taught, that when the ordeal is over, we will be strengthened, with our Faith enlarged, and our trust in God deepened to a greater degree. But even when that happens, and we rejoice in Victory, we must remember, that the Evil One will be allowed to come *"again."* As such, it is a never ending process, at least until the Trump sounds, or the Lord calls us home, all for our good.

SATAN

It is difficult for most Believers to understand that Satan, at least at times, has access to Heaven, and above all, to the very Throne of God. But we see here in these Passages that he most definitely does.

We see also in II Chronicles 18:18-22 that evil spirits as well have access to Heaven, and once again, even to the Throne of God. Why the Lord allows this, that particular information we aren't given. The following we do know:

Very soon Satan, along with all of his cohorts of darkness are to be cast out of Heaven, and allowed admittance no more. The Scripture says:

"*And there was war in Heaven* (pertains to the *'Mystery of God'* being finished [Rev. 10:7]): *Michael and his Angels fought against the dragon; and the dragon fought and his Angels* (this pertains to Satan and all the Angels who followed him being cast out of Heaven, which will take place at the midpoint of the Great Tribulation; why the Lord, as stated, has allowed Satan and his minions to remain in Heaven all of this time, we aren't told; it is a *'Mystery,'* but it will now be finished),

"*And prevailed not* (Satan will then be defeated; incidentally, it is not Satan who instigates this war, but rather the Archangel Michael at the Command of God); *neither was their place found anymore in Heaven* (joins with the close of the Book of Revelation, where the Evil One has no more place on Earth as well, but rather the place of torment forever and ever (Rev. 20:10).

"*And the great dragon was cast out, that old serpent, called the Devil, and Satan* (he is referred to as *'the Great Dragon'* because of his propensity to *'steal, kill, and destroy'* (Jn. 10:10); he is the *'old serpent'* because in his first appearance in the Bible, he chose to work through a serpent; thereby, he is what the curse caused the serpent to be, wryly, subtle, and treacherous), *which deceives the whole world* (deception is his greatest weapon; he deceives, and is himself deceived): *he was cast out into the earth, and his Angels were cast out with him* (pronounces the beginning of the end for this evil monster).

"*And I heard a loud voice saying in Heaven* (presents the white-robed wearers of Rev. 6:10-11), *Now is come Salvation, and Strength, and the Kingdom of our God* (presents the triumph of Christ), *and the power of His Christ* (refers to the fact that Christ will rule this world, not Satan): *for the accuser of our Brethren is cast down, which accused them before our God day and night.* (This implies that either Satan or one of his fallen Angels is before the Throne of God, accusing the Brethren constantly [Job, Chpts. 1-2]).

"*And they overcame him by the Blood of the Lamb* (the power to overcome and overwhelm the kingdom of Satan is found exclusively in the Blood of the Sacrifice of the Son of God, and our Faith in that Finished Work [Rom. 6:3-5, 11, 14] *and by the Word of our Testimony* (the *'testimony'* must pertain to the fact that the Object of our Faith is the Cross, and exclusively the Cross, which then gives the Holy Spirit latitude to work within our lives); *and they loved not their lives unto the death.* (This refers to the fact that the Believer must not change his testimony regarding the Cross to something else, even if it means death.)

"*Therefore rejoice, you Heavens, and you who dwell in them.* (Heaven rejoices because Satan has no more access to those portals.) *Woe to the inhabitants of the earth and of the sea! for the Devil is come down unto you, having great wrath* (the *'woe'* mentioned here is the third and final woe, and pertains to Satan being cast out of Heaven, down to this Earth; he will have great anger), *because he knows that he has but a short time* (in order to carry out his plan; failing that he is doomed!)

"*And when the dragon saw that he was cast into the Earth, he persecuted the woman which brought forth the man child.* (That's when, as stated, the Antichrist will break his seven year Covenant with Israel, attacking and defeating her)" (Rev. 12:7-13).

As stated, all of these things concerning Satan being cast out of Heaven, along with all of his demon spirits and Angels, will take place at the midpoint of the Great Tribulation.

THE ULTIMATE END OF SATAN

Despite the fact that God is omnipotent, omniscient, and omnipresent and, as well, the Creator, Satan still believes that he can win this conflict. He has deceived himself into believing this and, thereby, makes it his business to deceive much of the world. The Word of God, however, pronounces his eternal doom. It says:

"And when the thousand years are expired (should have been translated *'finished'*), *Satan shall be loosed out of his prison* (is not meant to infer a mere arbitrary act on the part of God; He has a very valid reason for doing this),

"And shall go out to deceive the nations which are in the four quarters of the Earth, Gog and Magog (the main reason the Lord allows Satan this latitude is, it seems, to rid the Earth of all who oppose Christ; George Williams says: *'The Creation Sabbath witnessed the first seduction, and the Millennial Sabbath will witness the last'*; the *'Gog and Magog'* spoken of by John is a Hebrew term expressive of multitude and magnitude; here it embraces all nations, *'the four quarters of the Earth'*), *to gather them together to battle; the number of whom is as the sand of the sea* (proclaims the fact that virtually all of the population at that particular time, which did not accept Christ during the Kingdom Age, will throw in their lot with Satan.

"And they went up on the breadth of the Earth, and compassed the camp of the Saints about, and the beloved city (pictures Satan coming against Jerusalem with his army, which will be the last attack against that city): *and fire came down from God out of Heaven, and devoured them.* (Stipulates that the Lord will make short work of this insurrection. In fact, very little information is given regarding this event, as is obvious.)

"And the Devil who deceived them was cast into the Lake of Fire and brimstone (marks the end of Satan regarding his influence in the world and, in fact, in any part of the Creation of God), *where the Beast and the False Prophet are* (proclaims the fact that these two were placed in *'the Lake of Fire and brimstone'* some 1,000 years earlier [Rev. 19:20]), *and shall be tormented day and night forever and ever.* (This signifies the eternity of this place. It is a matter of interest to note that Satan's first act is recorded in Gen., Chpt. 3 [the Third

NOTES

Chapter from the beginning], whereas his last act on a worldwide scale is mentioned in Rev., Chpt. 20 [the Third Chapter from the end])" (Rev. 20:7-10).

So, Satan's final doom, along with all of his fallen Angels and demon spirits, will be the Lake of Fire, in which it will last forever and forever.

WITHOUT CAUSE

Our Word of Faith friends, which actually is no faith at all, at least that God will recognize, claimed that Job suffered this terrible trial because of fear. They base their hypotheses on the statement made by Job when he said, *"For the thing which I greatly feared is come upon me, and that which I was afraid of is come unto me"* (Job 3:25).

But yet, the Lord said of Job, even as He spoke to Satan, *"Have you considered My Servant Job, that there is none like him in the Earth, a perfect and an upright man, one who fears God, and hates evil? and still he holds fast his integrity, although you move me against him, to destroy him without cause"* (Job 2:3). Note the words, *"without cause!"*

This plainly tells us that the Lord plainly states that the reason for Job's great trial had nothing to do with Job himself personally. In other words, there was no *"cause"* that would precipitate such a situation, as our Word of Faith friends claim.

Of course, these same people claim that if Job had had the faith they have, he would never have had to undergo such difficulties.

They miss the whole point of the Book of Job.

As we have previously stated, it explains the problem of why good men are afflicted. It is in order to effect our Sanctification. It is very interesting that this difficult question should be first taken up and answered in the Bible.

Job had to discover, and do so the hard way, even as it is with most of us, the worthlessness of self, which is the first step in the Christian experience, that is, if we are to advance in the Lord. And then he had to discover the worthfulness of Christ, which is actually the last step in this great experience.

Job does not symbolize an unconverted

man, but rather a converted man. It was necessary that one of God's Children should be chosen for this trial; for the subject of the Book of Job is not the conversion of the sinner, but the consecration of the Saint. It is evident that an unconverted person needs to be brought to the end of himself; but that a man who feared God, who was perfect in all his ways, and who hated evil, should also need this, is not so very clear to us (Williams[1]).

As we shall see, Job finally came to the place that he saw himself for what he really was, and at the same time he saw God. The comparison was not a pretty picture, to say the least.

So, the Book of Job lets us know what man is, even the most consecrated man such as Job, and it lets us know what the Lord is. That's the reason that every Believer needs to read this Book, understand this Book, inasmuch as it will show the Believer what he actually is and, thereby, his need for the Lord Jesus Christ, and what Christ did for us at Calvary's Cross.

Man doesn't like to admit what he is, and religious man likes it least of all. But it is necessary, even as Job, to have this understanding, as unsavory as it might be. We can never really know the Lord as we should know Him, without this knowledge.

SAVE HIS LIFE

Life and death are solely in the domain of the Lord. To be sure, the Evil One would kill every single Child of God in the world, and would do so instantly, that is if he had the power to do so. He does not have that power and, in fact, will never have that power. While death is in his domain, simply because death was brought about by the Fall, and is caused in its origination by sin, still, the Lord reserves the right of finality. So, the Lord will tell Satan exactly as to what he can do, and what he cannot do. Satan dare not cross those boundaries then, and he dare not cross those boundaries now. The idea is:

No Believer is taken out of this world, until his work is finished. Now all type of situations may enter into that, such as our consecration or the lack thereof, but the fact remains, it is the Lord and the Lord Alone Who does the doing.

Job *"sitting down among the ashes,"* presents a position of mourning. In a sense, it means that one has been reduced to ashes, which means that everything has been lost.

Even as we have previously said, while we in reading this Book, know the end from the beginning, Job knew nothing. The Lord did not bother to explain the situation to him, in fact, gave him no clue at all as to what was happening, or why it was happening. In fact, the Lord very seldom ever explains to us at the beginning as to why certain things are taking place.

THE MANNER IN WHICH THE LORD DEALS WITH US

Everything the Lord does with us, even as it was with Job, is to teach us lessons that we need to learn, and to increase our Faith, to increase our trust in Him. It is always all for our good, irrespective as to what it might be. It may not seem to be good for the moment, but even as Paul said, it will *"afterward yield the peaceable fruit of Righteousness"* (Heb. 12:11).

Please understand, the Lord never punishes His Children. While He most definitely will chastise us, it is always for our correction, for our edification.

Punishment is given to inflict pain, but such is not done to God's Children, simply because Jesus bore our punishment at the Cross.

Unfortunately, many modern Christians seemingly enjoy seeing other Christians punished, and will join in the process if given the opportunity. The Holy Spirit through James addressed that by saying:

"Speak not evil one of another, brethren (refers to self-appointed Judges [Mat. 7:1-5]). *He who speaks evil of his brother, and judges his brother, speaks evil of the Law, and judges the Law* (pertains to the Law of Moses, to which James is pointing; when a Believer judges another, he has taken himself out from under Grace and placed himself under Law, where he will only find condemnation)*: but if you judge the Law, you are not a doer of the Law, but a Judge.* (In other words, such a person has placed himself in the position of God.)

"There is one Lawgiver, Who is able to save and to destroy (presents God as the only One Who can fill this position)*: who are you who judges another?* (The Greek actually says, 'but you — who are you?' In other words, 'who do you think you are?')" (James 4:11-12).

Someone said the following in a message preached many, many years ago:

• When you hear something bad about a fellow Christian, you must understand that you are hearing gossip, and must treat it accordingly.

• Even if you have understanding of the facts regarding the situation, still, you have little knowledge of the Spiritual warfare involved.

• If you had faced the same situation in the same way, would you have done any better, or even as well?

(9) "THEN SAID HIS WIFE UNTO HIM, DO YOU STILL RETAIN YOUR INTEGRITY? CURSE GOD, AND DIE.

(10) "BUT HE SAID UNTO HER, YOU SPEAK AS ONE OF THE FOOLISH WOMEN SPEAKS. WHAT? SHALL WE RECEIVE GOOD AT THE HAND OF GOD, AND SHALL WE NOT RECEIVE EVIL? IN ALL THIS DID NOT JOB SIN WITH HIS LIPS."

The synopsis is:

1. (Vs. 9) In essence, Job's wife said, *"Why do you hold on to your religious profession? Throw your idol god aside; there is no eternity; you need not be afraid to die; there is nothing behind death. This religion of Abel, Noah, and Abraham is a fairy tale!"*

2. This proclaims to us that Job's wife did not share his consecration and dedication to the Lord. In other words, this terrible trial that her husband was undergoing was showing what her Faith really was. She no longer believed!

3. (Vs. 10) This man, who had been the richest man in the east, which means he had been the most powerful, now is reduced to total poverty, his body full of sores, with even his wife condemning him. But yet, he did not blame God. What an example!

THIS TRIAL WOULD PROVE THE HEARTS OF ALL

As we are seeing and shall see, this great trial was not only for Job, but for his wife, for his friends, and for everyone. The sadness is, all failed with the exception of Job.

His wife evidently lost her Faith. She didn't understand at all as to why her family had been attacked in this fashion. All of her children were dead, and her husband reduced to abject poverty and, as well, what looked like to be a sickness unto death. Evidently she grew angry at God, blamed God, lost her Faith, consequently telling Job he might as well curse God and die. This just may have been the hardest blow of all as it regards Job.

A man's wife means everything to him. If he loses her confidence, her respect, there isn't much that could be worse.

On a personal basis, I have faced some dark days in my life and living for the Lord. But never one time did I lose the confidence of Frances. She stood with me, held me up, encouraged me, and despite the hurt and the pain, which she endured, she never once wavered in her Faith. If anything, she grew closer and closer to the Lord. Without that, I'm not sure if I would have made it.

But Job did not have that encouragement, that security, that confidence. How horrible it must have been for this man, sitting in a bed of ashes, a million questions filling his mind, and now his own wife tells him to *"curse God and die."* She has grown bitter at Job, bitter at God, and bitter at life.

This is one of the reasons that the Lord allows trials and tests. It is to bring out what is actually in us. Will we quit? Will we curse God? Will we grow disillusioned? Will we throw over our Faith? Or will we push closer to the Lord? Will we cling even more steadfastly to Him? Will we throw ourselves even more so on His Mercy and Grace?

JOB DID NOT SIN WITH HIS LIPS

He answered his wife by saying, *"You speak as one of the foolish women speaks. What? Shall we receive good at the Hand of God, and shall we not receive evil?"*

There are some who claim that Job evidenced a bad confession here, *"Shall we receive good at the Hand of God, and shall we not receive evil?"*

Was it a bad confession? Emphatically

not! The Holy Spirit said of Job, *"In all this did not Job sin with his lips."*

In fact, the entire confession message as it is presently proposed is unscriptural. The idea that we as Believers can begin to confess whatever it is we want, and God is bound to deliver it, holds no place in the Word of God whatsoever. We must ever understand, that God's Word cannot be used against Himself, i.e., *"against His Will."* And to be certain and sure, God has a Will, a Perfect Will as it regards anything and everything. If we have good sense, we will seek what His Will is, and then endeavor with all of our strength to follow it.

A PERSONAL EXPERIENCE

A young preacher acquaintance of mine resigned his Church in a particular Midwestern state. In talking with him, I happened to ask, *"Where are you going next?"*

"I'm not sure," he answered!

I then stated to him, *"You had better seek the Lord graphically so, deriving His Will as it regards this most important matter."*

He quickly turned toward me and said, *"Anywhere I go will be the Will of God!"*

I had not realized that he had been greatly influenced by the Word of Faith doctrine, as have millions to say the least and, therefore, he had the idea in his mind that whatever he decided was the Will of God. In other words, he was acting as his own god.

He went to a particular city, got in trouble and had to leave. He then went elsewhere, ran afoul of the law, and wound up in the penitentiary. So much for his will instead of God's Will.

Please remember, it is never a bad confession to tell the truth.

I remember once speaking to someone over the phone, whose name I forget at this particular time. It was obvious that they had a head cold. I made mention of it in passing, and they quickly retorted, *"Oh no, I don't have a cold."* They were putting forth their *"good confession,"* despite the fact that they most definitely did have a head cold, which was obvious. Did lying about it help them any? The answer to that should be very obvious!

Some may argue that it was not the Lord, but rather Satan who inflicted this terrible ordeal on Job and, therefore, Job was remiss in attributing such to God by saying, *"And shall we not receive evil?"*

While it was Satan that delivered the blows, but it was only by the permission of God. God was in control of everything from beginning to the end. So, the Holy Spirit through the writer of this great Book states, *"In all this did not Job sin with his lips."*

Now you can take the Word of the Holy Spirit, or you can take the prattle of foolish individuals who think they know more than God.

(11) "NOW WHEN JOB'S THREE FRIENDS HEARD OF ALL THIS EVIL THAT WAS COME UPON HIM, THEY CAME EVERY ONE FROM HIS OWN PLACE; ELIPHAZ THE TEMANITE, AND BILDAD THE SHUHITE, AND ZOPHAR THE NAAMATHITE: FOR THEY HAD MADE AN APPOINTMENT TOGETHER TO COME TO MOURN WITH HIM AND TO COMFORT HIM.

(12) "AND WHEN THEY LIFTED UP THEIR EYES AFAR OFF, AND KNEW HIM NOT, THEY LIFTED UP THEIR VOICE, AND WEPT; AND THEY RENT EVERY ONE HIS MANTLE, AND SPRINKLED DUST UPON THEIR HEADS TOWARD HEAVEN.

(13) "SO THEY SAT DOWN WITH HIM UPON THE GROUND SEVEN DAYS AND SEVEN NIGHTS, AND NONE SPOKE A WORD UNTO HIM: FOR THEY SAW THAT HIS GRIEF WAS VERY GREAT."

The overview is:

1. (Vs. 11) These three men represent the world of religion that attempts to serve God by means other than Christ and the Cross. The truth is, they were very religious, but very lost, because their faith, even as we shall see, was in the wrong things.

2. (Vs. 12) Job was so disfigured by the disease that they failed to recognize him. When he was recognized, they instantly realized that the situation was far worse than they could even begin to contemplate.

3. (Vs. 13) We must remember that Job, at least at this time, had absolutely no knowledge as to what was going on. So the question must have loomed large and furious in his mind. In fact, this was one of the greatest tests of Faith that one has ever engaged.

JOB'S THREE FRIENDS

The three men named here seemed to have been individuals with whom Job had been contemporary, and with whom he frequently associated. All three seemed to live a distance from Job, and even a distance apart among themselves.

It was probably about two months that had passed before word came to them of Job's plight, and they then agreed to pay him a visit, and to do so together. More probably, these individuals were considered to be men of wisdom, but before Job's trial and test, more than likely, they always deferred to him.

So, when they said that they would go to him in order to *"mourn with him and to comfort him,"* they had something else in mind altogether that was different than what they would encounter.

First of all, until they saw him, they had absolutely no idea of the severity of the situation. Seeing that severity, the terrible condition in which Job now finds himself, they automatically jump to conclusions, conclusions incidentally, which were totally wrong, even as we will ultimately see. These *"three friends,"* albeit some of the wisest men in the world, held no help for Job. They would basically only accuse him, which would ultimately arouse the Anger of God.

This should be a note of great interest to the modern church in its quest for humanistic psychology as the panacea for the ills of man. As these *"three friends,"* knowledgeable as they may have been, were of no help whatsoever to Job, but rather harmful, likewise, modern psychology offers no help whatsoever, but only harm. When will man ever learn that man cannot cure man of man's problems incurred in man's rebellion? Psychology is the HIV of the modern church.

We will find that these three men argued from different viewpoints. They are as follows:

• Eliphaz the Temanite: He argued from the standpoint of *"human experience."* The record of what he said took up four Chapters (4, 5, 15, and 22).

• Bildad the Shuhite: This man argued from the standpoint of *"human tradition."* His statements are found in three Chapters (8, 18, and 25).

• Zophar the Naamathite: He argued from the standpoint of *"human merit."* His statements take up two Chapters (11 and 20).

Many would feel God unjust in allowing the holiest man on Planet Earth to be placed in such a condition; nevertheless, in this episode three things will take place:

1. God will be glorified;
2. Satan will be defeated; and,
3. Man will be blessed.

God requires nothing of anyone of such nature but that He amply rewards for such faithfulness. As well, considering the great love that God has for humanity in the giving of His Only Begotten Son to die for a fallen race, one should be honored to suffer in any capacity that would bring Glory to God and, thereby, aid the Cause of Christ.

JUDGING ONE WHO IS USED OF GOD

As a Believer, we must be very careful as to what we say about someone, irrespective of their present difficulty or problems, who is obviously being used by God. This is not meaning in any way that sin should be condoned, so do not misunderstand the statement. Sin is sin, irrespective as to who commits it; however, situations are seldom as they seem to be. And if God is truly using someone, and that person fails, we had best be very careful as to what we say or do toward that individual.

Admittedly, Job did not fail the Lord, but still, the situation is the same.

Concerning such, Jesus said, and I quote from THE EXPOSITOR'S STUDY BIBLE:

"I Am the True Vine (the True Israel, as He is the True Church, and the True Man; more specifically, He Alone is the Source of Life), *and My Father is the Husbandman* (refers to God the Father not simply as the Vinedresser, but also the Owner so to speak).

"Every branch (Believer) *in Me* (to have Salvation, we must be *'in Christ,'* which refers to trusting in what He did at the Cross) *that bears not fruit* (the Holy Spirit Alone can bring forth fruit within our lives, and He does such through the Finished Work of Christ, which demands that the Cross ever be the Object of our Faith) *He takes away* (if the Believer refuses the Cross, ultimately, he will be taken out of the Body of

Christ): *and every branch that bears fruit* (has some understanding of Christ and the Cross), *He purges it* (uses whatever means necessary to make the Cross the total Object of one's Faith), *that it may bring forth more fruit* (only when the Cross becomes the total Object of one's Faith can the Holy Spirit perform His Work of bringing forth proper fruit)" (Jn. 15:1-2).

For one who is truly being used of God, our Lord plainly said here that He will *"purge him,"* all in order *"that he may bring forth more fruit."*

Job being closer to God than any man on the face of the Earth, he in no way realized that there were still many things in his life that were not proper. As well, all the things that he did, and rightly so, could not bring him to the place that he ought to be. It is the same with us presently!

While the Lord may use the loss of everything as with Job to deal with him, and while He might use failure in the life of another, even though He in no way is the cause of such failure, the outcome is meant to be the same. We must ever remember, while we can easily see what is happening, many times we little know what is actually going on.

We will learn from Job's three friends, as to how easy it is to be totally wrong when it looks so right at the beginning. We should take a lesson from them, although, regrettably, it seems that few do.

When these *"three friends"* saw Job, they were so stricken by what they saw, this man who had been the greatest man of the east, now reduced to this condition, was beyond their comprehension. So, *"they sat down with him upon the ground seven days and seven nights, and none spoke a word unto him."*

During those seven days and nights evidently they surmised that Job's condition must be caused by great sin on his part, as secret as it may have been, which they will be quick to expostulate very shortly.

Again, we must always remember that what we see is not altogether what is.

"According to Your gracious Word,
"In meek humility,
"This will I do, my dying Lord,
"I will remember Thee."

NOTES

"Your Body, broken for my sake,
"My bread from Heaven shall be;
"Your Cup of Blessing I will take,
"And thus remember Thee."

"Can I Gethsemane forget?
"Or there Your Conflict see,
"Your Agony and bloody Sweat,
"And not remember Thee?"

"When to the Cross I turn my eyes,
"And rest on Calvary,
"Oh Lamb of God,
"My Sacrifice,
"I must remember Thee."

"Remember Thee, and all Your Pains,
"And all Your Love to me;
"Yea, while a breath, a pulse remains,
"Will I remember Thee."

"And when these failing lips grow dumb,
"And mind and memory flee,
"When You shall in Your Kingdom come,
"Jesus, remember me."

CHAPTER 3

(1) "AFTER THIS OPENED JOB HIS MOUTH, AND CURSED HIS DAY.

(2) "AND JOB SPOKE, AND SAID,

(3) "LET THE DAY PERISH WHEREIN I WAS BORN, AND THE NIGHT IN WHICH IT WAS SAID, THERE IS A MAN CHILD CONCEIVED.

(4) "LET THAT DAY BE DARKNESS; LET NOT GOD REGARD IT FROM ABOVE, NEITHER LET THE LIGHT SHINE UPON IT.

(5) "LET DARKNESS AND THE SHADOW OF DEATH STAIN IT; LET A CLOUD DWELL UPON IT; LET THE BLACKNESS OF THE DAY TERRIFY IT.

(6) "AS FOR THAT NIGHT, LET DARKNESS SEIZE UPON IT; LET IT NOT BE JOINED UNTO THE DAYS OF THE YEAR, LET IT NOT COME INTO THE NUMBER OF THE MONTHS.

(7) "LO, LET THAT NIGHT BE SOLITARY, LET NO JOYFUL VOICE COME THEREIN.

(8) "LET THEM CURSE IT WHO CURSE THE DAY, WHO ARE READY TO RAISE UP THEIR MOURNING.

(9) "LET THE STARS OF THE TWILIGHT THEREOF BE DARK; LET IT LOOK FOR LIGHT, BUT HAVE NONE; NEITHER LET IT SEE THE DAWNING OF THE DAY:

(10) "BECAUSE IT SHUT NOT UP THE DOORS OF MY MOTHER'S WOMB, NOR HID SORROW FROM MY EYES."

The pattern is:

1. (Vs. 1) Job cursed his day of birth. The word *"cursed"* doesn't speak of profanity, but rather a negativism regarding his birth.

2. (Vs. 3) In other words, Job is saying that the birth of a baby boy should have been a great blessing, but it seems as it regards Job's thinking it wasn't. Job could not have been more wrong!

3. (Vs. 6) Job wishes the day of his birth in this night of his conception to be utterly blotted out from the calendar. But, aware that this is impossible, he subsides into a milder class of imprecations.

4. (Vs. 7) In essence, Job says, *"Considering what has happened to me, my birth was definitely not the case of joy."* But again, how wrong Job was!

All of this is meant to show us, as Believers, that we cannot look at circumstances, irrespective as to how negative they may presently seem to be.

5. In Verse 8 Job, in essence, is saying, *"Let those who curse life add my name to their list."*

JOB KNEW WHAT WAS HAPPENING BUT HE DID NOT KNOW WHAT WAS GOING ON

It seems for seven days and nights that Job's friends sat and looked at him. It was the custom in those days that when visitors came, the host was to speak first. Inasmuch as Job said nothing this length of time, the three friends said nothing either. Finally, Job speaks.

Why did he wait so long before he spoke?

Maybe it was acute embarrassment! Or maybe he saw something in the countenances of his friends which revealed, at least somewhat, their thoughts. Pharisaism finds it very difficult to conceal itself. Often it manifests itself, without a word spoken, and that most offensively. Pharisaism is more so a spirit than it is an attitude, and can definitely be felt.

We only venture such thinking because of the posture they took when they finally did begin to speak. It was not positive or pleasant to say the least!

It is very easy for us to look at the situation and form conclusions as it regards what Job should have said or not have said; however, hindsight is always perfect sight. Job had no idea as to why he was in this condition. He had no idea of the conversation that had taken place in Heaven between God the Father and Satan Himself. All of these things became clear to him later, but during the time of his trial, no hint of this was forthcoming.

As we've already stated, this great trial included not only Job, but as well, his three friends, his wife, and even the entirety of the population who knew Job. The only one, even as we shall ultimately see, who would pass the test, would be Job.

Someone has well said that all too often, famous people have friends according to what he can do for them or to them. Job was now reduced to a position to where he could do nothing for anyone, and neither could he do anything to anyone. That being the case, none had any fear of Job.

When one is down and unable to defend himself, and anyone can do any negative thing to him they so desire, and not fear being reprimanded but rather applauded, one finds out very quick just how many good Christians there actually are. Regrettably, there aren't many! Many take advantage of such a situation to exact vengeance for slights real or imagined.

As we said in our heading, Job knew what was happening, it was obvious all around him, but he did not know what was going on.

What was going on was the greatest trial in human history, instigated by Satan, but allowed by the Lord. In fact, Job had been the topic of conversation in Heaven. But, of course, Job at this time knew none of that. We should take that into account as well!

As a Believer, it's easy to look at circumstances, and to see what is happening, but we must remember, that something is going on in Heaven, which very well may be totally different than what is happening on Earth. At any rate, if we belong to the Lord, anything that He allows to happen, no matter how negative it may seem to be at the beginning, will always be for our good. We may not can see that presently, but we must have confidence that most definitely such is true.

Would Job have said all the things he did had he known that everything would be written down, and that untold millions would read every word he spoke, at least that which the Lord desired that we see?

JOB AND THE HOLY SPIRIT

Every Believer since the Cross has the Holy Spirit abiding within our hearts and lives, and doing so permanently (Jn. 14:15-18). Job did not have that then, neither did any Believer before the Cross. To be sure, the Holy Spirit presently is a tremendous help in all that we say, think, or do. Again, Job did not have that. While the Holy Spirit was with him, He definitely was not in him. A great difference is here enjoined.

Due to the fact that the blood of bulls and goats could not take away sins, meaning that the sin debt remained, even with the greatest stalwarts of the Old Covenant, this made it impossible for the Holy Spirit to come in to abide permanently. In fact, Jesus addressed this not long before His Crucifixion, saying:

"And I will pray the Father, and He shall give you another Comforter ('Parakletos,' which means 'One called to the side of another to help'), that He may abide with you forever (before the Cross, the Holy Spirit, as stated, could only help a few individuals, and then only for a period of time; since the Cross, He lives in the hearts and lives of all Believers, and does so forever);

"Even the Spirit of Truth (the Greek says, *'The Spirit of The Truth,'* which refers to the Word of God; actually, He does far more than merely superintend the attribute of Truth, as Christ *'is Truth'* [I Jn. 5:6]); *Whom the world cannot receive* (the Holy Spirit cannot come into the heart of the unbeliever until that person makes Christ his or her Saviour; then He comes in), *because it sees Him not, neither knows Him* (refers to the fact that only Born-Again Believers can understand the Holy Spirit and know Him): *but you know Him* (would have been better translated, *'but you shall get to know Him'*); *for He dwells with you* (before the Cross), *and shall be in you* (which would take place on the Day of Pentecost and forward, because the sin debt has been forever paid by Christ on the Cross, changing the disposition of everything).

"I will not leave you comfortless (helpless): *I will come to you* (through the Person of the Holy Spirit)" (Jn. 14:16-18).

In essence, at least as it regards the Holy Spirit, Job was *"comfortless,"* which means that he was *"helpless."* Understanding that, it is easy to see why he gave vent to his frustrations, which amounts to a gross understatement.

Job said a lot of things he should not have said, but none of it would be constituted as sin. While he voiced a lot of negative things concerning himself, he did not say anything derogatory about God. When the trial was over, even as we will ultimately see, the Lord would say to Eliphaz the Temanite: *"My wrath is kindled against you, and against your two friends: for you have not spoken of Me the thing that is right, as My servant Job has"* (Job 42:7).

THE CROSS OF CHRIST, THE HOLY SPIRIT, AND THE BELIEVER

Even though, since the Cross, the Holy Spirit abides permanently in the heart and life of every Believer, still, most Believers, not knowing or understanding how the Holy Spirit works, which refers to the Cross, receives very limited benefit from Him, and because that their Faith has as its object things other than the Cross of Christ (Rom. 8:2; Gal. 2:21).

That being the case, many modern Christians, although living in this great Dispensation of Grace, will say and do things that they would not say and do, if they only understood how the Spirit works.

I look back personally on my life before the understanding was given to me as it regards the Cross of Christ, and the way the Holy Spirit works, and I still remember the same frustration, even agony, which then I did not understand.

Even though the Holy Spirit was most definitely in my life and, in fact, was greatly helping me to reach much of the world for Christ, still, as it regarded my own personal life and living, in other words, my daily walk before God, I simply did not understand how to live for God. I thought I did, but in looking back, it was overly obvious that I didn't.

In such a state, Believers will say many things they regret saying, and to be sure, will do things they most definitely regret that they have done. It's all because our Faith is in something other than the Cross of Christ, which constitutes spiritual adultery, in which the Holy Spirit cannot function, which greatly limits Him in His Help towards us. Regrettably, that is the sad state of most modern Christians. They do not understand the Cross of Christ as it regards life and living, thinking it pertains only to Salvation and, as a result, they live so far beneath the Spiritual Privileges they ought to have, for which Christ paid such a price.

What I'm trying to say is, while all Believers most definitely have the Holy Spirit abiding within, they are receiving only a fraction of the help they could receive, if they only knew how He works.

(I would strongly recommend that the reader get for yourself our Study Guides on this very subject: "How The Holy Spirit Works, *The Cross Of Christ Series*" and "God's Prescribed Order Of Victory (Romans, Chapter 6, *The Cross Of Christ Series."* These two Study Guides are approximately 100 pages each, giant print, and will open up this great truth.)

JOB ASKS FOR DEATH

Many of God's greats have asked for death. Elijah was one, so was Moses. Even Paul said that it was better for him to die.

Strangely enough, Elijah hasn't died even unto this present time, having been translated. As well, while Job would eventually die, it would be many, many years later, in fact, about 140 years later. So, that oftentimes which we think is our ruin, falls out to be a Blessing, and a great one at that.

There are many things in life that can happen to us, which makes it seem like it's worse than death; however, I think I can say that Scripturally, such never is the case.

As Job looked at himself, all of his material possessions gone, reduced from the greatest man of the east to abject poverty, his body full of sores and he in great pain, and then having stood before ten caskets as the entirety of his family were lowered into the ground, it was very easy for him to wish for death.

While death will come in God's Time, at least until the Trump sounds, still, we have this life to live until that time does come.

We must remember, as it regards Job, not only did he not have the Holy Spirit living within him, as well, he did not have the Bible either, for that wouldn't begin until the time of Moses, and neither did he have Christ to look to, as we think of such presently. He had but one thing, and that was his naked Faith in God, and to be sure, that was being tested greatly, which, even though he did not know it at the time, was the very purpose of this trial. But we will find that Job's Faith, even though he did not have the anchor points we presently have, was enough to see him through.

(11) "WHY DIED I NOT FROM THE WOMB? WHY DID I NOT GIVE UP THE GHOST WHEN I CAME OUT OF THE BELLY?

(12) "WHY DID THE KNEES PREVENT ME? OR WHY THE BREASTS THAT I SHOULD SUCK?

(13) "FOR NOW SHOULD I HAVE LAIN STILL AND BEEN QUIET, I SHOULD HAVE SLEPT: THEN HAD I BEEN AT REST,

(14) "WITH KINGS AND COUNSELLORS OF THE EARTH, WHICH BUILD DESOLATE PLACES FOR THEMSELVES;

(15) "OR WITH PRINCES WHO HAD GOLD, WHO FILLED THEIR HOUSES WITH SILVER:

(16) "OR AS AN HIDDEN UNTIMELY BIRTH I HAD NOT BEEN; AS INFANTS WHICH NEVER SAW LIGHT.

(17) "THERE THE WICKED CEASE FROM TROUBLING; AND THERE THE WEARY BE AT REST.

(18) "THERE THE PRISONERS REST TOGETHER; THEY HEAR NOT THE VOICE OF THE OPPRESSOR.

(19) "THE SMALL AND GREAT ARE THERE; AND THE SERVANT IS FREE FROM HIS MASTER."

The structure is:

1. Perhaps this one word, *"Why?"* as given in Verse 11, looms as the largest word in any language!

2. (Vs. 11) The Holy Spirit allows the *"Why?"* because this teaches us trust. With God, everything is a lesson. His desire is that we learn the lesson. All of us desire immediate answers; nevertheless, they are not always immediately forthcoming. True love will truly trust (I Jn. 4:18).

3. (Vs. 12) The culture of that time placed a newborn child upon the knees of the father, which means he accepted it as his own, and pledged himself to provide for it.

4. (Vs. 17) The *"wicked cease from troubling,"* and *"the weary be at rest,"* only if they make the Lord their eternal Saviour; otherwise, no matter how bad life has been, at death the real Hell begins!

5. (Vs. 19) True freedom as briefly mentioned in Verse 19, is found only in Christ, of which Job would have had only a dim view at that time.

WHY?

Job had once been *"the greatest of all the men of the east."* Now, he is reduced not only to poverty, but to humiliation, shame, and great pain.

He had thought surely that God was pleased with him inasmuch as the Lord had blessed him greatly. But now all is gone. Job's biggest problem is the question, *"Why?"* What reasons were there? Why did God do such a thing?

As previously stated, perhaps this one word, *"Why,"* looms as the largest word in any language!

Having God's Word presently as we do, and having the Holy Spirit living within us as Believers, and due to the fact that the Cross of Christ is a Finished Work, there is really no reason why we should question the Lord. With Job having none of this, in actuality, only the Promise that God had given to Abraham, we certainly should understand his consternation.

BLAMING GOD!

Many modern Christians, shallow in the Word, and with very little relationship with the Lord, if any, are told by psychologists that if they think that God hasn't treated them right, they should go to prayer, and *"forgive God."*

Such advice is ridiculous to say the least! In the first place, the Lord has not done anything negative to anyone. So, for a psychologist, or anyone for that matter, to encourage such wrong thinking, can only lead to worse difficulties for the individual, whomever that person might be. But sadly, the modern church has embraced humanistic psychology in totality. As the result of such, the Cross is now all but totally ignored, if not altogether. So, most modern Christendom is Christianity in name only. It is definitely not Biblical Christianity, which means that it's something devised and instituted by man, which means that it's no more now than a religion.

Every Believer should understand, that the Lord either causes or allows every single thing that happens to us. While, of course, He does not cause us to sin in any fashion as ought to be obvious, still, He does allow it, that is, if we are so foolish to do so. Even then, He merits out the chastisement personally. We must always understand, that everything that happens to us, unless we have done wrong ourselves, will turn out to be a Blessing. Every Believer is very special in the Eyes of God. He has only our welfare at heart. He wants to do us good, and if we will cooperate with Him, most definitely we will be blessed.

But even in the midst of such, if He allows a trial or test, it is always meant to do us good in the long run, which it always will.

So, even though all of us have voiced the question, *"Why?"* at various times, the truth is, it's not a word that we should use as it regards the Lord's dealings with us. We ought to know better.

(20) "WHEREFORE IS LIGHT GIVEN TO HIM WHO IS IN MISERY, AND LIFE UNTO THE BITTER IN SOUL;

(21) "WHICH LONG FOR DEATH, BUT IT COMES NOT; AND DIG FOR IT MORE THAN FOR HID TREASURES;

(22) "WHICH REJOICE EXCEEDINGLY, AND ARE GLAD, WHEN THEY CAN FIND THE GRAVE?

(23) "WHY IS LIGHT GIVEN TO A MAN WHOSE WAY IS HID, AND WHOM GOD HAS HEDGED IN?

(24) "FOR MY SIGHING COMES BEFORE I EAT, AND MY ROARINGS ARE POURED OUT LIKE THE WATERS.

(25) "FOR THE THING WHICH I GREATLY FEARED IS COME UPON ME, AND THAT WHICH I WAS AFRAID OF IS COME UNTO ME.

(26) "I WAS NOT IN SAFETY, NEITHER HAD I REST, NEITHER WAS I QUIET; YET TROUBLE CAME."

The pattern is:

1. (Vs. 20) In essence, Job asks the question as to why the Lord would give life, if it's going to be such misery. Due to his circumstances, I would surely trust that one can understand Job's present frame of mind.

2. (Vs. 21) Some of God's greatest have longed for death; however, they were not right in doing so!

3. (Vs. 22) Inspiration guarantees that Job made these statements, but inspiration does not guarantee that they are right. In fact, much of what Job is saying here is wrong. The Holy Spirit allowed it to be put in the Sacred Text in order that we as Believers may understand that something is always behind what is taking place. We presently have the benefit of Job's experience, whereas Job didn't have that benefit. So, we shouldn't be hard on him.

4. (Vs. 25) Many have claimed that it was *"fear"* which caused Job's problems. However, the Bible doesn't say such, in fact, there is no hint that Job did anything that caused the hedge to come down. It was purely a matter of God allowing the test and the trial, which would be of great benefit to coming generations, and would, as well, turn out to be a great blessing to Job.

5. The idea of Verse 26 is, *"I don't know why this has happened to me!"*

FEAR?

A short time ago Frances and I were in Tulsa, Oklahoma. Our first great-grandson was being born to Matthew and Joanna. Matthew is our grandson and is a year younger than our other grandson Gabriel.

It had turned a little cool, and Gabe had not brought a coat with him, and so we drove up to one of the stores for him to get a jacket.

While he went into the store, I waited in the car, and turned on the radio. I found a Gospel Station, and listened for a few minutes to a particular preacher with whom I was not acquainted.

He was teaching on Job, and his idea was, which probably came from the Word of Faith people, that none of these tests and trials would have come upon Job, had he not allowed fear to captivate his heart. He then quoted Verse 25, *"For the thing which I greatly feared has come upon me."*

Is that correct?

No!

From the Hebrew, the meaning of Job's statement is not that the affliction which has come upon him is a thing which he had feared when he was prosperous, but it is rather something that plagues him now in his present condition. So there will be no misunderstanding, let's say it again:

There was no fear in Job's life before this terrible thing came upon him. That being the case, it could not have been fear that caused his problem, which is ludicrous to say the least! Now in his present condition, he is beset with fears, as should be obvious. As we have asked, *"Why is the Lord doing this?" "Is He greatly displeased with me?"*

As we have already stated, Job had absolutely no inkling whatsoever as to what was happening to him, or why it was happening to him. I think that fear would grip the heart of anyone who had been reduced to such circumstances as Job.

So, to properly understand what Job is saying, and from the original Hebrew, throws an entirely different light on the subject, and puts to rest the allegations of the Word of Faith people.

YET TROUBLE CAME!

The translation of Verse 26 which says, *"I was not in safety, neither had I rest, neither was I quiet; yet trouble came,"* probably does not properly explain what Job actually said.

The idea is, Job did not take his prosperity for granted. He did not rest upon the idea that he felt in his heart that he was doing exactly what God wanted, and was, therefore, in safety. In other words, he did not take for granted the great Blessings which had come upon him. He was conscious of no instance in which he had relaxed from his obligations to the Lord. He feared God and he loved the Lord. Yet trouble came!

The great Patriarch is perplexed, he doesn't understand what has happened, and if we think we could have done any better, we need to think again.

"Guide me, O Thou great Jehovah,
"Pilgrim through this barren land;
"I am weak, but You are Mighty;
"Hold me with Your powerful Hand."

"Open now the crystal fountain,
"Whence the healing stream shall flow;
"Let the fire and cloudy pillar,
"Lead me all my journey through."

"When I tread the verge of Jordan,
"Bid my anxious fears subside;
"Death of death, and Hell's destruction,
"Land me safe on Canaan's side."

CHAPTER 4

(1) "THEN ELIPHAZ THE TEMANITE ANSWERED AND SAID,

(2) "IF WE ASSAY TO COMMUNE WITH YOU, WILL YOU BE GRIEVED? BUT WHO CAN WITHHOLD HIMSELF FROM SPEAKING?

(3) "BEHOLD, YOU HAVE INSTRUCTED MANY, AND YOU HAVE STRENGTHENED THE WEAK HANDS.

(4) "YOUR WORDS HAVE UPHOLDEN HIM WHO WAS FALLING, AND YOU HAVE STRENGTHENED THE FEEBLE KNEES.

(5) "BUT NOW IT IS COME UPON YOU, AND YOU FAINT; IT TOUCHES YOU, AND YOU ARE TROUBLED.

(6) "IS NOT THIS YOUR FEAR, YOUR CONFIDENCE, YOUR HOPE, AND THE UPRIGHTNESS OF YOUR WAYS?

(7) "REMEMBER, I PRAY YOU, WHOEVER PERISHED, BEING INNOCENT? OR WHERE WERE THE RIGHTEOUS CUT OFF?

(8) "EVEN AS I HAVE SEEN, THEY WHO PLOW INIQUITY, AND SOW WICKEDNESS, REAP THE SAME.

(9) "BY THE BLAST OF GOD THEY PERISH, AND BY THE BREATH OF HIS NOSTRILS ARE THEY CONSUMED.

(10) "THE ROARING OF THE LION, AND THE VOICE OF THE FIERCE LION, AND THE TEETH OF THE YOUNG LIONS, ARE BROKEN.

(11) "THE OLD LION PERISHES FOR LACK OF PREY, AND THE STOUT LION'S WHELPS ARE SCATTERED ABROAD."

The structure is:

1. (Vs. 2) The argument of Eliphaz will be from human experience, which will prove to be totally wrong.

2. (Vs. 3) It is true that Job helped many who needed help when he was the most powerful man of the east. Now Eliphaz is telling him that what he counseled was wrong. However, it is Eliphaz who is wrong!

3. (Vs. 5) *"Your condition,"* Eliphaz says, *"proves that you were wrong, or else this trouble would not have come upon you."*

4. (Vs. 7) Eliphaz, upon hearing Job curse the day that he was born, had heard enough to convince him that, regardless of Job's past outward goodness in helping the poor, instructing the needy, and upholding the weak, he was a wicked man, who had committed many sinful acts in secret, and now was reaping what he had sown.

5. (Vs. 7) This *"friend"* continues to argue that all of Job's past, public, and private acts of goodness were for show, and to cover up his real self. He called attention to the fact that, by observing what had happened to other wicked men, one could see that Job's reaping was only normal, and something to be expected, or so Eliphaz presumed!

6. (Vs. 8) Eliphaz is claiming that Job is reaping what he has sowed. He fails to

understand that many times problems come to those who have not *"plowed iniquity"* or *"sown wickedness"* (II Cor. 11:23-27).

7. (Vs. 11) Eliphaz is referring to Job as an *"old lion,"* who is about done in; in fact, Job is 70 years old at the time, and will live to be 210. So, whatever now seems to be the case is not the case; in fact, every Believer should take a lesson from this.

THE ERRONEOUS DOCTRINE OF ELIPHAZ

Eliphaz was very much like our Word of Faith friends. If trouble came, it was because the individual had done something wrong, it may have been in secret, still, God saw it, and now the punishment has come.

With Eliphaz, the answer to this so-called great perplexity is really very simple. Job is a secret sinner, or so he presumes! Everyone knows, *"Whoever perished being innocent? Or where were the righteous cut off?"* The fact that Job is suffering this terrible calamity, or so Eliphaz claims, proves that Job is a secret sinner. In other words, while Job may have helped the poor, helped the needy, strengthened the feeble knees, etc., still, it was all for show. There was nothing sincere about it, it was done in order to hide what he really was.

It is only evil-doings, according to Eliphaz, which brings down calamities upon men and that, therefore, where calamities fall, there must be precedent wickedness.

One would think that Eliphaz, who evidently was aged of years, would have seen by his own observation that good and evil, prosperity and adversity, are not necessarily distributed in this life according to moral desert. So it is argued that when affliction seems to fall on a good man, the truth is, his goodness is not real goodness. It is rather a counterfeit, a sham — the fabric of moral excellence, so fair to view, but yet is honeycombed by secret vices.

Of course, if the afflictions were abnormal, extraordinary, then the secret sins must be a most heinous and horrible kind to deserve such a terrible retribution. This is what Eliphaz hints to be the solution of Job's case. God has seen his secret sins, and is now punishing them openly. Consequently, Job

NOTES

should humble himself before God, confess his many sins, and then repent. Then, and then only, may he hope that God will remove his Hand, and put an end to his sufferings.

Some friend!

THE ACCOUNT OF JOB

One would think, would you not, that the modern church has surely learned some things from reading this great Book of Job. Regrettably, that doesn't seem to be the case.

If one has been on the biting end of the self-righteous, then one can somewhat understand Job's feelings, at this terrible time of his life. Regrettably, he would not get any comfort from his *"friends."*

As if Job's sufferings aren't enough, his friends will heap upon him accusations that will only tend to deepen his misery. At a time of this nature, one longs to hear a kind word! If one is forthcoming, it is treasured, to be sure, as the Goodness of God.

As we go down through this great Book of Job, we will see the results of self-righteousness. Job was in terrible straits, and his friends had not been touched, at least not with adversity. So they felt perfectly comfortable in passing judgment on the great Patriarch. Unfortunately, their kind have not ceased on the Earth!

It's not a pleasant thing to be called a hypocrite, to be labeled as false, to be ridiculed. And if someone does venture to say a kind word about you, they are quickly silenced! But Job it seems didn't have anyone to say anything kind about him.

(12) "NOW A THING WAS SECRETLY BROUGHT TO ME, AND MY EAR RECEIVED A LITTLE THEREOF.

(13) "IN THOUGHTS FROM THE VISIONS OF THE NIGHT, WHEN DEEP SLEEP FALLS ON MEN,

(14) "FEAR CAME UPON ME, AND TREMBLING, WHICH MADE ALL MY BONES TO SHAKE.

(15) "THEN A SPIRIT PASSED BEFORE MY FACE; THE HAIR OF MY FLESH STOOD UP:

(16) "IT STOOD STILL, BUT I COULD NOT DISCERN THE FORM THEREOF: AN IMAGE WAS BEFORE MY EYES, THERE WAS SILENCE, AND I HEARD A

VOICE, SAYING,

(17) "SHALL MORTAL MAN BE MORE JUST THAN GOD? SHALL A MAN BE MORE PURE THAN HIS MAKER?

(18) "BEHOLD, HE PUT NO TRUST IN HIS SERVANTS; AND HIS ANGELS HE CHARGED WITH FOLLY:

(19) "HOW MUCH LESS IN THEM WHO DWELL IN HOUSES OF CLAY, WHOSE FOUNDATION IS IN THE DUST, WHICH ARE CRUSHED BEFORE THE MOTH?

(20) "THEY ARE DESTROYED FROM MORNING TO EVENING: THEY PERISH FOREVER WITHOUT ANY REGARDING IT.

(21) "DOES NOT THEIR EXCELLENCY WHICH IS IN THEM GO AWAY? THEY DIE, EVEN WITHOUT WISDOM."

The diagram is:

1. (Vs. 12) Eliphaz will now relate a personal experience, a vision he claims to have had.

2. (Vs. 17) Was this vision that Eliphaz had from the Lord, or from an evil spirit? The Fifteenth Verse says that it was *"a spirit,"* which means that it was not of God. To be sure, Satan and his spirits at times tell the truth, but only to make a big lie bigger. And that's what is happening here.

3. (Vs. 21) As we shall see at the end of this Book, the direction of all of Job's friends is totally wrong. While they may say some right things, their right things basically come from human wisdom, and not from a true knowledge of God.

A VISION

There is one thing that the Believer must learn, all things from the supernatural aren't from God. Eliphaz was claiming that this vision he had, was from God and that it gave him the right to make his claims. So, somewhat because of this so-called vision he claims a oneness with God that Job evidently doesn't have, at least in the thinking of Eliphaz.

Unfortunately, Believers even presently, are swayed by that which is claimed to be of God in the form of visions, etc. While it is true that the Lord definitely at times gives visions, and for purpose, the Believer must ever understand, that all things in the spirit world aren't from God.

NOTES

Paul addressed this for modern Christians by saying:

"For such are false apostles, deceitful workers (they have no rightful claim to the Apostolic Office; they are deceivers), *transforming themselves into the Apostles of Christ.* (They have called themselves to this Office.)

"And no marvel (true Believers should not be surprised)*; for Satan himself is transformed into an Angel of light.* (This means he pretends to be that which he is not.)

"Therefore it is no great thing if his ministers (Satan's ministers) *also be transformed as the ministers of righteousness* (despite their claims, they were 'Satan's ministers' because they preached something other than the Cross [I Cor. 1:17-18, 21, 23; 2:2; Gal. 1:8-9])*; whose end shall be according to their works* (that 'end' is spiritual destruction [Phil. 3:18-19])" (II Cor. 11:13-15).

THE WORD OF GOD IS TO BE THE CRITERIA

Everything is to be measured by the Word. Is it Scriptural? If it's not Scriptural, then it's not of God. Whenever a Preacher claims to have had a revelation from the Lord, but then will say, *"But you won't find it in the Bible,"* that's a sure sign that what he has is not from God. It may have been a revelation or a vision, but it was not from the Lord.

Concerning all things, Jesus said: *"Man shall not live by bread alone, but by every Word that proceeds out of the Mouth of God"* (Mat. 4:4).

But Job didn't have the Word of God, at least to the capacity that we now lay claim. He had only that which had been given to Abraham, and had been passed down to his great-grandfather Isaac, and then to his grandfather Jacob, and then to his father Issachar, and then to him. The Lord had told Abraham, and I quote from THE EXPOSITOR'S STUDY BIBLE:

"Now the LORD had said unto Abram (referring to the Revelation, which had been given to the Patriarch a short time before; this Chapter is very important, for it records the first steps of this great Believer in the path of Faith)*, Get thee out of your country* (separation)*, and from your kindred*

(separation), *and from your father's house* (separation), *unto a land that I will show you* (refers to the fact that Abraham had no choice in the matter; he was to receive his orders from the Lord, and go where those orders led him)*:*

"And I will make of you a great Nation (the Nation, which God made of Abraham has changed the world, and exists even unto this hour; in fact, this Nation *'Israel'* still has a great part to play, which will take place in the coming Kingdom Age)*, and I will bless you, and make your name great* (according to Scripture, *'to bless'* means *'to increase'*; the builders of the Tower of Babel sought to *'make us a name,'* whereas God took this man, who forsook all, and *'made his name great'*)*; and you shall be a blessing:* (Concerns itself with the greatest blessing of all. It is the glory of Abraham's Faith. God would give this man the meaning of Salvation, which is *'Justification by Faith,'* which would come about through the Lord Jesus Christ, and what Christ would do on the Cross. Concerning this, Jesus said to Abraham, *'Your father Abraham rejoiced to see My day: and he saw it, and was glad'"* [Jn. 8:56]).

"And I will bless them who bless you (to bless Israel, or any Believer, for that matter, guarantees the Blessings of God)*, and curse him who curses you* (to curse Israel, or any Believer, guarantees that one will be cursed by God)*: and in you shall all families of the Earth be blessed.* (It speaks of Israel, which sprang from the loins of Abraham and the womb of Sarah, giving the world the Word of God, and, more particularly, bringing the Messiah into the world. Through Christ, every family in the world who desires blessing from God can have that Blessing, i.e., *'Justification by Faith'*)*"* (Gen. 12:1-3).

Evidently, Eliphaz was not aware of this great Promise given to Abraham, the great-great-grandfather of Job. Or else it had been revealed to him by Job and, if so, he evidently little believed what he heard. Had he believed it, he would not have cursed Job, but would have blessed him.

This, of which I have given, is the only Word of God that Job had. But, if inspected closely, it is quite a Word. It is as follows:

• The Lord had given a great Revelation to Abraham.

• He had, in essence, promised Abraham a great land, which his offspring would ultimately occupy.

• He would make of Abraham a great nation, of which Job was a part.

• He would bless Abraham, and all who followed him, and make his name great.

• Abraham and all who followed him, which included Job, would be a great blessing to the entirety of the world.

• These people, who would come from the loins of Abraham and the womb of Sarah, would be so loved of the Lord, that God would bless all who bless them.

• At the same time, those who would try to do harm to these whom God had raised up, would be cursed by God.

• Through Abraham, all the families of the Earth would be blessed, which spoke of the coming Redeemer, in essence, God becoming Man, Who would atone for all sin by going to the Cross.

I am certain that Job cherished this great Word, and did so constantly. In fact, he, no doubt, attributed the great Blessings which God had bestowed upon him to this Promise. We do know, as well, from some of the things that Job will say in this Book, that he understood that through Abraham, a Redeemer was coming.

But, Job doesn't see his present plight in these great Promises of God. Yet, it is connected, which he will ultimately see.

He will find out that good men can at times be greatly afflicted, and through no fault of their own, all for their Sanctification. It would not be a lesson easily learned, but it would be a lesson most definitely learned, at least by the great Patriarch. God help us to learn it as well!

No, what Eliphaz saw as it regards his vision, was not from God. In fact, the Fifteenth Verse, as stated, says through his own mouth, that it was a *"spirit which passed before my face."* This means that it was an evil spirit, even though Eliphaz did not realize such.

"O Christ, what burdens bowed Your Head!
"Our load was laid on Thee;

"You stood in the sinner's stead,
"Did bear all ill for me.
"A Victim led, Your Blood was shed;
"Now there's no load for me."

"Death and the curse were in our cup,
"O Christ, 'twas full of Thee!
"But You have drained the last dark
    drop,
"'Tis empty now for me.
"That bitter cup — love drank it up;
"Now Blessings draught for me."

"Jehovah lifted up His Rod,
"O Christ, it fell on Thee!
"You were sore stricken of Your God;
"There's not one stroke for me.
"Your Tears, Your Blood, beneath it
    flowed;
"Your bruising heals me."

"The tempest's awful voice was heard,
"O Christ, it broke on Thee!
"Your open Bosom was my ward,
"It braved the storm for me.
"Your Form was scarred, Your Visage
    marred;
"Now cloudless peace for me."

"Jehovah bade His Sword awake,
"O Christ, it woke against Thee!
"Your Blood the flaming blade must
    slake;
"Your Heart its sheath must be,
"All for my sake, my peace to make;
"Now sleeps that sword for me."

"For me, Lord Jesus, You have died,
"And I have died in Thee;
"You are risen: my bands are all
    untied,
"And now You live in me.
"When purified, made white, and tried,
"Your Glory then for me!"

CHAPTER 5

(1) "CALL NOW, IF THERE BE ANY WHO WILL ANSWER YOU; AND TO WHICH OF THE SAINTS WILL YOU TURN?

(2) "FOR WRATH KILLS THE FOOLISH MAN, AND ENVY SLAYS THE SILLY ONE.

(3) "I HAVE SEEN THE FOOLISH TAKING ROOT: BUT SUDDENLY I CURSED HIS HABITATION.

(4) "HIS CHILDREN ARE FAR FROM SAFETY, AND THEY ARE CRUSHED IN THE GATE, NEITHER IS THERE ANY TO DELIVER THEM.

(5) "WHOSE HARVEST THE HUNGRY EATS UP, AND TAKES IT EVEN OUT OF THE THORNS, AND THE ROBBER SWALLOWS UP THEIR SUBSTANCE.

(6) "ALTHOUGH AFFLICTION COMES NOT FORTH OF THE DUST, NEITHER DOES TROUBLE SPRING OUT OF THE GROUND;

(7) "YET MAN IS BORN UNTO TROUBLE, AS THE SPARKS FLY UPWARD."

The diagram is:

1. (Vs. 1) Certain ones in Roman Catholicism have tried to use Verse One to authorize prayers to the Saints. The argument, however, of this Verse is to show the uselessness of such prayer.

2. (Vs. 1) Eliphaz' argument will now become more pointed, more direct, more cutting. He will now pour sarcasm upon Job. He is taunting Job, claiming that it's not even possible for Job to get his prayers answered. In other words, Job has sinned so terribly, he says, that God will not even hear him any longer.

3. (Vs. 1) As well, there is not another Believer (Saint) to whom he can turn. All the Saints, according to Eliphaz, know of Job's hypocrisy.

4. (Vs. 2) Job is foolish and silly, according to Eliphaz, if he thinks that anyone will hear him now!

5. (Vs. 4) Inasmuch as Job's ten children were instantly killed, in effect, Eliphaz is saying that Job is to blame. To judge what seems to be obvious is, most of the time, wrong, just as here.

6. (Vs. 6) Eliphaz is saying that Job is in the condition he's in simply because he has been secretly wicked.

THE SAINTS

It is claimed by some expositors that Eliphaz when using the word *"Saints,"* is speaking of Angels; however, from the accompanying Texts such is doubtful. But irrespective as to whether he was speaking of Angels or fellow Believers, still, the end result was the same. There was no one, absolutely no one, as far as Believers of that day was concerned, who stood up for Job. All automatically jumped to conclusions. As far as we know, not a single soul encouraged him, not one said a kind word.

Job had been known for his philanthropy, his helping the poor, the downtrodden, the unfortunate, but none of these came forward.

In effect, Eliphaz was saying to Job, no one is going to say a kind word to you, or help you in any way, because they know that you are a hypocrite, a secret sinner, etc.

Job had to undergo the insults of his *"friends,"* had to look in vain for help from anyone, which blow was probably as bad as the loss that he had suffered.

There is a particular Church Denomination with which I am acquainted, that if one of their Preachers has a problem, it is their policy to always speak to him, that is if they do so at all, in biting, bitter terms. In other words, they are not to evidence one word of kindness of any nature.

Now I don't mean that's the attitude of one or two in their ranks, I mean that is their Church policy, unwritten, but nevertheless adhered to strictly. Job knew how that felt.

What we're seeing here, both in the ancient and the modern is self-righteousness, one of the ugliest sins that could ever capture anyone. While no one is to ever condone sin, still, biting vituperation has never helped anyone.

If a Christian has, in fact, sinned and if he shows any inclination at all toward making things right with the Lord, he should be given every aid possible. All must remember that there are no perfect ones among us. While we may not be guilty of the same sin committed by the individual in question, whomever that might be, still, in the Eyes of God, sin is sin. While there certainly are some sins worse than others, all sin, no matter how small it may seem to be in our eyes, is enough in the eyes of God to cause a person to be eternally lost. So, that means that all of us exist because of the Mercy and the Grace of God. It is certainly not because of any perfection on our part.

We must remember how much the Lord has forgiven us, how much He has helped us, how much He has not dealt with us after our sins, for if He did, none of us would be alive. Consequently, we should keep these things in mind when dealing with others.

While in some cases, and due to rebellion on the part of the particular individual, fellowship may have to be withdrawn; however, if that is the case, it is not to be done with bitterness or unkindness, but always with a hope that the erring individual will see his erroneous ways, and make things right with God. In other words, we are not to be a stumbling stone for the person, but rather a help, at least as it lies within our power.

THE FAMILY CURSE

Eliphaz insinuates that Job's children were killed because of his sins. He said, *"His children are far from safety, and they are crushed in the gate, and neither is there any to deliver them."* He is meaning that the sins of the fathers are visited upon the children.

How this must have cut Job! How it must have hurt!

In the first place, such thinking is totally unscriptural. The Scripture says in regard to this:

"The Word of the LORD came unto me again, saying,

"What do you mean, that you use this Proverb concerning the land of Israel, saying, The fathers have eaten sour grapes, and the children's teeth are set on edge? (The miseries suffered by the people in Jerusalem because of the Babylonian war were declared by them to be due to their father's sins, for they themselves were righteous, so they claimed. Hence, their Proverb of Verse 2, repeated in Verse 19, was insisted upon in Verses 25 and 29. That is, they charged God with injustice, for man always throws the blame upon God, as did Adam [Gen. 3:12; Ex. 20:5]).

"As I live, says the Lord GOD, you shall not have occasion anymore to use this Proverb in Israel. (Actually, this Proverb declared, even in a roundabout way, that there was unrighteousness with God. They were taking a Proverb which had a measure of truth

in it and distorting it into a falsehood.)

"Behold, all souls are Mine; as the soul of the father, so also the soul of the son is Mine: the soul that sins, it shall die. (Emphatically, the Lord through the Prophet declares that these people are suffering for their own sins, not the sins of their fathers. *'The soul that sins, it shall die,'* proclaims the truth that God judges each person upon his own actions, not upon the actions of others)" (Ezek. 18:1-4).

The Prophet further says, as it regards a wicked father and his son, if the son serves God, *"he shall not die for the iniquity of his father, he shall surely live"* (Ezek. 18:17).

This places the responsibility upon the individual involved. The father is not responsible, spiritually speaking, for the sins of his son, as the son is not responsible for the sins of the father. Each person, in the Eyes of God, is responsible for his own sins.

IS THERE SUCH A THING AS A FAMILY CURSE?

Yes, there is!

In the giving of the Ten Commandments to Moses and to Israel, the Lord said, *"You shall not bow down yourself to them* (to idols), *nor serve them: for I the LORD your God am a jealous God, visiting the iniquity of the fathers upon the children unto the third and fourth generation of them who hate me"* (Ex. 20:5).

However, it must be quickly understood, that the moment a person gives their heart and life to Christ, the family curse, if there is one, and all other curses for that matter, are immediately broken and lifted. Paul said, *"Christ has redeemed us from the curse of the Law* (He did so on the Cross), *being made a curse for us* (He took the penalty of the Law, which was death): *for it is written, Cursed is everyone who hangs on a tree* (Deut. 21:23):

"That the Blessing of Abraham (Justification by Faith) *might come on the Gentiles through Jesus Christ* (what He did at the Cross); *that we might receive the Promise of the Spirit through Faith.* (All sin was atoned at the Cross, which lifted the sin debt from believing man, making it possible for the Holy Spirit to come into the life of the Believer and abide there forever)" (Gal. 3:13-14).

Considering what was done at the Cross, and considering that these benefits will last forever, Paul also said: *"Therefore if any man be in Christ* (Saved by the Blood), *he is a new creature* (a new creation): *old things are passed away* (what we were before Salvation); *behold, all things are become new.* (The old is no longer usable, with everything given to us now by Christ as *'new.'*)

"And all things are of God (all these new things), *Who has reconciled us to Himself by Jesus Christ* (which He was able to do as a result of the Cross), *and has given to us the Ministry of Reconciliation* (pertains to announcing to men the nature and conditions of this Plan of being reconciled, which is summed up in the *'preaching of the Cross'* [I Cor. 1:21, 23])" (II Cor. 5:17-18).

Even under the Law, the Lord added immediately after Exodus 20:5, *"And showing mercy unto thousands of them who love Me, and keep My Commandments"* (Ex. 20:6).

For a preacher or anyone for that matter, to claim that a Believer still has a curse hanging over him because of something their great-great grandfather did years ago, presents an insult to Christ of unprecedented proportions. It says that what He did at the Cross was not a Finished Work, was not valid, was not able to set the captive free, was not able to break this curse, etc. I hope the reader can see and understand how wicked that such a position actually is.

No, these preachers who are telling Christians that the reason for their problem, whatever it might be, is because there is a family curse on them, and that they have to go to a preacher who knows about these things, who will lay hands on them and rebuke the curse, and then they will be free.

As stated, there's absolutely nothing like that in the Bible. While it is true that people in an unsaved state have all kinds of curses upon themselves, the truth is, the moment that person comes to Christ, whoever that person might be, and whatever has happened in the past, it is all instantly washed away and changed by the Power of God. Paul also said:

"Do you not know that the unrighteous shall not inherit the Kingdom of God? (This

shoots down the unscriptural doctrine of Unconditional Eternal Security.) *Be not deceived* (presents the same Words of our Lord, *'let no man deceive you'* [Mk. 13:5]): *neither fornicators, nor idolaters, nor adulterers, nor effeminate, nor abusers of themselves with mankind* (the proof of true Christianity is the changed life),

"Nor thieves, nor covetous, nor drunkards, nor revilers, nor extortioners, shall inherit the Kingdom of God (refers to those who call themselves *'Believers,'* but yet continue to practice the sins mentioned, whom the Holy Spirit says are not Saved, irrespective of their claims).

"And such were some of you (before conversion)*: but you are washed* (refers to the Blood of Jesus cleansing from all sin), *but you are sanctified* (one's position in Christ), *but you are justified* (declared not guilty) *in the Name of the Lord Jesus* (refers to Christ and what He did at the Cross, in order that we might be Saved), *and by the Spirit of our God* (proclaims the Third Person of the Triune Godhead as the Mechanic in this great Work of Grace)" (I Cor. 6:9-11).

SO WHAT IS THE SOLUTION TO OUR PROBLEMS?

While it is definitely true that many Believers are having problems, and of every description. While nothing can be done to eliminate all problems for all time, because the Bible does not promise such, still, many, if not most, Christians are suffering problems they simply don't have to suffer.

Many problems in the life of the Believer are caused by the Believer not understanding how to live for God. I realize that's quite a statement, but it is true.

Of course, most every Believer would claim, and loudly, that they most definitely do know how to live for God. But the truth is they don't!

When the Believer places his or her faith in something other than the Cross of Christ, Satan to be sure, will take full advantage of such a position, and cause such a Believer untold problems. Considering that the modern church knows virtually nothing about the Cross of Christ as it regards our Sanctification, i.e. our everyday living for God, this means that they have opened themselves up for all type of difficulties.

Jesus said, *"You shall know the Truth and the Truth shall make you free"* (Jn. 8:32).

WHAT IS THE TRUTH?

In simple terms, the Truth is, *"Jesus Christ and Him Crucified."* Paul also said concerning this:

"But we preach Christ Crucified (this is the Foundation of the Word of God and, thereby, of Salvation), *unto the Jews a stumblingblock* (the Cross was the stumblingblock), *and unto the Greeks foolishness* (both found it difficult to accept as God a dead Man hanging on a Cross, for such Christ was to them)" (I Cor. 1:23).

Jesus Christ is the Source of all things that we receive from God, and the Cross is the Means by which these things are received, all superintended by the Holy Spirit (Rom. 8:1-2, 11).

So, the Believer doesn't need some preacher to rebuke a family curse over them, but rather simply needs to know the Truth of the Gospel, which is the Cross of Christ, and which we have given here in simple terms.

HOW IS THE CROSS OF CHRIST THE ANSWER TO OUR DIFFICULTIES?

It was at the Cross where Jesus atoned for all sin, thereby, removing the legal right that Satan had to hold man captive. That's what Paul was talking about when he said, *"When He ascended up on high* (the Ascension), *He led captivity captive* (liberated the souls in Paradise; before the Cross, despite being Believers, they were still held captive by Satan because the blood of bulls and goats could not take away the sin debt; but when Jesus died on the Cross, the sin debt was paid, and now He makes all these His Captives), *and gave Gifts unto men.* (These *'Gifts'* include all the Attributes of Christ, all made possible by the Cross.)

"(Now that He ascended (mission completed), *what is it but that He also descended first into the lower parts of the earth?* (Immediately before His Ascension to Glory, which would be done in total triumph, He first went down into Paradise, as stated, to deliver all the believing souls in

"*He Who descended is the same also Who ascended* (this is a portrayal of Jesus as Deliverer and Mediator) *up far above all Heavens* (presents His present location, never again having to descend into the nether world), *that He might fill all things.*) (He has always been the Creator, but now He is also the Saviour)" (Eph. 4:8-10).

The short phrase, *"He led captivity captive,"* is somewhat strange. But as we've already stated, it simply means that every single Believer before the Cross, when they died, went down into Paradise, which Jesus referred to as *"Abraham's Bosom"* (Lk. 16:22).

They could not then be taken to Heaven, simply because the blood of bulls and goats could not lift the sin debt. To be sure, these people were Saved, and Saved exactly as we are today by Faith, but it was all predicated on Jesus going to the Cross. But when He went to the Cross, thereby, atoning for all sin, then He could legally remove all of these people from Paradise and take them with Him to Heaven. Now, when Believers die, they instantly, in their soul and spirit form, go to be with the Lord Jesus Christ (Phil. 1:23).

THE CROSS OF CHRIST WAS AND IS A LEGAL WORK

It is so much so that it is actually referred to by the Holy Spirit as a *"Law."* Paul said:

"For the Law of the Spirit of life in Christ Jesus . . ." (Rom. 8:2).

When we mention Law in this fashion, we are referring to Laws which the Godhead has derived in eternity past. Satan hasn't made any laws, nor have any of his fallen Angels. It is God Who devises the Laws, and we speak of the Laws, which govern this Universe in every capacity. Sin is the breaking of the Law of God against that dread malady. It is referred to as *"the Law of Sin and Death"* (Rom. 8:2). The only Law that will answer the Law of Sin and Death is, as stated, *"The Law of the Spirit of Life in Christ Jesus,"* which, in effect, is *"The Law of the Atonement,"* which Jesus carried out at the Cross. So, His Work on the Cross was a legal Work. Man had broken the Law of God, so God became Man, in what we refer to as the Incarnation, and went to the Cross, which paid the price demanded by the Law of Sin and Death, actually and, as stated, a Law devised by God.

All of this was affected at the Cross. This is where the price was paid, this was where the Law of sin and death was addressed, which satisfied the Righteousness and the Nature of a thrice-Holy God. That's the reason that Paul preached the Cross, taught the Cross, held up the Cross as the answer to man's dilemma, etc. (Rom. 6:1-14; 8:1-2, 11; I Cor. 1:17-18, 21, 23; 2:2; Gal. 2:20-21; Gal., Chpt. 5; 6:14; Eph. 2:13-18; Col. 2:14-15; Gen. 3:15; 15:6; Ex. 12:13). To be frank, the entirety of the Bible, all the way from Gen. 1:1 through Rev. 22:21, presents the Story of Jesus Christ and Him Crucified. One might say that the entirety of the story of the Bible is the Story of Christ and Him Crucified, i.e., *"man's Redemption."*

Remove the Cross from Christianity, and you have nothing left but a vapid philosophy. Regrettably, the church has almost succeeded in doing just that, removing the Cross completely from our thinking, our theology, in effect, our interpretation of the Bible. To be frank, the Bible itself is being shoved aside in favor of man's pathetic thoughts. How stupid can we be!

Until the preacher comes to the place where he understands that the Cross of Christ is not only an absolute necessity for Salvation, but as well, for Sanctification, we cannot be truly said to be preaching the Cross. Let me say it again:

Jesus Christ is the Source of all things that we receive from God, while the Cross is the Means by which those things are received, all superintended by the Holy Spirit (Rev. 5:6).

(8) "I WOULD SEEK UNTO GOD, AND UNTO GOD WOULD I COMMIT MY CAUSE:

(9) "WHICH DOES GREAT THINGS AND UNSEARCHABLE; MARVELLOUS THINGS WITHOUT NUMBER:

(10) "WHO GIVES RAIN UPON THE EARTH, AND SENDS WATERS UPON THE FIELDS:

(11) "TO SET UP ON HIGH THOSE THAT BE LOW; THAT THOSE WHICH MOURN MAY BE EXALTED TO SAFETY.

(12) "HE DISAPPOINTS THE DEVICES OF THE CRAFTY, SO THAT THEIR HANDS CANNOT PERFORM THEIR ENTERPRISE.

(13) "HE TAKES THE WISE IN THEIR OWN CRAFTINESS: AND THE COUNSEL OF THE FROWARD IS CARRIED HEADLONG.

(14) "THEY MEET WITH DARKNESS IN THE DAYTIME, AND GROPE IN THE NOONDAY AS IN THE NIGHT.

(15) "BUT HE SAVES THE POOR FROM THE SWORD, FROM THEIR MOUTH, AND FROM THE HAND OF THE MIGHTY.

(16) "SO THE POOR HAS HOPE, AND INIQUITY STOPS HER MOUTH.

(17) "BEHOLD, HAPPY IS THE MAN WHOM GOD CORRECTS: THEREFORE DESPISE NOT YOU THE CHASTENING OF THE ALMIGHTY:

(18) "FOR HE MAKES SORE, AND BINDS UP: HE WOUNDS, AND HIS HANDS MAKE WHOLE.

(19) "HE SHALL DELIVER YOU IN SIX TROUBLES: YES, IN SEVEN THERE SHALL NO EVIL TOUCH YOU.

(20) "IN FAMINE HE SHALL REDEEM YOU FROM DEATH: AND IN WAR FROM THE POWER OF THE SWORD.

(21) "YOU SHALL BE HID FROM THE SCOURGE OF THE TONGUE: NEITHER SHALL YOU BE AFRAID OF DESTRUCTION WHEN IT COMES.

(22) "AT DESTRUCTION AND FAMINE YOU SHALL LAUGH: NEITHER SHALL YOU BE AFRAID OF THE BEASTS OF THE EARTH.

(23) "FOR YOU SHALL BE IN LEAGUE WITH THE STONES OF THE FIELD: AND THE BEASTS OF THE FIELD SHALL BE AT PEACE WITH YOU.

(24) "AND YOU SHALL KNOW THAT YOUR TABERNACLE SHALL BE IN PEACE; AND YOU SHALL VISIT YOUR HABITATION, AND SHALL NOT SIN.

(25) "YOU SHALL KNOW ALSO THAT YOUR SEED SHALL BE GREAT, AND YOUR OFFSPRING AS THE GRASS OF THE EARTH.

(26) "YOU SHALL COME TO YOUR GRAVE IN A FULL AGE, LIKE AS A SHOCK OF CORN COMES IN IN HIS SEASON.

(27) "LO THIS, WE HAVE SEARCHED IT, SO IT IS; HEAR IT, AND KNOW YOU IT FOR YOUR GOOD."

The diagram is:

1. The Eighth Verse, in essence, says that Job should confess to God what he really is.

2. (Vs. 12) Job is judged by Eliphaz to be *"crafty,"* but God, so says Eliphaz, sees through Job's craftiness.

3. (Vs. 16) According to Eliphaz, Job's mouth has now been stopped, and the *"poor"* can rest in ease. The truth is, Job has been a great benefactor to the poor.

4. (Vs. 17) Eliphaz claims that Job is under the chastising Hand of God. However, the Lord is not really correcting Job, at least not as Eliphaz thinks.

5. In Verse 19, the idea is expressed by Eliphaz that if one is walking in righteousness that *"no evil will touch you."* So, Job is judged to be unrighteous!

6. (Vs. 21) Since many people are now speaking evil of Job, this means that Job must be wicked.

7. (Vs. 24) It is obvious that Job now has no peace, so that means he, according to Eliphaz, has sinned. However, the Lord has said differently (1:10, 22).

8. (Vs. 25) Eliphaz reasons that inasmuch as Job's ten children were killed, this only furnishes more proof of Job's wickedness, according to Eliphaz.

9. (Vs. 27) Eliphaz in concluding this part of his discourse, claims that his word is law and gospel; the Truth is, it is anything but.

THE EDIFICATION OF THE BELIEVER

Everything that these men will say to Job is wrong, with actually the Lord clarifying such (Job 42:7). So, why did the Holy Spirit think it desirable to record all of the things these men said?

He did so in order that we might see how deficient that human reasoning is. Furthermore, all of these discourses given by these men were, in effect, from the wisest of the wise, at least as far as the world's wisdom is concerned. This shows us, as well, how deficient this is.

The Holy Spirit through Paul deals with this question as well. The great Apostle said:

"For it is written (Isa. 29:14), *I will destroy the wisdom of the wise, and will bring to nothing the understanding of the*

prudent (speaks to those who are wise in their own eyes, in effect, having forsaken the Ways of the Lord).

"*Where is the wise?* (This presents the first of three classes of learned people who lived in that day.) *where is the Scribe?* (This pertained to the Jewish Theologians of that day.) *where is the disputer of this world?* (This speaks of the Greeks, who were seekers of mystical and metaphysical interpretations.) *has not God made foolish the wisdom of this world?* (This pertains to what God did in sending His Son to redeem humanity, which He did by the Cross. All the wisdom of the world couldn't do this!)

"*For after that in the Wisdom of God the world by wisdom knew not God* (man's puny wisdom, even the best he has to offer, cannot come to know God in any manner), *it pleased God by the foolishness of preaching* (preaching the Cross) *to save them who believe.* (Paul is not dealing with the art of preaching here, but with what is preached.)

"*For the Jews require a sign* (the sign of the Messiah taking the Throne and making Israel a great Nation once again), *and the Greeks seek after wisdom* (they thought that such solved the human problem; however, if it did, why were they ever seeking after more wisdom?):

"*But we preach Christ Crucified* (this is the Foundation of the Word of God and, thereby, of Salvation), *unto the Jews a stumblingblock* (the Cross was the stumblingblock), *and unto the Greeks foolishness* (both found it difficult to accept as God a dead Man hanging on a Cross, for such Christ was to them);

"*But unto them who are called* (refers to those who accept the Call, for the entirety of mankind is invited [Jn. 3:16; Rev. 22:17], *both Jews and Greeks* (actually stands for both '*Jews and Gentiles*'), *Christ the Power of God* (what He did at the Cross atoned for all sin, thereby, making it possible for the Holy Spirit to exhibit His Power within our lives), *and the Wisdom of God.* (This Wisdom devised a Plan of Salvation, which pardoned guilty men and at the same time vindicated and glorified the Justice of God, which stands out as the wisest and most remarkable Plan of all time.)

NOTES

"*Because the foolishness of God is wiser than men* (God achieves the mightiest ends by the humblest means); *and the weakness of God is stronger than men* (refers to that which men take to be weak, but actually is not — the Cross).

"*For you see your calling, brethren* (refers to the nature and method of their Heavenly Calling), *how that not many wise men after the flesh, not many mighty, not many noble, are Called* (are Called and accept):

"*But God has chosen the foolish things of the world to confound the wise* (the preaching of the Cross confounds the wise because it falls out to changed lives, which nothing man has can do); *and God has chosen the weak things of the world to confound the things which are mighty* (the Cross is looked at as weakness, but it brings about great strength and power, regarding those who accept the Finished Work of Christ);

"*And base things of the world, and things which are despised, has God chosen* (it is God working in the base things and the despised things which brings about miraculous things), *yes, and things which are not, to bring to naught things that are* (God can use that which is nothing within itself, but with Him all things become possible):

"*That no flesh* (human effort) *should glory in His Presence.*

"*But of Him are you in Christ Jesus* (pertains to this great Plan of God, which is far beyond all wisdom of the world; we are '*in Christ Jesus,*' by virtue of the Cross — what He did there), *Who of God is made unto us Wisdom, and Righteousness, and Sanctification, and Redemption* (we have all of this by the Holy Spirit, through Christ and what He did at the Cross; this means the Cross must ever be the Object of our Faith):

"*That, according as it is written* (Jer. 9:23), *He who glories, let him glory in the Lord.* (He who boasts, let him boast in the Lord, and not in particular preachers)" (I Cor. 1:19-31).

THE CROSS OF CHRIST

If it is to be noticed, the Apostle Paul points Believers away from the wisdom of this world, to the Lord Jesus Christ, and more specifically, to "*Christ and Him Crucified,*" which opens up the Ways of God to believing man. The idea is this:

• As it regards life and living, the world has no wisdom that can make any contribution toward this all important task.

• Everything we must have for life and living comes from the Lord (II Pet. 1:3-4).

• More specifically, it comes to us from the Lord by the means of the Cross. This means, that the Believer cannot fully understand the Lord or His Word outside of the Cross (I Cor. 1:17-18; 2:2). The understanding that believing man has of the Lord, which means to understand His Word, can only come by the means of the Cross. We must never forget that.

• The maturity of the Believer is predicated solely on the Believer's understanding of the Cross. Little understanding, little maturity! Much understanding, much maturity!

• The answer for everything in life and living is found in the Cross of Christ and the Cross of Christ alone. That being the case, I think it would be prudent of the Believer to avail himself of every opportunity to understand the Finished Work of Christ to a greater degree.

All of this means that all of the pontificating of Job's three friends was to no avail as it regards help. In fact, most everything they said fell out to the hurt of Job, most definitely, not to his help. The Holy Spirit, as we have previously stated, desired that all of this be recorded, and that we would read it and see the absolute helplessness of man in his own wisdom. And we must remember, these individuals were some of the wisest men of their day, at least according to the standard of the world. But yet, they held no help for Job whatsoever, and neither can the modern variety.

Regrettably and sadly, the modern church is leaving the Ways of the Lord, rather opting for the ways of the world. Instead of the wisdom, which is from above, they have opted for the wisdom of this world, which is *"earthly, sensual, devilish"* (James 3:15). What a sad trade!

This is at least one of the reasons that this great Book of Job is so very important. It shows man's ways, even his best ways, his most educated ways, his most learned ways, up beside the Ways of God, which presents

NOTES

no contest. The Ways of the Lord are found in the Word of God, and the Word of God exclusively!

"When I survey the wondrous Cross
"On which the Prince of Glory died,
"My richest gain I count but loss,
"And pour contempt on all my pride."

"Forbid it, Lord, that I should boast,
"Save in the Cross of Christ my God:
"All the vain things that charm me most,
"I sacrifice them to His Blood."

"See from His Head, His Hands, His Feet,
"Sorrow and love flow mingled down;
"Did e'er such love and sorrow meet,
"Or thorns compose so rich a crown?"

"His dying crimson, like a robe,
"Spreads o'er His body on the tree;
"Then am I dead to all the globe,
"And all the globe is dead to me."

"Were the whole realm of nature mine,
"That were a present far too small;
"Love so amazing, so Divine,
"Demands my soul, my life, my all."

CHAPTER 6

(1) "BUT JOB ANSWERED AND SAID,

(2) "OH THAT MY GRIEF WERE THOROUGHLY WEIGHED, AND MY CALAMITY LAID IN THE BALANCES TOGETHER!

(3) "FOR NOW IT WOULD BE HEAVIER THAN THE SAND OF THE SEA: THEREFORE MY WORDS ARE SWALLOWED UP.

(4) "FOR THE ARROWS OF THE ALMIGHTY ARE WITHIN ME, THE POISON WHEREOF DRINKS UP MY SPIRIT: THE TERRORS OF GOD DO SET THEMSELVES IN ARRAY AGAINST ME.

(5) "DOES THE WILD ASS BRAY WHEN HE HAS GRASS? OR LOWES THE OX OVER HIS FODDER?

(6) "CAN THAT WHICH IS UNSAVOURY BE EATEN WITHOUT SALT? OR IS THERE ANY TASTE IN THE WHITE OF

AN EGG?

(7) "THE THINGS THAT MY SOUL REFUSED TO TOUCH ARE AS MY SORROWFUL MEAT.

(8) "OH THAT I MIGHT HAVE MY REQUEST; AND THAT GOD WOULD GRANT ME THE THING THAT I LONG FOR!

(9) "EVEN THAT IT WOULD PLEASE GOD TO DESTROY ME; THAT HE WOULD LET LOOSE HIS HAND, AND CUT ME OFF!

(10) "THEN SHOULD I YET HAVE COMFORT; YES, I WOULD HARDEN MYSELF IN SORROW: LET HIM NOT SPARE; FOR I HAVE NOT CONCEALED THE WORDS OF THE HOLY ONE.

(11) "WHAT IS MY STRENGTH, THAT I SHOULD HOPE? AND WHAT IS MY END, THAT I SHOULD PROLONG MY LIFE?

(12) "IS MY STRENGTH THE STRENGTH OF STONES? OR IS MY FLESH OF BRASS?

(13) "IS NOT MY HELP IN ME? AND IS WISDOM DRIVEN QUITE FROM ME?"

The exegesis is:

1. (Vs. 3) Job struggles to find words to express his sorrow. He has no understanding as to the reasons for these happenings in his life. And, at this time, God does not choose to reveal to him the cause or the reason. He will later.

2. (Vs. 3) It would seem to the unbeliever, or even to the carnal Christian, that the Almighty is unjust and cruel for allowing such to happen to Job. And make no mistake about it, God was the One Who allowed Satan to do these things.

3. (Vs. 3) The reasons were many. First of all, Job had to discover the worthlessness of self. Then, he had to discover the worthfulness of Christ. And that he would!

4. (Vs. 8) Many Believers are pressed to the point that they will request of God that which is not God's Will. Job wanted to die; that was his request. God would not answer this prayer. He had something far better for Job than death.

5. (Vs. 10) Job falls back on the Word of God. While none of it had yet been written as of this time (that began with Moses, who was probably then alive, and maybe even helped Job write this Book), still, all the great things of the Lord had been passed down from the very beginning by word of mouth, which could be repeated word-for-word and in detail.

6. (Vs. 12) *"There is only so much a human being can stand,"* is the thought of Job.

7. (Vs. 13) Job is at the end of his resources and, considering what the man has been through, it is no wonder! And yet, all of this is necessary in order to bring Job to the end of himself. Satan had one thing in mind, but God had entirely another. Through Job, and the terrible trial that he endured, we will learn God's Way, which is not man's way.

JOB'S REPLY TO ELIPHAZ

Some think that Job's trial lasted for approximately nine months to a year. It probably was not much longer than that.

In this trial and tremendous test of Faith, the Lord opens up the spirit world as never before; consequently, many questions are answered regarding God's control of the Universe and all therein. Some of the things learned are:

• We learn that Satan can only do what God allows him to do.

• We also learn that there is a hedge built about every Child of God.

• We learn, as well, that this hedge cannot be removed except under special circumstances, such as unconfessed sin, or by the Will of God, or by wicked self-will.

• In this scenario the Child of God learns *"trust,"* which is perhaps the greatest lesson of all.

• We also learn that God amply rewards the Believer for the suffering that has been enjoined.

THE LIMITS OF THE HUMAN SPIRIT

Job wants to die, and prays to do so, but thankfully, this is a prayer the Lord will not answer, and rightly so. Job had lost the following:

• His material possessions.
• His place and position in society.
• He had lost his health, and was at the point to die, or so he thought.
• He had lost his self-respect.
• He had lost his ten children, which was worse than all the loss of his material

possessions, etc.

- In a sense he came close to losing his Faith, even though he never blamed God.

- Due to the fact that he had tried his best to obey the Lord, and in all things, he had lost his confidence in himself. *"What had he done wrong?"* was the question that plagued his mind.

We learn from Job the limit of human endurance, where the person is left without recourse or hope. We will find that the Lord had far more in mind than this tryst with Satan. While that certainly entered into it, the Lord would teach a lesson not only to Job, but to all who would follow Him, including you and me. Perhaps this great lesson could be summed up in the following phrase:

THE WORTHLESSNESS OF SELF AND THE WORTHFULNESS OF CHRIST

As we've already stated, considering that the Book of Job is the First Book written as it regards the Canon of Scripture, and was probably written by Moses in collaboration with Job; and considering that the first subject taken up was the Sanctification of the Saint, we are made to learn just how important this subject actually is.

This is shown extensively in the writings of the Apostle Paul as well. Of the Fourteen Epistles the great Apostle wrote, over ninety percent of his teaching is given over to this subject of Sanctification. We must remember, that it was to Paul that the meaning of the New Covenant was given by our Lord (Gal. 1:12). Considering that the Holy Spirit delegated this much space in this man's Epistles to this subject of Sanctification, and taking Job into account, we should learn the significance of all of this.

What do we mean by the worthlessness of self?

As someone has well said, when Jesus died on the Cross, He did so to save us from sin and, as well, to save us from self.

Some years ago, reading the remarks by one English preacher on this very subject, his statements startled me. He said, *"The Child of God must repent not only of the bad that he has done, but, as well, the good."*

Repenting of the bad is understandable,

NOTES

but not so understandable regarding the good.

What did the preacher mean?

He was speaking of the good, whatever it might be, in which we Believers depend, which God cannot accept. So, we must repent of our dependence on these good things, whatever they might be. This certainly doesn't mean that we are to cease carrying out the good, but it does mean, our Faith must not be in that, but always in Christ and what Christ has done for us at the Cross.

GOD DOES NOT ADDRESS BELIEVERS FROM THE VIEWPOINT OF GOOD AND EVIL

Of course, and as should be understandable, the *"good"* is what we do and should continue to do, and the *"evil"* is what we should not do, which should be overly obvious. But, if God dealt with us on that basis, all of us would be lost.

He deals with us exclusively on the basis of our Faith, and I speak of our Faith being in Christ and what Christ has done for us at the Cross. That and that alone is the basis on which God judges us. That's the reason that He said to us through Paul: *"Examine yourselves, whether you be in the Faith* (the words, *'the Faith,'* refer to *'Christ and Him Crucified,'* with the Cross ever being the Object of our Faith); *prove your own selves.* (Make certain your Faith is actually in the Cross, and not other things.) *Know you not your own selves, how that Jesus Christ is in you* (which He can only be by our Faith expressed in His Sacrifice), *except you be reprobates?* (Rejected)" (II Cor. 13:5).

We may think of ourselves as being very holy, very righteous, etc. However, if the Lord judged us on the basis of good and evil, and remember, He cannot accept anything less than perfection, that being the case, we would be eternally lost. Because in the best of us, whomever that might be, there are things that portend toward evil, which necessitates our constant need of the Intercession of Christ (Heb. 7:25).

THE CROSS OF CHRIST, THE ONLY WAY TO VICTORY

Since the Lord in 1997 opened up to me the great Message of the Cross, and continues to do so unto this very hour, and I trust will ever continue to do so, the attitude of our detractors is most noticeable. It's very similar to that which was leveled against Paul, although with a little different twist.

Some of Paul's detractors claimed that he was teaching that sin didn't really matter, because Grace was so much greater than sin. He had made the great statement, and inspired by the Holy Spirit, *"Moreover the Law entered, that the offense might abound* (the Law of Moses, that the offense might be identified). *But where sin abounded, Grace did much more abound* (where sin increased, Grace super-abounded, and then some on top of that):

"That as sin has reigned unto death (sin reigns as an absolute monarch in the being of the unredeemed), *even so might Grace reign through Righteousness unto Eternal Life by Jesus Christ our Lord.* (Grace reigns unto Life, but it reigns *'through Righteousness,'* i.e., because of God's Righteous Judgment of sin at Calvary executed in the Person of His Son Jesus Christ)" (Rom. 5:20-21).

The great Apostle answered that accusation by saying: *"What shall we say then?* (This is meant to direct attention to Rom. 5:20.) *Shall we continue in sin, that Grace may abound?* (Just because Grace is greater than sin doesn't mean that the Believer has a license to sin.)

"God forbid (presents Paul's answer to the question, 'Away with the thought, let not such a thing occur'). *How shall we, who are dead to sin* (dead to the sin nature), *live any longer therein?* (This portrays what the Believer is now in Christ)" (Rom. 6:1-2).

No, the Message of the Cross is the only means by which the Believer can get Victory over sin; therefore, those who claim that we tell people they can sin all they want to and then just go to the Cross and everything is alright, are saying such out of a heart of animosity. In fact, they know what they are saying is wrong.

As we've already stated, what we are teaching, and I continue to speak of the Message of the Cross, is the only way, and I mean the only way, that one can have Victory over sin. It cannot be gained by any other method or way.

NOTES

WHAT DO WE MEAN BY THE WORTHLESSNESS OF SELF?

Jesus in Luke 9:23 told us to *"deny ourselves."* What did He mean by that?

First of all, He wasn't speaking of asceticism, as many think, but rather that the Believer must not depend on self in any capacity. This means that whatever we hope to gain from the Lord, cannot be gained by our ability, talent, strength, education, motivation, intellectualism, etc. It can only be gained by one denying all of these particular things, and I'm speaking of denying them in the capacity of trying to reach God through that means, but rather to look to Christ exclusively and what He did for us at the Cross.

The Message of the Cross is the most simple, and easy to understand Doctrine in the Bible. Where it gets complicated is when we try to insert self into the picture.

We Believers are quick to point out the sins, aberrations, perversions, and faults of the unsaved; however, we like to think of ourselves in a totally different light. Now don't misunderstand, the Lord cleaned us up immeasurably when we were Saved. But still, we aren't perfect, and as we have previously stated, God cannot accept anything less than perfection. So, that being the case, how can God accept us, considering that none of us are perfect?

THE PERFECTION OF CHRIST

He accepts us solely on the basis of our Faith in Christ and what Christ has done for us at the Cross. Christ is Perfect in all things. When He came to this world, he came as our Substitute, the Last Adam, the Second Man, our Representative. In other words, everything He did was in its entirety for us.

He kept the Law perfectly in every respect, never failing even one time, whether in word, thought, or deed. As stated, He did that for us, all on our behalf. He then went to the Cross, in order to address the broken Law, of which all of us were guilty. And this is what Paul said about that:

"Blotting out the handwriting of Ordinances that was against us (pertains to the

Law of Moses, which was God's Standard of Righteousness that man could not reach), *which was contrary to us* (Law is against us, simply because we are unable to keep its precepts, no matter how hard we try), *and took it out of the way* (refers to the penalty of the Law being removed), *nailing it to His Cross* (the Law with its decrees was abolished in Christ's Death, as if Crucified with Him)" (Col. 2:14).

Christ was Perfect in His Life, was Perfect in His Death, was Perfect in His Atonement, was Perfect in all things. Our Faith in Him, and in Him exclusively and what He did for us at the Cross, grants to us His Perfection, which makes it possible for God to accept us. It is all by Faith, but more particularly, Faith in Christ and what He did for us at the Cross.

The Believer must come to the place that he recognizes the worthlessness of self, and the worthfulness of Christ. Until that is done, with him then placing his Faith exclusively in Christ and the Cross, he will never know the Victory that such can bring, and such alone can bring.

We will find that this great Book of Job will teach us this.

THE WORDS OF THE HOLY ONE

Job said in Verse 10, *"For I have not concealed the Words of the Holy One."* This portrays to us the fact that Job fell back on the Word of God. As we have previously stated, at that time there was no written Bible, for Moses a few years later would be the first one to write down the Word of God. In fact, and as we have also previously stated, this Book of Job was probably the first one written, and was written by Moses in collaboration with Job.

However, the Word of God had been given to Adam in the beginning, and then to Abel, and then to Enoch, and then on to Noah, and Abraham, and had been guarded with perfect memory. These Divine experiences had, no doubt, been related and retold countless times. As well, much of it had probably been written down. Moses would later compile it inspired by the Holy Spirit and would write the first Books, which first of all was, no doubt, this Book of Job, and then Genesis. A little later he wrote Exodus, Leviticus, Numbers, and Deuteronomy. This was the beginning of the Written Word of God (Lk. 24:27).

The Bible, being the oldest Book in the world, and the only revealed Truth in the world, means that it's by far the most important work on the face of the Earth. It is that because it is the Word of God. This means that it does not merely contain the Word of God, but, in fact, is the Word of God, all the way from Genesis 1:1 through Revelation 22:21. It is the road map for life and living, the blueprint for eternity. Every Believer should do all within his power to understand the Word.

If the Reader doesn't have THE EXPOSITOR'S STUDY BIBLE, then I would strongly encourage you to obtain your copy. Virtually every Scripture is explained. Jesus said that we would *"know the Truth, and the Truth would make us free"* (Jn. 8:32). But as someone has well said, it is only the Truth, which we know that will make us free.

The story of the Bible is the story of the Redemption of man, all carried out by Christ and the Cross. In fact, Jesus Christ is the Living Word. He is on every page of the Bible and, in fact, in every Scripture, in one way or the other.

In essence, Job by using the phrase, *"For I have not concealed the Words of the Holy One,"* is saying, that even though he doesn't understand what has happened to him, or why it has happened, still, he will stand on the Word, whatever the outcome. That would be one of the greatest statements that he made in this entire scenario.

IS THERE ENOUGH STRENGTH IN THE HUMAN BEING?

Job asked two questions in Verse 13. He said, *"Is not my help in me? and is wisdom driven quite from me?"*

The world of psychology states that an individual has the resources down deep within himself or herself, to overcome any and every problem, whatever it might be. Consequently, they say, the alcoholic can reach way down within himself and find enough strength to quit drinking, or the gambler to quit gambling, or the drug addict to stop taking drugs.

Is that true?

No!

While some few may quit drinking, or quit gambling, etc., the truth is, the bondage remains. That's the reason that Alcoholics Anonymous tells people to say, *"I am a recovering alcoholic,"* and, in fact, they are to say that the rest of their life.

This means the desire for alcohol is still there, the desire to gamble is still there, the desire for drugs is still there, the desire for pornography is still there, etc. In effect, such a person is in a prison.

To be sure, we are thankful for those that would quit drinking, etc.; however, that by no means constitutes freedom. Jesus said, and in quote from THE EXPOSITOR'S STUDY BIBLE:

"If the Son therefore shall make you free (Christ Alone can make one free, and He does so through and by what He did at the Cross, and our Faith in that Finished Work), *you shall be free indeed* (a freedom which the world cannot give and, in fact, doesn't even understand)*"* (Jn. 8:36).

And how does the Lord make one free?

Jesus also said: *"And you shall know the Truth, and the Truth shall make you free* (this is the secret of all Abundant Life in Christ; the *'Truth'* is *'Jesus Christ and Him Crucified,'* which alone is the answer to the problems of man)*"* (Jn. 8:32).

WHAT IS TRUTH?

The Scripture tells us what Truth is:

• Jesus Christ is Truth: He said, *"I am the Way, the Truth, and the Life: no man comes unto the Father, but by Me"* (Jn. 14:6).

• The Word of God is Truth: Jesus also said, *"Sanctify them through Your Truth: Your Word is Truth"* (Jn. 17:17).

• John the Beloved said: *"And it is the Spirit Who bears witness, because the Spirit is Truth"* (I Jn. 5:6).

So this means that *"Truth"* is not a philosophy, or merely a principal. In fact, it is a Person, the Lord Jesus Christ.

The *"Truth"* that mankind is to know and understand is Jesus Christ and Him Crucified. If the person gives their heart to Christ, places their Faith exclusively in Christ and what He did for us at the Cross, and doesn't allow it to be moved elsewhere, the Holy Spirit Who is God, and Who can do anything, and Who lives in the hearts and lives of all Believers (I Cor. 3:16), will then begin to evidence His mighty Power, giving the Believer Victory over the world, the flesh, and the Devil. As stated, there is nothing that He cannot do. In fact, there have been multiplied, multiplicities of millions who have been instantly set free by the Power of God. Conversely, there has never been one single soul set free by humanistic psychology, or by any of the religions of the world. All life, all Victory, all freedom is found exclusively in Christ and what Christ did at the Cross. That is the Truth that Christ wants us to know and understand. That's the reason that Paul said to the Church at Corinth, and to you and I as well, *"And I, Brethren, when I came to you, came not with excellency of speech or of wisdom* (means that he depended not on oratorical abilities, nor did he delve into philosophy, which was all the rage of that particular day), *declaring unto you the Testimony of God* (which is Christ and Him Crucified).

"For I determined not to know anything among you (with purpose and design, Paul did not resort to the knowledge or philosophy of the world regarding the preaching of the Gospel), *save Jesus Christ, and Him Crucified* (that and that alone is the Message, which will save the sinner, set the captive free, and give the Believer perpetual Victory)*"* (I Cor. 2:1-2). And please understand, if the Church does not hold up the great Message of Jesus Christ and Him Crucified, this means that the world has no Deliverance at all. And I'm afraid that the modern church has long since abandoned the Cross, in favor of humanistic psychology. As such, there is no freedom, there is no victory and, in fact, there is no Salvation.

THE TERRIBLE PROBLEM OF SIN

The terrible power of darkness is greater than the power of man. It is greater because of the Fall of man which took place a long, long time ago. Concerning this, Paul said: *"For to be carnally minded is death* (this doesn't refer to watching too much television, as some think, but rather, to trying to live for God outside of His Prescribed Order; the results will be sin and separation from God); *but to be Spiritually minded is life and peace* (God's Prescribed Order is the Cross; this demands our constant Faith in that Finished Work, which is the Way of the Holy Spirit).

"Because the carnal mind is enmity against God (once again, this refers to attempting to live for God by means other than the Cross, which places one *'against God'*): *for it is not subject to the Law of God, neither indeed can be* (in its simplest form a means that what is being done, whatever it may be, is not in God's Prescribed Order, which is the Cross).

"So then they that are in the flesh cannot please God (refers to the Believer attempting to live his Christian Life by means other than Faith in Christ and the Cross).

"But you are not in the flesh (in one sense of the word is asking the question, 'Since you are now a Believer and no longer depending on the flesh, why are you resorting to the flesh?'), *but in the Spirit* (as a Believer, you now have the privilege of being led and empowered by the Holy Spirit; however, He will do such for us only on the premise of our Faith in the Finished Work of Christ), *if so be that the Spirit of God dwell in you* (if you are truly Saved). *Now if any man have not the Spirit of Christ, he is none of His* (Paul is saying that the Work of the Spirit in our lives is made possible by what Christ did at Calvary, and the Resurrection).

"And if Christ be in you (He is in you through the Power and Person of the Spirit [Gal. 2:20]), *the body is dead because of sin* (means that the physical body has been rendered helpless because of the Fall; consequently, the Believer trying to overcome by willpower presents a fruitless task); *but the Spirit is life because of Righteousness* (only the Holy Spirit can make us what we ought to be, which means we cannot do it ourselves; once again, He performs all that He does within the confines of the Finished Work of Christ).

"But if the Spirit (Holy Spirit) *of Him* (from God) *Who raised up Jesus from the dead dwell in you* (and He definitely does),

NOTES

He Who raised up Christ from the dead shall also quicken your mortal bodies (give us power in our mortal bodies that we might live a victorious life) *by His Spirit Who dwells in you* (we have the same Power in us, through the Spirit, that raised Christ from the dead, and is available to us only on the premise of the Cross and our Faith in that Sacrifice)" (Rom. 8:6-11).

In these Passages, the Apostle Paul tells us how that we can overcome the world, the flesh, and the Devil. He bluntly and plainly tells us that we cannot do it by our own strength and power, even though we are Saved and even Spirit-filled. The reason is simple:

Because of the Fall, the physical body has been weakened to such an extent, that it cannot function in the manner in which God originally created it. This will all change at the Resurrection of Life when we put on the Glorified Body; however, it will not change until then. That's the reason we must have the Power of the Holy Spirit to function in our lives. And He functions on the premise, as stated, of the Finished Work of Christ, i.e., *"the Cross,"* which demands our Faith in that finished product (Gal. 6:14).

No, despite the fact that Job was *"a perfect and an upright man, one who feared God, and hated evil,"* and despite the fact, *"that there was none like him in the earth,"* still, he did not have it within himself to affect that which he needed, which was to climb out over this terrible problem that he now faces, and neither can you!

The answer is in Christ Alone, and what He did for us at the Cross.

A PERSONAL ILLUSTRATION

Some time back I saw a program over television, featuring the testimony of a man who had been delivered from gambling.

In fact, this man held a Ph.D. in humanistic psychology, and was in charge of the rehabilitation programs in the particular state where he resided. If I remember correctly, he also taught a course in psychology at the University in his city.

In giving his testimony, he went on to relate as to how at a particular time he was visited by some friends. There was a casino in the city, and his guest suggested that they go out to the casino for a few hours of entertainment.

The host, who had never been in a casino, quickly volunteered to take them.

All of them went out, and for the first time in his life, he put some quarters into a slot machine. Several hours later he was still there. In that short period of time, he was hooked.

To make the story brief, and as he told it, he gambled away his life savings, his automobile, and then his home.

The irony about it was, he applied to himself all the psychological methods that were supposed to work on those who were hooked. To be sure, he was hooked! Sadly, none of it worked.

At a particular time, he drove the old car to which he had been reduced to drive, out to a place of privacy, with a determination to take his life. He reached in the glove compartment of the car, where there was supposed to be a pistol, but found that it was now gone.

When he arrived back home an hour or so later, he told his wife, *"You saved my life today!"* She looked at him in surprise, and asked how?

He then told her what had happened. She mentioned that she had taken the pistol a couple of days before, and had sold it in order to pay the light bill. That's how desperate their situation was. Incidentally, he had now lost his position with the State, all because of his addiction.

A few days later, as he gave his testimony, he said that he drove back out to the place of privacy where he had gone previously to take his life, but this time there was a difference.

He parked the car, got out, and began to walk under the trees, and for the first time in his life, he prayed.

He repented before the Lord, asking God to forgive him of the terrible things he had said about Him, and how that he had made fun of those who claimed to serve God.

God is a merciful God, and in a few moments time, this man was gloriously and wondrously Saved. In his prayer, he at the same time asked the Lord to give him a miracle — in fact, he had once laughed at the notion of Biblical Miracles. But here he was, asking for one.

"Lord will you break this bondage of gambling in my life?"

I heard him stand there that day, this man with a Ph.D. in humanistic psychology, and tell all and sundry, that even though he held the highest educational degree that could be obtained in the field of humanistic psychology, that it did him no good whatsoever. I heard him give all the Glory to the Lord Jesus Christ, for Saving him, and setting him free.

Such a story has been repeated untold millions of times down through the centuries, all because of what Jesus did at the Cross of Calvary. That is the only answer and, in fact, there is no other answer, as there can be no other answer.

(14) "TO HIM WHO IS AFFLICTED PITY SHOULD BE SHOWN FROM HIS FRIEND; BUT HE FORSAKES THE FEAR OF THE ALMIGHTY.

(15) "MY BRETHREN HAVE DEALT DECEITFULLY AS A BROOK, AND AS THE STREAM OF BROOKS THEY PASS AWAY;

(16) "WHICH ARE BLACKISH BY REASON OF THE ICE, AND WHEREIN THE SNOW IS HID:

(17) "WHAT TIME THEY WAX WARM, THEY VANISH: WHEN IT IS HOT, THEY ARE CONSUMED OUT OF THEIR PLACE.

(18) "THE PATHS OF THEIR WAY ARE TURNED ASIDE; THEY GO TO NOTHING, AND PERISH.

(19) "THE TROOPS OF TEMA LOOKED, THE COMPANIES OF SHEBA WAITED FOR THEM.

(20) "THEY WERE CONFOUNDED BECAUSE THEY HAD HOPED; THEY CAME THITHER, AND WERE ASHAMED.

(21) "FOR NOW YOU ARE NOTHING; YOU SEE MY CASTING DOWN, AND ARE AFRAID."

The composition is:

1. (Vs. 14) Job looked for pity from his friend, but found none. The Patriarch says that his friend has overstepped his bounds, and has shown, by his attitude, that he has no fear of God. Regrettably, most of Christendom thinks little of roundly accusing or

condemning that of which it has no knowledge and no understanding. They do so because they, as well, have precious little fear of God. The reason is self-righteousness.

2. (Vs. 15) These three friends came to Job as if they desired to comfort and to help him; instead, they accused and condemned him. As they would soon see, the Lord did not look kindly on their action.

3. (Vs. 20) Job implies that he is ashamed of having looked for compassion and kindness from his friends; he should have been wiser and known better.

4. (Vs. 21) These *"friends"* thought that Job was an object of Divine vengeance, and feared, if they would show him sympathy, they might involve themselves in his punishment.

LET US HELP OUR BROTHER ON THE JOURNEY OF LIFE

As we have previously stated, *"when a Brother or Sister is down, and cannot defend themselves in any way, and anyone can do any negative thing to them they so desire, and have no fear of being reprimanded, but rather applauded, then one finds out just how many good Christians there actually are."*

I pray that you the reader never find yourself in such a position. But if you are unfortunate enough to do so, you will find as Job, precious little help from others.

Those who would desire to help you, and know they need to, will be fearful of doing so, because it might incur the wrath of your enemies, etc.

My prayer is, that the Lord will help me to be a blessing to others on this journey of life, and not be a hindrance. Job needed a friend at this time, but did not find even one.

When we face another who has failed, it is very easy to push him down further, and one will probably be applauded for doing so, but it is true Godliness to pick him up. Some have the mistaken idea, that to do such means that we are condoning sin. What if the Lord looked at us in that fashion.

Is He condoning sin when He shows mercy to us? Helps us? Forgives us?

Jesus had something to say about this:

"A certain man went down from Jerusalem to Jericho, and fell among thieves, which stripped him of his raiment, and wounded him, and departed, leaving him half dead.

"And by chance there came down a certain Priest that way: and when he saw him, he passed by on the other side (selfishness is the commanding force in human nature).

"And likewise a Levite (spoke of those who were of the tribe of Levi), *when he was at the place, came and looked on him, and passed by on the other side* (proclaims this man at least looking on, while the Priest did not even bother with that).

"But a certain Samaritan (the Samaritans and the Jews normally were enemies), *as he journeyed, came where he was* (where the wounded Israelite was): *and when he saw him, he had compassion on him,*

"And went to him, and bound up his wounds, pouring in oil and wine (in those days, a wound was cleansed with grape-juice with oil then applied, which aided healing), *and set him on his own beast, and brought him to a inn, and took care of him* (tells us that this wounded traveler was not rich and, therefore, could not possibly repay the kindness extended to him).

"And on the morrow when he (the good Samaritan) *departed, he took out two pence, and gave them to the host, and said unto him, Take care of him; and whatsoever you spend more, when I come again, I will repay you.*

"Which now of these three (the three men who came in contact with the wounded traveler) *do you think, was neighbor unto him who fell among the thieves?*

"And he said, He who showed mercy on him. Then said Jesus unto him, Go, and do thou likewise (another lesson taught in this Parable is that some need to be placed in the position of the wounded traveler in order that they may be willing to receive help from anyone, even the hated Samaritan)" (Lk. 10:30-37).

Why did these three friends conduct themselves toward Job as they did?

Why do so many presently follow in the same train?

SELF-RIGHTEOUSNESS

The problem is self-righteousness.

If the Believer doesn't have his Faith

anchored supremely in Christ and what Christ did at the Cross, which insures the Righteousness of Christ given to such a person, the individual without fail will be encumbered by self-righteousness. And to be sure, this sin, and it is a sin, a terrible sin, is one of the worst that could attach itself to an individual. This is the sin — self-righteousness — that nailed Christ to the Cross. It wasn't the gamblers or the thieves or the immoral, as wicked as they were, who crucified Christ, but rather the religious leaders of Israel. What a travesty!

One cannot really understand oneself, or others, or the Lord for that matter, unless one has his Faith anchored supremely in Christ and the Cross. When he sees the Cross, understands the Cross, he will then begin to understand himself. And to be sure, what he sees about himself will not be a pretty picture, hence, his dire need for the Cross of Christ. Understanding himself, he will tend to have greater pity on others, because he fully realizes the pity that the Lord has had on him.

Those who do not know the Cross, who do not look to the Cross, who ignore it, or else repudiate it, do not really know the Love of God, for such cannot know the Love of God. In fact, they love themselves, because they know nothing about the Righteousness that's afforded by Christ.

They glory in their so-called *"good works,"* in their place and position, in their religiosity, which is the definition of self-righteousness. Let us say it again, because it is so very, very important:

The only way that one can have the Righteousness of Christ, is by placing his Faith exclusively in Christ and the Cross, otherwise, it will be self-righteousness.

Sadly and regrettably, and due to the fact that the modern church has all but abandoned the Cross of Christ, the problem of self-righteousness is pandemic, to say the least.

As someone has well said, *"the world is slow to forgive, and the Church forgives not at all."* It is because of self-righteousness.

Self-righteousness concludes that God is punishing some people, and that if they help them, they, as well, will suffer the punishment of God.

PUNISHMENT?

The Lord does not punish His Children, He rather chastises us. Punishment is for the purpose of inflicting hurt and pain, while chastisement is for the purpose of correcting us, in other words, getting us to the right path. One is for hurt and the other is for help.

Every single Believer, that is if they are a true Believer, experiences chastisement from the Lord. The Scripture says: *"For whom the Lord loves He chastens* (God disciplines those He loves, not those to whom He is indifferent), *and scourges every son whom He receives.* (This refers to all who truly belong to Him.)

"If you endure chastening, God deals with you as with sons (chastening from the Lord guarantees the fact that one is a Child of God); *for what son is he whom the father chastens not?* (If an earthly father truly cares for his son, he will use whatever measures necessary to bring the boy into line. If an earthly father will do this, how much more will our Heavenly Father do the same?)

"But if you be without chastisement whereof all (all true Believers) *are partakers, then are you bastards, and not sons.* (Many claim to be Believers while continuing in sin, but the Lord never chastises them. Such shows they are illegitimate sons, meaning they are claiming faith on a basis other than the Cross. The true son, without doubt, will be chastised at times)" (Heb. 12:6-8).

(22) "DID I SAY, BRING UNTO ME? OR, GIVE A REWARD FOR ME OF YOUR SUBSTANCE?

(23) "OR, DELIVER ME FROM THE ENEMY'S HAND? OR, REDEEM ME FROM THE HAND OF THE MIGHTY?

(24) "TEACH ME, AND I WILL HOLD MY TONGUE: AND CAUSE ME TO UNDERSTAND WHEREIN I HAVE ERRED.

(25) "HOW FORCIBLE ARE RIGHT WORDS! BUT WHAT DOES YOUR ARGUING REPROVE?

(26) "DO YOU IMAGINE TO REPROVE WORDS, AND THE SPEECHES OF ONE WHO IS DESPERATE, WHICH ARE AS WIND?

(27) "YES, YOU OVERWHELM THE

FATHERLESS, AND YOU DIG A PIT FOR YOUR FRIEND.

(28) "NOW THEREFORE BE CONTENT, LOOK UPON ME; FOR IT IS EVIDENT UNTO YOU IF I LIE.

(29) "RETURN, I PRAY YOU, LET IT NOT BE INIQUITY, YES, RETURN AGAIN, MY RIGHTEOUSNESS IS IN IT.

(30) "IS THERE INIQUITY IN MY TONGUE? CANNOT MY TASTE DISCERN PERVERSE THINGS?"

The pattern is:

1. (Vs. 24) Job's friends claim he has sinned, so they reason that they should tell him what he has done!

2. (Vs. 26) In essence, Job says, your words and accusations should not be dignified by a response.

3. (Vs. 27) All of this tells us, when one is down, condemnation is of no value; a helping hand is what is needed (Gal. 6:1-2).

4. As it regards Verse 30, Job will ultimately find that there is iniquity in his tongue, as there is with all; however, it has nothing to do with these *"friends,"* and what they have said.

THE TONGUE

That to which Job refers as it regards the tongue, proclaims him as being correct. There is no record up to this time, that there was iniquity in his tongue, in other words, that he had said things he should not have said; however, that will change!

Even though Job would not say anything about the Lord that he should not have said (42:7), still, when the time for the trial to end had come, he would say himself, *"therefore have I uttered that I understood not"* (42:3).

Concerning the tongue, James said the following:

"For in many things we offend all. (This refers to the universality of sin and failure, even among Believers.) *If any man offend not in word, the same is a perfect man, and able also to bridle the whole body.* (The Holy Spirit Alone can control the Believer's tongue.)

"Behold, we put bits in the horses' mouths, that they may obey us; and we turn about their whole body. (The Holy Spirit is saying our mouths should obey us, instead of us obeying our mouths.)

"Behold also the ships, which though they be so great, and are driven of fierce winds, yet are they turned about with a very small helm, whithersoever the governor lists. (This refers here to the 'helm' being likened to the 'tongue.')

"Even so the tongue is a little member (it is small, but it exerts a powerful influence), *and boasts great things* (responsible for great things, whether good or bad). *Behold, how great a matter a little fire kindles!* (The image projected here by James is the picture of a vast forest in flames, all begun by the falling of a single spark.)

"And the tongue is a fire (speaks of fire in a negative way, that which destroys), *a world of iniquity* (the tongue in some way is responsible for all the iniquity in the world): *so is the tongue among our members* (body members), *that it defiles the whole body* (constantly speaking in a negative way can bring about physical illness in the body), *and sets on fire the course of nature* (the tongue sets us on a particular path, and in this case the wrong path); *and it is set on fire of hell.* (By using the word 'hell,' we are made to understand not only the wickedness of the tongue, but, as well, its destructive power.)

"For every kind of beasts, and of birds, and of serpents, and of things in the sea, is tamed, and has been tamed of mankind (a proven fact):

"But the tongue can no man tame (this is the Word of the Lord; however, the tongue can most definitely be tamed by the Holy Spirit; the way it is done has to do with the Cross of Christ; the Holy Spirit works within the parameters of the Finished Work of Christ on the Cross; He demands that we ever make the Cross the Object of our Faith, and then He can do mighty things within our lives [Rom. 8:1-2, 11]); *it is an unruly evil, fool of deadly poison.* (The Believer must realize this. It means that just because he is Saved, such doesn't necessarily guarantee a change in this problem. As stated, it definitely can be and, in fact, must be changed, but it can only be so by and through the Cross.)

"Therewith bless we God, even the Father; and therewith curse we men (proclaims

the inconsistency, to say the least, of blessing God one moment and cursing men the next), *which are made after the similitude of God.* (In a sense, when we curse men, which refers to wishing them hurt, we are cursing God. To curse the Creation is to curse the Creator.)

"Out of the same mouth proceeds blessing and cursing (presents the tongue devoted to uses so different). *My Brethren, these things ought not so to be.* (If the Lord has His Way in our hearts and lives, they won't be.)

"Does a fountain send forth at the same place sweet water and bitter? (Of necessity, this question must be answered in the negative.)

"Can the fig tree, my Brethren, bear olive berries? either a vine, figs? so, can no fountain both yield salt water and fresh. (This speaks of nature; however, man can do what nature cannot do)" (James 3:1-12).

"Glory, Glory be to Jesus,
"Glory to His precious Name;
"Sweet it is to sound His praises,
"Blest it is to spread His Fame."

"In the place of His rejection,
"Where He suffered, where He died,
"Bursts of holy praise ascending,
"Greets the glorious Crucified."

"Here was marred His blessed Visage,
"Here His Brow was wreathed with thorn,
"Here the object of derision,
"Bitter taunt and mocking scorn."

"Yes, triumphant hallelujahs,
"Still arise to greet His Name;
"Sweet it is to sound His praises,
"Blest it is to spread His Fame."

CHAPTER 7

(1) "IS THERE NOT AN APPOINTED TIME TO MAN UPON EARTH? ARE NOT HIS DAYS ALSO LIKE THE DAYS OF AN HIRELING?

(2) "AS A SERVANT EARNESTLY DESIRES THE SHADOW, AND AS AN HIRELING LOOKS FOR THE REWARD OF HIS WORK:

(3) "SO AM I MADE TO POSSESS MONTHS OF VANITY, AND WEARISOME NIGHTS ARE APPOINTED TO ME.

(4) "WHEN I LIE DOWN, I SAY, WHEN SHALL I ARISE, AND THE NIGHT BE GONE? AND I AM FULL OF TOSSINGS TO AND FRO UNTO THE DAWNING OF THE DAY.

(5) "MY FLESH IS CLOTHED WITH WORMS AND CLODS OF DUST; MY SKIN IS BROKEN, AND BECOME LOATHSOME.

(6) "MY DAYS ARE SWIFTER THAN A WEAVER'S SHUTTLE, AND ARE SPENT WITHOUT HOPE.

(7) "O REMEMBER THAT MY LIFE IS WIND: MY EYE SHALL NO MORE SEE GOOD.

(8) "THE EYE OF HIM WHO HAS SEEN ME SHALL SEE ME NO MORE: YOUR EYES ARE UPON ME, AND I AM NOT.

(9) "AS THE CLOUD IS CONSUMED AND VANISHES AWAY: SO HE WHO GOES DOWN TO THE GRAVE SHALL COME UP NO MORE.

(10) "HE SHALL RETURN NO MORE TO HIS HOUSE, NEITHER SHALL HIS PLACE KNOW HIM ANY MORE."

The overview is:

1. (Vs. 1) Job, under tremendous pressure, now resorts to cynicism. He has asked to die, and now he thinks he really will die; and, to die in this state makes it seem as though his life has had no purpose. He sees nothing except destruction and hurt, little knowing what is taking place in the spirit world.

2. (Vs. 1) I doubt that there has ever been another human being whom the Lord has tested as He did Job. So this means that it was not only for Job's benefit, but for ours, as well. There is far more here than meets the eye.

3. (Vs. 4) One can well imagine the consternation that filled Job's heart and mind, as it regarded his situation. There was no rest night or day.

4. (Vs. 5) Regarding the type of disease which gripped Job, tumors would develop on the skin, followed by a discharge of a virulent and loathsome character.

5. (Vs. 6) Regarding his loathsome situation; physically, domestically, and financially,

he reasons that there is no hope!

6. (Vs. 7) Job was wrong on all counts. Through Job's situation, the Lord is showing us that no matter how bad the situation might be, if we know the Lord, there is nothing that He cannot change.

7. (Vs. 9) All that Job can see ahead of him is death! Little does he realize that, in a sense, his life is just beginning.

MAN'S APPOINTED TIME ON EARTH

The idea is, even as Job puts it, and he is right, that to each man, and we speak of Believers, a certain work is appointed for him to do, and a certain limited time assigned him within which to do it. That time can be shortened or lengthened according to disobedience or obedience as it regards the Word of the Lord. But, if a person is doing the Will of God, he will not be taken, and, in fact, cannot be taken until he has finished his work. Concerning this, the Scripture says: *"Walk in wisdom toward them who are without* (refers to 'ordering one's behavior'), *redeeming the time* (make wise and sacred use of every opportunity to present Christ)" (Col. 4:5).

Unbelievers are at the whim of nature and circumstances. While the Lord will definitely deal with some of them according to the prayers of loved ones, otherwise, there is no safety or protection. But with the Saints, every Believer is bought with a price, and we speak of what Christ did at Calvary. As a result, we have a great Salvation that has been given unto us, and we are to use it as wisely as possible. Concerning this, our Lord said:

THE PARABLE OF THE TALENTS

"For the Kingdom of Heaven is as a man traveling into a far country, who called his own servants, and delivered unto them his goods (represents Christ at His First Advent).

"And unto one he gave five talents, to another two, and to another one; to every man according to his several abilities; and straightway (immediately) *took his journey* (every single Believer, none excluded, is given a proper Ministry).

"Then he who had received the five talents went and traded with the same, and made them other five talents (the talents were awarded according to faithfulness).

"And likewise he who had received two, he also gained other two (he was faithful with what he had).

"But he who had received one went and dug in the earth, and hid his lord's money (he wasn't faithful).

"After a long time the lord of those servants comes, and reckons with them (service for the lord ends at death; however, the reckoning is reserved for the Rapture).

"And so he who had received five talents came and brought other five talents, saying, lord, you delivered unto me five talents, behold, I have gained beside them five talents more (this will take place at the Judgment Seat of Christ).

"His lord said unto him, Well done, thou good and faithful servant: you have been faithful over a few things, I will make you ruler over many things: enter thou into the joy of your lord (as is obvious, it is faithfulness here that is being rewarded; contrary to popular thought, God hasn't called us to be successful, but rather to be faithful).

"He also who had received two talents came and said, lord, you delivered unto me two talents: behold, I have gained two other talents beside them (faithfulness as well!)

"His lord said unto him, Well done, good and faithful servant; you have been faithful over a few things, I will make you ruler over many things: enter thou into the joy of your lord (if it is to be noticed, both received equal rewards; as stated, the criterion is faithfulness and not other things).

"Then he who had received the one talent came and said, lord, I know you and that you are an hard man, reaping where you have not sown, and gathering where you have not planted (pure and simple, his statements constitute a lie):

"And I was afraid, and went and hid your talent in the earth: lo, there you have that which is Yours (the purpose of the 'talent' was not preservation, but rather, multiplication; his action proclaims not only indolence, but, as well, insolence; untold numbers, who claim to be Christians, fall into this category).

*"His lord answered and said unto him,

You wicked and slothful servant, you knew that I reap where I sowed not, and gather where I have not planted (if you really believed that, you would not have done what you did):

"You ought therefore to have put my money to the exchangers, and then at my coming I should have received my own with usury (regrettably, the majority of professors or religion, fall into this category).

"Take therefore the talent from him, and give it unto him who has ten talents (this is the law of the faithful; light rejected is light taken, and given to the one who already has an abundance of light).

"For unto every one who has shall be given, and he shall have abundance: but from him who has not shall be taken away even that he has (in fact, this happens unnumbered times, every single day; observe religious denominations, which have rejected light!).

"And cast you the unprofitable servant into outer darkness: there shall be weeping and gnashing of teeth (these individuals do not merely lose reward, but rather their soul; all of this, as should be overly obvious, completely refutes the unscriptural doctrine of unconditional eternal security)" (Mat. 25:14-30).

Tragically, there are millions who claim to be Saved, but in reality, and according to these Passages, aren't! There is nothing in the world worse than a false way of Salvation.

BELIEVERS AND OUR WORK FOR GOD

Considering all of this, every Believer should take inventory as to where he is, what he is, and what he is supporting. Millions are supporting churches which have long since left the Word of God, meaning that they are supporting that which is not of the Lord.

It's not enough to merely give money or time, above all we should know what we are supporting, making doubly sure that it is according to the Word of God.

If one studies Paul's Epistles to any degree, one soon comes upon the realization that the Judaizers caused the Apostle great difficulties.

The Judaizers were Jews from Jerusalem or Judea, who claimed that if Gentiles were to truly be Saved, they had to also keep the Law. Of course, these individuals placed no stock whatsoever in the Cross of Christ, but rather on the Law. As stated, Paul had more difficulty with these individuals, than any other thing he faced.

To make a bad matter worse, there were some of the people in some of the Churches he had founded, people incidentally who had been Saved under his ministry, who were supporting these false apostles.

It should be understood, to support that which is not of God, is actually supporting Satan's ministers (II Cor. 11:13-15).

Understanding that, it is for certain that the Lord would not bless money given to these individuals, whoever they may have been, especially considering that they were supporting the work of Satan. Consequently, the modern Believer should seek the Lord incessantly as it regards his support.

JOB THINKS HE IS DYING

And no wonder! He cannot see any way out. He has lost everything, which is a great perplexity to him, as should be obvious.

His health is gone, and he doesn't see how he can recover.

I do not wonder at the things he said, but rather that he didn't say much more.

It's so easy to criticize the man, thinking we would have done better. What a foolish thought!

It is said that every man has a breaking point! I suppose that is true.

One could easily say that Job finally broke; however, I don't think so! He was bent terribly bad, but I don't think he broke. When it was all over, the Lord said of him, when speaking to Job's so-called friends, *"for you have not spoken of Me the thing that is right, as My Servant Job has"* (Job 42:7).

This means, I think, that Job, despite his terrible ordeal, did not break. What a testimony!

Once again I state, that it is easy for us to see the situation, simply because we know the end from the beginning and the beginning from the end; however, Job knew none of that, only knowing what he could see presently. It was not a pretty sight! He thinks he is dying, and yet he feels in his heart that he has not finished his course of life on this Earth, he has not accomplished that which he believes the Lord wants him to do. He says: *"My days are swifter than a weaver's shuttle, and are spent without hope."*

He has lost all hope, and one doesn't wonder why!

(11) "THEREFORE I WILL NOT REFRAIN MY MOUTH; I WILL SPEAK IN THE ANGUISH OF MY SPIRIT; I WILL COMPLAIN IN THE BITTERNESS OF MY SOUL.

(12) "AM I A SEA, OR A WHALE, THAT YOU SET A WATCH OVER ME?

(13) "WHEN I SAY, MY BED SHALL COMFORT ME, MY COUCH SHALL EASE MY COMPLAINT;

(14) "THEN YOU SCARE ME WITH DREAMS, AND TERRIFY ME THROUGH VISIONS:

(15) "SO THAT MY SOUL CHOOSES STRANGLING, AND DEATH RATHER THAN MY LIFE.

(16) "I LOATHE IT; I WOULD NOT LIVE ALWAYS: LET ME ALONE; FOR MY DAYS ARE VANITY.

(17) "WHAT IS MAN, THAT YOU SHOULD MAGNIFY HIM? AND THAT YOU SHOULD SET YOUR HEART UPON HIM?

(18) "AND THAT YOU SHOULD VISIT HIM EVERY MORNING, AND TRY HIM EVERY MOMENT?

(19) "HOW LONG WILL YOU NOT DEPART FROM ME, NOR LET ME ALONE TILL I SWALLOW DOWN MY SPITTLE?

(20) "I HAVE SINNED; WHAT SHALL I DO UNTO YOU, O YOU PRESERVER OF MEN? WHY HAVE YOU SET ME AS A MARK AGAINST YOU, SO THAT I AM A BURDEN TO MYSELF?

(21) "AND WHY DO YOU NOT PARDON MY TRANSGRESSION, AND TAKE AWAY MY INIQUITY? FOR NOW SHALL I SLEEP IN THE DUST; AND YOU SHALL SEEK ME IN THE MORNING, BUT I SHALL NOT BE."

The pattern is:

1. In essence, the Eleventh Verse means, *"What difference does it now make what I say?"* Perhaps this is the trying point for all Christians. Lacking understanding in the happenings of our life, we are prone to give vent to our emotions. Every time this happens, it is a lack of faith because of unbelief. And yet, the Lord will have amazing patience with Job, and with us.

2. (Vs. 14) Along with the terrible affliction of his body, and the loss of all his material goods, Satan, no doubt, terrified Job with demonic dreams and visions. Job thought it was God doing it and, in effect, the Lord was allowing Satan to use this method; so, Job's terrible predicament was not only the loss of his possessions and his physical health, but also the terror of his soul.

3. (Vs. 16) Job says to the Lord, *"Let me alone."* Fortunately, the Lord will not let us alone, and thank God He won't! If He did, we would be eternally lost.

4. (Vs. 17) Job's question, *"What is man, that You should magnify him?"* presents the great question of life. It would ultimately be answered by God. It would be given to David about 600 years later (Ps. 8:4-6).

5. (Vs. 17) It was very difficult for Job to see God's ultimate purpose in the creation of man, especially when he sat in an ash heap with sore boils all over his body, scraping himself with a potsherd.

6. (Vs. 18) The whole life of man is a probation, not merely particular parts of it. God *"tries us every moment."* Everything is a test!

7. (Vs. 19) To the natural mind, the thought is intolerable that God's watchful Eye should scrutinize every action; but, to the mind enlightened by and subjected to the Holy Spirit, the fact is delightful.

8. (Vs. 21) Whatever the problem, in Job's mind, it is now too late! However, let the Reader understand that with God, at least as long as there is breath, it is never too late!

IT MATTERS WHAT WE SAY

Job has now come to the place that he says, *"Therefore I will not refrain my mouth; I will speak in the anguish of my spirit; I will complain in the bitterness of my soul."*

His thoughts are, *"What's the use!"*

Little did he realize that millions upon millions of people, down through the many centuries, would read his every word, look into his mind, even as he was undergoing this terrible trial. That should be a lesson to us!

There is never a time that the Believer is off-duty, so to speak.

Seemingly, we come to the place of acute distress, thereby, occasioning faithless words, a long, long time, before Job reached that point. In fact, Job is meant to be a lesson to us.

WHAT IS MAN?

Man is the highest Creation of God, even higher than the Angels.

I realize it's not easy to see that presently, and because we observe man in his fallen condition. But the manner in which God originally created man, and that which he will ultimately be, proclaims the truth of what we have said.

God has given man the power to create, although from substance already created. Only God can create something from nothing.

In fact, it was originally the intention of God, even as He gave man and woman the power of procreation, which refers to bringing offspring into the world, that such would be brought in the Image of God (Lk. 3:38). The EXPOSITOR'S STUDY BIBLE says in regard to this:

"Adam was a son of God by creation, and not by the Born-Again experience; it was the intention of God that humanity bring sons and daughters of God into the world, which they could do by procreation; however, due to the Fall, children cannot be born in the likeness of God, but rather in the likeness of Adam, i.e., the sinful nature (Gen. 5:3); as wonderful as being in the genealogy of Christ was, some, if not many, of these individuals listed in Luke, Chapter 3 were not Saved; and, in fact, some of them were ungodly; this proves that Salvation does not come by inheritance or genealogy; it comes only by accepting Christ as one's Saviour (Jn. 3:16)."

The Lord would answer this question as posed by Job (Vs. 17) approximately 600 years later. The answer would be given to David, the sweet singer of Israel. The Holy Spirit through him said: *"What is man, that You are mindful of him? And the son of man that You visit him?*

"For You have made him a little lower than the Angels, and have crowned him with glory and honor (the Hebrew word *'Elohim'* here translated *'Angels'* should have been translated *'God,'* or *'the Godhead,'* for that's what the word actually means; there is no place in the Old Testament where *'Elohim'* means *'Angels'*; this means that man was originally created higher than the Angels, and through Christ will be restored to that lofty position [Rom. 8:14-17]).

"You made him to have dominion over the works of Your Hands; You have put all things under his feet. (In their fullness, these words given here are true only of the God-Man, Jesus Christ [Mat. 28:18]; Christ has been exalted to a place higher than Angels or any other being except the Father; redeemed man is to be raised up to that exalted position with Him [Eph. 2:6-7])" (Ps. 8:4-6).

SIN

The translation of the Twentieth Verse, *"I have sinned,"* would probably have been better translated, *"granting that I have sinned,"* or, *"suppose that I have sinned."*

Job is not saying that he has sinned, but is saying that it certainly is possible.

He then asks, *"If, in fact, I have sinned, why do You not pardon my transgression, and take away my iniquity?"*

He now surmises that anyway it is too late. He is about to die, or so he thinks!

I don't think it's possible for us to even begin to understand the agony of this man. He speaks, but it's not so much an answer to the accusations of Eliphaz, but rather the cry of his heart. Why has this happened to him? And now he thinks it's too late for any help to be forthcoming.

While Job was a sinner, as all men are born in sin, still, the cause of his terrible situation was not personal sin on his part. But to be sure, one could not convince his friends of that. They surmised that he must be the greatest of sinners, especially considering what has happened to him. Little do they know or realize what was taking place. As we have said, they knew what was happening, but they didn't know what was going on.

"Alas! And did my Saviour bleed?

*"And did my Sovereign die?
"Would He devote that sacred Head,
"For such a worm as I?"*

*"Was it for crimes that I had done,
"He groaned upon the tree?
"Amazing pity! Grace unknown!
"And love beyond degree!"*

*"Well might the sun in darkness hide,
"And shut His glories in,
"When Christ, the mighty Maker, died,
"For man the creature's sin."*

*"Thus might I hide my blushing face,
"While His dear Cross appears,
"Dissolve my heart in thankfulness,
"And melt my eyes to tears."*

*"But drops of grief can ne'er repay,
"The debt of love I owe;
"Here, Lord, I give myself away,
"'Tis all that I can do."*

CHAPTER 8

(1) "THEN ANSWERED BILDAD THE SHUHITE, AND SAID,

(2) "HOW LONG WILL YOU SPEAK THESE THINGS? AND HOW LONG SHALL THE WORDS OF YOUR MOUTH BE LIKE A STRONG WIND?

(3) "DOES GOD PERVERT JUDGMENT? OR DOES THE ALMIGHTY PERVERT JUSTICE?

(4) "IF YOUR CHILDREN HAVE SINNED AGAINST HIM, AND HE HAS CAST THEM AWAY FOR THEIR TRANSGRESSION;

(5) "IF YOU WOULD SEEK UNTO GOD BETIMES, AND MAKE YOUR SUPPLICATION TO THE ALMIGHTY;

(6) "IF YOU WERE PURE AND UPRIGHT; SURELY NOW HE WOULD AWAKE FOR YOU, AND MAKE THE HABITATION OF YOUR RIGHTEOUSNESS PROSPEROUS.

(7) "THOUGH YOUR BEGINNING WAS SMALL, YET YOUR LATTER END SHOULD GREATLY INCREASE.

(8) "FOR ENQUIRE, I PRAY YOU, OF THE FORMER AGE, AND PREPARE YOURSELF TO THE SEARCH OF THEIR FATHERS:

(9) "(FOR WE ARE BUT OF YESTERDAY, AND KNOW NOTHING, BECAUSE OUR DAYS UPON EARTH ARE A SHADOW:)

(10) "SHALL NOT THEY TEACH YOU, AND TELL YOU, AND UTTER WORDS OUT OF THEIR HEART?

(11) "CAN THE RUSH GROW UP WITHOUT MIRE? CAN THE FLAG GROW WITHOUT WATER?

(12) "WHILE IT IS YET IN HIS GREENNESS, AND NOT CUT DOWN, IT WITHERS BEFORE ANY OTHER HERB."

The construction is:

1. (Vs. 1) As Eliphaz argued from the position of *"experience,"* Bildad argues from the position of *"tradition."* He would have nothing good to say about Job.

2. (Vs. 2) It was not very encouraging for Job, while sitting in an ash heap, to hear this man say that his words were no more than *"hot air."*

3. (Vs. 3) As Eliphaz, Bildad knew some things about God, but not the things that really mattered.

4. (Vs. 6) Bildad was really saying that if Job were as pure and upright as he (Bildad) was, then he too would be prosperous, and not in this condition. If one will notice carefully, the entirety of the discourses of these three *"friends"* will subtly extol their righteousness while proclaiming Job's unrighteousness. In truth, Job was *"pure and upright,"* but only in the Eyes of God. Still, isn't that all that counts?

5. (Vs. 7) *"Your latter end,"* says Bildad, *"shows that your beginning was all wrong as well."*

6. In the Eighth Verse Bildad is speaking of *"human tradition."* Some traditions are good; most are not (Mat. 15:6).

7. The Tenth Verse says in other words, *"Job, if you had even a modicum of intelligence, you would know the answer to your questions."*

HUMAN TRADITION

As we have previously stated, Eliphaz answers Job from *"human experience,"* while Bildad now answers him from the position of *"human tradition."* His words will be much harsher than that of Eliphaz. In fact, he will have nothing good to say about Job. Nevertheless, as the *"human experience"* was no reliable guide for Eliphaz, likewise, *"human tradition"* is no reliable guide for Bildad.

In fact, almost all of humanity bases its reasoning on that of Job's three friends. It is:
- Human experience;
- Human tradition; and,
- Human merit.

Even though these individuals knew some things about God, still, their answers and their judgment were not based on the Word of God but on man's human reasonings. This is the blight, sadly, of the human race, and even of the church.

JEWISH TRADITION

The word *"tradition"* does not occur in the Old Testament, but between the Testaments much teaching in explanation of the Old Testament was added by the Rabbis. Tradition pertains to teaching that is handed down from teacher to pupil, and by Jesus' day had assumed a place equal to Scripture. This equation of human commentary with Divine Revelation was condemned by our Lord. By such tradition the Word of God was *"transgressed,"* meaning, *"made of none effect."* Therefore, it was to be laid aside and rejected. In fact, the doctrines taught by tradition were *"the commandments of men"* (Mat. 15:9; Mk. 7:6-7).

Commentary on the Scripture is encouraged in the Bible, but is always meant to explain the Scripture, instead of formulating that which claims to be truth apart from Scripture.

CHRISTIAN TRADITION

Jesus placed His Own teaching alongside the Word of God as an authoritative commentary, which He handed down to His Disciples. Thus, in the Sermon on the Mount Jesus quoted from the Law, but put beside it His Own Words, *"But I say to you"* (Mat. 5:22, 28, 32, 34, 39, 44; 6:25). His justification for so doing is found in His Person.

As the Spirit-anointed Messiah, the Word made flesh, He alone could make a valid and authoritative commentary on the Spirit-inspired Word of God. Likewise the Epistles emphasize the Person of Christ in contrast to tradition. In Colossians 2:8 Paul warns against falling prey to *"philosophy and empty deceit... according to human tradition... and not according to Christ."* So in Galatians 1:14, 16, Paul abandoned the elders' tradition when God revealed His Son in him; Christ not only created the true tradition but constitutes it.

Christian tradition in the New Testament has three elements:

1. The facts of Christ (I Cor. 11:23; 15:3; Lk. 1:2).

2. The Theological interpretation of those facts, correlated in I Corinthians 15.

3. The manner of life which flows from them (I Cor. 11:2; II Thess. 2:15; 3:6-7). In Jude 3 the *"Faith... once for all delivered"* covers all three elements.

THE APOSTOLIC TESTIMONY

Christ was made known by the Apostolic Testimony to Him; the Apostles, therefore, claim that their tradition was to be received as authoritative (I Cor. 11:2; II Thess. 2:15; 3:6). Christ told the Apostles to bear witness of Him because they had been with Him from the beginning; He also promised the Gift of the Spirit Who would lead them into all truth (Jn. 15:26-27; 16:13). This combination of eyewitness testimony and Spirit-guided witness produced a *"tradition"* that was a true and valid compliment to the Old Testament. So, I Timothy 5:18 and II Peter 3:16 placed apostolic tradition alongside Scripture and described it as such.

THE METHOD OF VALID TRADITION

During Old Testament times, and during the time of Christ, actually up to the invention of the printing press, methods such as learning by heart, memorizing the actual words of the teacher, condensing the material into short text, and the use of notebooks were common in the days of Christ. The Apostles and the Early Church were also seriously concerned with a conscious handing down of a valid tradition of Christ and not just with an unconscious transmission of a diluted tradition through preaching. When the uniqueness of Jesus in the eyes of the Early Church is also taken into account, the likelihood of additions to the story becomes even more suspect. In the light of that, the environment in which the Gospels were originally written was deeply concerned for the correct handing on of tradition and not as interested in supplementing fact with imagined improvement, as some scholars believe. The exhortations of Paul regarding the *"tradition"* gained added significance in this context.

The Apostolic Office was limited to eyewitnesses, and, as only eyewitnesses could bear a faithful witness to Christ as He lived and died and rose again, true tradition must also be Apostolic. This was recognized by the Church in later years when the Canon of the New Testament was eventually produced on the basis of the Apostolic nature of the Books concerned.

Apostolic tradition was at one time oral, but for us it is crystallized in the Apostolic writings containing the Spirit-guided witness to the Christ of God.

Other teaching, while it may be instructive and useful and worthy of serious consideration, still, cannot claim to be placed alongside Old Testament and New Testament as authoritative without manifesting the same defects as condemned Jewish tradition in the Eyes of our Lord.

(The above material on *"tradition"* was derived in part from the New Bible Dictionary.[1])

So, one can be certain presently that the Bible held in one's hands, at least as it regards the King James Version, is authentic, and in every capacity. In other words, it does not merely contain the Word of God, but in reality, is the Word of God.

Once again, and tragically so, modern preachers are doing that which Israel of old did in the time of Christ. They are:

• Placing the ideas of man alongside the Word of God.

• In many cases, adding to the Word.

• Placing greater significance in their words than even the Word of God.

• In many cases, completely ignoring the Word of God, subscribing instead to the mere words of man.

I hear the Words of our Lord, echoing through the ages of time, *"Man shall not live by bread alone, but by every Word that proceeds out of the Mouth of God"* (Mat. 4:4).

NOTES

If one wants to know the value of man's words as it pertains to life and living, one need only to study carefully the ramblings of Eliphaz, Bildad, and Zophar. And then we hear the Word of God as it relates to these three men when He said, *"My wrath is kindled against you . . . for you have not spoken of Me the thing that is right"* (Job 42:7).

In 42:8 they were then instructed to go to the Cross. Please understand, the admonition is still the same now as it was then, *"Go to the Cross!"* When one goes to the Cross, one goes directly to the Word of God, for the Bible is the Story of Jesus Christ and Him Crucified.

THE WISDOM OF MAN AND THE WISDOM OF GOD

James contrasted these two sources of wisdom, by saying that the wisdom of man is *"earthly, sensual, and devilish."* He said that the Wisdom of God is *"pure, peaceable, gentle, and easy to be entreated, full of mercy and good fruits, without partiality, and without hypocrisy"* (James 3:15-17).

These three men, who were supposed to be Job's friends, were given up in that day to be some of the wisest men in the world. But yet, their wisdom, contrasted with that of Job, was that of the world. As we have stated, they knew some things about God, things which were true, but the true Ways of God they did not know nor understand and, therefore, there was no way they could speak that of Him which was right.

As we have also previously stated, the Holy Spirit allowed all of their ramblings to be placed in the Sacred Text, in order that we may know and understand that the very best the world has to offer, is woefully insufficient. In fact, it holds no validity at all, at least as it regards life and living. Peter said:

"Grace and Peace be multiplied unto you through the knowledge of God, and of Jesus our Lord (this is both Sanctifying Grace and Sanctifying Peace, all made available by the Cross),

"According as His Divine Power has given unto us all things (the Lord with large-handed generosity has given us all things) *that pertain unto life and godliness* (pertains to the fact that the Lord Jesus has

given us everything we need regarding life and living), *through the knowledge of Him Who has called us to Glory and Virtue* (the *'knowledge'* addressed here speaks of what Christ did at the Cross, which alone can provide *'Glory and Virtue'*):

"Whereby are given unto us exceeding great and Precious Promises (pertains to the Word of God, which alone holds the answer to every life problem)*: that by these* (Promises) *you might be partakers of the Divine Nature* (the Divine Nature implanted in the inner being of the believing sinner becomes the source of our new life and actions; it comes to everyone at the moment of being *'Born-Again'*), *having escaped the corruption that is in the world through lusts.* (This presents the Salvation experience of the sinner and the Sanctification experience of the Saint)" (II Pet. 1:2-4).

There was a time that the Word of God was the Queen of the sciences in our universities; presently, it is humanistic psychology.

Once the Word of God was the Queen of our life and living in the churches; presently, it is humanistic psychology.

What a sorry trade!

(13) "SO ARE THE PATHS OF ALL WHO FORGET GOD; AND THE HYPOCRITE'S HOPE SHALL PERISH:

(14) "WHOSE HOPE SHALL BE CUT OFF, AND WHOSE TRUST SHALL BE A SPIDER'S WEB.

(15) "HE SHALL LEAN UPON HIS HOUSE, BUT IT SHALL NOT STAND: HE SHALL HOLD IT FAST, BUT IT SHALL NOT ENDURE.

(16) "HE IS GREEN BEFORE THE SUN, AND HIS BRANCH SHOOTS FORTH IN HIS GARDEN.

(17) "HIS ROOTS ARE WRAPPED ABOUT THE HEAP, AND SEES THE PLACE OF STONES.

(18) "IF HE DESTROY HIM FROM HIS PLACE, THEN IT SHALL DENY HIM, SAYING, I HAVE NOT SEEN YOU.

(19) "BEHOLD, THIS IS THE JOY OF HIS WAY, AND OUT OF THE EARTH SHALL OTHERS GROW.

(20) "BEHOLD, GOD WILL NOT CAST AWAY A PERFECT MAN, NEITHER WILL HE HELP THE EVIL DOERS:

(21) "TILL HE FILL YOUR MOUTH WITH LAUGHING, AND YOUR LIPS WITH REJOICING.

(22) "THEY WHO HATE YOU SHALL BE CLOTHED WITH SHAME; AND THE DWELLING PLACE OF THE WICKED SHALL COME TO NOUGHT."

The pattern is:

1. (Vs. 13) Bluntly, Bildad calls Job a *"hypocrite."* The truth of the matter was that Job was no hypocrite, but Eliphaz, Bildad, and Zophar were. Their hypocrisy was the hypocrisy of self-righteousness, which is the worst hypocrisy of all.

2. (Vs. 13) Men are fond of judging their righteousness by comparing it to others. It made Bildad feel superior to point out Job's alleged shortcomings. He did not dream that while he was judging Job, God was judging him.

3. (Vs. 20) How ironclad is the argument of Bildad. He thinks, if Job had been a *"perfect man,"* God would not have cast him away; likewise, God not helping him proves that he is an *"evildoer."* How smug Bildad feels in his summation.

4. Verse 21 actually has in other words, Bildad saying to Job, *"If you will confess your evil, the Lord will fill your mouth with laughing."*

5. (Vs. 22) Whenever man, working from human reasoning, begins to judge, almost invariably he will call *"unholy"* what God calls *"holy,"* and *"holy"* what God calls *"unholy"*!

HYPOCRITE

A hypocrite as it regards living for the Lord, is one who puts on a pious face outwardly, but inwardly has no desire to live for God, is not trying to live for God, but is rather living a life of evil.

It does not refer to Believers, who are struggling with a problem of sin in their life, whatever it might be, in effect, trying to gain victory.

Jesus referred to the Pharisees as *"hypocrites."* He said:

"But woe unto you, Scribes and Pharisees, hypocrites! (The first of eight woes, and said to their faces. There could be no greater insult to them than being called *'hypocrites'*!) *for you shut up the Kingdom*

of Heaven against men (is the first scheme of Satan, and is carried out through religion): *for you neither go in yourselves, neither suffer you them who are entering to go in* (they refused to accept Christ, and stood in the door to bar access to any and all who would attempt to come in).

"*Woe unto you, Scribes and Pharisees, hypocrites! for you devour widows' houses, and for a pretense make long prayer* (projects a false piety, which deceives people, and the most helpless at that): *therefore you shall receive the greater damnation* (this tells us that religious wickedness is the greatest wickedness of all).

"*Woe unto you, Scribes and Pharisees, hypocrites! for you compass sea and land to make one proselyte* (working zealously to draw people to themselves, instead of the Lord), *and when he is made, you make him twofold more the child of Hell than yourselves* (religious people are the hardest of all to bring to the Lord).

"*Woe unto you, Scribes and Pharisees, hypocrites! for you make clean the outside of the cup and of the platter* (outward show), *but within they are full of extortion and excess* (the heart).

"*Even so you also outwardly appear righteous unto men, but within you are full of hypocrisy and iniquity*" (Mat. 23:13-15, 25, 28).

THE PROBLEM OF SIN IN THE LIFE OF CHRISTIANS

If the Believer doesn't understand the Message of the Cross as it refers to Sanctification, i.e., how we live for God, which means the object of his faith is something else other than the Cross of Christ, such a person will be ruled by the sin nature, no matter how hard he or she tries to do and be the opposite. The Seventh Chapter of Romans succinctly bears this out. The great Apostle said:

"*For that which I do* (the failure) *I allow not* (should have been translated, '*I understand not*'; these are not the words of an unsaved man, as some claim, but rather a Believer who is trying and failing): *for what I would, that do I not* (refers to the obedience he wants to render to Christ, but rather fails; why? as Paul explained, the Believer is married to Christ, but is being unfaithful to Christ by spiritually cohabiting with the Law, which frustrates the Grace of God; that means the Holy Spirit will not help such a person, which guarantees failure [Gal. 2:21]); *but what I hate, that do I* (refers to sin in his life, which he doesn't want to do, and, in fact, hates, but finds himself unable to stop; unfortunately, due to the fact of not understanding the Cross as it refers to Sanctification, this is the plight of most modern Christians)" (Rom. 7:15).

The Apostle went on to say, "*For the good that I would I do not* (if I depend on self, and not the Cross): *but the evil which I would not* (don't want to do), *that I do* (which is exactly what every Believer will do no matter how hard he tries to do otherwise, if he tries to live this life outside of the Cross [Gal. 2:20-21])" (Rom. 7:19).

To be sure, when Paul wrote this, giving us a glimpse into his life after his conversion and after being baptized with the Holy Spirit, most definitely he now knew God's Prescribed Order of Victory. But he is letting us see his life before this great Revelation was given to him. Regrettably and sadly, the things he said about himself are the lot and life of most modern Christians.

As we have stated, these are people who love the Lord, and are trying with all of their strength not to fail, but simply because they do not understand the Message of the Cross, which is how the Holy Spirit works, they cannot overcome. These people aren't hypocrites!

IS AN ACT OF SIN SIMPLY A MATTER OF SAYING "*YES*" OR "*NO*"?

The answer to the question of the heading is a resounding "*no*"!

Frances and I were with a particular Pentecostal denomination for years, and preaching meetings in their churches all over the nation, at times the subject would be approached respecting some particular preacher or a layman who had had some type of problem. Countless times I heard preachers say about these particular individuals, whomever they may have been, "*All they had to do was to say 'no,' and walk away!*"

They were stating that the matter of sin was simply a *"yes"* or *"no,"* meaning that if a Believer yielded to the temptation, whatever the temptation would be, that means the person was no good to begin with, and the church or the denomination would be better off without them.

As a young Preacher, I would hear these statements, and I wondered about them in my mind. These preachers were older than I, had much more experience, so I did not question what they said, but just simply locked it away.

Was the matter of sin that simple? I was to find out that it was not that simple.

I'm going to make some statements that some of you have never heard, but I know they are true, because the Bible says so. Please read the heading very carefully.

IF A BELIEVER DOESN'T UNDERSTAND GOD'S PRESCRIBED ORDER OF VICTORY, SATAN CAN FORCE THAT BELIEVER TO DO SOMETHING AGAINST THEIR WILL

Listen again to Paul, as I quote from THE EXPOSITOR'S STUDY BIBLE:

"For I know that in me (that is, in my flesh,) dwells no good thing (speaks of man's own ability, or rather the lack thereof in comparison to the Holy Spirit, at least when it comes to spiritual things): *for to will is present with me* (Paul is speaking here of his willpower; regrettably, most modern Christians are trying to live for God by means of willpower, thinking falsely that since they have come to Christ, they are now free to say 'no' to sin; that is the wrong way to look at the situation; the Believer cannot live for God by the strength of willpower; while the will is definitely important, it alone is not enough; the Believer must exercise Faith in Christ and the Cross, and do so constantly; then he will have the ability and strength to say *'yes'* to Christ, which automatically says, *'no'* to the things of the world); *but how to perform that which is good I find not* (outside of the Cross, it is impossible to find a way to do good)" (Rom. 7:18).

Clearly and plainly in this Eighteenth Verse, Paul tells us, while the will is important as should be obvious, it is not within itself strong enough to resist the powers of darkness. But yet, most modern Christians are trying to live for God by the means of willpower alone. Let me say it again:

Show me the best Christian, the most consecrated Christian that you know. If that person doesn't understand God's Prescribed Order of Victory, which means he will little have the help of the Holy Spirit, Satan can force that person to do something he or she is trying not to do, doesn't want to do, is struggling not to do, but will find themselves doing it anyway, whatever it might be. That means, that the problem of sin is not merely a *"yes"* or *"no"* affair, as should be obvious.

WHAT IS GOD'S PRESCRIBED ORDER OF VICTORY?

Let me give this little formula that might help us to understand it even more. It's very simple, but I think it will suffice.

• FOCUS: The Lord Jesus Christ (Jn. 14:6).
• OBJECT OF FAITH: The Cross of Christ (Rom. 6:3-5).
• POWER SOURCE: The Holy Spirit (Rom. 8:1-2, 11).
• RESULTS: Victory (Rom. 6:14).

In very abbreviated form we have given you God's Prescribed Order of Victory. If any Believer will do what is given there, such a Believer can walk in Victory, and I speak of Victory over the world, the flesh, and the Devil. In fact, this is the only manner in which one can walk in Victory. The Lord doesn't have five ways or even two ways, only one way, and that is the Way of the Cross.

Let's turn around this same formula and use it the way that it is basically being used in the Christian world at present. Please read it carefully:

• Focus: Works
• Object of Faith: Performance
• Power Source: Self
• Results: Defeat

There is only one answer for sin and that is the Cross of Christ.

HOW IS THE CROSS OF CHRIST THE ANSWER FOR SIN?

When we say the *"Cross,"* of course, we

are not speaking of the wooden beam, but rather that which Jesus did there, the Victory He won, the price He paid. So we're not speaking of wearing the Cross around one's neck, or as a bracelet, or a charm, which should go without saying.

As well, we aren't really speaking of the death that Jesus died. While that was absolutely necessary, and actually the very reason He came to this world, and that which satisfied the Righteousness of a thrice-Holy God, still, Jesus died in weakness (II Cor. 13:4). But to be sure, it was a contrived weakness. In other words, He had the Power to call down twelve legions of Angels if He so desired, but He refused to use that power, and rightly so. So, the Victory of the Cross is not so much in the death of Christ, even though it was His Death which made possible the Victory.

The power of the Cross is actually in the domain of the Holy Spirit.

The Holy Spirit works exclusively within the legal confines, if one would use that terminology, of the Cross of Christ. In other words, it is the Cross and what Jesus did there in the giving of Himself in Sacrifice, which satisfied the demands of a thrice-Holy God, thereby, satisfying the claims that God had against man, because of the broken Law. Concerning that, Paul also wrote:

"Christ has redeemed us from the curse of the Law (He did so on the Cross), *being made a curse for us* (He took the penalty of the Law, which was death)*: for it is written, Cursed is everyone who hangs on a tree* (Deut. 21:22-23)*:*

"That the blessing of Abraham (Justification by Faith) *might come on the Gentiles through Jesus Christ* (what He did at the Cross)*; that we might receive the Promise of the Spirit through Faith.* (All sin was atoned at the Cross, which lifted the sin debt from believing man, making it possible for the Holy Spirit to come into the life of the Believer and abide there forever [Jn. 14:16-17])*"* (Gal. 3:13).

Satisfying the curse of the broken Law meant that the terrible sin debt was lifted from man, at least for all who will believe (Jn. 3:16).

This made it possible for the Holy Spirit to come into the hearts and lives of Believers, which He does instantly at conversion. The Power is in the Holy Spirit, but it was all made possible by the Cross. That's what Paul was also speaking of when he said:

"For the preaching (Message) *of the Cross is to them who perish foolishness* (spiritual things cannot be discerned by unredeemed people, but that doesn't matter; the Cross must be preached just the same, even as we shall see)*; but unto us who are Saved it is the Power of God.* (The Cross is the Power of God simply because it was there, as stated, that the total sin debt was paid, giving the Holy Spirit, in Whom the Power resides, latitude to work mightily within our lives)*"* (I Cor. 1:18).

If the Cross of Christ is preached, people will be Saved, Believers will be filled with the Spirit, the sick will be healed, miracles will come about, people will be delivered from bondages of sin and darkness, the Fruit of the Spirit will be evident in the lives of Believers, the Gifts of the Spirit will be evident in hearts and lives, the Believer will grow in Grace and the knowledge of the Lord, victorious over the world, the flesh, and the Devil. This is God's Way.

If any other way is entertained, no matter how good it may seem to be on the surface, none of the things mentioned above will happen. While there might be great religious machinery in operation, still, absolutely nothing will truly be done for God. The Church must preach the Cross, must sing the Cross, must think the Cross, understanding that every single Doctrine in the Bible, if it is to be legitimate, must be built squarely on the foundation of the Cross of Christ. Otherwise it will be specious (I Pet. 1:18-19).

"Lamb of God! Our souls adore Thee,
"While upon Your Face we gaze;
"There the Father's Love and Glory,
"Shine in all their brightest rays;
"Your Almighty Power and Wisdom,
"All Creation's works proclaim;
"Heaven and Earth alike confess Thee,
"As the ever great 'I Am.'"

"Lamb of God! Your Father's Bosom,
"Ever was Your Dwelling Place;
"His delight, in Him rejoicing,

"One with Him in Power and Grace;
"Oh, what wondrous Love and Mercy!
"You did lay Your Glory by;
"And for us did come from Heaven,
"As the Lamb of God to die."

"Lamb of God! When we behold Thee,
"Lowly in the manger laid,
"Wandering as a homeless stranger,
"In the world Your Hands have made;
"When we see You in the Garden,
"In Your agony of blood;
"At Your Grace we are confounded,
"Holy, Spotless Lamb of God!"

"When we see You, as the Victim,
"Bound to the accursed tree,
"For our guilt and folly stricken,
"All our judgment borne by Thee,
"Lord, we own, with hearts adoring,
"You have loved us unto blood;
"Glory, glory everlasting,
"Be to You, Thou Lamb of God."

"Lamb of God, You soon in Glory,
"Will to this sad Earth return;
"All Your foes shall quake before Thee,
"All who now despise You mourn;
"Then Your Saints all gather to Thee,
"With You in Your Kingdom reign;
"Yours the praise and Yours the glory,
"Lamb of God, for sinners slain!"

CHAPTER 9

(1) "THEN JOB ANSWERED AND SAID,

(2) "I KNOW IT IS SO OF A TRUTH: BUT HOW SHOULD MAN BE JUST WITH GOD?

(3) "IF HE WILL CONTEND WITH HIM, HE CANNOT ANSWER HIM ONE OF A THOUSAND.

(4) "HE IS WISE IN HEART, AND MIGHTY IN STRENGTH: WHO HAS HARDENED HIMSELF AGAINST HIM, AND HAS PROSPERED?

(5) "WHICH REMOVES THE MOUNTAINS, AND THEY KNOW NOT: WHICH OVERTURNS THEM IN HIS ANGER.

(6) "WHICH SHAKES THE EARTH OUT OF HER PLACE, AND THE PILLARS THEREOF TREMBLE.

(7) "WHICH COMMANDS THE SUN, AND IT RISES NOT; AND SEALS UP THE STARS.

(8) "WHICH ALONE SPREADS OUT THE HEAVENS, AND TREADS UPON THE WAVES OF THE SEA.

(9) "WHICH MAKES ARCTURUS, ORION, AND PLEIADES, AND THE CHAMBERS OF THE SOUTH.

(10) "WHICH DOES GREAT THINGS PAST FINDING OUT; YES, AND WONDERS WITHOUT NUMBER.

(11) "LO, HE GOES BY ME, AND I SEE HIM NOT: HE PASSES ON ALSO, BUT I PERCEIVE HIM NOT.

(12) "BEHOLD, HE TAKES AWAY, WHO CAN HINDER HIM? WHO WILL SAY UNTO HIM, WHAT ARE YOU DOING?"

The exegesis is:

1. The answer to Job's question of Verse 2 is found in Romans, Chapter 3.

2. (Vs. 3) If God questions us, we cannot even answer one question out of a thousand, at least out of our own ability, no matter how educated we might be.

3. (Vs. 8) God is the Creator of all things and, thereby, has control of all things, and can change their function as He so desires.

4. Verse 9 shows that the rotundity of the Earth was known at that time, which was about 3,700 years ago.

5. Job says the things recorded in Verse 11 in the heat of this tremendous trial. Some things he says are right and some are wrong. In fact, Job does perceive the Lord, but he is now questioning his own experience. In other words, he is saying, *"Considering what has happened to me, I'm not sure if my perception is right or not."*

6. (Vs. 12) Job is saying that the Lord has taken away all that he has and, in a sense, that is true, and there was nothing that Job could do to stop or change the situation. Furthermore, he doesn't even know why!

JUSTIFICATION BY FAITH

Job asks the question, *"How shall man be just with God?"*

Even though Job had no Bible as we do today, which means that his knowledge would have been extremely limited, still, the knowledge of God that he did have was purely by Revelation and by experiences that others had before him, others such as Abraham, Isaac, and his grandfather Jacob.

It is certain that Job knew of his great-great grandfather Abraham's great experiences. He had, no doubt, heard the story told scores of times of how Abraham believed God, *"And He counted it to him for Righteousness"* (Gen. 15:6).

However, there is another side to this *"spiritual warfare"* that we must examine. In this Chapter we will find that Job questions his Faith and his theology. In truth, a great spiritual crisis will force the examination of one's faith. I think that Job did understand *"Justification by Faith,"* at least as far as Old Testament Believers could understand it. Or, quite possibly, he is asking the question out of frustration and despair. More than likely this is correct.

Taking everything into consideration, we must believe that Job did actually believe that he was *"just with God"*; however, circumstances make it seem otherwise, and in view of God's Power, who can contend with Him?

Of all the things that man receives from God, Faith is the bedrock of God's Gifts. Every attack by Satan, irrespective of its nature, is but for one purpose, and that is to destroy our Faith in God, or at least to seriously weaken it. Satan's attack on Job was for that very purpose, *"to destroy Job's Faith."*

WHAT EXACTLY IS JUSTIFICATION BY FAITH?

Justification is the act of a thrice-Holy God, Who declares in a moment's time an obviously guilty sinner, as perfectly righteous. He does this and, in fact, can do this, on the basis of the sinner exercising Faith in Christ, Who has paid the price for man's Redemption at Calvary's Cross. In fact, Justification can be received from God only on the basis of Faith exercised, which Faith must without question be in Christ and what Christ has done for us at the Cross. If one seeks Justification on the basis of merit or so-called good works, such a person will be instantly rejected. That's why Paul wrote:

"For by Grace (the Goodness of God) *are you Saved through Faith* (Faith in Christ, with the Cross ever as its Object)*; and that not of yourselves* (none of this is of us, but all is of Him)*: it is the Gift of God* (anytime the word *'Gift'* is used, God is speaking of His Son and His Substitutionary Work on the Cross, which makes all of this possible)*:*

"Not of works (man cannot merit Salvation, irrespective what he does), *lest any man should boast* (boast in his own ability and strength; we are allowed to boast only in the Cross [Gal. 6:14])" (Eph. 2:8-9).

The great Apostle also said: *"Therefore being justified by Faith* (this is the only way one can be justified; refers to Faith in Christ and what He did at the Cross), *we have peace with God* (justifying peace) *through our Lord Jesus Christ* (what He did at the Cross):

"By Whom also we have access by Faith into this Grace (we have access to the Goodness of God by Faith in Christ) *wherein we stand* (wherein alone we can stand), *and rejoice in hope* (a hope that is guaranteed) *of the Glory of God* (our Faith in Christ always brings Glory to God; anything else brings glory to self, which God can never accept)" (Rom. 5:1-2).

HOW CAN A RIGHTEOUS GOD HONESTLY JUSTIFY AN OBVIOUSLY UNRIGHTEOUS SINNER, AND RETAIN HIS INTEGRITY?

In other words, how can God be *"just,"* and at the same time be the *"Justifier"* of an obvious sinner?

Paul addresses this by saying:

"Being justified freely by His Grace (made possible by the Cross) *through the Redemption that is in Christ Jesus* (carried out at the Cross)*:*

"Whom God has set forth to be a propitiation (Atonement or Reconciliation) *through Faith in His Blood* (again, all of this is made possible by the Cross), *to declare His Righteousness for the remission of sins that are past* (refers to all who trusted Christ before He actually came, which covers the entirety of the time from the Garden of Eden to the moment Jesus died on the Cross), *through the forbearance* (tolerance) *of God* (meaning that God tolerated the situation before Calvary, knowing the debt would be fully

paid at that time);

"*To declare, I say, at this time His Righteousness* (refers to God's Righteousness, which must be satisfied at all times, and is in Christ and only Christ)*: that He* (God) *might be just* (not overlooking sin in any manner), *and the Justifier of him which believes in Jesus* (God can justify a believing [although guilty] sinner, and His Holiness not be impacted, providing the sinner's Faith is exclusively in Christ; only in this manner can God be *'just'* and at the same time *'justify'* the sinner)" (Rom. 3:24-26).

In essence, Paul is saying that God can justify an obviously guilty sinner, and maintain His Integrity, on the basis of justice satisfied by Christ at Calvary's Cross, and the sinner's obvious Faith in Christ, which is an absolute necessity.

That's why the term is used *"Justification by Faith."* It cannot be by works, it cannot be by merit, it cannot be by self effort, it can only be by Faith in Christ and what He has done for us at the Cross.

Justification by Faith brings to an end the hostility between God and man, caused by man's sin. Concerning this, Paul also said:

THE REMOVAL OF HOSTILITY BETWEEN GOD AND MAN

"*Having abolished in His Flesh* (speaking of His Death on the Cross, by which He redeemed humanity, which also means He didn't die spiritually, as some claim) *the enmity* (the hatred between God and man, caused by sin), *even the Law of Commandments contained in Ordinances* (pertains to the Law of Moses, and more particularly the Ten Commandments); *for to make in Himself of twain* (of Jews and Gentiles) *one new man, so making peace* (which again was accomplished by the Cross); *and that He* (Christ) *might reconcile both* (Jews and Gentiles) *unto God in one body* (the Church) *by the Cross* (it is by the Atonement that men ever become reconciled to God), *having slain the enmity thereby* (removed the barrier between God and sinful man)" (Eph. 2:15-16).

As the Scripture said, and we have just quoted, it was the Cross of Christ, where our Lord paid the price by the giving of Himself as a Perfect Sacrifice, which was accepted by God that removed the terrible barrier between God and man, caused by man's sin.

Because of that sin, man cannot approach God in any capacity, except by Faith in Christ and what Christ did at the Cross. The reason for this is simple, it was at the Cross that the price was paid, in essence, the ransom which man owed to God was forever paid, and paid by Christ. To acquire all the benefits of what Jesus did there, all that sinful man has to do is simply register Faith in Christ, and in the doing so, everything for which Jesus paid such a price will be granted freely, and we speak of a perfect Righteousness, to the believing sinner. This is the great Plan of Redemption, all wrapped up in Christ and what Christ did at the Cross.

That's the reason that we preach the Cross! Preach the Cross! Preach the Cross! (I Cor. 1:23).

THAT WHICH THE LORD GAVE TO PAUL

Paul maintains that God justifies sinners on a just ground: namely, that Jesus Christ, acting on their behalf, has satisfied the claims of God's Law upon them. He was *"born under the Law"* (Gal. 4:4) in order to fulfill the precept and bear the penalty of the Law in our stead. By His *"Blood"* (His Death) He put away our sins (Rom. 3:25; 5:9). By His obedience to God He won for all His People the status of *"Law-keepers"* (Rom. 5:19). He became *"obedient unto death"* (Phil. 2:8); His Life of Righteousness culminated in His dying the death of the unrighteous, bearing the Law's penal curse (Gal. 3:13; Isa. 53:4-12). In His Person on the Cross, the sins of His People were judged and expiated. Through this *"one act of Righteousness"* — His sinless Life and sinless Death — *"the free gift came unto all men to Justification of Life"* (Rom. 5:18). Thus, Believers become the Righteousness of God in and through Him Who knew no sin personally, but was representatively *"made sin"* (treated as a sinner, and judged, as it regards death) in our place (II Cor. 5:21). Thus, Paul speaks of *"Christ Jesus, Whom God made . . . our Righteousness"* (I Cor. 1:30).

On the basis of justice satisfied, and done

so by Christ on the Cross, God accounts sinners who believe in Christ as perfectly righteous, not because He accounts us to have kept His Law personally (which would be a false judgment), but because He accounts us to be *"in the One Who kept God's Law representatively,"* which is a true Judgment.

So, when God justifies sinners on the ground of Christ's Obedience and Death, He acts justly. So far from compromising His Judicial Righteousness, this method of Justification actually exhibits it. It is designed *"to show God's Righteousness,"* because in His Divine forbearance He has passed over former sins (in Old Testament times). It was to prove at the present time that He Himself is righteous and that He justifies him who has Faith in Jesus (Rom. 3:25).

IS FAITH THE GROUND OF JUSTIFICATION?

In a word, no!

If faith was the ground of justification, it would be a meritorious work, and Paul would not be able to term the Believer, as such, *"one who does not work"* (Rom. 4:5). Nor could he go on to say that Salvation by Faith rests on Grace, for Grace absolutely excludes works (Rom. 11:6). So, what is the ground of Justification?

The ground for Justification on the part of God is the Cross of Christ, and the Cross of Christ alone. That's why Paul said, and which we have just quoted, *"And that He (Christ) might reconcile both (Jews and Gentiles) unto God in one body (the Church) by the Cross* (it is by the Atonement only that men ever become reconciled to God), *having slain the enmity thereby* (removed the barrier between God and sinful man, and did so by the Cross)" (Eph. 2:16).

QUESTIONING GOD!

Job said, and speaking about the Lord, *"Behold, He takes away, who can hinder Him? Who will say unto Him, what are you doing?"*

The desire to question God as to why or what, is perhaps one of the greatest temptations or desires that a Believer may have. The Lord very seldom sees fit to explain to us, or to show to us, as to why He does certain things, or why we are affected as we are. That is not without design and purpose. He wants us to trust Him, believe Him, look to Him, lean on Him, in essence, to trust Him implicitly, and without having to know the reason why. That is not all the time easy to do.

The Lord never does things in a haphazard way. He always has a purpose and a reason for everything He does. A purpose and reason that is for our benefit, that is, if we are serving Him. Why does He allow things to happen as they do?

Sometimes He sees fit to relate to us the reason immediately, and then at other times He waits for a length of time, even years.

A PERSONAL EXPERIENCE

If I remember correctly, the year was 1954. I had just started preaching. The occasion at hand, was a Sunday night Service at our little home Church in Ferriday, Louisiana. Probably there were only 15 or 20 people present that Sunday night, if that.

As I began to preach, it seemed like there was a bondage in the Service, and I soon realized I was getting nowhere fast. I was stumbling over the words I was trying to pronounce, almost incoherent with my thoughts. All of a sudden in the midst of all of this, I quoted the words of an old song that I had sung many times.

> *"Hallelujah what a thought,*
> *"Jesus full Salvation bought,*
> *"Victory, yes Victory.*
> *"Let the powers of sin assail,*
> *"Heaven's Grace shall never fail,*
> *"Victory, yes Victory."*

The moment I quoted that Verse, the Spirit of God instantly fell in that little building, with the entirety of the complexion of the Service instantly changing. I remember looking out and seeing people raising their hands worshipping God as the Spirit of the Lord filled my heart, and theirs as well.

I did not understand at all why the Lord did what He did that night, and really there was no reason for me to question what had happened, only to receive it, which I did, and be glad.

Many years passed, which helped us to see

the world touched for Christ with hundreds of thousands brought to a Saving knowledge of Jesus Christ, for which we give the Lord all the praise and glory. But yet, there were some extremely difficult times in the midst of this; times, which I did not think that I would weather, but I did.

Again, if I remember correctly, the year was 1998, over 40 years since that occasion in the little Church that Sunday night in 1954.

In one of our morning Prayer meetings here at the Ministry, as I was seeking the Lord that morning, the Holy Spirit brought to my mind that occasion that took place those many, many years before. He relived it for me. I could see the Church, the people inside, feel the struggle as I was trying to preach, and then the quoting of the Verse of the song, and then how the Spirit of God fell instantly. And then the Lord spoke to my heart.

He said, *"Do you remember that night so long ago?"* And yes, I did!

And then He said, *"Do you remember the song that you quoted which contained the words:*

"Let the powers of sin assail,
"Heaven's Grace can never fail?"

And yes, I remembered it vividly! And then the Lord spoke to my heart again, saying,

"The powers of sin did assail, but my Grace did not fail, did it?!"

I sat there on the floor with tears rolling down my cheeks, reliving that scene, and rejoicing in the great fact that Heaven's Grace did not fail, will never fail, and, in fact, cannot fail.

It was over 40 years before that the Lord revealed to me the reason for that moment in that little Church so long ago.

Why so long?

It would have done no good for Him to have related to me the reason whenever His Spirit first Moved upon me that Sunday night in 1954. I would not have understood what He was talking about. In fact, it would not have made any sense. But when He did choose to bring to my mind that occasion which happened so long before, a great Truth was revealed to me.

Why would the Lord conduct Himself toward me in that fashion so many years before the fact?

That I cannot say!

Perhaps it is to let us know that He knows the beginning from the end, and the end from the beginning; consequently, nothing is a surprise to Him.

What a delight it is to serve our Lord Who is full of Grace and full of Mercy.

(13) "IF GOD WILL NOT WITHDRAW HIS ANGER, THE PROUD HELPERS DO STOOP UNDER HIM.

(14) "HOW MUCH LESS SHALL I ANSWER HIM, AND CHOOSE OUT MY WORDS TO REASON WITH HIM?

(15) "WHOM, THOUGH I WERE RIGHTEOUS, YET WOULD I NOT ANSWER, BUT I WOULD MAKE SUPPLICATION TO MY JUDGE.

(16) "IF I HAD CALLED, AND HE HAD ANSWERED ME, YET WOULD I NOT BELIEVE THAT HE HAD HEARKENED UNTO MY VOICE.

(17) "FOR HE BREAKS ME WITH A TEMPEST, AND MULTIPLIES MY WOUNDS WITHOUT CAUSE.

(18) "HE WILL NOT SUFFER ME TO TAKE MY BREATH, BUT FILLS ME WITH BITTERNESS.

(19) "IF I SPEAK OF STRENGTH, LO, HE IS STRONG: AND IF OF JUDGMENT, WHO SHALL SET ME A TIME TO PLEAD?

(20) "IF I JUSTIFY MYSELF, MY OWN MOUTH SHALL CONDEMN ME: IF I SAY, I AM PERFECT, IT SHALL ALSO PROVE ME PERVERSE.

(21) "THOUGH I WERE PERFECT, YET WOULD I NOT KNOW MY SOUL: I WOULD DESPISE MY LIFE.

(22) "THIS IS ONE THING, THEREFORE I SAID IT, HE DESTROYS THE PERFECT AND THE WICKED.

(23) "IF THE SCOURGE SLAY SUDDENLY, HE WILL LAUGH AT THE TRIAL OF THE INNOCENT.

(24) "THE EARTH IS GIVEN INTO THE HAND OF THE WICKED: HE COVERS THE FACES OF THE JUDGES THEREOF; IF NOT, WHERE, AND WHO IS HE?"

The exposition is:

1. (Vs. 13) Considering Job's circumstances, surely God, he thinks, must be angry with him. So, all of this tells us that it's very

difficult for us to discern the Lord or His Ways. Unless He reveals His Purpose to us, as He did to Job a little later, almost all the time our assumptions are wrong.

2. As it regards Verse 14, Job is saying that he did not know how to pray; in fact, he didn't even know what to say. Living under the Old Covenant, Job did not have the privilege of the infilling of the Holy Spirit as we do today under the New Covenant. Truly our New Covenant is based on better Promises (Heb. 8:6).

3. (Vs. 15) God is my Judge; prayer is the only rightful attitude of even the best man before his Maker — prayer for Mercy, pardon, Grace, prayer for advance in holiness.

4. (Vs. 16) Job reasons, and wrongly we might add, that due to his condition, God would not hearken unto him.

5. According to Verse 17, Job doesn't understand that there is a cause regarding his situation, he, therefore, said that God was multiplying his wounds without cause. There was a cause, but not in the realm which Job could comprehend, or anyone else at that time for that matter; the *"cause"* was not Job or anything he had done, but rather the *"spirit world."*

6. As it regards Verse 20, about ourselves, there is nothing we can say; in fact, it's what God says that counts; He has already made a gracious statement about Job, but unknown to the Patriarch (2:3).

7. (Vs. 22) While Job is not concluding himself to be perfect, in effect, he is saying, *"It wouldn't matter if I were, it would do me no good"*; in that he is wrong!

8. (Vs. 24) Inasmuch as God has to allow things to be done before they can be done, and irrespective as to what they are, still, there is a reason why God does all things, and that reason is valid; the Judge of all the Earth will do right! (Gen. 18:25).

THE CAUSE

Job said, as it regards the Lord, *"For He breaks me with a tempest, and multiplies my wounds without cause."*

One cannot blame Job for his attitude and the statement he makes here. He does not understand what is happening to him or why it has happened. Irrespective as to what his so-called friends might say, he knows that he has done his very best to live a godly life, in other words, to bring glory to the Lord. So, as far as he is concerned, what is happening to him is without cause.

He is right in one sense of the word that the *"cause"* is not attributed to him per se. While he is the main point of all that is happening, still it is not because He did something wrong that has brought about this terrible trial. But there is a cause!

To be sure, this *"cause"* is of far greater consequence, than anyone at that time could ever begin to know. Little did Job realize in the midst of this trial (he would later), what had actually taken place. He could not visualize Satan himself appearing before God with Job becoming the subject matter of the conversation. He didn't understand that what was happening was being played out before the entirety of the spirit world, which included every Angel both good and evil, and even Satan himself. He will find this out later as the Lord will reveal such to him, but at the present time, he doesn't have a clue.

Every Believer must understand that every single thing that happens to us is either caused or allowed by the Lord. Every Believer is monitored closely! This means there are no accidents with the people of God. There may be many things which look like an accident, but it isn't! Nothing just happens to a Child of God. In fact, everything that happens to a Believer has first been looked at very closely by the Lord of Glory, and judged as to how it will affect us as Believers.

To be sure, we bring many adverse things on ourselves by our lack of consecration, by self-will with the latter being the greatest culprit of all, but still, all Believers come under the canopy of the protection of God and in every capacity. While there may be negative things that happen to us, and even some things that look catastrophic, even as with Job, still, the Lord is monitoring all things.

To be sure, many adverse things (not all), can be shunned aside by our proper relationship with the Lord, meaning that we should ever seek to make that relationship greater and closer.

THE CONDITION OF THE WORLD

Job said, *"The Earth is given into the hand of the wicked: he covers the faces of the judges thereof; if not, where, and who is he?"*

Questions concerning the omnipotence of God, meaning that He is all-mighty, meaning that He can do anything, and if so, why all the evil in the world? Why do hundreds of millions go to bed hungry each night? Possibly there would be reasons for the adults, but why the innocent children?

Why all the sickness and suffering? Why the starvation? Why the war? Why man's inhumanity to man?

The questions fly thick and fast, so untold millions reason, as they consider such, that there is no God. So as the philosopher Bertrand Russell said, and I paraphrase his words, *"If there is a God, and He is Almighty, and allows the innocent to suffer, I do not want any part of such a God."*

When man fell in the Garden of Eden, Satan became the *"god of this world."* Paul said:

"In whom the god of this world (Satan) *has blinded the minds of them which believe not* (a willful blindness), *lest the light of the Glorious Gospel of Christ* (the Message of the Cross) *Who is the Image of God* (Who Alone is the Image of God), *should shine unto them.* (If men reject the Cross, they have, in effect, rejected Christ)" (II Cor. 4:4).

Paul also said:

"And you has He quickened (made alive), *who were dead in trespasses and sins* (total depravity due to the Fall and original sin);

"Wherein in time past you walked according to the course of the this world (refers to the fact that the unredeemed order their behavior and regulate their lives within this sphere of trespasses and sins), *according the prince of the power of the air* (pertains to the fact that Satan heads up the system of this world), *the spirit that now works in the children of disobedience* (the spirit of Satan, which fills all unbelievers, thereby working disobedience)" (Eph. 2:1-2).

Satan, along with all fallen Angels and demon spirits, control the systems of this present world. His motif is to *"steal, kill, and destroy"* (Jn. 10:10).

Now, of course, the question is, God being Almighty, why has He allowed Satan the latitude to do what he has done, which has filled this Earth with graves, and caused sorrow and heartache that knows no bounds?

The only answer that can be given presently is the Bible, as previously stated, refers to this as a *"mystery."* John the Beloved wrote concerning this, *"But in the days of the voice of the seventh Angel, when he shall begin to sound* (proclaims the beginning of the last half of the Great Tribulation, which will be worse than ever), *the Mystery of God should be finished* (this *'Mystery'* pertains to the reason God has allowed Satan to continue his reign over this Earth for these thousands of years [II Cor. 4:4], as He has declared to His Servants the Prophets [Isa. 14:12-20; Ezek. 28:11-19])" (Rev. 10:7).

This we do know, God does all things well, meaning that He has allowed Satan to continue this long for a reason; however, we are very near the time when God is going to step in, and as the song says, *"turn this thing around."*

It will take place at the Second Coming, when Jesus Christ personally will set up a kingdom on this Earth, and will rule the world Personally for a thousand years. Then this world will see peace, prosperity, and freedom as it has never known before.

At that time, Satan along with all his fallen Angels and demon spirits, will be locked away in the bottomless pit. The Scripture says:

"And I saw an Angel come down from Heaven (continues with the idea that Angels are very prominent in the Plan and Work of God), *having the key of the bottomless pit* (speaks of the same place recorded in Rev. 9:1; however, there the key is given to Satan, but this Angel of Rev. 20:1 *'has the key,'* implying that he has had it all along; more than likely, God allows this Angel to give the key to Satan in Rev. 9:1) *and a great chain in his hand* (should be taken literally).

"And he laid hold on the dragon, that old serpent, who is the Devil, and Satan (as a *'dragon,'* he shows his power; as a *'serpent,'* he shows his cunning; as the *'Devil,'* he is the accuser; and as *'Satan,'* he is the adversary),

and bound him a thousand years* (refers to being bound by the great chain carried by the Angel),

"*And cast him into the bottomless pit, and shut him up, and set a seal upon him* (speaks of the abyss being sealed to keep him there), *that he should deceive the nations no more, till the thousand years should be fulfilled: and after that he must be loosed a little season.* (At the end of the thousand-year period, Satan will be loosed out of his prison. He will make another attempt to deceive the nations, in which he will not succeed. We aren't told how long this *'little season'* will be)" (Rev. 20:1-3).

THE FINAL DOOM OF SATAN

The Scripture then says, "*And when the thousand years are expired* (should have been translated, *'finished'*), *Satan shall be loosed out of his prison* (is not meant to infer a mere arbitrary act on the part of God; He has a very valid reason for doing this),

"*And shall go out to deceive the nations which are in the four quarters of the Earth, Gog and Magog* (the main reason the Lord allows Satan this latitude is, it seems, to rid the Earth of all who oppose Christ; George Williams says: *'The Creation Sabbath witnessed the first seduction, and the Millennial Sabbath will witness the last'*; the *'Gog and Magog'* spoken of by John is a Hebrew term expressive of multitude and magnitude; here it embraces all nations, *'the four quarters of the Earth'*), *to gather them together to battle: the number of whom is as the sand of the sea* (proclaims the fact that virtually all of the population at that particular time, which did not accept Christ during the Kingdom Age, will throw in their lot with Satan).

"*And they went up on the breadth of the earth, and compassed the camp of the Saints about, and the beloved city* (picture Satan coming against Jerusalem with his army, which will be the last attack against that city): *and fire came down from God out of Heaven, and devoured them.* (Stipulates that the Lord will make short work of this insurrection. In fact, very little information is given regarding this event, as is obvious.)

"*And the Devil who deceived them was

NOTES

cast into the Lake of Fire and brimstone* (marks the end of Satan regarding his influence in the world, and, in fact, in any part of the Creation of God), *where the Beast and the False Prophet are* (proclaims the fact that these two were placed in *'the Lake of Fire and brimstone'* some one thousand years earlier [Rev. 19:20]), *and shall be tormented day and night forever and ever.* (This signifies the eternity of this place. It is a matter of interest to note that Satan's first act is recorded in Gen., Chpt. 3 [the Third Chapter from the beginning], whereas his last act on a worldwide scale is mentioned in Rev., Chpt. 20 [the Third Chapter from the end])" (Rev. 20:7-10).

THE NEW HEAVEN AND THE NEW EARTH

At this time, after the last insurrection by Satan, with him now being locked away in the Lake of Fire, the heavens and the Earth will be renovated by fire. Peter said:

"*But the Day of the Lord will come as a thief in the night* (the conclusion of the Millennium; what will happen at that time will be unexpected, and for a variety of reasons); *in the which the Heavens shall pass away with a great noise, and the elements shall melt with fervent heat, the Earth also and the works that are therein shall be burned up.* (This does not speak of annihilation, but rather passing from one condition to another.)

"*Seeing then that all these things shall be dissolved* (the present is temporal), *what manner of persons ought you to be in all holy conversation* (lifestyle) *and Godliness* (pertains to the correct view of things),

"*Looking for and hasting unto the Coming of the Day of God* (concerns the coming eternal, perfect Earth, which will last in that condition forever and forever), *wherein the Heavens being on fire shall be dissolved, and the elements shall melt fervent heat?* (*'The Day of God'* will be ushered in by the cataclysmic events of this Verse. There must be no sin left in the Universe.)

"*Nevertheless we* (Believers), *according to His Promise* (the Lord has promised that a new day is coming [Isa. 65:17]), *look for new Heavens* (this is the Promise!) *and a new *earth, wherein dwells Righteousness.* (This proclaims the condition of the coming *'New Heavens and New Earth')"* (II Pet. 3:10-13).

As it regards the new Heaven and the new Earth, John said: *"And I saw a New Heaven and a New Earth* (*'New'* in the Greek is *'kainos,'* and means *'freshness with respect to age'*; when it is finished, it will be new, as is obvious, but the idea is it will remain new and fresh forever and forever because there is no more sin): *for the first Heaven and the first Earth were passed away* (refers to the original Creation, which was marred by sin; *'passed away'* in the Greek is *'parerchomai,'* and means *'to pass from one condition to another'*; and never means annihilation); *and there was no more sea* (refers to the giant oceans, such as the Pacific and the Atlantic; however, there will continue to be lakes, bodies of water, rivers, streams, etc.).

"And I John saw the Holy City, New Jerusalem (presents a New City for this New Earth) *coming down from God out of Heaven* (in effect, God will change His Headquarters from Heaven to Earth), *prepared as a bride adorned for her* (proclaims the Eternal Home of the Redeemed as a dwelling place)" (Rev. 21:1-2).

Concerning this place and what it will be like, the Scripture further says: *"Behold, the Tabernacle of God is with men, and He will dwell with them, and they shall be His people, and God Himself shall be with them, and be their God.* (Finally proclaims that which God intended from the beginning.)

"And God shall wipe away all tears from their eyes (actually says in the Greek, *'every teardrop,'* and refers to tears of sorrow); *and there shall be no more death, neither sorrow, nor crying, neither shall there be any more pain* (addresses sin and all of its results): *for the former things are passed away* (refers to the entire effect of the Fall).

"And He Who sat upon the Throne said (presents, for the second time in this Book, God Himself as the Speaker), *Behold, I make all things new* (refers to the fact of changing from one condition to another). *And He said unto me, Write: for these words are true and faithful.* (All said is *'true,'* and God will be *'faithful'* to bring it all to pass as well)" (Rev. 21:3-5).

NOTES

THE NEW JERUSALEM

Incidentally, the Scripture says that the New Jerusalem will descend down from God out of Heaven, with God then making Planet Earth His Headquarters, and for Eternity (Rev. 21:10-27).

The Scripture says that this city is 12,000 furlongs square, which translates to about 1,500 miles per side. That means, if the southeast corner is situated in Dallas, Texas, the southwest corner would be in Los Angeles, California, and with the northwest corner in Vancouver, B.C., Canada, with the northeast corner in Minneapolis, Minnesota. Needless to say, that's quite a city!

But above all of that, the city is not only about 1,500 miles to the side, it is also 1,500 miles high (Rev. 21:16).

The password for admittance is to be *"born again,"* which means to accept Christ as one's personal Saviour (Jn. 3:3, 16).

THE LAMB OF GOD

In the last two Chapters of Revelation, which describes the Perfect Age to come, incidentally, the Age that will never end, and which will be occupied by every Born-Again Believer who has ever lived, Jesus is referred to seven times as the *"Lamb"* (Rev. 21:9, 14, 22-23, 27; 22:1, 3).

Why?

Of course, the name *"Lamb,"* refers to the Sacrifice of Calvary. The Holy Spirit refers to Him seven times in this respect, in order to let us know, that all of this glory and grandeur, which is coming, was made possible by what Jesus did at the Cross. This we must never forget!

(25) "NOW MY DAYS ARE SWIFTER THAN A POST: THEY FLEE AWAY, THEY SEE NO GOOD.

(26) "THEY ARE PASSED AWAY AS A THE SWIFT SHIPS: AS THE EAGLE THAT HASTENS TO THE PREY.

(27) "IF I SAY, I WILL FORGET MY COMPLAINT, I WILL LEAVE OFF MY HEAVINESS, AND COMFORT MYSELF:

(28) "I AM AFRAID OF ALL MY SORROWS, I KNOW THAT YOU WILL NOT HOLD ME INNOCENT.

(29) "IF I BE WICKED, WHY THEN

LABOUR I IN VAIN?

(30) "IF I WASH MYSELF WITH SNOW WATER, AND MAKE MY HANDS NEVER SO CLEAN;

(31) "YET SHALL YOU PLUNGE ME IN THE DITCH, AND MY OWN CLOTHES SHALL ABHOR ME.

(32) "FOR HE IS NOT A MAN, AS I AM, THAT I SHOULD ANSWER HIM, AND WE SHOULD COME TOGETHER IN JUDGMENT.

(33) "NEITHER IS THERE ANY DAYSMAN BETWIXT US, WHO MIGHT LAY HIS HAND UPON US BOTH.

(34) "LET HIM TAKE HIS ROD AWAY FROM ME, AND LET NOT HIS FEAR TERRIFY ME:

(35) "THEN WOULD I SPEAK, AND NOT FEAR HIM; BUT IT IS NOT SO WITH ME."

The pattern is:

1. According to his statement made in Verse 28, Job reasons, *"if all of this is happening to me, then it stands to reason that I'm not innocent"*; specifically, he was right; particularly, he was wrong!

2. (Vs. 31) *"It doesn't matter what I have done to try to live right, the only conclusion to which I can arrive is that 'the Lord abhors me.'"* Once again, the great Patriarch was looking at circumstances. He knew what was happening, but he didn't know what was going on.

3. As it regards Verse 32, what a plea for the coming Redeemer! True, God is not a man, but God would become Man, and then God and Man would *"come together in Judgment."*

4. (Vs. 33) Job did not understand the coming Work of Christ as Mediator between God and man (I Tim. 2:4-5), but he knew in his heart that the need for such was great. Thank God Jesus Christ has come as the Mediator, i.e., *"Daysman."*

5. (Vs. 34) Little did Job realize that this prayer, no doubt half uttered, would be answered so fully and wondrously in Christ.

THE DAYSMAN

The Patriarch said, *"Neither is there any Daysman betwixt us, that might lay his hand upon us both."*

NOTES

He was right, at that time there was no Daysman, i.e., *"Mediator."* But there was One coming. His name would be, *"The Lord Jesus Christ."*

Before the Law was given, which time Job lived, there were no Priests as such, as would be in the time of the Law, who served as Mediators. In fact, the head of each house, as it pertains to those who served Jehovah, in effect, served as the Priest of the house. So, in effect, Job served as the Priest of his house, but there was none who stood for him, and now he most definitely sees the need for such.

The Priests under the Mosaic Law were very frail specimens as Mediators between God and man, because they were human.

When Christ came, Who is our Mediator, He came as both God and Man. He was very God and very Man. Concerning this, Paul said:

"For there is one God (manifested in three Persons — God the Father, God the Son, and God the Holy Spirit), *and one Mediator between God and men, the Man Christ Jesus* (He can only be an adequate Mediator, Who has sympathy with and understanding of both parties, and is understandable by and clear to both; in other words, Jesus is both God and Man, i.e., 'Very God and Very Man');

"Who gave Himself a ransom for all (refers to the fact that our Lord's Death was a spontaneous and voluntary Sacrifice on His Part; the word 'ransom' refers to the price He paid, owed by man to God, which was His Precious Blood [I Pet. 1:18-20]), *to be testified in due time.* (This refers to the planning of this great Work, which took place *'before the foundation of the world,'* unto the *'due time'* of its manifestation, which refers to when Christ was Crucified)" (I Tim. 2:5-6).

All of this means that Jesus is our Mediator in the sense that He is both God and Man. That's the reason Paul also said:

"Seeing then that we have a Great High Priest (Christ acts on our behalf to God), *Who is passed into the Heavens* (has to do with a legal process), *Jesus the Son of God* (presents the fact that Jesus is not only Man, but is God as well), *let us hold fast our profession.* (Let us hold fast to Christ and the Cross, which was necessary for our Lord to

be our High Priest.)

"For we have not an High Priest which cannot be touched with the feeling of our infirmities (being Very Man as well as Very God, He can do such)*; but was in all points tempted like as we are, yet without sin* (His temptation, and ours as well, was to leave the prescribed Will of God, which is the Word of God; but He never did, not even one time.)

"Let us therefore come boldly unto the Throne of Grace (presents the Seat of Divine Power, and yet the Source of boundless Grace), *that we may obtain Mercy* (presents that which we want first), *and find Grace to help in time of need.* (Refers to the Goodness of God extended to all who come, and during any *'time of need'*; all made possible by the Cross)" (Heb. 4:14-16).

"'Man of sorrows,' what a name,
"For the son of God Who came,
"Ruined sinners to reclaim!
"Hallelujah! What a Saviour!"

"Bearing shame and scoffing rude,
"In my place condemned He stood;
"Sealed my pardon with His Blood:
"Hallelujah what a Saviour!"

"Guilty, vile and helpless, we:
"Spotless Lamb of God was He:
"'Full Atonement!' can it be?
"Hallelujah! What a Saviour!"

"'Lifted up' was He to die,
"'It is finished,' was His cry;
"Now in Heaven exalted high:
"Hallelujah! What a Saviour!"

"When He comes, our glorious King,
"All His ransomed home to bring,
"Then anew this song we'll sing:
"Hallelujah! What a Saviour!"

CHAPTER 10

(1) "MY SOUL IS WEARY OF MY LIFE; I WILL LEAVE MY COMPLAINT UPON MYSELF; I WILL SPEAK IN THE BITTERNESS OF MY SOUL.

(2) "I WILL SAY UNTO GOD, DO NOT CONDEMN ME; SHOW ME WHEREFORE YOU CONTEND WITH ME.

(3) "IS IT GOOD UNTO YOU THAT YOU SHOULD OPPRESS, THAT YOU SHOULD DESPISE THE WORK OF YOUR HANDS, AND SHINE UPON THE COUNSEL OF THE WICKED?

(4) "HAVE YOU EYES OF FLESH? OR DO YOU SEE AS MAN SEES?

(5) "ARE YOUR DAYS AS THE DAYS OF MAN? ARE YOUR YEARS AS MAN'S DAYS,

(6) "THAT YOU ENQUIRE AFTER MY INIQUITY, AND SEARCH AFTER MY SIN?

(7) "YOU KNOW THAT I AM NOT WICKED; AND THERE IS NONE WHO CAN DELIVER OUT OF YOUR HAND.

(8) "YOUR HANDS HAVE MADE ME AND FASHIONED ME TOGETHER ROUND ABOUT; YET YOU DO DESTROY ME.

(9) "REMEMBER, I BESEECH YOU, THAT YOU HAVE MADE ME AS THE CLAY; AND WILL YOU BRING ME INTO DUST AGAIN?

(10) "HAVE YOU NOT POURED ME OUT AS MILK, AND CURDLED ME LIKE CHEESE?

(11) "YOU HAVE CLOTHED ME WITH SKIN AND FLESH, AND HAVE FENCED ME WITH BONES AND SINEWS.

(12) "YOU HAVE GRANTED ME LIFE AND FAVOUR, AND YOUR VISITATION HAS PRESERVED MY SPIRIT.

(13) "AND THESE THINGS HAVE YOU HID IN YOUR HEART: I KNOW THAT THIS IS WITH YOU."

The composition is:

1. (Vs. 1) It is very easy to condemn Job for his statements and actions. However, if any one of us had been placed in his position, would we have done any better, or even as well?

2. In the Second Verse, Job is, in essence, asking the Lord, *"Why do You contend with me?"* Very shortly, the Lord will answer that prayer, and in a far greater way than Job can now imagine.

3. (Vs. 4) The Lord does not see as man sees, but infinitely greater, which means that He knows all things.

4. (Vs. 8) There are times when it seems that God is destroying us. During these times, Satan desires that we throw up our

hands and quit, and, in effect, *"curse God."* God desires that we throw ourselves at the foot of the Cross and draw ever closer to Him, which is what this trial is all about.

5. (Vs. 9) Job has already stated that God can deliver him if He so desires, or else He can kill him. He has the power to do both. Which will it be?

6. (Vs. 12) Job was a man who had walked with God, who has experienced countless *"visitations,"* and who has known God's Power and even God's Grace. He has been favored, but only because he favored God.

JOB'S CONTENTION WITH GOD

In all the things that Job said, the Lord, even as we shall see when this trial ends, did not seemingly take exception to Job's remarks.

We do learn from this, that Job had a deep relationship with the Lord, which is obvious in the things that he says. And the Lord said about him, that there was *"none like him in all the Earth."* What an accolade! What a statement! What a compliment, at least, if one would refer to such as that.

While reading Job's statements in answer to his *"friends,"* which really did not have a lot to do with them, they mostly came from a broken heart. Still, considering what this man was called upon to undergo, considering his present state and position, Job does not blame God, but rather states what he knows about the Lord.

WHAT IS GOD LIKE?

If one wants to know what God is like, one only has to look at the Lord Jesus Christ.

Concerning this, Jesus said:

"If you had known Me, you should have known My Father also (means *'if you had learned to know Me Spiritually and experientially, you should have known that I and the Father are One,'* i.e., One in essence and unity, and not in number)*: and from henceforth you know Him, and have seen Him* (when one truly sees Jesus, one truly sees the Father; as stated, they are *'One'* in essence).

"Phillip said unto Him, Lord, show us the Father and it suffices us (like Phillip, all, at least for the most part, want to see God, but the far greater majority reject the only manner and way to see Him, which is through Jesus).

NOTES

"Jesus said unto him, Have I been so long with you, and yet have you not known Me, Phillip? (Reynolds says, *'There is no right understanding of Jesus Christ unless the Father is actually seen in Him.'*) *He who has seen Me has seen the Father* (presents the very embodiment of Who and what the Messiah would be; if we want to know what God is like, we need only look at the Son)*; and how do you say then, Show us the Father?*

"Do you believe not that I am in the Father, and the Father in Me? (The key is *'believing'*) *the words that I speak unto you I speak not of Myself* (the words, which came out of the mouth of the Master are, in fact, those of the Heavenly Father)*: but the Father Who dwells in Me, He does the works* (the Father does such through the Holy Spirit).

"Believe Me that I am in the Father, and the Father in Me (once again places Faith as the vehicle and Jesus as the Object)*: or else believe Me for the very works' sake* (presents a level, which should be obvious to all, and includes present observation as well)" (Jn. 14:7-11).

(14) "IF I SIN, THEN YOU MARK ME, AND YOU WILL NOT ACQUIT ME FROM MY INIQUITY.

(15) "IF I BE WICKED, WOE UNTO ME; AND IF I BE RIGHTEOUS, YET WILL I NOT LIFT UP MY HEAD. I AM FULL OF CONFUSION; THEREFORE SEE YOU MY AFFLICTION;

(16) "FOR IT INCREASES, YOU HUNT ME AS A FIERCE LION: AND AGAIN YOU SHOW YOURSELF MARVELLOUS UPON ME.

(17) "YOU RENEW YOUR WITNESSES AGAINST ME, AND INCREASE YOUR INDIGNATION UPON ME; CHANGES AND WAR ARE AGAINST ME."

The composition is:

1. (Vs. 14) God forgives only on the basis of one's Faith in the Atonement of Christ, which was symbolized in the Sacrifices of Job's day.

2. (Vs. 15) At the end, the Lord does not condemn Job for his confusion. Job was asked to undergo what few, if any, had ever undergone. He was asked to do so without explanation, so his confusion is understandable.

3. (Vs. 17) Job, no doubt, was wondering what was coming next, as blow after blow came to him. He doesn't know nor understand that all of this has been delegated by God, with boundaries drawn.

THE ATONEMENT

Sin can be forgiven by God only on the basis of satisfaction made, which was done at the Cross of Calvary, which alone is recognized by God.

Actually, the Atonement was not devised after the fact, meaning after the Fall. Through foreknowledge God knew He would make man, and that man would Fall. So, even before the foundation of the world, it was deemed necessary by the Godhead, that man would be redeemed by God becoming man, Who would be the Lord Jesus Christ, and Who would go to the Cross and there pay the price.

The following is the way the Atonement progressed after the Fall:

• The first Prophecy concerning the Atonement was given by God and directed at Satan through the serpent. The Lord said: *"And I will put enmity* (animosity) *between you and the woman* (presents the Lord now actually speaking to Satan, who had used the serpent; in effect, the Lord is saying to Satan, *'You used the woman to bring down the human race, and I will use the woman as an instrument to bring the Redeemer into the world, Who will save the human race'*) *and between your seed* (mankind which follows Satan) *and her Seed* (the Lord Jesus Christ)*; it* (Christ) *shall bruise your head* (the Victory that Jesus won at the Cross [Col. 2:14-15]), *and you shall bruise His Heel* (the sufferings of the Cross)" (Gen. 3:15).

• The Lord then made coats of skins in order to cover the nakedness of Adam and Eve, which the fig leaves could not cover. The Scripture says:

"And the eyes of them both were opened, and they knew that they were naked; and they sewed fig leaves together, and made themselves aprons" (Gen. 3:7). The Scripture then says:

"Unto Adam also, and to his wife did the LORD God make coats of skins, and clothed them (in the making of coats of skins, God, in effect, was telling Adam and Eve that their fig leaves were insufficient; as well, He was teaching them that without the shedding of blood, which pertained to the animals that gave their lives, which were Types of Christ, is no remission of sin; in this first sacrifice was laid the foundation of the entirety of the Plan of God as it regards Redemption; also, it must be noticed that it is the *'Lord God'* Who furnished these coats, and not man himself; this tells us that Salvation is altogether of God and not at all of man; the Life of Christ given on the Cross, and given as our Substitute, provides the only covering for sin; everything else must be rejected)" (Gen. 3:21).

• The Lord introduced the Sacrificial system, which pertained to an innocent animal, a lamb that would serve as a substitute until the Redeemer could come. This information was given to the First Family, and was the means, despite their Fall, that they could have forgiveness of sins, and communion with God. It was all a type of Calvary. The Scripture says:

"And Abel, he also brought of the firstlings of his flock and of the fat thereof (this is what God demanded; it was a blood sacrifice of an innocent victim, a lamb, which proclaimed the fact that Abel recognized his need of a Redeemer, and that One was coming Who would redeem lost humanity; the Offering of Abel was a Type of Christ and the price that He would pay on the Cross of Calvary in order for man to be redeemed). *And the LORD had respect unto Abel and to his offering:* (As stated, this was a Type of Christ and the Cross, the only Offering which God will respect. Abel's Altar is beautiful to God's Eye and repulsive to man's. Cain's altar is beautiful to man's eye and repulsive to God's. These *'altars'* exist today; around the one, that is Christ and His atoning Work, few are gathered, around the other, many. God accepts the slain lamb and rejects the offered fruit; and the offering being rejected, so of necessity is the offerer)" (Gen. 4:4).

• The Sacrificial system remained with each individual family until the Law was given by Moses, a time frame of approximately 2,500 years. When the Law was given, the Sacrificial system was greatly enlarged, even with a Priesthood developed (Lev., Chpts. 1-9).

• The Sacrificial system was meant to be temporary, meaning that it was to last until the Lord Jesus would come, with Him giving His Life on the Cross of Calvary, which was the Plan of God all along (Mat. 27:33-56). What His Death and Resurrection actually meant, such information was given to the Apostle Paul, which he gave to us in his fourteen Epistles.

The Cross of Christ will never be understood unless it is seen that thereon the Saviour was dealing with the sins of all mankind.

In doing this He fulfilled all that the old sacrifices had foreshadowed, and the New Testament writers love to think of His death as a Sacrifice. Jesus Himself referred to His Blood as *"Blood of the Covenant"* (Mk. 14:24), which points us to the Sacrificial Rites for its understanding.

THE VICARIOUS ASPECT OF THE ATONEMENT

It is agreed by most that Christ's Death was Vicarious. If in one sense He died *"for sin"*, in another He died *"for us"*. But *"vicarious"* is a term which may mean much or little. It is better to be more precise. Most scholars today accept the view that the Death of Christ is representative. That is to say, it is not that Christ died and somehow the benefits of that death became available to men, it is rather that He died specifically for us. He was our representative as He hung on the Cross. This is expressed succinctly in II Corinthians 5:14, *"One died for all; and therefore, all have died."* The death of the Representative counts as the death of those He represents. When Christ is spoken of as our *"Advocate with the Father"* (I Jn. 2:1) there is the plain thought of representation. The passage immediately goes on to deal with His Death for sin it is relevant to our purpose.

The Epistle to the Hebrews has Christ as our Great High Priest as one of its major themes. The thought is repeated over and over. Now whatever else may be said about a High Priest, he represents men. The thought of representation may be said to be very strong in this Epistle.

NOTES

Whatever can be said, it must be understood that when Christ died on the Cross, He dealt fully with man's sin. Nothing was left undone.

All of this means that we are not to overlook the fact that the Atonement represents more than something negative. We have been concerned to insist on the place of Christ's Sacrifice of Himself in the putting away of sin. But that opens up the way to a new life in Christ. And that new life, the fruit of the Atonement, is not to be thought of as an insignificant detail. It is that to which all the rest leads.

(18) "WHEREFORE THEN HAVE YOU BROUGHT ME FORTH OUT OF THE WOMB? OH THAT I HAD GIVEN UP THE GHOST, AND NO EYE HAD SEEN ME!

(19) "I SHOULD HAVE BEEN AS THOUGH I HAD NOT BEEN; I SHOULD HAVE BEEN CARRIED FROM THE WOMB TO THE GRAVE.

(20) "ARE NOT MY DAYS FEW? CEASE THEN, AND LET ME ALONE, THAT I MAY TAKE COMFORT A LITTLE,

(21) "BEFORE I GO WHENCE I SHALL NOT RETURN, EVEN TO THE LAND OF DARKNESS AND THE SHADOW OF DEATH;

(22) "A LAND OF DARKNESS, AS DARKNESS ITSELF; AND OF THE SHADOW OF DEATH, WITHOUT ANY ORDER, AND WHERE THE LIGHT IS AS DARKNESS."

The exegesis is:

1. The Eighteenth Verse proclaims the great Patriarch as wishing that he had died at birth.

2. Verse 20 constitutes a prayer that Job would be very glad the Lord didn't answer.

3. (Vs. 21) At the time of Job, the understanding of the Resurrection was very dim.

LIFE AND LIVING

Job rues the day that he was born, actually desiring to die. Immediately, we tend to fault him; however, before we do this, once again we should attempt to put ourselves in his shoes. He doesn't know why his situation has come about as it has. He doesn't understand why the Lord has allowed this to happen to him. He has lost everything, and is being humiliated as few human beings ever have. He doesn't see any way out, doesn't see any light at the end of this proverbial tunnel, doesn't see how that it can change, so he wishes to die.

Other great men of God have at times wished the same; however, there is nothing in the Word of God that substantiates such desire. Life is precious, even at its worst. It is meant to be lived to glorify God, which brings the utmost joy and happiness. If adverse circumstances come our way, so difficult that we see no point in living, then our trust in God is put to the test.

On a personal level, I know what it is to be humiliated, to where my name is a joke all over the world. Someone has well said, that public humiliation, is like the skin has been pulled from the body with every nerve exposed. They are right!

Of course, the immediate retort of most people is that if someone does something wrong, then they deserve whatever it is they get.

While wrongdoing is always and without exception the fault of the perpetrator, and while wrongdoing will always bring negative results, still, none of this is as simple as some make it out to be. The matter of trusting the Lord is the same in any case. Whether it is with Job who did nothing wrong to warrant such action upon his person, or whether the individual has failed the Lord in some respect, still, the only answer to the situation is Faith in God.

Of course, many modern Believers, so-called, claim that if wrongdoing has been committed, then the Lord will not hear such a person when they pray, etc.

People who think such know little about the Lord or His Word. The Lord will hear anyone, will answer anyone, will attend anyone, irrespective as to what they have done, if they will turn to Him with humility and brokenness. The Scripture plainly says: *"The Sacrifices of God are a broken spirit: a broken and a contrite heart, O God, You will not despise"* (Ps. 51:17).

John the Beloved also wrote as the Holy Spirit inspired him: *"If we confess our sins, He is faithful and just to forgive us our sins, and to cleanse us from all unrighteousness"* (I Jn. 1:9).

Now the Lord is either true to His Word, or He isn't. I know that He is.

Whatever the Lord allows, whether humiliation on a worldwide scale, or anything else of any nature, it is the intention of the Lord to bring us to the place He desires us to be, whatever the price might be.

THE SANCTIFICATION OF THE SAINT

The Sanctification of the Saint is the business of the Holy Spirit. Whatever He has to allow, whatever He has to do, He will always work toward that end.

As far as Satan was concerned, the matter of Job was only a contest. Could Job be squeezed hard enough that he would curse God, or would he continue to praise the Lord? But with God the matter was entirely different.

While the statements just made entered into the situation as would be obvious, still, the Lord had something far greater in mind than winning a contest. He wanted to show Job something that the great Patriarch did not then know, which would stand as a test for all time, as it regards the Sanctification of the Saint.

For all of Job's efforts to live the life he ought to live, and to please God, the Lord desired to show him and, in fact, did show him, and you and me, as well, that for all of Job's efforts, what was truly needed in the heart and life of this man, and every Believer, could only be brought about by the Holy Spirit. Of course, the Holy Spirit then was very limited as to what He could do since Jesus had not yet gone to the Cross. But still, the lesson that was taught, had to be taught, and was applicable to all Believers and for all time.

As we've already stated, it is remarkable that this subject of Sanctification, considering that the Book of Job is the first Book written as it regards the Bible, is the Sanctification of the Saint. This shows us how all-important this subject is, and how difficult it is at the same time.

Since the Cross, all Believers have something that neither Job nor any Believer had before the Cross. At the Cross the sin debt was totally and completely paid, making it possible for the Holy Spirit to come into our hearts and lives, and to remain, and to do so forever, which those before the Cross did not have. So, as we read this great Book of Job, let us understand the following:

The Holy Spirit, as we have previously stated, allowed all the ramblings of these three friends to be inscribed, so we would see the fruitlessness of man's wisdom and, as well, that He would allow Job's statements to be given to us in full, so that we Believers might learn many lessons that we desperately need to learn. Some of those lessons are:

• God is directing everything as it regards Believers.

• Nothing can happen to us unless either the Lord causes it or allows it.

• We will find through life that the Sanctification experience is an ongoing process and, in fact, will never end, at least until the trump sounds or the Lord calls us home.

• Whatever is needed within our lives, we cannot, by our own machinations, bring it to pass, that work will be carried out only by the Holy Spirit.

• In order for our Sanctification, the Lord will use many things, even Satan as the Book of Job portrays.

• Whatever comes our way, if it draws us closer to the Lord, the price paid is worth it.

DEATH

When God originally created Adam and Eve there was no intention of them ever dying. True, their physical bodies were made of clay, which is very perishable, but still, they had access to the Tree of Life, and as such, could remain youthful and young forever. When they partook of the forbidden fruit, the Tree of the Knowledge of Good and Evil, the Judgment of death came upon them. First of all, it was spiritual death, which means separation from God, which eventually led to physical death.

Medical science does not really understand presently why the organs of the physical body age, or contract disease, and eventually quit. They state that the physical body of the human being somewhat rejuvenates itself every seven years, or rather tries to do so. They state that the physical organs should last forever.

NOTES

In these things they are correct, but we know that the cause of the bodily organs aging and eventually wearing out, or contracting disease, is all because of original sin. Even then, the physical body was so wondrously made, that it took over 2,000 years to wear it down to where it is presently. When you read in Genesis, Chapter 5 of the individuals who lived astounding numbers of years, you are reading the truth. Adam lived to be 930 years old, *"and he died."* Seth lived to be 912 years old, *"and he died."* Enos lived to be 905 years old, *"and he died."* As stated, these are not fables, but facts. Abraham was 175 years old when he died, which was about 2,000 years after Adam. Job was 210 when he died, but his added years were the fulfillment of a Promise made by God to the Patriarch.

By the time of David, nearly 3,000 years after Adam, the sweet singer of Israel died at 70 years of age. That age, on an international basis, has pretty much held true from then until now. While some countries enjoy a longer life span on the average than 70, due to other countries going in the opposite direction, it averages out at approximately 70 years of age for the life span.

While there will be death in the coming Kingdom Age; however, it will be a rarity. Actually, the indication is that it will only be those who are executed because they refuse to obey the Laws of the Lord. Every indication is that the entirety of the world at the time, will partake of the medicine designed by the Lord, which will, no doubt, stop sickness, and aging beyond a certain point. The Scripture says:

"And by the River upon the bank thereof, on this side and on that side, shall grow all Trees for meat, whose leaves shall not fade, neither shall the fruit thereof be consumed: it shall bring forth new fruit according to his months, because their waters they issued out of the Sanctuary: and the fruit thereof shall be for meat, and the leaf thereof for medicine" (Ezek. 47:12).

The notes from THE EXPOSITOR'S STUDY BIBLE give us this information regarding this particular Passage. It says:

"Now Ezekiel is shown the purpose of these miracle Trees which grow on either

side of these Rivers. These 'Trees' shall perpetually bring forth new fruit because they are nourished by waters issuing from the Sanctuary. The fruit will heal as well as nourish. Such is the character of a Life and Ministry based upon Calvary, and energized by the Holy Spirit.

"In fact, the population of the world (which will include all, with the exception of the Glorified Saints) *will continue to live perpetually by the means of the 'fruit' and the 'leaf' of these Trees. In other words, the aging process will be halted.*"

And then when it comes to the new Heavens and the new Earth the Scripture says, and I quote from THE EXPOSITOR'S STUDY BIBLE:

"And He showed me a pure River of Water of Life, clear as crystal (symbolic of the Holy Spirit [Jn. 7:37-39]), *proceeding out of the Throne of God and of the Lamb.* (This 'Water of Life' is made possible by what Jesus did at the Cross, hence, the word 'Lamb.')

"In the midst of the street of it (proclaims the fact that this 'pure River of Water of Life, clear as crystal' flows in the middle of this street of pure gold), *and on either side of the river, was there the Tree of Life* (the fruit of this Tree of Life must be eaten every month, and we're speaking of the part of the population who don't have Glorified Bodies), *which bear twelve manner of fruits, and yielded her fruit every month* (we have the number '12' again, which signifies the Government of God as it relates to the manner of Eternal Life; there are twelve different types of fruit, but we aren't told what they are)*: and the leaves of the tree were for the healing of the nations.* (This pertains to the stopping of any type of sickness before it even begins. As stated, the population on Earth, which will never die and will not have Glorified Bodies, will need these things. These are they who were Saved during the Kingdom Age, and thereafter)" (Rev. 22:1-2).

In that Perfect Age to come, which will never end, there will be no more sickness or no more dying. The babies that are born, and babies will be born at that time, will come to a certain age, and then cease to continue aging, and will live forever by virtue of the Tree of Life which grows beside the River, which will bring forth particular fruits, and coupled with the leaves will sustain life forever. This means that in this coming Perfect Age there will be two types of people on the Earth, in effect, exactly as it will be in the Kingdom Age. They are:

• The Glorified Saints of God: these are the ones who will have part in the first Resurrection of Life, and will have Glorified Bodies. The only thing we know about Glorified Bodies is what we know about Christ after His Resurrection, for He had a Glorified Body at that time, and will keep such forever. We know it's a body of flesh and bone, but it seems that there will be no blood in that particular body, with it being sustained by the Holy Spirit. Presently, the life of the flesh is in the blood, but when Jesus mentioned His Glorified Body, He used the statement, *"Behold My Hands and My Feet, that it is I Myself: handle Me, and see for a spirit has not flesh and bones, as you see Me have"* (Lk. 24:39). He didn't mention blood, signifying that the Glorified Body will not have blood, but as stated, will be sustained by the Holy Spirit.

As well, the Glorified Body is not bound by natural boundaries, as we understand Christ. In other words, it can appear and disappear at will and, at the same time, pass through walls, etc. (Lk. 24:36; Jn. 20:19, 26; Lk. 24:31). So, the Glorified Body we know will have properties that the present physical body doesn't have.

• Natural people: every evidence is, in the New Jerusalem, and in the new Earth, which will be forever and forever, every evidence is that there will be families with children born just exactly as there are presently, but with the great difference of not having a curse over this world, which has plagued mankind since the Fall. Concerning that coming glad day, the Scripture says: *"And the nations of them who are Saved shall walk in the light of it: and the kings of the Earth do bring their glory and honor into it"* (Rev. 21:24). The notes in THE EXPOSITOR'S STUDY BIBLE state: *"Should have been translated, 'And the nations shall walk by means of its light'; the words 'of them who are Saved' are not actually in the best manuscripts; in fact, there will be no one in* the world in that day who isn't Saved."

The Scripture then says, *"And they shall bring the glory and honor of the nations into it,"* and speaking of the New Jerusalem (Rev. 21:26).

All of this speaks of activity such as we presently have in the world, with the exception of sin and shame, which will make a difference of unprecedented proportions, for the Scripture also says: *"And there shall be no more curse: but the Throne of God and of the Lamb shall be in it; and His servants shall serve Him"* (Rev. 22:3).

A curse was placed on the Earth at the Fall; it is being said here that there will be no more curse because there will be no more sin. The authority of rulership will be as great with God the Son as it is with God the Father; in fact, by the use of the word *"Lamb,"* we are made to realize that all of this is made possible because of what Jesus did at the Cross. The idea is that every Believer in the Perfect Age to come will so love the Lord and the Lamb that they will gladly *"serve Him."*

POSSIBLE EXPANSION

Peter said, and concerning the time immediately following the Kingdom Age: *"But the Day of the Lord will come as a thief in the night* (the conclusion of the Millennium; what will happen at that time will be unexpected, and for a variety of reasons)*; in the which the Heavens shall pass away with a great noise, and the elements shall melt with fervent heat, the Earth also and the works that are therein shall be burned up.* (This does not speak of annihilation, but rather passing from one condition to another.)

"Nevertheless we (Believers), *according to His Promise* (the Lord has Promised that a new day is coming [Isa. 65:17]), *look for new Heavens* (this is the Promise!) *and a new Earth, wherein dwells Righteousness.* (This proclaims the condition of the Coming 'New Heavens and New Earth' [Rev., Chpts. 21-22])" (II Pet. 3:10, 13).

There is a great possibility, considering that the Perfect Age outlined in Revelation, Chapters 21 and 22 will never end, that the Lord, considering again that the entirety of the Universe has been made new, will reach

NOTES

out and colonize other Planets.

Why not?! He has the Power, and with that Power, such could easily be done.

The Scripture says: *"But as it is written* (Isa. 64:4), *Eye has not seen, nor ear heard, neither have entered into the heart of man* (the purpose is to show that we cannot come to a knowledge of God through these normal ways of learning), *the things which God has prepared for them who love Him.*

"But God has revealed them unto us by His Spirit (tells us the manner of impartation of Spiritual Knowledge, which is by Revelation)*: for the Spirit searches all things, yes, the deep things of God.* (The Holy Spirit is the only One amply qualified to reveal God because He is God, and He is the member of the Godhead Who deals directly with man)" (I Cor. 2:9-10).

BEFORE THE CROSS

During the time of Job, which, of course, was long before the Cross, death was an enigma. There was very little information given at that time as to what death was, or as it regards the coming Resurrection. We will find that Job believed in a coming Resurrection, still, that, as well, was very dim.

As we have previously stated, before the Cross and due to the fact that the blood of bulls and goats could not take away sins, when Believers died, such as Job eventually would, their soul and their spirit went down into Paradise, and even though they were then comforted, they were still held captive by Satan. In fact, and according to the Words of our Lord, they were very close to the burning side of Hell, being separated only by a great gulf (Lk. 16:23-31). Their release from this place was predicated solely upon the Sacrifice of Christ on the Cross, which would pay this terrible sin debt, and bring them out from under the domain of Satan, which was done.

Concerning this, the Apostle Paul said, *"Wherefore He said* (Ps. 68:18), *When He ascended up on high* (the Ascension), *He led captivity captive* (liberated the souls in Paradise; before the Cross, despite being Believers, they were still held captive by Satan because the blood of bulls and goats could not take away the sin debt; but when Jesus died on the Cross, the sin debt was paid, and now He makes all these His Captives), *and gave Gifts unto men.* (These *'Gifts'* include all the Attributes of Christ, all made possible by the Cross.)

"(Now that He ascended [mission completed], *what is it but that He also descended first into the lower parts of the earth?* [Immediately before His Ascension in Glory, which would be done in total triumph, He first went down into Paradise to deliver all the believing souls in that region, which He did!]

"He Who descended is the same also Who ascended [this is a portrayal of Jesus as Deliverer and Mediator] *up far above all Heavens* [presents His present location, never again having to descend into the nether world], *that He might fill all things).* (He has always been the Creator, but now He is also the Saviour)" (Eph. 4:8-10).

Job referred to death as *"the land of darkness and the shadow of death."* But Jesus by His Sacrificial Atoning Sacrifice on Calvary's Cross took away the sting of death. Paul also said: *"So when this corruptible* (sin nature) *shall have put on incorruption* (the Divine Nature in total control by the Holy Spirit), *and this mortal* (subject to death) *shall have put on immortality* (will never die), *then shall be brought to pass the saying that is written, Death is swallowed up in Victory* [Isa. 25:8], the full benefits of the Cross will then be ours, of which now have only the Firstfruits)" (Rom. 8:23).

"O death, where is your sting? (This presents the Apostle looking ahead, and exulting in this great coming victory. Sin was forever atoned at the Cross, which took away the sting of death.) *O grave, where is your victory?* (Due to death being conquered, the *'grave'* is no more and once again, all because of what Christ did at the Cross)" (I Cor. 15:53-55).

"Awake, and sing the song,
"Of Moses and the Lamb;
"Wake, every heart and every tongue;
"To praise the Saviour's Name."

"Sing of His dying Love;
"Sing of His risen Power;
"Sing how He intercedes above,
"For those whose sins He bore."

"You pilgrims, on the road,
"To Zion's City, sing;
"Rejoice ye in the Lamb of God,
"In Christ the Eternal King."

"There shall each raptured tongue,
"His endless praise proclaim;
"And sweeter voices tune the song,
"Of Moses and the Lamb."

CHAPTER 11

(1) "THEN ANSWERED ZOPHAR THE NAAMATHITE, AND SAID,

(2) "SHOULD NOT THE MULTITUDE OF WORDS BE ANSWERED? AND SHOULD A MAN FULL OF TALK BE JUSTIFIED?

(3) "SHOULD YOUR LIES MAKE MEN HOLD THEIR PEACE? AND WHEN YOU MOCK, SHALL NO MAN MAKE YOU ASHAMED?

(4) "FOR YOU HAVE SAID, MY DOCTRINE IS PURE, AND I AM CLEAN IN YOUR EYES.

(5) "BUT OH THAT GOD WOULD SPEAK, AND OPEN HIS LIPS AGAINST YOU;

(6) "AND THAT HE WOULD SHOW YOU THE SECRETS OF WISDOM, THAT THEY ARE DOUBLE TO THAT WHICH IS! KNOW THEREFORE THAT GOD EXACTS OF YOU LESS THAN YOUR INIQUITY DESERVES."

The pattern is:

1. (Vs. 1) Zophar, another *"friend,"* now speaks.

2. (Vs. 3) He argues from the position of *"human merit."*

3. (Vs. 3) Job has been called a hypocrite, now Zophar calls him a liar.

4. (Vs. 6) It is ironical, everything that Zophar knew about Job was good, and yet he now feels perfectly free to claim that Job was the worst kind of sinner.

THE POSITION OF HUMAN MERIT

As we have previously said and will elaborate on more fully, the argument as presented by Zophar is a perfect example of what passes for knowledge of God without relationship with God. In fact, all of these three *"friends"* fell into the same category. As we have previously stated:

• Eliphaz argued from the position of *"human experience."*

• Bildad argued from the position of *"human tradition."*

• Zophar argues from the position of *"human merit."*

If it is to be noticed, one can easily follow the increase of harshness.

• *"Human experience"* basically comes from intellectualism.

• *"Human tradition"* stems from religion.

• *"Human merit"* stems from self-righteousness.

It is amazing how glibly that Zophar answered Job, and why not? The healthy man always has the answer for the sick man. The self-righteous man always has the answer for the unrighteous man; the rich man always has the answer for the poor man. Most of the time their answers are exactly as Zophar's.

Zophar said, *"Should not the multitude of words be answered? And should a man full of talk be justified?"*

It is easy to see that Zophar doesn't have the faintest idea as to the meaning of *"Justification by Faith."* Consequently, he deals from *"human merit,"* which is no Salvation at all. Sadly, his questions of Verse 2 characterize the majority of the modern Church world.

Job has been called a hypocrite, and now he is called a liar. No wonder Zophar arouses the anger of God. It is very easy to call a man a liar who is in Job's position; however, what Zophar's kind never seem to realize is that when he called Job a liar, he was actually calling God a liar.

The idea that Job claimed his doctrine to be *"pure"* and his life to be *"clean"* was a mockery to one such as Zophar. Self-righteousness can never agree with such; therefore, Zophar thusly considered Job's claims.

In just a little while God will speak, but Zophar will not enjoy that which would be said. The Lord will *"open His lips,"* but it will not be against Job; it will be against Job's *"three friends."*

Let this be an example and a lesson to all who would be righteous in their own eyes, and ignore the Word of God, thereby feeling free to condemn and judge others. Ultimately, God will speak, and what He will say will not be pleasant to the self-righteous.

Zophar now says, *"Know therefore that God exacts of you less than your iniquity deserves."*

What a statement! What blatant judging! He knew precious little of Job's life, and what he did know was good. At the same time, he had no idea of any iniquity that Job had committed, if any at all. And yet, he felt perfectly free to claim that Job was some kind of great sinner. He must be according to Zophar's reasoning because of the condition that he was in.

SELF-RIGHTEOUSNESS

Self-righteousness has no pity, compassion, or love. Religion, which characterizes self-righteousness, and which, sad to say, characterizes the majority of that which is called *"the church,"* is without feeling. It feels no pang of conscience, nor compassion of heart, even while uttering the cruelest of statements. Sadly, when you hear the prating, babbling of *"this Zophar,"* you are hearing the majority of the religious, self-righteous, holier-than-thou modern church world.

It must be remembered, that it was self-righteousness which nailed Christ to the Cross. The gamblers, immoral, drunkards, as vile as those sins might be, did not put Christ on the Cross. It was religion that put Him there. In fact, Satan does his best work in this field.

Mankind has two roads he can travel. One is the road of the Cross, which guarantees the Righteousness of Christ, and the other is man-devised roads, which always falls out to self-righteousness. Let me say it in another way:

If the Believer doesn't understand the Cross of Christ as it regards our Sanctification, if the Believer doesn't understand the Cross of Christ as it regards life and living, if the Believer doesn't understand the Cross of Christ as it regards victory over the world, the flesh, and the Devil, then such a Believer is going to embrace self-righteousness. There is no other alternative. It's either the Cross and Righteousness, which is the

Righteousness of Christ, or else it's man's way, which is self-righteousness. Those are the two paths, and they are the only paths. So that means that every single so-called Believer in the world today is on one path or the other. And knowing that most of the modern church knows little or nothing about the Cross of Christ as it regards our everyday life and living, this means, sad to say, that the majority of the church is on the road of self-righteousness.

PERSONAL

I look at my own life and Ministry. I speak of the years before I knew and understood this great Revelation of the Cross, which the Lord in His Mercy and Grace has afforded this unworthy Evangelist. Self-righteousness was very much evident within my life during those days. I look back now with shame, I look back with sorrow, I look back with hurt, because now, since the Cross, it has become so obvious.

If it is to be noticed, Jesus had much to say about self-righteousness. Read carefully this Parable that He gave us:

"*And He spoke this Parable unto certain which trusted in themselves* (self-righteousness) *that they were righteous, and despised others* (the twin curse of self-righteousness):

"*Two men went up into the Temple to pray* (only one would be heard by God, who would probably be the very opposite of the one most men would choose); *the one a Pharisee* (a fundamentalist, who claimed to believe the entire Bible), *and the other a Publican* (a tax-collector, referred to by Israel as traitors and, thereby, beyond Salvation).

"*The Pharisee stood and prayed thus with himself* (meaning that his prayer went no further than himself; even though it was directed toward God, it was not heard by God), *God, I thank You, that I am not as other men are, extortioners, unjust, adulterers, or even as this Publican* (he put himself on a much higher plane than the Publican; he actually asked the Lord for nothing, and that's exactly what he received; as far as he was concerned, he had everything, '*have need of nothing*' [Rev. 3:17]).

"*I fast twice in the week, I give tithes of all that I possess* (Verse 11 portrays relative righteousness and this Verse portrays works righteousness, both rejected by the Lord).

"*And the Publican standing afar off* (means that he did not feel free to come close to the Temple appointments as had the Pharisee), *would not lift up so much as his eyes unto Heaven* (refers to him realizing and admitting just how unclean he actually was), *but smote upon his breast saying, God be merciful to me a sinner* (brought instant results because the plea was based upon Atonement and not on self-righteousness; every afternoon at three o'clock the evening Lamb was offered up as a propitiation for the sins of that day; the Publican pleaded forgiveness and acceptance because of the merit of that atoning blood; it foreshadowed the Atoning Death of the Lamb of God, Who was Himself the Propitiation, i.e., the '*Mercy-Seat*').

"*I tell you, this man went down to his house justified* (declared a righteous man; there are no degrees in Justification; one is either justified totally, or not justified at all!) *rather than the other* (the Pharisee who depended on his self-righteousness was not justified and, therefore, lost): *for everyone who exalts himself shall be abased* (rejected); *and he who humbles himself shall be exalted* (proclaims the basis for acceptance by God)" (Lk. 18:9-14).

Now Jesus gives us another object lesson as to our total dependence, which must be on God and God Alone.

UNLESS YOU BECOME AS A LITTLE CHILD

"*And they brought unto Him also infants, that He would touch them: but when His Disciples saw it, they rebuked them* (erroneously thinking that Jesus should not be bothered with such).

"*But Jesus called them unto Him* (called the parents with their infants), *and said, Suffer little children to come unto Me, and forbid them not: for of such is the Kingdom of God* (Jesus is presenting an object lesson; a little child is completely dependent on its parents or guardians; likewise, we are to be totally dependent in the same manner on the Lord).

"*Verily I say unto you, Whosoever shall*

not receive the Kingdom of God as a little child shall in no wise enter therein (the greatest hindrance to entering the *'Kingdom of God'* is the refusal of many to humble themselves before God; it is the pride factor, which is the opposite of little children)" (Lk. 18:15-17).

Total dependence on the Lord, and for everything, is the complete opposite of self-righteousness. Such presents the understanding that whatever it is we need, we cannot of ourselves provide it. If we are to have it at all, it must be given to us by the Lord.

(7) "CAN YOU BY SEARCHING FIND OUT GOD? CAN YOU FIND OUT THE ALMIGHTY UNTO PERFECTION?

(8) "IT IS AS HIGH AS HEAVEN; WHAT CAN YOU DO? DEEPER THAN HELL; WHAT CAN YOU KNOW?

(9) "THE MEASURE THEREOF IS LONGER THAN THE EARTH, AND BROADER THAN THE SEA.

(10) "IF HE CUT OFF, AND SHUT UP, OR GATHER TOGETHER, THEN WHO CAN HINDER HIM?

(11) "FOR HE KNOWS VAIN MEN: HE SEES WICKEDNESS ALSO; WILL HE NOT THEN CONSIDER IT?

(12) "FOR VAIN MEN WOULD BE WISE, THOUGH MAN BE BORN LIKE A WILD ASS'S COLT."

The exposition is:

1. (Vs. 7) These questions (Vss. 7-8, 10-11) are sometimes used as proof that God is so great that the most learned cannot comprehend Him, but this is an improper use of the questions. While one cannot learn about God by scientific methods, so-called, one can definitely learn about Him from His Word, and by Revelation.

2. (Vs. 11) The idea as Zophar erroneously puts it, is that God is so great that there is no point in men trying to find out anything about Him. Were that true, the Lord would not have given us His Word, or sent the Messiah!

3. In the Twelfth Verse, Zophar refers to Job as *"vain."*

WHAT IS GOD LIKE?

We know from the Word of God, that there is one God, but manifested in three Persons, *"God the Father, God the Son, and God the Holy Spirit."* These Three are One in essence, but yet there are certain things that can be said about one that cannot be said about the other.

For instance, it was God the Son Who paid the price on Calvary's Cross. While He did the Will of the Father, and while He was helped greatly by the Holy Spirit, still, it was not the Father or the Spirit Who died on the Cross, except that in a sense they were in Christ, which was most definitely the case. The Scripture says:

"To wit, that God was in Christ (by the agency of Christ), *reconciling the world unto Himself* (represents the Atonement as the work of the Blessed Trinity and the result of love, not of wrath), *not imputing their trespasses unto them* (refers to the fact that the penalty for these trespasses was imputed to Christ instead); *and has committed unto us the Word of Reconciliation.* (All Believers are to preach the Cross in one way or the other [I Cor. 1:18])" (II Cor. 5:19).

If one wants to know Who God is, and what He is like, one need only look at Christ. Everything He did was the Will of the Father. So, one need look no further than the Lord Jesus Christ to understand the Father, to comprehend the Father.

While all Three of the Godhead minister in a sense in the same capacity, still, their work is somewhat different. For instance, it is the Holy Spirit Who baptizes the believing sinner into Christ at conversion (Jn. 3:3-8). When the Believer is baptized in the Spirit, it is the very opposite. Whereas at conversion, the Spirit baptizes the believing sinner into Christ, at the infilling of the Spirit, it is Jesus Who baptizes with the Spirit (Mat. 3:11).

WILL WE SEE ALL THREE MEMBERS OF THE GODHEAD IN HEAVEN?

I personally believe that we will.

In Revelation 4:2-3, we are given a picture by John the Beloved of the Throne of God, with John mentioning God the Father sitting on that Throne. In Revelation 5:6, we see Christ portrayed symbolically as a Lamb, with the Scripture then saying about our Lord, *"You are worthy to take the Book, and to open the Seals thereof: for You were slain, and have redeemed us to God by Your Blood"* (Rev. 5:9). This, of course, is the Lord Jesus Christ.

The Holy Spirit is pictured in Revelation 5:6 symbolically as well. Also, Jesus referred to Him before His Crucifixion, by personal pronouns. He said:

"Howbeit when 'He', the Spirit of Truth, is come, 'He' will guide you into all Truth: for 'He' shall not speak of 'Himself'; but whatsoever 'He' shall hear, that shall 'He' speak: and 'He' will show you things to come.

"'He' shall glorify Me: for 'He' shall receive of Mine, and shall show it unto you" (Jn. 16:13-14).

In those two Verses, the Holy Spirit is referred to Personally some nine times. If the Holy Spirit was merely an emanation from the Father, as claimed by some, our Lord would have been in error referring to Him Personally as He did.

The Holy Spirit, if language means anything, and it most definitely does, is God. He is, as we state, the Third Person of the Godhead. In fact, everything done on this Earth by the Godhead has been done by and through the Office, Ministry, Power, and Person of the Holy Spirit, with the exception of the Ministry of Christ in His Life and Atonement. And even then, the Holy Spirit superintended it from beginning to conclusion.

The Word of God opens by saying, *"And the Spirit of God moved upon the face of the waters"* (Gen. 1:2). It closes with the *"Spirit"* bidding men to come and *"take the Water of Life freely"* (Rev. 22:17).

DOES GOD HAVE A BODY?

Jesus Christ does have a physical body, albeit Glorified. There is evidence, that He will retain this physical body forever and forever.

Before His Incarnation, which refers to the time that he became a human being, the Scripture says that He *"dwelt in the Light which no man can approach unto"* (I Tim. 6:16).

Regarding the Incarnation, the Scripture also says: *"Sacrifice and Offering You would not* (refers to the fact that He would pay for sin, but not with animal sacrifices), *but a Body have You prepared Me* (God became man with the full intention that His Perfect Physical Body was to be offered up in Sacrifice on the Cross, which it was; the Cross was ever His Destination)" (Heb. 10:5).

As we have stated, He was given this Perfect Physical Body for one purpose, and that was to offer it up in Sacrifice, which was necessary in order that the Righteousness of God would be satisfied, meaning that the ransom owed by man to God would be paid, and paid by Christ.

As stated, there is every evidence that He will dwell in this physical body forever. At the Second Coming, the Prophet Zechariah prophesied, *"And one shall say unto Him, What are these wounds in Your Hands? Then He shall answer, Those with which I was wounded in the house of My friends"* (Zech. 13:6).

The idea is, what Christ did at the Cross is of such magnitude, such moment, such wonder, that the traces of it as it regards the wounds in His Hands will remain with Him forever. Those wounds will be obvious forever, always as a sign of the price that was paid for our Redemption. We must never forget that! That's the reason we preach the Cross! Preach the Cross! Preach the Cross!

There is evidence that God the Father and God the Spirit have spirit bodies.

When John the Beloved said, *"And I saw in the Right Hand of Him Who sat on the Throne a Book written . . ."* that is not merely, as some claim, an anthropomorphic statement as some claim (Rev. 5:1).

The word *"anthropomorphic"* refers to statements used in Scripture concerning God, in order that we might understand what is being said. In other words, those who believe that claim that the Lord doesn't really have a right hand, etc., but that this term is merely used, and scores of others in the Word of God attributing bodily parts to God, that we might have some comprehension of Him. I don't believe that is correct.

I don't think the Holy Spirit would have inspired John to attribute a *"Right Hand"* to God, if He didn't have such.

As we have stated, there are scores of similar Passages in the Word of God describing God the Father. When Ezekiel had a Vision of the Lord, he said that He had *"the likeness* as the appearance of a man" (Ezek. 1:26).

Concerning *"Moses and Aaron, along with Nadab and Abihu, with 70 of the Elders of Israel,"* the Scripture says that *"they saw the God of Israel: and there was under His Feet as it were a paved work of a sapphire stone, and as it were the body of Heaven in His clearness.*

"And upon the nobles of the Children of Israel He laid not His Hand: also they saw God, and did eat and drink" (Ex. 24:9-11).

The Tenth Verse says that He has feet. Again, I do not believe that this is merely an anthropomorphic statement. Some say this was a preincarnate appearance of Christ. It may very well have been. But it reads as if this is God the Father.

A spirit body, which I personally believe that God the Father and God the Spirit has, is exactly what it says, spirit and not flesh. As such, it has astounding capabilities so far beyond our thinking as to defy description. It can probably take any form it likes, but at the same time I believe there is enough Scriptural evidence to proclaim the fact that the form is as a man most of the time.

When God created man, He said: *"Let Us make man in Our Image, after Our Likeness"* (Gen. 1:26).

Whereas *"Image and Likeness"* actually refer to true Righteousness and Holiness (Eph. 4:24), as well, it contains a natural meaning also.

The word *"image"* in the Hebrew is *"Tselem,"* and means *"resemblance."* The word *"likeness"* in the Hebrew is *"Dmuwth,"* and means *"resemblance and shape."* So, there must be some resemblance to man and God in the natural sense, even though man has a physical body, and God has a Spirit Body.

(13) "IF YOU PREPARE YOUR HEART, AND STRETCH OUT YOUR HANDS TOWARD HIM;

(14) "IF INIQUITY BE IN YOUR HAND, PUT IT FAR AWAY, AND LET NOT WICKEDNESS DWELL IN YOUR TABERNACLES.

(15) "FOR THEN SHALL YOU LIFT UP YOUR FACE WITHOUT SPOT; YES, YOU SHALL BE STEDFAST, AND SHALL NOT FEAR:

(16) "BECAUSE YOU SHALL FORGET YOUR MISERY, AND REMEMBER IT AS WATERS THAT PASS AWAY:

(17) "AND YOUR AGE SHALL BE CLEARER THAN THE NOONDAY: YOU SHALL SHINE FORTH, YOU SHALL BE AS THE MORNING.

(18) "AND YOU SHALL BE SECURE, BECAUSE THERE IS HOPE; YES, YOU SHALL DIG ABOUT YOU, AND YOU SHALL TAKE YOUR REST IN SAFETY.

(19) "ALSO YOU SHALL LIE DOWN, AND NONE SHALL MAKE YOU AFRAID; YES, MANY SHALL MAKE SUIT UNTO YOU.

(20) "BUT THE EYES OF THE WICKED SHALL FAIL, AND THEY SHALL NOT ESCAPE, AND THEIR HOPE SHALL BE AS THE GIVING UP OF THE GHOST."

The pattern is:

1. The Thirteenth Verse proclaims the fact, that here, as always, we have the self-righteous telling the righteous how to seek the Lord. What a travesty!

2. (Vs. 14) Zophar so much believes that Job is full of iniquity; self-righteousness always assumes such. The facts are that Zophar is full of iniquity, and Job is not.

3. Zophar declares that Job must be wicked or he would not be suffering like the wicked. What conceit! What self-righteousness!

BITING ACCUSATION

Having absolutely no idea as to what has happened to Job, with Job himself also having absolutely no idea as to what has happened to him, the question must quickly be asked as to how these three friends can come to the conclusion to which they have arrived? That conclusion being, that Job is a wicked man, and such, they think, is obvious, because of the terrible situation in which he now finds himself. Self-righteousness always jumps to conclusions. It always has the answer, and the fault is always on the head of the victim whomever he or she might be.

No Believer, that is if he will take the time to look at himself closely, has the right to criticize another individual personally. While we as Believers most definitely have the right, and actually the obligation, to judge all doctrine, which we are told to do (Mat. 7:15-20), that is not to extend to the individual personally.

If the evidence becomes obvious that an individual is living in a state of sin, and condoning the sin, and we speak of Believers, then fellowship must be withdrawn. But even then, we should pray for the person, asking the Lord to keep dealing with them, that they may come to their spiritual senses.

As it regards wrongdoing, which God cannot abide in any capacity, it's very easy for one Believer to ridicule another Believer because of failure, when it's something that does not bother him, while he conveniently overlooks that which does bother him. However, all of us have a tendency to quickly point out the failures of others, while conveniently overlooking our own failures.

The fact is, sin is a terrible thing, and that speaks of any type of sin. It is so bad that our Lord had to go to the Cross for this terrible problem to be properly addressed. To be sure, if the Believer doesn't take his sin to the Cross, he will never know Victory over sin.

Zophar has the perfect solution for Job, or so he thinks. He urges him to repent and quit sinning, and then God will bless him.

Ultimately we will come to the place that God will appear, and will strongly reprimand these *"three friends,"* and then I wonder what their thoughts were. All of this tells us that every one of us is going to have to answer to the Lord for the decisions we make, the things we say, and the things we do regarding others.

"O my Saviour crucified!
"Near Your Cross would I abide,
"Gazing with adoring eye,
"On Your dying agony."

"Jesus bruised and put to shame,
"Tells the glories of God's Name:
"Holy Judgment there I found,
"Grace did there over sin abound."

"God is love I surely know,
"In the Saviour's depth of woe;
"In the Sinless, in God's Sight,
"Sin is justly brought to light."

"In His spotless soul's distress,
"I have learned my guiltiness;
"Oh how vile my low estate,
"Since my ransom was so great."

"Rent the veil that closed the way,
"To my home of heavenly day,
"In the flesh of Christ the Lord;
"Ever be His Name adored!"

"Yet in sight of Calvary,
"Contrite should my spirit be,
"Rest and holiness there find,
"Fashioned like my Saviour's Mind."

CHAPTER 12

(1) "AND JOB ANSWERED AND SAID,

(2) "NO DOUBT BUT YOU ARE THE PEOPLE, AND WISDOM SHALL DIE WITH YOU.

(3) "BUT I HAVE UNDERSTANDING AS WELL AS YOU; I AM NOT INFERIOR TO YOU: YES, WHO KNOWS NOT SUCH THINGS AS THESE?

(4) "I AM AS ONE MOCKED OF HIS NEIGHBOUR, WHO CALLS UPON GOD, AND HE ANSWERS HIM: THE JUST UPRIGHT MAN IS LAUGHED TO SCORN.

(5) "HE WHO IS READY TO SLIP WITH HIS FEET IS AS A LAMP DESPISED IN THE THOUGHT OF HIM WHO IS AT EASE.

(6) "THE TABERNACLES OF ROBBERS PROSPER, AND THEY WHO PROVOKE GOD ARE SECURE; INTO WHOSE HAND GOD BRINGS ABUNDANTLY."

The pattern is:

1. Verse Two proclaims Job using sarcasm, actually saying the opposite of what he means.

2. (Vs. 3) These men were treating Job as though he had no understanding of God's Ways and God's Actions. While it was true that Job did not understand the present situation, still, quite possibly at this present time, there were few men on the face of the Earth, if any, who had the knowledge of God and the relationship with God that Job had.

3. (Vs. 4) Because the modern church little understands *"Justification by Faith,"* as well, *"the just upright man is laughed to scorn."*

4. Verse 5 could read: *"A lamp is for him who is ready to fall, but is despised by him who thinks himself safe"*; this was a rebuke

to the self-confidence and self-righteousness of his *"three friends."*

5. (Vs. 6) These *"three friends"* asserted that prosperity would always follow the one who was right with God. Job replies to this assertion by pointing out that robbers and rebels often prosper.

SARCASM

Job has come to the place that his patience is wearing thin with these *"friends."* He quickly tells them, even though he has lost everything he has, and his body is full of sores with him sitting in an ash heap scraping himself, still, he has no confidence in the things they are saying. He quickly informs them that he has understanding as well, and despite his condition, is not inferior to them. One thing we do know, the Lord when He finally did appear, did not reprimand Job for his statements. In fact, he verified everything Job had said about these individuals.

The Book of Job should be a great lesson for all of us, the ones undergoing a trial, and the ones observing those who are undergoing a trial. But I think the majority of the time, the lesson is all but lost on us.

THE JUST UPRIGHT MAN

Who is the *"just upright man"*?

He is the individual who has placed his faith, his confidence, in Christ and what Christ has done for us at the Cross. Regardless of the past, the Lord judges such a one as *"just and upright."* Regrettably, and all too often, the modern church laughs at the faith of such a one, just as those of Job's day laughed at him, which they, no doubt, did.

A PERSONAL EXPERIENCE

Some time ago, a Christian attorney called me about a particular situation in which he desired to carry forth. He was not a preacher, and did not claim to be one. As stated, he was an attorney at law, and made his living practicing law.

But observing a particular situation, he reasoned in his mind, if sensible men could get together, the situation could be resolved. He asked me the names of several men who pastored very large churches in that particular denomination, which I gave to him.

NOTES

Together they were to go to the powers that be, in order to rectify the situation. He felt certain that he could succeed.

Knowing the situation better than he did, I warned him that while his quest was commendable, and Christlike, I feared that it would come to no good end. At any rate, he was determined to try.

So he and the preachers went to the leaders in question, and laid their case before them.

He called me a few days later and said with exclamated surprise, *"Brother Swaggart, those men believe in penance!"*

"I tried to tell you that," I answered!

And that's the case with most modern Christians. From the heads of denominations on down, even those who claim to believe all the Bible, they actually believe in penance. The Catholic Church is open about their advocating such, while the Protestant world doesn't openly advocate penance, actually, this is what they believe.

If a person does something wrong, they have got to *"pay for it."*

This automatically states several erroneous things.

PENANCE

• First and foremost, penance actually states that what Jesus did at the Cross is not enough, and has to have something added.

• Penance, in essence, states that one can earn forgiveness by carrying forth certain works.

• Penance completely abrogates the Grace of God, simply because Grace cannot function alongside penance.

• Penance also abrogates Justification by Faith.

• Penance, plain and simple, is a sin.

THE WORD OF GOD

John the Beloved said: *"If we confess our sins He is faithful and just to forgive us our sins, and to cleanse from all unrighteousness"* (I Jn. 1:9).

The Apostle continued by saying, *"My little children, these things write I unto you, that you sin not. And if any man sin, we have an Advocate with the Father, Jesus Christ the Righteous:*

"And He is the propitiation for our sins:

and not for ours only, but also for the sins of the whole world" (I Jn. 2:1-2).

Our Lord is the *"propitiation"* (satisfaction) for our sins, through the Sacrificial Offering of Himself at the Cross of Calvary, which paid the price that man could not pay, and a price that God did accept.

Paul said: *"For by Grace* (the Goodness of God) *are you Saved through Faith* (Faith in Christ, with the Cross ever as its Object)*; and that not of yourselves* (none of this is of us, but all is of Him)*: it is the Gift of God* (anytime the word *'Gift'* is used, God is speaking of His Son and His Substitutionary Work on the Cross, which makes all of this possible)*:*

"Not of works (man cannot merit Salvation, irrespective what he does), *lest any man should boast* (boast in his own ability and strength; we are allowed to boast only in the Cross)" (Eph. 2:8-9).

DOES ECONOMIC PROSPERITY ALWAYS FOLLOW THE FAITHFUL?

In a relative sense, I think that one can say *"yes."* But yet, prosperity, as well, even as Job said, at times comes to the wicked.

The chief aim of the Believer, however, must be toward Righteousness and Holiness.

Jesus, with His Sermon on the Mount, said much about giving and, as well, our receiving from God (Mat. 6:1-4, 19-21; 7:7-11). But yet, when he began the Message by the giving of the Beatitudes, the following is what He said, which must be that which Believers should seek. It is:

"Blessed (happy) *are the poor in spirit* (conscious of moral poverty)*: for theirs is the Kingdom of Heaven* (the moral characteristics of the citizens of the Kingdom of the heavens; and so it is apparent that the New Birth is an absolute necessity for entrance into that Kingdom [Jn. 3:3]; this Kingdom is now present spiritually, but not yet physically).

"Blessed are they who mourn (grieved because of personal sinfulness)*: for they shall be comforted* (what the Holy Spirit will do for those who properly evaluate their spiritual poverty).

"Blessed are the meek (the opposite of the self-righteous; the first two Beatitudes guarantee the *'meekness'*)*: for they shall inherit the Earth* (speaks of the coming Kingdom Age, when the *'Kingdom of Heaven'* will be brought down to Earth, when the Saints will rule, with Christ as its Supreme Lord.

"Blessed are they which do hunger and thirst (intense desire) *after Righteousness* (God's Righteousness, imputed by Christ, upon Faith in His Finished Work)*: for they shall be filled.* (But first of all must be truly empty of all self-worth)" (Mat. 5:3-6).

If the first four Beatitudes are properly addressed, the others will likewise fall into place.

This is where the emphasis must be, and not on material things. And yet at the same time, all Believers should give to the Lord unsparingly, and at the same time, should expect Him to bless them. In fact, all Believers, that is if they are functioning according to the Word of God, should expect Blessings from the Lord, and on an unending basis. His Word tells us to ask and we would receive (Mat. 18:18-19; 21:22; Mk. 11:23-24; Jn. 15:7, etc.).

(7) "BUT ASK NOW THE BEASTS, AND THEY SHALL TEACH YOU; AND THE FOWLS OF THE AIR, AND THEY SHALL TELL YOU:

(8) "OR SPEAK TO THE EARTH, AND IT SHALL TEACH YOU: AND THE FISH OF THE SEA SHALL DECLARE UNTO YOU.

(9) "WHO KNOWS NOT IN ALL THESE THAT THE HAND OF THE LORD HAS WROUGHT THIS?

(10) "IN WHOSE HAND IS THE SOUL OF EVERY LIVING THING, AND THE BREATH OF ALL MANKIND.

(11) "DOES NOT THE EAR TRY WORDS? AND THE MOUTH TASTE HIS MEAT?

(12) "WITH THE ANCIENT IS WISDOM; AND IN LENGTH OF DAYS UNDERSTANDING.

(13) "WITH HIM IS WISDOM AND STRENGTH, HE HAS COUNSEL AND UNDERSTANDING.

(14) "BEHOLD, HE BREAKS DOWN, AND IT CANNOT BE BUILT AGAIN: HE SHUTS UP A MAN, AND THERE CAN BE NO OPENING.

(15) "BEHOLD, HE WITHHOLDS THE WATERS, AND THEY DRY UP: ALSO HE SENDS THEM OUT, AND THEY OVERTURN

THE EARTH.

(16) "WITH HIM IS STRENGTH AND WISDOM: THE DECEIVED AND THE DECEIVER ARE HIS.

(17) "HE LEADS COUNSELLORS AWAY SPOILED, AND MAKES THE JUDGES FOOLS.

(18) "HE LOOSES THE BOND OF KINGS, AND GIRDS THEIR LOINS WITH A GIRDLE.

(19) "HE LEADS PRINCES AWAY SPOILED, AND OVERTHROWS THE MIGHTY.

(20) "HE REMOVES AWAY THE SPEECH OF THE TRUSTY, AND TAKES AWAY THE UNDERSTANDING OF THE AGED.

(21) "HE POURS CONTEMPT UPON PRINCES, AND WEAKENS THE STRENGTH OF THE MIGHTY.

(22) "HE DISCOVERS DEEP THINGS OUT OF DARKNESS, AND BRINGS OUT TO LIGHT THE SHADOW OF DEATH.

(23) "HE INCREASES THE NATIONS, AND DESTROYS THEM: HE ENLARGES THE NATIONS, AND STRAITENS THEM AGAIN.

(24) "HE TAKES AWAY THE HEART OF THE CHIEF OF THE PEOPLE OF THE EARTH, AND CAUSES THEM TO WANDER IN A WILDERNESS WHERE THERE IS NO WAY.

(25) "THEY GROPE IN THE DARK WITHOUT LIGHT, AND HE MAKES THEM TO STAGGER LIKE A DRUNKEN MAN."

The synopsis is:

1. The Tenth Verse proclaims the fact that all of Creation shows that there is a Creator.

2. (Vs. 16) God has not only the wisdom to design the course of events, but the Power and ability to carry out all that He designs.

3. (Vs. 17) The wise of the Earth (wise in their own eyes) cannot resist or escape Him; He frustrates their designs and overthrows them.

4. (Vs. 19) While some men may be mighty, still, God is Almighty; there is a vast difference!

5. (Vs. 23) The Lord sets up some kingdoms, and then tears down some kingdoms; all are at His Mercy.

6. (Vs. 25) When men forsake the Lord, He allows them to pursue a devious course instead of a straight one.

REVELATION

Job said of the Lord, and rightly so, *"He discovers deep things out of darkness."*

This means that God reveals truths to man that are beyond his power of understanding. This, I think, could be said to always be an illumination of the Word. In other words, everything that God wants us to know is found in His Word; however, our understanding of His Word is always deficient, which means there is much more to be learned, no matter how much we have learned previously. In fact, the Word of God, and because it is the Word of God, cannot be exhausted.

In 1997 the Lord opened up the Message of the Cross. Due to the fact that I've already alluded to this Revelation, I will be brief.

THE SIN NATURE

First of all, He showed me the cause of failure as it regards the life and living of the Believer. He took me to the Sixth Chapter of Romans, which is the great Chapter where Paul explains this great Truth. If the Believer doesn't understand God's Prescribed Order of Victory, which is the Cross of Christ, and the Cross of Christ exclusively, in some way, the sin nature is going to rule such a person, making life a whole lot less than it is intended to be. The Truth is, millions of Christians are struggling to live a righteous life, and are failing almost on a daily basis. And the facts are, if you pull the truth out of them, they simply do not know why they are failing. They're doing everything they know to do, and everything that other preachers are telling them to do, all to no avail. The problem is the preachers do not know what to tell them, and whatever they do tell them, most of the time is wrong. Also, the preachers are having the same problems the laity is having. The idea is, the modern church simply does not know how to live for God.

THE CROSS OF CHRIST

A few days after the Lord showed me the cause of the problem, which is the sin nature. He also showed me the cure for that problem, which is the Cross of Christ. He took me back to the Sixth Chapter of Romans and said to me that day in the prayer meeting the following:

• The answer for which you seek is found in the Cross.

• The solution for which you seek is found in the Cross.

• The answer for which you seek is found only in the Cross.

In other words, there is no other answer for sin, no other answer for the sin nature, no other answer for acts of sin, no other answer for bondage, no other answer for perversion, no other answer for spiritual darkness, no other answer for whatever it is that we might need, other than the Cross of Christ. This is given to us in Romans 6:3-5.

This Sixth Chapter of Romans pertains to the Sanctification of the Saint, and the part the Cross of Christ plays in that great Work. In fact, the Cross doesn't merely play a part, it is all in all as it regards life and living. Tragically, most Believers understand some things about the Cross as it regards Salvation, but nothing at all as it regards Sanctification. The Believer must understand the following:

"Christ is the Source of all things that we receive from God, and the Cross is the Means by which those things are received, all superintended by the Holy Spirit" (Rom. 8:2).

THE HOLY SPIRIT

A few weeks later, the Lord showed me how the Holy Spirit works in all of this.

He showed me that the Holy Spirit works exclusively within the legal framework of the Finished Work of Christ, in other words, what Christ did for us at the Cross, the great victories He there purchased with His Own shed Blood.

The Holy Spirit doesn't demand much of us, but He does demand that our Faith be exclusively in Christ and what He did for us at the Cross. The following is the Word of God on this Subject which He gave to me, and I quote from THE EXPOSITOR'S STUDY BIBLE:

"For the Law (that which we are about to give is a Law of God, devised by the Godhead in eternity past [I Pet 1:18-20], this Law, in fact is *'God's Prescribed Order of Victory'*) *of the Spirit* (Holy Spirit, i.e., *'the way the Spirit works'*) *of Life* (all life comes from Christ, but through the Holy Spirit [Jn. 16:13-14]) *in Christ Jesus* (any time Paul uses this term or one of its derivatives, he is, without fail, referring to what Christ did at the Cross, which makes this *'life'* possible) *has made me free* (given me total Victory) *from the Law of Sin and Death* (these are the two most powerful Laws in the Universe; the *'Law of the Spirit of Life in Christ Jesus'* alone is stronger than the *'Law of Sin and Death'*; this means that if the Believer attempts to live for God by any manner other than Faith in Christ and the Cross, he is doomed to failure)" (Rom. 8:2).

I started studying the Bible when I was eight years old. I've read it through over 50 times; however, unless the Holy Spirit had revealed to me that which I just gave to you, there is no way that I could have understood it, unless it had come from another preacher, which it didn't.

As well, every Believer should understand that any Revelation from the Lord is always based strictly on the Word of God. It will not add to the Word, or take from the Word. Revelation illuminates the Word, in other words, explaining it more fully to the individual.

Any time a preacher, or anyone, claims they've had a Revelation from the Lord, but it cannot be found in the Bible, then you'd better mark that one off.

"There is a green hill far away,
"Outside a city wall,
"Where the dear Lord was crucified,
"Who died to save us all."

"We may not know, we cannot tell,
"What pains He had to bear;
"But we believe it was for us,
"He hung and suffered there."

"He died that we might be forgiven,
"He died to make us good,
"That we might go at last to Heaven,
"Saved by His precious Blood,"

"There was no other good enough,
"To pay the price of sin;

"He only could unlock the gate,
"Of Heaven, and let us in."

"O dearly, dearly has He loved,
"And we must love Him too,
"And trust in His redeeming Blood,
"And try His Works to do."

CHAPTER 13

(1) "MY EYE HAS SEEN ALL THIS, MY EAR HAS HEARD AND UNDERSTOOD IT.

(2) "WHAT YOU KNOW, THE SAME DO I KNOW ALSO: I AM NOT INFERIOR UNTO YOU.

(3) "SURELY I WOULD SPEAK TO THE ALMIGHTY, AND I DESIRE TO REASON WITH GOD.

(4) "BUT YOU ARE FORGERS OF LIES, YOU ARE ALL PHYSICIANS OF NO VALUE.

(5) "O THAT YOU WOULD ALTOGETHER HOLD YOUR PEACE! AND IT SHOULD BE YOUR WISDOM.

(6) "HEAR NOW MY REASONING, AND HEARKEN TO THE PLEADINGS OF MY LIPS.

(7) "WILL YOU SPEAK WICKEDLY FOR GOD? AND TALK DECEITFULLY FOR HIM?

(8) "WILL YOU ACCEPT HIS PERSON? WILL YOU CONTEND FOR GOD?

(9) "IS IT GOOD THAT HE SHOULD SEARCH YOU OUT? OR AS ONE MAN MOCKS ANOTHER, DO YOU SO MOCK HIM?

(10) "HE WILL SURELY REPROVE YOU, IF YOU DO SECRETLY ACCEPT PERSONS.

(11) "SHALL NOT HIS EXCELLENCY MAKE YOU AFRAID? AND HIS DREAD FALL UPON YOU?

(12) "YOUR REMEMBRANCES ARE LIKE UNTO ASHES, YOUR BODIES TO BODIES OF CLAY.

(13) "HOLD YOUR PEACE, LET ME ALONE, THAT I MAY SPEAK, AND LET COME ON ME WHAT WILL."

The pattern is:

1. (Vs. 2) Job says that whatever these friends claim to know about God, he knows as well. Actually, Job is far superior in knowledge!

2. (Vs. 3) Job, realizing that God is his only hope, addresses himself to that conclusion. These *"friends"* cannot help.

3. Any Preacher who stands behind a pulpit and holds up anything but the Lord Jesus Christ, and what He did at the Cross, as the answer to the ills of man falls into the same category of that which is said in Verse 4.

4. (Vs. 6) As his *"friends"* have not kept silence, but have spoken, Job claims the right also to be heard!

5. (Vs. 7) It is sad but true that the majority of those who stand behind pulpits *"speak wickedly for God"* and *"talk deceitfully for Him."* They do so because they substitute their own human reasoning for the Word of God.

PHYSICIANS OF NO VALUE

Anybody who proposes any solution to the problems of mankind, other than the Cross of Christ, must be put in the category of *"physicians of no value."*

The Word of God is replete with this solution, all the way from Genesis 1:1 through Revelation 22:21. In fact, the story of the entirety of the Bible is *"Jesus Christ and Him Crucified"* (I Cor. 1:23; Gal. 6:14; Rev. 22:17). But, the world ignores the Bible, continuing to try to formulate solutions of its own, which never work.

Regrettably and sadly, the church, which ought to know better, follows suit with the world. It keeps proposing one solution after the other, which is not the Cross, not after the Cross, and doesn't pertain to the Cross. Even though they may be religious solutions, and in fact most are, still, there is no help or hope from that source.

It is sad to say, that in most churches, the man who stands behind the pulpit, is a *"physician of no value."* He's not preaching the Gospel, so whatever it is he is proposing, is of no consequence.

"LEST THE CROSS OF CHRIST BE OF NONE EFFECT"

Paul said, *"Christ sent me not to baptize, but to preach the Gospel, not with *enticing words of man's wisdom, lest the Cross of Christ should be made of none effect"* (I Cor. 1:17).

Satan is ever trying to change the Message from the Cross, that is if the Message has ever been the Cross, to something else.

At the Church at Corinth, false teachers were coming in promoting Water Baptism, and even beyond that, particular individuals who had done the baptizing. In other words, they were saying, that if you were baptized by Simon Peter... or Apollos... or of Paul, this meant, according to which one was being promoted, that your baptism was greater, etc. It seems that Believers are ready and willing to believe anything and everything except the Message of the Cross. Some of the most preposterous things can be advocated, and Christians by the tens of thousands will fall for it, but when the Cross of Christ is mentioned, it is instantly dismissed.

Why?

WHY THE CROSS OF CHRIST IS IGNORED

There are many and varied reasons why this happens, none legitimate. Some of them are:

- Many Believers think of the Cross as being elementary.
- Many Believers think they already know all about the Cross, when in reality, they know very little.
- Many, according to the Word of Faith doctrine, actually repudiate the Cross, claiming it is of no consequence.
- The Cross of Christ is an offense, simply because it exposes self-righteousness.
- Many ignore the Cross, simply because they have not been taught properly regarding the Cross.
- Satan fights the Message of the Cross as he fights nothing else. And he does it mostly through preachers.
- The Message of the Cross is singular. In other words, it cannot be the Cross plus....
- Works appeal to pride, while Faith appeals to the Cross.
- Jesus Christ is the Source of all Blessings from God, while the Cross is the Means. Far too many preachers desire that other things be the means.
- The Cross of Christ is the only thing standing between mankind and eternal Hell. There is nothing else to which man can look.

SPEAKING WICKEDLY FOR GOD

Job asks of his three friends, *"Will you speak wickedly for God? And talk deceitfully for Him?"*

It is sad but true that the majority of those who stand behind pulpits *"speak wickedly for God, and talk deceitfully for Him."* They do so because they substitute their own human reasoning for the Word of God, exactly as these three *"friends."*

If men, even anyone, claim to speak for God, then we had best know what we are saying. Even as the account is given in the Book of Job concerning the three friends, and even Job himself, the Lord keeps a record of all that is said presently, and by everyone. We must remember that!

Point number two to this scenario proclaims the fact that the only way that a Believer can speak rightly of God, is by and through the Lord Jesus Christ and what He did for us at the Cross. If man tries to approach God, tries to appeal to God, tries to speak for God on any basis other than the Cross of Christ, what he says cannot be accepted, and could even bring the Judgment of God on the head of such a person. Let it be understood, that man has no access to God except through the Cross of Christ. Only through the Cross are we allowed to *"Come boldly unto the Throne of Grace* (presents the Seat of Divine Power, and yet the Source of boundless Grace), *that we may obtain Mercy* (presents that which we want first), *and find Grace to help in time of need* (refers to the Goodness of God extended to all who come, and during any *'time of need'*; all made possible by the Cross)" (Heb. 4:16).

A PERSONAL EXPERIENCE

As I look at my own life, going back to those days and years before the Revelation of the Cross, the difference in then and now is beyond belief. To be sure, the Lord greatly helped me and blessed me in those days, for which I will ever be thankful, and because He knew that I was reaching out after Him in every capacity, even though I did not understand the Cross as it regards Sanctification. The Believer must understand that the Lord loves us. He's not trying to wash us out, but rather to bring us in. He uses His infinite patience with us, infinite longsuffering, for which we should be so grateful. Were it not for His patience and longsuffering, you and I would not be here today.

In those days, I knew something was wrong, but I did not know what it was, and not knowing what it was, I did not know how to address it. But irrespective of my sincerity, irrespective of my zealousness, irrespective to the degree that God was using me to touch half the world with the Gospel by television, still, not knowing and understanding God's prescribed order of victory, there was no way that I could live the life that I should live, and neither can anyone else. Let's say it again:

GOD'S PRESCRIBED ORDER OF VICTORY

The little diagram that we will now give, and possibly even give it again in this Volume, and because of its great significance, even though brief, will, we think, adequately explain *"God's Prescribed Order of Victory."* Please understand, a person can be Saved and not understand this of which we say; however, a Believer, no matter his zealousness, no matter his sincerity, cannot live a victorious life without understanding the Message of the Cross. It simply cannot be done. The Cross is God's Way of Salvation, and His only Way of Salvation, and His Way of Sanctification, and His only Way of Sanctification. We must never forget that! So, please look at this diagram carefully, and even though it is brief, I think the truth of what is presented will be obvious.

FOCUS: The Lord Jesus Christ (Jn. 14:6).
OBJECT OF FAITH: The Cross of Christ (Rom. 6:3-5).
POWER SOURCE: The Holy Spirit (Rom. 8:1-2).
RESULTS: Victory (Rom. 6:14).

Now let's use the same formula, but apply a different method. You'll see, I think, the way that most in the Church are trying to live this life, which regrettably and sadly, leads to disaster.

Focus: Works.
Object of Faith: Performance.
Power Source: Self.
Results: Defeat.

The two diagrams listed above, portray, *"God's Prescribed Order of Victory,"* and *"man's way of victory,"* of which the latter contains no victory at all.

WHAT DOES IT MEAN TO EMBRACE THE CROSS?

• We must first of all understand that Jesus Christ is the Source of all that we receive from God, and the Cross is the Means of us receiving it, with the Holy Spirit superintending all things (Rom. 8:1-2, 11).

• We must understand that it was at the Cross where every sin was atoned, past, present, and future, at least for those who will believe (Jn. 3:16), and, consequently, Satan plus all of his minions of darkness, were totally and completely defeated (Col. 2:14-15).

• We must understand that all victory is found in the Cross, and only in the Cross!

• God will not deal with man in any capacity except through the Cross of Christ.

• The object of Faith of every Believer has to be the Cross of Christ and the Cross of Christ exclusively. This is absolutely imperative (I Cor. 1:17-18, 21, 23; 2:2).

• Our Faith must be explicitly in Christ and the Cross, which eliminates everything else. Unfortunately, this is not too agreeable with many Believers (Gal. 6:14).

• The Believer must understand that the entirety of the Story of the Bible centers up in *"Jesus Christ and Him Crucified"* (Jn. 1:1-2, 14, 29).

• We must understand that the Cross of Christ is the only means of Salvation for the sinner, and the only means of Sanctification for the Saint (Rom. 6:1-14).

• The Believer must understand that the only means of victory over the sin nature, is Faith in the Cross of Christ, which then gives the Holy Spirit latitude to work within our lives (Rom. 8:1-2, 11).

• One must understand that while one can be a Christian, and not understand the Cross as it regards Sanctification, there is no way that one can walk in victory, and I speak of victory over the world, the flesh, and the Devil, without embracing the Cross of Christ, and the Cross of Christ alone (Eph. 2:13-18).

(14) "WHEREFORE DO I TAKE MY FLESH IN MY TEETH, AND PUT MY LIFE IN MY HAND?

(15) "THOUGH HE KILL ME, YET WILL I TRUST IN HIM: BUT I WILL MAINTAIN MY OWN WAYS BEFORE HIM.

(16) "HE ALSO SHALL BE MY SALVATION: FOR AN HYPOCRITE SHALL NOT COME BEFORE HIM.

(17) "HEAR DILIGENTLY MY SPEECH, AND MY DECLARATION WITH YOUR EARS.

(18) "BEHOLD NOW, I HAVE ORDERED MY CAUSE, I KNOW THAT I SHALL BE JUSTIFIED."

The exegesis is:

1. (Vs. 14) Now Job makes his appeal to God and God Alone; but Job prefaces it by excusing his boldness.

2. Verse 15 where Job says, *"Though He kill me, yet will I trust in Him,"* presents a tremendous statement of Faith.

3. The Sixteenth Verse proclaims the fact that these *"friends"* held no Salvation for Job; as well, he states here that he is not a hypocrite, as they have contended.

THOUGH HE SLAY ME, YET WILL I TRUST HIM

This was not a bad confession as some claim, but rather a confession of Faith which was approved by God (Job 42:7).

The statement, *"Though God slay me, yet will I trust Him,"* presents the fact that God is not to be blamed. As well, whatever God decides to do, Job is saying that he will acquiesce to the Will of God.

Job reasons that everything has been taken from him. We speak of his wealth, his children, his health, and there is nothing left but his life. As well, he knows that God has allowed this to be done, even though he does not understand why.

We find from all of this, that even though Job didn't have a Bible as we have today, still, he had a far greater knowledge of God, and the way that God functioned and worked, than even do most in this age of Grace in which we presently live. You don't find Job

NOTES

"forgiving God," as the world of humanistic psychology, i.e., *"Christian Psychology,"* recommends. Likewise, one doesn't find Job, as previously stated, blaming God. He doesn't know why he's in the situation he's in, and because he doesn't know of any sin that's in his life which would displease the Lord. So, there is a great question in his mind as to the reason for all of this, which is perfectly obvious, and for which the Lord did not reprimand him at all.

Satan had claimed that Job was serving God only for what he could get out of God. In other words, God had blessed Job abundantly, and this is the reason that Job was serving Him. *"Take away all that he has,"* Satan claimed, *"and he will curse You to Your face."* Well we find the opposite taking place.

Instead of cursing God, Job finds no fault with his Creator, and if fault is found, he finds it with himself.

In history, I think one can say without fear of contradiction, there's never been a trial quite like this trial, never been a situation quite like this situation, and yet we see God's man coming forth, even as a champion.

WHAT WAS THE REASON FOR ALL OF THIS?

Even though we've already addressed this after a fashion, it is so very important, that I think we should look at it from every angle.

The Lord had far more in mind as it regards this scenario than winning an argument with Satan. While he most definitely would win that argument, still, what took place, even as the Lord planned it, would serve as an example for every generation and for all time.

Satan would be proven a liar in every capacity, meaning that his accusations concerning Job were no more than blow and bluster. As well, the consecration and dedication of a man to God and His Ways would be proven out before the whole world, and beyond the shadow of a doubt.

But above all of that, the Lord would use this in order to affect the Sanctification process in the heart and life of Job. He would show the great Patriarch, that even though he was closer to God than any man on the earth at that time, and was actually the topic of conversation in Heaven, still, even though this pleased God, the Lord would show him that what he really needed, which was more and more of the Lord, could not be obtained by his own efforts and strength. It could only be done God's Way.

As we've already stated, that God would choose the most perfect man on Earth to teach us this manifold lesson, should be a tremendous example to us.

WHAT DOES IT SHOW US?

It should show us, and is meant to show us, that within ourselves, referring to our own power, education, intellect, strength and ability, that we cannot bring about in our lives that which is so desperately needed, and I speak of Righteousness and Holiness. The Holy Spirit Alone can do this which needs to be done. As well, we must learn that the Holy Spirit works exclusively by and through the means of the Cross of Christ, which actually gives Him the legal right to do all that He does. This requires Faith on our part, and I am speaking of Faith exclusively in Christ and the Cross. As we have previously stated, the Holy Spirit doesn't demand much of us, and in fact, if He did, we couldn't function too very well, but He does demand that our Faith be exclusively in Christ and His Sacrificial, Atoning Work.

So, the lesson taught in Job is invaluable to say the least! Even though he would suffer as few men have suffered, still, the end result would be that which only the Lord would do. He would give the great Patriarch twice what had been taken from him. As should be understood, this was a blessing of untold proportions. In fact, the Lord never asks anything of anyone, but that He reciprocates in kind, and even many times more.

AN EXAMPLE!

The Scripture says:

"*And it came to pass, that, as the people pressed upon Him to hear the Word of God, He stood by the Lake of Gennesaret* (the Sea of Galilee),

"*And saw two ships standing by the lake* (two among the many): *but the fishermen were gone out of them, and were washing their nets* (Peter, Andrew, James, and John had fished all night and caught nothing).

"*And He entered into one of the ships, which was Simon's* (proclaims Jesus borrowing this vessel to serve as a platform or pulpit), *and prayed him that he would thrust out a little from the land. And He sat down* (the custom then), *and taught the people out of the ship.*

"*Now when He had left speaking* (had finished preaching and teaching), *He said unto Simon, Launch out into the deep, and let down your nets for a draught* (came as a surprise to these fishermen; they had fished all night and caught nothing, so they must have wondered as to what He was doing; in effect, He will pay for the use of the boat; God will owe man nothing).

"*And Simon answering said unto Him, Master, we have toiled all the night, and have taken nothing: nevertheless at Your Word, I will let down the net* (the idea is that Peter would not have bothered himself to have let down the net on the word of anyone else other than Jesus).

"*And when they had this done, they enclosed a great multitude of fishes: and their net broke* (so many fish that it broke the net).

"*And they beckoned unto their partners* (Peter and Andrew beckoned to James and John), *who were in the other ship, that they should come and help them. And they came, and filled both the ships, so that they began to sink* (Christ had the same power over the fish of the sea as He had over the frogs, lice, and locusts of Egypt)" (Lk. 5:1-7).

The Lord, as amply stated, borrowed the boat to use as a platform to preach to the people. He will now pay for the use of that boat by giving them a great catch of fish.

As stated, the Lord will owe no man anything. Anyone who does anything for Him will always be paid for whatever was done, and in fact, many times over.

(19) "WHO IS HE WHO WILL PLEAD WITH ME? FOR NOW, IF I HOLD MY TONGUE, I SHALL GIVE UP THE GHOST.

(20) "ONLY DO NOT TWO THINGS UNTO ME: THEN WILL I NOT HIDE MYSELF FROM YOU.

(21) "WITHDRAW YOUR HAND FAR FROM ME: AND LET NOT YOUR DREAD

MAKE ME AFRAID.

(22) "THEN YOU CALL, AND I WILL ANSWER: OR LET ME SPEAK, AND YOU ANSWER ME.

(23) "HOW MANY ARE MY INIQUITIES AND SINS? MAKE ME TO KNOW MY TRANSGRESSION AND MY SIN.

(24) "WHEREFORE HIDE YOU YOUR FACE, AND HOLD ME FOR YOUR ENEMY?

(25) "WILL YOU BREAK A LEAF DRIVEN TO AND FRO? AND WILL YOU PURSUE THE DRY STUBBLE?

(26) "FOR YOU WRITE BITTER THINGS AGAINST ME, AND MAKE ME TO POSSESS THE INIQUITIES OF MY YOUTH.

(27) "YOU PUT MY FEET ALSO IN THE STOCKS, AND LOOK NARROWLY UNTO ALL MY PATHS; YOU SET A PRINT UPON THE HEELS OF MY FEET.

(28) "AND HE, AS A ROTTEN THING, CONSUMES, AS A GARMENT THAT IS MOTH EATEN."

The diagram is:

1. (Vs. 21) Job now appeals to the Lord. He asks the Lord to help him not to fear. And his greatest fear is that he has displeased the Lord.

2. (Vs. 23) He went on to tell the Lord, *"These friends have claimed that I am a great sinner; I will only take Your Word for that, not theirs."*

3. (Vs. 24) Job believes that the Lord will vindicate him. But he asks if there is a present alienation, and desires to be made acquainted with the cause of it, if, in fact, it does exist.

4. (Vs. 25) Job compares himself to two of the weakest things in nature — a withered leaf and a morsel of dry stubble.

5. As it regards Verse 26, in considering what the indictment against him might be, he can only suppose that these old and long-forgotten sins of his youth are being remembered and brought up against him.

6. The Twenty-seventh Verse presents a figure of speech on Job's part, meaning that it seemed as if God had made him a captive to his terrible plight.

JOB PLEADS WITH THE LORD

To be sure, the Lord heard every word said by Job, and although He did not answer immediately, most definitely He would ultimately answer.

Job had a close relationship with the Lord, and of that I think it should be obvious; however, this made his situation even more grievous. Why had the Lord allowed this to happen to him? Why did not the Lord vindicate him? What sin had he committed, that would have brought the Judgment of God down upon him, or so he thinks? His *"three friends"* were very busy telling him what a hypocrite he was, and what great secret sins he had obviously committed, and to be sure, that stung very, very badly.

The Salvation of Job was that he knew better. He knew what his life was! He knew there were no secret sins in his life! And that is what sustained him, but it did not answer the questions as it regards why the Lord had allowed all of this to happen. That confuses him greatly and rightly so!

None of this is to say that Job was perfect, for as it regards moral perfection, no human being, even the one closest to God, can claim such. *"All have sinned, and come short of the Glory of God"* (Rom. 3:23).

The idea of this Text is that even the most Righteous among us continue to come short of the Glory of God, even on a continuing basis. That's the reason that we need the constant intercession of Christ. Paul said:

"Wherefore He (the Lord Jesus Christ) *is able also to save them to the uttermost* (proclaims the fact that Christ Alone has made the only true Atonement for sin; He did this at the Cross) *who come unto God by Him* (proclaims the only manner in which man can come to God), *seeing He ever lives to make intercession for them.* (His very Presence by the Right Hand of the Father guarantees such, with nothing else having to be done [Heb. 1:3])" (Heb. 7:25).

But yet, Job had tried, and was still trying to live a life for the Lord that would be pleasing to the Lord, and of that the Lord honored greatly.

"O sacred Head, once wounded,
"With grief and shame bowed down,
"Now scornfully surrounded,
"With thorns, Your only Crown.
"O sacred Head, what glory,

"What bliss till now was Thine!
"Yet, though despised and gory,
"I joy to call You Mine."

"What Thou, my Lord, has suffered,
"Was all for sinners' gain;
"Mine, mine was the transgression,
"But Thine the deadly pain:
"Lo, here I fall, my Saviour!
"'Tis I deserve Your place;
"Look on me with Your favour,
"Vouchsafe to me Your Grace."

"What language shall I borrow,
"To thank You, dearest friend,
"For this Your dying sorrow,
"Your pity without end?
"O make me Yours forever;
"And should I fainting be,
"Lord, let me never, never,
"Outlive my love for Thee."

"Be near me when I'm dying,
"O show Your Cross to me,
"And to my succour flying,
"Come, Lord, and set me free.
"These eyes, new faith receiving,
"From Jesus shall not move,
"For he, who dies believing,
"Dies safely through Your Love."

CHAPTER 14

(1) "MAN WHO IS BORN OF A WOMAN IS OF FEW DAYS AND FULL OF TROUBLE.

(2) "HE COMES FORTH LIKE A FLOWER, AND IS CUT DOWN: HE FLEES ALSO AS A SHADOW, AND CONTINUES NOT.

(3) "AND DO YOU OPEN YOUR EYES UPON SUCH AN ONE, AND BRING ME INTO JUDGMENT WITH YOU?

(4) "WHO CAN BRING A CLEAN THING OUT OF AN UNCLEAN? NOT ONE.

(5) "SEEING HIS DAYS ARE DETERMINED, THE NUMBER OF HIS MONTHS ARE WITH YOU, YOU HAVE APPOINTED HIS BOUNDS THAT HE CANNOT PASS;

(6) "TURN FROM HIM, THAT HE MAY REST, TILL HE SHALL ACCOMPLISH, AS AN HIRELING, HIS DAY.

(7) "FOR THERE IS HOPE OF A TREE, IF IT BE CUT DOWN, THAT IT WILL SPROUT AGAIN, AND THAT THE TENDER BRANCH THEREOF WILL NOT CEASE,

(8) "THOUGH THE ROOT THEREOF WAX OLD IN THE EARTH, AND THE STOCK THEREOF DIE IN THE GROUND;

(9) "YET THROUGH THE SCENT OF WATER IT WILL BUD, AND BRING FORTH BOUGHS LIKE A PLANT.

(10) "BUT MAN DIES, AND WASTES AWAY: YES, MAN GIVES UP THE GHOST AND WHERE IS HE?

(11) "AS THE WATERS FAIL FROM THE SEA, AND THE FLOOD DECAYS AND DRIES UP:

(12) "SO MAN LIES DOWN, AND RISES NOT: TILL THE HEAVENS BE NO MORE, THEY SHALL NOT AWAKE, NOR BE RAISED OUT OF THEIR SLEEP.

(13) "O THAT YOU WOULD HIDE ME IN THE GRAVE, THAT YOU WOULD KEEP ME SECRET, UNTIL YOUR WRATH BE PAST, THAT YOU WOULD APPOINT ME A SET TIME, AND REMEMBER ME!

(14) "IF A MAN DIE, SHALL HE LIVE AGAIN? ALL THE DAYS OF MY APPOINTED TIME WILL I WAIT, TILL MY CHANGE COME."

The synopsis is:

1. Due to the Fall in the Garden of Eden by our original parents, the statement made in Verse 1 is true.

2. (Vs. 2) The phrase, *"He comes forth like a flower, and is cut down,"* is used quite frequently in Scripture (Ps. 103:15; Isa. 28:1, 4; James 1:10-11; I Pet. 1:24).

3. The question of Verse 3 is actually the age-old question of man. Why would God, Who is able to create whatever He desires, go to such lengths and trouble to redeem *"such an one"*?

4. Verse 4 presents a question that addresses itself directly to the inability of man to save himself; therefore, Salvation had to be outside of man, and that it was, in Christ Jesus.

5. (Vs. 5) The life span of every individual is fixed by God; however, it can be cut short or prolonged, according to disobedience or obedience.

6. The idea of Verse 6 is, when the life span

is over, man should have accomplished that which was intended; regrettably, only a precious few accomplish their appointed task.

7. Verse 7 tells us that even if a man does fall on hard times, if he will believe God, the fallen tree can sprout and grow again.

8. (Vs. 10) Before Christ, and even before the Law, the eternal abode of man was only dimly understood.

9. In Verse 12, Job is not addressing himself to the Resurrection, as some think, but rather to the brevity of this life.

10. Plainly Verse 14 proclaims the coming Resurrection, although dimly understood at that time; correct understanding would come only with Christ and the Truth He would ultimately give to the Apostle Paul (I Cor. 15:51-57).

FEW DAYS AND FULL OF TROUBLE

Job is exactly right when he said, *"Man that is born of a woman is of few days and full of trouble."*

This was not originally intended to be. God intended for man to live in bliss, in a veritable Paradise, actually that which was given to him at Creation, and without sickness or dying. He only had to do one thing, and that was to obey the Lord.

Concerning this obedience, the Scripture says: *"And the LORD God took the man, and put him into the Garden of Eden to dress it and to keep it.*

"And the LORD God commanded the man, saying, Of every tree of the Garden you may freely eat (as stated, before the Fall, man was vegetarian):

"But of the Tree of the Knowledge of Good and Evil, you shall not eat of it (as for the *'evil,'* that was obvious; however, it is the *'good'* on this tree that deceives much of the world; the *'good'* speaks of religion; the definition of religion pertains to a system devised by men in order to bring about Salvation, to reach God, or to better oneself in some way; because it is devised by man, it is unacceptable to God; God's Answer to the dilemma of the human race is *'Jesus Christ and Him Crucified'* [I Cor. 1:23]): *for in the day that you eat thereof you shall surely die* (speaks of spiritual death, which is separation from God; let it be understood that the Tree of the Knowledge of Good and Evil was not the cause of Adam's Fall; it was a failure to heed and obey the Word of God, which is the cause of every single failure; spiritual death ultimately brought on physical death, and has, in fact, filled the world with death, all because of the Fall)" (Gen. 2:15-17).

THE FALL OF MAN

As it regards the Fall, the Biblical account is, and I continue to quote from THE EXPOSITOR'S STUDY BIBLE:

"Now the serpent was more subtle than any beast of the field which the LORD God had made (the word *'subtle,'* as used here, is not negative, but rather positive; everything that God made before the Fall was positive; it describes qualities such as quickness of sight, swiftness of motion, activity of self-preservation, and seemingly intelligent adaptation to its surroundings). *And he said unto the woman* (not a fable; the serpent before the Fall had the ability of limited speech; Eve did not seem surprised when he spoke to her!), *Yes, has God said, You shall not eat of every tree of the Garden?* (The serpent evidently lent its faculties to Satan, even though the Evil One is not mentioned. That being the case, Satan spoke through the serpent, and questioned the Word of God.)

"And the woman said unto the serpent (proclaims Satan leveling his attack against Eve, instead of Adam; his use of Eve was only a means to get to Adam), *We may eat of the fruit of the trees of the Garden* (the trial of our First Parents was ordained by God, because probation was essential to their Spiritual development and self-determination; but as He did not desire that they should be tempted to their Fall, He would not suffer Satan to tempt them in a way that would surpass their human capacity; the tempted might, therefore, have resisted the tempter):

"But of the fruit of the tree which is in the midst of the Garden, God has said, You shall not eat of it, neither shall you touch it, lest you die (Eve quoted what the Lord had said about the prohibition, but then added, *'neither shall you touch it'*).

"And the serpent said unto the woman, You shall not surely die (proclaims an

outright denial of the Word of God; as God had preached to Adam, Satan now preaches to Eve; Jesus calls Satan a liar, which probably refers to this very moment [Jn. 8:44])*:*

"For God does know that in the day you eat thereof, then your eyes shall be opened (suggests the attainment of higher wisdom), *and you shall be as gods, knowing good and evil.* (In effect, says, *'you shall be Elohim.'* It was a promise of Divinity. God is Omniscient, meaning that His Knowledge of evil is thorough, but not by personal experience. By His very Nature, He is totally separate from all that is evil. The knowledge of evil that Adam and Eve would learn would be by moral degradation, which would bring wreckage. While it was proper to desire to be like God, it is proper only if done in the right way, and that is through Faith in Christ and what He has done for us at the Cross.)

"And when the woman saw that the tree was good for food (presents the lust of the eyes), *and that it was pleasant to the eyes* (the lust of the flesh), *and a tree to be desired to make one wise* (the pride of life), *she took of the fruit thereof, and did eat* (constitutes the Fall), *and gave also unto her husband with her; and he did eat* (refers to the fact that evidently Adam was an observer to all these proceedings; some claim that he ate of the forbidden fruit, which she offered him out of love for her; however, no one ever sins out of love; Eve submitted to the temptation out of deception, but *'Adam was not deceived'* [I Tim. 2:14]; he fell because of unbelief; he simply didn't believe what God had said about the situation; contrast Verse 6 with Luke 4:1-13; both present the three temptations, *'the lust of the flesh, the lust of the eyes, and the pride of life'*; the first man falls, the Second Man conquers).

"And the eyes of them both were opened (refers to the consciousness of guilt as a result of their sin), *and they knew they were naked* (refers to the fact that they had lost the enswathing light of purity, which previously had clothed their bodies)*; and they sewed fig leaves together, and made themselves aprons* (sinners clothe themselves with morality, sacraments, and religious ceremonies; they are as worthless as Adam's apron of fig leaves)*"* (Gen. 3:1-7).

NOTES

THE TROUBLE

Now, because of the Fall, the state of man will be that of *"trouble,"* and even more so *"full of trouble."*

So, the terrible plight of the human race as seen today and has been seen through some 6,000 years of recorded history is the result of man's rebellion against God and accepting Satan as Lord (Gen. 3:8).

When Adam and Eve fell, two distinct things happened:

Satan at that time became the *"god of this world"* (II Cor. 4:4), and the *"prince of the powers of the air"* (Eph. 2:2).

What does that mean?

It means that Satan controls the system of this world, hence, all the wars, starvation, superstition, and man's inhumanity to man. One day soon, even as we have stated previously in this Volume, Satan will be locked away forever and forever (Rev. 20:10).

WHAT EXACTLY HAPPENED TO MAN AT THE FALL?

In the first place, he fell from total God-consciousness, down to the far, far lower level of total self-consciousness. The sin nature now rules fallen man, which means that everything he does in some way is from the viewpoint of sin, i.e., *"disobedience to God."* In other words, unredeemed man is ruled by the sin nature and constantly.

What exactly does that mean?

While sin originates in the heart, we must understand what is meant by that statement (Mat. 15:18-19).

When the Lord spoke of the *"heart"* of man, He wasn't speaking of the physical organ that beats within our breast, thereby, keeping us alive. He was rather speaking of the soul and the spirit of the individual. Presently, many tend to divide a human being into isolated functions, such as: the Spiritual, the intellectual, the emotional, the rational, and the volitional. But Biblical thought maintains the unity of the person. It looks at a human being as a whole and expresses all of these and other inner human functions by use of the word *"heart."* In the Bible the heart is thus the *"conscious self,"* the inner person with every function that makes a person human, i.e., *"the soul and the spirit."*

WHAT IS THE SIN NATURE?

The sin nature pertains to the very nature of man as a result of the Fall, which is taken over by sin. In other words, due to Adam's Fall, each of us were born in original sin, meaning that our very nature was that of sin. It is in man to transgress the Word of God, to disobey the Word of God, to rebel against the Word of God. As stated, it is his very nature.

Sin begins in the very soul and spirit of the individual, which refers to the nature of the person, which produces sin.

Paul addressed this by saying that the sin nature seeks to exhibit its desires of evil through the faculties of the human body. The Apostle said:

"Let not sin (the sin nature) *therefore reign* (rule) *in your mortal body* (showing that the sin nature can once again rule in the heart and life of the Believer, if the Believer doesn't constantly look to Christ and the Cross; the 'mortal body' is neutral, which means it can be used for Righteousness or unrighteousness), *that you should obey it in the lusts thereof* (ungodly lusts are carried out through the mortal body, if Faith is not maintained in the Cross [I Cor. 1:17-18]).

"Neither yield you your members (of your mortal body) *as instruments of unrighteousness unto sin* (the sin nature): *but yield yourselves to God* (we are to yield ourselves to Christ and the Cross; that alone guarantees Victory over the sin nature), *as those who are alive from the dead* (we have been raised with Christ in 'Newness of Life'), *and your members as instruments of Righteousness unto God* (this can be done only by virtue of the Cross and our Faith in that Finished Work, and Faith which continues in that Finished Work from day-to-day [Lk. 9:23-24])" (Rom. 6:12-13).

All unsaved people are ruled by the sin nature 24 hours a day, seven days a week, i.e., forever, unless they come to Christ.

However, when the believing sinner comes to Christ, the sin nature is at that time made dormant, meaning that it is made ineffective. But, if the Believer doesn't understand God's Way of Victory, which refers to overcoming life and living, the sin nature will once again begin to rule in such a person, causing untold difficulties. This doesn't mean the person loses their soul, but it does mean that life is a whole lot less than what it ought to be.

The means by which the Believer is to live a victorious, overcoming, Christian life, victorious over the world, the flesh, and the Devil, is according to God's Prescribed Order. What is that order?

GOD'S PRESCRIBED ORDER OF VICTORY

The Believer is to understand that Christ is the Source of all things that we receive from God, and the Cross is the Means by which these things are given to us, or rather made possible to us, all superintended by the Holy Spirit (Rom. 8:1-2, 11).

This means that the Believer is to place his faith exclusively in Christ and the Cross, understanding that this is the key to all Victory, and never allow it to be moved elsewhere. To be sure, Satan will fight with all of his might to try to get the Believer to make something else the object of his faith. To be sure, Satan doesn't care too very much about what the other thing is, just so it's not the Cross. He was defeated at the Cross, and defeated totally (Col. 2:14-15).

As the Believer maintains his Faith in Christ and what Christ did for us at the Cross, never allowing it to be moved, then the Holy Spirit, Who works exclusively within the parameters of the Finished Work of Christ, will begin to work within our hearts and lives, developing His Fruit, thereby, making us what we ought to be (Rom. 6:1-14; 8:1-2, 11; I Cor. 1:17-18, 21, 23; 2:2).

THE CORRECT OBJECT OF FAITH

Everything is by faith, yet, for it to be Faith that God will recognize, it must have the Cross of Christ as its Object (I Cor. 1:17-18; 2:2).

Every Christian talks about faith, and rightly so; however, most Christians do not understand what we're talking about when we speak of the correct Object of Faith.

If most Christians were asked as to what the object of their faith was, most would probably say, *"the Word of God."* To be frank, that is correct; however, that which says too much actually concludes by saying precious little at all.

Let's look at it a little closer.

The Story of the Bible is the Story of Jesus Christ and Him Crucified (Jn. 1:1-2, 14, 29). In a sense, Jesus Christ is on every Page of the Bible, virtually every Chapter, actually every Scripture, in one way or the other. He came to this world but for one Purpose. Paul said:

"But when the fullness of time was come (which completed the time designated by God that should elapse before the Son of God would come), *God sent forth His Son* (it was God Who acted; the Law required man to act; this requirement demonstrated man's impotency; the Son of God requires nothing from man other than his confidence), *made of a woman* (pertains to the Incarnation, God becoming man), *made under the Law* (refers to the Mosaic Law; Jesus was subject to the Jewish legal economy, which He had to be, that is if He was to redeem fallen humanity; in other words, He had to keep the Law perfectly, which no human being had ever done, but He did),

"To redeem them who were under the Law (in effect, all of humanity is under the Law of God, which man, due to his fallen condition, could not keep; but Jesus came and redeemed us by keeping the Law perfectly, and above all satisfying its penalty on the Cross, which was death), *that we might receive the adoption of sons* (that we could become the sons of God by adoption, which is carried out by Faith in Christ and what He did at the Cross)" (Gal. 4:4-5).

So, when we say that our Faith is in the Word of God, we must understand the Purpose of the Word of God, which is to portray Christ, Who Alone is our Redeemer, and our Redeemer by virtue of the Cross. All of this means that the Cross of Christ, which was the destination of Christ, even before the foundation of the world, is to ever be the Object of our Faith. Then and only then can the Holy Spirit Work unfettered within one's heart and one's life.

To be sure, that which we need to be in Christ, no matter how hard we try within our own capabilities, we cannot accomplish the task. We must have the Work of the Holy Spirit within our lives, and considering that He Works exclusively within the legal framework of the Cross of Christ, this means that our Faith must ever be in Christ and what He did for us at the Cross.

Only then can man find life and living as it ought to be. It is all in Christ and His Sacrificial, Atoning Death.

To sum up the reasons for God's eternal Interest in man, at least in part, see the following:

• The Love of God: because of His Love, God could not allow man to remain in this terrible state of depravity. Love created man, and love demands that man be redeemed.

• The original Creation of man: what men see today regarding man is not that which God originally created. What is seen is the result of the Fall. In fact, one must look at Jesus Christ to observe what the Lord originally desired man to be and what man could have been other than the Fall.

• God must redeem fallen humanity because to not do so would, in effect, declare Satan the winner of this terrible struggle between good and evil. God has never been defeated and, in fact, will never be defeated.

• God did redeem fallen humanity, and did so by Jesus, God's Son going to the Cross, and did so, at least in part, to teach the Angelic Host that the accusation of Satan, that man will not voluntarily live for God, is a lie (I Pet. 1:12).

MAN CANNOT REDEEM MAN

In Verse 4, Job asks, *"Who can bring a clean thing out of an unclean?"* He then answered, *"Not one."* In the question asked by Job in the fourth Verse, the Patriarch acknowledges his faults, his sinfulness, and even his depravity, asking how he could be otherwise, coming from a fallen race.

This Verse of Scripture should be a warning to all those who have tried to effect the redemption of man through the efforts of man. Man has ever tried; man has ever failed. This is at least one of the reasons that humanistic psychology is such a fraud. It is impossible to bring the clean out of the unclean; in other words, it is impossible for sickness to heal sickness, for sin to save from sin, for darkness to dispel darkness, for fallen man to redeem fallen man.

In effect, psychology states that man holds the answer to man's problems. It is not a new claim. Satan has been making the same claim from day one. Sadly, the Bible is no longer the yardstick for the modern church. Instead, psychology has become its religion and the psychologist its saviour.

One of the most popular preachers over television, popular because he tells people what they want to hear instead of what they need to hear, refuses to preach the Cross, refuses to preach against sin, because he claims, if such is done, it would offend people. To be frank, his preaching, that is if you would call it that, carries no convicting Power of the Holy Spirit, because unless the Word of God is faithfully preached, there can be no convicting Power of the Spirit, which means that no one is truly Saved who responds to his appeals, whatever those appeals might be.

The idea is, not only in his church, but untold thousands of churches, sinners are to come into the church, mix and mingle with Believers, if, in fact, there are any Believers there, and then somehow they will gradually evolve into Redemption.

There is absolutely nothing worse than a false way of Salvation. Untold millions are in Hell today because they believed a false way. Other millions, even hundreds of millions, are on their way there, simply because they are believing a false message. Let the Reader understand the following:

GOD'S PLAN OF SALVATION

For man to be Saved he has to be Born-Again. Jesus, without mincing words, told Nicodemus, incidentally, one of the religious leaders of Israel, *"Verily, verily, I say unto you, Except a man be born again, he cannot see the Kingdom of God"* (Jn. 3:3).

We don't find Jesus patting Nicodemus on the back, insinuating that everything was alright with this religious leader. We find the very opposite.

Then Jesus told this religious leader how to be Born-Again by saying, *"And as Moses lifted up the serpent in the wilderness, even*

NOTES

so must the Son of Man be lifted up: that whosoever believes in Him should not perish, but have Eternal Life" (Jn. 3:14-15).

When Jesus mentioned the serpent being lifted up in the wilderness, which account is found in Numbers 21:5-9, He was speaking of the Cross, which was an absolute necessity if man was to be Saved. In other words, Jesus preached the Cross to Nicodemus. Had he not done so, this religious leader could have never been Born-Again. It has not changed from then until now.

The Truth must be preached to fallen man. That Truth is *"Jesus Christ and Him Crucified"* (I Cor. 1:23). The Cross of Christ is not one of several ways of Salvation, it is the only Way. That's the reason that Job asked the question, *"Who can bring a clean thing out of an unclean?"*

THE MANNER OF REDEMPTION

When Jesus died on the Cross, He shed His Life's Blood, which was untainted by sin or failure of any nature, which means He poured out His Life. In the Incarnation, Christ partook of the *"flesh and blood"* of humanity. In His Death on the Cross, He shed His Blood and suffered in His Flesh, thereby, defeating Death and *"him who had the power of death, that is, the Devil."*

All of the Biblical writers assert that it is Jesus' physical Death that atones for sin and redeems man from death. It is evident from the usage of *"blood"* in the Bible that it is a symbol of physical life given in death, particularly sacrificial and violent death. The Atonement of Christ was a physical act involving the shedding of His Blood in bodily Crucifixion. The writer to the Hebrews, for example, teaches that the whole Levitical system is expressed in the statement that *"all things are cleansed with blood and without the shedding of blood there is no forgiveness"* (Heb. 9:22-23).

With the Levitical sacrifices in mind, Peter tells his readers they are redeemed *"with precious blood, as of a lamb unblemished and spotless, the Blood of Christ"* (I Pet. 1:19). Likewise, Luke refers to Believers as *"the Church, which He purchased with His Own Blood"* (Acts 20:28). Paul states that *"We have Redemption through His Blood, the forgiveness of our trespasses"* (Eph. 1:7). John tells us that Christ *"released us from our sins by His Blood"* (Rev. 1:5). In referring to the "blood," all of these Biblical witnesses point to the fact that the Atonement of Christ was an overtly physical act, which took place on the Cross of Calvary, which means that Redemption was complete with the Death of Christ on the Cross. The Resurrection, as important as it was, the Ascension as important as it was, the Exaltation of Christ as important as it was, were all made possible, however, by what Jesus did at the Cross. So let me say it again:

If the preacher is not preaching the Cross, is not preaching the Blood, is not preaching the Sacrificial, Atoning, Vicarious, Efficacious Death of Christ on the Cross for our sins, then whatever it is he is preaching, is not the Gospel. And then Paul had the following to say about the preaching of another gospel:

LET HIM BE ACCURSED

The Holy Spirit through the great Apostle said:

"I marvel that you are so soon removed from Him (the Holy Spirit) *Who called you into the Grace of Christ* (made possible by the Cross) *unto another gospel* (anything which doesn't have the Cross as its Object of Faith):

"Which is not another (presents that fact that Satan's aim is not so much to deny the Gospel, which he can little do, as to corrupt it); *but there be some who trouble you, and would pervert the Gospel of Christ* (once again, to make the object of Faith something other than the Cross).

"But though we (Paul and his associates), *or an Angel from Heaven, preach any other gospel unto you than that which we had preached unto you* (Jesus Christ and Him Crucified), *let him be accursed* (eternally condemned; the Holy Spirit speaks this through Paul, making this very serious).

"As we said before, so say I now again (at some time past, he had said the same thing to them, making their defection even more serious), *If any man preach any other gospel unto you* (anything other than the Cross) *than that you have received* (which Saved your souls), *let him be accursed* ('eternally condemned,' which means the loss of the soul).

"For do I now persuade men, or God? (In essence, Paul is saying, *'Do I preach man's doctrine, or God's?'*) *or do I seek to please men?* (This is what false apostles do.) *for if I yet please men, I should not be the Servant of Christ* (one cannot please both men and God at the same time)*"* (Gal. 1:6-10).

WHAT IS THE GOSPEL?

Paul also identified and did so exactly, as to what the Gospel of Jesus Christ is. He said:

"For Christ sent me not to baptize (presents to us a Cardinal Truth), *but to preach the Gospel* (the manner in which one may be Saved from sin): *not with wisdom of words* (intellectualism is not the Gospel), *lest the Cross of Christ should be made of none effect.* (This tells us in no uncertain terms that the Cross of Christ must always be the emphasis of the Message.)*"*

He then said, *"For the preaching* (Message) *of the Cross is to them who perish foolishness* (spiritual things cannot be discerned by unredeemed people, but that doesn't matter; the Cross must be preached just the same, even as we shall see); *but unto us who are Saved it is the Power of God.* (The Cross is the Power of God simply because it was there that the total sin debt was paid, giving the Holy Spirit, in Whom the Power resides, latitude to work mightily within our lives)*"* (I Cor. 1:17-18).

This means, as stated, if the preacher is not preaching the Cross as the answer, and the sole answer for man's terrible dilemma, then whatever it is he is preaching, it's not the Gospel of Jesus Christ.

There are scores of preachers who claim to preach the Cross, but it's never mentioned, because it doesn't fit their motif. Some claim that it may offend people. The truth is, they don't believe in the Cross of Christ as the answer for man's dilemma, but in something else altogether. Whoever has the misfortune to sit under such leadership is unfortunate indeed! Such direction will cause a person to lose their soul.

Getting back to the original Text, it is impossible for man by his own strength and ability to *"bring a clean thing out of an unclean."* Yet, unredeemed man seems to never learn that, and, sadly, most in the modern church follow suit. Let's say it one more time:

"But this Man (this Priest, Christ Jesus), *after He had offered One Sacrifice for sins forever* (speaks of the Cross), *sat down on the Right Hand of God* (refers to the great contrast with the Priests under the Levitical system, who never sat down because their work was never completed; the Work of Christ was a *'Finished Work,'* and needed no repetition)" (Heb. 10:12).

This tells us in no uncertain terms that there is only one answer to man's dilemma, and that goes for all men, and for all time, and that one solution is the Cross of Christ. Considering that is true, and it most definitely is, doesn't it behoove us to preach the solution, and to preach it without compromise?

Paul also said, *"For after that in the Wisdom of God the world by wisdom knew not God* (man's puny wisdom, even the best he has to offer, cannot come to know God in any manner), *it pleased God by the foolishness of preaching* (preaching the Cross) *to save them who believe.* (Paul is not dealing with the art of preaching here, but with what is preached.)"

The great Apostle then said: *"For the Jews require a sign* (the sign of the Messiah taking the Throne and making Israel a great Nation once again), *and the Greeks seek after wisdom* (they thought that such solved the human problem; however, if it did, why were they ever seeking after more wisdom?):

"But we preach Christ Crucified (this is the Foundation of the Word of God and, thereby, of Salvation), *unto the Jews a stumblingblock* (the Cross was the stumblingblock), *and unto the Greeks foolishness* (both found it difficult to accept as God a dead Man hanging on a Cross, for such Christ was to them)" (I Cor. 1:21-23).

THE NUMBER OF MAN'S DAYS

Job said, *"Seeing his days are determined, the number of his months are with You, You have appointed his bounds that he cannot pass."*

All of this tells us that God minutely directs the life of each person, in other words,

NOTES

as to exactly how long they are to live upon this Earth. But yet, man by disobedience or obedience can either shorten or lengthen his life. The Fifth Commandment says, *"Honor your father and your mother: that your days may be long upon the land which the LORD your God gives you"* (Ex. 20:12).

This statement, as is obvious, tells us that our days can be shortened or lengthened according to the disobedience or obedience as it regards this particular Commandment. But, at any rate, it is God Who makes the determination and, thereby, appoints man his days on Earth.

Medical science is now claiming that shortly it will be possible for man to live to be 150 years old, etc. Medical science, they say, will find a way to slow the aging process, etc.

After the Fall, and even though death was decreed, still, the physical body of man was so wondrously made that it took about 1,000 years for sin to wear down this most excellent specimen. In other words, when one reads the Fifth Chapter of Genesis concerning the astounding numbers of years that people lived, that is not a fable, but a fact.

By the time of Abraham, who died at 175 years old, we can see the length of days beginning to be shortened, and all because of the Fall, i.e., *"original sin."* By the time of David, who died at 70 years of age, even though ages fluctuate in some countries, and because of variables, still, 70 years of age is about the median of mankind presently. The Psalmist said:

"The days of our years are threescore years and ten; and if by reason of strength they be fourscore years, yet is their strength labor and sorrow; for it is soon cut off, and we fly away" (Ps. 90:10).

It's not so much the question of how long we live, but rather what we're doing with the years that God does give us.

Paul said: *"Redeeming the time* (take advantage of the opportunities that present themselves), *because the days are evil.* (The Cross must be our Foundation. Only then can we overcome the *'evil,'* and carry out that which the Lord has called us to do.)

"Wherefore be ye not unwise (time is precious because God has given us only a few

short days to make choices that will bring eternal consequences), *but understanding what the Will of the Lord is.* (We can do this as we look exclusively to Christ and the Cross)" (Eph. 5:16-17).

A PERSONAL EXPERIENCE

I was speaking with a man some time ago who had vast business interests, which meant, as well, that he was very wealthy. I made mention to him, that when he stands before the Lord, those business interests will never be mentioned, with the exception of how well he used them, if at all, to further the Work of God. All of us should keep that in mind.

Things on this Earth that we feel are so very, very important, will have little bearing at the Judgment Seat of Christ. The little rhyme says:

"One life will soon be past,
"Only what's done for Christ will last."

THE HOPE OF A TREE

Verses 7, 8, and 9 give us a tremendous Promise. They say:

"For there is hope of a tree, if it be cut down, that it will sprout again, and that the tender branch thereof will not cease.

"Though the root thereof wax old in the earth, and the stock thereof die in the ground;

"Yet through the scent of water it will bud, and bring forth boughs like a plant."

Job was talking about the life and death of an individual; however, he has just uttered a great truth here, even though at the moment, he doesn't seem to realize what he has said.

Even though it is certainly true that when a man dies his life has ended, at least as far as this life is concerned; however, the truth that Job has uttered pertains to this present life.

In essence, Job had given up as it regards his restoration. Considering his present condition, he could not see how in the world that could be changed. He felt he was about the die. And, in fact, if he had to go on living like this, he would rather die.

But the Lord is saying through him, even though he doesn't seem to understand it at the time, that as a tree is cut down, and it looks like it's gone, still, *"it will sprout again."* As that tree is restored, he is going to likewise be restored, even though at the time he doesn't see that. This Passage also holds a tremendous truth for all Believers, whoever they might be.

Unfortunately, there can come in any life tremendously adverse circumstances, where it seems like all is lost. But the Holy Spirit through the great Patriarch is telling us, that the tree can grow again. When the *"water of the word"* is applied to the stump, so to speak, *"it will bud, and bring forth boughs like a plant."* But it must be remembered, that only the Lord can do this.

Even though man is a Believer, meaning that he is Born-Again, still, within himself, he cannot effect any change within his life. It's hard for us to come to grips with that, but it is the truth. Change can be brought about only by the Holy Spirit, Who stands ready to accomplish the task.

HOW DOES THE HOLY SPIRIT ACCOMPLISH THAT TASK?

As we've already said several times in this Volume, the Holy Spirit, Who is God, and Who can do anything, works exclusively, however, within the parameters of the Finished Work of Christ, i.e., *"the Cross."* In other words, it is the Cross which has given the Holy Spirit the legal right to all that He does within our lives. It was at the Cross that all sin was atoned, making it possible for the Holy Spirit to do these things (Rom. 8:1-2, 11).

As we've also said several times in this Volume, while the Lord doesn't demand much of us, He does demand one thing, and that without fail, and that is that the Cross of Christ ever be the Object of our Faith.

Now that's a very simple thing and, in fact, very easy to be accomplished; however, it proves to be, regrettably, very difficult for most Believers.

Why?

THE CROSS OF CHRIST, THE OBJECT OF OUR FAITH

Satan doesn't too much care what the object of our faith is, just as long as it isn't the Cross of Christ. In fact, he makes it very easy for us to place our Faith in our church, our religious denomination, a particular preacher, our good works, etc., just as long as it's not in the Cross of Christ. In Truth, everything other than the Cross of Christ constitutes religion, which refers to that which is devised by man, which God can never accept. So, the social position, economic position, and domestical position, are all centered up in the object of our Faith. Therefore, if the Believer says, *"My Faith from henceforth is exclusively in Christ and the Cross,"* he will find much opposition. Many times his friends will turn against him, even his family at times will turn against him. He might even be told to leave his church, and more than likely will be told such. Consequently, he finds the journey at times very lonely, and very difficult. That's why Jesus said the following:

"And He said to them all, if any man will come after Me (the criteria for Discipleship), *let him deny himself* (not asceticism as many think, but rather that one denies one's own willpower, self-will, strength, and ability, depending totally on Christ), *and take up his cross* (the benefits of the Cross, looking exclusively to what Jesus did there to meet our every need) *daily* (this is so important, our looking to the Cross; that we must renew our Faith in what Christ has done for us, even on a daily basis, for Satan will ever try to move us away from the Cross as the Object of our Faith, which always spells disaster), *and follow Me* (Christ can be followed only by the Believer looking to the Cross, understanding what it accomplished, and by that means alone [Rom. 6:3-5, 11, 14; 8:1-2, 11; I Cor. 1:17-18, 21, 23; 2:2; Gal. 6:14; Eph. 2:13-18; Col. 2:14-15])*.

"For whosoever will save his life shall lose it (try to live one's life outside of Christ and the Cross)*: but whosoever will lose his life for My Sake, the same shall save it* (when we place our Faith entirely in Christ and the Cross, looking exclusively to Him, we have just found *'more abundant life'* [Jn. 10:10])" (Lk. 9:23-24).

Jesus then said: *"If any man come to Me* (no exceptions), *and hate* (prefer) *not his father, and mother, and wife, and children, and brethren, and sisters, yea, and his own life also* (no affection, however strong, must be permitted to compete with or displace Christ) *he cannot be My Disciple* (once again, no exceptions!)" (Lk. 14:26).

The Cross of Christ is God's Way, and His only Way, because no other way is needed.

IF A MAN DIE, SHALL HE LIVE AGAIN?

Evolution says that man is an animal and, consequently, will live and die as an animal, and after death will be no more.

Reincarnation says that man will live again in the form of another person or even an animal. Both evolution and reincarnation are lies fostered by Satan.

Before the First Advent of Christ, even though Resurrection was known and understood, at least by ardent Believers, still, the view of that great spectacle was dim. Only when the Cross was a fact could the Lord give the total meaning of Resurrection, which was given to the Apostle Paul, who gave it to us in the Fifteenth Chapter of I Corinthians. Job declared, even before the Law was given, that Resurrection was expected, but, as stated, precious little was known of this great subject.

The *"change"* that Job addressed was the Resurrection of Life. Actually, two Resurrections await the whole of humanity. They are as follows:

THE RESURRECTION OF LIFE

The Resurrection of Life is at times referred to as *"the First Resurrection"* (Rev. 20:6; Dan. 12:2; Jn. 5:28-29).

This is the Resurrection of all the just, the blessed, and the holy, all the way from Adam to the Millennium. It covers the period of time from Christ's Resurrection to the Resurrection of the Tribulation Saints and the two witnesses, and includes the various companies of redeemed.

Actually, the word *"Resurrection"* and *"Rapture,"* refer to the same event. As it regards the First Resurrection, it might be said to be in four parts, i.e., *"four Raptures."* They are as follows:

1. *". . . Afterward they who are Christ's at His Coming"* (I Cor. 15:23; Jn. 14:1-3; Lk. 21:34-36; I Thess. 4:13-17; II Thess. 2:1, 7).

Everyone in Christ, dead or alive, all the way from Abel, will be translated at this time. Not one person will be left on Earth who is truly *"in Christ,"* for that is the requirement to be ready (I Thess. 4:16-17). This is what is referred to as the main Rapture.

2. The 144,000 Jews Saved in the first three and a half years of Daniel's seventieth week, which will be at the midpoint of the Great Tribulation (Rev. 7:1-8). They will be caught up as the man child in the middle of this week or three and a half years before the Second Advent (Rev. 12:5; 14:1-5; Isa. 66:7-8; Dan. 12:1).

3. The great multitude of Tribulation Saints who will come to Christ during the Great Tribulation (Rev. 6:1-19; 21). The first martyrs of this period are told to rest until the balance of them are killed (Rev. 6:9-11). All of these will be Raptured during the Great Tribulation, but in time for the Marriage Supper of the Lamb (Rev. 7:9-17; 15:2-4; 20:4-6). This means that those who will be martyred by the Antichrist the last three and a half years of this seven year period of the Tribulation will, as well, have part in the First Resurrection (Rev. 20:4-6). This proves that their Rapture will be in time for the Marriage Supper (Rev. 19:1-10), and in time to come back with Christ at the Second Coming (Rev. 19:11-21; Jude 14; Zech. 14:5).

4. The Rapture of the two witnesses (Rev. 11:7-11): this will end the First Resurrection of Life.

There are some who claim that the Saints taken from Paradise to Heaven, at the time of the Resurrection of Christ, actually constitute the first group resurrected; however, there is no record that they are given a Glorified Body at that time. The truth is they will be included in the general Rapture, so they cannot be said to be a Resurrection or Rapture of their own.

The Fifteenth Chapter of I Corinthians tells us what will take place at the time of the Rapture (Resurrection), and those things did not take place with those Saints who were transferred from Paradise to Glory. There is no record they were changed, that is, given a Glorified Body at that time. To be sure, they will be given such at the time of the general Rapture, which will include, up to that time, every Saint of God who has ever lived (I Thess. 4:13-17).

In the First Resurrection of Life, the Greek expression, *"ek nekron,"* which means, *"out of the dead,"* is used 49 times and teaches a select Resurrection from the dead — the righteous selected from among the wicked — but it does not teach a select Resurrection of some righteous from among the remaining righteous.

The theory that a few of the righteous will be selected from among the righteous is a mere human invention based upon a couple of quotes from the Old Testament, which were never intended as types.

Actually, all the dead and living in Christ will be in the First Resurrection — not just a few of those in Christ. There is no such thing as a partial Justification. If a person is Saved, they are totally justified, because there can be no such thing as a partial Justification. While some Christians are most definitely closer to the Lord than others, the Truth is, if a person is Born-Again, irrespective of their particular consecration at the time, they will go in the Rapture.

The truth is, there are millions in churches who claim to be Saved, but actually aren't. They either never have been, or else they have lost their way. While they may remain religious after a fashion, that doesn't mean that they are Saved.

The criteria for Salvation is Faith in Christ and what He has done for us at the Cross (Jn. 3:3, 16; Rom. 5:1-2). As well, if one has proper Faith in Christ and the Cross, there will be suitable Fruit that will be evident in their lives. In other words, a mere mental ascent is not enough. There must be an acceptance of Christ from the heart and, as stated, which will always result in a changed life.

THE SECOND RESURRECTION OF DAMNATION
(Dan. 12:3; Jn. 5:28-29; Rev. 20:6)

This is the Resurrection of all the wicked from Adam to the end of the Millennium. It will take place after the Millennium and will also include those wicked who died during the Millennium (Rev. 20:4-6, 11-15).

The wicked dead will be raised with

immortal bodies to be tormented in Hell forever (Mat. 10:28; Jn. 5:28-29; 12:24; Dan. 12:2; Acts 24:15; I Cor. 15:21, 34-50; Rev. 14:9-12; 19:20; 20:4-6, 11-15).

The theory that only the righteous will be raised to immortality is false, not being founded on one Scripture. The method of the Resurrection of the just and unjust is plainly taught and illustrated by a grain of wheat or any other grain. So what makes the difference between the two Resurrections?

Does not a bad or a poisonous seed reproduce in the same way that a good seed does? Do not both go through the same process? The Resurrection of men follows the same process, the only difference being in the Glory of one over the other. Both the Saved and the unsaved will be immortal as is plainly taught in all Scripture. The wicked bodies will exist in conscious torment forever.

Paul explained the Resurrection of the dead by likening it as a grain of wheat (I Cor. 15:35-38).

So, Job, even in those early days before the Law, knew that there would be a Resurrection and that man would ultimately be changed — some to immortality of Eternal Life, some to immortality of eternal damnation.

(15) "YOU SHALL CALL, AND I WILL ANSWER YOU; YOU WILL HAVE A DESIRE TO THE WORK OF YOUR HANDS.

(16) "FOR NOW YOU NUMBER MY STEPS: DO YOU NOT WATCH OVER MY SIN?

(17) "MY TRANSGRESSION IS SEALED UP IN A BAG, AND YOU SEW UP MY INIQUITY.

(18) "AND SURELY THE MOUNTAINS FALLING COME TO NOUGHT, AND THE ROCK IS REMOVED OUT OF HIS PLACE.

(19) "THE WATERS WEAR THE STONES: YOU WASH AWAY THE THINGS WHICH GROW OUT OF THE DUST OF THE EARTH; AND YOU DESTROY THE HOPE OF MAN.

(20) "YOU PREVAIL FOR EVER AGAINST HIM, AND HE PASSES: YOU CHANGE HIS COUNTENANCE, AND SEND HIM AWAY.

(21) "HIS SONS COME TO HONOUR, AND HE KNOWS IT NOT; AND THEY ARE BROUGHT LOW, BUT HE PERCEIVES IT NOT OF THEM.

(22) "BUT HIS FLESH UPON HIM SHALL HAVE PAIN, AND HIS SOUL WITHIN HIM SHALL MOURN."

The structure is:

1. (Vs. 15) This one Passage tells us that the great Creation of God, as it regards man, will not be lost; that which the Lord originally intended will ultimately be carried out.

2. Verse 16 proclaims the fact that the Lord minutely records and catalogs everything about man.

3. (Vs. 17) The transgression of man can be erased only by Faith in the shed Blood of Christ (Eph. 2:13-18).

4. (Vs. 20) Man cannot prevail against God, irrespective as to what he might do.

5. Verse 21 answers the question of whether the Saints of God in Heaven know what is transpiring with their loved ones on Earth. In effect, it says that they know nothing of the things that happen on Earth. So this destroys the Catholic myth of praying to Saints in Heaven.

6. The statement given in Verse 22 is based on Job's present situation. Inspiration guarantees that these things were said, and by the ones to whom they are attributed. However, inspiration does not guarantee that all that is said is true. In fact, virtually all that is said by the friends of Job would have to be concluded as being incorrect. Most of what Job says is true.

THE WORSHIP OF SAINTS AND IMAGES

Job said in Verse 21, and speaking of knowledge after death, *"His sons come to honor, and he knows it not; and they are brought low, but he perceives it not of them."*

As we have stated, this Passage answers the question of whether the Saints of God in Heaven know what is transpiring concerning their loved ones on Earth. In effect, it says they know nothing of the things that happen on Earth. They are even unconscious of that which happens to their own children in this world, knowing not whether they be honored or degraded. This fact destroys the Roman Catholic dogma of the intercession of Saints. For if a righteous man, such as

God Himself declared Job to be, would in the spirit world be unconscious in regard of those so near to him as his own children, what hope could strangers have of his help?

Unfortunately, the worship of Saints and images is an integral part of the Roman Catholic religion. Let us examine it as the Roman Catholic Church teaches and proclaims it — and then let us look at it in the light of the Word of God.

THE TEACHING OF THE ROMAN CATHOLIC CHURCH TODAY

The Roman Catholic Church teaches the following:
- That Saints function as mediators between the faithful and God.
- We should address prayers to the Saints and kneel before them to obtain their favor.
- The Saints are pleased to see their images venerated and adorned with costly treasures, and they will recompense the faithful who are generous in their worship.
- The images of the Blessed Virgin and the Lord Jesus Christ may be venerated under different names. This can give rise to competition between different images of the same person.
- According to the Catholic position, *"Saints"* are individuals of the New Testament (or later martyrs or notable persons of the Church) who have died and subsequently been declared to be Saints by the Pope.

A GREAT PROBLEM

In this enlightened age it is difficult to realize that the majority of Catholics are unaware of the direct contradiction between a belief in an Omnipotent God and the worship of Saints as advocates and intercessors.

In a conversation between an Evangelical and several Roman Catholics, the following inquiry was raised:

"Everyone accepts that the Saints are finite beings — not only on earth, but in Heaven as well, so how can finite beings hear the prayers of men who are on the earth? If one would stop to think about this, it would seem impossible for a finite being to hear the prayers of not just two or three people, but those of multiplied thousands who are all praying at the same time.

"The only way they could hear so many thousands of prayers, and discern the heart attitudes of all of these people, is if they were both Omniscient and Omnipresent. In other words, each Saint would have to be God in order to accomplish this."

When this question was put to the Roman Catholic representatives, they did not know how to reply. Finally, after a whispered conference, one of them offered:

"There is no difficulty. Even if the Saints can't hear our prayers, God can and He could reveal them to the Saints."

Dare we anticipate the resulting conclusion in this dialogue?

This would then mean that we would be approaching the Saints through God — instead of God through the Saints.

The idea becomes more absurd the further we pursue it.

The very thought of individuals speaking to frail and finite humans — and expecting them to carry their ideas to God — is ludicrous. The Word of God states clearly that we can go directly to the Father, at any time, in the Name of the Lord Jesus Christ (Jn. 16:23).

WHERE DID THE CATHOLIC WORSHIP OF SAINTS AND IMAGES ORIGINATE?

The Catholic system of Patron Saints is nothing more or less than a continuation of ancient heathen beliefs in gods devoted to days, occupations, and the various needs of human life. Since the worship of Saints is really a perpetuation of these false gods, Romanism is patently guilty of worshipping other gods — a practice that is condemned repeatedly in Scripture.

25,000 THOUSAND

By the Tenth Century some 20,000 to 25,000 Saints had been canonized by the Roman Catholic Church. Of course, by this time Rome had hopelessly insinuated pagan religions into Christianity.

SUBSTITUTE A CHRISTIAN-SOUNDING NAME

To make the apostasy less obvious, the leaders of the Roman Catholic Church substituted Christian-sounding names that were similar to the original pagan names.

For example, the goddess Victoria of the Bass-Alps was renamed St. Victoire. The pagan god Osiris was named St. Onuphris. Apollo was renamed St. Apollinaris, and the heathen god Mars became St. Martine.

We are told that one of the best preserved of the ancient temples in Rome is the Pantheon, which was originally dedicated to *"Jove and all the gods."* It was reconsecrated, however, by Pope Boniface IV to the *"Mother of God and all the Saints."* An edifice formally consecrated to the Greek god Apollo now is displayed proudly as the church of St. Apollinaris.

Where the ancient temple of Mars once stood, we now find the church of St. Martine. Rome simply adopted the heathen gods into the so-called Christian church, renaming them as their worship continued uninterrupted.

Just as the pagans worshipped idols or statues of their gods, so does the Roman Catholic Church utilize statues in their worship.

In many cases the same statue that was worshipped as a pagan god was re-christened with the name of a Christian Saint, and worship continued. The statue of Jupiter, for example, was slightly changed and re-titled *"Peter."*

Through the centuries more and more statues have been crafted (and venerated) until today there are churches in Europe that contain as many as several thousand statues! However, whether in a great Cathedral, a small chapel, or on the dashboard of an automobile, these are still idols and are absolutely forbidden by the Word of God.

NOT THE HINT OF SUCH IN SCRIPTURE OR IN THE EARLY CHURCH

It was not until the Fifth Century that pictures of Mary, Christ, and the Saints were made and used as objects of worship.

Scripture specifically condemns idol worship in countless places, as there is not a hint or a suggestion in the Word of God that the Early Church deviated from these age-old injunctions.

THE VOICE OF THE ELDERS IN THE EARLY CHURCH

Irenaeus (about A.D. 130-202), a pupil of Polycarp (who sat at the feet of the Apostle John), said:

"As the Church has received liberally from the Lord, so let it minister liberally, and not ask to do anything through the invocation of Angels or through enchantments and other perverse rarities, but let prayers be addressed purely, clearly, and openly to the Lord, from Whom are all things, invoking the Name of our Lord Jesus Christ."

Clement of Alexandria, a Greek theologian (about A.D. 150-215), said:

"It is the height of foolishness to pray as though to gods to those who are no gods at all, for there is but one good God, to Him only do we and the Angels pray."

In another place he said:

"Every image or statue should be called an idol, for it is nothing but vile and profane material, and for this reason, and to remove idolatry by the roots, God has forbidden the use of any image or likeness of anything in heaven or on earth, and has also forbidden the making of such images, and for this reason we Christians have none of these material representations."

Origen, Greek teacher and writer (about A.D. 185-254), said:

"The Angels are greatly interested in your Salvation. They have been given as helpers to the Son of God, but all prayers to God, whether they are supplications or thanksgiving, should be raised to Him through Christ, the High Priest, Who is above all Angels ... men do not know the Angels so it is unreasonable to address prayers to them instead of to Christ Who is known of men. And even were we to know the Angels, we should not be allowed to address our prayers to anyone except to God, the Lord of all creation, who is sufficient for all, and we come to Him through our Saviour, the Son of God."

The same writer said in another place:

"In the reproof of those who trust in the Saints, I would say, 'cursed be the man who trusts in man' (Jer. 17:5), and 'it is better to trust in the Lord than to put confidence in man' (Ps. 118:8). If it is necessary for us to have confidence in anyone, let us leave all others and trust in the Lord."

Cyprian (martyred about A.D. 258), Bishop of Carthage (about 248-258), declared:

"Why bow down before images? Lift up your eyes and heart to Heaven; that is the place where you should seek God."

Athanasius, a Bishop of Alexandria and the father of orthodoxy (about A.D. 300-373), said:

"It is written, 'God is my rock; in Him will I trust; He is my shield, and the horn of my salvation' (II Sam. 22:3), and 'the Lord also will be a refuge for the oppressed, a refuge in times of trouble' (Ps. 9:9). And how many similar words do we find in the Sacred Scriptures! Should anyone reply that these are prophecies that apply to the Son, which may be true, then let them admit that the Saints do not venture to call any created being their help and refuge."

Elsewhere he declared:

"The invocation of idols is a sin, and anything that is sinful at the beginning can never be good later."

Augustine, Bishop of Hippo (about A.D. 354-430), said:

"Let not our religion be the worship of the dead, for if they lived a holy life, it is impossible to imagine that they desire such honors, rather they would wish that we should render our worship to Him through Whom we should be partakers with them of Salvation. Therefore we should honor them by imitating them — not by worshipping them.

"The only image of Christ that we should make for ourselves is to keep before us His humility, patience, and kindness, and endeavor to make our lives like His in all things. Those who go in search of Jesus and the Apostles in mural paintings, far from conforming to Scripture, fall into error."

Jerome (about 343-420), who translated the Old Testament directly into Latin from Hebrew (the Vulgate Bible), quoted a letter from an Epiphanius in which he stated the following:

"In a part of the country that I visited I found a candle placed in the door of a Church over which was painted an image of Christ and another of a Saint. I was displeased that, in this defiance of Holy Scripture, the image of a man should be hung up in the Church of Christ, and I cut the candle down, advising the sacristan that it would be put to better use at the funeral of some poor person."

THE USE OF IMAGES CONDEMNED BY MANY

The use of images was condemned by all in the Early Church and even condemned as late as the Synod of Elvira (A.D. 305), the Council of Frankfort (A.D. 794), and the Council of Rouen (A.D. 1445).

This latter assembly in its seventh Canon condemned the practice of praying before images with names such as Our Lady of Piety, Our Lady of Help, and Our Lady of Consolation.

It said:

"Such practices tend to lead to superstition, as though there was more power in some than in others."

Desiderius Erasmus of Rotterdam (about 1466-1536), a Dutch Scholar held in high esteem by the Roman Catholic Church, was right when he said:

"No one who bows before an image or looks at it intentionally is free from some kind of superstition; and not only so, but if he only prays before an image."

WHAT DOES THE BIBLE SAY?

• "You shall make you no idols nor graven image, neither rear you up a standing image, neither shall you set up any image of stone in your land, to bow down unto it: for I am the LORD your God" (Lev. 26:1).

• "Be not deceived: neither fornicators, nor idolators . . . shall inherit the Kingdom of God" (I Cor. 6:9-10).

• "For there is one God, and one Mediator between God and men, the Man Christ Jesus" (I Tim. 2:5).

• "Neither is there Salvation in any other: for there is none other Name under Heaven given among men, whereby we must be Saved" (Acts 4:12).

With regard to the worship of Saints we read:

• "And as Peter was coming in, Cornelius met him, and fell down at his feet, and worshipped him. But Peter took him up, saying, Stand up; I myself also am a man" (Acts 10:25-26).

• "And I John saw these things, and

heard them. *And when I had heard and seen, I fell down to worship before the feet of the Angel which showed me these things. Then said he unto me, see you do it not: for I am your fellow servant, and of your brethren the Prophets, and of them which keep the sayings of this Book: worship God"* (Rev. 22:8-9).

ALL TRUE CHRISTIANS ARE SAINTS

There is no indication in the Word of God that a person becomes a Saint after he dies. In fact, it is not the Pope who makes someone a Saint, it is God. In Scripture, Saints are always living people — never the dead.

For example, when Paul wrote to the Ephesians, his letter was addressed *"to the Saints who are at Ephesus"* (Eph. 1:1).

Likewise, the Book of Philippians was written *"to all the Saints in Christ Jesus who are at Philippi"* (Phil. 1:1).

The early Christians in the Church at Rome were called *"Saints"* (Rom. 1:7; 16:15, as were the Christians who lived at Corinth [I Cor. 1:2; II Cor. 1:1]).

Consequently, if a person wants a Saint to pray for him, he should find a Christian and ask him to join him in prayer, for all true Christians are Saints.

Anytime a person tries to contact people who have died, it is a form of spiritualism. The Bible repeatedly condemns any attempt to commune with the dead.

• *"There shall not be found among you . . . an enchanter* (one who uses incantations), *or a witch, or a charmer, or a consulter with familiar spirits, or a wizard, or a necromancer* (one who entreats the spirits of the dead). *For all who do these things are an abomination unto the LORD . . ."* (Deut. 18:10-12).

• *"When they shall say unto you, Seek unto them who have familiar spirits, and unto wizards that peep, and that mutter: should not a people seek unto their God? for the living to the dead? . . . if they speak not according to this Word, it is because there is no light in them"* (Isa. 8:19-20).

WHAT ABOUT THE MIRACLES AND THE SHRINES?

I am sure, after reading this, that some will say, *"But what about the miracles that have been performed by the intercession of the Saints?"*

These consist of statues that weep, from tears on faces, or produce (alleged miracles). The Virgin of Lourdes is the most publicized.

Actually, there is absolutely nothing in the Word of God that even hints at such a thing. God has never healed or performed miracles or done any kind of good works through inanimate objects, except in the case of Paul's handkerchiefs and aprons as described in Acts 19:12. And this one isolated case is not an example of worshiping or venerating an idol or image.

If a person were to visit Lourdes today, as many do, he would be appalled by the carnival atmosphere. This is, of course, totally foreign to the Word of God and the Work of God. There are no miracles at Lourdes, no healings or cures or anything else of this nature. There may be emotional reactions, but that is as far as it goes.

However, this should be said as well. Satan, who causes sicknesses by demon oppression (Acts 10:38; Lk. 13:11-16) can take off what he puts on without opposing himself or casting himself out. When he can damn a soul by getting a person to deny the essentials of the Bible that will save the soul, then it is to his advantage to deceive by taking away the sickness.

SATAN DECEIVES PEOPLE

Many accept false religions that promise healing and other benefits. Satan cooperates with these religions which he himself has founded to deceive men. He can even bring about a withdrawal of the sickness from the people without God being involved in the process. Such people naturally think they are in the true religion. They reject Christ and see no need of being Saved from sin or of following the Bible. They will be damned for doing so, Satan having won their souls.

One of the major works of Satan is the work of deception and, in this vein, along with other efforts, he is leading much of the world astray.

For instance, Pope John Paul II claimed

to have had a vision of Mary when he was a young man, who told him that he would be Pope. Now some would hear that, and would think that inasmuch as he became Pope, this surely must have been a visitation from Mary.

It wasn't!

I have no doubt that this man had a vision, but it was not given by God, but rather by a familiar spirit impersonating Mary. As we have stated, there is no such thing in the Bible of contacting the dead, or the dead contacting those who are alive.

The Catholic Church under John Paul II, already deep into Mary worship, went even deeper under this particular man. In fact, he attempted to have Mary declared as a co-redemptress with our Lord, which was gross blasphemy. Thankfully, he was talked out of it by wiser heads, but still, he would have done this thing had he had the support of other higher ups in the Catholic Church. Let us say it again:

Under his leadership, the Catholic Church was taken even deeper into idol worship, and Mary worship, which would be abhorrent to the Mother of our Lord, if she, in fact, knew such a thing.

Yes, we do believe in miracles. We believe in healing. We believe that God answers prayer. We believe that at times the Lord gives visions. But we believe that it comes about in a Biblical way.

Jesus said a long time ago:

"*Come unto Me* (Jesus Himself — not some Angel or dead Saint) *. . . and I will give you rest. Take My yoke upon you, and learn of Me* (not some Angel or dead Saint) *. . . and you shall find rest unto your souls*" (Mat. 11:28-29).

IN CLOSING

The worship of Saints and images has absolutely no foundation in the Word of God. It is an excursion into superstition and paganism, which will further enfold its web of deceit around the followers of Roman Catholicism.

"*In that day you shall ask me nothing. Verily, verily, I say unto you, Whatsoever you shall ask the Father in My Name, He will give you it. Hitherto have you asked nothing in My Name: ask, and you shall receive, that your joy may be full.*

"*For the Father Himself loves you, because you have loved Me, and have believed that I came out from God*" (Jn. 16:23-24, 27).

"*Behold the Man! How glorious He!*
"*Before His Foes He stands unawed,*
"*And without wrong or blasphemy,*
"*He claims equality with God.*"

"*Behold the Man! By all condemned,*
"*Assaulted by hosts of foes;*
"*His Person and His Claims condemned,*
"*A Man of sufferings and of woes.*"

"*Behold the Man! He stands alone,*
"*His Foes are ready to devour;*
"*Not one of all His friends will own,*
"*Their Master in His trying Hour.*"

"*Behold the Man! Though scorned below,*
"*He bears the greatest Name Above;*
"*The Angels at His Footstool bow,*
"*And all His Royal Claims approve.*"

CHAPTER 15

(1) "THEN ANSWERED ELIPHAZ THE TEMANITE, AND SAID,

(2) "SHOULD A WISE MAN UTTER VAIN KNOWLEDGE, AND FILL HIS BELLY WITH THE EAST WIND?

(3) "SHOULD HE REASON WITH UNPROFITABLE TALK? OR WITH SPEECHES WHEREWITH HE CAN DO NO GOOD?

(4) "YES, YOU CAST OFF FEAR, AND RESTRAIN PRAYER BEFORE GOD.

(5) "FOR YOUR MOUTH UTTERS YOUR INIQUITY, AND YOU CHOOSE THE TONGUE OF THE CRAFTY.

(6) "YOUR OWN MOUTH CONDEMNS YOU, AND NOT I: YES, YOUR OWN LIPS TESTIFY AGAINST YOU.

(7) "ARE YOU THE FIRST MAN WHO WAS BORN? OR WERE YOU MADE BEFORE THE HILLS?

(8) "HAVE YOU HEARD THE SECRET OF GOD? AND DO YOU RESTRAIN WISDOM TO YOURSELF?

(9) "WHAT DO YOU KNOW, THAT WE DON'T KNOW? WHAT UNDERSTANDING DO YOU HAVE, WHICH IS NOT IN US?

(10) "WITH US ARE BOTH THE GRAY-HEADED AND VERY AGED MEN, MUCH ELDER THAN YOUR FATHER.

(11) "ARE THE CONSOLATIONS OF GOD SMALL WITH YOU? IS THERE ANY SECRET THING WITH YOU?

(12) "WHY DOES YOUR HEART CARRY YOU AWAY? AND WHAT DO YOUR EYES WINK AT,

(13) "THAT YOU TURN YOUR SPIRIT AGAINST GOD, AND LET SUCH WORDS GO OUT OF YOUR MOUTH?

(14) "WHAT IS MAN, THAT HE SHOULD BE CLEAN? AND HE WHICH IS BORN OF A WOMAN, THAT HE SHOULD BE RIGHTEOUS?

(15) "BEHOLD, HE PUTS NO TRUST IN HIS SAINTS; YES, THE HEAVENS ARE NOT CLEAN IN HIS SIGHT.

(16) "HOW MUCH MORE ABOMINABLE AND FILTHY IS MAN, WHICH DRINKS INIQUITY LIKE WATER?"

The pattern is:

1. In the Second Verse, Eliphaz says here that everything that Job has said is nothing but wind.

2. In the Fourth Verse, he now belittles Job's faith.

3. (Vs. 6) Eliphaz is repeatedly condemning Job while claiming he isn't. The self-righteous enjoy putting words into the mouths of those whom they condemn.

4. According to Verse 9, Eliphaz is plainly agitated at the statements made by Job.

5. In the Sixteenth Verse, it cannot be doubted that Job is individually pointed at here, and not mankind in general. Eliphaz could not be more wrong.

THE SECOND SPEECH OF ELIPHAZ

After Job had answered all three of his so-called friends in turn, it was time for the second round of discourses, so Eliphaz, who had spoken first, began his speech.

He accused Job of fifteen sins and mentioned twenty judgments of God upon the wicked, coming to the conclusion that Job must be wicked because of suffering the judgments of the wicked.

NOTES

Eliphaz' second address was not so polite as the first. He claims to be a man of science (of intellect) and as such will judge from facts seen and experienced by himself. He will say as much in Verse 17.

Eliphaz accuses Job of all type of sins, when in reality, Job was guilty of none of this. But Eliphaz and his self-righteousness will have little difficulty in making his condemnations.

I wonder what his accusations would have been had he known that God would record every single word he uttered, with multiple millions of human beings reading them in future centuries, and, thereby, learning of his gross ignorance of God and even his stupidity.

SELF-RIGHTEOUSNESS IS A WICKED SIN

The whole of the speeches given by these three *"friends,"* smack of self-righteousness.

This malady, self-righteousness, claims Righteousness from God on the basis of good things being done, supposedly, or bad things not being done. It is a form of righteousness which in the Eyes of God is no righteousness at all, which God can never accept. He cannot accept anything that man produces in the realm and sense of what man concludes holiness or righteousness to be. The only Righteousness that God can accept is that which is afforded by Christ, and made possible by the Cross, and obtained by the faith of the individual.

The idea, in the mind of the self-righteous, that God can impute Righteousness instantly to an individual who is obviously unrighteous, is completely unacceptable in their minds. So, the Righteousness which Christ Alone can give, and will do so without fail to the believing sinner, is completely unacceptable! So, we have here two types of righteousness that is tendered by man, which God will not accept, and that which is tendered by God, which the self-righteous man will not accept.

THE PLIGHT OF THE MODERN CHURCH

That plight has to do with Salvation and Sanctification.

Some of the Church accepts the Righteousness of Christ as it regards the initial Salvation experience. They will preach and teach, at least some of them, that God will freely impute a perfect Righteousness to the believing sinner upon Faith in Christ. But, when it comes to Sanctification, that's something else again.

The problem with the Churches in Galatia was, even though they had accepted Salvation by Faith, upon the advent of the Judaisers, who were bitterly opposed to Paul, they were being swayed toward sanctification by self, which can never be. And that's the plight of the modern church.

It tries to sanctify itself by its good works, by its supposed merit, and at the same time, refuses to accept Sanctification on the basis of Faith in Christ and what He did at the Cross. I find that the same problem exists now that existed in the time of Paul.

Paul preached Faith and Grace as it regards Sanctification, meaning that the Believer's Faith must ever be anchored in Christ and the Cross, which then gives the Holy Spirit latitude to work. Upon the correct Object of Faith, the Holy Spirit can then perfect His Fruit in our hearts and lives, thereby, perfecting Righteousness and Holiness. But, the self-righteous in the realm of Sanctification, will not accept that; therefore, they twist what is being said to try to make it mean something else. Let me give an example:

As Paul preached Grace, stating, *"Where sin abounded, Grace did much more abound"* (Rom. 5:20), some were taking that into license. They were saying that inasmuch as Grace was much more powerful than sin, it really didn't matter how much one sinned. All they had to do, or so they were saying, was simply to express Faith in Christ and the Cross, and it really didn't matter how much they sinned. Paul's answer to that is as follows:

"What shall we say then? (This is meant to direct attention to Rom. 5:20). *Shall we continue in sin, that Grace may abound?* (Just because Grace is greater than sin doesn't mean that the Believer has a license to sin.)

"God forbid (presents Paul's answer to the question, *'Away with the thought, let not such a thing occur')*. *How shall we, who are dead to sin* (dead to the sin nature), *live any longer therein?* (This portrays what the Believer is now in Christ)" (Rom. 6:1-2).

GRACE AND FAITH IS THE ONLY WAY TO HAVE VICTORY OVER SIN

What Paul was teaching was, in effect, the only way that a Believer could have Victory over sin. That doesn't mean sinless perfection, but it does mean that sin (the sin nature), is to no longer have dominion over the individual. In fact, if any Believer tries to have Victory over sin by any other method than the Cross of Christ, and it doesn't really matter what the method is, such a Believer will find that the very opposite takes place. In other words, he will find himself being ruled by the sin nature, with sin becoming worse and worse within his life. Let us say it again:

The only way, and I mean the only way, that the Believer can have Victory over the sin nature, which means that it no longer rules in his heart and life, is by placing his Faith exclusively in Christ and what Christ has done for us at the Cross, which gives the Holy Spirit latitude to work within our lives. That is God's Way, and one might describe it as, *"God's Prescribed Order of Victory"* (Rom. 6:1-14; 8:1-2, 11; I Cor. 1:17-18, 21, 23; 2:2; Eph. 2:13-18; Col. 2:14-15).

SANCTIFICATION BY WORKS TRANSLATES INTO SELF-RIGHTEOUSNESS

If the heading is true, that Sanctification by works translates into self-righteousness, and it most definitely is true, then this leaves the modern church in a serious dilemma.

The modern church knows almost nothing as it regards the Cross of Christ respecting the Sanctification experience or, in effect, how we live for God. As a result, it is trying to effect Righteousness by works, by merit, etc. The end result of such a direction, and the only end result is self-righteousness, which is one of the most evil and wicked sins that can attach itself to an individual. This is the sin that nailed Jesus to the Cross! This is the sin of which Paul was so guilty, when he was finally stricken down on the road to Damascus, and had the Vision of Christ, and there gave his heart to Christ. This is the sin that caused him to drag Believers into prison cells, with some of them losing their lives in the process. It is the sin that is the greatest hindrance to the Work of God presently. This is the sin that has stained the earth with blood, that murdered hundreds of thousands if not millions during the Dark Ages, when the Catholic Church demanded allegiance to the Pope. This is the sin that has taken untold millions to Hell, and continues to do so. It is the sin of self-righteousness, perhaps one of, if not the worst sin that a person can commit, with the exception of blaspheming the Holy Spirit. And to be sure, this is the sin that leads up to blaspheming the Holy Spirit, which, in effect, is the cause of such blasphemy. That's how dangerous, how volatile, how ugly that it is!

This is the sin of the three *"friends"* who attacked Job with such venom. There is no mercy in self-righteousness, only law!

(17) "I WILL SHOW YOU, HEAR ME; AND THAT WHICH I HAVE SEEN I WILL DECLARE;

(18) "WHICH WISE MEN HAVE TOLD FROM THEIR FATHERS, AND HAVE NOT HID IT:

(19) "UNTO WHOM ALONE THE EARTH WAS GIVEN, AND NO STRANGER PASSED AMONG THEM.

(20) "THE WICKED MAN TRAVAILS WITH PAIN ALL HIS DAYS, AND THE NUMBER OF YEARS IS HIDDEN TO THE OPPRESSOR.

(21) "A DREADFUL SOUND IS IN HIS EARS: IN PROSPERITY THE DESTROYER SHALL COME UPON HIM.

(22) "HE BELIEVES NOT THAT HE SHALL RETURN OUT OF DARKNESS, AND HE IS WAITED FOR OF THE SWORD.

(23) "HE WANDERS ABROAD FOR BREAD, SAYING, WHERE IS IT? HE KNOWS THAT THE DAY OF DARKNESS IS READY AT HIS HAND.

(24) "TROUBLE AND ANGUISH SHALL MAKE HIM AFRAID; THEY SHALL PREVAIL AGAINST HIM, AS A KING READY TO THE BATTLE.

(25) "FOR HE STRETCHES OUT HIS HAND AGAINST GOD, AND STRENGTHENS HIMSELF AGAINST THE ALMIGHTY.

(26) "HE RUNS UPON HIM, EVEN ON HIS NECK, UPON THE THICK BOSSES OF HIS BUCKLERS:

(27) "BECAUSE HE COVERS HIS FACE WITH HIS FATNESS, AND MAKES COLLOPS OF FAT ON HIS FLANKS.

(28) "AND HE DWELLS IN DESOLATE CITIES, AND IN HOUSES WHICH NO MAN INHABITS, WHICH ARE READY TO BECOME HEAPS.

(29) "HE SHALL NOT BE RICH, NEITHER SHALL HIS SUBSTANCE CONTINUE, NEITHER SHALL HE PROLONG THE PERFECTION THEREOF UPON THE EARTH.

(30) "HE SHALL NOT DEPART OUT OF DARKNESS; THE FLAME SHALL DRY UP HIS BRANCHES, AND BY THE BREATH OF HIS MOUTH SHALL HE GO AWAY.

(31) "LET NOT HIM WHO IS DECEIVED TRUST IN VANITY: FOR VANITY SHALL BE HIS RECOMPENCE.

(32) "IT SHALL BE ACCOMPLISHED BEFORE HIS TIME, AND HIS BRANCH SHALL NOT BE GREEN.

(33) "HE SHALL SHAKE OFF HIS UNRIPE GRAPE AS THE VINE, AND SHALL CAST OFF HIS FLOWER AS THE OLIVE.

(34) "FOR THE CONGREGATION OF HYPOCRITES SHALL BE DESOLATE, AND FIRE SHALL CONSUME THE TABERNACLES OF BRIBERY.

(35) "THEY CONCEIVE MISCHIEF, AND BRING FORTH VANITY, AND THEIR BELLY PREPARES DECEIT."

The exposition is:

1. (Vs. 17) Eliphaz now proclaims his judgment upon Job.

2. (Vs. 18) He claims great wisdom; however, this was worldly wisdom, and not wisdom from above (James 3:15).

3. (Vs. 29) Eliphaz claims that the hypocrisy of Job is now being found out.

4. (Vs. 31) He says that Job is deceived so all his trust and faith are of no consequence.

5. (Vs. 35) The Lord allowed the prattle of these *"friends"* to be included in the Sacred Text, even as wrong as it was, in order to show us that circumstances rarely present the true picture. Understanding

this, we had best withhold judgment.

HYPOCRISY

In the Thirty-fourth Verse, Eliphaz accuses Job of hypocrisy. The word *"hypocrisy"* refers to a person who is *"acting under a false part."* It refers to a person putting on a face to others, which is not what they really are. This means they aren't really even trying to live for God, only pretending to do so.

Jesus referred to the Pharisees as *"hypocrites"* (Mat. 23:13-15, 23, 25, 27, 29).

The scary part about all of this is self-righteousness will ultimately lead to hypocrisy. It is impossible to live a clean life by trusting in works and merit. So, as the sin nature begins to rule in such a person, which it most definitely will, many times such an individual will try to make excuses for the failure, or else try to hide it. So, in effect, such a person is living a double life.

HYPOCRISY AND THE TRUE BELIEVER

If the true Believer doesn't understand the Message of the Cross as it refers to Sanctification, such a person will be overcome by sin, and despite all of his efforts to do otherwise. Such a person is not a hypocrite; however, if his sin is found out, as it is oftentimes, he will most definitely be accused of being a hypocrite. But the truth is he isn't. He is not trying to live a double life, but rather to walk in victory; however, he continues to fail, as fail he must, and because his faith is in the wrong object. In one way or the other, every single Believer who has ever lived, has functioned in the capacity of which we have just spoken. Not understanding the Message of the Cross, they have tried to live for God in all the wrong ways. Even though such a person is sincere, still, their sincerity will not bring about victory.

The truth is, Job's three friends would much closer come under the web of hypocrisy. There was no hypocrisy about Job at all!

"And did the Holy and Just,
"The Sovereign of the skies,
"Stoop down to wretchedness and dust,
"That guilty man might rise?"

"Yes, the Redeemer left His Throne,
"His radiant Throne on high

"Surprising Mercy! Love unknown!
"To suffer, bleed, and die."

"To dwell with misery here below,
"The Saviour left the sky,
"And sunk to wretchedness and woe,
"That worthless man might rise."

"He took the dying traitor's place,
"And suffered in his stead;
"For sinful man — oh wondrous Grace!
"For sinful man He bled."

"O Lord, what heavenly wonders dwell
"In Your Atoning Blood!
"By this are sinners Saved from Hell,
"And rebels brought to God."

CHAPTER 16

(1) "THEN JOB ANSWERED AND SAID,

(2) "I HAVE HEARD MANY SUCH THINGS: MISERABLE COMFORTERS ARE YOU ALL.

(3) "SHALL VAIN WORDS HAVE AN END? OR WHAT EMBOLDENS YOU THAT YOU ANSWER?

(4) "I ALSO COULD SPEAK AS YOU DO: IF YOUR SOUL WERE IN MY SOUL'S STEAD, I COULD HEAP UP WORDS AGAINST YOU, AND SHAKE MY HEAD AT YOU.

(5) "BUT I WOULD STRENGTHEN YOU WITH MY MOUTH, AND THE MOVING OF MY LIPS SHOULD ASSWAGE YOUR GRIEF.

(6) "THOUGH I SPEAK, MY GRIEF IS NOT ASSWAGED: AND THOUGH I FORBEAR, WHAT AM I EASED?

(7) "BUT NOW HE HAS MADE ME WEARY: YOU HAVE MADE DESOLATE ALL MY COMPANY.

(8) "AND YOU HAVE FILLED ME WITH WRINKLES, WHICH IS A WITNESS AGAINST ME: AND MY LEANNESS RISING UP IN ME BEARS WITNESS TO MY FACE.

(9) "HE TEARS ME IN HIS WRATH, WHO HATES ME: HE GNASHES UPON ME WITH HIS TEETH; MY ENEMY SHARPENS HIS EYES UPON ME.

(10) "THEY HAVE GAPED UPON ME

WITH THEIR MOUTH; THEY HAVE SMITTEN ME UPON THE CHEEK REPROACHFULLY; THEY HAVE GATHERED THEMSELVES TOGETHER AGAINST ME.

(11) "GOD HAS DELIVERED ME TO THE UNGODLY, AND TURNED ME OVER INTO THE HANDS OF THE WICKED.

(12) "I WAS AT EASE, BUT HE HAS BROKEN ME ASUNDER: HE HAS ALSO TAKEN ME BY MY NECK, AND SHAKEN ME TO PIECES, AND SET ME UP FOR HIS MARK.

(13) "HIS ARCHERS COMPASS ME ROUND ABOUT, HE CLEAVES MY REINS ASUNDER, AND DOES NOT SPARE; HE POURS OUT MY GALL UPON THE GROUND.

(14) "HE BREAKS ME WITH BREACH UPON BREACH, HE RUNS UPON ME LIKE A GIANT."

The pattern is:

1. (Vs. 5) From what the Lord said about Job (42:7), there is every evidence, if the tables were reversed, that Job would truly have comforted his *"friends."*

2. Job's statements as given in Verse 9 are incorrect; there was no wrath of God against Job, which he will ultimately see.

3. What Job said in the Tenth Verse is correct! In fact, these statements are very similar to some used about the Lord (Ps. 35:16; 37:12).

4. While it was Satan who actually did the things mentioned in Verse 14, still, it was the Lord Who allowed him to do so. So, in essence, Job wasn't wrong in this particular statement.

MISERABLE COMFORTERS

This great test that God gave Job by allowing Satan to afflict him was not only a test for Job, but for his friends as well. Also, it was a test for Job's wife. It seems that all failed the test, and miserably so, except Job.

We should learn from this that every test that comes to a Child of God is not only a test for the person in question, whatever that test might be, but is, as well, for others of the Body of Christ.

Why were these *"friends"* miserable comforters? The answers are obvious:

• The teachings of human wisdom can neither strengthen the heart, nor mitigate the sufferings of a person so mysteriously afflicted as Job.

• The Holy Spirit is really the only Comforter Who can actually strengthen and help the Child of God in times of difficulty (Jn. 14:26).

JOB MAKES STATEMENTS CONCERNING GOD:

• Destroyed all the witnesses that Job could have produced to prove his innocence — his children and his servants.

• Shriveled up his body with a horrible disease, which seemed an evidence of his guilt.

• Rent him in anger, persecuted him, and gnashed upon him with his teeth as an enemy sharpens his eyes upon him.

• He permitted evil men to mistreat Job.

• The ungodly and the wicked were given power over him.

• God Himself dashed him to the ground, and then, broken as he was, set him up as a target.

• That the archers, Job's *"three friends,"* might attack him.

DELIVERED TO THE UNGODLY

Job said, *"God has delivered me to the ungodly, and turned me over into the hands of the wicked."*

Did the Lord do that?

While, of course, some can say that Satan is the one who did this, which would be correct; however, he had to have permission from the Lord to do so. Once again we must understand that Satan can do nothing unless he gets permission from the Lord to do it, and even then, the Lord draws the boundaries on all things. The Lord is never subservient to Satan, but Satan is always subservient to the Lord.

So why would the Lord allow Job to be delivered to the ungodly and turned over into the hands of the wicked?

God has a reason for all that He does. In other words, He does nothing capriciously. Every act is with design and purpose, all, no matter how negative it may seem to be at the present, for our good.

A PERSONAL EXPERIENCE

In 1988 the Lord allowed me personally

to be *"delivered to the ungodly, and turned over into the hands of the wicked."*

I go back in my mind's eye to an early morning just before daylight during the month of April, 1988, that is, if I remember the time period correctly.

I had slept very little, if any at all, that night. Actually, I had left out of our bedroom and gone downstairs trying to sleep, but to no avail.

Sometime at about daylight, I was importuning the Lord, and I said to Him, *"Lord, why did You have to do this as You did it? Why did it have to be so shameful, so public, so humiliating? You are God and can do anything, could it not have been done another way?"*

Sometimes the Lord does not answer our petitions immediately, but that time He did. The answer was almost instant. He said to me:

"You asked Me as to why I did what I did, and why I did it in the way that it was done?" And then He added, *"I had to cripple you as I crippled Jacob."*

That was the answer that He gave me.

A VISION

If I remember correctly, the year was 1982. It was a Saturday morning. I do not really remember the month, but it must have been sometime in July.

I had gone to a secluded spot by the Mississippi River, which is not so very far from our home, where I went occasionally to pray. I would spend most of that Saturday in prayer, alternately studying the Word of God and seeking the Lord.

That morning after seeking the Lord for approximately an hour or so, the Spirit of the Lord came upon me heavily, stating that I must deliver a message to the Catholic people all over the world.

At that time, our Telecast was aired all over Central and South America, translated into Spanish and then Portuguese for Brazil. As well, we were on Television in the Philippines, which is heavily Catholic, plus parts of Europe and Africa. In those days, we were translating the Telecast into Spanish, Portuguese, French, German, and several other languages. Actually, in 1989 we would begin to translate also in Russian.

At any rate, the Lord told me that I was to deliver the Message through our Telecast to Catholics. The message was simple, *"The Just Shall Live By Faith."*

CATHOLIC CHARISMATICS

To be frank, at that time, I knew little or nothing about Catholicism. Beside that, Catholic Charismatics were sending our Ministry hundreds of thousands, if not millions, of dollars each year, which we desperately needed for the Work of God. Having been raised in North Louisiana where there are very few Catholics, I was woefully deficient as it regarded the meaning of Catholic doctrine.

The Lord then spoke to my heart, stating that I was to deliver a particular word to the denominational world (they must come to the Holy Spirit), and to the Pentecostal and Charismatic world (they must come back to the Holy Spirit).

The Lord then told me, if I obeyed Him, as I should, that I could lose everything. He emphatically stated to me *"your own will turn against you."* He was speaking of the Pentecostals, etc.

The Pentecostal world turning against me came to pass exactly as the Lord said it would. I'm glad at the time that I didn't know nor understand the degree of what the Lord had said. If I had, I'm not certain if I could have carried it out.

OUR MINISTRY AT THAT TIME

At the time the Lord dealt with me in 1982, our Ministry was by far the largest in the world, at least of its kind. We were airing Television over a great part of the world and, as stated, with the program translated into several languages. We were conducting crusades all over the world, which would shortly be the largest that the world had ever known, at least on a continuing basis. Family Worship Center in Baton Rouge was growing by proverbial leaps and bounds. Actually, at that time we were in the process of building a new structure that would seat over 5,000 people. The Bible College was just beginning, with hundreds of students. But then the Lord had said, *"You may very well lose it all."*

And then He asked me, *"Are you willing to lose everything and to start over?"*

When the Lord spoke that to my heart, I did not answer immediately. In fact, all the things I've just mentioned, the Ministry in its totality, came before my eyes, but I knew what the Lord told me that I must do.

After seeking His Face further for a period of time, I then said, *"Lord, I will do my best to carry out what You have instructed me to do irrespective of the cost."*

As I've just stated, I really did not at that time fully understand, not at all, what that cost would be.

In a sense, it all happened exactly as the Lord told me it would. While we didn't lose everything, we lost a great deal.

At any rate, when I wrote the first article regarding Catholicism, and after months of prayer, entitled, *"A Letter To My Catholic Friends"* that's when it all began.

Our magazine, *"The Evangelist,"* then went into 800,000 homes monthly in America and Canada. The reaction was immediate.

I then made statements over Television, actually very simple statements, such as *"the just shall live by Faith,"* and speaking to our Catholic friends, which means that the Church cannot save, but very pointedly.

We were, I think, the subject of every newspaper columnist in America, demanding that we be taken off the air, etc.

Ironically enough, our greatest opposition came from our own, and I speak of the Pentecostal Denominations.

Why?

THE POLICY OF THE PENTECOSTAL AND CHARISMATIC WORLDS

I had stated in my article, *"A Letter To My Catholic Friends"* that while many Catholics were giving their hearts to Christ, and actually that many were also being baptized with the Holy Spirit, the truth was and is, that being the case, they were going to have to leave the Catholic Church. In other words, they could not stay in that unscriptural system and maintain what they had in the Lord. That is what caused the furor.

The policy of the Pentecostal and Charismatic worlds was that the Catholics who had come to Christ must stay in that denomination and *"do missionary work,"* as it was put. I remember one Charismatic leader wrote me, stating, that my Message had torn down what he had taken 20 years to build.

I answered him very kindly, but I thought in my heart, that if one Message from me could cause that type of difficulty, he must not have built very much in that 20 years.

I am certain that there were many preachers in the Pentecostal and Charismatic worlds who did not subscribe to that policy at that time, but most of the leadership did. And now I come along stating that this is wrong, and that there is no way that Catholics can stay in that nefarious system and maintain their walk with the Lord; to be sure, such didn't set very well.

Right in the middle of the initial furor when every newspaper was screaming for my head, and most of the religious world had turned against me, we were scheduled to preach a Crusade in Guatemala City, Guatemala.

Frances and I didn't want to leave, but we had no choice, the meeting had to be conducted. In fact, we would have a tremendous meeting, with the stadium filled, and with thousands coming to Christ, for which we gave and give the Lord all the glory.

THE THRESHINGFLOOR

If I remember correctly, we arrived in Guatemala City on a Thursday. The Crusade would begin Friday night. At any rate, at about 1 a.m. Friday morning, I arose out of bed, and went to the adjoining room to pray.

I was greatly troubled over the situation at home. With all the great powers arrayed against us, I was concerned that we might lose much of our Television Network, in other words, that we would be taken off the air. I was greatly troubled about all of this, and did the only thing I could do, which was to take it to the Lord in prayer.

That night as I began to seek the Face of the Lord, crying to Him to give us wisdom as to what to do regarding the situation at hand, at a point in time, the Spirit of the Lord came heavily upon me.

I remember standing beside the window, for our rooms were on the top floor of the hotel, looking out over the sprawling metropolis of Guatemala City. And then I saw it.

I personally believe that it was a Vision. At any rate, the city faded from view, and in front of my eyes I saw a threshingfloor. To be frank, in the natural I had never seen such, so I could only see what it seemed to be in Bible times.

It was a large round rock that stood up a little bit above the ground. In the vision I saw a man with a type of pitchfork in his hand pitching the grain up in the air, with the wind blowing the husk over the side and the grain falling back to the floor.

In the Vision, I did not see how that the grain was separated from the husk in the many ways that it was done in those days. When the Vision appeared, it had passed that stage.

As I watched the man pitching the grain up in the air, and the wind blowing the husks to the side, and the grain falling back to the floor, I also saw that the husks on the outside of the threshingfloor were on fire. In fact, John the Baptist had referred to this very thing. He said:

"I indeed baptize you with water unto Repentance: but He Who comes after me is mightier than I, Whose shoes I am not worthy to bear: He shall baptize you with the Holy Spirit and with fire: Whose fan is in His Hand, and He will thoroughly purge His Floor, and gather His wheat into the garner; but He will burn up the chaff with unquenchable fire" (Mat. 3:11-12).

As in the Vision I watched the flames consuming the husks, I asked the Lord, *"Why is it necessary to burn the husks, when it's no longer mixed with the grain, and in fact, it's not even any longer on the threshingfloor?"*

The answer from the Lord came back immediately, *"The husk represents the flesh, and there must be nothing remaining of the flesh. It must all be of My Spirit."*

To be frank, at that time, I didn't understand the Vision. I was seeking the Lord concerning the problems at home, but the Lord seemed to ignore my request in that capacity, rather giving me the Vision of the threshingfloor.

THE VISION WAS FOR ME PERSONALLY

I came to know later, actually several years later, as to what the Vision was all about.

Actually, we lost only one Television Station in the hundreds over which we were then televising the program, which incidentally was owned by a Charismatic. But what the Lord told me that night as it regards the Vision of the threshingfloor, pertained to me personally.

He, in effect, as I was to later learn, was telling me that there was much *"flesh"* in my life and experience, flesh which must be removed. I was to find out, that those things do not come about quickly or easily.

While Job was closer to the Lord, even according to the Word of the Lord, than any other individual on Earth, still, there was much *"flesh"* in his life as well, which he found to be the case as the great trial progressed. Job found that the flesh could not be removed by the flesh, it was a work that only the Holy Spirit could do. I was to find out the same thing. What I had to go through in order for this to be revealed to me, and to be carried out in my life, which, incidentally, is a continuing process, a process actually that will never end, at least this side of Glory, was carried out in my case, humiliatingly before the entirety of the world.

The separation of the grain from the husk in Old Testament times was, in fact, a violent process. It was carried out by several methods, sometimes it was tramped down by people walking over the grain, and sometimes by an ox pulling a cart with its wheels performing the task. Then and then only can it be separated, and even then, the husk must be burned, that there be no trace of such left, with only the grain remaining.

WHAT IS THE FLESH?

Paul used the term *"flesh"* often (Rom. 7:5, 18, 25; 8:1, 3-5, 8, etc.).

The word *"flesh"* as the Holy Spirit used the term through Paul, refers to the ability of the human being, as it regards personal talent, strength, power, education, motivation, intellectualism, etc. While these things within themselves aren't necessarily wrong, the idea is that by their use, we cannot effect the things of God within our lives. In other words, mankind cannot produce anything within himself that God can accept, no matter who that person is, or how consecrated he might be. Whatever is done in our hearts and lives as it regards the Lord, must be carried out without fail by the Holy Spirit. If we try to perfect Sanctification, Holiness, Righteousness, etc., by our own efforts, i.e., *"the flesh,"* which all of us has tried to do at one time or the other, it is an effort that God cannot condone. The Lord can accept and, in fact, will only accept, that which is carried out by the Holy Spirit. And then for the Holy Spirit to do the work that He alone can do, the Faith of the Believer must be anchored exclusively in the Cross of Christ.

THE CROSS OF CHRIST AND THE HOLY SPIRIT

The Believer must understand, that from eternity past into eternity future, everything has always depended on the Cross of Christ. In fact, all who were Saved before the Cross, were Saved one might say on credit. In other words, before the Cross believing sinners were Saved by looking forward to that coming great Work. Now, believing sinners are Saved by looking backward to a Work already finished, but having continued results, results incidentally, which will never be discontinued.

Everything the Holy Spirit has done, is doing, and shall do, depends totally and completely on the Finished Work of Christ, which gave and gives the Holy Spirit the legal means to do all that He does. That's the reason it is referred to as *"The Law of the Spirit of Life in Christ Jesus"* (Rom. 8:2). In fact, the Fifth Chapter of Revelation proclaims to us in that which is glaringly obvious, the proximity of the Holy Spirit relative to Christ and the Cross. It says:

"And I beheld, and, lo, in the midst of the Throne and of the four Beasts, and in the midst of the Elders, stood a Lamb as it had been slain (the Crucifixion of Christ is represented here by the word *'Lamb,'* which refers to the fact that it was the Cross that redeemed mankind; the slain Lamb Alone has redeemed all things), *having seven horns* (horns denote dominion, and *'seven'* denotes total dominion; all of this was done for you and me, meaning that we can have total dominion over the powers of darkness, and in every capacity; so there is no excuse for a lack of victory) *and seven eyes* (denotes total, perfect, pure, and complete illumination of all things spiritual, which is again made possible for you and me by the Cross; if the Believer makes the Cross the Object of his Faith, he will never be drawn away by false doctrine), *which are the Seven Spirits of God sent forth into all the Earth* (signifying that the Holy Spirit, in all His Perfection and universality, functions entirely within the parameters of the Finished Work of Christ; in other words, it is required that we ever make the Cross the Object of our Faith, which gives the Holy Spirit latitude, and guarantees the *'dominion,'* and the *'illumination'* [Isa. 11:2; Rom. 8:2])" (Rev. 5:6).

SPIRITUAL GROWTH

As it regards *"growing in Grace and in the knowledge of the Lord"* (II Pet. 3:18), this is predicated on three things. They are:

1. The Holy Spirit: Anything and everything that's done within our hearts and lives regarding the Lord can only be done by the Holy Spirit. God will accept nothing else. If we try to bring about the attributes of the Lord by our own means, it is referred to in the Word of God as *"the flesh,"* which the Lord can never accept (Rom. 8:8). So the Believer must understand that. In fact, this, the flesh, which relates to efforts and ingenuity from the means of man, presents itself as the bane of the Church. Every one of us has tried to perfect righteousness and holiness in our lives by the means of religious laws, which again, the Lord can never accept. The Holy Spirit Alone can bring about these great attributes, can develop them within our hearts and lives, and can perfect our growing process.

2. The Cross of Christ: The Holy Spirit, even as we've already stated, works exclusively within the parameters of the Finished Work of Christ (Rom. 8:2). In fact, it is the Cross which gave and gives the Holy Spirit the legal right, which refers to the legal means to do all that He does within our

hearts and lives. Actually, the Holy Spirit and the Cross of Christ are so closely intertwined, even as we have just portrayed to you regarding Revelation, Chapter 5, that one might say They are indivisible, which means inseparable. Paul said, *"The preaching of the Cross is to them who perish foolishness, but to we who are Saved it is the Power of God"* (I Cor. 1:18). In truth, there was no power in the Cross as a wooden beam, and there was not even any power in the death of Christ, as it regards death per se. The power is in the Holy Spirit (Acts 1:8), but He is able to use that power on our behalf, only because of the Cross of Christ. The Holy Spirit is God, and can do anything; however, it is the Cross, as stated, which gives Him the legal liberty and latitude to work within our hearts and lives (Rom. 8:2).

3. Our Faith: For the Christian to merely proclaim that he has Faith in God, while a correct statement, still, doesn't say very much. It is the correct Object of Faith which is so very, very important (Rom. 6:1-14; 8:1-2, 11; I Cor. 1:17-18, 21, 23; 2:2; Col. 2:14-15). Satan doesn't too much care what the object of faith is regarding the Believer, just so it isn't the Cross. It was at the Cross that he and all of his minions of darkness were totally and completely defeated (Col. 2:14-15). And this is where he fights the hardest. When the Christian places his faith exclusively in Christ and the Cross, understanding that Christ is the Source of all things we receive from God, and that the Cross is the Means by which these things are carried out, this gives the Holy Spirit latitude and liberty to work within our hearts and lives, thereby, to bring about our Spiritual Growth. This is God's Way, and one might say His *"Prescribed Order of Victory."* He has no other way, simply because no other way is needed.

So, we have the Holy Spirit, the Cross of Christ, and our Faith in the Cross, which gives us the continued results of all for which Jesus paid such a price.

(15) "I HAVE SEWED SACKCLOTH UPON MY SKIN, AND DEFILED MY HORN IN THE DUST.

(16) "MY FACE IS FOUL WITH WEEPING, AND ON MY EYELIDS IS THE SHADOW OF DEATH;

(17) "NOT FOR ANY INJUSTICE IN MY HANDS: ALSO MY PRAYER IS PURE.

(18) "O EARTH, COVER NOT THOU MY BLOOD, AND LET MY CRY HAVE NO PLACE.

(19) "ALSO NOW, BEHOLD, MY WITNESS IS IN HEAVEN, AND MY RECORD IS ON HIGH.

(20) "MY FRIENDS SCORN ME: BUT MY EYE POURS OUT TEARS UNTO GOD.

(21) "O THAT ONE MIGHT PLEAD FOR A MAN WITH GOD, AS A MAN PLEADS FOR HIS NEIGHBOUR!

(22) "WHEN A FEW YEARS ARE COME, THEN I SHALL GO THE WAY WHENCE I SHALL NOT RETURN."

The pattern is:

1. The Fifteenth Verse proclaims the fact that Job at this time doesn't see any way out. He thinks he is dying.

2. (Vs. 17) Job repudiates the charge of rapine and robbery which Eliphaz has brought against him (15:28, 34); neither has he been guilty of hypocrisy.

3. (Vs. 19) In his mind he thinks that after he is dead, he wants the Earth to cry out against the injustice done to him, typifying that of Abel (Gen. 4:10). He believes that he will be vindicated, even if it's after his death.

4. Job once again, according to Verse 21, pleads for a true Mediator. That prayer will ultimately be answered in Christ.

GOD IS MY REFUGE

Pulpit says, *"It is not to his friends, or companions, or comforters, or any human aid, that Job turns in his distress. God alone is his Refuge."*[1]

Looking to man instead of God is the bane of the modern church. Whether it be in the realm of humanistic psychology, or whether other Believers, precious little help will come from those sources.

Believing man is obligated to proclaim the Word of the Lord to our fellow human beings, which, in essence, teaches us to look exclusively to the Lord. I value the advice and counsel of my fellow Believers, at least as long as the advice and counsel they give is strictly according to the Word. But when it comes to help, no help is forthcoming, even from the godliest of men and women, outside of being pointed to the Word of God exclusively. In other words, your fellowman can help you, if he points you to the Word and the Word alone, which means he will point you to the Cross. Man, even the godliest, being a poor, finite human being, can do precious little as far as actual help is concerned. The Lord Alone can do what needs to be done.

COVERING

One of the catch phrase questions prominent at this particular time is, *"Who is your covering?"*

Whoever asks such a question normally is referring to some prominent preacher, or denominational heads, who act as a covering. In other words, the idea is, they, whomever they might be, vouch for the credibility of the individual. And, as the idea continues, if the individual does not have this type of *"covering,"* this means that he is trying to hide something.

To be truthful, the exact opposite is the case.

Men can fool other men, and do so constantly, but God cannot be fooled, as should be overly obvious.

Beside that, to claim some poor, frail, pitiful human being as one's covering, no matter who that human being might be, presents an insult to Christ of unprecedented proportions. In fact, it speaks of man's pitiful fig leaves.

Christ Alone is our Covering and, in fact, He had better be our Covering, and our sole Covering, or the truth is, we have no covering.

I remember once looking at a particular Christian Telecast, so-called, which featured an entertainer and a preacher. The entertainer whose name is very well-known, had lost his way, had made a rock-and-roll album, and was now trying to defend it, despite the fact that he was about 40 years past the age of rock-and-roll, which as a Christian, should have been an abomination to him.

The preacher by his side, also well-known, finally spoke up and said to the television audience, that he was the *"covering"* of this entertainer, and irrespective as to what he did, this gave him credibility.

What a travesty!

Let me say it again.

Anytime a Believer claims some poor mortal as his covering, he is sinning greatly against Christ. And any time any individual claims to be the covering of someone else, they have just put themselves into the place of Christ, a role that no man can fill except Christ. Our Lord Alone paid the price on Calvary's Cross that He might wash our sins away, which He Alone can do. To claim anyone else, or anything else, as a *"covering,"* is an abomination before God.

The great Prophet Isaiah, whom incidentally Jesus quoted more than any other Prophet, stated: *"Woe to the rebellious children, says the LORD, who take counsel, but not of Me, and who cover with a covering, but not of My Spirit, that they may add sin to sin"* (Isa. 30:1).

Concerning this Verse, notes from THE EXPOSITOR'S STUDY BIBLE say: "In the preceding Chapter, the design of the Jewish rulers to seek the alliance of Egypt was covertly looked at and condemned; now it is openly declared and rebuked.

"*'Counsel'* which is not of the Word of God is also not from God.

"As well, only the Spirit of God can cover someone, which He does through the Word, which speaks of what Jesus did for us at the Cross. Actually, the *'covering'* comes for each Believer through Christ, Who Alone can actually cover. And He does so by the Spirit through the Cross. Christ is the Source, while the Cross is the Means.

"Any poor mortal who thinks he can be the *'covering'* for another presents spiritual and Scriptural ignorance."

A MEDIATOR

The Patriarch said, *"Oh that one might plead for a man with God, as a man pleads for his neighbor."*

All of these statements by Job proclaim the fact, that these three so-called friends were useless. They could not serve as a covering and, in fact, would not serve as a covering. They reasoned Job to be a hypocrite, who was getting what he deserved. So much for the wisdom of the world!

Job cries for a mediator who could plead man's case with God, which he recognized as that which was sorely needed. That prayer, which was offered by Job, would be answered, but it would be about 1,500 years into the future.

Jesus Christ is that Mediator and, in fact, the only Mediator between God and men. The Scripture says:

"For there is one God (manifested in three Persons — God the Father, God the Son, and God the Holy Spirit), *and one Mediator between God and men, the Man Christ Jesus* (He can only be an adequate Mediator Who has sympathy with and an understanding of both parties, and is understandable by and clear to both; in other words, Jesus is both God and Man, i.e., 'Very God and very Man');

"Who gave Himself a ransom for all (refers to the fact that our Lord's Death was a spontaneous and voluntary Sacrifice on His Part; the word *'ransom'* refers to the price He paid, owed by man to God, which was His Precious Blood [I Pet. 1:18-20]), *to be testified in due time.* (This refers to the planning of this great Work, which took place *'before the foundation of the world'* [I Pet. 1:18-20], unto the *'due time'* of its manifestation, which refers to when Christ was Crucified)" (I Tim. 2:5-6).

In fact, Jesus Alone could act as such, because He is both Man and God. As well, and as should be obvious, this addresses the *"covering"* as well. To deny this, and look to some poor mortal, I hope one can see is an insult to Christ and what He has done for us.

In regard to Jesus as our Mediator, Paul further said: *"For we have not an High Priest Who cannot be touched with the feeling of our infirmities* (being Very Man as well as Very God, He can do such); *but was in all points tempted like as we are, yet without sin* (His Temptation, and ours as well, was to leave the Prescribed Will of God, which is the Word of God; but He never did, not even one time.)

"Let us therefore come boldly unto the Throne of Grace (presents the Seat of Divine Power, and yet the Source of boundless Grace), *that we may obtain Mercy* (presents that which we want first), *and find Grace to help in time of need* (refers to the Goodness of God extended to all who come, and during any *'time of need'*; all made possible by the Cross)" (Heb. 4:15-16).

It is the Cross which made it possible for Christ to serve as the Mediator between God and men. That's at least one of the reasons that the Cross must ever be the Object of our Faith.

"You we adore, Eternal Word!
"The Father's equal Son;
"By Heaven's obedient host adored,
"Ere time its course begun."

"The first Creation has displayed,
"Your energy Divine;
"For not a single thing was made,
"By other hands than Thine."

"But ransomed sinners, with delight,
"Sublimer facts survey,
"The all-creating Word unites,
"Himself to dust and clay."

"Creation's Author now assumes,
"A creature's humble form:
"A man of grief and woe becomes,
"And trod on like a worm."

"The Lord of Glory bears the shame,
"To vile transgressors due;
"Justice the prince of life condemns,
"To die in anguish too."

"God overall, forever blest,
"The righteous curse endures;
"And thus, to souls with sin distressed,
"Eternal bliss insures."

"What wonders in Your Person meet,
"My Saviour, all Divine!
"I fall with rapture at Your feet,
"And would be wholly Thine."

CHAPTER 17

(1) "MY BREATH IS CORRUPT, MY DAYS ARE EXTINCT, THE GRAVES ARE READY FOR ME.

(2) "ARE THERE NOT MOCKERS WITH ME? AND DOES NOT MY EYE CONTINUE IN THEIR PROVOCATION?

(3) "LAY DOWN NOW, PUT ME IN A

SURETY WITH YOU; WHO IS HE WHO WILL STRIKE HANDS WITH ME?

(4) "FOR YOU HAVE HID THEIR HEART FROM UNDERSTANDING: THEREFORE SHALL YOU NOT EXALT THEM.

(5) "HE WHO SPEAKS FLATTERY TO THIS FRIENDS, EVEN THE EYES OF HIS CHILDREN SHALL FAIL.

(6) "HE HAS MADE ME ALSO A BYWORD OF THE PEOPLE; AND AFORETIME I WAS AS A TABRET.

(7) "MY EYE ALSO IS DIM BY REASON OF SORROW, AND ALL MY MEMBERS ARE AS A SHADOW."

The exegesis is:

1. (Vs. 1) The accusations of these *"friends"* were contributing as much as his physical disability toward Job's possible death. We as Believers should take a lesson from all of this.

2. The Third Verse, in essence, says, *"Lord, You are the only One to Whom I can look."*

3. According to Verse 6, Job had become a joke in the entirety of that part of the world.

WHAT HELP CAN WE PROVIDE A FELLOW BELIEVER?

Job feels that he is about to die; however, not only is his physical body wracked with sickness, and acutely so, as well, his spirit, which is probably more dangerous than the physical, has been crushed by these *"friends,"* and others. Job said that he had become *"a byword of the people,"* meaning that he had become a joke.

Most people make snap judgments on outward appearances. Situations in the world are seldom judged as they actually are, but as people perceive them to be. So, people perceive Job at this time to be evil. So now he will be little more than a *"byword."* In Job's day there did not seem to be anyone in Job's proximity who had Spiritual Discernment; likewise, there seems to be precious few today as well!

As we have previously said in this Volume, when a person is down and cannot defend themselves, and anyone can do any negative thing to them they so desire, and will not only not be reprimanded, but rather applauded, one then sees just how many good Christians there actually are. Regrettably, there aren't many.

This is not a plea to condone sin. God forbid! But at the same time, when another has failed, we had best take stock as to how much the Lord has pardoned us, and if we will look at it as we should, we will quickly realize that we have no right to condemn others.

Now please understand, it is the obligation of every Believer, preacher, or otherwise, to judge doctrine, but that is far different than judging the motivation of the individual. No human being can do the latter. As it regards judging the motivation of others, and the doctrine of others, our Lord had much to say on the matter. We will deal first of all with motivation, and use THE EXPOSITOR'S STUDY BIBLE as reference:

"Judge not, that you be not judged (this statement by Christ harks back to Verses 25 through 34 of Matthew, Chapter 6. The idea is, God may permit poverty to test His Child, but fellow Believers are not to err, as Job's friends did, and believe the trial to be a judgment for secret sin. As well, the word, *'judging,'* as used here, covers every aspect of dealing with our fellowman).

"For with what judgment you judge, you shall be judged (whatever motive we ascribe to others, such motive will ultimately be ascribed to us): *and with what measure you mete, it shall be measured to you again* (a double emphasis is given here in order to proclaim the seriousness of the Words of our Lord; when we judge others, we are judging ourselves).

"And why do you behold the mote that is in your brother's eye (the Believer is not to be looking for fault or wrongdoing in the lives of fellow Believers), *but consider not the beam that is in your own eye?* (We have plenty in our own lives which needs eliminating without looking for faults in others. The *'mote'* and *'beam'* are contrasted! The constant judging of others portrays the fact that we are much worse off than the one we are judging.)

"Or how will you say to your brother, Let me pull out the mote out of your eye (the seriousness of setting ourselves up as Judge, jury, and executioner)*; and, behold, a beam is in your own eye?* (Once again draws attention to the fact that the person

doing the judging is in far worse spiritual condition than the one being judged.)

"*You hypocrite* (aptly describes such a person), *first cast out the beam out of your own eye; and then you shall see clearly to cast out the mote out of your brother's eye* (the very fact that we do not address ourselves, but rather others, portrays the truth that our personal situation is worse. When we properly analyze ourselves, then, and only then, can we *'see clearly.'* This is speaking of character assassination and the not the correction of doctrine)" (Mat. 7:1-5).

Jesus then dealt with false prophets. He said:

FALSE PROPHETS

"*Beware of false prophets, who come to you in sheep's clothing, but inwardly they are ravening wolves* (*'beware of false prophets'* is said in the sternest of measures! There will be and are false prophets, and are some of Satan's greatest weapons).

"*You shall know them by their fruits* (this is the test as given by Christ as it regards identification of false prophets and false apostles). *Do men gather grapes of thorns, or figs of thistles?* (It is impossible for false doctrine, generated by false prophets, to bring forth good fruit.)

"*Even so every good tree brings forth good fruit; but a corrupt tree brings forth evil fruit* (the good fruit is Christlikeness, while the evil fruit is self-likeness).

"*A good tree cannot bring forth evil fruit, neither can a corrupt tree bring forth good fruit* (the *'good tree'* is the Cross, while the *'corrupt tree'* pertains to all of that which is other than the Cross).

"*Every tree that brings not forth good fruit is hewn down, and cast into the fire* (Judgment will ultimately come on all so-called gospel, other than the Cross [Rom. 1:18]).

"*Wherefore by their fruits you shall know them* (the acid test)" (Mat. 7:15-20).

AGAINST MERE PROFESSION

Again, we quote from THE EXPOSITOR'S STUDY BIBLE:

"*Not everyone who says unto Me, Lord, Lord, shall enter into the Kingdom of Heaven* (the repetition of the word *'Lord'* expresses astonishment, as if to say: *'Are we to be disowned?'*); *but he who does the Will of My Father Who is in Heaven* (what is the Will of the Father? Matthew, Chapter 7, Verse 23 tells us).

"*Many will say to Me in that day, Lord, Lord, have we not prophesied in Your Name? and in Your Name have cast out devils? and in Your Name done many wonderful works?* (These things are not the criteria, but rather Faith in Christ and what Christ has done for us at the Cross [Eph. 2:8-9, 13-18]. The Word of God alone is to be the judge of doctrine.)

"*And then will I profess unto them, I never knew you* (again we say, the criteria alone is Christ and Him Crucified [I Cor. 1:23])*: depart from Me, you who work iniquity.*

• We have access to God only through Christ.

• And access to Christ only through the Cross.

• And access to the Cross only through a denial of self [Lk. 9:23];

"Any other Message is judged by God as *'iniquity,'* and cannot be a part of Christ [I Cor. 1:17])" (Mat. 7:21-23).

THE WISE MAN AND THE FOOLISH MAN

Jesus now goes on to say the following, in effect, telling us what the Will of the Father actually is, as demanded in Verse 21 above.

"*Therefore whosoever hears these sayings of Mine, and does them, I will liken him unto a wise man, who built his house upon a rock* (the *'Rock'* is Christ Jesus, and the Foundation is the Cross [Gal. 1:8-9])*:*

"*And the rain descended, and the floods came, and the winds blew, and beat upon that house; and it fell not; for it was founded upon a rock* (the Foundation of our belief system must be Christ and Him Crucified [Gal. 6:14]).

"*And everyone who hears these sayings of Mine, and does them not, shall be likened unto a foolish man, who built his house upon the sand* (but for the foundation, this house looked the same as the house that was built upon the rock)*:*

"*And the rain descended, and the floods came, and the winds blew, and beat upon that house; and it fell: and great was the fall of it* (while the sun shines, both houses look good; but, when adversity comes, and come it shall, Faith, which is alone in Christ and Him Crucified will stand [I Cor. 1:18])" (Mat. 7:24-27).

(8) "UPRIGHT MEN SHALL BE ASTONIED AT THIS, AND THE INNOCENT SHALL STIR UP HIMSELF AGAINST THE HYPOCRITE.

(9) "THE RIGHTEOUS ALSO SHALL HOLD ON HIS WAY, AND HE WHO HAS CLEAN HANDS SHALL BE STRONGER AND STRONGER.

(10) "BUT AS FOR YOU ALL, DO YOU RETURN, AND COME NOW: FOR I CANNOT FIND ONE WISE MAN AMONG YOU.

(11) "MY DAYS ARE PAST, MY PURPOSES ARE BROKEN OFF, EVEN THE THOUGHTS OF MY HEART.

(12) "THEY CHANGE THE NIGHT INTO DAY: THE LIGHT IS SHORT BECAUSE OF DARKNESS.

(13) "IF I WAIT, THE GRAVE IS MY HOUSE: I HAVE MADE MY BED IN THE DARKNESS.

(14) "I HAVE SAID TO CORRUPTION, YOU ARE MY FATHER: TO THE WORM, YOU ARE MY MOTHER, AND MY SISTER.

(15) "AND WHERE IS NOW MY HOPE? AS FOR MY HOPE, WHO SHALL SEE IT?

(16) "THEY SHALL GO DOWN TO THE BARS OF THE PIT, WHEN OUR REST TOGETHER IS IN THE DUST."

The composition is:

1. Referring to Verse 8, Job is saying that even upright men, upon viewing his terrible plight, will be astonished and will surely think him guilty. Even the innocent (little children) will think he is a hypocrite. Perhaps this was the heaviest load of all to bear.

2. Verse 9 is uttered by Faith. Job will not allow these individuals, whoever they might be, to deter him from his hold on God, no matter how much they hurt. In fact, the accusations will only make his Faith stronger.

3. Verse 10 proclaims Job, in effect, saying that these *"friends"* can repeat their arguments as often as they wish; even so, not a wise word has yet been uttered, because it was not the Word of God.

4. Verse 12 proclaims the fact that doubt, unbelief, accusations, and condemnation, as offered by these *"friends,"* actually do the work of Satan.

5. Verse 13 proclaims the fact that if Job listens to these people, their words will kill him. Are our words to others a blessing or a curse?

6. (Vs. 15) Job's *"friends"* are saying that he has no hope in God. There is no greater sin that a person can commit than the sin of denying the hope of the Word of God to any individual.

WORDS AND WOUNDS

As we said under the last heading, Job's problem was not only physical, but, as well, the accusations of his *"friends,"* had crushed his spirit. To be frank, had not Job had a strong hold on the Lord, their words most definitely would have killed him.

What are we saying to others to help them along the way?

Are our words helping them or hurting them?

The crushing of one's spirit, which can easily be done with ill placed words, almost always comes from the world of self-righteousness. How many of us have been to the place at times, where we long for someone to say something kind to us? It's not a question of whether it's true or false, just because it's true, doesn't necessarily mean that it needs to be said. Giving a person hope can be done with words, and taking away hope can be done by words. Let us say it again:

If Job had not been totally consecrated to the Lord and, thereby, held a great relationship with the Lord, his friends would have killed him.

Solomon said: *"Pleasant words are as an honeycomb, sweet to the soul, and health to the bones"* (Prov. 16:24).

He also said: *"The words of a talebearer are as wounds, and they go down into the innermost parts of the belly"* (Prov. 18:8).

HOPE

The Patriarch asked the question, *"And where is now my hope? As for my hope, who shall see it?"*

As long as a person has hope, he also has

life. If hope is taken away, life is, as well, taken away.

As well, if our hope is in anything except Christ and what He has done for us at the Cross, which is the Word of God, then it's a fool's hope. If men hope in other men, disappointment will be the conclusion. If men hope in God, one way or the other, their hope is always realized.

Job was coming to the place that he was losing hope. He could see no way out of his dilemma. If he had some understanding as to why all of this was happening, perhaps he would have something on which to base hope. But he understands nothing, and then on top of all of that, his *"friends"* are busy biting him, so to speak, every opportunity they get.

Unfortunately, the self-righteous will do all within their power to try to steal one's hope. They deny God to the one whom they are attacking, they deny His Word to them, and they seem to delight in pronouncing destruction. It is only the Believer who has his hope in Christ and the Cross that can offer hope to others. Such a person, due to the Cross, understands himself. As well, he understands the Lord, at least as far as a poor human can understand Him. Also, he understands God's Word. Having a correct understanding of these things, such a person can offer hope, and the hope offered is that which is found in Christ and Christ Alone.

"When I consider the Works of Your
  Hands,
"The mountains innumerable, sovereignly stand,
"Against the horizon, the heavens
  above,
"Speak of Your infinite Mercy and
  Love."

"When I consider Your Own Holy Son,
"Who left Your Own Glory to die for
  this one,
"My heart starts to tremble, as clearly
  I see,
"He Who knew no sin became sin for
  me."

"Suffering terrors, His Life flowing
  down,
"A Man torn and broken, with thorns
  He was crowned,
"The darkness did gather, the veil it
  was rent,
"A cry 'it is finished,' my Lord's Life
  was spent."

"Laid in the tomb, wrapped in linen
  and myrrh,
"My Lord's Body stilled with my judgment incurred,
"Apart from the living, that I might
  not be,
"He, tasted that bitter cup and drank
  it for me."

"The third day He's risen, the stone
  rolled away.
"To His Throne He's ascended to live
  there alway.
"He's promised me one thing and thus
  it shall be,
"To take me to Glory His Own Face to
  see."

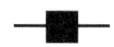

CHAPTER 18

(1) "THEN ANSWERED BILDAD THE SHUHITE, AND SAID,

(2) "HOW LONG WILL IT BE ERE YOU MAKE AN END OF WORDS? MARK, AND AFTERWARDS WE WILL SPEAK.

(3) "WHEREFORE ARE WE COUNTED AS BEASTS, AND REPUTED VILE IN YOUR SIGHT?

(4) "HE TEARS HIMSELF IN HIS ANGER: SHALL THE EARTH BE FORSAKEN FOR YOU? AND SHALL THE ROCK BE REMOVED OUT OF HIS PLACE?

(5) "YES, THE LIGHT OF THE WICKED SHALL BE PUT OUT, AND THE SPARK OF HIS FIRE SHALL NOT SHINE.

(6) "THE LIGHT SHALL BE DARK IN HIS TABERNACLE, AND HIS CANDLE SHALL BE PUT OUT WITH HIM.

(7) "THE STEPS OF HIS STRENGTH SHALL BE STRAITENED, AND HIS OWN COUNSEL SHALL CAST HIM DOWN.

(8) "FOR HE IS CAST INTO A NET BY HIS OWN FEET, AND HE WALKS UPON A SNARE.

(9) "THE GIN SHALL TAKE HIM BY THE HEEL, AND THE ROBBER SHALL PREVAIL AGAINST HIM.

(10) "THE SNARE IS LAID FOR HIM IN THE GROUND, AND A TRAP FOR HIM IN THE WAY."

The pattern is:

1. Multiple tens of millions the world over separate themselves and seek to learn the wisdom of the ages without the Bible. Such presents itself as a fruitless exercise.

2. The *"fool"* of Verse 2 is the one who constantly tries to find *"himself."* Proper *"understanding"* of oneself can only be found in the Bible.

3. The less one values the Bible, the less *"contempt"* one will have for the way of *"the wicked."*

4. The worldly wisdom of man is like a brackish pool that quickly dries up; however, for the man who knows and understands the Bible, his *"mouth"* will be as *"deep waters."*

5. The only correct *"judgment"* in the world is that which comes from *"the righteous."* Mostly, and with great loss, they are ignored.

6. Spiritually, the *"fool"* is the one who does not know the Bible; because of his lack of true knowledge, he will quickly find trouble. His *"mouth"* will guarantee his destruction.

7. A *"talebearer"* in this Passage is likened to a slanderer. His *"words"* are as morsels that go down into the heart of the listener and cause *"wounds."*

8. The *"great waster"* of Verse 9 is one who does not properly care for that which is entrusted to him.

9. The correct Spiritual Posture for the Christian is to fear Satan and in no way attempt to face him in one's own strength, but, instead, quickly run to Christ. Only there is one guaranteed safety.

THE FRUITLESS WISDOM OF THE WORLD

One may read these statements given by Bildad and conclude them to be correct. For instance, he says, *"Yes, the light of the wicked shall be put out and the spark of his fire shall not shine."*

NOTES

Yet, the Lord, when He finally did appear, said about Bildad, as well as all the other so-called friends of Job, *"You have not spoken of Me the thing that is right, as My servant Job has"* (Job 42:7).

The idea is this:

Bildad was actually making these statements about Job, saying that he was *"wicked,"* and that his *"light would be put out,"* etc.

Of course, Job was not wicked and, as well, his light would not be put out. In fact, at the end of this trial, his *"light"* would shine brighter than ever.

If one reads the Book of Job carefully, it very quickly comes to the surface that Job has a right relationship with God, while these *"friends"* don't! They have worldly wisdom, but that's all it is, worldly wisdom. Such cannot find out about God, cannot know God, cannot have any relationship with God. But regrettably, that's where most of the modern church is heading.

It is obvious that the world, and despite its lofty degrees, has no knowledge of the Lord whatsoever, which means that whatever knowledge they do have is faulty. Let us make it very clear, unless one knows the Lord and His Word, one cannot have true Wisdom, no matter the degrees he might have from prestigious universities. The Scripture plainly says, and rightly so:

"The fear of the LORD is the beginning of wisdom: a good understanding have all they who do His Commandments" (Ps. 111:10).

Even though all true Wisdom is found in the Bible, still, the unredeemed man, who is dead spiritually, cannot understand the Word of God, therefore, cannot understand its wisdom. Paul said and regarding this:

"But the natural man receives not the things of the Spirit of God (speaks of the individual who is not Born-Again)*: for they are foolishness unto him* (a lack of understanding)*: neither can he know them* (fallen man cannot understand Spiritual Truths), *because they are spiritually discerned* (only the regenerated spirit of man can understand the things of the Spirit)*"* (I Cor. 2:14).

The Apostle also said: *"Because the foolishness of God is wiser than men* (God achieves the mightiest ends by the humblest means)*; and the weakness of God is stronger than men* (refers to that which men take to be weak, but actually is not — the Cross).

"For you see your calling, brethren (refers to the nature and method of their Heavenly Calling), *how that not many wise men after the flesh, not many mighty, not many noble, are Called* (are Called and accept):

"But God has chosen the foolish things of the world to confound the wise (the preaching of the Cross confounds the wise because it falls out to changed lives, which nothing man has can do); *and God has chosen the weak things of the world to confound the things which are mighty* (the Cross is looked at as weakness, but it brings about great strength and power, regarding those who accept the Finished Work of Christ);

"And base things of the world, and things which are despised, has God chosen (it is God working in the base things and the despised things which brings about miraculous things), *yes, and things which are not, to bring to naught things that are* (God can use that which is nothing within itself, but with Him all things become possible):

"That no flesh (human effort) *should glory in His Presence.*

"But of Him are you in Christ Jesus (pertains to this great Plan of God, which is far beyond all wisdom of the world; we are *'in Christ Jesus,'* by virtue of the Cross — what He did there), *Who of God is made unto us Wisdom, and Righteousness, and Sanctification, and Redemption* (we have all of this by the Holy Spirit, through Christ and what He did at the Cross; this means the Cross must ever be the Object of our Faith):

"That, according as it is written (Jer. 9:23), *He who glories let him glory in the Lord.* (He who boasts, let him boast in the Lord, and not in particular preachers)" (I Cor. 1:25-31).

The great Apostle also said: *"But what things were gain to me* (Paul was speaking of his privileges as a Jew), *those I counted loss for Christ.* (All must be given up for Christ, and Christ is worth all we give up, and a thousand times more.)

"Yes doubtless, and I count all things but loss for the excellency of the knowledge of Christ Jesus my Lord (the knowledge of the Lord Jesus, which Paul gained through the experience of intimate companionship and communion with Him)*: for Whom I have suffered the loss of all things* (*'for Whose Sake I have been caused to forfeit'*), *and do count them but dung, that I may win Christ* (next to Christ, everything else is nothing)" (Phil. 3:7-8).

THE APOSTLE PAUL

Paul was one of the most educated men used of God to write the Sacred Text, which he did in his fourteen Epistles, almost half the New Testament. In fact, he was being groomed to take the place of the great Jewish teacher, Gamaliel (Acts 5:34). In other words, he would be the darling of the Pharisees.

Also, there are some who believe that he, as well, attended the University of Tarsus, which was noted to be one of the greatest in the world of its day. But, he renounced all of that in favor of Christ.

When he left Athens to come to Corinth, where the Holy Spirit had led him, there to plant a Church, it seems that his mind was troubled. Corinth had produced some of the greatest philosophers in the world and, as well, was one of the most jaded cities of vice found in the entirety of the Roman Empire. It had over 100 temples dedicated to Greek gods, staffed by hundreds, if not thousands, of both female and male prostitutes, which played their part in the worship of these paganistic gods. No doubt, the great Apostle wondered as to how he could break through this shell of heathenistic philosophy, and of heathenistic vice, a double-barreled effort of Satan, so to speak.

He had not had great success in Athens and he, no doubt, wondered as to how he could reach these Corinthians, especially as jaded and vice-ridden as they were.

As he was coming into Corinth quite possibly the Holy Spirit whispered to him, *"Preach the Cross!" "Preach the Cross!"*

And that's exactly what the great Apostle did.

While he could undoubtedly have addressed himself to philosophy, which was the rage of that particular time, still, he said in his first letter to the Corinthians, that is after the Church had been established, *"And I, brethren, when I came to you, came not with excellency of speech or with wisdom* (means that he depended not on oratorical abilities, nor did he delve into philosophy, which was all the rage of that particular day), *declaring unto you the Testimony of God* (which is Christ and Him Crucified).

"For I determined not to know anything among you (with purpose and design, Paul did not resort to the knowledge or philosophy of the world regarding the preaching of the Gospel), *save Jesus Christ and Him Crucified* (that and that alone is the Message, which will save the sinner, set the captive free, and give the Believer perpetual Victory).

"And I was with you in (personal) *weakness* (an expression of utter dependence on God), *and in fear* (fear that he might not properly preach the Cross), *and in much trembling.* (He realized the significance of what he was preaching, and his inadequacy regarding his own person.)

"And my speech and my preaching was not with enticing words of man's wisdom (he knew that would not set anyone free; the modern church should take a lesson from this), *but in demonstration of the Spirit and of Power* (which speaks of what the Holy Spirit can do in the hearts and lives of Believers, if the Cross is properly preached)*:*

"That your Faith should not stand in the wisdom of men (speaks of any proposed way other than the Cross), *but in the Power of God* (made possible only by the Cross).

"Howbeit we speak wisdom among them who are perfect (only the spiritually mature can understand the Wisdom of God, which is the Cross)*: yet not the wisdom of this world* (the Wisdom of God pertaining to Salvation has absolutely no relationship whatsoever to the *'wisdom of this world'*), *nor of the princes of this world, that come to naught* (the great Sages and Philosophers of the world contributed nothing to Paul, nor do they to us as well)*:*

"But we speak the Wisdom of God in a mystery, even the hidden wisdom (God's Wisdom leads sinful men to the great Sacrifice of history, the offering up of Jesus on the Cross of Calvary, which paid the terrible sin debt of man, at least for all who will believe), *which God ordained before the world unto our glory* (in the Mind of God, Christ was offered up on the Cross even before the foundation of the world)*"* (I Cor. 2:1-7).

THE PREACHING OF THE CROSS

Why did Paul say, *"For I determined not to know anything among you, save Jesus Christ and Him Crucified"* (I Cor. 2:2)?

Actually, the answer to that is very simple. The great Apostle knew that the only hope of man, and irrespective as to who the man might be, is Jesus Christ and what He did for us at the Cross.

Since we started preaching the Cross, in essence, teaching and preaching the Revelation which the Lord gave us in 1997, I have been appalled at the ignorance represented in the Christian community, regarding this all-important subject.

To address the lesser of the two evils first, some people think that we're talking about the wooden beam on which Jesus died. Let it be understood, that this wooden beam, i.e., *"the Cross,"* on which Jesus died, contained no power whatsoever. In fact, if the actual Cross was found somehow to have survived, and it could be proven to be the real item, it would have no more power than another piece of wood. This means, that people wearing crosses around their necks as charms or amulets, or anything of this nature, contains no properties of help whatsoever. The wooden beam, on which Jesus died, just happened to be the instrument used by God. It had absolutely nothing to do with what was there done.

SUFFERING

The real culprit, as it regards the Cross, is that people think when the Cross is mentioned, that we are speaking of suffering. In other words, the more the individual suffers, and in whatever capacity, this, they think, is *"bearing the Cross."*

Please understand, while Jesus most definitely suffered on the Cross, and did it for you and me, the Cross of Christ within itself, has absolutely nothing to do with the Believer suffering. For a Christian to think that, they are actually saying, whether they understand it or not, that what Jesus did at the Cross is not sufficient, and that we have to add our suffering to His suffering. Not so!

While it is definitely true that at times Believers do suffer, and for whatever reason, it has absolutely nothing to do with the Cross of Christ. So, the Believer should get it out of his or her mind that the Cross of Christ is somehow connected with our suffering and our suffering is somehow connected with the Cross. In fact, that's one of the reasons that most Christians don't know anything about the Cross, and are not interested too very much in finding out anything about it. And if I believed what they did, I would feel the same way.

WHAT DOES THE CROSS ACTUALLY MEAN?

The Apostle Paul, to whom the meaning of the New Covenant was given (Gal. 1:12), used the term *"the Cross,"* to explain the entire embodiment of New Testament Christianity, and a fulfillment of the Old. In fact, several words are used in this capacity, such as *"the Faith,"* or *"the Way,"* or *"the Cross!"* (I Cor. 1:17-18; Gal. 6:14). Other Passages say the same thing, without actually using the term *"the Cross"* (I Cor. 1:21, 23; 2:2).

It is what Jesus accomplished on the Cross by the giving of Himself in Sacrifice, which proclaims what this Message of the Cross is all about.

On the Cross our Lord atoned for all sin, past, present, and future, at least for all who will believe (Jn. 3:16). In atoning for all sin, this lifted the sin debt that hung over the entirety of the human race, as well, for all who would believe. This made it possible for the Holy Spirit to come into the heart and life of the Believer and to abide there permanently (Jn. 14:16).

With all sin atoned, i.e., the sin debt lifted, once again for all who will believe, this took away Satan's legal right to hold man captive. That's the reason that we are to look to Christ exclusively, and what He did for us at the Cross, placing our Faith entirely in Him and His Finished Work, which then grants us the great Victory that He purchased for us. In fact, we are to understand, that every victory that we have, in fact, everything we receive from the Lord Jesus Christ is the Source of all these things, while the Cross is the Means by which it was and is given to us, all superintended by the Holy Spirit (Rom. 6:1-14; 8:1-2, 11).

What the church must understand is, the Cross of Christ, as we have already stated, is the means by which all of the Blessings of God come to us. This demands that our Faith be exclusively in Christ and the Cross (Rom. 6:1-14; 8:1-2, 11; Eph. 2:13-18; Col. 2:14-15). This is the reason that we keep saying that the Cross of Christ must ever be the Object of our Faith. This is what the Apostle Paul taught (Gal. 2:20-21; 5:6).

THE GREAT STRUGGLE

This is where the great struggle commences, the battle between the flesh and the Spirit, the struggle between the carnal nature and the Divine Nature. Paul used the term *"flesh,"* to describe this, and did so constantly (Rom. 8:1, 8).

When Paul used the term *"flesh,"* he was speaking of human ability, human talent, human power, human motivation, human intellect, human education, etc. Now these things within themselves aren't necessarily wrong; however, where the wrong comes in is when we place our Faith in those things, which automatically brings about defeat. The Holy Spirit wants us to place our faith exclusively in Christ and what He did for us at the Cross. But inasmuch as we are human beings, there is something in us that automatically wants to resort to the flesh, i.e., human ability.

Why is it that the Lord doesn't want us to do this?

The Apostle said: *"So then they who are in the flesh cannot please God"* (Rom. 8:8).

So, once again, why cannot we please God by the use of our own ability, talent, education, etc.?

The following will tell us why!

THE BODY IS DEAD BECAUSE OF SIN

The great Apostle said, *"And if Christ be in you* (He is in you through the Power and Person of the Spirit [Gal. 2:20]), *the body is dead because of sin* (means that the physical body has been rendered helpless because of the Fall; consequently, the Believer trying to overcome by willpower presents a fruitless task); *but the Spirit is life because of Righteousness* (only the Holy Spirit can make us what we ought to be, which means we cannot do it ourselves; once again, He performs all that He does within the confines of the Finished Work of Christ)" (Rom. 8:10).

What did the Apostle mean by the statement, *"the body is dead because of sin."*

He is speaking of the physical body with its attributes, talents, and compliments, whatever they might be.

When he said that it is *"dead,"* he is meaning that because of the Fall in the Garden of Eden with our First Parents, the physical body was rendered helpless. The reason is because of *"sin."*

The word *"sin"* in this Tenth Verse is a noun instead of a verb, so in actuality, it refers to the sin nature. It means that the very nature of the human being became that of sin, because of the Fall. This means that every action, every direction, every thought, is tainted by sin in such an individual.

When the believing sinner comes to Christ the sin nature is automatically made dormant. It is not removed, but rather made ineffective. It is like an electric appliance that is unplugged. It is supposed to remain that way, but unfortunately it never does.

When the new convert sins, as all of us have done, the shocking realization of such demands attention by the Believer, with every effort being made that this act not be repeated. Not understanding the Cross, every single time, the person in some way will resort to the flesh. This refers to his own efforts and ability to try to overcome sin. He fails as fail he must.

While the sin itself does not occasion a revival of the sin nature, the placing of one's faith in something other than the Cross of Christ most definitely does. Here is what happens!

When the Believer resorts to the flesh, which refers to the manner in which one attempts to live for God, this greatly limits the Holy Spirit. In fact, such a person is actually living in a state of spiritual adultery (Rom. 7:1-5). This means they are looking to something other than Christ and His

NOTES

Cross to bring about victorious living. Such a direction guarantees continued failure, with the sin nature once again beginning to rule the Child of God.

The only answer for the sin nature is the Cross of Christ, and our Faith in that Finished Work.

WHAT IS THE SIN NATURE?

As we've already explained, the sin nature is what developed in the heart and life of Adam and Eve upon their failure, i.e., *"their disobedience of the Word of God."* Their entire nature became that of sin. Where the Divine Nature ruled them before the Fall, now they are ruled by the sin nature, which occasions every type of perversion, transgression, man's inhumanity to man, etc.

Due to the Fall, Adam and Eve could not bring sons and daughters of God into the world, thereby condemned to bring sons and daughters in the likeness of Adam into the world, meaning, that the sin nature of Adam passed down to all who have followed thereafter, which includes every single person who has ever lived, with the exception of the Lord Jesus Christ. His conception was in a Virgin, who was Mary, which means that He was not born with a sin nature.

The only way the Christian can have Victory over the sin nature, is by us placing our Faith exclusively in Christ and what He did for us at the Cross, and doing so on a constant basis (Lk. 9:23; 14:27).

Even then, it's not going to be easy. This is the reason that the only hope the Believer has is the Cross of Christ. Due to the Fall, man is so hopelessly messed up, so to speak, that unfortunately, the clinging vines of the Fall continue to attach themselves to us even after we have come to Christ, and have been Spirit-filled.

What God demands of us, with such a direction given in the Ten Commandments, the human being, at least within ourselves, simply cannot accomplish.

THE SPIRIT OF GOD

Paul also said, in answer to the sin nature, *"But the Spirit is Life because of Righteousness."* In other words, the only way that we as a Believer are going to have Righteousness within our hearts and lives, is by and through the Work of the Holy Spirit. All *"life"* flows from Christ, but through the Spirit. As well, the Holy Spirit works exclusively within the capacity of the Finished Work of Christ and, in fact, will function in no other manner. It is what Christ did at the Cross which gives the Holy Spirit the latitude that He has, in other words, the legal means to do all that He does (Rom. 8:2).

So, whatever it is we need to be in the Lord, and I refer to Righteousness, Holiness, the Fruit of the Spirit, Victory over the world, the flesh, and the Devil, can only be brought about in our lives, not at all by the flesh, but only by and through the Holy Spirit. We must understand that! We must get that in our minds! What needs to be done, we simply cannot do it, and irrespective as to how hard we try.

Some have contended that the word *"Spirit"* used in this Tenth Verse pertains to the human spirit. I do not think so, and because the Eleventh Verse is speaking of the Holy Spirit, and that is undeniable. If it is the Holy Spirit in Verse 11, then it is the Holy Spirit, as well, in Verse 10.

For instance, it is the Holy Spirit Who *"quickens our mortal bodies."* What is meant by that?

As Paul has already told us in the Tenth Verse, the physical body is rendered ineffective because of sin. Then Paul tells us that it can be *"quickened"* by the Holy Spirit, which means to be made alive. In other words, what we need to do in our physical body, which refers to conducting ourselves morally and righteously, can only be done by the Power of the Holy Spirit.

HOW DOES THE HOLY SPIRIT QUICKEN OUR MORTAL BODY?

Most Believers do not have the foggiest idea as to how the Holy Spirit works within our hearts and lives. And let me say this first of all:

We believe and teach from the Word of God that the Baptism with the Holy Spirit is a distinct Work separate and apart from Salvation. The receiving of this experience, which is always and without exception, accompanied by the speaking with other Tongues, does not, however, make one more Saved. Whenever one comes to Christ, one is as Saved as one will ever be. Justification by Faith cannot be improved upon. The Baptism with the Spirit is given to us as a source of Power and, as well, opens up our heart to the Leading and Guidance of the Holy Spirit in all things. Let the following be understood:

If our Lord, God manifest in the flesh, needed the Holy Spirit in His earthly Ministry, and He most definitely did, then don't you think that we need Him also (Lk. 4:18)?

However, the Baptism with the Holy Spirit, with the evidence of speaking with other Tongues, within itself, will not give the individual Victory over sin. That is not His Place and Position. The sin matter was handled exclusively at the Cross. While the Holy Spirit will help us in all things, and that includes Victory over sin, He does so only by and through the Sacrifice of Christ. While we've already quoted the following in this Volume, due to the seriousness of the matter, please allow us the latitude of doing so again.

The great Apostle said in connection with the Holy Spirit and how He works: *"For the Law* (that which we are about to give is a Law of God, devised by the Godhead in eternity past [1 Pet. 1:18-20]; this Law, in fact, is *'God's Prescribed Order of Victory'*) *of the Spirit* (Holy Spirit, i.e., *'the way the Spirit works'*) *of Life* (all life comes from Christ, but through the Holy Spirit [Jn. 16:13-14]) *in Christ Jesus* (any time Paul uses this term or one of its derivatives, he is, without fail, referring to what Christ did at the Cross, which makes this *'life'* possible) *has made me free* (given me total Victory) *from the Law of Sin and Death* (these are the two most powerful Laws in the Universe; the *'Law of the Spirit of Life in Christ Jesus'* alone is stronger than the *'Law of Sin and Death'*; this means that if the Believer attempts to live for God by any manner other than Faith in Christ and the Cross, he is doomed to failure)" (Rom. 8:2).

Whenever we as Believers place our faith exclusively in Christ and what Christ did for us at the Cross, and not allow it to be moved to other things, in other words, not making other things the object of our faith, the Holy Spirit Who works exclusively within the parameters of the Finished Work of Christ, will then begin to function in our physical bodies, enabling us to do the things we ought to do, and in the way they ought to be done. In other words, He will help us to obey God. However, when we place our Faith in something other than the Cross of Christ, this constitutes spiritual adultery, and greatly hinders the Holy Spirit (Rom. 7:1-5). Thankfully, the Holy Spirit doesn't leave us, and thank God a million times over He doesn't, still, He is greatly hindered. In other words, we take the matter out of His Hands, which, in effect, nullifies all that Christ has done for us at the Cross.

THE SUBJECT OF WILLPOWER

Most Christians not knowing or understanding how the Holy Spirit works, in other words, that He works exclusively by and through the Cross of Christ, somehow thinks that when they come to Christ, that the Lord greatly strengthens their willpower. As one man told me the other day, *"When I was unsaved, I couldn't say no to drugs, now I can."*

No he can't!

If one tries to live for God in that manner, which regrettably is the manner in which most modern Believers are attempting to live for God, failure is the inevitable result.

While the willpower is important, *"whosoever will . . ."* still, that is not the manner in which one lives for God and overcomes sin. Listen again to Paul:

"For I know that in me, (that is, in my flesh,) dwells no good thing (speaks of man's own ability, or rather the lack thereof in comparison to the Holy Spirit, at least when it comes to spiritual things)*: for to will is present with me* (Paul is speaking here of his willpower; regrettably, most modern Christians are trying to live for God by means of willpower, thinking falsely that since they have come to Christ, they are now free to say *'no'* to sin; that is the wrong way to look at the situation; the Believer cannot live for God by the strength of willpower; while the will is definitely important, it alone is not enough; the Believer must exercise Faith in Christ and the Cross, and do so constantly; then he will have the ability and strength to say *'yes'* to Christ, which automatically says, *'no'* to the things of the world)*; but how to perform that which is good I find not* (outside of the Cross, it is impossible to find a way to do good)" (Rom. 7:18).

Sadly, most modern Christians are attempting to live for God by the means of willpower alone. It cannot be done!

Paul also said: *"If Righteousness come by the Law, then Christ is dead in vain"* (Gal. 2:21).

In other words, if we could live this life by the means of willpower, then Christ didn't need to come down here and die on a Cross. All He needed to have done was to give us a little more power regarding the will, and the task would be accomplished. As we have stated, while the will is definitely important, it is important only in the capacity in which the Lord originally gave it.

The *"will"* is to be used in that our desire is that we have the things of God. We *"will"* to please Him! We *"will"* to live the life He wants us to live!

The *"desire"* is as far as it goes. The Holy Spirit has to take over thereafter, and in doing so, He *"quickens our mortal bodies,"* which means that He gives us the necessary strength to do what we need to do and be what we need to be. But always remember, He does this strictly through what Christ has done for us at the Cross, which demands that the Cross of Christ ever be the Object of our Faith (Rom. 6:1-14; I Cor. 1:17-18, 23; 2:2; Gal., Chpt. 5; 6:14; Eph. 2:13-18; Col. 2:14-15).

(11) "TERRORS SHALL MAKE HIM AFRAID ON EVERY SIDE, AND SHALL DRIVE HIM TO HIS FEET.

(12) "HIS STRENGTH SHALL BE HUNGERBITTEN, AND DESTRUCTION SHALL BE READY AT HIS SIDE.

(13) "IT SHALL DEVOUR THE STRENGTH OF HIS SKIN: EVEN THE FIRSTBORN OF DEATH SHALL DEVOUR HIS STRENGTH.

(14) "HIS CONFIDENCE SHALL BE ROOTED OUT OF HIS TABERNACLE, AND IT SHALL BRING HIM TO THE KING OF TERRORS.

(15) "IT SHALL DWELL IN HIS TABERNACLE, BECAUSE IT IS NONE OF HIS: BRIMSTONE SHALL BE SCATTERED UPON HIS HABITATION.

(16) "HIS ROOTS SHALL BE DRIED UP BENEATH, AND ABOVE SHALL HIS BRANCH BE CUT OFF.

(17) "HIS REMEMBRANCE SHALL PERISH FROM THE EARTH, AND HE SHALL HAVE NO NAME IN THE STREET.

(18) "HE SHALL BE DRIVEN FROM LIGHT INTO DARKNESS, AND CHASED OUT OF THE WORLD.

(19) "HE SHALL NEITHER HAVE SON NOR NEPHEW AMONG HIS PEOPLE, NOR ANY REMAINING IN HIS DWELLINGS.

(20) "THEY WHO COME AFTER HIM SHALL BE ASTONISHED AT HIS DAY, AS THEY WHO WENT BEFORE WERE AFFRIGHTED.

(21) "SURELY SUCH ARE THE DWELLINGS OF THE WICKED, AND THIS IS THE PLACE OF HIM WHO KNOWS NOT GOD."

The exegesis is:

1. (Vs. 13) Imagine how Job must have felt listening to all of this, and because it is actually being directed to him. In other words, the statements of Bildad were personal.

2. (Vs. 17) Bildad said that Job's remembrance would perish from the Earth; however, the truth is, Job not only has not been forgotten, but, to the contrary. Few men on the face of the Earth, and through all time, have been remembered as Job is remembered, because he placed his trust and Faith in God, and not in man.

3. (Vs. 17) Bildad also stated that Job's name would be forgotten. To the contrary, Job's name is famous, because it is linked to patience, Faith, and trust in God. He is looked to as an example by every single person who has ever had to undergo a trial of any nature — and that includes the entirety of the human race.

4. (Vs. 19) Quite the contrary to him having no son or nephew to continue his name, the Lord gave him *"seven more sons and three more daughters"* (42:13).

5. (Vs. 21) How difficult it must have been for Job, especially in his weakened condition, to hear his *"friend"* say to him that he did not know God. The only thing that a man really has is his Faith. And now all will deny that Faith. Thankfully, even though they tried, Job never lost his Faith.

THE REASONING OF THE HOLY SPIRIT

Of course, all the reasons the Holy Spirit had for including these speeches by these individuals, irrespective that everything they said was wrong, is, I think, in order that we may understand, as previously stated, that the wisdom of this world is of no consequence. And the worst spectacle of all, is religious individuals using the wisdom of the world, thinking it is God. And that's what we have in these three *"friends"* and, no doubt, all others who had congregated to make fun of Job, which the Bible does not address.

What greater evidence could it be concerning the futility of such an effort as this provided in the Holy Scriptures as it regards Job and his three friends? All of their pontificating, and we speak of the *"friends,"* was against Job, which is the tact that self-righteousness always takes.

While Job had no idea as to the cause of his predicament, to be sure, they knew exactly the reason why, or at least so they thought! They had an answer for everything, and they felt very free to pontificate on any and every subject.

Yet, while the lesson is so very clear before us as it regards this great Book of Job, regrettably, the majority of the modern church little heeds the lessons here taught. Perhaps to fully understand it, one has to have at least a modicum of experience similar to that of Job.

"The Cross it stands fast,
"Hallelujah, hallelujah!
"Defying every blast,
"Hallelujah, hallelujah!
"The winds of Hell have blown,
"The world its hate has shown,
"Yet it is not overthrown,
"Hallelujah, for the Cross!"

"It is the old Cross still,
"Hallelujah, hallelujah!
"Its triumph let us tell,
"Hallelujah, hallelujah!
"The Grace of God here shown,

"Through Christ the blessed Son,
"Who did for sin atone,
"Hallelujah for the Cross!"

"'Twas here the debt was paid,
"Hallelujah, hallelujah!
"Our sins on Jesus laid,
"Hallelujah, hallelujah!
"So round the Cross we sing,
"Of Christ our offering,
"Of Christ our Living King,
"Hallelujah for the Cross!"

CHAPTER 19

(1) "THEN JOB ANSWERED AND SAID,

(2) "HOW LONG WILL YOU VEX MY SOUL, AND BREAK ME IN PIECES WITH WORDS?

(3) "THESE TEN TIMES HAVE YOU REPROACHED ME: YOU ARE NOT ASHAMED THAT YOU MAKE YOURSELVES STRANGE TO ME.

(4) "AND BE IT INDEED THAT I HAVE ERRED, MY ERROR REMAINS WITH MYSELF.

(5) "IF INDEED YOU WILL MAGNIFY YOURSELVES AGAINST ME, AND PLEAD AGAINST ME MY REPROACH:

(6) "KNOW NOW THAT GOD HAS OVERTHROWN ME, AND HAS COMPASSED ME WITH HIS NET.

(7) "BEHOLD, I CRY OUT OF WRONG, BUT I AM NOT HEARD: I CRY ALOUD, BUT THERE IS NO JUDGMENT.

(8) "HE HAS FENCED UP MY WAY THAT I CANNOT PASS, AND HE HAS SET DARKNESS IN MY PATHS.

(9) "HE HAS STRIPPED ME OF MY GLORY, AND TAKEN THE CROWN FROM MY HEAD.

(10) "HE HAS DESTROYED ME ON EVERY SIDE, AND I AM GONE: AND MY HOPE HAS HE REMOVED LIKE A TREE.

(11) "HE HAS ALSO KINDLED HIS WRATH AGAINST ME, AND HE COUNTED ME UNTO HIM AS ONE OF HIS ENEMIES.

(12) "HIS TROOPS COME TOGETHER, AND RAISE UP THEIR WAY AGAINST ME, AND ENCAMP ROUND ABOUT MY TABERNACLE."

The pattern is:

1. Verse 2 proclaims the fact that the accusations and condemnation of his *"friends"* only added to his hurt.

2. Job's statement of Verse 3 concerning *"ten times,"* must be a figurative expression, meaning a number of times, for literally they have not answered him ten times.

3. (Vs. 6) Bildad insinuates that Job has fallen into his own snare (18:7-9). Job replies that the snare in which he is taken is from God, and in that he was right.

4. (Vs. 7) Up to now, all Job's appeals to God have elicited no reply from Him.

5. (Vs. 8) Nothing vexes him so much as his inability to understand why he is so afflicted.

6. (Vs. 11) The actual afflictions take second place to the cause of why he is afflicted, which he thinks is the wrath of God; it isn't!

WHY HAS THE LORD DONE THIS?

Basically, everything that Job says here about the Lord is correct. He reasons that no force in the world could bring this upon him except God. He is not perplexed or confused as to the source. Where his contention is, is why the Lord has done this. Job cannot know, at least at this stage, as to the magnitude of what has happened and is happening to him. He doesn't realize at this time that the great lesson being taught, pertains to our Sanctification, and will show mankind for ages to come, that even one as consecrated to the Lord as was Job, cannot sanctify himself. And this is the mystery of this Book, as to why the Lord would choose the most perfect man on Earth, the most consecrated man on Earth, to teach this invaluable lesson. Once we come to an understanding as to what the Lord is saying and doing, we then understand that it had to be a man of Job's caliber to properly teach this great lesson.

The Sanctification of the Saint, which is the first subject taken up in the Bible, continues to be a mystery unto this hour. We keep thinking that we can sanctify ourselves, and do so by religious works. It's very difficult for us to come to the place that we understand that all that we do, all of our consecration, all of our love for God, as pure as it might be, cannot bring about that which is needed within our hearts and lives. The Holy Spirit Alone can accomplish this, and sometimes, even as Job, we have to be brought to a place to where it seems all hope is gone before we will turn loose and place our Faith fully and solely in Christ, and what He has done for us at the Cross.

SANCTIFICATION

Sanctification, in its most simple form, means that one is set apart exclusively for the Lord. That within itself is not a difficult thing to understand. Every good Christian wants this. Yet, we try to bring it about in all the wrong ways. We do good things, and then more good things, and we think fully that this will bring about that which is desired. It's hard for us to learn that it won't. The history of God working with His People is replete with these conclusions.

It took Abraham some 25 years before he and Sarah finally learned God's Way. It took Moses 40 years, 40 years at the back side of a desert, 40 years of asking the question *"why?"* 40 years of loneliness, before he was finally ready to do what God wanted. It took the great Apostle Paul any number of years, with him finally saying, *"O wretched man that I am! Who shall deliver me from the body of this death?"* (Rom. 7:24). The flesh dies hard, and it dies slowly. We cover it over with religious favor, and we think surely this is exactly what the Lord desires. It's hard for us to come to the place that we fully understand that He cannot accept anything of the flesh. Why?

Despite being Born-Again, despite becoming a new creation in Christ Jesus, despite former things passing away and all things becoming new, despite us being an heir of God, and joint heir with Jesus Christ, still, God cannot use anything that we can produce, that is, by the means of the flesh, i.e., *"our own ingenuity."*

A NEW TESTAMENT EXAMPLE

Just days before the Crucifixion, Jesus came to Bethany the home of Simon the leper, and his two sisters, Mary and Martha.

NOTES

The Scripture says:

"And being in Bethany (a small village, actually a suburb of Jerusalem, to the east of the city) *in the house of Simon the leper* (a man whom Jesus had healed), *as he sat at meat, there came a woman* (probably refers to Mary, the sister of Lazarus [Jn. 11:1-2]) *having an alabaster box of ointment of spikenard very precious* (the Greek word, *'pistikos,'* is used, meaning that it was genuine, not imitation or adulterated; it was very costly); *and she broke the box, and poured it on His head* (she broke the seal that kept the fragrance preserved; the pouring upon Him, spoke of her anointing Him for His Burial; anointing Him now, which was generally done after death, testified to her belief in the Resurrection; she seems to have been the only one who did believe in His Resurrection before the fact).

"And there were some who had indignation within themselves (pertained to some, if not all, of the Disciples but with Judas Iscariot taking the lead), *and said, Why was this waste of the anointment made?* (It is believed by some that this ointment would have been worth about $12,000 in 2008 currency. The truth is, nothing given to Christ is wasted, while much of the world's resources used otherwise are, in fact, wasted.)

"For it might have been sold for more than 300 pence, and have been given to the poor (originated with Judas [Jn. 12:4-6]; he probably had other things in mind, such as stealing it). *And they murmured against her* (no case of murmuring has ever been justified or sanctioned by God in Scripture regardless of how right the cause; and to make matters worse, this cause wasn't right).

"And Jesus said, Let her alone (it appears from Jn. 12:7 that Jesus here addressed Himself pointedly to Judas); *why trouble ye her?* (Concerns the murmuring.) *she has wrought a good work on Me* (even though they didn't understand it, her actions showed her Faith in His Resurrection).

"For you have the poor with you always (regrettably, portrays a condition resulting from the Fall in the Garden of Eden), *and whensoever you will you may do them good* (the two, Himself and the poor, are equivalent in His Sight [Mat. 25:40-45]): *but Me*

you have not always (speaking of His present position, which was soon to change).

"*She has done what she could* (she had been moved by the Holy Spirit to do this)*: she is come aforehand to anoint My Body to the burying* (His Body had been prepared by God for Sacrifice [Heb. 10:5]).

"*Verily I say unto you, Wheresoever this Gospel shall be preached throughout the whole world* (a prediction that it would go throughout the whole world, which it has), *this also that she has done shall be spoken of for a memorial of her* (this act is connected with her and will never be forgotten)" (Mk. 14:3-9).

The idea of all of this is, this *"box of anointment"* very precious, is symbolic of Believers. But, for this ointment to serve its purpose, the box had to be broken. Likewise, for us to be what we ought to be in Christ, to honor Him even as did Mary, we must be broken. It's not a simple process, and it will be criticized by others. But if we are to be of value to the Kingdom of God, it must be. This is the only way that God can use us.

It refers to the flesh being broken, where Christ can become all in all.

ANOTHER EXAMPLE

This concerns Jesus feeding the five thousand men, beside the women and children, with five loaves and two fishes. The Scripture says:

"*And they say unto Him, We have here but five loaves, and two fishes* (little is much if God be in it!).

"*He said, Bring them hither to Me* (the secret is Christ! we are to bring what little to Him).

"*And He commanded the multitude to sit down on the grass* (this presents order and a method by which the distribution was made)*, and took the five loaves and the two fishes, and looking up to Heaven, He blessed, and break, and gave the loaves to His Disciples, and the Disciples to the multitude*" (Mat. 14:17-19).

The order is this:

• He took the five loaves: this symbolizes Him taking you and me from the field of sin.

• He blessed the five loaves: when we come to Christ, Blessings generally follow and in great abundance.

• He then broke the loaves: the blessing is followed by the breaking. This means that the Believer must be broken.

• And then He gave the loaves to His Disciples, and the Disciples to the multitude. Before we can properly be given to others, we must first be broken. The blight on the modern church is us being given to the world without first being broken. All of this, one might say, stems back to Job.

Job didn't think that he needed breaking, but the results were that he did.

All of us like the blessing. None of us like the breaking. But if the blessing is to continue, the breaking must take place.

HOW DOES THE BREAKING COME ABOUT?

It is possible by only one manner, and that is the Cross. The Cross must be the Object of our Faith, for in reality, this is a work of Faith. We must come to the place, and sometimes that place is not easy to arrive at. The Cross of Christ is the goal and, in fact, Jesus said if this wasn't done, then we could not be His Disciple (Lk. 14:27).

The Cross is not the problem, not at all! The problem is our coming to the Cross, making it the sole Object of our Faith. This means that all the schemes and plans of religious men have to go. Denominationalism is gone! Our own efforts at holiness must be laid aside. Our Faith must be placed totally and completely in Christ and the Cross, never allowing it to depart from that Object, which alone will bring us to the place desired by the Lord. Let us say it again:

It's not the Cross that's the problem, the flesh is the problem. It has to be broken, and that process, as stated, is not cheap, nor speedy.

THE FIERY TRIAL

Peter said: "*Beloved, think it not strange concerning the fiery trial which is to try you* (trials do not merely happen; they are designed by wisdom and operated by love; Job proved this), *as though some strange thing happened unto you* (your trial, whatever it is, is not unique; many others are experiencing the same thing!)*:*

"But rejoice (despite the trial), *inasmuch as you are partakers of Christ's sufferings* (refers to suffering for Righteousness' sake); *that, when His Glory shall be revealed* (refers to His Second Coming), *you may be glad also with exceeding joy.* (There will be great joy in the heart of every Saint when we come back with the Lord at the Second Coming)" (I Pet. 4:12-13).

So it's not to be misunderstood, let's say it again:

The Cross itself is not the affliction. It's what it takes to get us there that portrays the affliction. As we have stated, the flesh dies hard. A perfect example is Abraham as it regards Ishmael.

ABRAHAM AND ISHMAEL

George Williams the English Preacher has an excellent statement regarding Abraham and Ishmael. He said, and I quote:

"The affect of the birth of Isaac was to make manifest the character of Ishmael. Ishmael hated him, and so did his mother. Prompted by her, he sought to murder Isaac (Gal. 4:29), *and with his mother was justly expelled. Both merited the severer sentence of death. Thus, the birth of Isaac, which filled Sarah's heart with mirth, filled Hagar's with murder.*

"Isaac and Ishmael symbolized the new and the old nature in the Believer. Sarah and Hagar typified the two covenants of works and Grace, of bondage and liberty (Gal. 4). *The birth of the new nature demands the expulsion of the old. It is impossible to improve the old nature. The Holy Spirit says in Romans 8 that 'it is enmity against God that it is not subject to the Law of God, neither indeed can be.' If, therefore, it cannot be subject to the Law of God, how can it be improved? How foolish, therefore, appears the doctrine of moral evolution! The Divine way of Holiness is to 'put off the old man' just as Abraham 'put off' Ishmael. Man's way of Holiness is to improve the 'old man,' that is, to improve Ishmael. The effort is both foolish and hopeless. Of course, the casting out of Ishmael was 'very grievous in Abraham's sight,' because it always costs a struggle to cast*

NOTES

out this element of bondage, that is, Salvation by works. For legalism is dear to the heart. Ishmael was the fruit, and to Abraham the fair fruit of his own energy and planning. But the Epistle to the Galatians states that Hagar, the bondwoman, represents the covenant of the Law, and that her son represents all who are of 'works of law,' that is, of all who seek, righteousness on the principle of works of righteousness. But the bondwoman cannot bring forth a free man! The Son alone makes free, and He makes free indeed. Sarah, the free-woman, symbolizes the covenant of grace and liberty. 'So then, we are not children of the bondwoman but of the free.'"[1]

(13) "HE HAS PUT MY BRETHREN FAR FROM ME, AND MY ACQUAINTANCE ARE VERILY ESTRANGED FROM ME.

(14) "MY KINSFOLK HAVE FAILED, AND MY FAMILIAR FRIENDS HAVE FORGOTTEN ME.

(15) "THEY WHO DWELL IN MY HOUSE, AND MY MAIDS, COUNT ME FOR A STRANGER: I AM AN ALIEN IN THEIR SIGHT.

(16) "I CALLED MY SERVANT, AND HE GAVE ME NO ANSWER; I INTREATED HIM WITH MY MOUTH.

(17) "MY BREATH IS STRANGE TO MY WIFE, THOUGH I INTREATED FOR THE CHILDREN'S SAKE OF MY OWN BODY.

(18) "YEA, YOUNG CHILDREN DESPISED ME; I AROSE, AND THEY SPOKE AGAINST ME.

(19) "ALL MY INWARD FRIENDS ABHORRED ME: AND THEY WHOM I LOVED ARE TURNED AGAINST ME.

(20) "MY BONE CLEAVES TO MY SKIN AND TO MY FLESH, AND I AM ESCAPED WITH THE SKIN OF MY TEETH."

The composition is:

1. (Vs. 13) Job had actual *"brothers"* (42:11), who forsook him and, *"dealt deceitfully"* with him (6:15) during the time of his adversity.

2. (Vs. 14) No one wanted to have anything to do with Job, neither his relatives, nor even his friends. In their thinking he was surely under the Judgment of God and, consequently, had done terrible things; therefore, they too joined in with accusations.

3. (Vs. 15) All, his kinfolk and even his servants, condemned him. There was not one person who stood up for him except God. What a lesson for us when we begin to judge others, especially of things that we know little or nothing about.

4. For a servant to ignore the entreaty of his master, as given in Verse 16, in eastern culture, is the worst of all insults.

5. His own wife turned against him. The last phrase of Verse 17 either speaks of his children who are now dead, or else, as some Scholars claim, his personal brothers and sisters, who also turned against him.

6. (Vs. 18) Young children, no doubt, had heard their parents speak against Job, so they followed suit.

THE MAJORITY AREN'T ALWAYS RIGHT

Evidently taking a cue from Job's *"three friends,"* all concerned felt free to voice their disapproval of the great Patriarch. Everyone, it seems, knew exactly as to why God was punishing Job. Evidently he had been a great sinner, and now he was reaping what he had sown.

Even those of menial status, such as the servants, even the little children, felt free to condemn Job, and to make fun of him. Why not, if God had turned against him, well then they felt perfectly free to do so as well.

As far as the Scripture portrays, not one single person stood up for Job. Not one individual whom he had befriended and helped, and he, no doubt, had helped scores, stood up for him at that time. What a terrible indictment of the human race! But again, this is the fruit of self-righteousness.

This was perhaps the unkindest cut of all! For one's relatives and close loved ones, even the closest of friends, to turn against one, breaks the heart more than anything.

Someone has said, *"That a man's friends are often such because of what he can do for them or to them."* This means that they aren't really friends at all.

All of these people, no doubt, thought that inasmuch as God had turned against Job, that they would be going against the wishes of God to help him in any way. So, they thought they were now doing God a service by throwing dirt in Job's face, so to speak.

NOTES

Unless one has been in such a place, and I have, one has no idea as to exactly how Job felt.

The only thing that was different, my family, and certain ones at Family Worship Center stood with me. Almost all of the balance of the religious world followed in the train of Job's friends.

I remember complaining to the Lord at one dark juncture, as to why the religious publications thought that they had to castigate me on every hand? *"Why, could not at least one article be written that had a modicum of kindness about it?"* We had seen literally tens of thousands of people brought to a Saving knowledge of Jesus Christ. Had seen multiple thousands baptized with the Holy Spirit. Had changed the face of entire countries from Roman Catholicism to the sure Message of the Word of God. We had filled the churches of certain denominations with untold numbers of people, with them experiencing the greatest growth in their history. We had built over 150 schools for children in Third World countries, and beside that, feeding tens of thousands each and every day of malnourished children. But not a word was said about any of that!

The Lord responded to my question by saying, *"You are in much greater danger when they praise you than when they curse you."* I've never forgotten that!

As we have stated, the flesh had to die, and it does not die quickly or easily. It is not a painless demise! But let the following be understood:

Whatever it takes to bring a person to the place of Sanctification, i.e., *"the Cross,"* is worth it. Job was and is the perfect example!

(21) "HAVE PITY UPON ME, HAVE PITY UPON ME, O YOU MY FRIENDS; FOR THE HAND OF GOD HAS TOUCHED ME.

(22) "WHY DO YOU PERSECUTE ME AS GOD, AND ARE NOT SATISFIED WITH MY FLESH?

(23) "OH THAT MY WORDS WERE NOW WRITTEN! OH THAT THEY WERE PRINTED IN A BOOK!

(24) "THAT THEY WERE GRAVEN WITH AN IRON PEN AND LEAD IN THE ROCK FOREVER!"

The exposition is:

1. The pathetic appeal of Verse 21 should have elicited sympathy, but it didn't!

2. In effect, and according to Verse 22, Job says, *"Isn't my condition enough punishment? Why do you want to persecute me more?"*

3. Job would have his prayer of Verse 23 answered. The Book of Job, in all of its detail that would give future generations untold direction and counsel, would be the result of his prayer.

4. That for which Job wished in Verse 24 was answered, and even greater than he could begin to anticipate. His words were placed as a part of the Word of God, and nothing could be greater than that!

PERSECUTION

Job asked the question of his friends, *"Why do you persecute me as God, and are not satisfied with my flesh?"* In essence, he is saying, are you not satisfied with my present condition? Do you want to make it worse? Sad to say, that's exactly what they did desire, to make it worse!

In their thinking, he was being persecuted by God, and they were doing God a service by helping the Lord to strike even more blows.

How so much we should learn from all of this.

First of all, we aren't qualified to act in the place of God in any circumstance. Why does it take us so long to realize this? As well, do we not know that *"whatever measure we mete, it will be measured to us again"* (Mat. 7:2)?

If we really believe that, I think we would have a second thought before adding our two cents worth! But whether we believe it or not, that which was said by our Lord will come to pass and exactly as He said it.

In the second place, no human being is worthy to punish another human being in the sense of what happened to Job. All men in a sense are spiritual lepers. And about the best that one can do is to brag that he only has 97 leprous spots on him, while the other fellow has 99. How stupid we are! How so heavy we tread on soil where Angels fear to tread.

THE BOOK OF JOB

While Job was sitting in an ash heap, his body covered with sores, having lost everything he had, with even his family and friends having turned against him, he says, *"Oh that my words were now written! Oh that they were printed in a Book!"*

That prayer was answered, and in a way that was miraculous to say the least. In fact, the Book of Job, probably written by Moses in collaboration with Job, was the very First Book written which was to be inserted in the Word of God, for it was the Word of God.

It seems that he knew something special was happening to him, but he had no idea as to exactly what it was. He would find out when the Lord ultimately appeared to him.

What must have been his thoughts, when this great Book was ultimately penned? What must he had thought when he held the scrolls in his hands?

Every one of us, who has seen the Lord answer prayer, is always astounded at what He does, and how He does it.

When he said, *"That they were graven with an iron pen and lead in the rock forever,"* the Lord would give him something even greater than that. Job wanted the account of his experience to be given to future generations. And oh how so much it has!

(25) "FOR I KNOW THAT MY REDEEMER LIVES, AND THAT HE SHALL STAND AT THE LATTER DAY UPON THE EARTH:

(26) "AND THOUGH AFTER MY SKIN WORMS DESTROY THIS BODY, YET IN MY FLESH SHALL I SEE GOD:

(27) "WHOM I SHALL SEE FOR MYSELF, AND MY EYES SHALL BEHOLD, AND NOT ANOTHER; THOUGH MY REINS BE CONSUMED WITHIN ME.

(28) "BUT YOU SHOULD SAY, WHY PERSECUTE WE HIM, SEEING THE ROOT OF THE MATTER IS FOUND IN ME?

(29) "BE YOU AFRAID OF THE SWORD: FOR WRATH BRINGS THE PUNISHMENTS OF THE SWORD, THAT YOU MAY KNOW THERE IS A JUDGMENT."

The overview is:

1. Even though Job would not have understood the term, *"the Lord Jesus Christ,"* actually, this is the One of Whom he was speaking in Verse 25. He knew the Redeemer was coming, even though he knew nothing about particulars.

2. In Verse 26, Job portrays here the fact of the Resurrection and the Glorified Body. This proves that God had made to primitive man a wonderfully full Revelation of some New Testament Truths.

3. Verse 27 proclaims the fact that Job would see the Lord, and *"not by proxy, or merely through faith, or in a vision, but really, actually, I shall see Him for myself."* Once again, Job proclaims the Resurrection.

4. In Verse 28, Job is telling his *"friends,"* that they had better be careful as to what they say about him. How right he was!

5. In Verse 29 he tells them that the sword of God's Justice will assuredly smite them, if they persecuted an innocent man. This they must not forget!

GREAT DOCTRINES

Several great Doctrines are found in Verses 25 through 29. They are:

• A Redeemer was ultimately coming, for man must have Redemption. That Redeemer would be the Lord Jesus Christ.

• The Second Coming is portrayed in the last phrase of Verse 25, *"And that He shall stand at the latter day upon the Earth."*

• Job believed in and taught a future Resurrection.

• The phrase, *"Yet in my flesh shall I see God,"* in essence, speaks of the Glorified Body. He would not have had knowledge of that coming work, but yet, in a sense, would see it dimly.

• One day he knew that he would feast his eyes upon this *"Redeemer,"* and so it has been, and so it shall be.

• Job saw a Judgment Day coming, whether *"the Judgment Seat of Christ,"* where all Believers will be judged for their motives and actions, not for sins, because that was done at Calvary (Rom. 14:10), and the Great White Throne Judgment, where all the unsaved will appear, and for all ages (Rev. 20:11-15).

Once again, Job uttered these words, given to him by the Holy Spirit, which spoke of the great Doctrines of the Bible, which would be fully fleshed out under the New Covenant, while sitting in an ash heap, in a totally destitute condition.

Was it worth it?

NOTES

I think if you were able to approach Job at this present time, he would tell you unequivocally, that it was worth it and much more.

"By Christ redeemed, in Christ restored,
"We keep the memory adored,
"And show the death of our dear Lord,
"Until He come."

"His Body broken in our stead,
"Is seen, in this memorial bread,
"And so our feeble love is fed,
"Until He come."

"The drops of His dread Agony,
"His life-blood shed for us, we see;
"The wine shall tell the mystery,
"Until He come."

"And thus that dark betrayal-night,
"With the last advent we unite,
"By one blest chain of loving rite,
"Until He come."

"Until the Trump of God be heard,
"Until the ancient graves be stirred,
"And with great commanding word,
"The Lord shall come."

"O blessed hope! With this elate;
"Let not our hearts be desolate,
"But, strong in Faith, in patience wait,
"Until He come."

CHAPTER 20

(1) "THEN ANSWERED ZOPHAR THE NAAMATHITE, AND SAID,

(2) "THEREFORE DO MY THOUGHTS CAUSE ME TO ANSWER, AND FOR THIS I MAKE HASTE.

(3) "I HAVE HEARD THE CHECK OF MY REPROACH, AND THE SPIRIT OF MY UNDERSTANDING CAUSES ME TO ANSWER.

(4) "DO YOU NOT KNOW THIS OF OLD, SINCE MAN WAS PLACED UPON EARTH,

(5) "THAT THE TRIUMPHING OF THE WICKED IS SHORT, AND THE JOY OF THE HYPOCRITE BUT FOR A MOMENT?

(6) "THOUGH HIS EXCELLENCY MOUNT UP TO THE HEAVENS, AND HIS HEAD REACH UNTO THE CLOUDS;

(7) "YET HE SHALL PERISH FOR EVER LIKE HIS OWN DUNG: THEY WHICH HAVE SEEN HIM SHALL SAY, WHERE IS HE?

(8) "HE SHALL FLY AWAY AS A DREAM, AND SHALL NOT BE FOUND: YES, HE SHALL BE CHASED AWAY AS A VISION OF THE NIGHT.

(9) "THE EYE ALSO WHICH SAW HIM SHALL SEE HIM NO MORE; NEITHER SHALL HIS PLACE ANY MORE BEHOLD HIM.

(10) "HIS CHILDREN SHALL SEEK TO PLEASE THE POOR, AND HIS HANDS SHALL RESTORE THEIR GOODS.

(11) "HIS BONES ARE FULL OF THE SIN OF HIS YOUTH, WHICH SHALL LIE DOWN WITH HIM IN THE DUST.

(12) "THOUGH WICKEDNESS BE SWEET IN HIS MOUTH, THOUGH HE HIDE IT UNDER HIS TONGUE;

(13) "THOUGH HE SPARE IT, AND FORSAKE IT NOT; BUT KEEP IT STILL WITHIN HIS MOUTH:

(14) "YET HIS MEAT IN HIS BOWELS IS TURNED, IT IS THE GALL OF ASPS WITHIN HIM.

(15) "HE HAS SWALLOWED DOWN RICHES, AND HE SHALL VOMIT THEM UP AGAIN: GOD SHALL CAST THEM OUT OF HIS BELLY."

The composition is:

1. (Vs. 2) Zophar brushes aside Job's warnings concerning judgment, and hastens to answer, again with venom.

2. (Vs. 3) In his self-righteousness, Zophar says that he admits he has reproached Job, but not nearly to the degree that he should have been reproached. Also, because he has great understanding of these matters, he has no choice but to answer.

3. (Vs. 5) Zophar continues to refer to Job as a *"hypocrite."*

4. (Vs. 7) The man insults Job, and further says that future generations will ask, *"What has become of him?"*

5. (Vs. 10) He now accuses Job of having gained his former riches by oppressing the poor.

6. (Vs. 13) Even though he won't admit to evil, Job, Zophar says, is full of evil.

7. The Fourteenth Verse proclaims Zophar now referring to Job as a snake, and a poisonous one at that.

8. (Vs. 15) The wicked man shall be made to disgorge his ill-gotten gains, which he claims that Job has had to do.

ZOPHAR CLAIMS TO HAVE ALL THE ANSWERS

James said that the wisdom of the world is *"earthly, sensual, devilish."* Where this type of wisdom prevails you will find *"envying and strife and confusion and every evil work"* (James 3:15-16).

However, that is one thing, and we see it evident on every hand. But the worst wisdom of all, even worse than we have just named, is religious wisdom. It is that which characterized the Pharisees, that which nailed Christ to the Cross, all fueled by self-righteousness. Job's three friends were characterized not only by earthly wisdom but, as well, religious wisdom, which presented a double-barreled evil.

The Scribes and the Pharisees of Jesus' day had impeccable reputations among the people, yet, hated Christ with a passion.

Let the following be understood:

Reputation is what people think you are, while character is what God knows you are. As stated, these Scribes and Pharisees had impeccable reputations, were thought of highly by most of the people, yet, there was no evil any worse than their evil. Jesus said of them, *". . . Verily I say unto you, That the publicans and the harlots go into the Kingdom of God before you* (He said this to their faces, and before the people; He could not have insulted them more, putting them beneath publicans, whom they considered to be traitors, and harlots).

"For John (John the Baptist) *came unto you in the way of righteousness, and you believed him not* (speaking to the religious leaders)*: but the publicans and the harlots believed him: and you, when you had seen it, repented not afterward, that you might believe him* (they saw the changed lives as a result of John's Gospel, but still wouldn't believe)*"* (Mat. 21:31-32).

JOB'S THREE FRIENDS AND THE PHARISEES OF JESUS' DAY

How were these similar?

All who do not have the wisdom of the Word of God, fall into the category just mentioned, irrespective if they lived before the Cross or after the Cross.

Before the Cross, most every Promise and Prediction pointed to the Redeemer Who was to come, Who would pay the price for man's sins. Faith in the coming One, typified by the sacrifices, is what brought Salvation to those at that time. In fact, every single soul that has ever been Saved has been Saved by Grace, whether before the Cross or after the Cross. Actually, the entirety of the Bible points exclusively to Christ and what He would do as it regards the Redemption of humanity. So, if Faith was properly placed in that coming Sacrifice, as it regards Job's three friends, they would have had understanding somewhat as to what was happening to Job. Even though before the Lord appeared, they would have had no knowledge whatsoever of the conversation between the Lord and Satan, yet, they would not have judged Job as they did. They did that because their wisdom was earthly and not Heavenly. As a result, they actually thought they had perfect understanding; therefore, they felt free to pontificate on all the great questions of life, but most of all to point a finger at Job. They said that *"his bones were full of the sin of his youth."* Once again, we go back to the problem of self-righteousness, which has plagued mankind from the very beginning.

WHAT IS SELF-RIGHTEOUSNESS?

Jesus gave us the answer to that by saying, *"And He spoke this Parable unto certain who trusted in themselves that they were righteous, and despised others"* (Lk. 18:9).

Self-righteousness is exactly that which describes itself. It's righteousness, or that which is referred to as righteousness, it's centered up in self, in other words, what self can do as it regards religious activity. And because of the individual performing these religious activities, whatever they might be, and placing their faith in them, this means they are trying to make themselves righteous by what they do or don't do.

To turn it around, this means that their faith is not in Christ and what Christ did at the Cross, all on our behalf, but rather in themselves. While they might use the Name of Jesus occasionally, and speak religiously on a constant basis, still, their faith is really not in Christ and the Cross, but rather their own works, i.e., *"themselves."*

The only true Faith that God will recognize, which automatically imputes to such a person the Perfect Righteousness of Christ, and instantly so, is that which is anchored solely in Christ and what Christ has done for us at the Cross (Rom. 5:1-2; Eph. 2:8-9).

Always and without exception, the self-righteous *"despise others."* They do not accept and, in fact, will not accept, Faith that is placed exclusively in Christ and the Perfect Price He paid for us. While they may possibly mouth the words that seem to be correct, their actions speak much louder than their words.

It's a strange thing, Repentance and Brokenness before God stops all ministry in the modern church. With God Repentance makes one's Ministry, whatever it might be, greater than ever. The problem is self-righteousness.

THE CROSS OF CHRIST

This is the reason that Satan opposes the Message of the Cross as he opposes nothing else. He knows that in the Cross of Christ is all Salvation, all Victory, all prosperity, all blessing, and all answers to prayer. He knows that all Righteousness is in the Cross, all Holiness is in the Cross, all Faith that God recognizes is that which is placed exclusively in the Cross. So, he does everything within his power to push the church away from the Cross, and he has been very successful in doing that.

UNDERSTANDING THE CROSS

Frances reads hundreds of e-mails each week, which come to us from virtually every nation under Heaven. I don't read but a handful, simply because I don't have the time. Really, she doesn't either, but she makes time, because it is important.

She was relating to me the other day that I was going to have to do my best to make the Message of the Cross more simple, more easy to understand, simply because most

Christians really don't know, as she stated, what we're talking about, when we speak of the Message of the Cross. Beyond, *"Jesus died for me,"* most of the modern church doesn't have a clue. In other words, most Christians, that is if they are truly Saved, have at least a modicum of understanding as it regards the Cross and Salvation, but when it comes to Sanctification, they draw a blank.

It may be a surprise to know that when many hear us talk about the Cross of Christ, they think we are speaking of the wooden beam on which Jesus died. We aren't! I suppose that's the reason that many people send us crucifixes, and in every shape, form, and fashion.

Please understand, there was no power in that wooden beam. In fact, if it was possible that the Cross on which Jesus died, would somehow have miraculously survived all these centuries, and would be found, and introduced to the world, it would hold no more power than any other piece of wood. So get it out of your mind that we're talking about a wooden beam. As stated, we aren't!

Second, and even more important, most Christians think that when one speaks of the Cross, they're speaking of suffering.

I read a Message the other day by a famous preacher, who gave his summation of the Cross. It basically had to do with the old Wesleyan concept of the Cross, as a place of suffering. In other words, if a Christian was to faithfully bear the Cross of Christ, even as we are commanded to do (Lk. 9:23; 14:27), this would entail much and great suffering.

It doesn't!

Of course, Christ suffered terribly on the Cross, as should be overly obvious. But He suffered for us, and strictly for us, that we would not have to suffer.

While Christians most definitely may suffer many things in this life's journey, still, the idea of suffering in order to avail oneself of the great Blessings of God is not found in the Bible. In effect, if suffering would entail Salvation or Blessing, this would mean that what Christ did on the Cross was an incomplete work; however, we know that His Work was a Finished Work, meaning nothing can be added, as nothing needs to be added.

Thinking that the Cross of Christ refers to suffering, and suffering on our part, most Christians, want no part of the Cross. One can certainly understand why!

One of the great Scriptures that is grossly misunderstood falls into this category. Jesus said:

". . . If any man will come after Me (the criteria for Discipleship), *let him deny himself* (not asceticism as many think, but rather that one denies one's own willpower, self-will, strength, and ability, depending totally on Christ), *and take up his cross* (the benefits of the Cross, looking exclusively to what Jesus did there to meet our every need) *daily* (this is so important, our looking to the Cross; that we must renew our Faith in what Christ has done for us, even on a daily basis, for Satan will ever try to move us away from the Cross as the Object of our Faith, which always spells disaster), *and follow Me* (Christ can be followed only by the Believer looking to the Cross, understanding what it accomplished, and by that means alone [Rom. 6:3-5, 11, 14; 8:1-2, 11; I Cor. 1:17-18, 21, 23; 2:2; Gal. 6:14; Eph. 2:13-18; Col. 2:14-15]).

"For whosoever will save his life shall lose it (try to live one's life outside of Christ and the Cross)*: but whosoever will lose his life for My Sake, the same shall save it* (when we place our Faith entirely in Christ and the Cross, looking exclusively to Him, we have just found *'more abundant life'* [Jn. 10:10])*"* (Lk. 9:23-24).

Satan has caused Believers to misinterpret these particular Scriptures just quoted, making them think that Jesus was talking about denying ourselves of everything that has any type of pleasure or comfort, and then having to suffer. No wonder people wouldn't want that.

The reality is, this is one of the greatest Scriptures found in the entirety of the Word of God. Taking up the Cross and following Christ is the source of all Salvation, all Victory, all Blessings, which actually means that we cannot have these things unless we understand the Cross.

Getting back to the original subject, if one misunderstands the Cross of Christ, self-righteousness will be the result, which is what plagued Job's three friends. We should take a lesson from this.

(16) "HE SHALL SUCK THE POISON OF ASPS: THE VIPER'S TONGUE SHALL SLAY HIM.

(17) "HE SHALL NOT SEE THE RIVERS, THE FLOODS, THE BROOKS OF HONEY AND BUTTER.

(18) "THAT WHICH HE LABOURED FOR SHALL HE RESTORE, AND SHALL NOT SWALLOW IT DOWN: ACCORDING TO HIS SUBSTANCE SHALL THE RESTITUTION BE, AND HE SHALL NOT REJOICE THEREIN.

(19) "BECAUSE HE HAS OPPRESSED AND HAS FORSAKEN THE POOR; BECAUSE HE HAS VIOLENTLY TAKEN AWAY AN HOUSE WHICH HE BUILT NOT;

(20) "SURELY HE SHALL NOT FEEL QUIETNESS IN HIS BELLY, HE SHALL NOT SAVE OF THAT WHICH HE DESIRED.

(21) "THERE SHALL NONE OF HIS MEAT BE LEFT; THEREFORE SHALL NO MAN LOOK FOR HIS GOODS.

(22) "IN THE FULNESS OF HIS SUFFICIENCY HE SHALL BE IN STRAITS: EVERY HAND OF THE WICKED SHALL COME UPON HIM.

(23) "WHEN HE IS ABOUT TO FILL HIS BELLY, GOD SHALL CAST THE FURY OF HIS WRATH UPON HIM, AND SHALL RAIN IT UPON HIM WHILE HE IS EATING.

(24) "HE SHALL FLEE FROM THE IRON WEAPON, AND THE BOW OF STEEL SHALL STRIKE HIM THROUGH.

(25) "IT IS DRAWN, AND COMES OUT OF THE BODY; YES, THE GLITTERING SWORD COMES OUT OF HIS GALL: TERRORS ARE UPON HIM.

(26) "ALL DARKNESS SHALL BE HID IN HIS SECRET PLACES: A FIRE NOT BLOWN SHALL CONSUME HIM; IT SHALL GO ILL WITH HIM THAT IS LEFT IN HIS TABERNACLE.

(27) "THE HEAVEN SHALL REVEAL HIS INIQUITY; AND THE EARTH SHALL RISE UP AGAINST HIM.

(28) "THE INCREASE OF HIS HOUSE SHALL DEPART, AND HIS GOODS SHALL FLOW AWAY IN THE DAY OF HIS WRATH.

(29) "THIS IS THE PORTION OF A WICKED MAN FROM GOD, AND THE HERITAGE APPOINTED UNTO HIM BY GOD."

NOTES

The synopsis is:

1. (Vs. 19) Once again, Job is accused of having gained his former riches by deceit and fraud, and especially by oppressing the poor.

2. (Vs. 20) Job was never satisfied, says Zophar, in that he continued to oppress the poor long after he was extremely wealthy.

3. (Vs. 21) Zophar continues by claiming that the Lord has taken everything away because of his terrible sin.

4. (Vs. 23) Many like Zophar seem to enjoy calling down the wrath of God on others.

5. (Vs. 27) He claimed that Heaven would reveal Job's iniquity; however, the very opposite happened. Heaven revealed his Righteousness, and men once again sought his help and advice.

6. (Vs. 29) Zophar's argument seemed plausible, enough so that the entirety of all who knew Job agreed with this summation and, therefore, soundly condemned Job themselves. Once again, it shows that the majority are not always right — in fact, they seldom are.

BARBS DIRECTED AT JOB

Self-righteousness and self-will heap up together as it regards these three so-called friends of Job's. It is amazing how the Holy Spirit allowed all of this verbiage, as wrong as it was, to be put in print, and inserted in the Sacred Text. And please understand, while inspiration does not guarantee that what is said is true, even as in this case, it does guarantee that it was said, and that we have verbatim that which was said.

Again as we have stated, the Holy Spirit, no doubt, allowed this for any number of reasons; however, the main reason of all, I think, is to help us to see that the wisdom of the world holds no answer for the Child of God. That as it relates to spiritual things, while it may sometimes say something that is correct, still, the origination of such wisdom is wrong, and its application must be wrong as well.

The type of wisdom of which we speak here pertains to life and living. It does not pertain to technological advancement, etc. Thankfully, the Lord has originated fixed laws as it regards technology, and even the most wicked of men must abide by these laws, or whatever it is they are trying to develop will not work. For instance, mathematics is one of those laws. This is a law that cannot be tampered with. Two and two is four, and it will never be anything else, etc. So, the engineers who build the airplanes in which we fly have to abide by these laws, or the airplane won't fly. It's just that simple!

When it comes to life and living, the Lord has also given us fixed laws that are just as secure as the laws of science. Unfortunately, man thinks he knows more than God, and tries to change these laws. It results in nothing but wreckage and heartache. Listen to Simon Peter, to which we have already recorded elsewhere in this Volume. But due to its great significance, please allow us this repetition:

"*According as His Divine Power has given unto us all things* (the Lord with large-handed generosity has given us all things) *that pertain unto life and godliness* (pertains to the fact that the Lord Jesus has given us everything we need regarding life and living), *through the knowledge of Him Who has called us to 'Glory and Virtue'* (the 'knowledge' addressed here speaks of what Christ did at the Cross, which alone can provide '*Glory and Virtue*')" (II Pet. 1:3).

Now either the Lord, as Simon Peter was inspired to say, did give us "*all things that pertain unto life and godliness,*" or else He didn't. If that is the case, then we must turn to the likes of Freud, Maslow, and Rogers, etc. I happen to believe that Simon Peter was led by the Holy Spirit when he made his statement, and I have accepted it as Law and Gospel.

I believe the Holy Spirit Who functioned in the Creation of mankind knows what man needs, irrespective of the time frame and the culture in which man lives.

WHAT IS THE KEY TO LIFE AND LIVING?

To be brief, Jesus Christ is the Source of all things that we receive from God, Who has every single thing that we need, and the Cross is the Means by which these things are given to us, all superintended by the Holy Spirit (Rom. 6:1-14; Gal. 6:14).

John said:

NOTES

"*In the last day, that great day of the Feast* (spoke of the eighth day of the Feast of Tabernacles), *Jesus stood and cried, saying, If any man thirst, let him come unto Me, and drink* (presents the greatest invitation ever given to mortal man).

"*He who believes on Me* (it is '*not doing*,' but rather, '*believing*'), *as the Scripture has said* (refers to the Word of God being the Story of Christ and Him Crucified; all the Sacrifices pointed to Christ and what He would do at the Cross, as well as the entirety of the Tabernacle and Temple and all their appointments), *out of his belly* (innermost being) *shall flow rivers of Living Water* (speaks of Christ directly, and Believers indirectly).

"*(But this spoke He of the Spirit* [Holy Spirit], *which they who believe on Him should receive* [it would begin on the Day of Pentecost]*: for the Holy Spirit was not yet given* [He has now been given]*; because that Jesus was not yet glorified.)* (The time of which John wrote was shortly before the Crucifixion. When Jesus died on the Cross and was Resurrected three days later, He was raised with a Glorified Body, which was one of the signs that all sin had been atoned, now making it possible for the Holy Spirit to come in a new dimension)" (Jn. 7:37-39).

HOW DO WE TAP INTO THIS LIVING WATER?

To understand this statement given by John concerning "*Living Water,*" and which was stated by Christ, we have to go back to the Seventeenth Chapter of Exodus. The Scripture says, and I quote from THE EXPOSITOR'S STUDY BIBLE:

"*And all the congregation of the Children of Israel journeyed from the wilderness of Sin, after their journeys, according to the Commandment of the Lord, and pitched in Rephidim: and there was no water for the people to drink.* (It might seem strange that God, Who professed to love Israel, should lead them into a desert, both foodless and waterless. But love led them there that they might learn the desperate unbelief of their own hearts, and the unfailing faithfulness of God's Heart.)

"*Wherefore the people did chide with*

Moses, and said, Give us water that we may drink. And Moses said unto them, Why chide you with me? wherefore do you tempt the Lord? (Only in a desert could God reveal what He can be to those who trust Him; for only there was Israel dependent upon Him for everything. Without God — nothing; with God — everything. When we criticize God's man we are, in essence, criticizing God. The questions of the wilderness are: *'What?' 'Where?' 'How?'* Faith has a brief but comprehensive answer to all three, namely, *'God!'*)

"And the people thirsted there for water; and the people murmured against Moses, and said, Wherefore is this that you have brought us up out of Egypt, to kill us and our children and our cattle with thirst? (First of all, they tempted the Lord, which is a want of Faith, and now they *'murmur,'* which proved to be one of their greatest sins because murmuring always exhibits unbelief.)

"And Moses cried unto the LORD saying, What shall I do unto this people? they be almost ready to stone me. (One of the most prominent traits of the character of Moses is that, at the occurrence of a difficulty, he always carried it straight to God [Ex. 15:25; 24:15; 32:30; 33:8; Num. 11:2, 11; 12:11; 14:13-19].)

"And the LORD said unto Moses, Go on before the people, and take with you of the Elders of Israel; and your rod, wherewith you smote the river, take in your hand, and go.

"Behold, I will stand before you there upon the Rock in Horeb; and you shall smite the Rock, and there shall come water out of it, that the people may drink. And Moses did so in the sight of the Elders of Israel. (This is one of the most beautiful Types found in the entirety of Scripture. The *'Rock'* was a Type of Christ [I Cor. 10:1-4]. The Rock being *'smitten'* typified the Cross [Isa. 53:4]. The *'water'* coming out of the Rock was a Type of the Holy Spirit [Jn. 7:37-39]. However, the water, i.e., *'the Holy Spirit,'* was not available until the Rock [Christ] was smitten [crucified — Jn. 14:16-20]. In fact, Christ, the Cross, our Faith, and the Holy Spirit constitute the basis of Christianity [Gal., Chpt. 5].)

NOTES

"And he called the name of the place Massah (contention), *and Meribah* (strife), *because of the chiding of the Children of Israel, and because they tempted the LORD, saying, Is the LORD among us, or not?* (This proclaims the fact that the smitten Rock, which gushed forth with a river of water, was not brought about because of the Righteousness and Holiness of the people, but strictly because of the Grace of God; however, for the Believer to stay on a wrong path of unbelief will ultimately bring total destruction [Rom. 8:12])" (Ex. 17:1-7).

It all comes down to the Cross of Christ!

The Believer taps into this *"Living Water,"* made possible by the Cross, and made possible only by the Cross, by placing his Faith exclusively in Christ and the Cross, and not allowing it to be moved elsewhere. In fact, Jesus said that this must be done even on a daily basis (Lk. 9:23).

WHAT DID JESUS MEAN BY *"DAILY"*?

This speaks of Luke 9:23, where Jesus said: *"If any man will come after Me, let him deny himself, take up his cross daily, and follow Me."*

A beautiful type of this found in the Old Testament is the Manna. It says: *"And when the dew that lay was gone up, behold, upon the face of the wilderness there lay a small round thing, as small as the hoar frost on the ground.*

"And when the Children of Israel saw it, they said one to another, It is Manna: for they wist not what it was. And Moses said unto them, This is the Bread which the LORD has given you to eat. (The Manna was so precious that it could not bear contact with the Earth. It fell upon the dew and had to be gathered before the sun came up. This teaches us that yesterday's Blessings will not do for today, nor today's Blessings for tomorrow. Thus, must the Christian feed upon Christ daily as He reveals Himself in the Scriptures.)

"This is the thing which the LORD has commanded, Gather of it every man according to his eating, an omer for every man, according to the number of your persons; take you every man for them who are in his tents. (In Egypt, Israel had slave food; in

the desert, Angel's food. The test quickly revealed that the natural man had little appetite for Heavenly things, for the people soon called it *'light food.'*)

"And the Children of Israel did so, and gathered, some more, some less. (Israel in the desert presented a striking picture! Egypt was behind them, Canaan was before them, the wilderness was around them, and the Manna was above them.)

"And when they did mete it with an omer (an *'omer'* is the equivalent of six pints; considering there were approximately three million people, this would play out to some eighteen million pints, or about thirteen and a half million pounds gathered daily; to help us understand it even more, it would take a train pulling forty-five cars, each car having in it fifteen tons, to take care of one day's supply; this means that approximately one and a half million tons of Manna were gathered annually by Israel; and let it be remembered that this continued for nearly forty years! Great is our God!), *he who gathered much had nothing over, and he who gathered little had no lack* (Christians who hoard money will find that it will not grow as they think; Christians who give generously to the Work of God will find that personally, and for their family, they will *'have no lack'*; God blesses us, in order that we may bless His Work); *they gathered every man according to his eating.* (That which the Lord gives to us as Believers should be used according to our need, and the balance be given to the Work of God; however, we must make certain that what we are supporting is truly the Work of God.)

"And Moses said, Let no man leave of it till the morning. (What they gathered, they were to eat. None was to be left over for the next day. This means that we must partake of Christ every day. As well, what we receive today from the Lord will not suffice for tomorrow. Tomorrow must, and will, bring a fresh enduement of power from on high.)

"Notwithstanding they hearkened not unto Moses; but some of them left of it until the morning, and it bred worms, and stank: and Moses was angry with them. (That which some Christians are trying to present to the world *'stinks,'* at least in the nostrils of God, because it is someone else's vision, or yesterday's blessing.)

"And they gathered it every morning, every man according to his eating: and when the sun waxed hot, it melted. (Thus, must the Christian feed upon Christ every day.)

"And it came to pass, that on the sixth day they gathered twice as much bread, two omers for one man; and all the rulers of the congregation came and told Moses. (They were allowed to gather twice as much on the sixth day, because the Manna would not fall on the seventh day)" (Ex. 16:14-22).

As the Manna was demanded to be gathered each day, which means they were not to try to gather several days in advance, likewise, we are to take up the Cross *"daily."* It's somewhat like our Faith being renewed each and every day in the great Finished Work of Christ.

No, there is no ceremony or ritual in which one has to engage, merely a mental position that our Faith for this day is in Christ and what He did for us at the Cross, and we are guaranteed that *"our strength shall be as our day,"* meaning that whatever is needed for the day, will be given to us.

The *"Living Water"* is available to any and all, but to have this which is provided, and done so daily, our Faith, as stated, must be exclusively in the Cross of Christ, which will then guarantee the help of the Holy Spirit, Who Alone can carry out that which is needed in our lives.

WRONG METHODS

The Cross covers every single thing that we need; however, the major purpose of the Cross was to defeat sin, which was done by Jesus atoning for all sin, past, present, and future, at least for all who will believe (Jn. 3:16). And make no mistake about it, sin is an ever present problem, which every Believer must face on a daily basis and, thereby, needs daily victory. That Victory can be found only in the Cross of Christ and no other place.

Unfortunately, we who believe in the Power of God have tried to address sin, and in whatever form, by various different means other than the Cross, which will afford no victory. Even though the particulars we will now list are Biblical, and are very helpful in their own right, the truth is, as valuable as they may be otherwise, victory cannot be found by these methods. They are:

• The laying on of hands: this is very Scriptural and, in fact, should be done constantly, and will help in any case, that is if the person's Faith is in Christ and the Cross. But unfortunately, many have tried to find victory over sin, by the laying on of hands. It cannot be done.

• Manifestations: others have thought that if the Lord would knock them off their feet by His Power, which is referred to as *"slain in the Spirit,"* which is valid, that is if it's truly of God, still, it will afford no victory over sin. Jesus said that we would *"know the Truth, and the Truth would set us free"* (Jn. 8:32). If individuals do not know the *"Truth"* even if the Lord does knock them off their feet, regrettably, they will get up the same way they fell, finding that their problem, whatever it is, is still with them.

• The Baptism with the Holy Spirit with the evidence of speaking with other Tongues: while the Holy Spirit most definitely plays a vital part in our overcoming experience, the mere fact of one being baptized with the Spirit, and even having Gifts of the Spirit, will not guarantee victory of any nature. In fact, there are multiple millions of Believers presently who are definitely Spirit-filled, but are still controlled by the sin nature. In fact, such is very confusing to them, because they feel that due to the fact that they are Spirit-filled, they should have victory. Sure, being Spirit-filled, is most definitely the first step in the victory process, but only the first step.

• Delivered from demon spirits: many have been led to believe that if they have a reoccurring bondage in their lives, whatever it might be, that it's caused by a demon spirit. While demon spirits most definitely are involved in any type of sin, it is Scripturally erroneous that such a person who is Spirit-filled is at the same time demon possessed. Demon oppressed, yes, demon possessed, no! unfortunately, down through the last several decades, scores have been told that if they have a temper problem, that it's a temper demon that's causing it, or a lust problem, that it's a lust demon that's causing it, etc.

NOTES

More than likely there most definitely are temper demons, and lust demons, etc.; however, it is impossible for the Child of God who is inhabited by the Holy Spirit, at the same time to be inhabited by demon spirits. There's nothing in the Word of God that substantiates such thinking.

When Believers do not have the truth, they resort to very foolish things.

Many are told to write all their sins down on a piece of paper, read them out aloud, and then tear the paper in little pieces, or else throw it into the fire, all the time shouting the praises of God, and this, they think, is supposed to deliver them.

It won't!

THE TRUTH SHALL SET YOU FREE

What is the Truth?

Jesus said, and we mentioned it earlier, *"And you shall know the Truth, and the Truth shall make you free"* (Jn. 8:32).

This *"Truth"* is the secret of all abundant Life in Christ. The *"Truth"* is *"Jesus Christ and Him Crucified,"* which alone is the answer to the problems of man.

The Scripture further says: *"And as Moses lifted up the serpent in the wilderness* (refers to Num. 21:5-9; the *'serpent'* represents Satan who is the originator of sin), *even so must the Son of Man be lifted up* (refers to Christ being lifted up on the Cross, which alone could defeat Satan and sin):

"That whosoever (destroys the erroneous hyper-Calvinistic explanation of predestination that some are predestined to be Saved, while all others are predestined to be lost; the word *'whosoever'* means that none are excluded from being lost, and none are excluded from being Saved) *believes in Him* (believes in Christ and what He did at the Cross; otherwise, one would perish) *should not perish, but have Eternal Life* (the Life of God, the Ever-Living One, Who has life in Himself, and Alone has immortality)" (Jn. 3:14-15).

Paul said: *"For I determined not to know anything among you* (with purpose and design, Paul did not resort to the knowledge of philosophy of the world regarding the preaching of the Gospel), *save Jesus Christ, and Him Crucified* (that and that alone is the Message, which will save the sinner, set the captive free, and give the Believer perpetual Victory)" (I Cor. 2:2).

Paul also said: *"But God forbid that I should glory* (boast), *save in the Cross of our Lord Jesus Christ* (what the opponents of Paul sought to escape at the price of insincerity is the Apostle's only basis of exultation), *by Whom the world is crucified unto me, and I unto the world.* (The only way we can overcome the world, and I mean the only way, is by placing our Faith exclusively in the Cross of Christ and keeping it there.)"

The Apostle went on to say: *"For in Christ Jesus neither Circumcision avails anything, nor uncircumcision* (blows all of man's religious ceremonies to pieces), *but a new creature* (new in every respect, which can only be brought about by trusting Christ and what He did for us at the Cross)" (Gal. 6:14-15).

The great Apostle also said: *"I am Crucified with Christ* (is the foundation of all Victory; Paul, here, takes us back to Rom. 6:3-5): *nevertheless I live* (have new life); *yet not I* (not by my own strength and ability), *but Christ lives in me* (by virtue of me dying with Him on the Cross, and being raised with Him in Newness of Life): *and the life which I now live in the flesh* (my daily walk before God) *I live by the Faith of the Son of God* (the Cross is ever the Object of my Faith), *Who loved me, and gave Himself for me* (which is the only way that I could be Saved).

"I do not frustrate the Grace of God (if we make anything other than the Cross of Christ the Object of our Faith, we frustrate the Grace of God, which means we stop its action, and the Holy Spirit will no longer help us): *for if Righteousness come by the Law* (any type of Law), *then Christ is dead in vain.* (If I can successfully live for the Lord by any means other than Faith in Christ and the Cross, then the Death of Christ was a waste)" (Gal. 2:20-21).

THE CROSS OF CHRIST AS A SYNONYM

There are two or three phrases, which are used in the Word of God as a synonym for the entirety of Biblical Christianity.

A *"synonym"* is a word or words of the same language that have the same or nearly the same meaning in some or all senses. It is a symbolic or figurative name.

The following are some synonyms used for Biblical Christianity. In other words, the word or words when used, if properly understood, explain in a nutshell, so to speak, what Biblical Christianity actually is.

• *"The Cross"*: Paul said: *"For the preaching of the Cross is to them who perish foolishness; but unto us which are Saved it is the Power of God"* (I Cor. 1:18).

• *"The Faith"*: Paul also said: *"Examine yourselves, whether you be in the Faith* (the words, 'the Faith,' refer to 'Christ and Him Crucified,' with the Cross ever being the Object of our Faith . . .)" (II Cor. 13:5).

• *"The Way"*: The Scripture says: *"And the same time there arose no small stir about that Way* ('that Way' is the 'Pentecostal Way,' which characterizes the entirety of the Book of Acts)" (Acts 19:23).

• *"The Gospel"*: *"For Christ sent me not to baptize, but to preach the Gospel: not with wisdom of words, lest the Cross of Christ should be made of none effect"* (I Cor. 1:17).

When any one of these four words is heard, the Christian should automatically know what they mean. They are a synonym, as stated, to define Biblical Christianity.

"Here, O my Lord, I see You Face-to-Face;
"Here would I touch and handle things unseen;
"Here grasp with firmer hand the eternal Grace,
"And all my helplessness upon You lean."

"Here would I feed upon the bread of God,
"Here drink with You the royal wine of Heaven;
"Here would I lay aside each earthly load,
"Here taste afresh the calm of sin forgiven."

"This is the hour of banquet and of song,
"This is the heavenly table spread for me;
"Here let me feast, and feasting, still prolong,

"The brief, bright hour of fellowship with Thee."

"Too soon we rise; the symbols disappear;
"The feast, though not the love, is past and gone;
"The bread and wine removed, but You are here,
"Nearer than ever; still my Shield and Sun."

"I have no help but Yours; nor do I need,
"Another arm save Yours to lean upon;
"It is enough, my Lord, enough indeed;
"My strength is in Your Might, Your Might alone."

"Feast after feast thus comes and passes by,
"Yet passing, points to the glad feast above,
"Giving sweet foretastes of the festal joy,
"The Lamb's great Bridal Feast of bliss and love."

CHAPTER 21

(1) "BUT JOB ANSWERED AND SAID,

(2) "HEAR DILIGENTLY MY SPEECH, AND LET THIS BE YOUR CONSOLATIONS.

(3) "SUFFER ME THAT I MAY SPEAK; AND AFTER THAT I HAVE SPOKEN, MOCK ON.

(4) "AS FOR ME, IS MY COMPLAINT TO MAN? AND IF IT WERE SO, WHY SHOULD NOT MY SPIRIT BE TROUBLED?

(5) "MARK ME, AND BE ASTONISHED, AND LAY YOUR HAND UPON YOUR MOUTH.

(6) "EVEN WHEN I REMEMBER I AM AFRAID, AND TREMBLING TAKES HOLD ON MY FLESH.

(7) "WHEREFORE DO THE WICKED LIVE, BECOME OLD, YES, ARE MIGHTY IN POWER?

(8) "THEIR SEED IS ESTABLISHED IN THEIR SIGHT WITH THEM, AND THEIR OFFSPRING BEFORE THEIR EYES.

(9) "THEIR HOUSES ARE SAFE FROM FEAR, NEITHER IS THE ROD OF GOD UPON THEM.

(10) "THEIR BULL GENDERS, AND FAILS NOT; THEIR COW CALVES, AND CASTS NOT HER CALF.

(11) "THEY SEND FORTH THEIR LITTLE ONES LIKE A FLOCK, AND THEIR CHILDREN DANCE.

(12) "THEY TAKE THE TIMBREL AND HARP, AND REJOICE AT THE SOUND OF THE ORGAN.

(13) "THEY SPEND THEIR DAYS IN WEALTH, AND IN A MOMENT GO DOWN TO THE GRAVE."

The pattern is:

1. (Vs. 3) Job says to his three *"friends,"* *"hear what I have to say and, if you do not agree, 'mock on'"*; and that's exactly what they did.

2. (Vs. 4) Job says, *"I'm not looking to man, but rather to God!"*

3. Verse 6 says, in essence, *"When I think of what has happened to me, I tremble with fear."*

4. (Vs. 7) Job says that sometimes the wicked live as long as the righteous, and are mighty in power, as well. So the argument of his *"friends"* doesn't hold water.

5. (Vs. 8) Oftentimes the children of the wicked are blessed, at least with worldly goods.

6. (Vs. 13) Many times the wicked die without suffering from any prolonged or severe illness.

WHY DO THE WICKED OFTENTIMES PROSPER?

This question plagues Job, and it has plagued untold millions from then until now.

All along Job's complaint has been to God. Of course, he has no idea as to the conversation that has gone on in Heaven between God and Satan; consequently, he does not, at least at this time, realize that one of the greatest contests in the world is being played out as a lesson for all eternity. All he knows is this:

He has done his best to live for God, and now it seems that God has deserted him, and, furthermore, has brought upon him great calamity. Such conclusions would not be hard to arrive at considering Job's destitute condition.

Furthermore, he says that he was not complaining to man, for if so, his spirit would be greatly troubled because man simply cannot help.

The wicked prosper for any number and a variety of reasons. Some of them are:

• God does not guide the destiny of the wicked, unless they impact in some way His Plan of Redemption.

• If they are smart enough to acquire great wealth, most of the time, the Lord allows such to be. They are not a part of His Program.

• The wicked are in a system that is controlled by Satan, with Satan sometimes helping some wicked to prosper and for his own devious means.

• As it regards the wicked, this is it. There is no Heaven for them.

• The truth is, while a few wicked by comparison to the whole do prosper, still, the far greater majority don't prosper at all.

• There is no lasting peace for the wicked, irrespective as to what front they may show to the world.

• For a Believer to get his eyes on the wicked, who seem to be prosperous, thereby, allowing Satan to talk to him, is not wise at all.

ENVYING THE WICKED

Asaph was the choir director, so to speak, for David as it regards Israel. He held one of the greatest and most Spiritual Positions in the entirety of the Plan of God at this particular time. In fact, he authored a number of Psalms, which actually are songs. But yet, Asaph had a problem, even as many millions of Christians have the same problem. Listen to what he said:

"Truly God is good to Israel, even to such as are of a clean heart.

"But as for me, my feet were almost gone; my steps had well nigh slipped (Asaph, as stated, was the leader of the choral worship under David [I Chron. 16:4-5]. So he held a very high Spiritual Position in Israel.)

"For I was envious at the foolish, when I saw the prosperity of the wicked. (Asaph, perplexed with the problem that the ungodly prosper and the children of the Kingdom suffer, learns the lesson that outside the Sanctuary, the mind is distracted and the heart fermented, but that inside, all is peace. Looking in confounds; looking out confuses; looking up comforts.

"Asaph's problem was *'self.'* Preoccupation with *'self'* always leads to spiritual distraction. Men have ever tried to improve self; men have ever failed. Even Christian man fails, when endeavoring to improve *'self.' 'Self'* can only be conquered when it is hidden in Christ [Jn. 14:20].)

"For there are no bands in their death: but their strength is firm. (When one becomes enamored with *'self,'* then one's Spiritual Judgment becomes flawed. Asaph fell into the age-old trap. First of all, *'prosperity'* is not the purpose of Redemption; Salvation is.

"Second, Asaph is wrong about the *'death of the wicked.'* It is anything but positive.)

"They are not in trouble as other men; neither are they plagued like other men. (The truth is, the system of this world is not of God; but of Satan; consequently, the Child of God is constantly *'plagued'* by that system.

"But considering that, still, the life of the follower of Christ is, by far, the most rewarding life there is. If there were no eternity, living for God would still be, by far, the greater choice.)

"Therefore pride compasses them about as a chain, violence covers them as a garment. (Asaph is saying that *'the wicked'* constantly engage themselves in *'violence,'* with few negative results. They are filled with *'pride,'* and, instead of it bringing destruction, it seems to reward them.)

"Their eyes stand out with fatness: they have more than heart could wish. (These statements show that Asaph has given this much thought. Due to his preoccupation with *'self,'* Satan has made great inroads into his soul. One of Satan's greatest weapons is to make the Christian think that, by living for God, he is truly missing out. Actually, the opposite is true. However, we must always remember that Satan is a liar and the father of lies.)

"They are corrupt, and speak wickedly

concerning oppression: they speak loftily. (The speech of the wicked is lofty concerning how they will oppress people, and no harm seems to come to them.)

"They set their mouth against the heavens, and their tongue walks through the Earth. (Everything they say is in opposition to the Word of God. They boast of what they will do, evil as it may be, and they seem to be able to do it without hindrance.)

"Therefore his people return hither: and waters of a full cup are wrung out to them. (They cause men who have been converted from a life of covetousness to return to it.)

"And they say, how does God know? and is there knowledge in the Most High? (In other words, they laugh at God, thinking they are getting by with their wickedness.)

"Behold, these are the ungodly, who prosper in the world; they increase in riches. (It is true that some of the ungodly *'prosper'* [financially], but, as a whole, it is not true. In fact, it is seldom true. Taking the whole world into consideration, for every one prosperous wicked man there are ten thousand who are the very opposite).

"Verily I have cleansed my heart in vain, and washed my hands in innocency. (Every attack that Satan levels against the Believer, irrespective of its direction, is for one purpose: to destroy the faith of the individual. In other words, Asaph is saying that there is no profit in living for God.

"How wrong he is! The rewards of the wicked, such as they are, are fleeting and temporal. The rewards of the righteous are eternal.)

"For all the day long have I been plagued, and chastened every morning. (The Lord is sorely displeased with complaints. This is the opposite of faith and appreciation for what the Lord has done for us. And yet, so many of us are guilty of this sin — thanklessness.)

"If I say, I will speak thus; behold, I should offend against the generation of Your children. (He knew that the evidence was against him. Wickedness was not profitable, and living for God is.)

"When I thought to know this, it was too painful for me (now Asaph realizes he is wrong; he knows he is sliding down a path

NOTES

that leads only to destruction; still, he does not know the answer to his dilemma);

"Until I went into the Sanctuary of God; then understood I their end. (How could the Sanctuary give him the answers? Because the Sanctuary is where God dwelt. Now, He no longer sees the alleged prosperity of the wicked, but the Glory of God. Then and only then do the flaws of the wicked become obvious. As well, when he sees the Lord, he no longer sees himself.)"

The worship leader goes on to say, *"Surely You did set them* (the wicked) *in slippery places: you cast them down into destruction.* (On the surface, the road of the wicked may look prosperous; however, upon closer inspection, it is easy to see that it is *'slippery.'* Being so, they will fall to their own *'destruction'*)

"How are they brought into desolation, as in a moment! they are utterly consumed with terrors. (Now Asaph begins to see what the situation really is. The wicked look as though they are so prosperous, and then, all of a sudden, they are bankrupt and *'brought into desolation'* — *'as in a moment!'*

"Now he sees that all of their boasting and clamor against God is but a façade. In a moment, they are *'utterly consumed with terrors.'*)"

ASAPH'S REPENTANCE

The choir director now says: *"As a dream when one awakes; so, O Lord, when You awake, You shall despise their image.* (At times, it may seem as though the Lord is asleep; however, after a short period, the Lord will *'awake.'* Then He will intrude into their *'evil dream.'*)

"Thus my heart was grieved, and I was pricked in my reins. (Now that Asaph has seen the Lord, he has come under Holy Spirit conviction. He is *'grieved,'* because of his sin. What he has done now dawns upon him, and he is cut to the core of his being.)

"So foolish was I, and ignorant: I was as a beast before You. (The Holy Spirit causes Asaph to see that the direction he had been traveling was foolish indeed! In fact, one of the chief ministries of the Spirit is to smite with conviction. Were it not that, the Christian would too often get off course, and

would not know how to get back on course.)

"Nevertheless I am continually with You: You have held me by my right hand. (The Lord does not cast us off when we begin to go astray. Rather, He deals with us, speaks to us, and attempts to pull us back to the right direction. In doing so, he will literally, spiritually speaking, hold us by the hand.)

"You shall guide me with Your counsel, and afterward receive me to Glory. (Asaph had previously been listening to the *'counsel'* of self-will. Now he tells the Lord, *'I will listen to Your counsel.'* God's *'counsel'* is His Word.)

"Whom have I in Heaven but You? and there is none upon Earth that I desire beside You. (After seeing the Lord and receiving a fresh touch from Glory, he realizes that his Salvation is not money, place, or position, but Christ. He now knows that Christ satisfies all.)

"My flesh and my heart fails: but God is the strength of my heart, and my portion forever. (When Asaph begins to lean on his own strength, which is woefully inadequate, he *'fails.'* But now he realizes that *'God is his strength.'* Also, he now knows that anything and everything he needs can be provided by God — *'my portion forever.'*)

"For, lo, they who are far from You shall perish: You have destroyed all them who go a whoring from You. (He now fully sees the position of the wicked. They *'shall perish.'*)

"But it is good for me to draw near to God: I have put my trust in the Lord GOD, that I may declare all Your works. (Some bad things have happened, but some *'good'* is coming out of this, as well. His perilous situation has caused him to *'draw near to God.'* Now, his *'trust'* is in the Lord, and not in the things of the world. Asaph vows that he will no longer talk about the prosperity of the wicked, but now will *'declare all Your works.'* This should be a great lesson to us!)" (Ps. 73:1-28).

Let us say it again: there is no peace for the wicked although some of them may be very prosperous. The peace that comes to the soul, is that alone which can be given by the Lord Jesus Christ. The wicked do not have that peace and, in fact, cannot have that peace.

THE PEACE THAT GOD ALONE CAN GIVE

Jesus said: *"Peace I leave with you (Sanctifying Peace), My Peace I give unto you* (there is a vast difference in *'Peace with God,'* which all Believers have, and *'The Peace of God'* of which Jesus here speaks)*: not as the world gives, give I unto you* (the peace of the world is but surface; that given by Christ is in the heart). *Let not your heart be troubled, neither let it be afraid.* (*'The Peace of God'* heals the troubled heart, and takes away fear)" (Jn. 14:27).

(14) "THEREFORE THEY SAY UNTO GOD, DEPART FROM US; FOR WE DESIRE NOT THE KNOWLEDGE OF YOUR WAYS.

(15) "WHAT IS THE ALMIGHTY, THAT WE SHOULD SERVE HIM? AND WHAT PROFIT SHOULD WE HAVE, IF WE PRAY UNTO HIM?

(16) "LO, THEIR GOOD IS NOT IN THEIR HAND: THE COUNSEL OF THE WICKED IS FAR FROM ME.

(17) "HOW OFT IS THE CANDLE OF THE WICKED PUT OUT! AND HOW OFT COMES THEIR DESTRUCTION UPON THEM! GOD DISTRIBUTES SORROWS IN HIS ANGER.

(18) "THEY ARE AS STUBBLE BEFORE THE WIND, AND AS CHAFF THAT THE STORM CARRIES AWAY.

(19) "GOD LAYS UP HIS INIQUITY FOR HIS CHILDREN: HE REWARDS HIM, AND HE SHALL KNOW IT.

(20) "HIS EYES SHALL SEE HIS DESTRUCTION, AND HE SHALL DRINK OF THE WRATH OF THE ALMIGHTY.

(21) "FOR WHAT PLEASURE HAS HE IN HIS HOUSE AFTER HIM, WHEN THE NUMBER OF HIS MONTHS IS CUT OFF IN THE MIDST?

(22) "SHALL ANY TEACH GOD KNOWLEDGE? SEEING HE JUDGES THOSE WHO ARE HIGH.

(23) "ONE DIES IN HIS FULL STRENGTH, BEING WHOLLY AT EASE AND QUIET.

(24) "HIS BREASTS ARE FULL OF MILK, AND HIS BONES ARE MOISTENED WITH MARROW.

(25) "AND ANOTHER DIES IN THE BITTERNESS OF HIS SOUL, AND NEVER EATS WITH PLEASURE.

(26) "THEY SHALL LIE DOWN ALIKE IN THE DUST, AND THE WORMS SHALL COVER THEM."

The composition is:

1. Verse 14 pretty well characterizes the attitude of most of the world. Hundreds of millions are steeped in heathenistic idolatry. Other hundreds of millions know about God, but do not want any part of Him.

2. Verse 15 proclaims the love of money being the root of all evil (I Tim. 6:10), unconverted man only thinks in terms of *"profit."* Not being Spiritually Minded, he has no idea as to the *"profit"* found in serving God and praying unto Him. In fact, this is the greatest *"profit"* of all.

3. Job says in Verse 16 that the wicked sometimes prosper without being judged by God in this life any more than the righteous. So the reasoning that he was a wicked man because of suffering the judgments of the wicked proved nothing in his case.

4. Verse 17 is actually a question. God at times does distribute sorrow upon the wicked, however, only at times. The real sorrow comes after death when Hell awaits them, and from that there will be no reprieve.

5. (Vs. 19) *"God,"* Job's opponents may say, *"punishes the wicked through their children."* Job does not deny that the Lord may do so, but suggests a better course in the latter phrase. Judgment at times is sent by the Lord on the wicked.

6. Verse 25 proclaims the fact that some have to suffer terribly before death comes to them, and their spirit is embittered by their misfortunes.

7. According to Verse 26, however different the circumstances of their lives, men are alike in their death. All die, and become the prey of worms, at least as it regards the physical body.

THE DESTINY OF THE WICKED

While some wicked may seem to fare well in this life, the truth is, this life is only a mere dress rehearsal for eternity. The soul and the spirit of man, awaiting the Resurrection of life for the just, and the resurrection of damnation for the unjust, are eternal. And one must understand, *"eternal or eternity"* presents a long, long time!

How stupid it is for man to tell the Lord to depart from him! And then it becomes more stupid for them to say, *"For we desire not the knowledge of Your Ways."*

The Ways of God are found in His Word, and constitute honesty, integrity, love, fairness, equality, Grace, and Blessing. Why is it that the majority of mankind doesn't want that?

While sin takes a deadly toll on its participants, still, man loves his sin. He can't have sin and God both, so he opts for sin. Every person has to make that choice. The following was said of Moses:

"By Faith Moses, when he was come to years (refers to him coming to the age of 40 [Ex. 2:11]), *refused to be called the son of Pharaoh's daughter* (in effect, he refused the position of Pharaoh of Egypt, for which he had been trained because he had been adopted by Pharaoh's daughter);

"Choosing rather to suffer affliction with the people of God (proclaims the choice Moses made; he traded the temporal for the Eternal), *than to enjoy the pleasures of sin for a season* (presents the choice which must be made, affliction or the pleasures of sin);

"Esteeming the reproach of Christ greater riches than the treasures in Egypt (he judged the reproach was greater than the throne of Egypt); *for he had respect unto the recompense of the reward.* (Moses habitually 'looked away' from the treasures in Egypt, and purposely fixed his eye on the Heavenly Reward.)

"By Faith he forsook Egypt (which, Spiritually speaking, every Believer must do), *not fearing the wrath of the king* (Pharaoh tried to kill him at that time [Ex. 2:15]): *for he endured, as seeing Him Who is invisible.* (This speaks of Christ, Whom Moses saw by Faith.)

"Through Faith he kept the Passover (means that he 'instituted the Passover' according to the Word of the Lord), *and the sprinkling of blood* (referred to the Blood of the Paschal Lamb on the lentils and doorposts of the houses [Ex. 12:22]), *lest He*

Who destroyed the firstborn should touch them. (Every Israelite's house was safe that night because of the blood being applied to the doorposts, a Type of the Blood of Christ applied to our hearts, which stops the Judgment of God)" (Heb. 11:24-28).

The truth is, whereas Moses chose the Lord and His Ways, the far greater majority of the world does the very opposite.

Jesus said: *"Enter you in at the strait gate* (this is the Door Who is Jesus [Jn. 10:1])*: for wide is the gate, and broad is the way, that leads to destruction, and many there be which go in thereat* (proclaims the fact of many and varied religions of the world, which are false, and lead to eternal hellfire)*:*

"Because strait is the gate, and narrow is the way, which leads unto life, and few there be who find it (every contrite heart earnestly desires to be among the *'few'*; the requirements are greater than most are willing to accept)" (Mat. 7:13-14).

WHAT IS THE ALMIGHTY, THAT WE SHOULD SERVE HIM?

What a stupid question for the wicked to ask!

The question is asked as to *"what"* God is? Perhaps the following will shed some light on the subject:

• God is the Creator of all things which are good: that means that, in essence, He owns all things. The Scripture says: *"The Earth is the LORD's, and the fullness thereof; the world, and they who dwell therein* (God created the Earth, so it legally belongs to Him; sadly, it is now in rebellion against Him, being dominated more or less by Satan and evil spirit forces [II Cor. 4:4; Eph. 2:2; I Jn. 5:19]; however, with the Second Coming, all of this will be rectified)*. For he has founded it upon the seas, and established it upon the floods* (founded it and established it above . . .)" (Ps. 24:1-2).

• God through His Son, the Lord Jesus Christ is the Saviour of man: the Scripture says: *"Paul, an Apostle of Jesus Christ, by the Commandment of God our Saviour, and the Lord Jesus Christ, which is our hope"* (I Tim. 1:1).

• God is our Judge: Once again He is our Judge through the Lord Jesus Christ.

NOTES

The idea is, man will face Jesus Christ at Calvary, where all sins are remitted, or he will face Him at the Great White Throne Judgment, but face Him he will (Acts 2:21; Rev. 20:11-15).

So, God is Creator, He is Saviour, and He is Judge.

IS THERE PLEASURE IN SIN?

Yes, there is pleasure in sin, but only for a short period of time. The Scripture says of Moses, which we quoted a little bit back, *"Choosing rather to suffer affliction with the people of God, than to enjoy the pleasures of sin for a season"* (Heb. 11:25).

If you'll notice it said *"for a season."* Virtually always the pleasure soon ends, and the bondage begins. In other words, it ceases to be fun, whatever it is, and now drives the person, with the individual becoming a slave to his or her passions.

We are told that there are twenty million alcoholics in this nation. Every one of them started to drink for fun and pleasure. But at a point in time, it ceased to be fun and pleasure, and became a need, a need so great, that the person cannot stop.

Job said, *"For what pleasure has he and his house after him, when the number of his months is cut off in the midst?"* (Job 21:21).

Outside of the Lord there is no true pleasure, no true enjoyment, no true satisfaction. Only in Christ is there *"more abundant life"* (Jn. 10:10).

(27) "BEHOLD, I KNOW YOUR THOUGHTS, AND THE DEVICES WHICH YOU WRONGFULLY IMAGINE AGAINST ME.

(28) "FOR YOU SAY, WHERE IS THE HOUSE OF THE PRINCE? AND WHERE ARE THE DWELLING PLACES OF THE WICKED?

(29) "HAVE YOU NOT ASKED THEM WHO GO BY THE WAY? AND DO YOU NOT KNOW THEIR TOKENS,

(30) "THAT THE WICKED IS RESERVED TO THE DAY OF DESTRUCTION? THEY SHALL BE BROUGHT FORTH TO THE DAY OF WRATH.

(31) "WHO SHALL DECLARE HIS WAY TO HIS FACE? AND WHO SHALL REPAY HIM WHAT HE HAS DONE?

(32) "YET SHALL HE BE BROUGHT TO THE GRAVE, AND SHALL REMAIN IN THE TOMB.

(33) "THE CLODS OF THE VALLEY SHALL BE SWEET UNTO HIM, AND EVERY MAN SHALL DRAW AFTER HIM, AS THERE ARE INNUMERABLE BEFORE HIM.

(34) "HOW THEN COMFORT YOU ME IN VAIN, SEEING IN YOUR ANSWERS THERE REMAINS FALSEHOOD?"

The pattern is:

1. (Vs. 27) Job, in essence, tells his friends, *"I know, what you think of me."*

2. (Vs. 30) Irrespective as to what type of life the wicked may enjoy on this Earth, destruction in eternity awaits them, unless they get right with God!

3. (Vs. 34) *"Your position,"* Job continues, *"that the godly always prosper, while the wicked always are afflicted and brought low, by experience, in other words by your own reckoning, proves false."*

THE GREAT WHITE THRONE JUDGMENT

Job said, *"Have you not asked them to go by the way? and do you not know their tokens, that the wicked is reserved to the day of destruction? they shall be brought forth to the day of wrath"* (Job 21:29-30).

Whether Job realizes it or not, and most likely he doesn't, he is speaking here of the coming Great White Throne Judgment.

The following are some particulars about this coming terrible event. They are:

• This Judgment will include every unsaved person who has ever lived. None of the redeemed will be present.

• It will take place at the conclusion of the Kingdom Age, and before the advent of the New Heaven and the New Earth.

• Jesus Christ personally will be the Judge.

• Every person will be shown their just deserts. The books will be opened, which contains everything they ever did. They will have no excuse.

• All will be consigned to the Lake of Fire, where they will remain forever.

"Amidst us our Beloved stands,
"And bids us view His pierced Hands;
"Points to the wounded Feet and Side,
"Blest emblems of the Crucified."

"What food luxurious loads the board,
"When, at His Table, sits the Lord!
"The wine how rich, the bread how sweet,
"When Jesus deigns the guests to meet!"

"If now, with eyes defiled and dim,
"We see the signs, but see not Him;
"O, may His Love the scales displace,
"And bid us see Him Face-to-face!"

"Though glorious Bridegroom of our hearts,
"Your present Smile Heaven imparts!
"O, lift the veil, if veil there be,
"Let every Saint Your Glory see!"

CHAPTER 22

(1) "THEN ELIPHAZ THE TEMANITE ANSWERED AND SAID,

(2) "CAN A MAN BE PROFITABLE UNTO GOD, AS HE WHO IS WISE MAY BE PROFITABLE UNTO HIMSELF?

(3) "IS IT ANY PLEASURE TO THE ALMIGHTY, THAT YOU ARE RIGHTEOUS? OR IS IT GAIN TO HIM, THAT YOU MAKE YOUR WAYS PERFECT?

(4) "WILL HE REPROVE YOU FOR FEAR OF YOU? WILL HE ENTER WITH YOU INTO JUDGMENT?

(5) "IS NOT YOUR WICKEDNESS GREAT? AND YOUR INIQUITIES INFINITE?

(6) "FOR YOU HAVE TAKEN A PLEDGE FROM YOUR BROTHER FOR NOUGHT, AND STRIPPED THE NAKED OF THEIR CLOTHING.

(7) "YOU HAVE NOT GIVEN WATER TO THE WEARY TO DRINK, AND YOU HAVE WITHHELD BREAD FROM THE HUNGRY.

(8) "BUT AS FOR THE MIGHTY MAN, HE HAD THE EARTH; AND THE HONOURABLE MAN DWELT IN IT.

(9) "YOU HAVE SENT WIDOWS AWAY EMPTY, AND THE ARMS OF THE FATHERLESS HAVE BEEN BROKEN.

(10) "THEREFORE SNARES ARE

ROUND ABOUT YOU, AND SUDDEN FEAR TROUBLES YOU;

(11) "OR DARKNESS, THAT YOU CANNOT SEE; AND ABUNDANCE OF WATERS COVER YOU.

(12) "IS NOT GOD IN THE HEIGHT OF HEAVEN? AND BEHOLD THE HEIGHT OF THE STARS, HOW HIGH THEY ARE!

(13) "AND YOU SAY, HOW DOES GOD KNOW? CAN HE JUDGE THROUGH THE DARK CLOUD?

(14) "THICK CLOUDS ARE A COVERING TO HIM, THAT HE SEES NOT; AND HE WALKS IN THE CIRCUIT OF HEAVEN.

(15) "HAVE YOU MARKED THE OLD WAY WHICH WICKED MEN HAVE TROD?

(16) "WHICH WERE CUT DOWN OUT OF TIME, WHOSE FOUNDATION WAS OVERFLOWN WITH A FLOOD:

(17) "WHICH SAID UNTO GOD, DEPART FROM US: AND WHAT CAN THE ALMIGHTY DO FOR THEM?

(18) "YET HE FILLED THEIR HOUSES WITH GOOD THINGS: BUT THE COUNSEL OF THE WICKED IS FAR FROM ME.

(19) "THE RIGHTEOUS SEE IT, AND ARE GLAD: AND THE INNOCENT LAUGH THEM TO SCORN.

(20) "WHEREAS OUR SUBSTANCE IS NOT CUT DOWN, BUT THE REMNANT OF THEM THE FIRE CONSUMES."

The synopsis is:

1. (Vs. 2) Eliphaz, annoyed by the introduction of inconvenient facts, becomes abusive and, whereas in his first two speeches he only hinted at Job's alleged evil conduct, in this, his last speech, he directly accuses Job of wickedness and wrongdoing.

2. (Vs. 3) In reply to Job's facts, Eliphaz advances the theory that man's goodness does not add to, nor man's badness take from, God's economy. Therefore, God does not prosper some and afflict others for His Own advantage, he says. The cause, therefore, of such action must be found in men themselves, so Job's calamities clearly prove his guilt.

3. (Vs. 4) In other words he is saying, the fact of your reproof is sure evidence of the fact of your guilt.

4. In Verses 5 through 9, Eliphaz openly accuses Job of the worst type of sin.

5. According to Verse 13, Eliphaz accuses Job of saying, *"How does God know?"* The truth is, Job had never said any such thing, but it suits the purpose of Eliphaz to malign and misrepresent Job.

6. According to Verse 15, Eliphaz puts Job into the seed of Cain before the Flood, who *"corrupted their way"* (Gen. 6:12).

7. (Vs. 17) He now places Job among the most evil, whom God had to destroy with a flood.

8. According to Verse 18, Eliphaz, in essence, says, *"Even though these particular wicked individuals prospered, I will not have any part with them,"* thereby, holding himself up as pious. This is the terminology of the self-righteous!

9. Verse 19 proclaims the fact that Eliphaz, in essence, says *"It is righteous for me to condemn you."*

10. And then in Verse 20, he, in essence, says, *"Because I am blessed, and you are severely cursed, proves my statements."*

THE STANDPOINT OF HUMAN EXPERIENCE

As we have previously stated, Eliphaz the Temanite argued from the position of human experience. The Temanites, in fact, were famous for their wisdom (Jer. 49:7). Of course, their so-called wisdom was not that of God, but rather that of the world.

Eliphaz, like some present-day professors of science and philosophy, annoyed by the introduction of inconvenient facts, become abusive and, whereas, in his first two speeches he only hinted at Job's supposed evil conduct, in this his last speech he directly accuses him of wickedness and wrongdoing, and actually of the worst kind.

What angers this man is Job's claimed relationship with God. He actually denies this relationship and, as well, denies that any man can have such a relationship with God. What Eliphaz knows about God he has learned from experience, or so he thinks, which, in effect, is actually man's wisdom concerning God, and which offers no explanation of God whatsoever. In other words, Eliphaz, despite his claims, had no knowledge of God. Any supposed knowledge was superficial at best!

What Job knew about God he had learned from relationship and Revelation, which is the only way that God can be understood.

Concluding his argument against Job's relationship with God, he says in the Fifth Verse, *"Is not your wickedness great? And your iniquities infinite?"* He seeks to disprove this claimed relationship by accusing him of the most terrible sins, even though he has no knowledge whatsoever of such sins. Once again, when one reads the words of Eliphaz, and the other two friends as well, he is reading the words of self-righteousness.

LAUGHING AT THE CALAMITY OF THE WICKED

Eliphaz says, *"The righteous see it, and are glad: and the innocent laugh them to scorn."*

This was the justification of Eliphaz and his *"friends"* and their present attitude toward Job. Their reasoning was: if the righteous in other ages, or so they claim, rejoiced in the destruction of the wicked, their own conduct had not been out of place in this instance.

In Job's day, there was no written Word of God, at least as we know it presently. In fact, this Book of Job would be the very First Book written, and as previously stated, was probably written by Moses in collaboration with Job. Actually, Job was still alive for some period of time while Moses was at the back side of the desert. More than likely Job visited Moses, related his experiences, with Moses writing it all down, with it ultimately being placed in the Canon of Scripture.

However, as it regards the action of Eliphaz, there is nothing in the Word of God that gives credence to the idea of Believers seeing the calamity of the wicked and then laughing them to scorn. There are two or three Scriptures in the Old Testament, which some have endeavored to twist and make it seem like such, but they really do not contain that meaning. They are as follows:

"The righteous shall rejoice when he sees the vengeance: he shall wash his feet in the blood of the wicked" (Ps. 58:10).

The *"righteous"* in this Verse pertains to Israel, who shall rejoice when the Antichrist is defeated in the Battle of Armageddon, and rightly so.

The Psalmist then said, *"The righteous shall see it, and rejoice: and all iniquity shall stop her mouth"* (Ps. 107:42).

The rejoicing that is done here by the righteous merely refers to praise that goes to the Lord because He has helped them. It does not refer to rejoicing over the calamity of the wicked.

Solomon said, *"When it goes well with the righteous, the city rejoices: and when the wicked perish, there is shouting"* (Prov. 11:10). Again, this refers to the triumph of the Lord, and not rejoicing because the wicked are perishing.

Actually the Scripture says regarding the destruction of the wicked, *"Say unto them, As I live, says the Lord GOD, I have no pleasure in the death of the wicked; but that the wicked turn from his way and live: turn you, turn you from your evil ways; for why will you die, O House of Israel?"* (Ezek. 33:11).

Further, the Scripture says, *"The Lord is not slack concerning His Promise as some men count slackness; but is longsuffering to us-ward, not willing that any should perish, but that all should come to Repentance. (The Dispensation of the Cross has been the longest of all, and it is that because God keeps after sinners to be Saved. He has made a way through the Cross for all to be Saved. Most, however, refuse His Way)"* (II Pet. 3:9).

And then there is one of the greatest Passages of all: *"For God so loved the world, that He gave His Only Begotten Son, that whosoever believes in Him should not perish, but have Everlasting Life"* (Jn. 3:16).

Eliphaz did what millions do. They devised statements, and claim that it is of God.

While Eliphaz may have had some excuse, considering there was no written Bible at the time, presently, there is no excuse whatsoever. But, men keep twisting the Word, perverting the Word, adding to or taking from the Word.

I would strongly recommend THE EXPOSITOR'S STUDY BIBLE to any and every Believer. It is the King James Version; however, the notes given with the Scriptures, explain the Word of God to a greater degree, we think, than anything that's available

(21) "ACQUAINT NOW YOUR SELF WITH HIM, AND BE AT PEACE: THEREBY GOOD SHALL COME UNTO YOU.

(22) "RECEIVE, I PRAY YOU, THE LAW FROM HIS MOUTH, AND LAY UP HIS WORDS IN YOUR HEART.

(23) "IF YOU RETURN TO THE ALMIGHTY, YOU SHALL BE BUILT UP, YOU SHALL PUT AWAY INIQUITY FAR FROM YOUR TABERNACLES.

(24) "THEN SHALL YOU LAY UP GOLD AS DUST, AND THE GOLD OF OPHIR AS THE STONES OF THE BROOKS.

(25) "YES, THE ALMIGHTY SHALL BE YOUR DEFENCE, AND YOU SHALL HAVE PLENTY OF SILVER.

(26) "FOR THEN SHALL YOU HAVE YOUR DELIGHT IN THE ALMIGHTY, AND SHALL LIFT UP YOUR FACE UNTO GOD.

(27) "YOU SHALL MAKE YOUR PRAYER UNTO HIM, AND HE SHALL HEAR YOU, AND YOU SHALL PAY YOUR VOWS.

(28) "YOU SHALL ALSO DECREE A THING, AND IT SHALL BE ESTABLISHED UNTO YOU: AND THE LIGHT SHALL SHINE UPON YOUR WAYS.

(29) "WHEN MEN ARE CAST DOWN, THEN SHALL YOU SAY, THERE IS LIFTING UP; AND HE SHALL SAVE THE HUMBLE PERSON.

(30) "HE SHALL DELIVER THE ISLAND OF THE INNOCENT: AND IT IS DELIVERED BY THE PURENESS OF YOUR HANDS."

The pattern is:

1. (Vs. 21) Eliphaz now implores Job to repent, when in reality, it is Eliphaz who needs to repent.

2. (Vs. 22) For Job to be insulted by Eliphaz in this manner must have been a bitter pill to swallow.

3. (Vs. 24) *"You'll get rich again,"* Eliphaz says, *"If you will only repent."* So, judgment was equated with poverty, while blessing was equated with riches.

4. (Vs. 25) *"Reduced to poverty,"* Eliphaz says, *"proves, Job, that God is against you."*

5. (Vs. 26) It's interesting that Eliphaz placed the entirety of his theology on riches and poverty. How so much like some presently.

6. (Vs. 30) Little did Eliphaz realize that shortly Job would deliver these *"friends"* from the wrath of God by his intercession (42:7-9).

PIOUS SELF-RIGHTEOUSNESS

Let us emphasize the fact once again, that the Holy Spirit allowed the prattle of these *"three friends"* plus the babble of Elihu, who will surface a little later, to be inserted in the Holy Writ, in order that we might see firsthand the spirit of self-righteousness. It should be a lesson to all of us. The tragedy is, it seems like all of the others of that particular time, whomever they may have been, and they, no doubt, numbered many, fell into the same category. All who approached Job at that time, all who commented on his dilemma, all who observed his suffering, all and without exception it seems, fell into the awful category of self-righteousness. Even the little children followed suit, because they, no doubt, heard the remarks of their parents. And, as well, the *"three friends"* were relating to all and sundry their thoughts and feelings about the situation, and were, no doubt, heard by all who cared to listen. What a terrible summation of that time!

How much different is it presently?

Considering that we now have the Bible and the Holy Spirit living in our hearts and lives, is there any excuse for self-righteousness? Yet, I think I can say without fear of contradiction, that every last one of us, at one time or the other, has been plagued by this terrible malady.

Before the Lord showed me the great Word of the Cross, I would have had to have stood in that line also.

THE CROSS OF CHRIST, THE ONLY ANSWER TO SELF-RIGHTEOUSNESS

If, in fact, the heading is true, that the only cure, the only defense against self-righteousness, is the Cross of Christ, then there would be precious few who would not fall into this category. Let me say it again:

The only answer to pride, self-will, a lack of humility, and self-righteousness, is the

Cross of Christ. There is no other!

HOW IS THE CROSS OF CHRIST THE ANSWER TO SELF-RIGHTEOUSNESS?

The Cross helps one to see oneself, and to be sure, what one sees will prove to be extremely unsavory. I now grieve at some of the positions that I once took, some of the statements I once made, some of the attitudes I once had. But I could only see the wrong of this through the Cross of Christ.

What exactly does one see when one properly sees oneself?

One will see arrogance, pride, self-will, a holier-than-thou attitude, in fact, ugliness of every sort. It's not a pretty picture! And one cannot properly see such, thereby, properly evaluating such, as one must, without first understanding the Cross of Christ.

In fact, when one properly sees the Cross, the first thing that happens, is that one begins to properly see the Lord. Only then, can one begin to properly see oneself. This is exactly what happened to Job.

He thought pretty well of himself until the Lord appeared on the scene. And then when he saw the Lord he said, *"Wherefore I abhor myself, and repent in dust and ashes"* (Job 42:6).

Quoting from THE EXPOSITOR'S STUDY BIBLE, the notes say, "In effect, Job had previously reported that he had not abhorred himself, but, on the contrary, thought well of himself and had held fast to his moral excellency. The discovery of the deep corruption of the heart is the most painful and humbling that a man can make.

"So the Patriarch had to crucify all his goodness as truly as all his badness, and sit in wood ashes as a public confession that he merited death because of his sin-defiled nature.

"This moral principle governs the Sanctification of the Saint as it governs the Salvation of the sinner."

As we will see when we come to the latter part of this Book, when the Lord appeared, all, the three friends and Job, were taken to the Cross, symbolized by the Sacrifices (42:7-9).

Only when one has properly seen the Lord, and one can only properly see the Lord by and through the Cross of Christ, will one then be able to properly see oneself. Otherwise, it is impossible!

When we consider that the Spirit of God works through the Cross and, in fact, works exclusively through the Cross, meaning He will work no other way, we then begin to see how important all of this is. That's the reason that Paul, when given the meaning of the New Covenant, said we *"preach the Cross"* (Rom. 6:3-5; 8:2; I Cor. 1:17-18, 23; 2:2; Gal. 2:20-21; 6:14; Eph. 2:13-18; Col. 2:14-15).

THE MEANING OF THE NEW COVENANT

The meaning of the New Covenant, in essence, is the Cross of Christ. It is all summed up in the Cross. There all sin was atoned, Satan and his cohorts were totally defeated, which means the sin debt was forever lifted, at least for those who will believe, making it possible for the Holy Spirit to come into our hearts and lives and to abide forever (Jn. 14:16-18).

Every Covenant that God ever made with man was broken by man almost instantly. But the New Covenant, even though a Covenant made between God and man, cannot be broken. In fact, it is impossible for it to be broken.

How is that so when it, as well, is a Covenant between God and man, especially considering that man has broken every Covenant into which he has entered?

It is because the New Covenant is entirely in Christ. Christ is both God and Man. He serves as our Representative Man in all things, Whom Paul labeled as *"the Last Adam,"* or the *"Second Man"* (I Cor. 15:45-47).

While you and I may forfeit the benefits of the Covenant by our actions, which will greatly affect us in an adverse way, still, the Covenant itself remains unaffected, because it is not in me and you, but rather all in Christ. As such, that is why the Apostle referred to this Covenant as *"the Everlasting Covenant"* (Heb. 13:20).

This Covenant will never have to be amended, will never have to be replaced, will never suffer loss, and because it is all in Christ. That's the reason the Cross is so very important, because this is where the

Covenant was consummated, where the Blood was shed!

A Covenant in olden times always consisted in some way, of the shedding of blood. It might be the finger of both parties pricked, with the blood then intermingled, or it might be a lamb that was slaughtered, with its blood being shed, but it was always in blood, because the life of the flesh is in the blood. So, it was at the Cross of Calvary where our Lord suffered, bled, and died. It was there where the Covenant was cut so to speak, thereby, made viable, and was accepted by God the Father in full. The Scripture says:

"God, Who at sundry times and in divers manners (refers to the many and varied ways) *spoke in time past unto the fathers by the Prophets* (refers to Old Testament Times),

"Has in these last days (the Dispensation of Grace, which is the Church Age) *spoken unto us by His Son* (speaks of the Incarnation), *Whom He has appointed Heir of all things* (through the means of the Cross), *by Whom also He made the worlds* (proclaims his Deity, as the previous phrase of Him being the 'Heir of all things' proclaims His humanity);

"Who being the brightness of His Glory (the radiance of God's Glory), *and the express Image of His Person* (the exact reproduction), *and upholding all things by the Word of His Power* (carries the meaning of Jesus not only sustaining the weight of the Universe, but also maintaining its coherence and carrying on its development), *when He had by Himself purged our sins* (which He did at the Cross, dealing with sin regarding its cause, its power, and its guilt), *sat down on the Right Hand of the Majesty on high* (speaks of the Finished Work of Christ, and that the Sacrifice was accepted by the Father)" (Heb. 1:1-3).

SELF-RIGHTEOUSNESS IN ACTION

Self-righteousness always concludes itself to be perfectly right with God, while at the same time concluding, through circumstances, that others aren't.

It's not a very pleasant thing to be labeled as a hypocrite, as was Job! It's not a very pleasant thing to be accused of every vile sin and crime that one could imagine, as was Job! As we have said previously:

"When a person is down, and someone, anyone, in fact, can do any negative thing to him they so desire, and not be reprimanded, but rather applauded, one then finds out how many good Christians there really are."

There aren't many!

The Word of God takes a very dim view of self-righteousness and, in fact, our Lord, and to be sure, castigated such individuals (Lk. 18:9).

WHAT IS RIGHTEOUSNESS?

In short, Righteousness is simply that which is right; however, it's that which is right in the sight of God, and not in the sight of man. In fact, that is the difference between Righteousness and self-righteousness, i.e., *"unrighteousness."*

The Hebrew word for Righteousness is *"tsadaq,"* and simply means as stated, *"that which is right."*

The Greek word for Righteousness is *"dikaiosune"* and also means *"that which is right."*

The struggle has ever been that man, and especially religious man, tries to usurp authority over God's Word, thereby, inserting his own. To be sure, this problem did not begin yesterday. It actually began on the first page of human history.

I speak of Cain and Abel, and the sacrifices which God demanded, which would be a Type of Christ. The Fourth Chapter of Genesis proclaims the fact that Abel offered up the right kind of Sacrifice, the slain lamb, which typified Christ, and it was accounted to him for Righteousness. On the other hand, Cain, while offering up a sacrifice, would not offer that which was demanded by God, but actually that of his own choosing, the labor of his hands, whatever that may have been.

As someone has well said, around Cain's altar there are many, and around Abel's Altar there are few. Cain's sacrifice was repulsive to God and beautiful to man, while Abel's sacrifice was beautiful to God, and ugly to man. It hasn't changed from then until now. The church keeps trying to institute something other than the Cross. As a result, there is no righteousness, as there can be no righteousness.

THE MODERN CHURCH

It is amazing, that the church produces one scheme after the other, which is a sacrifice of its own hands, thereby, ignoring the Cross, and the false way will most of the time be eagerly accepted.

Some time back, my wife asked me to read the book, *"The Purpose Driven Life"*, which she handed to me as we were seated in our den at home.

I read a few pages of it and laid it down. She came in a little later and asked me had I read it?

I replied that I had read a few pages, but it was no point in going further.

"Why?" she asked!

My comment to her was, that I didn't need to read the entire book. I knew that it was spurious, because whatever it is they were proclaiming, it was not the Cross of Christ. And if it's not the Cross of Christ, no matter how slickly produced, no matter how glibly spoken, no matter how cleverly designed, it will do no one any good whatsoever.

The modern church is giving a drowning man a new suit of clothes, when he needs a life raft. That life raft is Christ and Him Crucified, and it is the only life raft, so to speak, in existence. There is no other!

"I will sing the wondrous Story,
"Of the Christ Who died for me;
"How He left His Home in Glory,
"For the Cross on Calvary."

"I was lost; but Jesus found me,
"Found the sheep that went astray;
"Threw His loving Arms around me,
"Drew me back into His Way."

"I was bruised: but Jesus healed me,
"Faint was I from many a fall;
"Sight was gone, and fears possessed me:
"But He freed me from them all."

"Days of darkness still come o'er me;
"Sorrows paths I often tread:
"But the Saviour still is with me,
"By His Hand I'm safely led."

"He will keep me till the river,
"Rolls its waters at my feet:
"Then He'll bear me safely over,
"Where the loved ones I shall meet."

CHAPTER 23

(1) "THEN JOB ANSWERED AND SAID,

(2) "EVEN TODAY IS MY COMPLAINT BITTER: MY STROKE IS HEAVIER THAN MY GROANING.

(3) "OH THAT I KNEW WHERE I MIGHT FIND HIM! THAT I MIGHT COME EVEN TO HIS SEAT!

(4) "I WOULD ORDER MY CAUSE BEFORE HIM, AND FILL MY MOUTH WITH ARGUMENTS.

(5) "I WOULD KNOW THE WORDS WHICH HE WOULD ANSWER ME, AND UNDERSTAND WHAT HE WOULD SAY UNTO ME.

(6) "WILL HE PLEAD AGAINST ME WITH HIS GREAT POWER? NO; BUT HE WOULD PUT STRENGTH IN ME.

(7) "THERE THE RIGHTEOUS MIGHT DISPUTE WITH HIM; SO SHOULD I BE DELIVERED FOR EVER FROM MY JUDGE."

The composition is:

1. (Vs. 2) Job's situation at present is so acute, and seemingly growing worse by the moment, that if God doesn't do something quickly, he feels he cannot last much longer. He has no idea, of course, as to what is really transpiring.

2. Verse 2 proclaims despair in its very words. Job knows now that he will receive no help from his *"friends,"* or even his loved ones. The only help that he will receive will come from God. Therefore, he longs for an audience with his Maker.

3. (Vs. 4) A short time later, the Lord will give Job exactly that which he has requested. However, his conduct will be far different than what he had imagined. Actually, he will little *"order his cause before Him."*

4. As it regards Verse 5, the Words that the Lord will say will be far beyond Job's ability to grasp or understand. However, the *"Words"* will be Words of comfort, strength, and deliverance, totally different from his *"friends."*

5. (Vs. 6) Job said that the Lord will put strength in him and, in fact, the Lord would do exactly that when He did appear.

6. (Vs. 7) Job is confident, and rightly so, that, if he can bring his cause before God, he will obtain an acquittal and deliverance.

OUR ONLY REFUGE IS THE LORD

Job's statement in this Chapter turns more toward God than toward his *"friends."* He has strikingly found out and, therefore, has come to the conclusion, that he will receive no help from them whatsoever. His only recourse is God! And to be sure, the only recourse of anyone is God, even though most in the modern church do not seem to realize that.

Little does the great Patriarch know that when he makes these statements, that his request will be honored and answered very shortly.

HUMANISTIC PSYCHOLOGY

In the 1950's, the Pentecostal world began to dabble in psychology. It was a slow process, but at the present time (2008 as I dictate these notes), psychology has actually become the religion of the Church. And please understand the following:

If humanistic psychology is embraced, even as it actually is, the Cross of Christ and the Moving and the Operation of the Holy Spirit must go. It is one or the other, it cannot be both! If humanistic psychology is embraced, the Cross and the Holy Spirit are abandoned, irrespective as to the claims made by preachers. If the Cross and the Holy Spirit are embraced, it will quickly become obvious that there is no place for humanistic psychology. In fact, psychology is the religion of humanism. It is man's answer, man's solution, for the ills, aberrations, and the perversions of modern man.

Is humanistic psychology bringing about the desired results?

No!

Today the people in our churches are suffering more nervous breakdowns, more divorces, more twisted and wrecked lives than ever before in the history of the Church. And yet, we have more trained psychiatrists and psychologists. What's wrong? Why aren't our carnal Philistine ways reducing these unfortunate statistics?

At least one of the problems is that all too many of our preachers today are receiving their education in secular schools, which, in reality, have turned their backs on God. Colleges and universities once existed for the purpose of training young people to develop a disciplined mind, and to learn how to study. Such discipline would lead to useful and fulfilled lives. It would help solve some of the problems of the day, and those so trained could be counted upon to become useful servants to God and their fellowman.

This no longer seems to be the purpose of higher learning. Colleges and universities seem to exist today for the sole purpose of subsidizing their professors' unfettered search for whatever it is they happen to view at the moment as *"truth."* One man has said that it seems students are now little more than a necessary evil, little more than a means of paying the freight on the professors' eternal quest for esoteric knowledge.

As a matter of fact, no one is considered to be truly educated today unless he believes that there is no such thing as absolute truth (and by extension, of course, the whole Bible is thus thrown into question — and disrepute). Even the word *"moral"* is a *"dirty word"* today in most educated circles.

A meeting was conducted not so long ago where hundreds of college and university presidents agreed that nothing is absolutely right and nothing is absolutely wrong — and of this they were absolutely sure! Of course, I am absolutely sure that they are absolutely wrong!

One professor said that colleges are educating people away from their common sense — and they're certainly educating them away from the Bible, which is the only true source of education the world has ever known.

MODERN PREACHERS

Sad to say, multiplied thousands of modern preachers have fallen for the secular way of helping individuals; consequently, I wonder if anyone is being helped. I think the answer to that is obvious, no they aren't!

The truth is, many, if not all, are being

harmed. The greatest problem facing this country today is not ignorance; it's believing things which aren't true!

It would seem that all of the religious, political, psychological, and sociological systems of today are based on philosophies and presuppositions. And if these preconceived ideas are false, then all doctrines and ideologies based upon them are false as well! Following such ideas will produce frustration, confusion, and the ultimate disintegration of any society or element that tries to accommodate them. In fact, this has been pulled over into the church as well.

CHRISTIAN PSYCHOLOGY?

Actually, in real terms, there is no such thing as Christian psychology. In other words, the psychology that is taught under the guise of *"Christian,"* is the same psychology that's taught in atheistic universities. It all comes from the same source. The word *"Christian"* is attached to such, to make a gullible Christian public believe that it's legitimate. It isn't!

Tragically, modern Bible Colleges and Seminaries, with most not even honestly being able to put the name *"Bible"* in their title, because the Bible is little taught anymore. You can look at the course offerings of these schools, and you will see that the majority of that being offered is in the field of psychology. And let the reader understand, it is not possible to wed the Bible with humanistic psychology. Those who claim to do so, are really fooling themselves, and above all, fooling fellow Believers. Either one cancels out the other.

The Word of God claims to hold all the answers to man's Spiritual and sociological needs. Peter said:

"Grace and peace be multiplied unto you through the knowledge of God, and of Jesus our Lord,

"According as His Divine Power has given unto us all things that pertain unto life and godliness, through the knowledge of Him Who has called us to Glory and Virtue:

"Whereby are given unto us exceeding great and precious Promises: that by these you might be partakers of the Divine Nature, having escaped the corruption that is in the world through lust" (II Pet. 1:2-4).

Now either the Holy Spirit meant what He said, when He gave these words to Simon Peter who gave them to us, or else He lied. I happen to believe that He told the truth!

When proposed preachers to be enter most Bible Colleges and Seminaries presently, they do not come out of those schools armed with the Word of God, which is the only answer for suffering humanity, but rather armed with psychological gimmicks that will help no one.

SIGMUND FREUD

Most of modern day psychology is based on the foolish assumptions of one Sigmund Freud — a man who was painfully insecure, who couldn't stand to have anyone look at him, and who had a markedly abnormal life, even to including a perverted relationship with his mother.

To compensate for his own hang-ups, he came up with all kinds of ridiculous assertions. For instance, he made sex a purely biological function and removed it from the realm of morality. The bottom line of such reasoning is that homosexuality (or any other type of perversion) isn't considered immoral. This is what is behind the efforts in this nation to legalize gay marriages so-called, which are an abomination in the eyes of God.

When one looks back at the history of empires, one finds that three sins were pandemic at the time of the fall of these empires, including the mighty Roman Empire. Those sins are:
- Homosexuality;
- Incest; and,
- Pedophilia.

As should be obvious, these sins are pandemic in this nation at the present time. And please understand, the Lord will allow such to continue only so long.

SOCIOLOGY

Sociologists would tell us that a man's problems are caused by his environment — failing to recognize that they are caused instead by an evil heart that has sinned against God, which is the result of the Fall.

That's what the statement means, *"man*

is a product of his society." Under this type of thinking, society is responsible for everything man does. But does God agree?

No!

God says that man alone is responsible for his actions; not society and not environment. Man's freedom from responsibility is the gospel of sociology — which makes secular humanism its religion.

I maintain that the Bible is the only true Book of preventive psychology ever written, that is if one wants to label it as such. Unfortunately, the church is forgetting this. The church, once again, needs to recall the difference between weakness and disease. It is impossible to reason with disease. You can't talk a person out of a case of smallpox. And — if mental problems are sicknesses (as liberal thinkers try to convince us they are), then why try talking to a psychiatrist at a $200 an hour rate? This is also what we try to do with alcoholics. We refer to alcoholism as a disease, when in reality it is a sin.

A DISEASE?

A disease is, by actual definition, an abnormal condition within an organism, as a consequence of infection or malfunction, which impairs the normal physiological activity. So what's the point of all this? The point is that counseling won't change a disease or sickness.

COUNSELING

Now, let's for a moment look at the word *"counseling."* This has become the mainstay of efforts to help most people within our churches today. It used to be that the preaching of the Gospel performed this task. It used to be that Altar Services, where God was dealing with individuals on an individual basis, were the key to mental health. No more. Counseling is now the great thruway that leads all to help and healing — be it pastoral or clinical counseling. In many of the larger churches, extensive staffs of trained psychologists are utilized to keep their parishioners healthy and happy. Dr. Edward Pinckney in his book, *"The Fallacy Of Freud And Psychoanalysis,"* states, *"there is a wealth of documented information to show that the results of psychoanalysis are not only unsuccessful, but, what is even worse, are harmful."*[1]

The good doctor went on to say that psychoanalysis is attractive to those who wish to be relieved of responsibility for their actions and failures. This seems to document very well the fact that psychoanalysis does more harm than good. In fact, it does no good at all.

SECULAR HUMANISM

Where does all this psychological mumbo-jumbo come from?

This entire program, which the church has little by little come to accept, stems directly from secular humanism. And secular humanism is, the most inhumane philosophy ever concocted on our Lord's Earth. It has, in fact, become the religion of sociology. Its basic tenant is that humanism looks at man as the basic building block of everything, and builds upon man a world (and cosmic) view and philosophy, which relentlessly proceeds to eliminate God in any Divine dimension.

Secular humanism is the summation of all that is anti-God. Actually, communism is merely secular humanism without a political format. Sociologists tell us that man can find happiness by merely seeking it. But we know happiness can only be achieved by serving one's fellowman and by voluntarily losing one's life for Christ's Sake, subsequently serving Him.

So the point I'm making is this: our preachers, who have majored in psychology or sociology and are trying to counsel people from this perspective, will be noneffective at best and harmful at worst.

I believe the so-called behavioral sciences (psychology, sociology, and psychiatry) are totally humanistic in content, with a foundation of inherent worldliness that denies God and the Bible, that does not recognize the cause of man's difficulties, and certainly does not know the cure. In essence, it only majors in *"effects."*

I'm little interested in anyone who tells me how I act when I already know how I act — but I don't know why I act like I act or who can keep me from acting like I act.

Consequently, any church or preacher who plans to help people by such methods will produce no lasting results. The answer must come back to what I originally pointed out.

THE CROSS OF CHRIST

The Cross of Christ alone is the answer to man's dilemma. There our Lord atoned for all sin, which removed Satan's legal right to hold men in bondage. Jesus Christ is, therefore, the Source of all things we receive from God, and the Cross of Christ is the Means by which these things are given to us, all superintended by the Holy Spirit. It remains for man to place his Faith exclusively in Christ and what Christ has done for us at the Cross, understanding that this is the answer and, in fact, the only answer for suffering humanity.

But, of course, the world is not interested in that solution at all, and regrettably and sadly neither is the modern church. In fact, the Cross of Christ has never been popular. As we have previously stated in this Volume, around Cain's altar many are gathered, while around Abel's Altar, few are gathered.

The Apostle Paul was trained in Mosaic Law as possibly few, if any, of his day. As well, it is believed by some Bible scholars, that Paul attended the University at Tarsus. So he was perfectly at home discussing philosophy, which was all the rage of his particular time. In fact, he was one of the most educated men to pen any of the Sacred Text. He wrote nearly half of the New Testament, as the Holy Spirit inspired him to do so.

The city of Corinth was one of the most jaded cities in the Roman Empire. It was plagued with the twin evils of vice and philosophy, having produced some of the famous philosophers of that era. So, when Paul was led by the Holy Spirit to plant a church in that great city, the evidence is that he wondered how in the world he could break through these twin shells that held these people in bondage — vice and philosophy.

The Holy Spirit gave him the answer. He said, in his First Letter to the Corinthians:

"And I, brethren, when I came to you, came not with excellency of speech or of wisdom, declaring unto you the Testimony of God.

"For I determined not to know anything among you, save Jesus Christ, and Him Crucified" (I Cor. 2:1-2).

He was determined not to know anything among them save Jesus Christ and Him Crucified because he knew that was the only answer for the Corinthians, and it's the only answer for all of mankind and for all time.

The Cross! The Cross! The Cross!

IS IT POSSIBLE TO MERGE BIBLICAL AND CLINICAL COUNSELING?

Is it possible to unite the Ark of the Covenant with Baal? Is it possible to join the Levitical Priesthood with the Philistines in the service of the Temple? Can one use worldly means to attain Spiritual results?

Youthful preachers are being spewed out of so-called Bible Colleges today, completely brainwashed in humanistic principles. The majority of these young people, sad to say, have lost their Faith in God and His Word. They persist in some type of religious orientation (in name only) or they may even adopt some *"fringe"* type of Christianity. Their system of values, however, is one totally at odds with the traditional Judeo-Christian concept. The foundation is so-called Christian humanism and the end result is destruction. But — thousands of preachers, even well-meaning ones, are coming out of schools filled with this so-called *"Christian humanism."*

Those so trained, and most are, are inclined to impose this on their congregation, thinking this is the *"help"* that is needed. Such *"preachers of the Gospel"* (and one must wonder what Gospel) are attempting an impossible feat of surgery: to graft secular humanistic beliefs onto those of the Bible, which will never work.

I have listened to psychologists and sociologists expound on the principles of their secular humanistic training and have watched them then tack on some obscure Bible reference, thinking they will thus add an element of righteousness to what they are promoting.

Some might well ask, *"Are you stating that all Psychologists, Sociologists, and Psychiatrists are of little use to individuals in the area of problem-solving?"* No, I'm not saying that. I am saying that they are of no use at all, and are probably of great harm.

GOD'S WAYS AND THE WORLD'S WAYS DON'T MIX

All kinds of ideas are presently being tried, but they're all doomed to failure without God. And again I must emphasize that we can't take the world's ungodly, humanistic, God-denying methods and try to mix them with the Word of God. The two will never mix.

The Lord does not need any help, and even the most elementary Christian should realize that.

Some have tried to claim that psychology is a science. No it isn't! not by even the greatest stretch of the imagination can it be labeled as such.

If it is a science, it is a science worthy of a Roman circus. And I don't think that's the definition of true science.

Science is knowledge covering general truths or the operation of general laws as obtained and tested through scientific methods. Psychology doesn't even remotely fall under that definition.

The world having denied God and His Word has to have something else on which to lean. So psychology is the religion of perverted man. That is understandable! However, what is not so understandable is that the church has as well adopted this same method.

Almost all the sermonizing today is laced with humanistic psychology. In fact, the most popular preachers over television are preaching no more than psychology. While they talk about the Lord occasionally, and throw in a Scripture or two, the fact is, they are teaching and preaching psychology. There is an exception here and there, and thank God for that, but those exceptions are few and far between. Let's go back to a statement previously made:

When the church began to adopt psychology, even as it did in the 1950's until now (2010) it is embraced in totality, at the same time, the Cross of Christ and the Holy Spirit have been abandoned. Let us say it again:

One cannot have both. If we embrace humanistic psychology, then we are denying the Cross and the Holy Spirit. If we embrace the Cross of Christ and the Holy Spirit, then we are denying psychology.

Paul said, *"For if we have been planted together* (with Christ) *in the likeness of His Death* (Paul proclaims the Cross as the instrument through which all Blessings come; consequently, the Cross must ever be the Object of our Faith, which gives the Holy Spirit latitude to work within our lives), *we shall be also in the likeness of His Resurrection* (we can have the *'likeness of His Resurrection,'* i.e., *'live this Resurrection Life,'* only as long as we understand the *'likeness of His Death,'* which refers to the Cross as the Means by which all of this is done)" (Rom. 6:5).

(8) "BEHOLD, I GO FORWARD, BUT HE IS NOT THERE; AND BACKWARD, BUT I CANNOT PERCEIVE HIM:

(9) "ON THE LEFT HAND, WHERE HE DOES WORK, BUT I CANNOT BEHOLD HIM; HE HIDES HIMSELF ON THE RIGHT HAND, THAT I CANNOT SEE HIM:

(10) "BUT HE KNOWS THE WAY THAT I TAKE: WHEN HE HAS TRIED ME, I SHALL COME FORTH AS GOLD.

(11) "MY FOOT HAS HELD HIS STEPS, HIS WAY HAVE I KEPT, AND NOT DECLINED.

(12) "NEITHER HAVE I GONE BACK FROM THE COMMANDMENT OF HIS LIPS; I HAVE ESTEEMED THE WORDS OF HIS MOUTH MORE THAN MY NECESSARY FOOD.

(13) "BUT HE IS IN ONE MIND, AND WHO CAN TURN HIM? AND WHAT HIS SOUL DESIRES, EVEN THAT HE DOES.

(14) "FOR HE PERFORMS THE THING THAT IS APPOINTED FOR ME: AND MANY SUCH THINGS ARE WITH HIM.

(15) "THEREFORE AM I TROUBLED AT HIS PRESENCE: WHEN I CONSIDER, I AM AFRAID OF HIM.

(16) "FOR GOD MAKES MY HEART SOFT, AND THE ALMIGHTY TROUBLES ME:

(17) "BECAUSE I WAS NOT CUT OFF BEFORE THE DARKNESS, NEITHER HAS HE COVERED THE DARKNESS FROM MY FACE."

The diagram is:

1. (Vs. 9) For every Believer, there are times when it seems that God has hidden Himself from us.

2. Verse 10 presents one of the greatest statements made in the entirety of the Word of God. In effect, Job is saying, *"even though I cannot 'perceive Him,' and it seems like He 'hides Himself,' still, He knows exactly what is happening to me and, when this trial is over, I shall come forth as gold!"*

3. Verse 11 proclaims the fact that Job continues to maintain his rightful direction, and rightly so!

4. Verse 12 proclaims the fact that to Job, the most important thing in the world was the *"Commandment of the Lord."* So there you have it, *"His Will and His Word."*

5. Verse 15 proclaims the fact as Job puts it, that the fear of an Eternal Being Who has an Eternal Plan, which we cannot doubt, is wise, even though it is inscrutable to us. It is fear mingled with confidence, as we go into the future.

6. Verse 17 proclaims the fact that Job doesn't understand the severity of this trial, and no wonder!

I SHALL COME FORTH AS GOLD

What a testimony!

By the statement, *"I shall come forth as gold,"* Job believes that whatever his present condition might be, ever how severe it may seem to be, ever how hopeless it may seem to be, that God has some type of plan in what He is doing, and that when it is all said and done, that *"he will come forth as gold."*

Job could not have been more right!

When things are going well, it is as though we can see God everywhere. When things are not going well, especially considering the condition that Job was in, it seems that God has forsaken us. Perhaps, every Christian has come to this place at one time or the other. Where is God? Why does He hide His Face from us?

Still, God is in the same place He was when Job was formerly being blessed. So often the modern Christian has been taught about God's Blessings but has been taught very little about God's Sanctification.

The Believer must understand, that Blessings from the Lord teach us about God; however, trial and adversity teaches us about our selves, without which we cannot learn what we need to know about ourselves.

As stated at the outset of this Book, the lesson here being taught is not about the conversion of the sinner but, instead, about the Sanctification of the Saint. The test of our Faith is small indeed during time of Blessing. It is only during times of great trial that our Faith really shines. To believe when it is easy is of little consequence; to continue to believe when nothing is easy is of great consequence.

Say it again, *"Even though I cannot perceive Him, and it seems like He hides Himself, still, He knows exactly what is happening to me, and when this trial is over, I shall come forth as gold."*

What a statement! What a declaration of Faith!

In fact, this statement as given by Job, should be the proclamation of every Child of God. In some way it seems that Job's statement proclaims that at least in some small measure he understands what God is doing. He is making of Job a better man. He is burning the dross out of his life — dross that Job did not previously think was there but, in fact, is in every Believer.

Let it be quickly said that the Sanctification process if followed to its conclusion will bring forth pure gold.

Peter said: *"That the trial of your Faith being much more precious than of gold that perishes, though it be tried with fire..."* (I Pet. 1:7).

Fire separates all the foreign and impure materials from gold. It loses nothing of its nature, weight, color, or any other property.

The Lord said through Isaiah, *"...I have chosen you in the furnace of affliction"* (Isa. 48:10).

It would be very difficult for one to describe the terrible tests of Faith that Job underwent as a *"Blessing,"* but, actually, it was. Too often the Blessings of God are defined only in the terms of *"money and health."* To be sure, those things could fall into that category; however, there is a far greater Blessing — our Sanctification. There are no shortcuts to that.

THE WORDS OF HIS MOUTH ARE MORE VALUABLE THAN MY NECESSARY FOOD

As we have stated, there was no Bible during Job's time. And yet, there may very well have been and, no doubt, was, accounts of the great things done by the Lord from the time of Creation, up to Job's day, a time frame of some 2,400 years. For instance, we know that Enoch, the father of Methuselah wrote several books concerning the Works of the Lord. It is positive also, that Noah kept an account of what took place with the awful event of the flood, and God's Dealings with him. Abraham, Isaac, Jacob, and Joseph, no doubt, did the same.

Considering that Jacob was Job's grandfather, and Isaac his great-grandfather, and Abraham his great-great-grandfather, the Patriarch had access to these writings, with, no doubt, many copies being made, of which Moses would put them into book form, in the account we refer to as *"Genesis."* In fact, the Book of Job and the Book of Genesis were, no doubt, written by Moses during his forty years at the back side of the desert.

Job relished in these accounts, loved God supremely, tried with all of his heart to please Him, and then stated, *"I have esteemed the Words of His Mouth more than my necessary food."*

How much hunger do we have for the Word of God as did Job?

Every Believer should read the Bible completely through at least once a year. And this I promise, if you will read THE EXPOSITOR'S STUDY BIBLE completely through in a year, you will have, I am positive, an understanding of the Word of God that you've never possessed before, and which will greatly strengthen your life and living for the Lord. And nothing could be greater than that!

What a beautiful statement, *"I have esteemed the Words of His Mouth more than my necessary food."* This is what saw Job through this terrible time of testing. This, *"the Words of His Mouth"* is what helped him to be able to say, *"When He has tried me, I shall come forth as gold."*

NOTES

The Word of God is the only revealed truth in the world and, in fact, ever has been. It is the road map for life, the blueprint for eternity.

SATAN'S ATTACK AGAINST THE BIBLE

The Evil One has always hated the Word of God as should be obvious. It was in the midst of the great attack by Satan against the Master in His Incarnation, when Jesus said, *"Man shall not live by bread alone, but by every Word that proceeds out of the Mouth of God"* (Mat. 4:4). This is how Job survived. He lived on the Word that came out of the Mouth of God.

Are you?

When I was a young Preacher just getting started, Satan of course was attacking the Bible then, as he always has; however, it was obvious as to what he was doing, and it really didn't fool many people, if any. He is, however, doing something different at the present!

He is not attacking the Word of God directly, but rather making an end run so to speak. He is rather producing scores of paraphrases, which are referred to as *"Bibles,"* such as the *"Message Bible,"* when in reality, these are not Bibles at all, but rather a collection of religious ideas.

The Believer should understand, that unless you have a *"word-for-word"* translation of the Bible, whatever it is you have, is not a Bible. For instance, the King James Version is a word-for-word translation. It means that the scholars of the Hebrew and Greek languages, when this Bible was translated, did their very best to bring the original Hebrew and Greek over into English. They did a very good job of it!

Of course, the King James Version has been edited several times from its original work. The reason is simple.

I have a page out of the Bible of its original printing when it was first translated in the early 1600's. The English is that which cannot be read presently. So, as the language gradually changed, the King James Version had to be edited, and rightly so. Actually, it has been edited several times, without losing the meaning of the Text.

ANCIENT MANUSCRIPTS

As the reader should know, there are no original Manuscripts remaining of the actual Texts of the Bible. The Passage of time caused them to be worn out or lost; however, thousands of copies were made, of entire Books of the Bible or parts thereof.

Scholarship states that if the original is lost but yet it has ten copies in existence, then such is rated as genuine. The Bible has far more copies than any other ancient work in the world.

Reading behind one excellent Greek scholar the other day, he made the statement in his book, that when one holds the King James Version in his hands, he can be absolutely certain that he is holding in his hands the Word of God.

So, whatever you the Believer might do, do not trade the Word of God, a word-for-word translation for a mere paraphrase that actually destroys the power of the Text.

I think if there was a certain medicine that you needed on a daily basis to keep you alive, you would not want that medicine tampered with! Would you? I think not!

Once again, we come back to the beautiful statement made by Job, *"I have esteemed the Words of His Mouth more than my necessary food."*

"Saved by the Blood of the Crucified One!
"Now ransomed from sin and a new work begun,
"Sing praise to the Father and praise to the Son,
"Saved by the Blood of the Crucified One!"

"Saved by the Blood of the Crucified One!
"The Angels rejoicing because it is done;
"A child of the Father, joint heir with the Son,
"Saved by the Blood of the Crucified One!"

"Saved by the Blood of the Crucified One!
"The Father, He spoke, and His Will, it was done;
"Great price of my pardon, His Own precious Son;
"Saved by the Blood of the Crucified One!"

"Saved by the Blood of the Crucified One!
"All hail to the Father, all hail to the Son,
"All hail to the Spirit, the great Three in One!
"Saved by the Blood of the Crucified One!"

CHAPTER 24

(1) "WHY, SEEING TIMES ARE NOT HIDDEN FROM THE ALMIGHTY, DO THEY WHO KNOW HIM NOT SEE HIS DAYS?

(2) "SOME REMOVE THE LANDMARKS; THEY VIOLENTLY TAKE AWAY FLOCKS, AND FEED THEREOF.

(3) "THEY DRIVE AWAY THE ASS OF THE FATHERLESS, THEY TAKE THE WIDOW'S OX FOR A PLEDGE.

(4) "THEY TURN THE NEEDY OUT OF THE WAY: THE POOR OF THE EARTH HIDE THEMSELVES TOGETHER.

(5) "BEHOLD, AS WILD ASSES IN THE DESERT, GO THEY FORTH TO THEIR WORK; RISING BETIMES FOR A PREY: THE WILDERNESS YIELDS FOOD FOR THEM AND FOR THEIR CHILDREN.

(6) "THEY REAP EVERY ONE HIS CORN IN THE FIELD: AND THEY GATHER THE VINTAGE OF THE WICKED.

(7) "THEY CAUSE THE NAKED TO LODGE WITHOUT CLOTHING, THAT THEY HAVE NO COVERING IN THE COLD.

(8) "THEY ARE WET WITH SHOWERS OF THE MOUNTAINS, AND EMBRACE THE ROCK FOR WANT OF A SHELTER.

(9) "THEY PLUCK THE FATHERLESS FROM THE BREAST, AND TAKE A PLEDGE OF THE POOR.

(10) "THEY CAUSE HIM TO GO NAKED WITHOUT CLOTHING, AND THEY TAKE AWAY THE SHEAF FROM THE HUNGRY;

(11) "WHICH MAKE OIL WITHIN THEIR WALLS, AND TREAD THEIR

WINEPRESSES, AND SUFFER THIRST.

(12) "MEN GROAN FROM OUT OF THE CITY, AND THE SOUL OF THE WOUNDED CRIES OUT: YET GOD LAYS NOT FOLLY TO THEM.

(13) "THEY ARE OF THOSE WHO REBEL AGAINST THE LIGHT; THEY KNOW NOT THE WAYS THEREOF, NOR ABIDE IN THE PATHS THEREOF.

(14) "THE MURDERER RISING WITH THE LIGHT KILLS THE POOR AND NEEDY, AND IN THE NIGHT IS AS A THIEF.

(15) "THE EYE ALSO OF THE ADULTERER WAITS FOR THE TWILIGHT, SAYING, NO EYE SHALL SEE ME: AND DISGUISES HIS FACE.

(16) "IN THE DARK THEY DIG THROUGH HOUSES, WHICH THEY HAD MARKED FOR THEMSELVES IN THE DAYTIME: THEY KNOW NOT THE LIGHT."

The structure is:

1. To make the language more clear to us as it regards Verse 1, Job is asking the question as to why the Almighty does not have set times to judge, or why His followers often do not see His interventions?

2. Verse 12 actually means that God at times, at least as Job then saw it, did not seem to punish wickedness quickly. And yet, God's Judgment will ultimately come for those who persist in their wickedness. It may be in this life or the next life, but come it will.

3. Verse 13 proclaims the fact that the wicked will not know, will not have anything to do with, the law of moral restraint.

4. Verse 16 proclaims the fact, that the wicked have no desire to know the Ways of the Lord.

WHY DOES GOD AT TIMES DELAY JUDGMENT?

The following will perhaps list some of the reasons:

• As a Believer, other people, at least as it regards Judgment, are not our concern. We must put them in the Hands of the Lord, and leave them there.

• We only know in part, while the Lord knows all things, past, present, and future. As a result, our judgments, of necessity, are faulty, while His are Perfect.

NOTES

• Who knows that such a person, no matter how evil they may be, may at some point give their heart to God, hence, the patience of the Lord in dealing with them. The Apostle Paul is an excellent case in point. Many Believers may have wished him dead before his conversion on the Road to Damascus, but that would have been a tremendous loss to the Kingdom of God.

• We should always desire that the Lord would be as merciful to others, as He has been to us. When we think of the Mercy and Grace, which He has shown to us, then it becomes easier for us to understand His Patience with those who are extremely wicked.

THE FEELINGS OF JOB!

Job is sitting in the middle of an ash heap, his body covered with sore boils, the pain severe to say the least, all of his prosperity gone, people making fun of him, and then he has conducted ten funerals as it regards his sons and daughters. As well, he has tried to do his very best to obey the Lord, and in every capacity. In reference to such, he does not know of anything in his life that would be detrimental to the Lord or His Word. And yet, despite all of this, the wicked go their merry way, continuing to take advantage of the poor and the helpless, but yet seemingly suffer no ill effect.

"Why is the Lord allowing this to happen to me?" must have been the great question of his heart at this time, hence, his statements of this Chapter.

It is obvious from the statements made, that Job has been a student of human character and actions. He is a man, seemingly so, who has given a clinical eye to all concerned, as to the character and nature of his fellowman. He, evidently, had carefully observed the wicked, and had done so for years and, as well, those who claimed righteousness.

At this juncture of his life, he is thoroughly confused. He has no answer for anything. The entirety of his theology has been upended. This is not the Way that God Works or so he thinks.

Perhaps in all of this, the test of this man's Faith, his love for God, his place and position in the Kingdom, have all come into question. Has he been wrong all along? Is

God totally unlike what He thinks he is?

Job will ultimately find that the Lord is exactly as he thought He was, and even more so, much more so. But that will be a little time in coming.

THE TEST OF FAITH

Every attack leveled at the Believer by Satan is for but one purpose, whether it be in the form of finances, physical, domestical or Spiritual, and that is to destroy, or at least, seriously weaken our Faith. It doesn't matter what form the attack takes, it is all but for one purpose.

Can Satan get the Believer to stop believing? Tragically, the Evil One has been successful with some, perhaps even many.

How many millions today are not living for God who once did, or else they have been seriously weakened in their consecration, all because in their heart, they harbor a feeling that God has done them wrong. He did not come to their rescue when He should have, or else they think that He has not been fair with them. The list is long!

The most precious attribute that an individual has is their Faith in God. Actually, that's the only thing the person can take with them when they die, is their Faith.

But sadder still, there are millions who, in fact, do have Faith, but it's in the wrong object. How many millions of Catholics have made Mary the object of their Faith? or the Pope? How many millions of Protestants have made their good works the object of their faith? or their particular church?

Satan does not bother these particular people, who number into the hundreds of millions, and for all the obvious reasons. While they do have faith, it's not that which God will recognize. In truth, the far greater majority of such people really aren't Born-Again. Nicodemus is an excellent case in point.

NICODEMUS

Nicodemus, in fact, was one of the religious leaders of Israel. He was a member of the vaunted Sanhedrin, which served as the Supreme Court of Israel, along with its spiritual leadership. It must be understood, that there was no separation of Church and State as it regarded Israel of old. It was a religious State from A to Z.

As well, Nicodemus was reputed to be one of the three richest men in Jerusalem, which in the eyes of Jews, constituted the favor of God. In truth, every evidence is that Nicodemus was extremely religious and scrupulous in his conduct. In other words, he had the most excellent reputation in all of Israel, but yet, he was not Born-Again.

To be sure, as far as good works were concerned, as far as reputation was concerned, as far as place and position in Israel were concerned, Nicodemus would have surpassed most today who claim to be Believers.

But yet, when Nicodemus said to Jesus, after the Master had explained the Born-Again experience to him, *"How can these things be? Jesus answered and said unto him, Are you a Master of Israel, and yet do not know these things?"* (Jn. 3:9-10).

Nicodemus most definitely had faith, but it was not at all in the right object. He had faith in his good works, in his place and position as a spiritual leader in Israel, in his money and power, which he identified as the Favor of God, but in the Eyes of the Lord none of that mattered!

Incidentally, it took the Cross of Christ to bring Nicodemus to a place of Repentance and, thereby, to be Born-Again. While he seemingly did not desire to identify with Christ while the Master was alive, when he saw the Cross, he then openly identified with Him, seemingly, irrespective as to what people may have thought.

It is ironic, every evidence is, Nicodemus, although he wouldn't accept Christ as the Messiah of Israel when He was alive, now that He is dead, he embraces Him totally as the Messiah. No, Nicodemus nor Joseph believed that Jesus would rise from the dead. Had they believed such, they would not have spent a large sum of money putting spices on His Body for His Burial. In fact, no one, not even His closest Disciples, believed that the Master would come from the dead, despite the fact that he had told them any number of times that He would rise again. This was a test of their faith of unimagined proportions. However, their faith or the lack thereof had no bearing whatsoever on His coming from the tomb after three days and nights of burial.

Actually, due to the fact that the wages of sin is death, had Jesus failed to atone for even one sin, even the smallest sin, He could not have risen from the dead. But He rose from the dead, simply because every sin in totality, past, present, and future, was atoned.

SIMON PETER

"And the Lord said, Simon, Simon, behold, Satan has desired to have you (portrays to us a glimpse into the spirit world, which was very similar to the same request made by Satan concerning Job), *that he may sift you as wheat* (Satan tempts in order to bring out the bad, while God tests in order to bring out the good; the simple truth is, God, at times using Satan as His instrument in addressing character, causes men to seek God's Holiness rather than their own.)

"But I have prayed for you, that your faith fail not (Satan's attack is always delivered against Faith, for if that fails all fails)*: and when you are converted, strengthen your brethren* (does not refer to being Saved again, but rather coming to the right path of trust and dependence on the Lord, instead of on self; that lesson learned, one is then able to strengthen the brethren)" (Lk. 22:31-32).

Did Peter's faith fail when he denied the Lord?

No it didn't!

While it was tested severely in his denial, had it failed, he would not have come back to Jesus. But we all know that He did come back to Jesus, and was totally and completely forgiven.

He most definitely sinned, and sinned greatly, but he never entertained the thought of quitting. To be sure, the Master's prayer was answered when He prayed that Peter's *"faith fail not."*

Faith is a powerful commodity. The truth is, it's not easy to turn out the light that the Holy Spirit has placed in our heart. It can be done, but not easily!

(17) "FOR THE MORNING IS TO THEM EVEN AS THE SHADOW OF DEATH: IF ONE KNOW THEM, THEY ARE IN THE TERRORS OF THE SHADOW OF DEATH.

(18) "HE IS SWIFT AS THE WATERS; THEIR PORTION IS CURSED IN THE EARTH: HE BEHOLDS NOT THE WAY OF THE VINEYARDS.

(19) "DROUGHT AND HEAT CONSUME THE SNOW WATERS: SO DOES THE GRAVE THOSE WHICH HAVE SINNED.

(20) "THE WOMB SHALL FORGET HIM; THE WORM SHALL FEED SWEETLY ON HIM; HE SHALL BE NO MORE REMEMBERED; AND WICKEDNESS SHALL BE BROKEN AS A TREE.

(21) "HE EVIL ENTREATS THE BARREN WHO BEARS NOT: AND DOES NOT GOOD TO THE WIDOW.

(22) "HE DRAWS ALSO THE MIGHTY WITH HIS POWER: HE RISES UP, AND NO MAN IS SURE OF LIFE.

(23) "THOUGH IT BE GIVEN HIM TO BE IN SAFETY, WHEREON HE RESTS; YET HIS EYES ARE UPON THEIR WAYS.

(24) "THEY ARE EXALTED FOR A LITTLE WHILE, BUT ARE GONE AND BROUGHT LOW; THEY ARE TAKEN OUT OF THE WAY AS ALL OTHER, AND CUT OFF AS THE TOPS OF THE EARS OF CORN.

(25) "AND IF IT BE NOT SO NOW, WHO WILL MAKE ME A LIAR, AND MAKE MY SPEECH NOTHING WORTH?"

The synopsis is:

1. In the Twentieth Verse, Job proclaims the fact that wickedness may thrive for a season, but ultimately it will be called to account.

2. Verse 23 proclaims Job as saying that at times it seems like even the most wicked are in safety, and they rest in their safety. He then says that it seems that God for a time watches the cruelties of oppressors without interference. In other words, He does not immediately punish their wicked conduct.

3. Job says in Verse 24 that it seems that many of the wicked live out their lives seemingly experiencing no interference from God, and even die as the righteous do, in other words, they die a natural death.

That is true; however, the moment the wicked die, irrespective of their life and living, they instantly go to Hell (Lk. 16:19-31).

4. In Verse 25, Job is saying that his words are true, and that even his three friends know it. In fact, Job's statements are correct. God does not contradict him. But, at last, when He does appear, He will contradict Job's three *"friends."*

5. (Vs. 25) God deals with each person on an individual basis, be they righteous or unrighteous. In effect, the Lord tells us that it is not our business how He deals with others.

INSPIRATION

The reader must understand some things as it regards the speeches given by Job's three friends, and even the speeches given by Job personally. While the Holy Spirit allowed it all to be taken down and printed, still, that doesn't mean at all that everything that was said is true. In fact, in the overall capacity of things, nothing the three friends said can be constituted as true. While a statement here and there may definitely be true within itself, the manner in which it is being used by these individuals, proclaims it falling out as that which is not true. When the Lord did finally appear, the Lord said of these three friends, *"My wrath is kindled against you . . . for you have not spoken of Me the thing that is right, as My Servant Job has"* (42:7).

As it regards that given by Job, while inspiration guarantees that he made the statements he made, even as it guarantees the statements of the three friends, it doesn't mean that everything Job uttered was inspired by the Holy Spirit. In fact, he said some things that were wrong. But in the final analysis, and in the overall sense, what he said about the Lord was correct. In fact, there were times that the Holy Spirit inspired him to proclaim a great Biblical Doctrine, or a great truth about his own situation. Some of those things are:

• *"Is there not an appointed time to man upon Earth?"* (7:1).
• *"What is man, that You should magnify him? and that You should set Your Heart upon him?"* (7:17).
• *"How should a man be just with God?"* (9:2).
• *"Neither is there any daysman betwixt us, who might lay his hand upon us both"* (9:33).
• *"Though He kill me, yet will I trust in Him"* (13:15).
• *"Man who is born of a woman is of few days, and full of trouble"* (14:1).
• *"For there is hope of a tree, if it be cut down, that it will sprout again, and that the tender branch thereof will not cease"* (14:7).
• *"If a man die, shall he live again? all the days of my appointed time will I wait, till my change come"* (14:14).
• *"For I know that my Redeemer lives, and that He shall stand at the latter day upon the Earth"* (19:25).
• *"And though after my skin worms destroy this body, yet in my flesh shall I see God"* (19:26).
• *"But He knows the way that I take: when He tries me, I shall come forth as gold"* (23:10).
• *"Neither have I gone back from the Commandment of His Lips; I have esteemed the Words of His Mouth more than my necessary food"* (23:12).
• *"He stretches out the north over the empty place, and hangs the Earth upon nothing"* (26:7).
• *"There is a path which no fowl knows, and which the vulture's eye has not seen"* (28:7).

While we have not listed all, we have listed some of the things that Job stated, which were definitely inspired by the Holy Spirit, and in some ways pointed to doctrine which would be ultimately brought about by the Cross.

THE REGION OF HELL

We as Believers should always remember that this life is but a dress rehearsal for eternity. While the wicked at times may seem to get by with their rebellion against God in this life, and even prosper in doing so, still, it's the eternal consequence that must be addressed.

The only thing that stands between man and eternal hell is the Cross of Christ. That's a startling statement, but it is true. All of our good works, all of our good intentions, all the things that might buy us time, are of little consequence. Let us say it again:

The only thing standing between man and eternal Hell is the Cross of Christ.

Understanding that, the preacher must preach the Cross, and the Believer, and I mean every Believer, must make the Cross of Christ the Object of his Faith (Jn. 3:16).

If a man dies, and irrespective as to what

he has done in life, and no matter the so-called good works, if he has not accepted Christ and what Christ did for him at the Cross, then he will die eternally lost. That means that his soul and his spirit instantly will go to Hell and, in fact, will be there forever and forever.

Jesus gave us a chilling account of the region of the underworld. The time of which He spoke, Paradise was in the heart of the Earth, actually next door to Hell so to speak. In fact, there was only a gulf that separated those in Hell from those in Paradise. This had to be simply because the blood of bulls and goats could not take away sins, meaning that the sin debt remained over all, even including the great Patriarchs and Prophets of old. This means that Satan continued to have a claim upon them, which claim would be made void by what Jesus did at the Cross. In other words, their deliverance from this place, and from being a captive of Satan, was solely dependent upon the great Work of Redemption, which Christ would carry out at the Cross.

At any rate, Jesus gave us a firsthand view of this place. I will copy directly from THE EXPOSITOR'S STUDY BIBLE.

THE PLACE CALLED HELL

"There was a certain rich man, who was clothed in purple and fine linen, and fared sumptuously every day (the Jews of Jesus' day concluded that riches were the favor of God, and poverty was the curse of God; therefore, this illustration given by Christ ripped to shreds their false doctrine)*:*

"And there was a certain beggar named Lazarus (many claim this is a Parable not to be taken literally; however, as it is to be noticed, Jesus uses names in this illustration, meaning that it's not a Parable, but actually, something that really happened; consequently, it is chilling indeed!), *which was laid at his gate, full of sores* (the rich man saw Lazarus constantly, but offered no help whatsoever; as stated, such concluded ones like Lazarus to be cursed of God, and to help such would be thwarting the Plan of God; how so much the Word of God is twisted by so many),

"And desiring to be fed with the crumbs which fell from the rich man's table (probably means that this rich man felt very good with himself in even allowing 'crumbs' to be given to this beggar)*: moreover the dogs came and licked his sores* (proclaims the fact that this man was not only poverty stricken, but, as well, was sick; he would not fit the mold of the modern prosperity gospel, which, in fact, is no Gospel at all; but he definitely did fit God's mold; we should consider all of this very carefully).

"And it came to pass, that the beggar died (more than likely, no one cared, but the Lord cared, as we shall see), *and was carried by the Angels into Abraham's bosom* (Paradise; where all Believers went before the Cross; as well, Jesus also tells us here that whenever a Believer dies, his soul and spirit are escorted by Angels into the Presence of God)*: the rich man also died, and was buried* (no Angels carried him away, for he died eternally lost; him being rich did not carry any weight as it regards his soul's Salvation)*;*

"And in Hell he lift up his eyes (Jesus plainly proclaims the Doctrine of eternal Hell; as well, He also proclaims the fact that the soul and the spirit immediately go to Heaven or Hell at the time of death, and that the soul and the spirit are totally conscious), *being in torments* (to say the least, Hell is not a pleasant place and, as stated, it is eternal), *and sees Abraham afar off, and Lazarus in his bosom* (all Believers before the Cross expressed faith in the Revelation given to Abraham by God as it regards Redemption and, in a sense, it is the same presently [Rom. 4:16]).

"And he cried and said, father Abraham, have mercy on me (there are no unbelievers in Hell, nor is there any Salvation there; the rich man repented, but too late), *and send Lazarus* (he had no concern for Lazarus back on Earth, but his conscience now recalls many things, but too late), *that he may dip the tip of his finger in water* (evidently there is no water there), *and cool my tongue; for I am tormented in this flame* (the Bible teaches that the fires of Hell are literal; Jesus said so!).

"But Abraham said, Son, remember that you in your lifetime received good things

(in no way does it mean that this was the cause of him being lost; it merely means that he was treated very well, but showed no thankfulness for his blessings), *and likewise Lazarus evil things* (the rich man didn't allow his blessings to bring him to the Lord, and Lazarus didn't allow his poverty to keep him from the Lord): *but now he is comforted* (because he had accepted the Lord), *and you are tormented* (the word *'now'* is that which is all-important; it speaks of the time after death; will it be one of *'comfort'* or *'torment'*?).

"*And beside all of this, between us and you there is a great gulf fixed* (this is in the heart of the Earth [Mat. 12:40]; before the Cross, even though all who went to Paradise were comforted, they were still captives of Satan, with him hoping that ultimately he would get them over into the burning pit [Eph. 4:8-9]; this means that when Believers died before the Cross, due to the fact that the blood of bulls and goats could not take away sins, the sin debt remained, and Satan still had a claim on them; so all those in Paradise were awaiting the Cross, which would deliver them): *so that they which would pass from hence to you cannot* (proclaims the fact that all opportunities for Salvation are on this side of the grave; this means that the Catholic doctrine of Purgatory is a *'fools hope'*; there is no such place); *neither can they pass to us, that would come from thence* (but yet it was possible for those in Hell to look over and see those in Paradise, and it seems to speak to them; that place, due to the Cross, is now empty, with all liberated by Christ after the price was paid [Eph. 4:8-9]).

"*Then he said, I pray thee therefore, father, that you would send him* (send Lazarus) *to my father's house* (this is the only example of praying to a dead Saint in Scripture; let those who do so remember that prayer to all other dead Saints will avail just as much as this prayer did — nothing):

"*For I have five brethren; that he may testify unto them* (these statements proclaim the fact that this man had a working knowledge of God and more than likely even professed Salvation before his death; but he wasn't Saved), *lest they also come into this place of torment* (he did not ask this grace for himself, for he knew that he was eternally entombed; it is easy to step into Hell, but impossible to step out).

"*Abraham said unto him, They have Moses and the Prophets; let them hear them* (doesn't mean that this event happened during the time of Moses, but that Abraham is referring to the Word of God; this tells us that at least a part of the Old Testament had then been written).

"*And he said, Nay, father Abraham: but if one went unto them from the dead, they will repent* (the Scriptures contain all that is necessary to Salvation; a returned spirit could add nothing to them; and a man who will not listen to the Bible will not listen to a multitude, if raised from the dead; in fact, a few days later, the Lord did raise a man named Lazarus from the grave, and the Pharisees went about to put him to death).

"*And he said unto him, If they hear not Moses and the Prophets, neither will they be persuaded, though one rose from the dead* (this illustration as given by Christ, actually happened and, in fact, presents a startling portrayal of life after death; we learn from this, and in stark reality, that the only thing that really matters in life is being right with God; there is a Heaven and there is a Hell, and every soul who has ever lived has gone or is going to one or the other; the only way to make Heaven one's eternal Home is to accept Christ; He Alone is the Door; everything else leads one to Hell, exactly as the rich man found out, and to his eternal dismay)" (Lk. 16:19-31).

"Praise, praise the Lamb, Who for sinners was slain;
"Who went down to the grave and ascended again;
"And Who soon shall return, when these dark days are o'er,
"To set up His Kingdom, in Glory and power."

"Then the Heavens and the Earth, and the sea shall rejoice;
"The field and the forest shall lift their glad voice;
"The sands of the desert shall flourish in green,

"And Lebanon's glory be shed o'er the scene."

"Her bridal attire, and her festal array,
"All nature shall wear on the glorious day;
"For her King comes down, with His People to reign,
"And His Presence shall bless her with Eden again."

CHAPTER 25

(1) "THEN ANSWERED BILDAD THE SHUHITE, AND SAID,
(2) "DOMINION AND FEAR ARE WITH HIM, HE MAKES PEACE IN HIS HIGH PLACES.
(3) "IS THERE ANY NUMBER OF HIS ARMIES? AND UPON WHOM DOES NOT HIS LIGHT ARISE?
(4) "HOW THEN CAN MAN BE JUSTIFIED WITH GOD? OR HOW CAN HE BE CLEAN WHO IS BORN OF A WOMAN?
(5) "BEHOLD EVEN TO THE MOON, AND IT SHINES NOT; YES, THE STARS ARE NOT PURE IN HIS SIGHT.
(6) "HOW MUCH LESS MAN, WHO IS A WORM? AND THE SON OF MAN, WHICH IS A WORM?"

The synopsis is:

1. Bildad's statement in Verse 2 contains the idea that Job cannot hope to reach God, considering who Job is, and considering Who God is.

2. Bildad in Verse 4 asks, *"How that a man can be justified with God?"* Man can be justified by Faith in God, which Job surely evidenced, but which Bildad evidently didn't believe.

3. As it regards Verse 6, I'm sure that Job got the point. He was being referred to by Bildad as a *"worm."*

HUMAN TRADITION

As previously stated, Bildad has addressed Job from the perspective of *"human tradition,"* which basically characterizes religion. As with all religion, some statements will be correct, and some gross error. His statements, as well as Eliphaz' and Zophar's, show that they know some things about God but have no relationship with God. Religion the world over basically falls into this category.

Some religions are closer to the truth than others and will, therefore, make more truthful statements than others. Some religions have no knowledge of God whatsoever. Christianity, incidentally, is not a religion. It is a relationship with a Man, the Man Christ Jesus.

Religions of the world are devised by men, and are basically made up of a code of ethics (do's and don'ts) which are of man's devisings in an attempt to reach God, or to better oneself in some way.

They all fail because man cannot reach God on his own. As a result of the Fall, man is depraved, and as such cannot concoct anything that God can accept. This means that God must reach man. That He has done through His Word and through the Lord Jesus Christ, by the Cross.

The problem is not so much unconverted man attempting to reach God by his own nefarious systems, which is understandable; the problem comes in, however, when the church follows suit.

It tries to save itself, by becoming religious, which means the churches are filled with people who have never really been Born-Again. And then, even those who are truly Born-Again, attempt to sanctify themselves, by one scheme after the other, all a product of the flesh, all which are rejected by God.

THE CROSS OF CHRIST

As we have stated, man, irrespective as to what he may attempt to do, cannot reach God on his own. God has to reach man, which He has done through His Word, and through the Lord Jesus Christ and what He did for us at the Cross of Calvary.

In fact, the only way that a thrice-Holy God could reach man, even religious man, is by and through the Cross of Christ. As we have said repeatedly, the Lord Jesus Christ is the Source of all things we receive from God, while the Cross is the Means by which those things are received, all superintended by the Holy Spirit (Jn. 7:37; Rom. 8:2; Gal. 2:20-21; 6:14).

If, in fact, the Cross of Christ is the Means, and the only Means by which God can reach man, doesn't it make sense that the preacher should preach the Cross? (I Cor. 1:23). Doesn't it make sense that the preacher should major in the Cross? (Gal. 6:14). And if the preacher preaches the Cross, due to the fact that *"Faith comes by hearing, and hearing by the Word of God,"* the people will then begin to see where their Salvation is, where their Victory is, where their power is and, in effect, where the Lord Jesus Christ is.

Of course, Christ is seated by the Right Hand of the Father; however, the passport from Christ to humanity is through the Cross, exactly as the passport for humanity to Christ is through the Cross, and the Cross alone (I Cor. 1:17-18; 2:2).

HOW CAN A MAN BE JUSTIFIED WITH GOD?

Actually, the heading presents the age-old question of mankind. A small segment of humanity denies there is a God. The far greater majority of humanity believes there is a God and try to reach Him in their own way. They are doomed to failure. Bildad asked this question because in his heart of hearts he knows that his religion (human tradition) cannot justify a man. Man can be justified in only one way, that is by accepting the Lord Jesus Christ and the price He paid at Calvary.

Before Calvary, men were Saved by looking forward to that great event. After Calvary, men are Saved by looking backward to that great event.

Bildad's question shows his lack of relationship with God for he does not seem to understand the Sacrificial Offerings which began with Adam immediately after the Fall, and which pointed to the coming Redeemer, the Lord Jesus Christ (Gen. 3:21; Gen., Chpt. 4).

Before Calvary, men, of course, knew nothing of the Lord Jesus Christ; however, they did know that the sacrifices of the lambs were representative of the coming Redeemer. It seems that Bildad did not understand this. God's dealings with the human family before Calvary are as follows:

THE FIRST PROMISE OF REDEMPTION

The Promise given to Adam and Eve in the Garden of Eden after the Fall was: *"And I will put enmity* (animosity) *between you and the woman* (presents the Lord now actually speaking to Satan, who had used the serpent; in effect, the Lord is saying to Satan, 'You used the woman to bring down the human race, and I will use the woman as an instrument to bring the Redeemer into the world, Who will save the human race'), *and between your seed* (mankind which follows Satan) *and her Seed* (the Lord Jesus Christ); *it* (Christ) *shall bruise your head* (the Victory that Jesus won at the Cross [Col. 2:14-15]), *and you shall bruise His Heel* (the sufferings of the Cross)" (Gen. 3:15).

Adam and Eve knew what this meant. Actually, when Cain was born, Eve thought that surely this was the promised Redeemer, because she said, *"I have gotten a man from the LORD"* (Gen. 4:1). She used the name *"LORD"* because it meant *"Covenant God;"* however, she would be greatly disappointed. Cain instead would be a murderer.

Some years later when Seth was born to her and Adam, Eve said, *"For God, said she, has appointed me another seed instead of Abel"* (Gen. 4:25).

By now Eve had lost hope, for she did not use God's Covenant Name of *"LORD"* but instead, used the name *"God,"* which showed that she had lost faith in the Covenant. She did not realize that it was impossible for fallen man to produce anything that God could accept; however, Seth would actually be the one through whose lineage the Messiah would ultimately come (Lk. 3:38).

THE COVENANT

"And God said, Sarah your wife shall bear you a son indeed; and you shall call his name Isaac (the name Isaac means 'laughter'): *and I will establish My Covenant with him for an Everlasting Covenant, and with his seed after him"* (Gen. 17:19).

Every person who remotely followed the Lord in those days knew of God's dealings with Abraham and of the great Promise given to Abraham by the Lord. It was passed down by word of mouth in its exact detail. Through Isaac the Promised Seed, the Lord Jesus Christ, would come.

This Covenant, the New Covenant, is referred to as *"an Everlasting Covenant,"* because it will never have to be amended, it will never have to be changed, and it will never have to be added to or subtracted from. In other words, and as previously stated in this Volume, it cannot be broken. It cannot be broken because it is all in Christ.

God has made many covenants with man down through the ages, with every one of them being broken by man almost as soon as they were made. But this Covenant cannot be broken, simply because it is all in Christ. Our Lord is both God and Man. As our substitutionary man, the Second Man and the Last Adam, even as Paul gave it to us (I Cor. 15:45-47), this Covenant will stand forever. While you and I may fail, it has no effect on the Covenant, because it's all in Christ. It's quite possible for a human being to forfeit their place and position in the Covenant, exactly as many of the Jews were doing during the time of Paul, which occasioned him to write the great Book of Hebrews; however, while I can reap the benefits of the Covenant, which we are intended to do through Christ, and while at the same time, if I so desire, I can leave the Covenant, but that does not impact the Covenant itself whatsoever. As stated, it is all in Christ, which means that it is unbreakable.

THE PROMISE

The Lord gave a Promise to Jacob. He said, *"The sceptre shall not depart from Judah* (the *'sceptre'* is defined as *'a staff of office and authority,'* which pertains to Christ), *nor a Lawgiver from between His Feet* (refers to the fact that Judah was meant to be a guardian of the Law, which they were; the Temple was in Jerusalem, which was a part of the Tribe of Judah, and which had to do with the Law), *until Shiloh come* (when Jesus came, typified by the name *'Shiloh,'* Who, in fact, was, and is, the True Lawgiver, He fulfilled the Law in totality by His Life and His Death, thereby satisfying all of its just demands); *and unto Him shall the gathering of the people be"* (Gen. 49:10).

• The only way to God the Father is through Christ the Son.

• The only way to Christ the Son is through the Cross.

• The only way to the Cross is through an abnegation of self (Lk. 9:23-24).

Now, it was known and should have been known by Bildad that the Redeemer Who would justify man would come from the Tribe of Judah.

Bildad did not understand *"Justification by Faith,"* even though through Job he most definitely had the opportunity to know what the Lord had given the Patriarchs.

Bildad, as the majority of the human race, attempts to be justified by works; consequently, those who would function from such, experience no change of heart. So, they attempt to cover up with self-righteousness. Self-righteousness is the product of religion.

THE CROSS OF CALVARY

Bildad said, *"How then can man be justified with God? or how can he be clean that is born of a woman?*

"Behold even to the moon, and it shines not; yes, the stars are not pure in His Sight.

"How much less man, who is a worm? and the son of man, which is a worm?"

Bildad knew that man was morally and physically corrupt. He knew there was a God, and he knew of God's greatness. He did not know how to bridge the two.

• It is said that Socrates the great philosopher surmised that there was such a thing as good and evil.

• His student Plato took up where Socrates left off. He said, as well, that there was good and evil, but that there was a great gulf between the two.

• Aristotle another great philosopher stated, there is good and evil, and there is a great gulf between the two. He also surmised that man is evil, but then he added, we have not found a way to bridge the gulf, in other words, to go from evil to good.

That same problem still plagues humanity presently, but let the whole world know, that the Lord Jesus Christ has bridged that great gulf. The song says:

"Oh, the Grace that drew Salvation's
   Plan,
"Oh, the Love that brought it down to
   man,
"Oh, the mighty gulf our God did span,
"At Calvary."

The Cross of Christ bridged that great gulf that man could not cross with all of his ingenuity and efforts. But, Jesus made a way for us. Unfortunately, many in the modern church are still attempting to function outside the boundaries of Calvary. It cannot be done!

Sometime back, Frances laid a book on the table before me entitled, *"The Purpose Driven Life"* and asked that I read it. She already knew that it was false doctrine, but she wanted my input.

I read a few pages and laid it down.

She asked me a little later if I had read it, and I said *"no!"*

I went on to state to her, *"I read a few pages, and it quickly became obvious that the man, who wrote this book, was not teaching and preaching the Cross."*

I then went on to say, *"Understanding that, whatever it is he is teaching, will not help anyone."*

In that book he stated, *"We need more than the Bible in order to grow; we need other Believers."*[1] He defined this statement better in *"The Purpose Driven Church"* book, Chapter 18, I'm told, by explaining how to develop mature members. He claims the statement, *"All you need is the Bible to grow,"* is a myth. He further states, *"Classroom Churches tend to be left-brain oriented rather than cognitive focused. They stress the teaching of the Bible content and doctrine, but give little, if any, emphasis to the Believer's emotional, experiential, and rational development."*[2]

As hopefully the reader will instantly recognize, what he is teaching is *"the felt needs of the individual,"* which is the sure road to destruction.

Church is not supposed to be a place where people are given what they think they need, hence, *"felt needs,"* it's supposed to be a place that they are given what they truly need, which is the Word of God. To be sure, many, even most, will not like that direction; nevertheless, what I've just stated is the truth.

To better understand the foolish statements made by Warren who wrote these particular books, he claims the following to be truth:

"Spiritual maturity is very practical, any Believer can grow to maturity if he or she will develop the habits necessary for spiritual growth. We need to take the mystery out of spiritual growth by breaking the components down into practical, everyday habits."[3]

Let me make a few statements regarding that ridiculous word given by Warren.

SANCTIFICATION

First of all, it is not possible for the Believer to sanctify himself, much less to do so by just simply developing new habits.

Sanctification is not merely a change of habits, or the development of a new process of living. There are two factors the Child of God must deal with. They are:

1. Sin: This has always been the problem, sin is the problem now, and sin will be the problem tomorrow. I realize according to this man's summation, sin need not be mentioned, because that might offend people. But, we come back to the age old truth, that before man can be Saved, he must first understand that he is lost, woefully lost!

And then after a person comes to Christ, they must know and understand that sin is still the problem, and that there is only one way that it can be conquered.

That one way is the Cross of Calvary, and by the Believer ever making such the Object of his Faith. Then the Holy Spirit, Who Alone can make us what we ought to be, and Who works explicitly within the parameters of the Finished Work of Christ, can begin to function within our hearts and lives, and give us Victory over the sin nature.

I'm sorry, but just because one is Saved, and even baptized with the Holy Spirit, of which Mr. Warren doesn't even believe in the latter, still, a sin nature is prevalent within the heart and life of every Believer (Rom. 6:1-14).

2. The flesh: Everything that Mr. Warren

is suggesting in his book stems from the flesh. In other words, it is something that is devised by man, whether himself or someone else in which the Holy Spirit can never sanction.

Mr. Warren boasted that *"spiritual maturity is demonstrated more by behavior than by beliefs."* What he doesn't seem to understand is that proper belief will produce proper behavior. And unless one has proper belief, which is proper Scriptural understanding, then one will not have proper behavior. Let's say it again:

All improper behavior stems from improper belief. And until the latter is corrected, the former will never be brought into line with that which the Holy Spirit demands.

Once again, we have man attempting to take the place of the Holy Spirit. We have man devising his schemes, and then claiming that the Lord will honor it and bless it. He won't!

ONE WAY

There is only one way in this Christian experience and, in fact, has always been, even from the first page of human history. That one way is, *"Jesus Christ and Him Crucified"* (I Cor. 1:23).

The only way that mankind can be Saved is by trusting in Christ and what He did at the Cross. Admittedly, unredeemed man doesn't know anything about the Cross whatsoever. In fact, he knows nothing about the Lord Jesus Christ. That's the reason that all one has to do to be Saved is simply, *"Call on the Name of the Lord"* (Rom. 10:13).

But after one is Saved, has become a new creation in Christ Jesus, and the Holy Spirit now lives in such a heart, the Lord now expects us to study His Word, and to be led by the Spirit. It's not an easy task, it's not a simple task, and it's not a quick task.

Invariably after the believing sinner comes to Christ, and if you will look back in your own life you will see what I'm saying is correct, at a point, the newly converted Saint will fail the Lord in some way. It will come as a shock, and as such, the Believer will set about to try to guarantee that the failure doesn't happen again. Invariably, as a new convert, he will try to effect victory within his own ability and strength. He will not understand that he is doing such within his own ability and strength, but that's the way it will be.

The failure will not cause a revival of the sin nature, but trusting in something other than the Cross of Christ most definitely will.

THE HOLY SPIRIT

The Holy Spirit works on only one premise. That is by and through the Finished Work of Christ. In other words, and as we have said over and over again, the Cross is what gives the Holy Spirit, Whom we must have operating within our lives, the legal right to do all that He does (Rom. 8:1-2, 11). When the new Believer begins to trust in something other than the Cross, even though he does it innocently, this greatly hinders the Holy Spirit, guarantees a revival of the sin nature, which will cause untold problems. All of this is perfectly epitomized in the great Seventh Chapter of Romans, where Paul gave us an excerpt from his own life and Ministry. One does not learn the Way of the Spirit easily or quickly. And to make matters worse, when it's never preached behind the pulpit, as it almost never is in the modern church, this leaves the Believer in a terrible dilemma. That's the reason that at the present time, virtually the entirety of the modern church, and I speak of the part that is truly Born-Again, is being ruled in some way by the sin nature. Such institutes a constant repetitiveness of sinning and Repentance, sinning and Repentance! Sinning and Repentance! Sinning and Repentance!

With such pandemic in the church, millions down through the ages just simply quit. They don't want to profess something that they really do not have, so they just stop living for God, which is the worst thing they can do. And then the other part doesn't quit, but they resign themselves to having to live a life that is far beneath that which in their heart of hearts they know that one ought to have. But they don't know how to have it.

SIN SHALL NOT HAVE DOMINION OVER YOU

While the Bible doesn't teach sinless

perfection, it most definitely does teach that the sin nature is not to dominate the Believer. Paul said, and I quote from THE EXPOSITOR'S STUDY BIBLE:

"For sin shall not have dominion over you (the sin nature will not have dominion over us if we as Believers continue to exercise Faith in the Cross of Christ; otherwise, the sin nature most definitely will have dominion over the Believer)*: for you are not under the Law* (means that if we try to live this life by any type of religious law, no matter how good that religious law might be in its own right, we will conclude by the sin nature having dominion over us), *but under Grace* (the Grace of God flows to the Believer on an unending basis only as long as the Believer exercises Faith in Christ and what He did at the Cross; Grace is merely the Goodness of God exercised by and through the Holy Spirit, and given to undeserving Saints)" (Rom. 6:14).

Even though Paul did not use the definite article in his statement, making it read *"For the sin shall not have dominion over you . . .",* nevertheless, he used the word *"sin"* as a noun instead of a verb. As such, it means the same thing, *"that the sin nature shall not have dominion over you."*

This is done, victory over the sin nature, by the Believer exercising Faith constantly in Christ and the Cross, not allowing it to be moved anywhere else.

DOMINION

The Greek word for *"dominion"* is *"kurieno,"* and means, *"to rule, to control, to exercise lordship over."*

I want the reader now to look at your own life for a moment. Is there a reoccurring sin in your life, something that you've struggled with for a long, long time, seemingly, unable to get the victory? If that is the case, then in some way the sin nature is controlling you.

You have asked the Lord any number of times, actually scores and scores of times, to forgive you of this thing, whatever it might be, and He, thank God, always does; however, as you have noticed, I'm sure, the problem is not getting better, but actually it's getting worse, and no matter how hard

NOTES

you try otherwise. This is what Paul was talking about referring to his own life, when he said the following:

"For that which I do (the failure) *I allow not* (should have been translated, *'I understand not'*; these are not the words of an unsaved man, as some claim, but rather a Believer who is trying and failing)*: for what I would, that do I not* (refers to the obedience he wants to render to Christ, but rather fails; why? As Paul explained, the Believer is married to Christ, but is being unfaithful to Christ by spiritually cohabiting with the Law, which frustrates the Grace of God; that means the Holy Spirit will not help such a person, which guarantees failure [Gal. 2:21]); *but what I hate, that do I* (refers to sin in his life, which he doesn't want to do, and, in fact, hates, but finds himself unable to stop; unfortunately, due to the fact of not understanding the Cross as it refers to Sanctification, this is the plight of most modern Christians)" (Rom. 7:15).

WHAT DO WE MEAN *"COHABITING WITH THE LAW"*?

While it's not the Law of Moses with which the modern Believer associates himself, nevertheless, it is law, i.e., *"religious law."*

What do we mean by that?

These are laws that we make up out of our own mind, or somebody else makes up, or our church devises, or our denomination, etc. While the religious law within itself might be good, it will not enable the individual to walk in victory.

Let me explain further.

When the Believer fails, he says to himself, I must not do that thing again, whatever it might have been. To guarantee that I don't do it again, I will do the following:

• I will read two Chapters a day in the Bible.

• I will be faithful to pray at least thirty minutes a day.

Now these things that the Believer says that he will begin to do, and be faithful, are what we refer to as *"disciplines."* In fact, these things are something that every good Christian ought to do and, in fact, must do, if we are to have a proper relationship with the Lord; however, using it in the way that

I've just mentioned, makes it a religious law, and although it's good and, as stated, something we should do, still, done in this fashion, will not bring victory over the sin problem in question.

In fact, this is something that all of us have done at one time or the other. While the religious laws may change, it all amounts to the same thing.

When we turn these good things, something we ought to do constantly, into a law, it then becomes the object of our faith, in which and with which the Holy Spirit, without Whom we cannot rightly function, cannot work. Listen again to Paul:

"I do not frustrate the Grace of God (if we make anything other than the Cross of Christ the Object of our Faith, we frustrate the Grace of God, which means we stop its action, and the Holy Spirit will no longer help us)*: for if Righteousness come by the Law* (any type of Law), *then Christ is dead in vain.* (If I can successfully live for the Lord by any means other than Faith in Christ and the Cross, which then gives the Holy Spirit latitude to work in my life, then the Death of Christ was a waste)" (Gal. 2:21).

WHAT DOES IT MEAN TO FRUSTRATE THE GRACE OF GOD?

Frustrating the Grace of God means that we stop its flow, or at least, seriously hinder it. This is what happens, when we devise our religious laws, and again I state, no matter how good they might be in their own right, thinking that doing such will bring us victory, won't.

Every Believer in the world is either under Law or Grace. While this most definitely is the Dispensation of Grace, still, we will not reap the benefits of Grace, if we function in Law of any nature.

Grace is simply the Goodness of God extended to undeserving people. To have this Grace flow to us twenty-four hours a day, seven days a week, uninterrupted, the Believer must place his Faith exclusively in Christ and the Cross, understanding it was there that every Victory was won, and then the Holy Spirit will begin to work within our lives, giving us Victory over these sins, which do so easily beset us.

NOTES

GOOD LAWS!

These things deceive us, because the religious laws we fashion in our lives, are good things. As we've already stated, they are things we ought to do and, in fact, will do if we are properly living for God; however, we must never make these things the object of our faith. Again, Paul said if such will bring victory, then Christ did not have to come down here and die on a Cross. Always remember, all Victory comes exclusively through the Cross of Christ, and not by any other means.

And because it's so very, very important, please allow me to say it again:

Inasmuch as these religious laws we devise are very good within themselves, this deceives us, making us think that the doing of such should bring victory. But remember, with the Believer it is not *"doing,"* but rather *"believing"* (Jn. 3:16; Rom. 5:1-2), but believing in the right thing, which is the Cross of Christ (I Cor. 1:17-18, 23; 2:2).

When the Believer gets things in proper perspective, gets his Faith anchored solely in the Cross of Christ, which then gives the Holy Spirit latitude to work within one's life, without which we cannot function properly, then the Believer will perform these disciplines, but do them in the right way. In other words, such a Believer will have a stronger prayer life than ever, will have a stronger Bible study time than ever, etc. But now he's doing it because he has victory, and not in order to obtain victory.

WHY IS IT SO HARD TO TRUST EXCLUSIVELY IN THE CROSS OF CHRIST?

In effect, it's not hard, but rather the most simple, the easiest thing in the world for one to do. But, where the problem comes in, is that Satan will fight this way more than anything else, because he knows the Cross of Christ is the place of Victory and, in fact, the only place of Victory. And, as well, law is very dear to our hearts, in other words, the things that we do.

As a perfect example, Abraham did not want to give up Ishmael. This young man was the product of the planning and scheming of both Abraham and Sarah. As such, Abraham loved this boy. But, the Lord tells him that Ishmael must go.

Why?

The traits of evil and wickedness in Ishmael did not show up until Isaac, with the latter being a product of the Spirit, was born. When Isaac was born, and the word came emphatically to Abraham that Isaac was to be the seed, in other words, would receive the inheritance of the firstborn and not Ishmael, this brought out the evil in Ishmael. In fact, Ishmael tried to kill Isaac. Paul said:

"But as then he who was born after the flesh (Ishmael) *persecuted him who was born after the Spirit* (Isaac), *even so it is now.* (Isaac and Ishmael symbolized the new and the old nature in the Believer. Hagar and Sarah typified the two Covenants of works and Grace, of bondage and Liberty, even as Paul is explaining here.)

"Nevertheless what says the Scripture? (Gen. 21:10). *Cast out the bondwoman and her son* (the birth of the new nature demands the expulsion of the old; it is impossible to improve the old nature; it must be cast out, i.e., 'placed in a dormant position'; this can only be done by the Believer evidencing constant Faith in the Cross, which then gives the Holy Spirit latitude to bring about this necessary work)*: for the son of the bondwoman shall not be heir with the son of the freewoman.* (Paul is giving a dramatic illustration of the irreconcilable conflict between Salvation by works and Salvation by Faith)" (Gal. 4:29-30).

The word *"persecuted"* as given in Verse 29 in the Greek is, *"dioko,"* and in this instance means, *"to murder."* So, Ishmael tried to murder Isaac.

The Jewish Targums say the way this was done was according to the following:

At this time Isaac was about four or five years old, and Ishmael was about twenty. Ishmael wanted the birthright, which would give him a double portion of Abraham's material goods when he died. But understanding that Abraham had decreed that Isaac was to be the one, although born after Ishmael, who would get the birthright, Ishmael was determined to obtain it himself. He would murder Isaac if he had to, in order to bring

NOTES

about that desired.

The Targums say that Ishmael would feign playing with Isaac, and would shoot an arrow in the distance, and then have the little boy run and get it. He was trying to hit the boy with the arrow and kill him, and then it could be passed off as an accident. That's the reason that the Lord told Sarah to tell Abraham that the bondwoman and her son must go (Gen. 21:9-10).

LEGALISM

Concerning this, the Scripture says: *"And the thing was very grievous in Abraham's sight because of his son.* (It is always a struggle to cast out this element of bondage, that is, Salvation by works, of which this is a type. For legalism is dear to the heart. Ishmael was the fruit, and, to Abraham, the fair fruit of his own energy and planning, which God can never accept.)

"And God said unto Abraham, Let it not be grievous in your sight because of the lad, and because of your bondwoman; in all that Sarah has said unto you, hearken unto her voice; for in Isaac shall your seed be called. (It is labor lost to seek to make a crooked thing straight. Hence, all efforts after the improvement of nature are utterly futile, so far as God is concerned. The *'flesh'* must go, which typifies the personal ability, strength, and efforts of the Believer. The Faith of the Believer must be entirely in Christ and what Christ has done at the Cross. Then, and then alone, can the Holy Spirit have latitude to work in our lives, bringing forth perpetual victory [Rom. 6:14]. It must ever be understood, *'in Isaac* [in Christ] *shall your seed be called.'*)

"And also of the son of the bondwoman will I make a nation, because he is your seed (out of this *'work of the flesh'* ultimately came the religion of Islam, which claims that Ishmael is the promised seed, and not Isaac).

"And Abraham rose up early in the morning, and took bread, and a bottle of water, and gave it unto Hagar, putting it on her shoulder, and the child, and sent her away: and she departed, and wandered in the wilderness of Beer-sheba. (This moment marks a distinct advance in the Spiritual

experience of Abraham. From this moment onwards all is strength and victory. He casts out the bondwoman and her son; he no longer fears the prince of this world [Abimelech], but reproves him; and now that the heir is come, Christ in Type, he knows himself to be the possessor of Heavenly, as well, as earthly promises)" (Gen. 21:11-14).

The idea is, all elements of the flesh, i.e., our own ability and strength, must go. Our Faith, our dependence, and confidence, must rest exclusively, solely in Christ and what Christ has done for us at the Cross. That is God's Way of Victory, and His only Way of Victory. He honors nothing except His Son, the Lord Jesus Christ, and what Christ did at Calvary, which He did entirely for us.

THE GREAT STRUGGLE

That which we have just given to you presents the great struggle with the Christian. It's never easy for us to give up the works that we perform, at least in the way they are being performed, and rely solely and totally on Christ and what He did at the Cross. We are constantly desiring to do something, which we think, will effect our victory. It won't!

A PERSONAL EXPERIENCE

Sometime ago, two preachers were invited as guests to be on our daily radio program, which airs over the SonLife Network, and at this stage, some 80 Stations. We were, in effect, studying this same subject.

One of our guests made the statement, *"When I have problems with sin, I fast three days and nights, and that settles the situation."*

I gently reminded him that while fasting is very important, and will definitely bless a person, still, that is not God's Way of Victory over sin. I went on to state that the Victory is solely in the Cross of Christ, and demands our Faith in that Finished Work.

I will never forget, the young man grew rather angry, clenched his fist and slammed it down on the table, saying, *"Well I'll have you know, that it works for me!"*

As stated, every one of us have invested much time, labor, and effort, into these religious laws, and it doesn't set too well with us when we are told, that it is all in vain. It's hard for us to accept that these things, which we have done and are doing, will have no positive results.

I wonder if the young man had ever thought that this was a reoccurring thing, in other words, that he was having to continue to fast three days and nights again and again.

I do not at all mean for my statements to be sarcastic, because I've been in the same place.

I can remember the day that the object of my faith was in my prayer life. To be sure, the Lord greatly blessed me in that endeavor, which I continue unto this hour, but still, I could not find victory in this capacity, no matter how hard I tried, and neither will you.

There is nothing more important than the prayer life of the Child of God, at least as it regards a Christian discipline. In fact, the Believer cannot have a proper relationship with Christ unless they have a proper prayer life; however, if we depend on that prayer life, making it the object of our faith, as wonderful as prayer within itself actually is, still, we will find that victory will be elusive. Let me say it again:

All Salvation is found in the Cross, even as all Sanctification is found in the Cross. Please note the following carefully:

JUSTIFICATION BY FAITH AND SANCTIFICATION BY FAITH

If the Believer doesn't properly understand Sanctification by Faith, he will have a jaundiced view of Justification by Faith as well. He may define Justification by Faith correctly, but then will turn around and try to earn something from God by the means of works.

The Apostle Paul wrote the Book of Galatians for this very reason. The Galatians had come to Christ under Paul's Ministry. So they knew the right way; however, the Judaisers, who were Jews that believed in Christ, but claimed that one had to keep the Law in order to be Saved, had come into their midst, preaching law. In other words, the Galatians were claiming Salvation by

Faith, which is exactly what they should have done, but then trying to effect Sanctification by self. In other words, they were trying to sanctify themselves, by their works, i.e., *"keeping religious laws."* Paul told them that if they did this they would *"fall from Grace"* (Gal. 5:4).

I'm sure that Paul's Letter set them straight, but unfortunately, in the modern church, Sanctification by self, in other words, by the obeying of religious laws, continues to go unchecked. *"The Purpose Driven Life"* book is a case in point. In fact, man is constantly coming up with one scheme after the other, which is supposed to give him victory. But let me say it again:

There is no victory outside of the Cross of Christ.

I have already inserted the following in this Volume, but because of the seriousness of the matter, please allow the repetition.

• FOCUS: The Lord Jesus Christ (Jn. 14:6).
• OBJECT OF FAITH: The Cross of Christ (Rom. 6:1-14).
• POWER SOURCE: The Holy Spirit (Rom. 8:1-2, 11).
• RESULTS: Victory (Rom. 6:14).

In a nutshell, that is God's Way; however, let's look at it now from man's way, using the same formula.

• Focus: Works.
• Object of faith: Performance.
• Power source: Self.
• Results: Defeat.

"Sing we the King Who is coming to reign,
"Glory to Jesus, the Lamb that was slain,
"Life and Salvation His Empire shall bring,
"Joy to the nations when Jesus is King."

"All men shall dwell in His marvelous Light,
"Races long severed His Love shall unite,
"Justice and Truth from His Sceptre shall spring,
"Wrong shall be ended when Jesus is King."

NOTES

"All shall be well in His Kingdom of peace,
"Freedom shall flourish and wisdom increase,
"Foe shall be friend when His triumph we sing,
"Sword shall be sickle when Jesus is King."

"Souls shall be Saved from the burden of sin,
"Doubt shall not darken His witness within,
"Hell has no terrors, and death has no sting,
"Love is victorious when Jesus is King."

"Kingdom of Christ, for Your coming we pray,
"Hasten, O Father, the dawn of the day,
"When this new song Your Creation shall sing,
"Satan is vanquished and Jesus is King."

CHAPTER 26

(1) "BUT JOB ANSWERED AND SAID,
(2) "HOW HAVE YOU HELPED HIM WHO IS WITHOUT POWER? HOW DO YOU SAVE THE ARM THAT HAS NO STRENGTH?
(3) "HOW HAVE YOU COUNSELLED HIM WHO HAS NO WISDOM? AND HOW HAVE YOU PLENTIFULLY DECLARED THE THING AS IT IS?
(4) "TO WHOM HAVE YOU UTTERED WORDS? AND WHOSE SPIRIT CAME FROM YOU?
(5) "DEAD THINGS ARE FORMED FROM UNDER THE WATERS, AND THE INHABITANTS THEREOF."

The pattern is:

1. In the Third Verse, Job is using irony. He rebukes the worthlessness of Bildad's human reasoning. In fact, all human reasoning, as it regards the Lord and His Work, is worthless.

2. The Fourth Verse presents the fact that

there is no inspiration on any words that come from man, even though so intellectual or lofty, unless they come from the Word of God. And, to be sure, the words of Bildad, and the other *"friends,"* as well, didn't come from God, but rather out of their own minds, as does so much presently.

3. The *"dead things"* of Verse 5 refer to the Rephaim, which was the result of the union of fallen Angels and women (Gen. 6:4).

THE WORTHLESSNESS OF
HUMAN REASONING

When we speak of *"human reasoning"* here we are speaking of life and living. We aren't speaking of technology, etc.

Sometime ago I saw over one of the major news networks, that which someone had conjectured is the answer to the inner city gangs. It was midnight basketball.

The idea was, if they could get the young men and young ladies playing basketball at midnight, then they wouldn't want to be in gangs, etc.

No, it didn't work, as nothing like that can ever work.

The federal government has spent hundreds of billions of dollars on drug prevention, with no success whatsoever. As well, they've spent hundreds of billions of dollars trying to rebuild the inner city, thinking that new apartments would solve the problem of crime, etc. Despite the fact that nothing they do works, they keep right on trying.

The only answer for fallen humanity is to be Born-Again. In fact, that's the very reason that man must be Born-Again. In his natural, fallen state, it is impossible for him to do right, to be right, to act right, and for a hundred obvious reasons. Unconverted man is ruled completely by the sin nature, and that means 24 hours a day, 7 days a week. Even the things he does, which he thinks are good, still, tend toward sin in some way, and we speak of impure motives, etc.

Jesus addressed the question of *"good,"* in answering the rich young ruler. The Scripture says:

"And, behold, one came and said unto Him, Good Master (addressed Him merely as a teacher)*, what good thing shall I do, that I may have eternal life?* (*'Doing'* is not the answer, but rather, *'believing'* [Jn. 3:16]).

"And He said unto him, Why do you call Me good? (You don't recognize Me as God) *there is none good but One, that is, God* (Jesus wasn't saying that He wasn't good; in fact, He definitely was good, because He is God)*: but if you will enter into life, keep the Commandments* (is meant to answer to man on the same grounds, which he has asked — the grounds of good works! He will show him that he, in fact, cannot attain to Eternal Life by *'keeping Commandments,'* i.e., *'good works'*).

"He said unto him, Which? (A ridiculous question!) *Jesus said, you shall not commit murder, you shall not commit adultery, you shall not steal, you shall not bear false witness* (Jesus didn't say keep one Commandment, but rather all of them, which the man had not done, nor any other man for that matter — except Christ),

"Honor your father and your mother: and, you shall love your neighbor as yourself (this latter Commandment is taken from Lev. 19:18; it was not a part of the original Ten, but actually summed up all the Commandments, which dealt with one's fellowman).

"The young man said unto Him, All these things have I kept from my youth up (he was mistaken; he had not)*: what lack I yet?* (This question proclaims the fact that something was wrong.)

"Jesus said unto him, If you will be perfect, go and sell that you have, and give to the poor, and you shall have treasure in Heaven: and come and follow Me (Jesus put His Finger on the two great Commandments of the Law and said: *'If you love your neighbor as yourself, then share your wealth with him; and if you love Jehovah your God with all your heart, then follow Me, for one only is good, that is God, and I am He'*).

"But when the young man heard that saying, he went away sorrowful: for he had great possessions (the Gospel makes mad, sad, or glad; Naaman went away in a rage; the rich ruler went away sorrowful; but Zacchaeus received Christ joyfully)*"* (Mat. 19:16-22).

Any *"good"* that any individual has, is all because of Christ, and what Christ has done for us at the Cross.

That's the reason Jesus also said: *"For whosoever will save his life shall lose it* (try to live one's life outside of Christ and the Cross)*: but whosoever will lose his life for My Sake, the same shall save it* (when we place our Faith entirely in Christ and the Cross, looking exclusively to Him, we have just found *'more Abundant Life' [Jn. 10:10])"* (Lk. 9:24).

THE GIANTS

We believe that the Bible teaches that before the Flood, and after the Flood, there was a corrupt union of fallen Angels with women on Earth that produced a race of giants. In fact, every evidence is that Goliath was one of those giants.

The Scripture says concerning this, and I quote from THE EXPOSITOR'S STUDY BIBLE:

"And it came to pass, when men began to multiply on the face of the Earth, and daughters were born unto them (the events of this Chapter probably began at about the time of Enoch, which was about a thousand years before the flood. There were, no doubt, several millions of people on the face of the Earth at that time. Verse 1 is not meant to imply that the births of baby girls were more than that of baby boys, but is rather meant to set up the narrative for that which is about to be said),

"That the sons of God saw the daughters of men that they were fair; and they took them wives of all which they chose (the *'sons of God'* portrayed here refer to fallen Angels, which had thrown in their lot with Lucifer, who led a revolution against God sometime in eternity past; in order to spoil the human lineage through which the Messiah would ultimately come, they would seek to corrupt that lineage, and to do so by marrying the *'daughters of men,'* thereby, producing a mongrel race, so to speak, of which at least some of these offspring turned out to be *'giants'*; at any rate, all who were the result of such a union were tainted; the term *'sons of God'* in the Old Testament, at least as it is used here, is never used of human beings, but always of Angels, whether righteous or fallen [Job. 1:6; 2:1]; in his short Epistle,

NOTES

Jude mentions these particular *'Angels.'* He said that they *'kept not their first estate, but left their own habitation'*; he then said what their sin was: *'going after strange flesh.'*

"Concerning this, Jude also said that God *'has reserved* [them] *in everlasting chains under darkness unto the Judgment of the Great Day' [Jude, Vss. 6-7]*).

"And the LORD said, My Spirit (Holy Spirit) *shall not always strive with man* (the Lord is speaking here of the man, Adam, and not mankind in general), *for that he also is flesh* (refers to the fact that even though the first man was created personally by God, he still was flesh, and because of the Fall must ultimately die): *yet his days shall be an hundred and twenty years* (from the time of this announcement, Adam was to be given 120 years to repent; there is no evidence that he did; many think that this hundred twenty years refer to the time limit to repent before the Flood; however, it has nothing to do with the Flood, as we will later prove).

"There were giants in the Earth in those days (as a result of the union of fallen Angels with the *'daughters of men'*); *and also after that* (*'those days'* speak of the time before the Flood, while *'also after that'* speaks of the time after the Flood; in fact, Goliath, as stated, who was killed by David, was one of those specimens), *when the sons of God came in unto the daughters of men, and they bore children to them, the same became mighty men which were of old, men of renown* (the terms, *'mighty men, men of renown'* shoot down the hypothesis of these terms referring merely to the lineage of Seth and the lineage of Cain).

"And God saw that the wickedness of man was great in the Earth (these *'men of renown,'* the giants, were developing more and more ways of wickedness), *and that every imagination of the thoughts of his heart was only evil continually* (due to this infestation, the evil began with the very thought processes, and incorporated every human being; this was a continuous action of evil which never let up, and constantly grew more degrading)" (Gen. 6:1-5).

Concerning this union of fallen Angels with women, Jude said, to which we have previously eluded:

"And the Angels who kept not their first estate, but left their own habitation (these particular Angels did not maintain their original position in which they were created, but transgressed those limits to invade territory foreign to them, namely the human race; they left Heaven and came to Earth, seeking to cohabit with women, which they did [Gen. 6:4]), *He* (the Lord) *has reserved in everlasting chains under darkness unto the Judgment of the Great Day* (these Angels are now imprisoned [II Pet. 2:4], and will be judged at the Great White Throne Judgment, then placed in the *'Lake of Fire'* where they will remain forever and forever [Rev. 20:10]).

"Even as Sodom and Gomorrha, and the cities about them in like manner (the Greek Text introduces a comparison showing a likeness between the Angels of Verse 6 and the cities of Sodom and Gomorrah; but the likeness between them lies deeper than the fact that both were guilty of committing sin; it extends to the fact that both were guilty of the same identical sin), *giving themselves over to fornication, and going after strange flesh* (the Angels cohabited with women; the sin of Sodom and Gomorrah, and the cities around them, was homosexuality [Rom. 1:27]), *are set forth for an example, suffering the vengeance of eternal fire* (those who engage in the sin of homosexuality and refuse to repent will suffer the vengeance of the Lake of Fire)" (Jude, Vss. 6-7).

(6) "HELL IS NAKED BEFORE HIM, AND DESTRUCTION HAS NO COVERING.

(7) "HE STRETCHES OUT THE NORTH OVER THE EMPTY PLACE, AND HANGS THE EARTH UPON NOTHING.

(8) "HE BINDS UP THE WATERS IN HIS THICK CLOUDS, AND THE CLOUD IS NOT RENT UNDER THEM.

(9) "HE HOLDS BACK THE FACE OF HIS THRONE, AND SPREADS HIS CLOUD UPON IT.

(10) "HE HAS COMPASSED THE WATERS WITH BOUNDS, UNTIL THE DAY AND NIGHT COME TO AN END.

(11) "THE PILLARS OF HEAVEN TREMBLE AND ARE ASTONISHED AT HIS REPROOF.

(12) "HE DIVIDES THE SEA WITH HIS POWER, AND BY HIS UNDERSTANDING HE SMITES THROUGH THE PROUD.

(13) "BY HIS SPIRIT HE HAS GARNISHED THE HEAVENS; HIS HAND HAS FORMED THE CROOKED SERPENT.

(14) "LO, THESE ARE PARTS OF HIS WAYS: BUT HOW LITTLE A PORTION IS HEARD OF HIM? BUT THE THUNDER OF HIS POWER WHO CAN UNDERSTAND?"

The diagram is:

1. (Vs. 6) Whereas the statements of Bildad and the other *"friends"* were not inspired, these particular statements concerning God, as given by Job, definitely are inspired.

2. Verse 7 proclaims the fact that it is the Power of God, evidenced in His fixed Laws, which upholds the Earth, and that alone.

3. (Vs. 8) Clouds have no texture, but yet, they hold great volumes of water. How? By the Power of God, once again, evidenced in fixed Laws.

4. (Vs. 9) It is evident now that man can fathom only a few of these laws; the evidence is, in the coming Kingdom Age, all of God's Laws of Creation will be revealed (Isa. 11:9-19).

5. The latter part of Verse 13 should be translated, *"His Hand has pierced the swift serpent,"* which refers to the defeat of Satan at the Cross, although that was then yet future; however, so sure was this coming event, that the Lord could speak of it in the past tense.

6. In the Fourteenth Verse, Job implies that he has not enumerated one-half of God's great Works — he has just hinted at them.

THE DEFEAT OF SATAN

Satan was totally and completely defeated at the Cross. Paul wrote, saying:

"Blotting out the handwriting of Ordinances that was against us (pertains to the Law of Moses, which was God's Standard of Righteousness that man could not reach), *which was contrary to us* (Law is against us, simply because we are unable to keep its precepts, no matter how hard we try), *and took it out of the way* (refers to the penalty of the Law being removed), *nailing it to His Cross* (the Law with its decrees was abolished in Christ's Death, as if Crucified with Him);

"And having spoiled principalities and powers (Satan and all of his henchmen were defeated at the Cross by Christ atoning for all sin; sin was the legal right Satan had to hold man in captivity; with all sin atoned, he has no more legal right to hold anyone in bondage), *He* (Christ) *made a show of them openly* (what Jesus did at the Cross was in the face of the whole universe), *triumphing over them in it.* (The Triumph is complete and it was all done for us, meaning we can walk in power and perpetual Victory due to the Cross)" (Col. 2:14-15).

When we speak of Jesus defeating Satan at the Cross, first of all the reader must understand that we're not speaking of anything physical. To be frank, Satan wants no part of Christ whatsoever. The only question, in fact, that Satan asks Christ when the Lord tells him to jump, so to speak, is *"how high?"*

So, how did Jesus actually defeat Satan?

As we've said in the notes accompanying the Texts, Jesus by atoning for all sin at the Cross, and doing so by giving Himself as a Perfect Sacrifice, removed Satan's legal right to hold man captive. That legal right was sin. With all sin atoned, Satan has no more legal right.

Even though the Victory of Christ was total and complete, and Satan was defeated in every capacity, and done so eternally, still, most of the world is still held captive by Satan.

Is there a contradiction here?

No!

The world is in bondage simply because they will not avail themselves of what our Lord has done. It is the age-old problem of *"unbelief,"* and *"deception."*

Now what we've just said is understandable by most Christians; however, the sad truth is, most Christians remain in bondage, as well, and we speak of bondage to the sin nature.

Why is this so?

Believers remain in bondage simply because their Faith is in something other than the Cross of Christ. As such, the Holy Spirit is very much limited as to what He can do for such Believers, with the sin nature then ruling them.

NOTES

It's a sad thing for Believers to trust Christ solely for their Salvation, but then try to bring about Sanctification by the efforts of *"self."* And regrettably, that is the status of most modern Christians.

One of the favorite sayings of Christians is, *"I can do all things through Christ Who strengthens me."*

Well, the truth is, Christ will not strengthen them, if their Faith is in something other than the Cross of Christ. And beside that, Believers, no matter that they are Born-Again, no matter that they are Spirit-filled, no matter that the Lord may even be using them, still, if their Faith is in something other than the Cross of Christ, they are living a defeated life.

The sad truth is, most preachers simply do not know how to tell people how to live for God. They simply don't know how themselves!

MOST CHRISTIANS DON'T KNOW HOW TO LIVE FOR THE LORD

Now, if most Christians were asked as to how that one should live for the Lord, the answers would probably be as varied as the individuals being asked. The truth is, modern Christians do not know how to live for God. As a result, they frustrate the Grace of God, which leaves such a Believer vulnerable to Satan, the flesh, and the world (Gal. 2:21).

The statements I am making, I have lived, so I know what I'm talking about. Countless times before the Lord gave me the great Revelation of the Cross, which is found in Romans, Chapter 6, I would cry to the Lord, telling Him that no human being could stand what I was having to undergo. The truth is, I was right. No human being can stand it, and actually, no human being is required to stand it. Jesus went to the Cross that we might walk in Victory, and I speak of Victory over the world, the flesh, and the Devil.

No, I am not meaning that the Believer can reach a certain place in the Lord that he'll never be tempted again, and there will never be another problem. The Bible does not teach that. To be frank, Satan will never stop in his efforts to steal, kill, and destroy.

But the facts are, and I speak of Scriptural facts, our Saviour, in the giving of Himself in Sacrifice on the Cross of Calvary, has made it possible for the Holy Spirit to come into our hearts and lives and there to abide forever (Jn. 14:16).

The Holy Spirit is God! There is nothing that He cannot do. Things which are hard for us, and even impossible, are nothing for Him, as we should understand.

GOD'S PRESCRIBED ORDER OF VICTORY

When the Believer places his Faith exclusively in Christ, and what Christ did for us at the Cross, this gives the Holy Spirit the legal right to work in our hearts and lives, bringing about that which He Alone can do. Please believe me, Satan is not afraid of us at all, at least as it regards our own personal strength. But he wants no part whatsoever of the Holy Spirit. But let me say the following:

Even with the Believer placing his Faith correctly in Christ and the Cross, and even with the Believer maintaining his Faith exclusively in Christ and the Cross, and even with the Holy Spirit abiding within our hearts and lives, and having the liberty to do and to work within us, to bring about the desired results, still, Paul referred to this experience, this journey of life, as *"war."* He said:

"For though we walk in the flesh (refers to the fact that we do not yet have Glorified Bodies), *we do not war after the flesh* (after our own ability, but rather by the Power of the Spirit)*:*

"(For the weapons of our warfare are not carnal [carnal weapons consist of those which are man-devised], *but mighty through God* [the Cross of Christ (I Cor. 1:18)] *to the pulling down of strongholds;)*

"Casting down imaginations (philosophic strongholds; every effort man makes outside of the Cross of Christ), *and every high thing that exalts itself against the Knowledge of God* (all the pride of the human heart), *and bringing into captivity every thought to the obedience of Christ* (can be done only by the Believer looking exclusively to the Cross, where all Victory is found; the Holy Spirit will then perform the task)" (II Cor. 10:3-5).

The Holy Spirit would not have used the word *"war,"* had He not desired to do so. It is war! And that means it's to the death!

There is only one way that the Believer can win in this conflict, a way that we have dealt with in every conceivable fashion, and that is by and through the Cross of Christ. In the Cross alone there is Victory. That's where Satan, as stated, was defeated. Consequently, that's where our Faith must reside — the Cross of Christ.

THE WEAPONS OF OUR WARFARE

What I am about to give has been given elsewhere in our Commentaries; but due to the manner in which most Commentaries are studied, I think it would be beneficial for us to relate this again.

The year was 1953. Frances and I had been married for about a year. Donnie would be born about a year later. Our domicile was a little mobile home, 32 feet long and 8 feet wide. I was just beginning to preach the Gospel.

Frances had gone to bed, and I had stayed up studying the Word for a period of time.

Sitting alone on the couch at the far end of that little mobile home, all of a sudden, a terrible oppressive spirit seemed to cover me. I tried to continue studying, but was unable to do so.

I left out of the little trailer, and started walking up and down the short road by which we were parked. There were no houses and it afforded a modicum of privacy. I was trying to pray, but once again it seemed like the heavens were brass.

I finally came back in, went to bed, and the Lord gave me a Dream.

THE HOUSE

I found myself in a house that was totally strange to me. I did not know why I was there, did not recognize anything there, and wondered actually how I had gotten there.

I was in the front room that was completely empty of all furniture. Neither did it have a window in the room, only a front door which led to the outside.

I hurriedly looked around, wondering what in the world I was doing here. Along with that, I felt a sinister spirit, and my first reaction was, *"I've got to get out of here."*

I turned toward the door, when all of a sudden there appeared in the doorway the most hideous looking creature I had ever seen. It must have stood about six or seven feet tall, and it had the face of a man and the body of a bear.

A DEMON SPIRIT

As I looked at the countenance of this thing, I don't think I've ever seen anything so evil. It seemed like all wickedness was etched on its face, and most of all the evil that was in its eyes. I've never seen anything that looked like that.

And then it began to descend on me. When I looked at that thing, such a spirit of fear gripped me that all my strength seemed to drain out of my body. I slumped to the floor, actually unable to stand.

As that thing descended on me with its arms outstretched, as if to say I have you now, I began to feel around over the floor to try to get something with which to defend myself. Of course, had I found something, what good would it have done? There was nothing there.

Looking back, the Lord was showing me that *"the weapons of our warfare aren't carnal, but mighty through God to the pulling down of strongholds"* (II Cor. 10:3-4).

IN THE NAME OF JESUS

Without premeditation, without contemplating anything, I screamed as loud as I could, *"In the Name of Jesus!"* However, even though I exerted all of my strength, still, my voice was barely above a whisper. That's how weak that I was.

But the moment I uttered that Name, the Name of Jesus, that thing screamed and clutched its head, just like somebody had hit it in the head with a ball bat. It began to stagger backward across the floor, all the time screaming.

I was made to realize, that the Power of that Name did not rest within my own personal strength. Even though I was so weak I could not stand, and so weak that my voice was barely above a whisper, still, with the mention of that Name, the Name of Jesus, the affect upon that terrible beast, was extremely obvious.

Now I began to gather strength, and stood to my feet. I said it again, *"In the Name of Jesus!"*

This time, the affect of that Name was just as powerful, or even more so. The beast slumped to the floor, actually writhing like a snake that had just received a death blow, all the time screaming and holding its head.

THE PROPHECY

Immediately after the Fall in the Garden of Eden, the Lord told Satan through the serpent, *"And I will put enmity between you and the woman, and between your seed and her Seed; it shall bruise your head . . ."* (Gen. 3:15).

In fact, that great Victory was won at Calvary, when Jesus defeated the *"head"* of all evil, Satan himself, and did so by atoning for all sin (Col. 2:14-15).

RENEWED STRENGTH, GREATER THAN EVER

And now as I stood over this thing as it writhed on the floor, I opened my mouth, and without any effort at all, said again, *"In the Name of Jesus!"*

As I used that mighty Name the third time, even though, as stated, I exerted no strength, still, it was as if though my voice was attached to a powerful public address system, even with my voice bouncing off the wall.

Now, instead of that thing towering over me, I was towering over it. In fact, it was at my feet.

The Scripture again says, *"And has put all things under His Feet, and gave Him to be the Head over all things to the Church, which is His Body, the fullness of Him that fills all in all"* (Eph. 1:22-23).

THE SOUND OF A RUSHING MIGHTY WIND

And then I heard it!

It was like a tornado that was coming, the sound of a *"rushing mighty wind,"* but yet, I saw nothing, only hearing the sound.

In the Dream, however, I knew that what I was hearing was the Holy Spirit (Acts 2:2).

Evidently, the Holy Spirit hit the beast on the floor, and it was knocked out the front door. As I ran out the door to see what happened. I saw nothing as it regards the *"rushing mighty wind,"* but I definitely saw the effects of it.

The last I saw of this terrible beast, it was being thrown through the air like a leaf, and then I awakened.

THE POWER OF GOD

Actually, I woke myself up praising the Lord in other Tongues.

I knew that the Lord had given me that Dream, but at the time, those many years ago, I did not actually know what it meant.

As time has passed, I believe I now know what the Dream meant.

• I believe the Lord, those many years ago, was giving me a preview as to how that Satan would attempt to destroy me.

• I believe He showed me in the Dream how that Satan could not be defeated by carnal means.

• He, as well, showed me the veracity and the Power of the Name of Jesus, and how that the use of that Name was not dependent upon my personal strength.

• He showed me in the Dream, that I would win the battle, although not by my own strength and power, but by the use of the Name of Jesus. It was all of Him and none of me.

• He showed me that I would regain my strength, and even in a greater way than ever.

• He let me hear the sound of the *"rushing mighty wind,"* which, of course, was the Holy Spirit.

• He showed me what the Name of Jesus and the Holy Spirit could accomplish, and which They Alone could accomplish.

• By me awakening myself praising the Lord in Tongues, with the Power of God all over me, He let me know that this Dream was definitely from the Lord.

I will say with Job, *"Lo, these are the parts of His Ways: but how little a portion is heard of Him? But the thunder of His Power who can understand?"*

"Jesus, Name of a matchless splendor!
"Name all other names above!

NOTES

"Glorious Son of God Incarnate,
"King of kings, and Lord of love!"

"Name that to our hearts is nearest,
"Here the stricken soul does hide;
"Name that to our hearts is dearest,
"As in Jesus we confide."

"Call Him Jesus! He shall save us,
"From the tyranny of sin;
"From its condemnation save us,
"From iniquity within."

"Thanks we give, and adoration,
"Every day and every hour,
"For an uttermost Salvation,
"Freedom from its guilt and power."

"Jesus! Sweetest note of any,
"In the lowly pilgrim's song;
"Jesus! The triumphant music,
"Of the bright angelic throng."

"Earth to Him her face upraises,
"Knows Him as the great I Am!
"Heaven resounds with Jesus' praises,
"Glory to the bleeding Lamb!"

CHAPTER 27

(1) "MOREOVER JOB CONTINUED HIS PARABLE, AND SAID,

(2) "AS GOD LIVES, WHO HAS TAKEN AWAY MY JUDGMENT; AND THE ALMIGHTY, WHO HAS VEXED MY SOUL;

(3) "ALL THE WHILE MY BREATH IS IN ME, AND THE SPIRIT OF GOD IS IN MY NOSTRILS;

(4) "MY LIPS SHALL NOT SPEAK WICKEDNESS, NOR MY TONGUE UTTER DECEIT.

(5) "GOD FORBID THAT I SHOULD JUSTIFY YOU: TILL I DIE I WILL NOT REMOVE MY INTEGRITY FROM ME.

(6) "MY RIGHTEOUSNESS I HOLD FAST, AND WILL NOT LET IT GO: MY HEART SHALL NOT REPROACH ME SO LONG AS I LIVE.

(7) "LET MY ENEMY BE AS THE WICKED, AND HE WHO RISES UP AGAINST ME AS THE UNRIGHTEOUS."

The diagram is:

1. The word *"parable"* as used in Verse 1, refers to a comparison of one thing with another, thereby, making it simpler to understand.

2. While it is true as given in Verse 2, that God did vex Job's soul, Job still doesn't know the reason yet.

3. Despite his problems, and according to Verse 3, he is still alive and the Spirit of God is still in him; he will now give a ringing defense of his own position.

4. (Vs. 4) He maintains his correctness of position, even from the beginning; when the Lord did finally appear, He did not contradict Job's statement.

5. (Vs. 5) The certainty of a position, irrespective of circumstances, can be maintained only if it is fully based on the Word of God.

6. (Vs. 6) Job says to his *"friends,"* that they have reproached him, but his heart hasn't.

7. Verse 7 constitutes a bold statement as given by Job, but yet, he is right; the truth of the matter is that the three *"friends,"* and not Job, were the wicked and, therefore, unrighteous.

RIGHTEOUSNESS

Righteousness before the Cross was somewhat different, actually a great deal different, than it is presently. In Truth, which we'll explain to a greater degree momentarily, going back to the beginning, it would be the same. But, as far as the individual was concerned, Righteousness before the Cross, consisted more, one might say, in *"doing,"* than presently as it refers to *"believing."*

Even before the Mosaic Law was given, individuals who desired to please God functioned somewhat according to Law.

• From the time of the Fall of Adam to the time of Noah, people functioned under the Law of Conscience.

• From Noah to Abraham, mankind functioned under the Law of Government.

• From Abraham to Moses, mankind functioned under the Law of Promise.

• From Moses to Christ, mankind functioned under the Mosaic Law.

But, these Laws could not save anyone and, in fact, were never meant to save anyone.

From the time of the Fall, the Lord showed the First Family how they could have fellowship with God and forgiveness of sins, despite their fallen condition. It would be through the Sacrificial system, the sacrificing of an innocent victim, namely a lamb (Gen., Chpt. 4).

As well, the sacrifices, although ordained by God, within themselves, did not save anyone. They were meant to serve as a stopgap measure, so to speak, thereby, pointing to the One Who was to come, namely the Lord Jesus Christ, Who in fact, could save. So, before the Cross, men were Saved by what the sacrifices represented, which was the coming Redeemer. They were to have Faith in what the sacrifices represented, which then perfected Salvation within their hearts and lives. In fact, there were millions who offered up sacrifices, actually what the Lord demanded to be offered up, but who were not Saved. Faith was always the workable component. It was the component before the Cross, and it is the component after the Cross.

Along with their faith, each Believer was to attempt to obey the Lord in every capacity, at least as far as was possible. This is where the *"doing"* came in, and was very important. Actually, this is what Job is maintaining:

THE PERSONAL RIGHTEOUSNESS OF JOB

Job knew that he had done his very best to obey the Lord as much as he knew how to do so, all of his life. In fact, I know that Jacob, his grandfather, would have been very, very proud of Job. That would have gone for his great-grandfather Isaac, and his great, great-grandfather, Abraham. Of course, this would have included his father Issachar, and his uncle Joseph.

No matter what his *"three friends"* said, or others might have said, Job maintained his righteousness, meaning that he had done his very best to please the Lord, and had done so for many, many years. He held to that, even as he should have. Irrespective as to what the *"three friends"* said, irrespective as to what others said, irrespective of the accusations made, still, Job maintained his righteousness. He would not allow the nay-sayers to take that from him.

A PERSONAL EXPERIENCE

In a small way, I have at least an inkling of personal knowledge as to that which Job faced.

I know what it is to be called a hypocrite, to be laughed at, to be denied anything of the Lord, at least by others. But I knew different. As such, I would not allow the nay-sayers to take from me, what I knew was rightfully mine. In fact, had I not had a strong hold on the Lord, there would have been no way that I could have stood the rejection, and the accusations.

As Paul said, I would say:

"*For the which cause* (to establish the Church) *I also suffer these things* (imprisonment, etc.)*: nevertheless I am not ashamed* (proclaims the fact that some were ashamed of Paul, regarding his imprisonment)*: for I know Whom I have believed* (refers to the Lord Jesus Christ)*, and am persuaded that He is able to keep that which I have committed unto Him against that day. (This refers to the soul with all its immortal interests)*" (II Tim. 1:12).

When most of the Church world was demanding penance of me, I knew this was Scripturally wrong, and would not acquiesce to their demands in that way. I knew my stand would bring upon my head further grief, nevertheless, I knew my only hope was the Lord, and to have His Blessings, I must obey His Word at any cost.

My following statements will be very strong, but I know them to be true.

There is nothing in the world more wicked, more ungodly, than institutionalized religion. Actually, one could say the same thing about religion in any capacity, institutionalized or not. This evil has sent more people to Hell, than all the dope dens of the world, or the alcohol distilleries.

I'll prove it from the Word of God.

Jesus addressed this, and I quote:

"*And when He was come into the Temple* (early in the morning)*, the Chief Priests and the Elders of the people* (religious leaders) *came unto Him as He was teaching* (interrupted His teaching)*, and said, By what authority do You do these things? and who gave You this authority?* (If He claimed that God gave Him this authority, that would have been admittance that He was the Messiah. This they wanted Him to do, in order to accuse Him of blasphemy.)

"*And Jesus answered and said unto them, I also will ask you one thing, which of you tell Me, I likewise will tell you by what authority I do these things* (in effect, by the question He will pose, will be the answer).

"*The Baptism of John* (of repentance)*, from where was it? from Heaven, or of men? And they reasoned with themselves, saying, If we shall say, from Heaven; He will say unto us, Why did you not then believe him?* (John introduced Christ as the Messiah.)

"*But if we shall say, Of men; and we fear the people; for all hold John as a Prophet* (whichever way they answered, put them in a dilemma; if they admitted that John was the predicted forerunner of Christ, then they were bound to receive Jesus as the Messiah).

"*And they answered Jesus, and said, We cannot tell* (this was untrue; they were the religious leaders of Israel and were supposed to know right from wrong)*. And He said unto them, Neither tell I you by what authority I do these things* (Jesus showed that they knew and were unwilling to answer; in effect He said, 'If you will not be honest with Me and the people, it is pointless to continue this conversation').

"*But what think you?* (This Parable and the next are directed to these religious leaders, as well as the people.) *A certain man had two sons; and he came to the first, and said, Son, go work today in my vineyard* (the 'certain Man' represents the Lord; the 'two sons' represent the unredeemed, who made no pretense at Salvation, while the second represented the Pharisees and their followers, who made every pretense of religion).

"*He answered and said, I will not: but afterward he repented, and went* (this represents the first son, who at the outset made no pretense at Salvation, but later repented).

"*And he came to the second, and said likewise. And he answered and said, I go, sir: and he went not* (this represents the Pharisees and their followers, who claimed much, but had nothing).

"*Which of the two did the will of his*

father? They say unto Him, The first (this proclaims the only answer that could be given; they little realized in their self-righteous piety that the Parable was directed at them; they were the ones who proclaim their allegiance to God and His Word, but in reality, had no allegiance at all!). *Jesus said unto them, Verily I say unto you, That the publicans and the harlots go into the Kingdom of God before you* (He said this to their faces, and before the people; He could not have insulted them more, putting them beneath publicans, whom they considered to be traitors, and harlots).

"*For John* (John the Baptist) *came unto you in the way of righteousness, and you believed him not* (speaking to the religious leaders)*: but the publicans and the harlots believed him: and you, when you had seen it, repented not afterward, that you might believe him* (they saw the changed lives as a result of John's Gospel, but still wouldn't believe)" (Mat. 21:23-32).

Jesus is addressing many of the religious leaders of Israel, and then He bluntly told them, that the publicans and harlots, as evil as their sins were, would go into the Kingdom of God before these religious leaders did.

No, He wasn't condoning the sins of the publicans and harlots at all, but actually saying, that when they heard the Gospel, some of them repented, and quit their evil ways. But these religious leaders would not repent. So, the publicans and harlots who had given their hearts to Christ, and had forsaken their former evil ways, would be admitted into the Kingdom, despite their past, while these religious leaders would be shut out altogether.

ANGRY RELIGIOUS LEADERS

To say that His Statements, and made to their faces at that, and in front of hundreds of people, angered them, would be a gross understatement. In fact, they hated Him for what He said, and would, thereby, crucify Him, when they had the opportunity to do so.

It must be remembered, it was not the publicans and harlots who nailed Christ to the Cross, but rather the religious leaders of Israel. One must see that, and understand that.

NOTES

As that was the greatest hindrance to the Work of God in the day of our Lord, it is the greatest hindrance to the Work of God presently.

In many of these denominations, the leadership oftentimes begins to equate that denomination with the Spirit of God. In other words, they look at it as one in the same. To be sure, it isn't!

In view of this, the decisions made, and the action taken, is not according to the Word of God at all, but in the direction of what they think will most benefit the institution.

I was speaking once with the leader of a particular Pentecostal denomination. He made a statement that I knew to be unscriptural. While I said it very kindly, I made the statement to him, *"My Brother, what you've just stated is not actually Scriptural."*

I was surprised at his answer!

He stumbled around for a few moments, then finally said, *"But that's our tradition."*

In other words, he did not at all deny what I said was correct, but, in effect, stated that it didn't matter what was Scriptural or unscriptural, what they were doing would benefit the denomination more so, so that's what would be done.

The truth is, when one disobeys the Word of God, the denomination or the institution are not benefited at all, but rather the opposite. In fact, when people leave the Word of God, they become blind to that which is the truth. They can only see one thing, and that's what self-will desires. They will follow it to their ruin.

RIGHTEOUSNESS AFTER THE CROSS

The Righteousness that now comes to Believers is all strictly by Faith.

As the individual expresses Faith in Christ that He is the Son of God, and that He died on Calvary in order to redeem humanity, at the moment of such Faith, a perfect, spotless Righteousness, the Righteousness of Christ, is instantly imputed to the believing sinner. It is all because of Christ, by Christ, and of Christ. In other words, an individual can be the worst type of sinner one moment, and upon believing Faith, can instantly be made Righteous.

So, how can a thrice-Holy God impute

to an obviously unrighteous person, a perfect Righteousness, thereby, declaring them righteous, and maintain His Integrity?

God can do such on the basis of Christ, Who has paid the price for all of humanity, at least for all who will believe, thereby, making it possible for the worst sinner to instantly be made righteous.

RIGHTEOUSNESS AND THE BELIEVER

What I've just stated, would be accepted by most in the church world who believes in Christ. But once the believing sinner has accepted Christ, all too often, such a person sets about, ignorantly I might quickly add, to try to earn his righteousness in some way.

He tries to earn it by belonging to a certain church, by doing certain things, or by not doing certain things, all which he thinks will perfect his righteousness.

It won't!

One might say it in this fashion:

While one can do nothing to make oneself righteous, except express Faith in Christ, one can do many things to make oneself unrighteous, and quickly. We make a grand mistake when we think that sin does not make one unrighteous. It does!

But the only answer for that, is for the Believer to instantly confess his sin to the Lord, in which we are assured that these sins will be forgiven, and righteousness, thereby, restored (I Jn. 1:9).

JUSTIFYING RIGHTEOUSNESS AND SANCTIFYING RIGHTEOUSNESS

One might say, as it regards the heading, that *"justifying righteousness"* never changes in the heart and life of the Believer, irrespective as to what he does or doesn't do, that is, if he maintains his Faith in Christ. But *"sanctifying righteousness"* is something else altogether.

While the righteousness is the same, the sanctifying aspect can change quickly, and all because of our actions. But, sanctifying righteousness being changed, does not in any way affect justifying righteousness.

Paul said: *"For we through the Spirit* (the Holy Spirit works exclusively within the parameters of the Sacrifice of Christ; consequently, He demands that we place our Faith exclusively in the Cross of Christ) *wait for the Hope of Righteousness* (which cannot come about until the Resurrection) *by Faith* (refers to Faith in Christ and what He did for us at the Cross)" (Gal. 5:5).

The *"Righteousness"* of which Paul here speaks, concerns *"sanctifying righteousness."*

In essence, he is saying that our *"sanctifying righteousness"* will not be perfect, until the coming Resurrection, when we shall be then gloriously changed. He then used the two words, *"by Faith."* It has a double meaning:

• We have Faith that this great Hope is coming.

• We have Faith that then we shall be totally and completely changed.

IS IT POSSIBLE FOR SANCTIFYING RIGHTEOUSNESS TO BE BROUGHT UP TO THE LEVEL OF JUSTIFYING RIGHTEOUSNESS?

No!

While the Holy Spirit constantly works within our hearts and lives, with every effort being made on His Part, to bring our *"sanctifying righteousness"* up to our *"justifying righteousness,"* while He is God, we aren't. Sanctifying righteousness will definitely be brought up to the level of justifying righteousness, but only when the Trump of God sounds, and then *"we shall be changed."*

"For this corruptible must put on incorruption, and this mortal must put on immortality." (I Cor. 15:52-53). When that happens, the sanctifying process will then become equal with the justifying process.

The Work of Christ is Perfect, which incorporates Justifying Righteousness. Being human, our efforts are somewhat less than perfect, which corresponds with sanctifying righteousness.

Even the great Paul said of himself, *"Not as though I had already attained, either were already perfect* (the Apostle is saying he doesn't claim sinless perfection)*; but I follow after* (to pursue), *if that I may apprehend* (Paul is pursuing absolute Christlikeness) *that for which also I am apprehended of Christ Jesus.* (He was Saved by Christ for the purpose of becoming Christlike, and so are we!)

"Brethren, I count not myself to have apprehended (in effect, repeats what he said in the previous Verse)*: but this one thing I do, forgetting those things which are behind* (refers to things the Apostle had depended upon to find favor with God, and the failure that type of effort brought about), *reaching forth unto those things which are before* (all our attention must be on that which is ahead, and not on what is past; *'those things'* consist of all the victories of the Cross),

"I press toward the mark (this represents a moral and spiritual target) *for the prize of the high calling of God* (Christlikeness) *in Christ Jesus* (proclaims the manner and means in which all of this is done, which is the Cross [I Cor. 1:17-18; 2:2])" (Phil. 3:12-14).

ENEMIES OF THE CROSS

In essence, the great Apostle is saying to us that the only way we can live this life, the only way we can be a true follower of Christ, the only way we can walk after the Spirit and, thereby, in the Spirit, is by placing our Faith exclusively in the Cross of Christ, thereby, trusting in what Christ has done for us, which we could not do for ourselves.

The great Apostle labeled anyone and everyone who opposed the Cross, as an enemy of the Cross. He said:

"Brethren, be followers together of me (be *'fellow-imitators'*) *and mark them which walk so as you have us for an example* (observe intently).

"(For many walk [speaks of those attempting to live for God outside of the Victory and rudiments of the Cross of Christ], *of whom I have told you often, and now tell you even weeping* [this is a most serious matter], *that they are the enemies of the Cross of Christ* [those who do not look exclusively to the Cross of Christ must be labeled *'enemies'*]*:*

"Whose end is destruction [if the Cross is ignored, and continues to be ignored, the loss of the soul is the only ultimate conclusion], *whose god is their belly* [refers to those who attempt to pervert the Gospel for their own personal gain], *and whose glory is in their shame* [the material things they seek, God labels as *'shame'*], *who mind earthly things.)* (This means they have no interest in Heavenly things, which signifies they are using the Lord for their own personal gain)" (Phil. 3:17-19).

THAT I MAY KNOW HIM

The great Apostle now tells us how to live for God. He said, and I quote:

"And be found in Him (to be united with Christ by a living Faith, which has as its Object the Cross of Christ), *not having my own Righteousness* (*'not having any Righteousness which can be called my own'*), *which is of the Law* (pertains to Law-keeping; he was done with that), *but that which is through the Faith of Christ* (what He did at the Cross), *the Righteousness which is of God by Faith* (a spotless Righteousness made possible by the Cross, and imputed by God to all who exhibit Faith in Christ and the Cross)*:*

"That I may know Him (referring to what Christ did at the Cross), *and the power of His Resurrection* (refers to being raised with Him in *'Newness of Life'* [Rom. 6:3-5]), *and the fellowship of His sufferings* (regarding our Trust and Faith placed in what He did for us at the Cross), *being made conformable unto His Death* (to conform to what He did for us at the Cross, understanding that this is the only means of Salvation and Sanctification)*;*

"If by any means I might attain unto the Resurrection of the dead. (This does not refer to the coming Resurrection, but rather the believing sinner being baptized into the Death of Christ [refers to the Crucifixion], and raised in *'Newness of Life,'* which gives victory over all sin)" (Phil. 3:9-11).

Back to our original subject, *"justifying righteousness"* is all of Christ and is all in Christ. Our faith grants us this perfection, which, as stated, never changes.

"Sanctifying righteousness" is that which is brought about by the Holy Spirit within our hearts and lives, but yet is predicated on our obedience or disobedience, hence, is mercurial, meaning up and down. In other words, the Holy Spirit can only perfect within our lives that which needs to be done, according to our working with Him as we should.

Working with Him as we should, is a place and position that is not arrived at easily or quickly. Even if it is arrived at, still, doing what we know we need to do is something else again. That's the reason I say, even with the best of us, whomever that might be, none can claim sinless perfection; therefore, all of us have to admit, that there is still very much work to be done. Thank the Lord that the Holy Spirit never quits. He never tires, He never loses patience, but ever seeks to bring us to the place that we ought to be.

The problem is, and with all of us, we have much more to learn than we realize, and none of it comes easy.

But yet, all of us must admit, that the Righteousness we now have in Christ, is so much greater than that which was obtained before the Cross. Paul said:

"But now (since the Cross) *has He* (the Lord Jesus) *obtained a more excellent Ministry* (the New Covenant in Jesus' Blood is superior, and takes the place of the Old Covenant in animal blood), *by how much also He is the Mediator of a Better Covenant* (proclaims the fact that Christ officiates between God and man according to the arrangements of the New Covenant), *which was established upon Better Promises.* (This presents the New Covenant, explicitly based on the cleansing and forgiveness of all sin, which the Old Covenant could not do.)

"For if that first Covenant had been faultless (proclaims the fact that the First Covenant was definitely not faultless; as stated, it was based on animal blood, which was vastly inferior to the Precious Blood of Christ), *then should no place have been sought for the Second* (proclaims the necessity of the New Covenant, which we now have)*"* (Heb. 8:6-7).

(8) "FOR WHAT IS THE HOPE OF THE HYPOCRITE, THOUGH HE HAS GAINED, WHEN GOD TAKES AWAY HIS SOUL?

(9) "WILL GOD HEAR HIS CRY WHEN TROUBLE COMES UPON HIM?

(10) "WILL HE DELIGHT HIMSELF IN THE ALMIGHTY? WILL HE ALWAYS CALL UPON GOD?

(11) "I WILL TEACH YOU BY THE HAND OF GOD: THAT WHICH IS WITH THE ALMIGHTY WILL I NOT CONCEAL.

(12) "BEHOLD, ALL YOU YOURSELVES HAVE SEEN IT; WHY THEN ARE YOU THUS ALTOGETHER VAIN?

(13) "THIS IS THE PORTION OF A WICKED MAN WITH GOD, AND THE HERITAGE OF OPPRESSORS, WHICH THEY SHALL RECEIVE OF THE ALMIGHTY.

(14) "IF HIS CHILDREN BE MULTIPLIED, IT IS FOR THE SWORD: AND HIS OFFSPRING SHALL NOT BE SATISFIED WITH BREAD.

(15) "THOSE WHO REMAIN OF HIM SHALL BE BURIED IN DEATH: AND HIS WIDOWS SHALL NOT WEEP.

(16) "THOUGH HE HEAP UP SILVER AS THE DUST, AND PREPARE RAIMENT AS THE CLAY;

(17) "HE MAY PREPARE IT, BUT THE JUST SHALL PUT IT ON, AND THE INNOCENT SHALL DIVIDE THE SILVER.

(18) "HE BUILDS HIS HOUSE AS A MOTH, AND AS A BOOTH THAT THE KEEPER MAKES.

(19) "THE RICH MAN SHALL LIE DOWN, BUT HE SHALL NOT BE GATHERED: HE OPENS HIS EYES, AND HE IS NOT.

(20) "TERRORS TAKE HOLD ON HIM AS WATERS, A TEMPEST STEALS HIM AWAY IN THE NIGHT.

(21) "THE EAST WIND CARRIES HIM AWAY, AND HE DEPARTS: AND AS A STORM HURLS HIM OUT OF HIS PLACE.

(22) "FOR GOD SHALL CAST UPON HIM, AND NOT SPARE: HE WOULD FAIN FLEE OUT OF HIS HAND.

(23) "MEN SHALL CLAP THEIR HANDS AT HIM, AND SHALL HISS HIM OUT OF HIS PLACE."

The composition is:

1. The Words of our Lord apply to Verse 8. He said, *"What shall it profit a man, if he shall gain the whole world, and lose his own soul?"* (Mk. 8:36).

2. (Vs. 10) Hypocrisy alienates God from us, and alienates us from God. Such cannot *"delight in the Almighty."*

3. In Verse 11, Job claims that his words now are inspired of the Lord. And so they were!

4. (Vs. 14) Some claim that these Passages contradict what Job said in Chapter 24. They do not! Chapter 24 proclaims what it often looks like outwardly regarding the wicked.

Chapter 27 tells us what is really happening.

5. Verse 20 tells us what is really going on in the heart of the unbeliever who has set himself against God. He has no protection from calamities, for the Lord is not his Father.

6. Verse 23 proclaims the fact that the greed that helped a certain individual get his riches is also in the hearts of others, who will rejoice at his downfall, which happens constantly!

THE HYPOCRITE

A hypocrite is one who puts on a face to appear to be something which he is not. In other words, he is playing a part.

As such regards the Lord, there are many who do not care for the Lord, have no desire to try to live for Him, but still think it worthwhile in some respect to put on a face of piety to others, so that others will think that the person is a Believer, when they really aren't.

On the other side of the coin, so to speak, there are millions of Believers, preachers included, who, in fact, do love the Lord, and are trying with all their might and strength to properly live for God. Yet, these same individuals, due to not knowing or understanding the Message of the Cross, have a besetting sin in their lives, which they are constantly trying to overcome, but seemingly are unable to do so. These individuals are not hypocrites, even though when their sin is found out, others may claim them to be.

A PERSONAL EXPERIENCE

Sometime back I happened to observe over a news program, information given as it regarded a preacher who had been caught in a homosexual situation. The reason it made the national news, was because his church was extremely large.

I had never heard of the man, but listened carefully as the news commentators hinted at his supposed hypocrisy.

The preacher stated, that he would cry himself to sleep many nights, promising God he would never commit this sin again, but then find himself doing the same thing all over again, which had gone on for a long period of time.

NOTES

Was that man a hypocrite?

No!

He didn't want to do what he was doing and, in fact, hated it. But pure and simple, he was unable to stop.

Why?

He evidently was trusting in his own willpower, his own personal strength, his own personal ability, which is always woefully insufficient. No one can overcome the powers of darkness in this fashion. It can only be done by such a Believer placing his Faith exclusively in Christ and the Cross, and not allow it to be moved, which then gives the Holy Spirit, Who is God, latitude to work in such a life and, thereby, to bring about certain Victory.

Even then, providing the individual knows and understands the Message of the Cross, it won't be easy. Sin is a powerful factor.

It has filled the Earth with graves, thereby, killing every human being who has ever lived, with the exception of Enoch and Elijah, who were translated. It has been the cause of every war, the cause of all of man's inhumanity to man, the cause of all sickness and sorrow, the cause of all heartache. It has made this world a bloody battlefield, and has swollen the stomachs of millions with hunger, even though they were innocent, and we speak of little children. It is referred to in the Bible as *"The Law of Sin and Death"* (Rom. 8:2).

There is only one other Law that is stronger than the Law of Sin and Death, and that is, *"The Law of the Spirit of Life in Christ Jesus"* (Rom. 8:2).

If anyone attempts to overcome the Law of Sin and Death by any other method than *"The Law of the Spirit of Life in Christ Jesus,"* such a person, irrespective as to whom they might be, and irrespective as to what they might do, will be unable to effect victory.

WHAT IS THE LAW OF THE SPIRIT OF LIFE IN CHRIST JESUS?

First of all, it is a Law devised by the Godhead some time in eternity past. Inasmuch as it is a *"Law,"* and that it was devised by the Godhead, this means that it's going to function exactly as it was devised to do so. As stated, this Law, *"The Law of the Spirit of*

Life in Christ Jesus" is the only Law that can defeat *"The Law of Sin and Death."*

Incidentally, the latter Law was devised by the Godhead as well, and will most definitely function exactly as it was formerly devised. In other words, the Lord has said that if one engages in sin; death and in several forms is going to be the inevitable result. Irrespective as to what man does, he will not be able to sidestep the effects of the Law of Sin and Death.

Men are ever trying to come up with one scheme after the other, thinking to ameliorate the effects of this Law. None have been successful thus far, and none will ever be successful.

THE HOLY SPIRIT

The Law of the Spirit of Life, refers to the Holy Spirit, Who is God, and the way that He Works. This is so very, very important.

It's a shame, but very few Christians know how the Holy Spirit works. They somehow take Him for granted, that is if He is given any shift at all.

And to be sure, and as we have stated, He will most definitely function within the boundaries of this Law that, in fact, He helped devise.

IN CHRIST JESUS

This Law, which is the way the Holy Spirit Works, is all entirely *"in Christ Jesus"* (Rom. 8:2).

What do we mean by that?

Whenever Paul used the statement, *"In Christ Jesus,"* or one of its derivatives such as *"in Him,"* or *"in the Lord,"* etc., without fail, he is speaking of that which Christ did at the Cross, all on our behalf.

All of this means that it is the Cross of Christ, what Jesus did there, the benefits which He perfected for us, which gives the Holy Spirit the legal right to do all that He does. When I say *"legal right,"* please understand, we're speaking here of a *"Law."*

All of this means that each and every Believer, irrespective as to whom they might be, irrespective as to how many times they have failed in the past, can have total and complete victory over every sin, every bondage, that would tend to place one in a spiritual prison. And sadly and regrettably, the far greater majority of the modern church is in a spiritual prison.

It only remains for the Believer to place his Faith exclusively in Christ and what Christ did at the Cross, which then gives the Holy Spirit, Who works entirely within the framework of the Sacrifice of Christ, to work on our behalf. This is God's Way, and His only Way!

IS IT THAT EASY?

In theory, yes! In practical application, no!

When we deal with human beings, as should be obvious, we are dealing with extremely complex creations. God made us that way! If every Believer understood the Cross of Christ perfectly, which is God's Prescribed Order of Victory, and could function perfectly, it would be easy; however, it is not easy, because we never function correctly all the time. We function correctly some of the time, but we do not function correctly all of the time. So, the Holy Spirit gradually leads us along, with us learning very slowly as to what the Lord wants within our hearts and lives, sometimes, seeming as if it's at a snail's pace.

It's perhaps a little easier to understand the complexity of Sanctification, when we also come to the understanding, as we've already stated, that the Book of Job, deals with the subject of Sanctification. Considering that it's the first Book that was penned, which went into the Bible, then we should understand the seriousness of the situation, the complexity of the matter and, thereby, the significance of that of which we are studying.

Someone said that we are creatures of habit. Perhaps that is right, but the bad thing about all of this is, concerning all the habits we develop, some of them, if not many of them, are bad habits.

Preachers argue over whether there is such a thing as a sin nature, and more so, does the sin nature remain in the Believer after the person has come to Christ?

Someone has readily answered that by stating, take a couple of two year olds, put them together in one playpen, with one rubber ducky, and you'll soon find out that there is a sin nature.

Hypocrisy, which is the subject of this part of the Twenty-seventh Chapter of Job, doesn't really care about these things. The hypocrite has no regard for pleasing God, only himself. To be sure, he cares what other people think, but that's the problem. So he conducts himself in a way that makes people think that which is wrong. But irrespective as to what people think, he is still a hypocrite.

As someone has well said, *"reputation is what people think you are, while character is what God knows you are."*

"Behold the glories of the Lamb,
"Amidst His Father's Throne;
"Prepare new honors for His Name,
"And songs before unknown."

"Let elders worship at His Feet,
"The Church adore around,
"With vials full of odors sweet,
"And harps of sweeter sound."

"Those are the prayers of the Saints,
"And these the hymns they raise;
"Jesus is kind to our complaints,
"He loves to hear our praise."

"Eternal Father, who shall look,
"Into Your secret Will?
"Who but the Son should take the Book,
"And open every seal?"

"He shall fulfill Your great Decrees,
"The Son deserves it well;
"Lo, in His Hand the sovereign keys,
"Of Heaven, and death, and Hell!"

"Now to the Lamb that once was slain,
"Be endless blessings paid;
"Salvation, glory, joy remain,
"Forever on Your Head."

"You have redeemed our souls with
   blood,
"Have set the prisoner free;
"Have made us kings and priests to
   God,
"And we shall reign with Thee."

"The worlds of nature and of Grace,
"Are put beneath Your Power;
"Then shorten these delaying days,
"And bring the promised hour."

NOTES

CHAPTER 28

(1) "SURELY THERE IS A VEIN FOR THE SILVER, AND A PLACE FOR GOLD WHERE THEY FINE IT.

(2) "IRON IS TAKEN OUT OF THE EARTH, AND BRASS IS MELTED OUT OF THE STONE.

(3) "HE SETS AN END TO DARKNESS, AND SEARCHES OUT ALL PERFECTION: THE STONES OF DARKNESS, AND THE SHADOW OF DEATH.

(4) "THE FLOOD BREAKS OUT FROM THE INHABITANT: EVEN THE WATERS FORGOTTEN OF THE FOOT: THEY ARE DRIED UP, THEY ARE GONE AWAY FROM MEN.

(5) "AS FOR THE EARTH, OUT OF IT COMES BREAD: AND UNDER IT IS TURNED UP AS IT WERE FIRE.

(6) "THE STONES OF IT ARE THE PLACE OF SAPPHIRES: AND IT HAS DUST OF GOLD.

(7) "THERE IS A PATH WHICH NO FOWL KNOWS, AND WHICH THE VULTURE'S EYE HAS NOT SEEN:

(8) "THE LION'S WHELPS HAVE NOT TRODDEN IT, NOR THE FIERCE LION PASSED BY IT.

(9) "HE PUTS FORTH HIS HAND UPON THE ROCK; HE OVERTURNS THE MOUNTAINS BY THE ROOTS.

(10) "HE CUTS OUT RIVERS AMONG THE ROCKS; AND HIS EYE SEES EVERY PRECIOUS THING.

(11) "HE BINDS THE FLOODS FROM OVERFLOWING; AND THE THING THAT IS HID BRINGS HE FORTH TO LIGHT."

The synopsis is:

1. (Vs. 2) Precious metals can be taken out of the earth, however, the Wisdom of God cannot be found in this manner.

2. (Vs. 3) Men mine for precious metals both day and night. If they would do so for such, surely we should be as diligent to find the things of the Lord, which can only be found in His Word.

3. (Vs. 4) The miner goes to great lengths to find precious metals; likewise, we should do no less in searching the things of God.

4. (Vs. 5) Fire is used to separate the gold from other metals; likewise, the Fire of the Holy Spirit is used to burn the chaff out of our lives (Mat. 3:11-12).

5. (Vs. 6) For those who ardently seek the Lord, they will find Spiritual sapphires and Spiritual gold.

6. The Seventh Verse proclaims the *"path of life,"* as it regards the Faith-filled Believer, which demons can never penetrate (Ps. 16:11).

7. According to Verse 8, the one who comes as a *"roaring lion,"* namely Satan, will not be able to trod it or pass by it. This is *"the secret place of the Most High"* (Ps. 91:1).

EARTHLY GOLD AND SPIRITUAL GOLD

In this Chapter, Job deals with precious metals, which are taken out of the earth, and for which man labors to secure these treasures. The idea is, as valuable as these things might be at the moment, they have their limitations; however, the things of God have no limitations.

If Believers would ardently seek the Lord, seek the knowledge of His Word, and in a sense would mine for this precious commodity, even as men mine the earth for its precious metals, what a blessing we would find.

For instance, the Word of God, i.e., *"the Bible,"* is the only revealed truth in the world and, in fact, ever has been. This means, that the Word of God is the most precious thing on Earth. That's why Jesus said:

"Man shall not live by bread alone, but by every Word that proceeds out of the Mouth of God" (Mat. 4:4). But, how many Believers ardently search the Word of God, and do so on an unending basis?! Worse yet, most Believers, and I think I can say that without fear of exaggeration, have never read the Bible through even once.

As strong as we are as it regards the Word of God at our Church (Family Worship Center), on a Wednesday night, some time ago, I haphazardly asked the congregation as to how many had read the Bible completely through? I was shocked at the number of people who did not raise their hands.

One of the men, who did not raise his hand, was a very close friend of mine. The next day I asked him about this.

His answer to me was revealing. He said, *"While I haven't read the Bible completely through, I am in the process of doing so."*

I asked him, *"How long do you think it's going to take you?"*

He had been Saved for over 20 years, and still had not read the Bible completely through.

The truth is, every single Believer ought to read the Bible completely through, starting with Genesis and going straight through to Revelation, at least once a year. The Word of God is the road map for life and living, the blueprint for eternity. And remember, there is only one Word of God, not ten, not five, not even two, only one.

A PERSONAL ILLUSTRATION

Every night I literally read myself to sleep.

I am presently going back and reading our Commentaries, beginning with Genesis. I am now in Isaiah, actually, almost having finished that great Book. Reading the Text, and then reading the notes that help explain the Text, gives one a new insight, and a broader understanding, I think, of the Word of God.

I think, if every Believer did the same thing, you would find your rest to be more relaxing, because your mind has been filled with the Word of God, and there is nothing greater than that.

THERE IS A PATH,
WHICH NO FOWL KNOWS

The literal meaning of Verses 7 and 8, is that the precious metals that are in the earth cannot be seen by the fowls of the heavens or by the animals that walk over them.

However, the Spiritual meaning is far different and has far greater implications. In the Spiritual sense, the *"path"* that is referred to is that which is designed by God.

• Jeremiah called it *"the old paths"* (Jer. 6:16).

• The Psalmist called it the *"path of life"* (Ps. 16:11).

• Isaiah called it the *"path of the just"* (Isa. 26:7).

• David called it the *"paths of Righteousness"* (Ps. 23:3).

• John the Baptist proclaimed *"make His Paths straight"* (Mat. 3:3).
• The writer of Hebrews called it *"straight paths for your feet"* (Heb. 12:13).
• Solomon said, *"And in the pathway there is no death"* (Prov. 12:28).

The *"vultures"* speak of demon spirits that will not have access to this *"path."*

As well, the one who comes as a roaring *"lion,"* namely Satan, will not be able to trod it or pass by it.

It is the Place in Christ that affords complete safety and protection.

HOW CAN THE BELIEVER FIND THIS PATH AND STAY ON THIS PATH?

Once again, we go back to the Cross. Satan, here represented as a lion, and demon spirits here represented as vultures, respect nothing but the Cross of Christ. They do not respect our so-called higher institutions of learning. They do not respect the wisdom of man. They do not respect any of the religions of the world. They respect one thing, and that is the Lord Jesus Christ, and what He did for us at the Cross.

A PERSONAL EXAMPLE

Preaching on a Sunday morning some time ago at Family Worship Center, and dealing with demon possession and demon oppression, all of a sudden it dawned on me that I had not experienced demonic oppression one single time since the Lord began to open up to me the Message of the Cross in 1997. From that time to the time I was ministering, was about 10 years.

Before the Message of the Cross was revealed to me, I experienced demonic oppression to the degree that at times I didn't think I would survive it.

Demon possession constitutes demons that inhabit an individual, and come from within. Incidentally, a Believer cannot be demon possessed.

Demon oppression comes from without, and probably every Christian has experienced such oppression at one time or the other. The only answer is the Cross of Christ.

As stated, since the Message of the Cross was revealed to me, I haven't experienced one moment of demonic oppression. Such

NOTES

oppression affects a person's emotional stability, brings about fear, nervous disorders, certain type of illnesses, and as should be obvious, it's not a very pleasant thing.

The only answer to this, even as we've already stated, and even as it is the answer for all things pertaining to life and living, is the Cross of Christ. The Believer must understand that the Lord has paid a terrible price for us, actually the Sacrifice of Himself. And to be sure, every single thing was addressed at the Cross.

I get amused at times, if one could label it as such, as some preachers claim that Divine Healing was not in the Atonement. They surmise that if Healing was in the Atonement, then Christians would never get sick. They should remember, that Redemption from sin was certainly in the Atonement, and regrettably, Christians still sin; however, that doesn't mean that what Jesus did there was insufficient.

The truth is, every single thing that man lost in the Fall was addressed in the Atonement. As well, even Satan's revolution against Christ was addressed in the Atonement. The Scripture says concerning that:

"Having made known unto us the mystery of His Will (refers to the secret purposes and counsels God intends to carry into effect in His Kingdom), *according to His good pleasure* (extended to Believers) *which He has purposed in Himself* (originated in His Own Mind)*:*

"That in the dispensation of the fullness of times (concerns itself with a well-ordered plan) *He might gather together in one all things in Christ* (the Atonement addressed not only man's Fall, but the revolution of Lucifer as well), *both which are in Heaven* (where the revolution of Lucifer began), *and which are on Earth* (the Fall of man)*; even in Him* (made possible by what Christ did at the Cross)*:*

"In Whom (Christ) *also we have obtained an inheritance* (the best Greek Texts have, 'we were designated as a heritage'; thus, the Saints are God's Heritage, His Possession through the Work of Christ at the Cross), *being predestinated according to the purpose of Him* (pertains to the inheritance being predestinated, not the individual who

would obtain the inheritance) *Who works all things after the Counsel of His Own Will (therefore, it is perfect)"* (Eph. 1:9-11).

The facts are, at this time, we only have the firstfruits of all that Jesus did in the Atonement. The Scripture also says concerning that:

"For we know that the whole Creation (everything has been affected by Satan's rebellion and Adam's Fall) *groans and travails in pain together until now* (refers to the common longing of the elements of the Creation to be brought back to their original perfection).

"And not only they (the Creation, and all it entails), *but ourselves also* (refers to Believers), *which have the Firstfruits of the Spirit* (even though Jesus addressed every single thing lost in the Fall at the Cross, we only have a part of that possession now, with the balance coming at the Resurrection), *even we ourselves groan within ourselves* (proclaims the obvious fact that all Jesus paid for in the Atonement has not yet been fully realized), *waiting for the Adoption* (should be translated, *'waiting for the fulfillment of the process, which Adoption into the Family of God guarantees'*), *to wit, the Redemption of our body* (the glorifying of our physical body that will take place at the Resurrection)" (Rom. 8:22-23).

The place of Victory is found only in the Cross of Christ. The Devil wants no part of the Cross, hence, it is a *"path which no fowl knows, and which the vulture's eye has not seen."*

(12) "BUT WHERE SHALL WISDOM BE FOUND? AND WHERE IS THE PLACE OF UNDERSTANDING?

(13) "MAN KNOWS NOT THE PRICE THEREOF; NEITHER IS IT FOUND IN THE LAND OF THE LIVING.

(14) "THE DEPTH SAYS, IT IS NOT IN ME; AND THE SEA SAYS, IT IS NOT WITH ME.

(15) "IT CANNOT BE GOTTEN FOR GOLD, NEITHER SHALL SILVER BE WEIGHED FOR THE PRICE THEREOF.

(16) "IT CANNOT BE VALUED WITH THE GOLD OF OPHIR, WITH THE PRECIOUS ONYX, OR THE SAPPHIRE.

(17) "THE GOLD AND THE CRYSTAL CANNOT EQUAL IT: AND THE EXCHANGE OF IT SHALL NOT BE FOR JEWELS OF FINE GOLD.

(18) "NO MENTION SHALL BE MADE OF CORAL, OR OF PEARLS: FOR THE PRICE OF WISDOM IS ABOVE RUBIES.

(19) "THE TOPAZ OF ETHIOPIA SHALL NOT EQUAL IT, NEITHER SHALL IT BE VALUED WITH PURE GOLD.

(20) "WHENCE THEN COMES WISDOM? AND WHERE IS THE PLACE OF UNDERSTANDING?

(21) "SEEING IT IS HID FROM THE EYES OF ALL LIVING, AND KEPT CLOSE FROM THE FOWLS OF THE AIR.

(22) "DESTRUCTION AND DEATH SAY, WE HAVE HEARD THE FAME THEREOF WITH OUR EARS.

(23) "GOD UNDERSTANDS THE WAY THEREOF, AND HE KNOWS THE PLACE THEREOF.

(24) "FOR HE LOOKS TO THE ENDS OF THE EARTH, AND SEES UNDER THE WHOLE HEAVEN;

(25) "TO MAKE THE WEIGHT FOR THE WINDS; AND HE WEIGHS THE WATERS BY MEASURE.

(26) "WHEN HE MADE A DECREE FOR THE RAIN, AND A WAY FOR THE LIGHTNING OF THE THUNDER:

(27) "THEN DID HE SEE IT, AND DECLARE IT; HE PREPARED IT, YES, AND SEARCHED IT OUT.

(28) "AND UNTO MAN HE SAID, BEHOLD, THE FEAR OF THE LORD, THAT IS WISDOM; AND TO DEPART FROM EVIL IS UNDERSTANDING."

The overview is:

1. Verse 12 proclaims the fact that as clever as man is in bringing to the light the wealth hidden in the darkness of the mine, he fails altogether to find out the place of wisdom, because the Wisdom of God cannot be found out by such methods.

2. (Vs. 13) The real value of Heavenly Wisdom cannot be estimated in terms of ordinary human calculations; in fact, a person is not truly educated until he is first educated in the Bible.

3. (Vs. 17) A proper understanding of the Word of God is of far greater value than all gold, silver, and jewels.

4. Verse 21 proclaims the fact that human intelligence cannot come by the Wisdom of God; it is revealed by the Spirit (I Cor. 2:7-12).

5. (Vs. 22) Heavenly Wisdom, i.e., *"the Word of God,"* alone answers the questions of death and destruction.

6. (Vs. 23) God Alone understands what True Wisdom is, and it is found in His Word.

7. Verse 25 pertains to the Laws of Creation, which God has made and, to be sure, everything functions according to these Laws.

8. Verse 26 means that God placed the fall of rain under fixed and unalterable Laws.

9. Verse 27 proclaims the fact that God foresaw all that was necessary to maintain His Universe in Perfect Order.

10. (Vs. 28) No amount of intelligence, no amount of cleverness, or of information or knowledge, or of worldly or scientific wisdom, will be of any true avail to man, unless he starts with this *"beginning of the fear of the Lord"* (Ps. 111:10; Prov. 1:7).

WHERE SHALL WISDOM BE FOUND?

Men can find many things by searching diligently and, by that, we speak of the method of human ingenuity; however, man cannot find the things of God by this method. Therefore, the path of intellectualism, of education, of riches, of power, and even of religion will not for all of its searching find God. The world over and for time beyond memory has tried to find God by such methods. All have failed as all must fail! The scientist's research cannot find God; the miner in digging in the bowels of the earth cannot find God; the astronaut in outer space cannot find God; the philosopher in his meanderings cannot find God.

Why?

God cannot be found of men in this fashion, but men can be found of God. Whenever we Believers talk about finding the Lord, the actual truth is, the Lord found us.

God has reached man by Revelation through His Word and through His Son, the Lord Jesus Christ. God is reached only by Faith and can be understood only by Faith. He does not seek to prove Himself. He only seeks to reveal Himself to the honest, seeking heart.

Jeremiah said: *"And you shall seek Me, and find Me, when you shall search for Me with all your heart"* (Jer. 29:13).

Paul taught, *"That they should seek the Lord, if haply they might feel after Him, and find Him, though He be not far from every one of us"* (Acts 17:27).

WISDOM AND KNOWLEDGE

Solomon, in his reign over Israel, made this Nation the most powerful on the face of the Earth, and did so without an army, or navy, or military conquest. He did it by wisdom, and his wisdom came from God. The nations of that day sent their Ambassadors to Solomon to prove him with hard questions, and he answered them all.

During the coming days of the Millennial Reign, of which Solomon's reign was a type, the Lord Jesus Christ, the greater than Solomon, will conquer the world in this same manner — not by military force, but by solving the problems that plague the human race.

It is somewhat amusing to hear the news pundits, and the Ph.D.'s of Harvard or Yale, etc., pontificate on the future of this Planet. Every type of weird prediction that one can make comes forth.

All they have to do is first of all give their hearts and lives to the Lord Jesus Christ, and then look into the Word of God, which will give them the answers to these questions. However, these individuals are far too smart, at least so they think, to even think about looking into the Word of God. In fact, they don't believe it is the Word of God.

The Bible tells us that there are some dark days coming, and they are just ahead.

Concerning this, Jesus said:

"For then shall be great tribulation (the last three and one half years), *such as was not since the beginning of the world to this time, no, nor ever shall be* (the worst the world has ever known, and will be so bad that it will never be repeated).

"And except those days should be shortened, there should no flesh be saved (refers to Israel coming close to extinction): *but for the elect's* (Israel's) *sake those days*

shall be shortened (by the Second Coming)" (Mat. 24:21-22).

At the conclusion of the Great Tribulation, the Battle of Armageddon will take place, which will precipitate the Second Coming of the Lord. Concerning this, the Scripture says:

THE COMING OF THE SON OF MAN

"*For as the lightning comes out of the east, and shines even unto the west* (is meant to proclaim the most cataclysmic event the world has ever known); *so shall also the coming of the Son of Man be* (no one will have to ask, is this really Christ; it will be overly obvious!).

"*For wheresoever the carcass is* (speaks of the Battle of Armageddon), *that there will the eagles be gathered together* (should have been translated, 'there will the vultures be gathered together' [refers to Ezek. 39:17]).

"*Immediately after the Tribulation of those days* (speaks of the time immediately preceding the Second Coming) *shall the sun be darkened, and the moon shall not give her light* (the light of these orbs will be dim by comparison to the light of the Son of God), *and the stars shall fall from Heaven* (a display of Heavenly fireworks at the Second Coming), *and the powers of the Heavens shall be shaken* (will work with the Son of God against the Antichrist, at the Second Coming):

"*And then shall appear the sign of the Son of Man in Heaven* (pertains to the Second Coming, which will take place in the midst of these Earth and Heaven shaking events): *and then shall all the tribes of the Earth mourn* (concerns all the nations of the world which possibly will see this phenomenon by television), *and they shall see the Son of Man* (denotes Christ and His human, Glorified Body) *coming in the clouds of Heaven with power and great glory* (lends credence to the thought that much of the world will see Him by television as He makes His Descent).

"*And He shall send His Angels* (they will be visible) *with a great sound of a trumpet* (announcing the gathering of Israel), *they shall gather together His elect* (Israel) *from the four winds, from one end of Heaven to the other* (Jews will be gathered from all over the world, and brought to Israel)" (Mat. 24:27-31).

When this time would come, Jesus also gave us another clue. He said:

THE PARABLE OF
THE FIG TREE

"*Now learn a Parable of the fig tree* (the Bible presents three trees, the fig, the olive, and the vine, as representing the Nation of Israel, nationally, spiritually, and dispensationally); *When his branch is yet tender, and puts forth leaves* (is meant to serve as the illustration of Israel nationally), *you know that summer is near* (refers to Israel as the greatest Prophetic Sign of all, telling us that we are now living in the last of the Last Days):

"*So likewise you* (points to the modern church), *when you shall see all these things* (which we are now seeing as it regards Israel), *know that it is near, even at the doors* (the fulfillment of Endtime Prophecies).

"*Verily I say unto you, This generation shall not pass* (the generation of Jews, which will be alive at the beginning of the Great Tribulation; as well, it was a prediction by Christ, that irrespective of the problems that Israel would face, even from His Day, they would survive), *till all these things be fulfilled* (there is no doubt, they will be fulfilled),

"*Heaven and Earth shall pass away* (doesn't refer to annihilation, but rather a change from one condition or state to another), *but My Words shall not pass away* (what the Word of God says, will be!).

"*But of that day and hour knows no man, no, not the Angels of Heaven, but My Father only*" (Mat. 24:32-36).

THE MILLENNIAL REIGN

This coming time, which will last for a thousand years, will be the most profitable, glorious, time of absolute freedom, prosperity and righteousness that the world has ever known. Some of the things that will take place are as follows:

• The Millennial Reign, or as it is sometimes referred to, the Kingdom Age, will commence immediately upon the Second

Coming of our Lord (Rev., Chpt. 19).

• Jesus Christ will personally rule from Jerusalem for the entirety of this time (Isa. 9:6).

• Jerusalem will be completely rebuilt, even as the Prophet Ezekiel described it in his Book (Ezek., Chpts. 40-48).

• Israel will then be the leading Nation of the world under Christ (Isa. 2:2).

• Her boundaries will then be what God originally promised Abraham. Those boundaries will include modern Lebanon, all of modern Syria, Iraq up to the river Euphrates, all of modern Jordan, as well as the Arabian Peninsula (Deut. 11:24).

• There will no more war (Isa. 2:4).

• Sickness will be a thing of the past (Ezek. 47:12).

• Death will, as well, be eliminated, with the exception of the few who will be executed, because they will insist upon rebelling against the Law of the Lord (Isa. 65:20).

• The world will experience a prosperity during this time that it has never known before. There will be no such thing then as poor nations, or poverty, etc. (Isa. 65:21-23).

• The nations of the world will constantly send their ambassadors to Jerusalem in order that they may consult Christ, thereby, ascertaining the answers to their questions, whatever those questions might be (Isa. 2:3).

• During this time, Satan, along with all his demon spirits and fallen Angels, will be locked away in the bottomless pit (Rev. 20:1-3). This means there will no more temptation.

• Every Saint of God at that time, who has ever lived, all the way from the very beginning will have Glorified Bodies, which will be impervious to limitations experienced presently. All these many Saints, which, as stated, will include every Born-Again Believer who has ever lived, will help Christ rule this Planet at this time (I Cor. 15:51-58; Rev. 20:4-6).

The following are a few of the Passages from the Word of God which describe this coming great day.

THE WORD OF GOD

"And many people shall go and say, Come you, and let us go up to the mountain of the LORD, to the House of the God of Jacob; and He will teach us of His Ways, and we will walk in His Paths: for out of Zion shall go forth the Law, and the Word of the LORD from Jerusalem. (The *'Law,'* as referred to here, has no reference to the Law of Moses, but rather to instruction, direction, and teaching. Again, this is the coming Kingdom Age, when the Messiah, *'The Greater than Solomon,'* will rule the world by Wisdom, Grace, and Love)" (Isa. 2:3).

And then the Prophet Isaiah said, *"And He shall judge among the nations, and shall rebuke many people: and they shall beat their swords into plowshares, and their spears into pruninghooks: nation shall not lift up sword against nation, neither shall they learn war any more.* (The words, *'judge among,'* should read *'arbitrate between,'* and *'rebuke'* would have been better translated *'decide the disputes of.'* Man's courts of arbitration are doomed to failure, but, to Messiah's Court, success is promised here)" (Isa. 2:4).

The Prophet continues: *"The wolf also shall dwell with the lamb, and the leopard shall lie down with the kid; and the calf and the young lion and the fatling together; and a little child shall lead them.* (The character and nature of the Planet, including its occupants and even the animal creation, will revert to their posture as before the Fall.)

"And the cow and the bear shall feed (feed together)*; their young ones shall lie down together: and the lion shall eat straw like the ox.* (This Passage plainly tells us that the carnivorous nature of the animal kingdom will be totally and eternally changed.)

"And the sucking child shall play on the hole of the asp, and the weaned child shall put his hand on the cockatrice' den. (Even though some of the curse will remain on the serpent in the Millennium, in that he continues to writhe in the dust, still, the deadly part will be removed [Gen. 3:14].)

"They shall not hurt nor destroy in all My Holy Mountain: for the Earth shall be full of the Knowledge of the LORD, as the waters cover the sea. (The *'Holy Mountain'* refers to the Dwelling Place of Christ during the Kingdom Age, which will be Jerusalem.

And from that vantage point shall go out the *'Knowledge of the LORD,'* which will cover the entirety of the Earth.)

"And in that day there shall be a root of Jesse, which shall stand for an ensign of the people; to which shall the Gentiles seek: and His rest shall be glorious. (The words, *'in that day,'* as in most cases, refer to the Great Tribulation, the Battle of Armageddon, the Second Coming of the Lord, and the coming Kingdom Age.

"The *'root of Jesse'* refers to David and the Promise made by the Lord to David in II Sam., Chpt. 7. Hence, Christ is really the *'root of Jesse,' 'the Son of David')"* (Isa. 11:6-10).

That's what the Bible tells us is coming in the future. And according to the Word of God, which gives us the signs of the times, these events are just ahead. Those signs are:

• The restoration of Israel is God's greatest Sign of all: In fact, Israel, as some have stated, is God's prophetic time clock. In other words, one can look at the Nation of Israel and tell what time it is prophetically (Mat. 24:32-33).

• The outpouring of the Holy Spirit, which commenced at approximately the advent of the Twentieth Century: It was the fulfillment of Joel's great Prophecies concerning the former and the latter rain (Joel 2:23). The *"former rain"* consisted of the beginning of the Early Church recorded in the Book of Acts. The *"latter rain"* consists of the outpouring presently. It is a sign of the last of the Last Days.

• The Apostasy of the Church: Regrettably and sadly, at the very end, and we speak of the end of the Church Age, the Scripture predicts the apostatizing of the church, which we have seen and are seeing before our very eyes (Rev. 3:14-22).

• Daniel's great Prophecy of knowledge being increased in the Last Days: This speaks of technological advancement and, as well, a greater knowledge of the Word of God. This has been fulfilled, and is being fulfilled before our very eyes (Dan. 12:4).

Now, you the reader can accept the ponderings of the intelligentsia, so-called, as it regards the future of this Planet, which prognostications change almost by the hour, or you can accept the Word of God. You cannot accept both!

"Redeemed, how I love to proclaim it!
"Redeemed by the Blood of the Lamb;
"Redeemed through His infinite Mercy,
"His Child, and forever, I am."

"Redeemed and so happy in Jesus,
"No language my rapture can tell;
"I know that the Light of His Presence,
"With me does continually dwell."

"I think of my blessed Redeemer,
"I think of Him all the day long;
"I sing, for I cannot be silent;
"His Love is the theme of my song."

"I know I shall see in His Beauty,
"The King in Whose Law I delight;
"Who lovingly guards my footsteps,
"And gives me songs in the night."

"Redeemed, redeemed,
"Redeemed by the Blood of the Lamb;
"Redeemed through His infinite Mercy,
"His Child, and forever I am."

CHAPTER 29

(1) "MOREOVER JOB CONTINUED HIS PARABLE, AND SAID,

(2) "OH THAT I WERE AS IN MONTHS PAST, AS IN THE DAYS WHEN GOD PRESERVED ME;

(3) "WHEN HIS CANDLE SHINED UPON MY HEAD, AND WHEN BY HIS LIGHT I WALKED THROUGH DARKNESS;

(4) "AS I WAS IN THE DAYS OF MY YOUTH, WHEN THE SECRET OF GOD WAS UPON MY TABERNACLE;

(5) "WHEN THE ALMIGHTY WAS YET WITH ME, WHEN MY CHILDREN WERE ABOUT ME;

(6) "WHEN I WASHED MY STEPS WITH BUTTER, AND THE ROCK POURED ME OUT RIVERS OF OIL;

(7) "WHEN I WENT OUT TO THE GATE THROUGH THE CITY, WHEN I PREPARED MY SEAT IN THE STREET!

(8) "THE YOUNG MEN SAW ME, AND HID THEMSELVES: AND THE AGED

AROSE, AND STOOD UP.

(9) "THE PRINCES REFRAINED TALKING, AND LAID THEIR HAND ON THEIR MOUTH.

(10) "THE NOBLES HELD THEIR PEACE, AND THEIR TONGUE CLEAVED TO THE ROOF OF THEIR MOUTH.

(11) "WHEN THE EAR HEARD ME, THEN IT BLESSED ME; AND WHEN THE EYE SAW ME, IT GAVE WITNESS TO ME:

(12) "BECAUSE I DELIVERED THE POOR THAT CRIED, AND THE FATHERLESS, AND HIM WHO HAD NONE TO HELP HIM.

(13) "THE BLESSING OF HIM WHO WAS READY TO PERISH CAME UPON ME: AND I CAUSED THE WIDOW'S HEART TO SING FOR JOY."

The construction is:

1. (Vs. 2) Job had yet to learn that *"self"* must die, whether it be prosperous self, afflicted self, or innocent self, and that he had to be brought to abhor himself, whether innocent or guilty. Entrance into the life more abundant can only be experienced when religious self is as heartily abhorred as irreligious self.

2. (Vs. 3) There is no light other than the Gospel of Jesus Christ; all else is darkness.

3. The *"Secret of God"* of Verse 4, was the *"Light of God,"* which was the *"Word of God,"* and was passed down then by word of mouth.

4. (Vs. 5) Although Job does not now know it, the Almighty is with him now even more than ever.

5. As it regards Verse 7, it was customary for Elders of the city to sit in the open place at the entrance of the gates. Judgment was meted out here, and many other activities were carried on as well.

6. Verse 8 proclaims the fact that all deferred to Job, and rightly so. The Touch of God on his life was obvious and evident to all.

7. (Vs. 13) Even though Job had helped so many, yet, none of these *"poor,"* or *"fatherless,"* or *"widows,"* would now speak a kind word for him. No doubt, he had helped thousands, or maybe even tens of thousands, but none remembered his kindness to them. Such is humanity!

NOTES

SELF

When we speak of *"self"* dying, we are referring to dependence on self. The fact is, everyone is a *"self,"* and will always be a *"self."*

It is the business of the Holy Spirit to *"sanctify self,"* which He does by us being placed *"in Christ"* (Jn. 14:20). It must be ever understood by the Believer and the unbeliever alike that *"carnal self"* cannot be improved upon. Man seeks to improve self by the false gospel of *"self-esteem,"* or *"self-actualization,"* or *"self-help,"* or *"self-betterment,"* all labeled as *"self-improvement."* Outside of Christ it cannot be done!

Man was born with no good in him but, instead, with all bad. It is hard for unconverted man to come to grips with that. It is even hard for converted man to come to grips with it. Man keeps thinking that he can improve *"self."* He ever fails as fail he must. Carnal self with its *"lusts"* and *"affections"* must be nailed to the Cross (Gal. 5:24). Quite readily, we are willing to *"crucify the flesh"* with its *"lusts;"* however, it is very difficult for the Believer to *"crucify the flesh"* with its *"affections."*

"Lusts" represent the sins of passion, which are the sins of the flesh. *"Affections"* represents the *"sins of pride,"* which are sins of the spirit and much more easily hidden under a cloak of self-righteousness. *"Affections"* represent the *"good side of the Tree of the Knowledge of Good and Evil."* *"Lusts"* represent the bad side of the *"Tree of the Knowledge of Good and Evil."*

Much preaching is aimed toward the *"lusts"* as it should be. Almost no preaching is aimed at the *"affections,"* which represent the *"good self."* It is very difficult for us to learn that there is no such thing as a *"good self."* As Job would come to the place where he would *"abhor self"* (42:6), likewise, we must do the same. Sadly, most Christians cannot be used by the Lord because to be used by Him and to truly represent Christ, *"self"* must be truly placed in Christ. The song says:

"Let me lose myself and find it Lord
   in Thee,
"May all self be slain, my friends see
   only Thee.

"Though it cost me grief and pain,
"I will find my life again.
"Let me lose myself and find it Lord
  in Thee."

THE PLACE AND POSITION OF JOB

The Blessings of the Lord upon Job played out in many areas. Not only was he an extremely wealthy individual, but, as well, he was noted for his wisdom, so much so, that when he appeared on the scene, *"the princes refrained talking, and laid their hand on their mouth."* In other words, no one second guessed Job! No one questioned his sagacity or wisdom.

As well, the poor knew they could go to him and find help. Also, the orphans knew that Job would stand up for them. In other words, the evidence is, that he had helped thousands of people, and in many and varied ways.

But now, not one soul, it seems, stands up for him, irrespective as it regards the thousands he has helped. And yet, this is the same Job, with the same wisdom now that he previously had, but now held up to ridicule.

Why?

The main reason is, precious few people of that time knew the Lord. So, in their thinking, Job, considering the condition he is now in, and considering that he has lost everything, cannot help them anymore. That being the case, they feel free to treat him like dirt.

TOTAL DEPRAVITY

All of this stems from total depravity, which is a result of the Fall. That's why Jesus said, and on which we have already commented, that there is none good but God.

Concerning man, and because of the Fall, the Scripture says:

"What then? are we better than they?" (Are Jews better than Gentiles?) *No, in no wise: for we have before proved both Jews and Gentiles, that they are all under sin* (points to the supposed claim of the Jews of superiority, which is refuted);

"As it is written (Ps. 14:1-3), *There is none righteous, no, not one* (addresses the complaint of the Jews and clinches the argument with the Scriptures, which the Jews could not deny):

"There is none who understands (proclaims total depravity), *there is none who seek after God* (man left on his own will not seek God and, in fact, cannot seek God; he is spiritually dead).

"They are all gone out of the Way (speaks of the lost condition of all men; the *'Way'* is God's Way), *they are together become unprofitable* (refers to the terrible loss in every capacity of wayward man); *there is none who does good, no, not one* (the Greek Text says, *'useless!'*).

"Their throat is an open sepulcher (the idea is of an open grave, with the rotting remains sending forth a putrid stench); *with their tongues they have used deceit* (speaks of guile, deception, hypocrisy, etc.); *the poison of asps is under their lips* (man cannot be trusted in anything he says):

"Whose mouth is full of cursing (wishing someone evil or hurt) *and bitterness* (bitter and reproachful language):

"Their feet are swift to shed blood (the world is filled with murder, killing, and violence):

"Destruction and misery are in their ways (all brought about by sin):

"And the way of peace have they not known (and cannot know until Christ returns):

"There is no fear of God before their eyes (there is no fear of God, because unbelieving man does not know God)" (Rom. 3:9-18).

Considering what the Holy Spirit has said about man, how is it that preachers think that man can be changed by changing a few habits, and above all, without being Born-Again?

NO SUCH THING AS MORAL EVOLUTION

What is moral evolution?

It is the idea that man can be changed, evil can be turned to good, unrighteousness to righteousness, hate to love, by changing man's environment, by education, by changing his habits, etc. In other words, placed in the right environment, and among the right people, he will change.

He won't!

That's the reason that Jesus plainly and

bluntly said, *"Verily, verily, I say unto you, except a man be born again, he cannot see the Kingdom of God."* The term, *"born again,"* means that man has already had a natural birth, but now must have a Spiritual Birth, which comes by Faith in Christ, and what He has done for us at the Cross, and is available to all.

Furthermore, without the New Birth, one cannot understand or comprehend the *"Kingdom of God."*

The *"Old Nature"* cannot be changed in man. It is impossible! Even the Lord does not change it. When an individual is Born-Again, that person receives a brand-new nature, referred to as *"the Divine Nature"* (II Pet. 1:4).

WHAT IS THE DIVINE NATURE?

The Divine Nature is actually the Nature or Character of God, which is imparted to all believing sinners once they come to Christ. This means that the Divine Nature implanted in the inner being of the believing sinner becomes the source of our new life and actions; it comes to everyone at the moment of being *"born again."*

When that happens, the potential is there for the following. The Scripture says:

"And beside this (Salvation), *giving all diligence* (refers to the responsibility we as Believers must show regarding the Christian Life), *add to your Faith Virtue* (this is Faith in the Cross, which will bring *'Virtue'*; the type of *'Virtue'* mentioned here is *'energy'* and *'power'*); *and to Virtue knowledge* (this is the type of knowledge which keeps expanding);

"And to knowledge temperance (self-control); *and to temperance patience* (our conduct must honor God at all times, even in the midst of trials and testing); *and to patience godliness* (being like God);

"And to godliness brotherly kindness (carries the idea of treating everyone as if they were our own flesh and blood *'brother'* or *'sister'*); *and to brotherly kindness charity* (love).

"For if these things be in you, and abound (continue to expand), *they make you that you shall neither be barren nor unfruitful in the knowledge of our Lord Jesus Christ.*

NOTES

(Once again, this *'knowledge'* refers to what Christ did at the Cross, all on our behalf)" (II Pet. 1:5-8).

As stated, this which the Holy Spirit gave to us through the Apostle Peter, presents that which is available. What the Believer does with these things, is something else again. As stated, the potential is there, but whether it will be realized or not, is up to the individual. Peter addressed this as well. He said:

"But he who lacks these things is blind, and cannot see afar off (the reason one may lack these things is he is spiritually blind; in other words, such a one has made something other than the Cross the Object of his Faith), *and has forgotten that he was purged from his old sins.* (Such a Believer is once again being ruled by the *'sin nature'* exactly as he was before conversion, which is always the end result of ignoring the Cross.)

"Wherefore the rather, Brethren, give diligence to make your calling and election sure (this is what Jesus was speaking of when He told us to deny ourselves and take up the Cross daily and follow Him [Lk. 9:23]; every day, the Believer must make certain his Faith is anchored in the Cross and the Cross alone; only then can we realize the tremendous benefits afforded by the Sacrifice of Christ): *for if you do these things, you shall never fall* (presents the key to Eternal Security, but with the Promise being conditional)" (II Pet. 1:9-10).

(14) "I PUT ON RIGHTEOUSNESS, AND IT CLOTHED ME: MY JUDGMENT WAS AS A ROBE AND A DIADEM.

(15) "I WAS EYES TO THE BLIND, AND FEET WAS I TO THE LAME.

(16) "I WAS A FATHER TO THE POOR: AND THE CAUSE WHICH I KNEW NOT I SEARCHED OUT.

(17) "AND I BROKE THE JAWS OF THE WICKED, AND PLUCKED THE SPOIL OUT OF HIS TEETH.

(18) "THEN I SAID, I SHALL DIE IN MY NEST, AND I SHALL MULTIPLY MY DAYS AS THE SAND.

(19) "MY ROOT WAS SPREAD OUT BY THE WATERS, AND THE DEW LAY ALL NIGHT UPON MY BRANCH.

(20) "MY GLORY WAS FRESH IN ME,

AND MY BOW WAS RENEWED IN MY HAND.

(21) "UNTO ME MEN GAVE EAR, AND WAITED, AND KEPT SILENCE AT MY COUNSEL.

(22) "AFTER MY WORDS THEY SPOKE NOT AGAIN; AND MY SPEECH DROPPED UPON THEM.

(23) "AND THEY WAITED FOR ME AS FOR THE RAIN; AND THEY OPENED THEIR MOUTH WIDE AS FOR THE LATTER RAIN.

(24) "IF I LAUGHED ON THEM, THEY BELIEVED IT NOT; AND THE LIGHT OF MY COUNTENANCE THEY CAST NOT DOWN.

(25) "I CHOSE OUT THEIR WAY, AND SAT CHIEF, AND DWELT AS A KING IN THE ARMY, AS ONE WHO COMFORTS THE MOURNERS."

The exegesis is:

1. The idea of Verse 17 is, if the wicked were going to defraud the poor, they would have to answer to Job!

2. The gist of Verse 21 is, before the calamity that came upon Job, he had the last word, because he had the wise word.

3. Verse 22 proclaims the fact that his judgments could not be improved upon.

4. Verse 24 proclaims the fact that when Job smiled on anyone, they were signally honored and blessed.

5. Verse 25 proclaims the fact that Job was the one to whom all looked in times of distress.

JOB'S POSITION BEFORE HIS CALAMITY

Despite all the thousands this man had helped, at this particular time, the public that once gave him adulation now ridicules and mocks him. And yet, as far as the Wisdom of God is concerned, nothing has changed with Job. Sadly, men judge more by what they perceive rather than by what really is.

Why will men change so quickly?

Most, sadly, follow the crowd, not desiring to oppose public opinion. To have spoken a kind word on Job's behalf at this time, would have brought ridicule from acquaintances, friends, and relatives; consequently, no one did.

With his great prosperity and the adulation of all who knew him, Job, before his trial, could only see continued prosperity ahead. Little did he realize that he would become a test of Faith that would span the ages, and, as well, that which would try his own Faith as possibly few men in history have been tried.

Now, no one seeks his advice or his counsel. No one brings their problems to him. No one feels that he knows anything about God.

Again, why is this?

Men mostly base their judgments on appearances; consequently, most of the time they are wrong. Job was no less wise now than he had been in the past. His *"counsel"* was no less needed now than then. But now he was mocked, laughed at, and even spit upon.

Job was vindicated, and greatly so; however, it seems that few pay any attention to this tremendously important Book of Job, which is actually the *"Word of God."* Then continue to repeat the same mistakes that Job's *"three friends"* made, plus all others.

"Years are spent in vanity and pride,
"Caring not my Lord was crucified,
"Knowing not it was for me He died,
"On Calvary!"

"By God's Word at last my sin I learned,
"Then I trembled at the Law I'd spurned,
"Till my guilty soul imploring turned,
"To Calvary."

"Now I've given to Jesus everything;
"Now I gladly own Him as my King;
"Now my raptured soul can only sing,
"Of Calvary."

"O, the Love that drew Salvation's Plan!
"O, the Grace that brought it down to man!
"O, the mighty gulf that God did span,
"At Calvary!"

"Mercy there was great, and Grace was free;
"Pardon there was multiplied to me;

"There my burdened soul found liberty,
"At Calvary."

CHAPTER 30

(1) "BUT NOW THEY WHO ARE YOUNGER THAN I HAVE ME IN DERISION, WHOSE FATHERS I WOULD HAVE DISDAINED TO HAVE SET WITH THE DOGS OF MY FLOCK.

(2) "YES, WHERETO MIGHT THE STRENGTH OF THEIR HANDS PROFIT ME, IN WHOM OLD AGE WAS PERISHED?

(3) "FOR WANT AND FAMINE THEY WERE SOLITARY; FLEEING INTO THE WILDERNESS IN FORMER TIMES DESOLATE AND WASTE.

(4) "WHO CUT UP MALLOWS BY THE BUSHES, AND JUNIPER ROOTS FOR THEIR MEAT.

(5) "THEY WERE DRIVEN FORTH FROM AMONG MEN, (THEY CRIED AFTER THEM AS AFTER A THIEF;)

(6) "TO DWELL IN THE CLIFFS OF THE VALLEYS, IN CAVES OF THE EARTH, AND IN THE ROCKS.

(7) "AMONG THE BUSHES THEY BRAYED; UNDER THE NETTLES THEY WERE GATHERED TOGETHER.

(8) "THEY WERE CHILDREN OF FOOLS, YES, CHILDREN OF BASE MEN: THEY WERE VILER THAN THE EARTH.

(9) "AND NOW AM I THEIR SONG, YES, I AM THEIR BYWORD.

(10) "THEY ABHOR ME, THEY FLEE FAR FROM ME, AND SPARE NOT TO SPIT IN MY FACE.

(11) "BECAUSE HE HAS LOOSED MY CORD, AND AFFLICTED ME, THEY HAVE ALSO LET LOOSE THE BRIDLE BEFORE ME.

(12) "UPON MY RIGHT HAND RISE THE YOUTH; THEY PUSH AWAY MY FEET, AND THEY RAISE UP AGAINST ME THE WAYS OF THEIR DESTRUCTION.

(13) "THEY MAR MY PATH, THEY SET FORWARD MY CALAMITY, THEY HAVE NO HELPER.

(14) "THEY CAME UPON ME AS A WIDE BREAKING IN OF WATERS: IN THE DESOLATION THEY ROLLED THEMSELVES UPON ME."

The synopsis is:

1. (Vs. 1) As high as Job had been in the estimation of others, as low he has fallen, but through no fault of his own.

2. According to Verse 4, from a king's table, Job is reduced to eating scraps.

3. Verse 9 proclaims the fact, that the lowest of the low ridiculed Job.

4. (Vs. 10) They mocked the Patriarch with ribald songs. Standing at a distance, they spat on him. Because God had loosed His Scourge and afflicted him, they too cast off all restraint in their persecution of him. As rabble they stood at his right hand to accuse him. They gave him no standing room in any court of justice and laid snares for him. They did their best to add to his sufferings, even though doing so brought them no personal profit.

5. (Vs. 11) They reasoned that if God had turned His Back upon Job, then he was now *"fair game."*

6. The Fourteenth Verse proclaims the fact, that when one began to taunt him, then they all began to taunt him.

A BYWORD

Job now becomes a song of derision. In other words, they made up bawdy songs about him, of which presented a studied insult. About 700 years later, the same thing was said of David.

"They who sit in the gate speak against me; and I was the song of the drunkards" (Ps. 69:12).

I turned cold all over, when I realized that songs in the same vein were made up of me as well!

As it regards Job and David, even though the songs were the same, songs of acute derision, still, the situation with each man was totally different. For purpose and reason I believe the Holy Spirit would have this delineated.

Job did nothing wrong as far as overt acts were concerned, while David committed two of the most dastardly crimes that could be committed, adultery, and the murder of the woman's husband, and in cold blood at that! But yet, in the Eyes of God, the derision heaped upon both men were the same, meaning that the Lord looked no more kindly upon the enemies of David than He did those of Job.

How could this be, considering that Job did not sin, at least that caused this problem, while David committed dastardly crimes?

Despite David's terrible crimes, both men belonged to the Lord. As such, the derision of one was just as evil as the derision of the other.

In David's day, the situation was a little different than in the time of Job. Job was probably the only one living for God at this particular place, or else one of the few. During the time of David, many, many in Israel claimed to be in the Covenant of Jehovah. But yet, even those who claimed Covenant relationship, at least for the most part, as well, derided David.

The failure of one of God's Servants, gives no room for ridicule on the part of others who claim Christ. About anything can be expected of the world, and to be sure, both situations probably fell into those ranks. However, Believers during the time of David, at least for the most part, were in sympathy with the songs of the drunkards.

One can expect anything from the world, but one expects more from those who claim Christ. But regrettably, oftentimes, there is more kindness shown by the world than even those who claim the Lord.

Why? How?

Self-righteousness is the reason! In fact, self-righteousness cannot do anything but sarcastically ridicule, and at the same time nod the head in approval, when one becomes the song of the drunkards.

But yet, despite Job's present condition, the Lord would restore him, actually making him greater than ever.

As it regards David, despite the terrible sins which he committed, and because of his Scriptural Repentance, the great Promises made to him by the Lord would be carried out in totality. Through his family the Messiah would come and, in fact, the Messiah would actually be referred to as *"the son of David!"* Only Mercy and Grace could restore Job and David, and do so without partiality.

NOTES

JUSTIFICATION BY FAITH

Let it be understood that no one gets by with sin. It always exacts its toll, and without fail. David is a perfect example of such. Because of his sin with Bathsheba, and the murdering of her husband, sorrow and heartache in every form would come to his house, thereby, taking its deadly toll. As we have stated, even though God forgives sin, and does so instantly and completely, at least upon proper confession of such, still, sin sets in motion a series of events which cause all type of heartache and suffering. This must never be forgotten.

But, at the same time, it is God Who measures out that which is chastisement, and not man. No man, irrespective of his proposed standing in Christ, has the right to punish another Believer. That is in the domain of the Lord only, and for many and varied reasons.

First of all, no Believer is worthy to punish another Believer. All Believers have to depend on the Grace and Mercy of God, and on a constant basis. So, as James said, *"Who do we think we are, thinking that we are qualified to punish another Believer?"* (James 4:11-12).

The brother of our Lord went on to say, *"There is one Lawgiver, Who is able to save and to destroy: who are you who judges another? (The Greek actually says, 'but you — who are you?' In other words, 'who do you think you are?')"* (James 4:12).

If a Believer attempts to condone sin in his life, thereby, continuing in that sin, and desiring to do so, fellowship will have to be withdrawn, but even then, prayer should continue to be made for the individual that they will ultimately come back to the right way.

But when someone has truly repented, even as did David, and then for others to think that they must exact their pound of flesh, so called, such presents itself as an awful sin in the Eyes of God. It makes a mockery of the Grace of God, and undermines the price that Jesus paid at Calvary's Cross, which no one in their right mind, should desire to do.

Whenever the Believer, even as David,

confesses their sin before the Lord, we have the Promise of God that the sin is instantly washed, cleansed, and forgiven. There is no penance to be carried out, no works to try to perform to atone for sin, that having been handled at Calvary.

The individual is to be treated as if they have never sinned, because that's the way that God treats the situation. And please understand, there has never been a human being in history, who hasn't had to go to the Lord many, many times, and ask forgiveness for sin. That's at least one of the reasons, that we have no right to hold forgiven sins over the head of an individual. If we do such, we can be assured that such will be done to us, and by no less than the Lord (Mat. 7:1-5).

(15) "TERRORS ARE TURNED UPON ME: THEY PURSUE MY SOUL AS THE WIND: AND MY WELFARE PASSES AWAY AS A CLOUD.

(16) "AND NOW MY SOUL IS POURED OUT UPON ME; THE DAYS OF AFFLICTION HAVE TAKEN HOLD UPON ME.

(17) "MY BONES ARE PIERCED IN ME IN THE NIGHT SEASON: AND MY SINEWS TAKE NO REST.

(18) "BY THE GREAT FORCE OF MY DISEASE IS MY GARMENT CHANGED: IT BINDS ME ABOUT AS THE COLLAR OF MY COAT.

(19) "HE HAS CAST ME INTO THE MIRE, AND I AM BECOME LIKE DUST AND ASHES.

(20) "I CRY UNTO YOU, AND YOU DO NOT HEAR ME: I STAND UP, AND YOU REGARD ME NOT.

(21) "YOU ARE BECOME CRUEL TO ME: WITH YOUR STRONG HAND YOU OPPOSE YOURSELF AGAINST ME.

(22) "YOU LIFT ME UP TO THE WIND, YOU CAUSED ME TO RIDE UPON IT, AND DISSOLVE MY SUBSTANCE.

(23) "FOR I KNOW THAT YOU WILL BRING ME TO DEATH, AND TO THE HOUSE APPOINTED FOR ALL LIVING.

(24) "HOWBEIT HE WILL NOT STRETCH OUT HIS HAND TO THE GRAVE, THOUGH THEY CRY IN HIS DESTRUCTION.

(25) "DID NOT I WEEP FOR HIM WHO WAS IN TROUBLE? WAS NOT MY SOUL GRIEVED FOR THE POOR?

(26) "WHEN I LOOKED FOR GOOD, THEN EVIL CAME UNTO ME: AND WHEN I WAITED FOR LIGHT, THERE CAME DARKNESS.

(27) "MY BOWELS BOILED, AND RESTED NOT: THE DAYS OF AFFLICTION PREVENTED ME.

(28) "I WENT MOURNING WITHOUT THE SUN: I STOOD UP, AND I CRIED IN THE CONGREGATION.

(29) "I AM A BROTHER TO DRAGONS, AND A COMPANION TO OWLS.

(30) "MY SKIN IS BLACK UPON ME, AND MY BONES ARE BURNED WITH HEAT.

(31) "MY HARP ALSO IS TURNED TO MOURNING, AND MY ORGAN INTO THE VOICE OF THEM WHO WEEP."

The overview is:

1. (Vs. 15) Not only is the physical and financial welfare of Job impugned, but he fears now for his soul.

2. (Vs. 18) Along with the insults, Job's physical condition seems to be deteriorating by the hour.

3. (Vs. 19) Perhaps it could be said that it's not possible for God to sanctify the *"carnal self"* without the individual, in some way, experiencing the *"dust and ashes."*

4. (Vs. 20) It is the worst of all calamities to be God-forsaken, as Job believed himself to be; however, he will soon find out that the Lord had not forsaken him.

5. According to Verse 22, the wind of adversity was allowed to blow against Job in full force.

6. As it relates to Verse 26, the Patriarch had been thinking that the situation would ultimately change, but instead, it has only gotten worse.

7. According to Verse 31, there is no more music in Job's soul!

WHEN I LOOKED FOR GOOD, EVIL CAME!

The sufferings from the Hand of God were dual with Job. They were:
- The silence of God to his prayer.
- The action of God in afflicting him.

Several things are said in Verses 23 through 25. Williams says the following:

- *"In Verse 23, Job declares his faith in a life beyond the grave.*
- *"In Verse 24, he states that God, having made a ruin of his physical frame, will not continue to afflict him in the spirit world when he dies.*
- *"In Verse 25, he argues that the Divine life in him which caused him to weep and grieve for those who were in trouble and in need, was an assurance to him that the Author of that compassion would ultimately act toward him, as he, moved by that Divine pity, had acted toward others."*[1]

I think it's virtually impossible for us to properly understand Job's feelings, and for all the obvious reasons. We know why this terrible trial came his way, and we know the conclusion of the matter. At the time he was uttering these words, he did not know why it had happened, in fact, he had no inkling, and circumstances at the time surely did not look like the Lord was going to intervene in any manner. In fact, Job thought he was dying.

He goes back in his thinking, back before this terrible trial commenced, to the time he was fully expecting the continuing of his great wealth and prosperity. And then this sudden shock of the calamity fell upon him. It was wholly unexpected and, therefore, the harder to bear.

WHEN I WAITED FOR LIGHT, THERE CAME DARKNESS

After this terrible ordeal began, Job knowing that he had done nothing wrong, expected the Lord to intervene at any time; consequently, he *"waited for light;"* however, instead, his situation became worse, hence, the words, *"there came darkness."*

As we have stated, very few people in history, if any, have been asked by the Lord to undergo what Job underwent.

The loss of his wealth, place, and position, was one thing; however, to lose all ten of his children, in other words, to have ten funerals at one time and, as well, to have all the people thinking of him as one that was wicked, hence, God bringing judgment upon him, was perhaps, at least one of the hardest cuts of all.

As we have previously stated in this

NOTES

Volume, Job was not the only one on trial. In fact, everyone else was on trial also. The truth is, Job is the only one who passed this test. All others failed it, and failed it miserably. We should take a lesson from this.

Anything that happens to others, whether it's little or large, whether we think so or not, the truth is, what will our reaction be? As someone has well said, *"It's not only how we act, but more than all, it's how we react."*

One could understand the people in Job's day conducting themselves as they did, simply because there was no Bible then, and Jehovah was only known in a limited way, and then only by a few. But now, with all the light that we are given, we should know as Believers, how to conduct ourselves. It might come as a surprise to us, that another person undergoing a tremendous trial, and whatever it might be, may include us as well, even though we have little knowledge of the situation.

Will we have compassion on the individual or not?

Are we secretly glad that it's happened to him or her? Whatever it may have been?

Do we have no feelings one way or the other?

Do we take this as an opportunity to exact our pound of flesh?

Do we surmise, *"I knew something was wrong all the time?"*

We need to think about these questions very carefully, because we are probably faced with them far more than we realize.

"Down at the Cross where my Saviour died,
"Down where for cleansing from sin I cried,
"There to my heart was the Blood applied;
"Glory to His Name!"

"I am so wondrously Saved from sin,
"Jesus so sweetly abides within,
"There at the Cross where He took me in;
"Glory to His Name!"

"O precious fountain that saves from sin,
"I am so glad I have entered in;

"There Jesus saves me and keeps me clean;
"Glory to His Name!"

"Come to this fountain so rich and sweet;
"Cast your poor soul at the Saviour's Feet;
"Plunge in today and be made complete;
"Glory to His Name!"

CHAPTER 31

(1) "I MADE A COVENANT WITH MY EYES: WHY THEN SHOULD I THINK UPON A MAID?
(2) "FOR WHAT PORTION OF GOD IS THERE FROM ABOVE? AND WHAT INHERITANCE OF THE ALMIGHTY FROM ON HIGH?
(3) "IS NOT DESTRUCTION TO THE WICKED? AND A STRANGE PUNISHMENT TO THE WORKERS OF INIQUITY?
(4) "DOES NOT HE SEE MY WAYS, AND COUNT ALL MY STEPS?
(5) "IF I HAVE WALKED WITH VANITY, OR IF MY FOOT HAS HASTED TO DECEIT;
(6) "LET ME BE WEIGHED IN AN EVEN BALANCE, THAT GOD MAY KNOW MY INTEGRITY.
(7) "IF MY STEP HAS TURNED OUT OF THE WAY, AND MY HEART WALKED AFTER MY EYES, AND IF ANY BLOT HAS CLEAVED TO MY HANDS;
(8) "THEN LET ME SOW, AND LET ANOTHER EAT; YES, LET MY OFFSPRING BE ROOTED OUT.
(9) "IF MY HEART HAS BEEN DECEIVED BY A WOMAN, OR IF I HAVE LAID WAIT AT MY NEIGHBOUR'S DOOR;
(10) "THEN LET MY WIFE GRIND UNTO ANOTHER, AND LET OTHERS BOW DOWN UPON HER.
(11) "FOR THIS IS AN HEINOUS CRIME; YES, IT IS AN INIQUITY TO BE PUNISHED BY THE JUDGES.
(12) "FOR IT IS A FIRE THAT CONSUMES TO DESTRUCTION, AND WOULD ROOT OUT ALL MY INCREASE.

NOTES

(13) "IF I DID DESPISE THE CAUSE OF MY MANSERVANT OR OF MY MAIDSERVANT, WHEN THEY CONTENDED WITH ME;"

The pattern is:
1. Job says in Verse 1 that he is not guilty of the sin of lust.
2. Verse 3 proclaims the fact that sin is the ruin of both soul and body.
3. (Vs. 6) The only *"even balance"* in the universe is that which is of God; all else is spurious.
4. (Vs. 7) It is to be remembered that Job had the testimony of God Himself to the fact that he was *"a perfect and upright man, one who feared God, and hated evil"* (2:3). This doesn't mean that Job was sinlessly perfect, for he wasn't; but it does mean that he was attempting to follow the Lord as closely as possible!
5. (Vs. 11) The crime of adultery subverts the family relation on which it has pleased God to erect the entire fabric of human society.
6. (Vs. 12) The sin of adultery lacking Repentance will bring down the wrath of God upon the person who commits such.
7. In the Thirteenth Verse, Job disclaims the oppression of his dependants; of which he had been accused by Eliphaz (22:5-9).

IMMORALITY

The Patriarch said, *"I made a covenant with my eyes: why then should I think upon a maid?"* In this Scripture Job lets us know that immorality had been a temptation at a particular time, but a temptation to which he never yielded.

Immorality, which comes in many shapes, forms, and sizes, presents itself as the plaguing sin of this age.

Due to the privacy of the Internet, this device probably affords the presentation of this form of immorality as nothing else.

A PERSONAL EXAMPLE

A friend of mine at one time in the past served on the board of one of the largest organizations in the world. They employ tens of thousands of people all over the world.

A poll was taken directed at the managerial section of this vast company. It numbered thousands of people.

Most of these individuals had a college education, with many professing to be Christians. As well, in this group there were quite a number of millionaires, etc.

The questionnaire did not require a signature which insured the truth being told.

He said that sixty percent of the thousands who filled out this report and, as stated, a report to which they did not have to sign their name, admitted to being hooked on Internet pornography.

When he said that to me, I did a double take, turned around and asked him to repeat what he had said. I thought I misunderstood.

He smiled, and said, *"I did the same thing."*

He then repeated what he had said, that sixty percent of the people in this position admitted to being hooked on Internet pornography.

I do not know exactly as to what was meant by the word *"hooked,"* unless they meant that they were driven to watch this stuff on a daily basis.

In television, even in the innocent sitcoms, so-called, the *"thou shalt nots . . ."* are gradually being eroded, until soft porn is now looked at as normal. In other words, we are becoming hardened to what we are seeing. What shocked us ten years ago, no longer shocks us.

Hollywood has done its very best to destroy the morals of this nation, and they have succeeded in doing so.

Abortion on demand is now the law of the land, even in many cases, to the time of the birth of the baby. Some have even suggested that if the child is not wanted, after it is born, it should be allowed to starve to death.

That's what the Holy Spirit through Paul was talking about when he said, *"For men shall be lovers of their own selves . . . without natural affection . . ."* (II Tim. 3:2-3).

HOMOSEXUALITY

As everyone knows, the nation is furiously plunging ahead toward legalizing *"gay marriages,"* ad nauseam. Whereas all immorality is an affront toward God, homosexuality and lesbianism are two of the worst sins on the Planet. As we stated in the notes above,

NOTES

"the crime of adultery or fornication, with the latter including homosexuality, subverts the family relation on which it has pleased God to erect the entire fabric of human society."

Many homosexuals claim they were born that way. They were not!

If they were born that way, how is it, that twins at times, who have the same genes, will turn out to one being straight, and the other being homosexual? Considering they have the same genes, whatever one is, the other would be, if they were born that way.

While it is to be admitted that different individuals are born with a greater proclivity toward certain things than others, that is obvious and is understood and, in fact, is a product of the Fall.

In other words, some people are born with a greater proclivity toward lying than others. Others would be born with a greater proclivity toward alcohol than others. As well, some are born with a greater proclivity toward homosexuality than others; however, that doesn't mean that God is the Author of such. As stated, this is a product of the Fall.

THE CROSS OF CHRIST

The answer to this abnormality, which incidentally plagues all in one way or the other, for all are born in sin, is the Cross of Christ. Now read those words very carefully, because they are very, very important.

There is only one answer for humanity, one answer for sin, one answer for perversion, one answer for every moral abnormality, whatever it might be, and that is the Cross of Jesus Christ.

When Jesus died on the Cross, He addressed every sin, and I mean every sin that plagues the human race. This means that He atoned for every one of these sins; past, present, and future, at least for all who will believe (Jn. 3:16).

CAN A HOMOSEXUAL BE SAVED?

When Jesus died on the Cross, He died for the whole of humanity, irrespective as to whom they might be, or what they have done. This includes homosexuals and homosexuality. He will save all who come to

Him. In fact, He said:

"Come now, and let us reason together, says the LORD: though your sins be as scarlet, they shall be as white as snow; though they be red like crimson, they shall be as wool" (Isa. 1:18).

There is no greater invitation found in the Bible than this one given by the Holy Spirit through the Prophet Isaiah.

In this Passage, sins are spoken of as *"scarlet."* Such has a reference to blood-guiltiness. All sin is murder in some form, hence, the blood-guiltiness.

This glorious Passage illustrates to us the eternal truth that irrespective of the evil, wickedness, deception, and weight of sin, the Lord stands ready, upon proper confession and Repentance to forgive all, and, therefore, to cleanse all. As stated, this is done exclusively by Faith in Christ and His shed Blood (Eph. 2:13-18).

But once the homosexual comes to Christ or the drunkard, or the gambler, or the drug addict, etc., those sins are to be laid aside, and forsaken. There is no such thing as the Lord Saving in sin. He saves from sin. And to be sure, homosexuality is sin and, in fact, one of the worst sins that one could think. Nevertheless, as stated, Jesus died for the homosexual as well as everyone else.

THE BONDAGE BROKEN

When some people come to Christ, instantly every bondage is broken, with no more desire for the thing, whatever it might have been. But with some, or with some particular things, one might say, there is a struggle at times, even a severe struggle.

A PERSONAL EXAMPLE

Two of the dearest friends that Frances and I have in this world are Roy and Beulah Chacon.

When Roy was Saved, he was an alcoholic. Plus, there were many other problems; however, when he came to Christ, every one of these problems dropped off and instantly with no more desire in that direction, with the exception of alcohol. He struggled with this thing for three years — yes, I said three years. He was prayed for, had hands laid on him, he fasted, he sought the Lord earnestly, but seemingly to no avail.

He knew that alcohol was wrong, terribly wrong. As well, he knew that he had to be free of this thing, but couldn't seem to find the way of victory.

And then one day it happened. The craving left, and it has never come back, and that has been at the time of this writing, nearly twenty years ago.

Now was Roy Saved during the time he was struggling with alcohol, and to be sure, failed again and again during those three years? Yes, most definitely he was Saved.

Many Christians would be quick to claim that he wasn't; however, the very ones who would say such are struggling with things in their own lives, things, incidentally, which are terribly wrong. But somehow they seem to conveniently forget that.

Roy wasn't trying to continue drinking. He wasn't trying to make excuses for his drinking. He was trying with everything within him to quit, and eventually, the Lord set him free.

Why did not the Lord take away alcohol immediately when he was Saved, exactly as the other vices fell away?

That I cannot answer. But I do know this, if the Believer will keep believing, and will place his Faith exclusively in Christ and the Cross, there will come an hour that Victory, and I mean total Victory, will be his. No, I'm not speaking of sinless perfection, for the Bible doesn't teach such; however, I am speaking of the dominion of sin. It will be broken and in its entirety (Rom. 6:14).

Homosexuality falls into the same category. In fact, any vice can fall into this category.

When the homosexual comes to Christ, it may very well happen that the craving for that ungodly passion may continue, with a great struggle ensuing to be free. But let me say it again, if such a Believer will place his Faith exclusively in Christ and the Cross, the Holy Spirit will see to the situation that it is resolved. It may take a while, but it will be done. We have the Promise of the Lord in that capacity. Paul said:

"For sin shall not have dominion over you: for you are no longer under Law but under Grace" (Rom. 6:14).

WHAT DOES IT MEAN TO BE UNDER GRACE AND NOT LAW?

The Holy Spirit works totally and completely within the parameters of Grace, which is the Goodness of God extended to undeserving Believers, and will, thereby, help the Believer to overcome. As we have stated, the only requirement for the Believer is that the Cross of Christ ever be the Object of our Faith. The reason why is simple!

The Holy Spirit works entirely within the parameters of the Finished Work of Christ, which gives Him the legal right to do all that He does and, in fact, will work no other way. That's the reason it is required of us that our Faith be entirely in Christ and the Cross (Rom. 6:1-14; 8:1-2, 11; I Cor. 1:17-18, 23; 2:2; Gal., Chpt. 5; 6:14; Eph. 2:13-18; Col. 2:14-15).

Now, *"Law"* is something else altogether. When Paul mentioned Law in Romans 6:14, he was speaking of the Law of Moses. Now many would read these words and automatically think, that the Law of Moses has long since been gone, and has no more affect on modern Believers. In a sense they are right. But the idea is, Paul is speaking not only of the Law of Moses, but any type of religious laws that we devise.

If the Believer tries to overcome in any capacity, and tries to do so by the means of religious laws, or the laws we devise ourselves, or others devise, or our Church devises, etc., there will be no victory, no deliverance. The Holy Spirit will not work in such an atmosphere. Paul also said:

"I do not frustrate the Grace of God: for if Righteousness come by the Law, then Christ is dead in vain" (Gal. 2:21).

WHAT DOES IT MEAN TO FRUSTRATE THE GRACE OF GOD?

As we have stated, the Grace of God is simply the Goodness of God extended to undeserving Believers.

The way to keep the Grace of God flowing to us in an uninterrupted manner is that our Faith be ever placed in Christ and the Cross. It is through the Cross of Christ that Grace is made possible for the Believer, and in no other way. We must never forget that!

NOTES

If we place our Faith in something other than the Cross of Christ, this stops the flow of Grace in our hearts and lives, thereby, guaranteeing our failure. Regrettably, this is where most of the modern church presently is. Even though this is the Age of Grace, the Dispensation of Grace, still, most modern Christians are recipients of precious little Grace, because they are frustrating this great Gift of God. So, if you try to live by religious law, and religious law of any kind, it frustrates the Grace of God, which guarantees failure.

That's why Paul said, that if Righteousness can be afforded to us by the means of Law, then Jesus did not have to come down here and die on a cruel Cross. But to be sure, He had to die on that Cross, simply because Law could not save anyone.

POWER

To overcome the powers of darkness, there has to be a greater power, and that greater Power is the Power of the Lord Jesus Christ, given to us through and by the Holy Spirit.

Sin is a powerful force, so powerful, in fact, that it is impossible to overcome this monster except by doing it God's Way.

When we devise religious laws, thinking that's going to help us be what we ought to be, the Holy Spirit cannot function in that capacity. And, to be sure, without Him, we are not going to see anything done in our lives.

Religious laws depend upon the personal ability, talent, motivation, strength, and character of the individual, which is always woefully lacking. Due to the Fall, the physical body of man was made ineffective, at least as far as overcoming the powers of darkness is concerned. No matter how hard we try in these capacities, we simply cannot do what needs to be done. We will fail every time. We might succeed for a while, but shortly we're going to fail.

As we have stated, it is the Cross of Christ that gives the Holy Spirit the legal right to do all that He does within our hearts and lives. Paul also said concerning this:

"For the preaching of the Cross is to them who perish foolishness; but to we who are Saved it is the Power of God" (I Cor. 1:18).

HOW IS THE CROSS THE POWER OF GOD?

It is the Power of God, simply because it is through that Finished Work of Christ, that the Holy Spirit works. In fact, the Power is registered in the Holy Spirit. But, it is the Cross of Christ, as stated, which gives Him the legal means to do all that He does in our hearts and lives. That's the reason that Paul also said:

"For the Law of the Spirit of Life in Christ Jesus has made me free from the Law of Sin and Death" (Rom. 8:2).

As we've already said in this Volume, if one is to notice, this Scripture is prefaced by the word *"Law."* It's not the Law of Moses, but rather a Law devised by the Godhead in eternity past. It is *"The Law of the Spirit* (the way the Spirit works) *of Life* (all life comes from Christ, but through the Holy Spirit), *in Christ Jesus* (pertaining to what Christ did for us at the Cross). . . ."

Please allow me the latitude of once again giving what we've already given in this Volume:

FOCUS: The Lord Jesus Christ (Jn. 14:6).

OBJECT OF FAITH: The Cross of Christ (Rom. 6:1-14).

POWER SOURCE: The Holy Spirit (Rom. 8:1-2, 11).

RESULTS: Victory (Rom. 6:14).

The little formula just given is the way and the means as to how the Holy Spirit works within our hearts and lives, thereby, giving us Victory, and irrespective as to what the problem may have been.

Whatever it is that binds humanity, even the worst vices of all, Jesus addressed it all at the Cross. But please understand, Victory is found in the Cross of Christ, and only in the Cross of Christ (I Cor. 1:17).

(14) "WHAT THEN SHALL I DO WHEN GOD RISES UP? AND WHEN HE VISITS, WHAT SHALL I ANSWER HIM?

(15) "DID NOT HE WHO MADE ME IN THE WOMB MAKE HIM? AND DID NOT ONE FASHION US IN THE WOMB?

(16) "IF I HAVE WITHHELD THE POOR FROM THEIR DESIRE, OR HAVE CAUSED THE EYES OF THE WIDOW TO FAIL;

(17) "OR HAVE EATEN MY MORSEL MYSELF ALONE, AND THE FATHERLESS HAS NOT EATEN THEREOF;

(18) "(FOR FROM MY YOUTH HE WAS BROUGHT UP WITH ME, AS WITH A FATHER, AND I HAVE GUIDED HER FROM MY MOTHER'S WOMB;)

(19) "IF I HAVE SEEN ANY PERISH FOR WANT OF CLOTHING, OR ANY POOR WITHOUT COVERING;

(20) "IF HIS LOINS HAVE NOT BLESSED ME, AND IF HE WERE NOT WARMED WITH THE FLEECE OF MY SHEEP;

(21) "IF I HAVE LIFTED UP MY HAND AGAINST THE FATHERLESS, WHEN I SAW MY HELP IN THE GATE:

(22) "THEN LET MY ARM FALL FROM MY SHOULDER BLADE, AND MY ARM BE BROKEN FROM THE BONE.

(23) "FOR DESTRUCTION FROM GOD WAS A TERROR TO ME, AND BY REASON OF HIS HIGHNESS I COULD NOT ENDURE.

(24) "IF I HAVE MADE GOLD MY HOPE, OR HAVE SAID TO THE FINE GOLD, YOU ARE MY CONFIDENCE;

(25) "IF I REJOICE BECAUSE MY WEALTH WAS GREAT, AND BECAUSE MY HAND HAD GOTTEN MUCH;

(26) "IF I BEHELD THE SUN WHEN IT SHINED, OR THE MOON WALKING IN BRIGHTNESS;

(27) "AND MY HEART HAS BEEN SECRETLY ENTICED, OR MY MOUTH HAS KISSED MY HAND:

(28) "THIS ALSO WERE AN INIQUITY TO BE PUNISHED BY THE JUDGE: FOR I SHOULD HAVE DENIED THE GOD WHO IS ABOVE."

The structure is:

1. Verse 15 proclaims the Spirit of God through Job ascertaining the equality of all men, irrespective of race, creed, or color.

2. (Vs. 17) Job claims to have always shared his bread with orphans and made them partakers of his abundance.

3. The Twenty-first Verse proclaims Job having done everything for the poor and the helpless that he had the power to do.

WHEN THE LORD VISITS, WHAT SHALL I ANSWER HIM?

Job enumerates the good things he had

done, and the bad things he had not done. In those days, these things carried more weight than they do presently. To be sure, the doing of good things or the not doing of bad things, did not constitute Salvation then, as it doesn't now. But, these type of things carried weight, and God honored it. And yet, men were Saved in those days, exactly as they are Saved now.

Then, Salvation consisted of Faith in the coming Redeemer, typified by the sacrifices. In truth, the sacrifices within themselves did not save anyone. Millions of Jews, when Israel became a Nation, offered up sacrifices constantly, but, which earned them nothing with God. They had no faith in the coming Messiah, in fact, could not have cared less about this all-important Doctrine. They were only interested in going through the ceremony and the ritual, thinking that pleased God, so they could go back to their sinning. In other words, at least in their thinking, the offered up sacrifices would account for their sins for the past week, giving them the freedom to continue in their sin the following week.

The Lord said through the Prophet Isaiah, *"Bring no more vain oblations* (sacrifices)*; incense is an abomination unto Me; the new moons and the sabbaths, the calling of assemblies, I cannot away with; it is iniquity, even the solemn meeting"* (Isa. 1:13).

This means that all the religious activity, which, in fact, was genuine and actually God-given, still, was emptied of all its significance, and became hateful to God — a mere form; consequently, it was, as stated, an *"abomination."*

He then said, *"Your new moons and your appointed feasts My soul hates: they are a trouble unto Me; I am weary to bear them"* (Isa. 1:14).

The Hebrew word for *"weary"* is *"la'ah,"* which means *"to be disgusted, grieved, loathe."*

Job presenting his case to the Lord was doing about all he knew to do. And, in fact, when the Lord would appear, He would not reprimand the Patriarch at all, but rather his *"three friends."* In essence, He complimented Job.

One might say, that we do good works because we are Saved, not in order to be Saved. This, I think, fit Job.

We must understand that during the time of Job, the only people on Earth living for God, those who knew Jehovah, constituted the family of Jacob. How many of them were actually living for God, is anyone's guess. In fact, Job lived before the Law of Moses was given. So his knowledge at that time was quite extensive, considering that every single Doctrine that we take for granted under the New Covenant, was understood then only in Shadow, and a darkened Shadow at that.

THE NEW COVENANT

Presently, and I'm speaking of the New Covenant, I think the Lord would take a rather dim view of anyone who endeavored to set his good works before the Lord, etc. Under the New Covenant, we have far more Light, as should be obvious, than Job of old. But I'm afraid that all too often, modern Believers avail themselves of precious little of the opportunity they have to properly learn the Word of God. So, the *"good works"* syndrome continues on, which God can never accept.

This doesn't mean that we're speaking in opposition to good works, for the truth is, every true Believer should, and without fail, carry out good works. But as we've already stated, these things ought to be done because we are Saved, not in order to be Saved.

At the present time when the Lord visits us, Job asks, *"What shall I answer Him?"* Now, we had better know what to answer Him!

WHAT WILL MY ANSWER BE?

Our answer should center up entirely in Christ. We plead no cause of our own, and surely no righteousness by the order of self.

A preacher had the misfortune to be in a terrible car wreck. When he was being rushed to the hospital, he heard one of the attendants say, *"It's no use, he's not going to make it."*

Whether he actually died or not is anyone's guess. At any rate, he found himself in a vision I suppose, standing before the Bar of God. The Lord looked down at him and asked the question, *"How do you plead, guilty or not guilty?"*

He saw Satan standing over in the corner observing the proceedings. He knew that if he answered *"not guilty,"* that Satan would instantly rise up and accuse him, and would be justified in doing so.

He knew if he answered *"guilty,"* this would keep him out of Heaven.

He stood there a few moments, whispering, *"Lord, help me to say the right thing!"*

He then looked back up at God the Father and said, *"I plead the Blood of Jesus Christ."*

In fact, that and that alone, *"The Blood of Jesus Christ,"* which was shed for you and me, is the right answer and, in fact, the only answer that the believing sinner can give.

We are Saved not because of the so-called good works we have done, or the bad things we have not done, but we are Saved because of the Sacrifice of Christ at Calvary's Cross, and our Faith in that Finished Work (Rom. 10:9-10, 13; Jn. 3:16).

I'M AS GOOD AS YOU ARE!

One of the favorite statements of individuals who have not accepted Christ and, in fact, have refused to accept Him, is the statement of our heading, *"I'm as good as you are!"* Of course, they are meaning that they are as good as Christians, etc.

The truth is, they very well might be, and as men label goodness, there is a possibility they are even judged by some as being better, in other words, more good. However, being good, as noble as that might be, is no passport to Heaven at all.

It would be about the same as a person going to a football game, and when they came to the man taking the tickets, they would hand him a spoon. Of course, inasmuch as the spoon might be a very valuable utensil when it comes to eating, it won't get the person into the game.

The ticket for Heaven, if we may be allowed to use such terminology, is Faith in Christ and what Christ has done for us at the Cross. That alone spends in God's Economy.

THE GOOD MAN AND THE BAD MAN

The other day I read of a man who lived in a particular city, who had been a great benefactor to the poor. He wasn't wealthy, which means he spent almost everything he made helping those who could not help themselves.

He drove an old pick-up truck that had long since worn out, because he used the money that could have purchased him a new truck, to help the poor. In fact, his own life was very Spartan, with everything he had going to this noble charity. When he died, there was hardly any building in the city large enough to seat the people who came to his funeral. As stated, he had helped thousands.

In relating this illustration, which was true, I placed up beside this man another individual who was the very opposite. He was a drunk, a wife beater, a fornicator, doing about everything that was bad that he was big enough to do. He was no benefit to society whatsoever, but rather a drag, one might say.

When he died, there was no one at his funeral except his immediate family, and for all the obvious reasons.

But then I went on to state to that great congregation that night in the Crusade, that if this man who had performed all the good deeds, had given himself totally and completely to helping others, yet had not accepted Jesus Christ as his Saviour, the truth is, he died eternally lost. The things he did were very good, and very commendable and, no doubt, very pleasing to the Lord; however, these good works within themselves did not purchase him admittance to Heaven.

On the other hand, let's say for the sake of argument, as it regards the man who was the drunk, in other words, the very opposite of the so-called good man who I've just mentioned, that on his death bed, he accepted the Lord Jesus Christ as his Saviour. The truth is, he went to Heaven. Let's say it again:

If the man doing all the good works did not accept Christ as his personal Saviour, then he died eternally lost. If the drunk in his last hours did, in fact, accept Christ, despite all the bad things he had done, he made Heaven his Eternal Home.

When I made that statement to that great congregation that night, a gasp went up from that crowd. Despite the fact that most of the people there, actually thousands, should have been more versed in the Bible than evidently they were, still had it in their mind, that the *"good works"* would give one an entrance into Heaven. They could not conceive of a man so evil and so wicked, who had been so hateful to his fellowman, and even to his loved ones, at the end crying to God for Salvation, and then making Heaven his Eternal Home. They couldn't seem to understand that! And neither could they understand the fact that the so-called good man if he did not accept Christ, despite all his good works, died eternally lost. Let us say it again:

Entrance into the Portals of Glory when we die, is allowed only on the premise of our Faith in Christ and what Christ did for us at the Cross. As the old song says, *"All else is sinking sand."*

(29) "IF I REJOICED AT THE DESTRUCTION OF HIM WHO HATED ME, OR LIFTED UP MYSELF WHEN EVIL FOUND HIM:

(30) "NEITHER HAVE I SUFFERED MY MOUTH TO SIN BY WISHING A CURSE TO HIS SOUL.

(31) "IF THE MEN OF MY TABERNACLE SAID NOT, OH THAT WE HAD OF HIS FLESH! WE CANNOT BE SATISFIED.

(32) "THE STRANGER DID NOT LODGE IN THE STREET: BUT I OPENED MY DOORS TO THE TRAVELLER.

(33) "IF I COVERED MY TRANSGRESSIONS AS ADAM, BY HIDING MY INIQUITY IN MY BOSOM:

(34) "DID I FEAR A GREAT MULTITUDE, OR DID THE CONTEMPT OF FAMILIES TERRIFY ME, THAT I KEPT SILENCE, AND WENT NOT OUT OF THE DOOR?

(35) "OH THAT ONE WOULD HEAR ME! BEHOLD, MY DESIRE IS, THAT THE ALMIGHTY WOULD ANSWER ME, AND THAT MY ADVERSARY HAD WRITTEN A BOOK.

(36) "SURELY I WOULD TAKE IT UPON MY SHOULDER, AND BIND IT AS A CROWN TO ME.

(37) "I WOULD DECLARE UNTO HIM THE NUMBER OF MY STEPS; AS A PRINCE WOULD I GO NEAR UNTO HIM.

(38) "IF MY LAND CRY AGAINST ME, OR THAT THE FURROWS LIKEWISE THEREOF COMPLAIN;

(39) "IF I HAVE EATEN THE FRUITS THEREOF WITHOUT MONEY, OR HAVE CAUSED THE OWNERS THEREOF TO LOSE THEIR LIFE:

(40) "LET THISTLES GROW INSTEAD OF WHEAT, AND COCKLE INSTEAD OF BARLEY. THE WORDS OF JOB ARE ENDED."

The structure is:

1. (Vs. 30) If those who hated Job during his prosperous times entered into adversity, the Patriarch proclaims the fact that he did not rejoice at their calamity. He left it all to the Lord.

2. (Vs. 34) Because of his integrity, Job had no fear of facing people.

3. The Thirty-fifth Verse proclaims the Patriarch desiring that one would hear him. To be sure, the Lord was definitely hearing Job, but not his adversaries.

4. (Vs. 40) In this Chapter, Job is not actually trying to justify himself before God, but merely answering the charges made against him by his *"friends."*

THE ALMIGHTY WILL ANSWER

The truth is, the Almighty very shortly most definitely did answer. He would vindicate Job and do so in totality; however, the three *"friends"* would not fare so well!

In a further comment on this Chapter and the significance of all that is said, it must be noted, that not committing these terrible sins does not constitute righteousness to any degree on the part of the innocent one. Righteousness must be imputed by God. In fact, whether we commit these sins or not, we are all unrighteous, for the Scripture says, *"There is none righteous, no, not one"* (Rom. 3:10).

At the same time, by not committing these dastardly sins one will save himself much grief, sorrow, and heartache.

The Thirty-first Chapter addresses itself to man's age-old problem, that he desires to claim his righteousness with God by things that he has either done or not done. Both are extremely important, but neither the *"not committing grave sins"* nor the *"doing of good things,"* as stated, bring upon the individual any Righteousness.

God has declared all men guilty, irrespective of their conduct; consequently, for men to receive from God, they must consider themselves guilty as well, and again, irrespective of their conduct.

Upon the basis of man admitting his guilt and repenting of his sin, God will freely impute Righteousness to the abased one. This great Truth of God which is the undergirding foundation of the entire Bible cannot be understood by a self-righteous Church, nor even accepted; consequently, the majority of the human race tries to earn their way with God, that is if they believe there is a God, by their conduct — *"not so bad," "not as bad as others," "good intentions," "I haven't done that," "I have done good things."*

Let us, as well, note that even though the not committing of certain sins does not earn one any Righteousness, still, the committing of sins will make one unrighteous quickly.

The argument that *"we did nothing to get in Grace, and we can do nothing to get out"* is fallacious indeed.

Grace covers sin, but only sin that is confessed and rejected. Grace does not cover unconfessed sin, neither will it forgive unconfessed sin. Sin must be properly confessed before God and forsaken (I Jn. 1:9).

WHAT HAPPENS WHEN A CHRISTIAN SINS?

First of all, and we mean immediately, the Holy Spirit convicts that individual of that sin, whatever it might be. And every single Believer who reads these words knows exactly what I'm talking about.

The Christian is to immediately, wherever he might be, confess his sin to the Lord, in which we are promised that the Lord will be *"faithful and just to forgive us our sins, and to cleanse us from all unrighteousness"* (I Jn. 1:9).

When that sin is forgiven, again whatever it might be, the Believer should understand as to why the sin was committed in the first place. No true Christian desires to sin. This means that most sin is committed, simply because the Believer's Faith has as its object something other than the Cross. When this happens, the Holy Spirit is greatly limited in what He can do for us, which makes us a fertile target for Satan.

The Believer should make certain that his Faith is now in the Cross of Christ, and only the Cross of Christ. In fact, and to which we have alluded, the sin was committed in the first place because the individual's faith was in something other than the Cross. If, in fact, the Believer does not place his faith exclusively in Christ and the Cross, he will find himself repeating that sin again and again, despite the fact that he is trying so hard not to commit the same sin again. In fact, millions of Christians are in this condition, committing the same sin over and over again, simply because their faith is in something except the Cross. That's what Paul was talking about when he said:

"Brethren, if a man be overtaken in a fault (pertains to moral failure, and is brought about because one has ignorantly placed himself under Law; such a position guarantees failure), *you who are Spiritual* (refers to those who understand God's Prescribed Order of Victory, which is the Cross), *restore such an one* (tell him he failed because of reverting to religious law, and that Victory can be his by placing his Faith totally in the Cross, which then gives the Holy Spirit latitude to work, Who Alone can give the Victory) *in the spirit of meekness* (never with an overbearing, holier-than-thou attitude); *considering yourself, lest you also be tempted* (the implication is that if we do not handle such a case Scripturally, we thereby, open the door for Satan to attack us in the same manner as he did the failing brother)" (Gal. 6:1).

The *"spiritual one"* in the Verse we have just quoted, pertains to the individual who knows and understands God's Prescribed Order of Victory, which is the Cross of Christ, and only the Cross of Christ! He then relates to the individual who has been overtaken in a fault the correct Scriptural answer, to get the person on the right track.

Now the reader must understand that when the Lord forgives, which He always will, He doesn't partially forgive. He forgives totally and completely. But, if the Believer doesn't place his faith correctly, which is the Cross of Christ, the same sin is going to be committed again and again and again, no matter how hard the individual tries for the thing not to happen. That's what Paul was talking about when he said:

"For the good that I would I do not: but the evil which I would not, that I do" (Rom. 7:19).

Of course, when Paul wrote these words, he full well understood God's Prescribed Order. He was merely reaching back in his previous experience before he knew and understood the Message of the Cross. In fact, it was to Paul that the meaning of the New Covenant was given, which, in effect, is the meaning of the Cross.

WHAT HAPPENS TO THE BELIEVER WHO DOES NOT COME TO THE TRUTH OF THE CROSS, AND FOR WHATEVER REASON?

Such a Believer will be ruled by the sin nature, making his Christian experience far less than it should be. It will be a case of committing the same sin over and over again, and asking the Lord's forgiveness over and over again.

Sin is abhorrent to a true Believer. So one can well imagine the damage it does when it occurs over and over again. Sadly, that is, however, the plight of most modern Christians, and simply because they do not know nor understand God's Prescribed Order of Victory, which is the Cross of Christ.

Many individuals facing this problem over and over again have simply quit. They felt they couldn't live it and, in fact, in the way they were trying to do so they were right, they could not successfully live for the Lord in that manner. And we speak of one placing one's faith in something other than the Cross of Christ.

While many do not quit, as stated, they live far beneath their rightful, Spiritual Privileges which they should have in Christ.

As well, sin hardens the individual. It takes a deadly toll on the person. Quite often, such a person goes into false doctrine, trying to make allowances for his sin, etc.

As we have stated over and over again, the only answer for sin is the Cross of Christ. Tragically and sadly, the modern church doesn't seem to know that. They keep trying to put forth one scheme after the other to address this problem, not the least being humanistic psychology. But let us say it again:

"But this Man (this Priest, Christ Jesus), *after He had offered One Sacrifice for sins forever* (speaks of the Cross), *sat down on the Right Hand of God* (refers to the great contrast with the Priests under the Levitical system, who never sat down because their work was never completed; the Work of Christ was a 'Finished Work,' and needed no repetition)" (Heb. 10:12).

"In loving kindness Jesus came,
"My soul and mercy to reclaim,
"And from the depths of sin and shame,
"Through Grace He lifted me."

"He called me long before I heard,
"Before my sinful heart was stirred,
"But when I took Him at His Word,
"Forgiven He lifted me."

"His Brow was pierced with many a thorn,
"His Hands by cruel nails were torn,
"When from my guilt and grief, forlorn,
"In love He lifted me."

"Now on a higher plane I dwell,
"And with my soul I know 'tis well;
"Yet how or why, I cannot tell,
"He should have lifted me."

"From sinking sand He lifted me,
"With tender Hand He lifted me,
"From shades of night to plains of light,
"O praise His Name, He lifted me!"

CHAPTER 32

(1) "SO THESE THREE MEN CEASED TO ANSWER JOB, BECAUSE HE WAS RIGHTEOUS IN HIS OWN EYES.

(2) "THEN WAS KINDLED THE WRATH OF ELIHU THE SON OF BARACHEL THE BUZITE, OF THE KINDRED OF RAM: AGAINST JOB WAS HIS WRATH KINDLED, BECAUSE HE JUSTIFIED HIMSELF

RATHER THAN GOD.

(3) "ALSO AGAINST HIS THREE FRIENDS WAS HIS WRATH KINDLED, BECAUSE THEY HAD FOUND NO ANSWER, AND YET HAD CONDEMNED JOB.

(4) "NOW ELIHU HAD WAITED TILL JOB HAD SPOKEN, BECAUSE THEY WERE OLDER THAN HE.

(5) "WHEN ELIHU SAW THAT THERE WAS NO ANSWER IN THE MOUTH OF THESE THREE MEN, THEN HIS WRATH WAS KINDLED.

(6) "AND ELIHU THE SON OF BARACHEL THE BUZITE ANSWERED AND SAID, I AM YOUNG, AND YOU ARE VERY OLD; WHEREFORE I WAS AFRAID, AND DID NOT SHOW YOU MY OPINION.

(7) "I SAID, DAYS SHOULD SPEAK, AND MULTITUDE OF YEARS SHOULD TEACH WISDOM.

(8) "BUT THERE IS A SPIRIT IN MAN: AND THE INSPIRATION OF THE ALMIGHTY GIVES THEM UNDERSTANDING.

(9) "GREAT MEN ARE NOT ALWAYS WISE: NEITHER DO THE AGED UNDERSTAND JUDGMENT.

(10) "THEREFORE I SAID, HEARKEN TO ME; I ALSO WILL SHOW MY OPINION."

The pattern is:

1. As it regards Verse 1, it should be noted that this is what these *"three men"* said, and not God. Actually, the reverse is true; it is the *"three friends"* who are *"righteous in their own eyes,"* not Job.

2. As it regards Verse 2, Job was not trying to justify himself in the Eyes of God, but rather he was stating his case. As it regards Elihu, it was his self-righteousness that caused his anger against Job.

3. (Vs. 4) Elihu would have been wiser yet to have said nothing.

4. (Vs. 7) In effect, Elihu says of Job, *"You are older than I am, so you should have more wisdom, but you don't."*

5. Some claim that Elihu was a type of Christ; however, that is contradicted by his statements in Verse 10. The Lord does not give *"His opinion,"* but rather *"Thus saith the Lord."*

THE IMPERTINENCE OF ELIHU

There are some who erroneously claim

NOTES

that Elihu is a type of Christ, with some even saying that he was Christ. Nothing could be further from the truth. Elihu was just another impertinent, self-righteous individual, who thought he had a right to reprimand Job. As stated, how impertinent! How ridiculous! How wrong!

The Second Verse says he grew very angry at Job. Why?

Job had never done anything to him or anyone else for that matter, so why should this upstart be angry at Job?

He claimed that Job was *"justifying himself rather than God."*

Job did no such thing. Elihu as well as the others desired that Job would confess that he was a great sinner, that he was wicked, etc. Had Job done that, he would have been lying, because he was not those things.

To be frank, had he done so, it would not have satisfied these individuals. Self-righteousness which characterized these three friends and Elihu, is never satisfied. Irrespective as to what one may do, they are never satisfied. They were not satisfied with David when he repented before God. They wanted to kill him! To be frank, it hasn't changed from then until now.

Dependence upon the Lord and dependence upon the Lord exclusively, is an affront to self-righteousness.

THE RIGHTEOUSNESS OF CHRIST

The Righteousness of Christ, which is the only Righteousness that God will recognize, is that which is given to anyone who will register Faith in Christ, and which will be done immediately. Self-righteousness cannot tolerate such. It has its own rules and regulations and it demands that these rules and regulations be obeyed. And don't misunderstand, even if they are obeyed, that will not, as well, satisfy self-righteousness. The truth is the following:

While self-righteousness conveniently overlooks its own faults and failings, the truth is, it cannot be satisfied at all with one who has failed. Failure embarrasses self-righteousness, and again we state, while it conveniently overlooks its own failures. What self-righteousness actually demands, is that the person be destroyed, to where they will never again have any opportunity to name the Name of Christ. They have no interest in so-called Restoration, but rather, destruction.

These *"three friends,"* along with Elihu, who, incidentally, the Lord completely ignored when He did appear, wanted Job totally and completely destroyed.

They had previously claimed to have been his friends. So, now his condition shames them, and they want the whole world to know that they are totally opposed to this man. And, to be sure, they will trumpet such loud and clear. They must distance themselves from him, and while doing so, must castigate him in the worst possible terms, and before all. This is for purpose.

In their minds, they think this makes them look good. It is obvious to all concerned that Job is a wicked sinner, or he would not be in this state. So he is fair game! Not only is he fair game, but we are compelled to let the world know just how we feel about the situation, that we may look good in their eyes. So, Elihu will insert his opinion into the fray as well.

(11) "BEHOLD, I WAITED FOR YOUR WORDS; I GAVE EAR TO YOUR REASONS, WHILE YOU SEARCHED OUT WHAT TO SAY.

(12) "YES I ATTENDED UNTO YOU, AND BEHOLD, THERE WAS NONE OF YOU WHO CONVINCED JOB, OR WHO ANSWERED HIS WORDS:

(13) "LEST YOU SHOULD SAY, WE HAVE FOUND OUT WISDOM: GOD THRUSTS HIM DOWN, NOT MAN.

(14) "NOW HE HAS NOT DIRECTED HIS WORDS AGAINST ME: NEITHER WILL I ANSWER HIM WITH YOUR SPEECHES.

(15) "THEY WERE AMAZED, THEY ANSWERED NO MORE: THEY LEFT OFF SPEAKING.

(16) "WHEN I HAD WAITED, (FOR THEY SPOKE NOT, BUT STOOD STILL, AND ANSWERED NO MORE;)

(17) "I SAID, I WILL ANSWER ALSO MY PART, I ALSO WILL SHOW MY OPINION.

(18) "FOR I AM FULL OF MATTER, THE SPIRIT WITHIN ME CONSTRAINS ME.

(19) "BEHOLD, MY BELLY IS AS WINE WHICH HAS NO VENT; IT IS READY TO BURST LIKE NEW BOTTLES.

(20) "I WILL SPEAK, THAT I MAY BE REFRESHED: I WILL OPEN MY LIPS AND ANSWER.

(21) "LET ME NOT, I PRAY YOU, ACCEPT ANY MAN'S PERSON, NEITHER LET ME GIVE FLATTERING TITLES UNTO MAN.

(22) "FOR I KNOW NOT TO GIVE FLATTERING TITLES; IN SO DOING MY MAKER WOULD SOON TAKE ME AWAY."

The exposition is:

1. (Vs. 15) The *"three friends"* were amazed at this young man's impertinence; so they answered him by saying nothing.

2. Had he known that his words were going to be placed in the Holy Text, and that untold millions would read them century after century, he would wish that he had kept his mouth shut. But self-righteousness cannot do that!

3. The Twenty-first Verse declares Elihu saying that he is not going to show Job any respect.

4. The Twenty-second Verse proclaims this young man foolishly placing himself spiritually far above Job. Once again, this is a perfect example of self-righteousness.

OPINIONS

Three times in this Thirty-second Chapter, Elihu talks about *"his opinion."* As we have previously stated, once again to refute the claim by some that Elihu was a type of Christ, the Lord doesn't give His Opinion. Such thinking is foolish. The Lord gives *"the Word,"* and not an opinion. Men have opinions, not God!

MAN'S WISDOM

Once again we bring forth the fact that God allowed all that the *"three friends"* said, plus that of *"Elihu,"* to be placed in the Sacred Text. He did not allow such because they actually had something to say that was worthwhile, but rather to show us that the wisdom of man has no validity as it regards the things of the Lord. In fact, this is at least one of the reasons that the world is in the mess that it's in presently.

The Word of God is the Wisdom of God.

Yet, the world cares not at all for this *"wisdom,"* but rather their own bloated opinions, which change with the wind.

As it regards Believers, the greatest insult of all, respecting the Lord, is when the Bible is abandoned and the ways of the world, with all its phoniness, are adopted. And that's exactly what is happening presently in the modern church.

HUMANISTIC PSYCHOLOGY

Psychology is the religion of humanism. Man without God has no answer, so he has turned to the ramblings of Freud, who was as mixed up himself as it was possible for a human to be. Yet, foolish Believers say that modern man is facing problems today that are not addressed in the Bible, so modern man, they continue to say, must have the help of psychology along with the Bible. The truth is, the Bible is now given no shift at all, with most all given over to humanistic psychology.

Whatever it is that religious leaders might say, the real truth as it regards their hatred for Jimmy Swaggart, is in this very category. They have embraced this nefarious system of the world, and they do not like it at all when someone stands up against it and boldly declares its error. That is the reason they hate us as they do!

When Family Worship Center was begun in 1980, my knowledge of psychology was pretty well non-existent. If I had thought about it at all, I would have thought that they are trying to help people, and considering that people need help, well then it must be a good thing. We even went so far as to hire two psychologists to serve on the staff of Family Worship Center.

The Ministry owned an A.M. Radio Station in Baton Rouge at the time, and I gave them thirty minutes of time each day on the Station, to minister to people. Once again, I thought this was a good thing.

I did not really have time to listen to their programming, so I actually did not know what they were saying.

One of our fellow Ministers came to me, and asked, *"Do you know what they're teaching?"*

I had to admit that I didn't, which was negligence on my part.

I tuned it in, and was shocked at what I was hearing. I called both of them into my office, a man and his wife, to discuss the situation. After dealing with them for a few minutes, I realized that we were on different sides of the table so to speak.

A short time later I dismissed them, and then began to look into this system called *"psychology."*

I found from my study that it was totally opposed to what the Bible said about man. I found that psychology doesn't actually believe in sin or a sin nature. In other words, the wisdom of psychology stems from the world, and as such, is *"earthly, sensual, devilish."*

The Scripture goes on to say that it will produce *"envying, strife, confusion, and every evil work"* (James 3:15-16). So, I felt that I had to take a stand against this unscriptural system.

At that time, we had the largest television audience in the world respecting Gospel. We were on television in mostly every city and town in the U.S., not only with our Sunday program, but our daily program, Monday through Friday, as well as many other countries, with the program translated into the respective language.

As I began to speak out against this system, the anger of religious leaders knew no bounds. And please remember and understand, whenever what is being stated cannot honestly be refuted, then they will seek to destroy the person, using any method at their disposal.

In fact, there is no wickedness in the world like religious wickedness. It is that which crucified Christ, and it is just as wicked today as it was then.

Had not the Lord appeared on the scene as it regards Job, which we will study when we arrive at that juncture, Job's *"friends"* would have done everything within their power to make certain that Job did not recover from his problem. Once again I state, self-righteousness must take this tact, and for all of the ungodly, and obvious reasons.

"I wandered in the shades of night,
"Till Jesus came to me.

"And with the sunlight of His Love,
"Bid all my darkness flee."

"Though clouds may gather in the sky,
"And billows round me roll,
"However dark the world may be,
"I've sunlight in my soul."

"While walking in the Light of God,
"I sweet communion find;
"I press with holy vigor on,
"And leave the world behind."

"I cross the wide extended fields,
"I journey o'er the plain,
"And in the sunlight of His Love,
"I reap the golden grain."

"Soon I shall see Him as He is,
"The Light that came to me,
"Behold the brightness of His Face,
"Throughout Eternity."

"Sunlight, sunlight in my soul today,
"Sunlight, sunlight all along the way;
"Since the Saviour found me, took away my sin,
"I have had the sunlight of His Love within."

CHAPTER 33

(1) "WHEREFORE, JOB, I PRAY YOU, HEAR MY SPEECHES, AND HEARKEN TO ALL MY WORDS.

(2) "BEHOLD, NOW I HAVE OPENED MY MOUTH, MY TONGUE HAS SPOKEN IN MY MOUTH.

(3) "MY WORDS SHALL BE OF THE UPRIGHTNESS OF MY HEART: AND MY LIPS SHALL UTTER KNOWLEDGE CLEARLY.

(4) "THE SPIRIT OF GOD HAS MADE ME, AND THE BREATH OF THE ALMIGHTY HAS GIVEN ME LIFE.

(5) "IF YOU CAN ANSWER ME, SET YOUR WORDS IN ORDER BEFORE ME, STAND UP.

(6) "BEHOLD, I AM ACCORDING TO YOUR WISH IN GOD'S STEAD: I ALSO AM FORMED OUT OF THE CLAY.

(7) "BEHOLD, MY TERROR SHALL NOT MAKE YOU AFRAID, NEITHER SHALL MY HAND BE HEAVY UPON YOU.

(8) "SURELY YOU HAVE SPOKEN IN MY HEARING, AND I HAVE HEARD THE VOICE OF YOUR WORDS, SAYING,

(9) "I AM CLEAN WITHOUT TRANSGRESSION, I AM INNOCENT; NEITHER IS THERE INIQUITY IN ME.

(10) "BEHOLD, HE FINDS OCCASIONS AGAINST ME, HE COUNTS ME FOR HIS ENEMY,

(11) "HE PUTS MY FEET IN THE STOCKS, HE MARKS ALL MY PATHS.

(12) "BEHOLD, IN THIS YOU ARE NOT JUST: I WILL ANSWER YOU, THAT GOD IS GREATER THAN MAN.

(13) "WHY DO YOU STRIVE AGAINST HIM? FOR HE GIVES NOT ACCOUNT OF ANY OF HIS MATTERS."

The composition is:

1. (Vs. 1) Elihu demands that Job hearken to all his words. The truth is, Elihu had nothing to say, so God will ignore all that he will say, thereby, tendering the worst insult of all. His own self-righteousness screams as loud as the *"three friends"* or even louder.

2. Verse 3 proclaims the fact that evidently, Elihu has a high opinion of himself. Consequently, according to Verse 4, he will come close to saying that the words he utters are from the Lord.

3. (Vs. 5) Job did not answer him, even as he should not have.

4. In essence, according to the Sixth Verse, Elihu is saying, *"Even though I am only a man, I can give you all the answers for which you have sought!"*

HEARKEN TO ALL MY WORDS?

The Lord did not hearken to any of Elihu's words, neither did Job. But the Lord most definitely did hearken to Job's words!

There are untold thousands of preachers every Sunday who stand behind pulpits all over the world and ask, or even demand, that their listeners *"hearken to all their words."*

The problem with the *"three friends"* and Elihu was that these *"words"* were out of their own minds, and did not come from the Lord. We've got Churches full of that, which provide no help whatsoever.

The preacher learns what to say, and the Born-Again Believer learns what to speak, by and through the Apostle Paul.

Why Paul?

We do not mean from this that every other writer in the Bible should be ignored. In fact, everything written in the Word of God is of vast significance, because it is the Word of God. As we have stated previously, while inspiration does not guarantee that all that is said is true and, in fact, things said by Satan and wicked individuals, most definitely aren't true, and the Bible carries a great deal of that; however, inspiration does guarantee that it was said, whether it is true or not. But everything that comes from the Lord, is not only true, but, as well, is *"Truth."* As we state constantly, the Bible is the only revealed Truth in the world today and, in fact, ever has been. It is the road map for life, and the blueprint for eternity.

As it regards the Apostle Paul, we single him out, because it was to Paul that the meaning of the New Covenant was given, which, in effect, is the meaning of the Cross. In fact, the Cross of Christ and the New Covenant are one and the same.

WHAT WORDS WILL CHANGE PEOPLE'S LIVES?

Paul said, *"We preach Christ Crucified"* (I Cor. 1:23).

He also said to the Church at Corinth, and to us as well, *"For I determined not to know anything among you, save Jesus Christ, and Him Crucified"* (I Cor. 2:2).

He also said, *"But God forbid that I should glory, save in the Cross of our Lord Jesus Christ, by Whom the world is Crucified unto me, and I unto the world"* (Gal. 6:14).

As well he stated, *"For the preaching of the Cross is to them who perish foolishness; but unto us who are Saved it is the Power of God"* (I Cor. 1:18).

As should be overly obvious, the Apostle Paul preached the Cross. And let us look at that for a moment.

THE CROSS OF CHRIST, THE ONLY ANSWER FOR MAN

The only thing that stands between mankind and eternal Hell is the Cross of Christ. If the Cross is rejected, there remains no more Salvation. That means that those who deny the Cross of Christ are eternally lost.

It also means that the preacher must preach the Cross. If he doesn't preach the Cross, then whatever it is he is preaching, might be clever, and might be appealing to the ears of man, but it will save no souls and change no lives. So, when the Preacher says, *"Hearken unto my words,"* you had better know as to what words he is proclaiming. Regrettably and sadly, only a precious few preachers around the world are preaching the Cross.

Some are preaching the Cross relative to Salvation, and thank God for that; however, very precious few know anything about the Cross as it regards Sanctification. That means that modern Christians simply do not know how to live for God. While they are Saved, still, so much for which Christ died escapes them, simply because, it is not preached. We must never forget the following:

"So then Faith comes by hearing (it is the publication of the Gospel, which produces Faith in it), *and hearing by the Word of God* (Faith does not come simply by hearing just anything, but rather by hearing God's Word, and believing that Word)*"* (Rom. 10:17).

For the Believer to live a victorious, overcoming, Christian life, which means Victory over the world, the flesh, and the Devil, the preacher must preach the Cross as it regards Sanctification, or the people will never know, and are doomed to live so far beneath their rightful, Spiritual Privileges.

WHAT DOES IT MEAN TO PREACH THE CROSS RELATIVE TO SANCTIFICATION?

In its most abbreviated form, it refers to the fact that the Believer must understand and believe the following:

• The Believer must understand that every single thing we receive from God comes exclusively from the Lord Jesus Christ (Jn. 14:6).

• The Believer must understand that the Cross of Christ is the legal means by which all of these things are received (Rom. 6:3-5; I Cor. 1:17-18, 23; 2:2; Gal. 6:14).

• The Believer must also understand that the Holy Spirit superintends all of this.

In fact, the Cross of Christ gives the Spirit the legal means to do all that He does for us. In other words, He takes that which is of Christ, which Christ has done at the Cross, and shows it to us (Rom. 8:1-2, 11; Jn. 16:13-15).

• Because the Cross is the Means, and the only Means by which we receive from the Lord, the Cross of Christ must ever be the Object of our Faith (Gal. 2:20-21; Chpt. 5; 6:14).

These are the words that Believers need to hear and, in fact, the only words, which will set the captive free.

(14) "FOR GOD SPEAKS ONCE, YES TWICE, YET MAN PERCEIVES IT NOT.

(15) "IN A DREAM, IN A VISION OF THE NIGHT, WHEN DEEP SLEEP FALLS UPON MEN, IN SLUMBERINGS UPON THE BED;

(16) "THEN HE OPENS THE EARS OF MEN, AND SEALS THEIR INSTRUCTION,

(17) "THAT HE MAY WITHDRAW MAN FROM HIS PURPOSE, AND HIDE PRIDE FROM MAN.

(18) "HE KEEPS BACK HIS SOUL FROM THE PIT, AND HIS LIFE FROM PERISHING BY THE SWORD.

(19) "HE IS CHASTENED ALSO WITH PAIN UPON HIS BED, AND THE MULTITUDE OF HIS BONES WITH STRONG PAIN:

(20) "SO THAT HIS LIFE ABHORS BREAD, AND HIS SOUL DAINTY MEAT.

(21) "HIS FLESH IS CONSUMED AWAY, THAT IT CANNOT BE SEEN; AND HIS BONES THAT WERE NOT SEEN STICK OUT.

(22) "YES, HIS SOUL DRAWS NEAR UNTO THE GRAVE, AND HIS LIFE TO THE DESTROYERS.

(23) "IF THERE BE A MESSENGER WITH HIM, AN INTERPRETER, ONE AMONG A THOUSAND, TO SHOW UNTO MAN HIS UPRIGHTNESS:

(24) "THEN HE IS GRACIOUS UNTO HIM, AND SAYS, DELIVER HIM FROM GOING DOWN TO THE PIT: I HAVE FOUND A RANSOM.

(25) "HIS FLESH SHALL BE FRESHER THAN A CHILD'S: HE SHALL RETURN TO THE DAYS OF HIS YOUTH:

(26) "HE SHALL PRAY UNTO GOD, AND HE WILL BE FAVOURABLE UNTO HIM: AND HE SHALL SEE HIS FACE WITH JOY: FOR HE WILL RENDER UNTO MAN HIS RIGHTEOUSNESS.

(27) "HE LOOKS UPON MEN, AND IF ANY SAY, I HAVE SINNED, AND PERVERTED THAT WHICH WAS RIGHT, AND IT PROFITED ME NOT;

(28) "HE WILL DELIVER HIS SOUL FROM GOING INTO THE PIT, AND HIS LIFE SHALL SEE THE LIGHT.

(29) "LO, ALL THESE THINGS WORKS GOD OFTENTIMES WITH MAN,

(30) "TO BRING BACK HIS SOUL FROM THE PIT, TO BE ENLIGHTENED WITH THE LIGHT OF THE LIVING.

(31) "MARK WELL, O JOB, HEARKEN UNTO ME: HOLD YOUR PEACE, AND I WILL SPEAK.

(32) "IF YOU HAVE ANYTHING TO SAY, ANSWER ME: SPEAK, FOR I DESIRE TO JUSTIFY YOU.

(33) "IF NOT, HEARKEN UNTO ME: HOLD YOUR PEACE, AND I SHALL TEACH YOU WISDOM."

The composition is:

1. In the Fourteenth Verse, Elihu is claiming that God has spoken to Job, but that Job is so lacking in spirituality that he didn't perceive it.

2. In the Nineteenth Verse, the young man claims that Job is being chastised by the Lord; that is not correct.

3. (Vs. 23) In effect, Elihu is telling Job that he is the *"messenger"* with the *"interpretation"* of Job's problems. He is saying, *"I am one among a thousand."* Only youthfulness, with its immaturity and ignorance, would dare make such a statement.

4. In the Twenty-fourth Verse the young man, in essence, is saying that if Job will listen to him, his soul will be settled, his physical body will be healed, and his joy will return.

5. (Vs. 26) So, to obtain God's Righteousness, all Job has to do is to listen to Elihu; such words sound greatly familiar!

6. In the Twenty-ninth Verse the young man is saying that Job's situation is not uncommon. He could not be more wrong! How many men in history have been the subject of a contest between God and Satan? Perhaps some, but not many!

7. In the Thirty-first Verse, it seems that Job at this juncture, may have attempted to answer the impertinence of this young man, but he is told by Elihu to keep quiet. Ignorance walks where Angels fear to tread!

8. In the Thirty-second Verse, Elihu claims that he is able to justify Job. The Patriarch evidently realizes that it would be foolish to dignify this young man's statements with an answer.

9. The Thirty-third Verse portrays great arrogance! Especially in his notion that he could *"teach Job wisdom!"*

ARROGANCE, IGNORANCE, AND SELF-RIGHTEOUSNESS

Why would the Lord include the ramblings of Elihu in the Sacred Text, when He doesn't mention him when He finally does appear to Job? He mentioned the *"three friends,"* but not Elihu.

Elihu has some head knowledge as it regards the Lord, with some of it being correct and some of it being incorrect; however, he has no heart knowledge at all. In other words, he has no real personal relationship with the Lord, as did Job. As a result, he is a perfect example of the man of the world who is religious, but not Born-Again.

So, the reason for all of these men being allowed into the Sacred Text, which includes the *"three friends"* as well as *"Elihu,"* is to portray the fact, and in glaring detail, as to the ineffectiveness of natural or religious wisdom. If an individual doesn't have a personal relationship with the Lord, even as Job had, there can be no proper knowledge of the Lord.

It becomes very easy in reading the Sacred Text, to compare the others with Job. It is obvious that Job has a tremendous relationship with the Lord, and that that relationship is of longstanding.

Personal relationship with the Lord is what separates the preachers, in other words, the ones who are a blessing to humanity, and the ones who just take up space. Most preachers, sad to say, have a head knowledge of the Lord, but very little heart knowledge. At least one of the reasons is that about half of the preachers in the land, or even more, do not believe in the Baptism with the Holy Spirit with the evidence of speaking with other Tongues.

THE BAPTISM WITH THE HOLY SPIRIT

The Baptism with the Spirit is totally different than being born of the Spirit. While the Holy Spirit is most definitely involved in both cases, still, there is a great difference than being born of the Spirit than being baptized with the Spirit. The following should be noted:

• The Baptism with the Spirit is an experience separate and apart from Salvation. In other words, one first has to be Born-Again before one can be Baptized with the Spirit (Jn. 14:17).

• Everyone who is baptized with the Spirit speaks with other Tongues as the Spirit of God gives the utterance. There are no exceptions (Acts 2:4; 10:44-46; 19:1-7).

• Speaking with other Tongues is very valuable to the Believer, inasmuch as it was predicted by the Prophet Isaiah 800 years before Christ (Isa. 28:11). It brings about *"rest"* and *"refreshing"* (Isa. 28:12), proclaims also by the Tongues being spoken, *"the wonderful Works of God"* (Acts 2:11), which edifies the Believer (I Cor. 14:4). Speaking in Tongues is one's spirit praying, which is a high form of petition (I Cor. 14:14), and is a sign to the unbeliever (14:22).

• The Baptism with the Spirit gives the Believer power to carry out the Work of the Lord, which, incidentally, is desperately needed (Acts 1:8).

• The Baptism with the Spirit gives one access to the Holy Spirit, and gives the Holy Spirit access to the Believer (Jn. 16:13-15).

Let us say it again, without the Baptism with the Holy Spirit, which is always accompanied by speaking with other Tongues, there can be very little personal relationship with the Lord. Most definitely there can be some, but not what is desired.

THE URGENT NEED OF BEING BAPTIZED WITH THE SPIRIT

• Some of the last instructions that Jesus gave to His Followers was that they were to first be baptized with the Spirit, which first took place on the Day of Pentecost (Acts 1:4, 8).

• This was so important, for them to be baptized with the Spirit, that Jesus *"Commanded them that they should not depart from Jerusalem, but wait for the Promise of the Father"* (Acts 1:4). In essence, He was saying, don't go witness for Me, and don't try to do anything for Me until you are first baptized with the Spirit.

• Are these instructions incumbent upon modern Believers? Most definitely they are, with two exceptions.

1. They were then told to *"wait for the Promise of the Father."* This was because the Holy Spirit had not yet come in the new dimension that He would come on the Day of Pentecost. Now inasmuch as He has come, we don't have to wait. The only requirement for being baptized with the Spirit is being Born-Again. That being the case, the person can then be baptized immediately with the Spirit.

2. They were then to go to Jerusalem, because that's where first the Spirit would fall. After that it is anywhere.

• When Philip preached the great revival in Samaria, many were Saved, but no one was baptized with the Spirit. When word came to Jerusalem as to what had happened, immediately Peter and John went to Samaria and preached the Holy Spirit to these new converts, and then prayed for them that they might receive. They did (Acts 8:14-17). If it is to be noticed, Peter and John didn't put this situation into the future. They responded immediately, because it was imperative that these Believers be baptized with the Spirit.

• When Paul was converted on the Road to Damascus, the Lord some three days later sent Ananias that he might pray for Paul to be filled with the Spirit (Acts 9:17).

• Paul, in speaking to the Ephesian Disciples, ascertained very soon that even though they were definitely Saved, they had not been baptized with the Spirit. He explained it to them, prayed for them, and they received (Acts 19:1-7).

It is clear from the Scriptures, that there is an urgency about all of this, and for purpose and reason. I think the evidence is clear that without the Baptism with the Holy Spirit, precious little is going to actually be done for the Lord.

WHAT ABOUT THE GREAT PREACHERS OF THE PAST WHO WERE NOT BAPTIZED WITH THE SPIRIT?

Yes, preachers such as D.L. Moody, Charles Finney, and Billy Sunday, to name a few, there is no record that they nor scores like them, were baptized with the Spirit with the evidence of speaking with other Tongues. However, there was a vast difference in these preachers, and those at the present time.

Those preachers in those days were walking in all the Light they had. In other words, they did not reject the Baptism with the Spirit, for the simple reason that they knew nothing about the Baptism with the Spirit. But today, preachers have to either accept or reject the Baptism with the Holy Spirit, with the evidence of speaking with other Tongues. And when Light is given, and then rejected, that is another matter altogether.

When the Prophet Joel gave his great Prophecy as it regards the Holy Spirit, he said:

"Be glad then, you children of Zion, and rejoice in the LORD your God: for He has given you the former rain moderately, and He will cause to come down for you the rain, the former rain, and the latter rain in the first month. (The phrase, *'Be glad then, you children of Zion,'* refers to Israel now restored as the premier Nation of the world, which is her rightful place. In other words, the world cannot be properly blessed until Israel is in her rightful place, which she will be not long after the Second Coming.

"The *'former rain'* and the *'latter rain'* refer to the two rainy seasons in Israel. The first, or *'former,'* coming in October, promoted the germination and growth of the seed previously sown; the *'latter,'* coming in April, matured the crops and got them ready for harvest. Spiritually speaking, the *'former rain'* speaks of the outpouring of the Holy Spirit on the Early Church. The *'latter rain'* speaks of the outpouring of the Spirit which began at approximately the turn of the Twentieth Century and which will continue on through the Millennial Reign [James 5:7]).

"And the floors shall be full of wheat, and the vats shall overflow with wine and oil. (This speaks of the harvest of prosperity which will be gathered in the coming Kingdom Age.)

"And I will restore to you the years that the locust has eaten, the cankerworm, and the caterpillar, and the palmerworm, My great army which I sent among you. (*'And I will restore to you the years,'* refers to that period of time which began with Nebuchadnezzar and which now has lasted for about 2,500 years. The mention of the *'locust,'* etc., is meant to be symbolic of the years lost to the *'times of the Gentiles.'* The phrase, *'My great army which I sent among you,'* speaks of the great empires which ruled Israel because of Israel's sin and refusal to repent.)

"And you shall eat in plenty, and be satisfied, and praise the Name of the LORD your God, Who has dealt wondrously with you: and My People shall never be ashamed. (Now, Israel will function as she should; as a result, they will *'eat in plenty, and be satisfied.'* As well, never again will God's People *'be ashamed.'*)

"And you shall know that I am in the midst of Israel, and that I am the LORD your God, and none else: and My People shall never be ashamed. (Once again, the Holy Spirit through the Prophet uses the phrase, *'And My People shall never be ashamed,'* because Israel, in fact, has lived in *'shame'* for over 2,500 years.)

"And it shall come to pass afterward, that I will pour out My Spirit upon all flesh; and your sons and your daughters shall prophesy, and your old men shall dream dreams, your young men shall see visions (the word *'afterward'* refers to the occurrences predicted in Verses 30 through 32. This Promise of the Spirit is placed out of chronological order in order to couple it with the material blessings of Verses 21 through 27 and to provide for Acts, Chpt. 2. In fact, the phrase, *'And it shall come to pass afterward that I will pour out My Spirit upon all flesh,'* even though beginning on the Day of Pentecost, still, will not be totally fulfilled until the coming Kingdom Age.

"'And your sons and your daughters shall prophesy,' refers to the Gifts of the Spirit, which accompanied the outpouring of the Holy Spirit during the time of the Early Church, and which continues to this hour [I Cor. 12:7-11]; however, and, as stated, this will have a complete fulfillment in the coming Kingdom Age. As well, the outpouring of the Spirit is for all — old and young, men and women):

"And also upon the servants and upon the handmaids in those days will I pour out My Spirit. (Even though the words, *'in those days,'* actually refer to the coming Kingdom Age, still, and according to what was said by the Apostle Peter, that which happened on the Day of Pentecost was the beginning of the *'pouring out of My Spirit,'* which continues unto this day and, as stated, will be fully realized in the coming Kingdom Age)" (Joel 2:23-29).

ACCEPTANCE OR REJECTION?

So, as stated in the notes, the great Prophet Joel predicted that there would be a *"Former Rain"* and a *"Latter Rain."* As we also stated, the Former Rain took place in the Early Church, of which we read about in the Book of Acts. The Latter Rain began at about the turn of the Twentieth Century. While most definitely there were people baptized with the Holy Spirit in the intervening time, still, it was miniscule by comparison to what has happened in the last 100 plus years.

It has been estimated that over five hundred million people from approximately the beginning of the Twentieth Century, have been baptized with the Holy Spirit with the evidence of speaking with other Tongues. Our Ministry (Jimmy Swaggart Ministries), in fact, had the opportunity and privilege of being a small part of this great outpouring.

When we first went on Radio, which was at the beginning of 1969, the Lord began to bless abundantly. In fact, in a short period of time, we were on some 600 Stations daily in this country, with the largest daily Gospel audience in the nation.

A PERSONAL EXPERIENCE

The Lord instructed me after a short period of time, to begin teaching on the Holy

Spirit, which we did. Our program, along with other efforts all instituted by the Holy Spirit, began to have a tremendous positive effect on the hearts and lives of many Believers. The Lord also told me to set aside at least one Service during the Crusades, to pray for Believers to be baptized with the Holy Spirit, which we did.

We saw thousands filled with the Spirit.

In prayer at one particular time, the Lord told me that if I would believe Him, He would fill 1,000 people or more in a single Service.

It happened, of all places, in Madison Square Garden, in New York City.

If I remember correctly, the coliseum at that time seated approximately 19,000 people. It was either completely filled that Sunday afternoon, or almost filled. At any rate, when I finished the Message, I gave the Altar Call for people to be Saved, and many responded.

After praying with these, I invited those who were Born-Again to come and be baptized with the Holy Spirit, that is if they were not already filled.

I think I can say without fear of exaggeration that thousands came forward, filling every isle all the way to the back of the auditorium. I asked a Spirit-filled Believer to stand beside each one. I gave them instructions, exactly as the Lord had told me to do, and then prayed for them to be filled. There was a mighty Moving of the Holy Spirit.

We left almost immediately after the Service that Sunday afternoon, to fly to London, England. We arrived there the next morning.

Our hotel was situated immediately beside Hyde Park. I told Frances that I was going out and walk in the Park a while, and seek the Lord, which I did.

As I was praying, the Lord brought back to my mind the Service the night before in Madison Square Garden. As stated, it had been a great meeting.

The Lord then brought to mind the Promise that He had given me several years before, that if I would obey Him, I would see 1,000 Believers baptized with the Holy Spirit in a single Service. He then asked me, *"How many came forward yesterday afternoon?"*

I thought for a moment, knowing that it was several thousands. He then said, *"I did yesterday afternoon exactly what I said that I would do. Over 1,000 were baptized with the Spirit."*

Regrettably and sadly, probably one would have to say that there are fewer people presently being baptized with the Holy Spirit than at any time since the turn of the Twentieth Century. It is little being preached in churches, that once majored in this all-important Gift. And let the following be understood:

The less the Presence of the Holy Spirit, the less that is done for God. The more the Operation of the Spirit, the more that is done for the Lord. The Holy Spirit, one might say, is the spark plug of the church. Remove that, and there is very little left that can accomplish anything.

The great Prophet Zechariah said: *". . . Not by might, nor by power, but by My Spirit, says the LORD of Hosts* (Zech. 4:6).

"The message of the Vision to Zerubbabel and also to all others, at least according to the need was, not by military might, nor by political power, but by spiritual energy, he would certainly complete the building of the Temple.

"'*Not by* (human) *might, nor by* (human) *power, but by My Spirit,*' presents God's Method of accomplishing His Work. Everything that has ever been done on this Earth, as it regards the Godhead, has been done by the Holy Spirit, with the exception of Christ and His Crucifixion; however, the Holy Spirit even superintended that from beginning to end (Lk. 4:18-19).

"If it is claimed to be for the Lord, whatever is being done must be done by the Moving, Operation, Power, and Person of the Holy Spirit through Believers. Otherwise, it will not be recognized by God; in fact, it will be constituted as a '*work of the flesh*' (Rom. 8:1).

"'*Says the LORD of Hosts,*' presents God's Supreme Personal Power over everything in the material and Spiritual universe. All are organized under His Command. As well, the word '*Hosts,*' as used here, is associated with warfare and relates to the word '*armies.*' In other words, He is the '*Lord of Armies.*'"

"There is a song in my heart today,
"Something I never had;
"Jesus has taken my sins away,
"O say, but I'm glad!"

"Wonderful, marvelous Love He brings,
"Into a heart that's sad;
"Through darkest tunnels the soul just sings,
"O say, but I'm glad!"

"Won't you come to Him with all your care,
"Weary and worn and sad?
"You too, will sing as His Love you share,
"O say, but I'm glad!"

"O say, but I'm glad, I'm glad,
"O say, but I'm glad!
"Jesus has come and my cup's overrun,
"O say, but I'm glad!"

CHAPTER 34

(1) "FURTHERMORE, ELIHU ANSWERED AND SAID,

(2) "HEAR MY WORDS, O YOU WISE MEN; AND GIVE EAR UNTO ME, YOU WHO HAVE KNOWLEDGE.

(3) "FOR THE EAR TRIES WORDS, AS THE MOUTH TASTES MEAT.

(4) "LET US CHOOSE TO US JUDGMENT: LET US KNOW AMONG OURSELVES WHAT IS GOOD.

(5) "FOR JOB HAS SAID, I AM RIGHTEOUS: AND GOD HAS TAKEN AWAY MY JUDGMENT.

(6) "SHOULD I LIE AGAINST MY RIGHT? MY WOUND IS INCURABLE WITHOUT TRANSGRESSION.

(7) "WHAT MAN IS LIKE JOB, WHO DRINKS UP SCORNING LIKE WATER?

(8) "WHICH GOES IN COMPANY WITH THE WORKERS OF INIQUITY, AND WALKS WITH WICKED MEN.

(9) "FOR HE HAS SAID, IT PROFITS A MAN NOTHING THAT HE SHOULD DELIGHT HIMSELF WITH GOD."

The construction is:

NOTES

1. (Vs. 2) The first Fifteen Verses of this Chapter are spoken to the *"three friends,"* with the remaining Verses spoken to Job.

2. The Third Verse proclaims a proverbial expression. It says, in essence, *"It is as much the business of the ear to discriminate between wise and foolish words, as of the palate to distinguish between wholesome and unwholesome food."*

3. (Vs. 5) While it is true that Job maintained his *"righteousness"* in a certain sense, still, he had not maintained his sinfulness, which seemed to have angered the three friends plus Elihu, because they concluded him to be a great sinner.

4. (Vs. 6) Job had maintained all along that transgressions were not the cause of his terrible condition. He was right!

5. (Vs. 9) Elihu claims that Job said, *"It profits a man nothing that he should delight himself with God."* Job had not said this!

ARROGANCE

The First Verse proclaims Elihu turning away from Job, even though his conversation is about Job, turning to others who were listening. No doubt, it included the *"three friends,"* plus others.

He makes the subject of his address to them regarding Job's conduct — scarcely a polite thing to do in Job's presence.

However, at this time, Job doesn't matter, at least in their eyes and thoughts. They can say anything about him they desire to say, and what can he do about it?

As we've said previously in this Volume, when a person is down, and anyone can do any negative thing to him he so desires, and not be reprimanded, but rather applauded, then we find out how many good Believers there really are. Job found out there were not many.

Appearances can be deceiving, and most of the time are. These men, not in the wildest stretch of their imagination, could have ever dreamed what was really taking place with Job. In fact, Job did not know himself, which he voiced over and over. So, they jumped to conclusions, adding insult to injury, making the situation which Job was undergoing, even worse! Little did they realize, that their words, which they now wished they could take back, would be read by millions and millions of people, century after century.

I would hope that they ended their life as a follower of the Lord. They thought they knew a lot about Job, but the truth was, they didn't!

As the Book of Job closes, there is some evidence that they made things right with God.

The Lord told them to offer up a *"Burnt Offering,"* which they evidently did. The Scripture also says that Job prayed for them. The Lord, of which we will have more to say when we arrive at the last Chapter, referred to the entirety of their efforts as *"folly."* He also stated that His *"Wrath was kindled against them."* Quite possibly this ordeal, especially with the Lord speaking to them, turned out well. It is certainly hoped that it did. One thing is certain, the Lord, as it respects the sacrifices, which were pictures of the coming Calvary, gave them every opportunity to repent. Prayerfully they did!

(10) "THEREFORE HEARKEN UNTO ME, YOU MEN OF UNDERSTANDING: FAR BE IT FROM GOD, THAT HE SHOULD DO WICKEDNESS; AND FROM THE ALMIGHTY, THAT HE SHOULD COMMIT INIQUITY.

(11) "FOR THE WORK OF A MAN SHALL HE RENDER UNTO HIM, AND CAUSE EVERY MAN TO FIND ACCORDING TO HIS WAYS.

(12) "YES, SURELY GOD WILL NOT DO WICKEDLY, NEITHER WILL THE ALMIGHTY PERVERT JUDGMENT.

(13) "WHO HAS GIVEN HIM A CHARGE OVER THE EARTH? OR WHO HAS DISPOSED THE WHOLE WORLD?

(14) "IF HE SET HIS HEART UPON MAN, IF HE GATHER UNTO HIMSELF HIS SPIRIT AND HIS BREATH:

(15) "ALL FLESH SHALL PERISH TOGETHER, AND MAN SHALL TURN AGAIN UNTO DUST."

The exegesis is:

1. In Verse 10, Elihu says that God is not wicked. That should be obvious!

2. (Vs. 15) Why did the Lord desire that the ramblings of this man be placed in the Sacred Text? Among other reasons, He did so to show us that intellectualism is not the answer. In fact, without a true Revelation from the Lord, one cannot understand the Lord or His Word (I Cor. 2:9-10).

3. Obviously, Elihu is very lifted up with himself. At a given point in time when the Lord would appear, all of his supposed wisdom would then have no answer.

PERSONAL RELATIONSHIP

To learn about the Lord is one thing, to know Him Personally is something else altogether. Job knew the Lord Personally. This means that he had a personal relationship with Him, gained over many years. Elihu, as stated, had some head knowledge of God which he had gained in some manner, but not personal relationship.

There are supposed to be two billion adherents to Christianity in the world presently. This includes about one billion Catholics, and about one billion Protestants. As to how many of these people have a true relationship with the Lord, is anyone's guess; however, the percentage is, no doubt, very small.

As with Elihu, it's very easy to be religious. In fact, virtually the entirety of mankind, and for all time, is religious. But that within itself means nothing.

Before anyone can have any type of relationship with the Lord, which is the greatest thing on Earth, first of all that person must be *"born again."* Jesus told Nicodemus, that without being Born-Again a person could not even see the Kingdom of God, much less be a part of such (Jn. 3:3).

After one is Born-Again, then such a person must be baptized with the Holy Spirit, which will always be accompanied by the speaking with other Tongues (Acts 2:4). While one certainly can have a relationship with the Lord without this experience, that relationship, to be sure, can be greatly expanded with the advent of the Spirit Baptism. However, there are millions who have definitely been baptized with the Spirit, but, due to a lack of consecration, have precious little relationship with the Lord. The potential is there, but whether that potential will be realized is something else again.

A PERSONAL EXPERIENCE

Just today as I dictate these notes (September 23, 2008) I have just come back from a prayer meeting in the Sanctuary of Family Worship Center. A group of us gather every Tuesday at noon.

As I began to seek the Lord, there was an obvious Moving of the Holy Spirit, but then it ceased. For a period of time, the powers of darkness, which could easily be felt, attempted to hinder. And then it happened: The Spirit of God began to move on all who were there. There was nothing loud that took place, but a deep Moving and Operation of the Spirit that was obvious to all.

All of a sudden, it seemed like I was in the very Presence of God. It was not a time for requests to be made and petitions to be offered. It was just a time to praise the Lord, which most did quietly.

When that prayer time ended, it was like I was walking on clouds. I wish I could say that something like this happened every day but it doesn't. But when it does happen, it's like you've been to the very Throne of God, and in a sense, that's exactly what has happened. It's like every care is gone, every difficulty, trouble, and problem seems to disappear. No, you find that they are still there, but somehow, they don't seem to be so menacing as before. During times like that, I find that much of my Praise and Worship are in other Tongues. The great Prophet Isaiah had something to say about this. He said:

"For with stammering lips and another tongue will He speak to this people. To whom He said, This is the rest wherewith you may cause the weary to rest; and this is the refreshing . . ." (Isa. 28:11-12).

This tells us that speaking with other Tongues brings about a *"rest"* from the tiredness of the journey of life, as well, speaking with other Tongues brings about a *"refreshing,"* which rejuvenates the person.

Many people ask, *"What good is there in speaking with other Tongues?"* This mentioned by Isaiah presents two Blessings, of which there are many. Regrettably, despite this tremendous gift given to the People of God, at least to those who will believe, like Judah of old, most *"will not hear,"* even as Paul quoted Isaiah (I Cor. 14:21).

Of course, not all of my praise and worship is in other Tongues, but much of it is, and I find that it brings the *"rest"* and the *"refreshing"* exactly as the Prophet said.

THE PRESENCE OF THE LORD

Once again, this comes about through a deep, personal relationship with the Lord, which, admittedly, doesn't come easily or quickly.

I know nothing about alcohol, never having taken a drink of any type of alcoholic beverage in my life. I know nothing about drugs as well, never having partaken of such. But I know what it is to be *"high"* on the Presence of God. As I have attempted to explain, it is the most wonderful feeling, the most wonderful experience that a Believer can have.

I wish I could say that it lasts indefinitely, but it doesn't. It wears off after a period of time, but once again it is the *"rest"* and the *"refreshing,"* and is ours for the asking.

A DREAM

Some years ago the Lord gave me a dream regarding Heaven.

A dear lady had been Saved through our Ministry, and then after a period of time found that she had contracted cancer. The doctors did all they could for her and, of course, we were praying for her daily. It quickly became obvious that the Lord was not going to heal her, but rather, would take her home.

She had not been Saved very long, but the Lord had performed a beautiful work within her heart and within her life. And yet, as I would call her from time to time to pray with her, she would voice her fears to me.

"What is death like?" she would ask! *"What will Heaven be like?"* she would continue!

Of course, I could only answer her according to the Word of God. But at a point in time, the Lord gave me a dream, which I believe was especially for her.

I dreamed that Frances and Frances' Mother, along with the dear lady in question, went with me across a particular chasm. I now know that that chasm was death.

At any rate, when we crossed the chasm we were in Heaven.

I remember turning to Zoe, for that was her name, and said to her, *"Zoe, this is yours!"*

I don't know how I knew that, but somehow I did. She looked at me and said, *"But I've only been Saved a short time, and I've done so little for the Lord. Do you mean I have all of this?"*

I answered in the affirmative.

I could see Angels in the distance, and they seemed to be everywhere, yet they did not disturb us as we stood there speaking with each other. As well, I could see the spires of buildings in the distance, but that was the extent of what I was able to see. But that was not the important part.

I remember, that the Presence of the Lord, the same Presence that I've just described to you which came into the Sanctuary in our prayer meeting, seemed to fill the air. You could literally breathe it in. It was the most wonderful, the most secure, the most glorious feeling I've ever experienced. And it didn't leave. It was like I was at home. It was like it was a place to where I belonged and had belonged all of my life. It was that Presence, the Presence of the Lord that made Heaven so wonderful, so grand, so glorious. It was so wonderful, that I didn't want to leave.

But then I knew that I had to go. I turned to Zoe and said to her, *"We have to leave now, but we'll be back before very long,"* and then the dream ended.

As I related that to her over the phone, just days before she died, it seemed to strengthen her greatly, even as I knew it would. In fact, I believe the Lord purposely gave me that dream just for her; however, it blessed me greatly as well.

There is nothing in the world like the Presence of God. It is Him saying, *"I approve of what is going on."* Or, *"You are where I am, and I am where you are."* Of course, it means many things and all of them good.

(16) "IF NOW YOU HAVE UNDERSTANDING, HEAR THIS: HEARKEN TO THE VOICE OF MY WORDS.

(17) "SHALL EVEN HE WHO HATES RIGHT GOVERN? AND WILL YOU CONDEMN HIM WHO IS MOST JUST?

NOTES

(18) "IS IT FIT TO SAY TO A KING, YOU ARE WICKED? AND TO PRINCES, YOU ARE UNGODLY?

(19) "HOW MUCH LESS TO HIM WHO ACCEPTS NOT THE PERSONS OF PRINCES, NOR REGARDS THE RICH MORE THAN THE POOR? FOR THEY ALL ARE THE WORK OF HIS HANDS.

(20) "IN A MOMENT SHALL THEY DIE, AND THE PEOPLE SHALL BE TROUBLED AT MIDNIGHT, AND PASS AWAY: AND THE MIGHTY SHALL BE TAKEN AWAY WITHOUT HAND.

(21) "FOR HIS EYES ARE UPON THE WAYS OF MAN, AND HE SEES ALL HIS GOINGS.

(22) "THERE IS NO DARKNESS, NOR SHADOW OF DEATH, WHERE THE WORKERS OF INIQUITY MAY HIDE THEMSELVES.

(23) "FOR HE WILL NOT LAY UPON MAN MORE THAN RIGHT; THAT HE SHOULD ENTER INTO JUDGMENT WITH GOD.

(24) "HE SHALL BREAK IN PIECES MIGHTY MEN WITHOUT NUMBER, AND SET OTHERS IN THEIR STEAD.

(25) "THEREFORE HE KNOWS THEIR WORKS, AND HE OVERTURNS THEM IN THE NIGHT, SO THAT THEY ARE DESTROYED.

(26) "HE STRIKES THEM AS WICKED MEN IN THE OPEN SIGHT OF OTHERS;

(27) "BECAUSE THEY TURNED BACK FROM HIM, AND WOULD NOT CONSIDER ANY OF HIS WAYS:

(28) "SO THAT THEY CAUSE THE CRY OF THE POOR TO COME UNTO HIM, AND HE HEARS THE CRY OF THE AFFLICTED.

(29) "WHEN HE GIVES QUIETNESS, WHO THEN CAN MAKE TROUBLE? AND WHEN HE HIDES HIS FACE, WHO THEN CAN BEHOLD HIM? WHETHER IT BE DONE AGAINST A NATION, OR AGAINST A MAN ONLY:

(30) "THAT THE HYPOCRITE REIGN NOT, LEST THE PEOPLE BE ENSNARED."

The overview is:

1. In Verse 16, the young man insults Job by saying that his words will be so wise

that Job possibly will not be able to understand them. In fact, they will actually be the very opposite.

2. In the Seventeenth Verse, he accuses Job of condemning God.

3. (Vs. 22) He then accuses Job of being full of iniquity and, therefore, trying to hide himself from God.

4. (Vs. 23) So, according to Elihu, what the Lord has done to Job is *"right,"* because Job is so wicked.

5. (Vs. 24) So Job was once mighty, and the Lord has now broken him in pieces. That is true, but not for the reasons that Elihu or the three friends have said.

6. According to the Thirtieth Verse, Elihu now calls the great Patriarch a hypocrite.

HYPOCRITE?

Probably of all the things they said, being referred to as a hypocrite, which the three friends and Elihu did, had to be the worst cut of all, that is as it regards their accusations.

No wonder that the Lord's Wrath was kindled against them.

While they were calling Job a hypocrite, the Lord was saying of him *". . . There is none like him in the Earth, a perfect and an upright man, one who fears God, and hates evil. and still he holds fast his integrity, although you* (Satan) *move Me against him, to destroy him without cause"* (Job 2:3).

In effect, Job's *"three friends,"* plus Elihu, and all others who may have joined in this fray, even though not recorded, were functioning on the part of Satan.

Whenever we get outside of the Word of God, then we are taking Satan's part. How many Christians have fallen into this trap? Things we don't know about, it would be best that we keep our mouth shut, and leave it to the Lord. Even things that we think we have great knowledge about, if it pertains to the hurt of someone else, no matter how wrong they may seem to be, once again, we would do well to pray for them, and let it go at that.

We must never forget that we are poor, finite, human beings, freighted with failure ourselves, and actually knowing so little even of that of which we think we have great knowledge. The Holy Spirit through Paul addressed this. He said:

"But as God is true, our word toward you was not yes and no (not fickle).

"For the Son of God, Jesus Christ, Who was preached among you by us (places the argument over Paul's integrity squarely on the Gospel he preached), *even by me and Silas and Timothy, was not yes and no, but in Him was yes* (carries the idea of One Who changes not [I Sam. 15:29; Mal. 3:6]).

"For all the Promises of God in Him (in Christ) *are yes, and in Him Amen* (means these Promises will not change), *unto the Glory of God by us* (our preaching the Cross to you will bring Glory to God)" (II Cor. 1:18-20).

Whatever the situation may seem to be, the *"Promises of God in Christ"* are always *"yes, and in Him Amen."*

This means that God does not change, and will never change. And this also means that a *"no"* can be turned into a *"yes,"* as it regards the Lord. In other words, He can take an empty net with which some of the Disciples had fished all night long and had taken nothing, and fill it to the brim. Never forget it, the Promises are *"yes."*

None of this leaves any room for gossip, for backbiting, for name calling, for criticism, of which these three friends of Job and Elihu, wished they never had engaged.

(31) "SURELY IT IS MEET TO BE SAID UNTO GOD, I HAVE BORNE CHASTISEMENT, I WILL NOT OFFEND ANY MORE:

(32) "THAT WHICH I SEE NOT TEACH YOU ME: IF I HAVE DONE INIQUITY, I WILL DO NO MORE.

(33) "SHOULD IT BE ACCORDING TO YOUR MIND? HE WILL RECOMPENSE IT, WHETHER YOU REFUSE, OR WHETHER YOU CHOOSE, AND NOT I: THEREFORE SPEAK WHAT YOU KNOW.

(34) "LET MEN OF UNDERSTANDING TELL ME, AND LET A WISE MAN HEARKEN UNTO ME.

(35) "JOB HAS SPOKEN WITHOUT KNOWLEDGE, AND HIS WORDS WERE WITHOUT WISDOM.

(36) "MY DESIRE IS THAT JOB MAY BE TRIED UNTO THE END BECAUSE OF HIS ANSWERS FOR WICKED MEN.

(37) "FOR HE ADDS REBELLION UNTO HIS SIN, HE CLAPS HIS HANDS AMONG US, AND MULTIPLIES HIS WORDS AGAINST GOD."

The pattern is:

1. In Verse 31, Elihu now tells Job to repent. If Repentance actually was needed, to be sure, Elihu was not the one to carry the message.

2. (Vs. 33) In his feigned piousness, Elihu gives an altar call for Job to get right with God.

3. According to Verse 34, in other words, he tells Job that *"if you have any wisdom you will hearken unto my words."*

4. In Verse 36, he desires that Job be afflicted even more, and because he is obviously so wicked!

5. (Vs. 37) So now, Elihu becomes more bold and more rash in his accusations against Job.

KNOWLEDGE, WISDOM, AND JOB

Elihu accused Job of speaking without knowledge, and of uttering words without wisdom. The truth is, Job had light years more knowledge than did the *"three friends"* or Elihu, and especially Elihu. As well, he had wisdom that came from above, in other words, from the Lord.

Elihu was looking at Job's present situation and judging him as most people of the world judge everything. If a man drives a big car, and lives in a big house, well then he must be a very smart individual. Unfortunately, the church seems to follow suit.

If the preacher has a big church with a lot of people attending that somehow denotes his greatness, or so it is thought.

The facts are, appearances are deceiving. As it regards the Work of the Lord, God has the final say in everything. While He allows some things with some that He doesn't allow with others, this portrays His unlimited Wisdom and Knowledge. Listen to the words of the Lord as He spoke to Samuel:

"And it came to pass, when they were come (Jesse and his sons), *that he* (Samuel) *looked on Eliab, and said, surely the LORD's anointed is before him.* (This was David's brother, and he looked the part of the king. This shows us that even a great Prophet like Samuel cannot trust his own intuition. To have done so would have been to have grossly violated the Will of God. We must ardently seek God concerning His Will, as it regards all things, both small and large.)

"But the LORD said unto Samuel, Look not on his countenance, or on the height of his stature; because I have refused him: for the Lord sees not as man sees; for man looks on the outward appearance, but the LORD looks on the heart (and only God knows the heart of man).

"Then Jesse called Abinadab, and made him pass before Samuel. And he said, Neither has the LORD chosen this.

"Then Jesse made Shammah to pass by. And he said, Neither has the LORD chosen this.

"Again, Jesse made seven of his sons to pass before Samuel. And Samuel said unto Jesse, The LORD has not chosen these.

"And Samuel said unto Jesse, Are here all your Children? And he said, There remains yet the youngest, and, behold, he keeps the sheep (a Type of Christ as the good Shepherd). *And Samuel said unto Jesse, Send and fetch him: for we will not sit down till he comes hither.* (David was the youngest, and apparently his father Jesse thought it would be useless to bring him into the house. Generally, those who are totally rejected by men are the very ones whom God chooses.)

"And he sent, and brought him in. Now he was ruddy (red-haired), *and withal of a beautiful countenance* (the Hebrew says, 'with beautiful eyes'), *and goodly to look to* (to look at, handsome). *And the LORD said, Arise, anoint him: for this is he.* (It is believed that David was probably about fifteen years of age at this time. It would be years before he would take the throne, but this is the beginning of the glory days of Israel.)

"Then Samuel took the horn of oil, and anointed him in the midst of his brethren (this was Samuel's last and crowning work; he would train the man who more nearly than any other approached unto the ideal of the theocratic king, and was to Israel the Type of their coming Messiah; it was Samuel's wisdom in teaching his young men

music which gave David the skill to be the sweet singer of the Sanctuary; and we may feel sure also that when David arranged the service of the House of God, and gave Priests and Levites their appointed duties [I Chron. 23:26], the model which he set before him was that in which he had so often taken part with Samuel at Ramah, with, of course, the Lord guiding it all): *and the Spirit of the LORD came upon David from that day forward* (which would be the means by which all things good were accomplished in David's life; David's name would be the very first human name in the New Testament and the very last human name in the New Testament; in fact, the Messiah would be referred to as *'the Son of David,'* because He would come through the lineage of David's family [II Sam., Chpt. 7]). *So Samuel rose up, and went to Ramah"* (I Sam. 16:6-13).

THE WAYS OF THE LORD

That's the reason that the Lord does things as He does. He sees the heart of all people, meaning He knows everything about that person, what they have done, what they are doing, and what they will do, whereas man, as stated, can only make judgments according to outward appearances.

Elihu looks at Job sitting in an ash heap, his body covered with sores and, as well, in great pain, with all of his riches gone, his place and position in society now reduced to an ash heap, and surmises, that surely Job must be an evil person with the curse of God coming upon him, to be in this condition. He could not have been more wrong.

Are we taking a lesson from all of this?

Are we learning from this great experience given to us in the Sacred Text?

"My soul in sad exile was out on life's sea,
"So burdened with sin and distress,
"Till I heard a sweet Voice saying,
"'Make Me your choice';
"And I entered the 'haven of rest.'"

"I yielded myself to His tender Embrace,
"And Faith taking hold of the Word,
"My fetters fell off, and I anchored my soul;

"The Haven of Rest is my Lord."

"The song of my soul, since the Lord made me whole,
"Has been the old Story so blest,
"Of Jesus who'll save whosoever will have,
"A home in the 'Haven of Rest.'"

"How precious the thought that we all may recline,
"Like John the Beloved and blest,
"On Jesus' strong Arm, where no tempest can harm,
"Secure in the 'Haven of Rest.'"

"O come to the Saviour, He patiently waits,
"To save by His Power Divine;
"Come, anchor your soul in the 'Haven of Rest,'
"And say, 'My Beloved is mine.'"

CHAPTER 35

(1) "ELIHU SPOKE MOREOVER, AND SAID,

(2) "DO YOU THINK THIS TO BE RIGHT, THAT YOU SAID, MY RIGHTEOUSNESS IS MORE THAN GOD'S?

(3) "FOR YOU SAID, WHAT ADVANTAGE WILL IT BE UNTO YOU? AND, WHAT PROFIT SHALL I HAVE, IF I BE CLEANSED FROM MY SIN?

(4) "I WILL ANSWER YOU, AND YOUR COMPANIONS WITH YOU.

(5) "LOOK UNTO THE HEAVENS, AND SEE; AND BEHOLD THE CLOUDS WHICH ARE HIGHER THAN YOU.

(6) "IF YOU SIN, WHAT DO YOU DO AGAINST HIM? OR IF YOUR TRANSGRESSIONS BE MULTIPLIED, WHAT DO YOU UNTO HIM?

(7) "IF YOU BE RIGHTEOUS, WHAT DO YOU GIVE HIM? OR WHAT RECEIVES HE OF YOUR HAND?

(8) "YOUR WICKEDNESS MAY HURT A MAN AS YOU ARE; AND YOUR RIGHTEOUSNESS MAY PROFIT THE SON OF MAN.

(9) "BY REASON OF THE MULTITUDE

OF OPPRESSIONS THEY MAKE THE OPPRESSED TO CRY: THEY CRY OUT BY REASON OF THE ARM OF THE MIGHTY.

(10) "BUT NONE SAYS, WHERE IS GOD MY MAKER, WHO GIVES SONGS IN THE NIGHT;

(11) "WHO TEACHES US MORE THAN THE BEASTS OF THE EARTH, AND MAKES US WISER THAN THE FOWLS OF HEAVEN?

(12) "THERE THEY CRY, BUT NONE GIVES ANSWER, BECAUSE OF THE PRIDE OF EVIL MEN.

(13) "SURELY GOD WILL NOT HEAR VANITY, NEITHER WILL THE ALMIGHTY REGARD IT.

(14) "ALTHOUGH YOU SAY YOU SHALL NOT SEE HIM, YET JUDGMENT IS BEFORE HIM; THEREFORE YOU TRUST IN HIM.

(15) "BUT NOW, BECAUSE IT IS NOT SO, HE HAS VISITED IN HIS ANGER; YET HE KNOWS IT NOT IN GREAT EXTREMITY:

(16) "THEREFORE DOES JOB OPEN HIS MOUTH IN VAIN; HE MULTIPLIES WORDS WITHOUT KNOWLEDGE."

The pattern is:

1. (Vs. 2) Elihu accuses Job of saying that his righteousness was more than God's. Job had said no such thing!

2. In the Fourth Verse the young man claims, at least in his own eyes, that he is wiser than all who are there.

3. In Verse 7 he makes a statement that he evidently thinks is very intelligent; however, the truth is, all of these things should be known by any sincere Believer.

4. The meaning of Verse 8 is, *"We cannot add to God, or take from Him, irrespective of our obedience or disobedience,"* which all Believers, as well, should know.

5. In Verse 9 the Patriarch is accused of oppressing others.

6. In Verse 13 he is accused of being *"vain."*

7. In Verse 14, in essence, Elihu is saying, *"You are in the condition you are in, because you have not trusted the Lord."* That wasn't true either!

8. (Vs. 15) According to Elihu, while God is angry at Job, due to the wickedness of the Patriarch, God should have been much angrier. Wrong again!

Job had not committed any wickedness and neither was the Lord angry with him. In fact, God was angry, but it was not at Job, but rather the three friends. In fact, the Lord, when He finally did appear, ignored Elihu, which was perhaps the greatest insult of all.

9. (Vs. 16) Once again, Elihu accuses Job of multiplying words without knowledge. The truth is, it is Elihu and the three friends who have multiplied words without knowledge, not Job.

ACCUSATIONS

Once again, we look for the reason for all of these accusations. The reason is acute self-righteousness, that which God hates.

As we have said elsewhere in this Volume, it was self-righteousness which rejected Christ as the Messiah of Israel. It was self-righteousness which denied that His Healings and Miracles were from God. It was self-righteousness that rejected Him out of hand, meaning they rejected everything about Him. It was self-righteousness that nailed Him to the Cross.

There is only one cure, one answer, one solution for self-righteousness, and that is the Cross of Christ. If the Cross is ignored, or rejected, or even if the Cross of Christ is ignored because of ignorance, still, the end result will be the same — self-righteousness.

The Beatitudes of our Lord begin with, *"Blessed are the poor in spirit: for theirs is the Kingdom of Heaven"* (Mat. 5:3). The words *"Poor in spirit,"* means *"conscious of moral poverty."* This is a telling blow against self-righteousness.

The Apostle Paul spelled out in no uncertain terms the reason for Israel's destruction. It was self-righteousness. He said:

ISRAEL AND SELF-RIGHTEOUSNESS

"Brethren, my heart's desire and prayer to God for Israel is, that they might be Saved (Israel, as a Nation, wasn't Saved, despite their history; what an indictment!).

"For I bear them record that they have a zeal of God (should read, *'for God'*; they had a zeal which had to do with God as its

Object), *but not according to knowledge* (pertains to the right kind of knowledge).

"*For they being ignorant of God's Righteousness* (spells the story not only of ancient Israel, but almost the entirety of the world, and for all time; '*God's Righteousness*' is that which is afforded by Christ, and received by exercising Faith in Him and what He did at the Cross, all on our behalf; Israel's ignorance was willful!), *and going about to establish their own righteousness* (the case of anyone who attempts to establish righteousness by any method other than Faith in Christ and the Cross), *have not submitted themselves unto the Righteousness of God* (God's Righteousness is ensconced in Christ and what He did at the Cross),

"*For Christ is the end of the Law for Righteousness* (Christ fulfilled the totality of the Law) *to everyone who believes* (Faith in Christ guarantees the Righteousness which the Law had, but could not give)" (Rom. 10:1-4).

As we've said previously, let us say again, if the Cross of Christ is not the Object of our Faith, then self-righteousness will be the result. This means that the modern church is regrettably and sadly eaten up with this terrible soul-destroying malady. It is self-righteousness.

"Gone from my heart the world and
 all its charms;
"Now through the Blood I'm Saved
 from all alarm;
"Down at the Cross my heart is bend-
 ing low;
"The precious Blood of Jesus cleanses
 white as snow."

"Once I was lost, and way down deep
 in sin;
"Once was a slave to passions fears
 within;
"Once was a afraid to meet an angry
 God,
"But now I'm cleansed from every
 stain through Jesus' Blood."

"Once I was bound, but now I am set
 free;
"Once I was blind, but now the Light
 I see;

"Once I was dead, but now in Christ
 I live,
"To tell the world around the peace
 that He does give."

CHAPTER 36

(1) "ELIHU ALSO PROCEEDED, AND SAID,

(2) "SUFFER ME A LITTLE, AND I WILL SHOW YOU THAT I HAVE YET TO SPEAK ON GOD'S BEHALF.

(3) "I WILL FETCH MY KNOWLEDGE FROM AFAR, AND WILL ASCRIBE RIGHTEOUSNESS TO MY MAKER.

(4) "FOR TRULY MY WORDS SHALL NOT BE FALSE: HE WHO IS PERFECT IN KNOWLEDGE IS WITH YOU.

(5) "BEHOLD, GOD IS MIGHTY, AND DESPISES NOT ANY: HE IS MIGHTY IN STRENGTH AND WISDOM.

(6) "HE PRESERVES NOT THE LIFE OF THE WICKED: BUT GIVES RIGHT TO THE POOR.

(7) "HE WITHDRAWS NOT HIS EYES FROM THE RIGHTEOUS: BUT WITH KINGS ARE THEY ON THE THRONE; YES, HE DOES ESTABLISH THEM FOREVER, AND THEY ARE EXALTED.

(8) "AND IF THEY BE BOUND IN FETTERS, AND BE HOLDEN IN CORDS OF AFFLICTION;

(9) "THEN HE SHOWS THEM THEIR WORK, AND THEIR TRANSGRESSIONS THAT THEY HAVE EXCEEDED.

(10) "HE OPENS ALSO THEIR EAR TO DISCIPLINE, AND COMMANDS THAT THEY RETURN FROM INIQUITY.

(11) "IF THEY OBEY AND SERVE HIM, THEY SHALL SPEND THEIR DAYS IN PROSPERITY, AND THEIR YEARS IN PLEASURES.

(12) "BUT IF THEY OBEY NOT, THEY SHALL PERISH BY THE SWORD, AND THEY SHALL DIE WITHOUT KNOWLEDGE.

(13) "BUT THE HYPOCRITES IN HEART HEAP UP WRATH: THEY CRY NOT WHEN HE BINDS THEM.

(14) "THEY DIE IN YOUTH, AND THEIR LIFE IS AMONG THE UNCLEAN.

(15) "HE DELIVERS THE POOR IN HIS AFFLICTION, AND OPENS THEIR EARS IN OPPRESSION.

(16) "EVEN SO WOULD HE HAVE REMOVED YOU OUT OF THE STRAIT INTO A BROAD PLACE, WHERE THERE IS NO STRAITNESS: AND THAT WHICH SHOULD BE SET ON YOUR TABLE SHOULD BE FULL OF FATNESS.

(17) "BUT YOU HAVE FULFILLED THE JUDGMENT OF THE WICKED: JUDGMENT AND JUSTICE TAKE HOLD ON YOU.

(18) "BECAUSE THERE IS WRATH, BEWARE LEST HE TAKE YOU AWAY WITH HIS STROKE: THEN A GREAT RANSOM CANNOT DELIVER YOU.

(19) "WILL HE ESTEEM YOUR RICHES? NO, NOT GOLD, NOR ALL THE FORCES OF STRENGTH.

(20) "DESIRE NOT THE NIGHT, WHEN PEOPLE ARE CUT OFF IN THEIR PLACE.

(21) "TAKE HEED, REGARD NOT INIQUITY: FOR THIS YOU HAVE CHOSEN RATHER THAN AFFLICTION.

(22) "BEHOLD, GOD EXALTS BY HIS POWER: WHO TEACHES LIKE HIM?

(23) "WHO HAS ENJOINED HIM HIS WAY? OR WHO CAN SAY, YOU HAVE WROUGHT INIQUITY?

(24) "REMEMBER THAT YOU MAGNIFY HIS WORK, WHICH MEN BEHOLD.

(25) "EVERY MAN MAY SEE IT; MAN MAY BEHOLD IT AFAR OFF."

The construction is:

1. (Vs. 1) If Elihu had been led by the Holy Spirit, he would not have even begun, much less proceeded.

2. (Vs. 4) His statement, *"He who is perfect in knowledge is with you,"* presents that which is the height of arrogance.

3. In the Sixth Verse, in essence, Elihu tells Job that his life is not going to be preserved. In other words, Job is going to die. The truth is, Job would live another 140 years, for a total of 210 years (42:16).

4. (Vs. 11) Elihu claims that if one fully obeys the Lord, *"They shall spend their days in prosperity, and their years in pleasures."* The truth is, the Righteous are told to expect tribulations and persecutions (Jn. 16:33; Acts 14:22; II Tim. 3:12; Heb. 12:1-11; I Pet. 4:12-13).

NOTES

5. In the Eighteenth Verse, the young man is saying that God is so angry with Job that He has taken away all his possessions, plus his health, and is now very close to taking his life — and there is nothing Job can do to stop it.

First of all, and as already stated, there was no wrath with God concerning Job; however, there definitely would be wrath from God concerning these individuals who judged Job (42:7).

6. In Verse 21, he accuses Job of choosing iniquity. The tragedy of Eliphaz, Bildad, Zophar, and now Elihu is that they actually were doing the work of Satan. All their accusations, judgmental attitudes, and approaches to Job were far more in keeping with the destructive work of Satan than of God.

7. In the Twenty-fifth Verse, Elihu says, in essence, that anyone could see how wrong Job is.

PERFECT IN KNOWLEDGE

What arrogance! Elihu claims to be perfect in knowledge. How much immaturity does one have to have in order to make such a statement?

If every human being would weigh their words very carefully, understanding that God hears all, knows all, and sees all, and that they will have to give account for what they say, fewer words would, no doubt, be spoken, or if spoken, would be said in a far different way.

Each one of these four men judged Job severely. Why?

• Self-righteousness: This terrible sin must defend itself and, as well, has all the answers for others.

• A lack of knowledge of the Word of God: As we have stated, these individuals knew about God, but had precious little, if any, relationship with God. Most of the erroneous actions of the Christian world are carried out because of not knowing the Word of God. There was a time that theology was the Queen of the Sciences; now, psychology holds that position. The Bible is, by and large, a neglected, unread, ignored Book.

• A lack of fear of God: Elihu would be ignored by God; however, the three friends would incur the wrath of God to such an extent that they would come close to eternal damnation. If they had feared God, they would have been very loath to voice their judgmental accusations. Sadly, there is very little of the fear of God in the world or in the church.

Elihu was pronouncing judgment and death on Job, which is exactly what Satan desired to do when God was about to pronounce Blessing and more Abundant Life.

HOW MANY CHRISTIANS ARE DOING THE WORK OF SATAN?

We are speaking of Christians being an *"accuser of the Brethren."* Listen to John the Beloved as he addresses this problem:

"And I heard a loud voice saying in Heaven (presents the white-robe wearers of Rev. 6:10-11), *Now is come Salvation, and strength, and the Kingdom of our God* (presents the triumph of Christ), *and the power of His Christ* (refers to the fact that Christ will rule this world, not Satan)*: for the accuser of our Brethren is cast down, which accused them before our God day and night.* (This implies that either Satan or one of his fallen Angels is before the Throne of God, accusing the Brethren constantly [Job, Chpts. 1-2].)

"And they overcame him by the Blood of the Lamb (the power to overcome and overwhelm the kingdom of Satan is found exclusively in the Blood of the Sacrifice of the Son of God, and our Faith in that Finished Work [Rom. 6:3-5, 11, 14]), *and by the word of their testimony* (the 'testimony' must pertain to the fact that the Object of our Faith is the Cross, and exclusively the Cross, which then gives the Holy Spirit latitude to work within our lives)*; and they loved not their lives unto the death.* (This refers to the fact that the Believer must not change his testimony regarding the Cross to something else, even if it means death)" (Rev. 12:10-11).

As a Believer, I am to judge doctrine as it is presented by all men, irrespective as to whom they might be; however, when it comes to their personal situation, in other words their victory or the lack thereof as it regards the world, the flesh, and the Devil, I am not to accuse them, irrespective of the failures. Of course, if there is sin being committed, and the individual shows no inclination toward ridding himself or herself of such, then fellowship would have to be withdrawn. But, if the person is trying, I, as a Believer, am to never join forces with Satan, as it regards accusing my Brother or Sister. Let us look at this a little closer:

THE EXAMPLE OF CORINTH

Paul said:

"It is reported commonly that there is fornication among you (fornication speaks of all types of immorality; it seemed to have been more widespread than just a case or two), *and such fornication as is not so much as named among the Gentiles* (meaning this type was not common among the Gentiles), *that one should have his father's wife* (refers to the man's stepmother; it also seems the father was alive [II Cor. 7:12].)

"And you are puffed up (it seems that some were attempting to say such was allowed under the guise of Christian liberty), *and have not rather mourned* (presents that which should have been the norm, but seemingly was not), *that he who has done this deed might be taken away from among you* (the idea is the individual repent, thereby, ceasing such activity or be disfellowshipped).

"For I verily, as absent in body, but present in spirit (means that even though he is not present personally in Corinth, the direction he will now give is still to be taken just as seriously as if he were there personally), *have judged already, as though I were present, concerning him who has so done this deed.* (Does not, as some think, contradict Jesus' instructions to not judge [Mat. 7:1-5]. Paul is judging an action here, as all Believers are called upon to do, i.e., 'Fruit' [Mat. 7:15-20].)

"In the Name of our Lord Jesus Christ (refers to Christ as the Head of the church), *when you are gathered together* (presents the authority of the local church), *and my spirit* (refers to Paul being there in spirit, even though he could not be there in the flesh), *with the Power of our Lord Jesus Christ.* (The authority is in the 'Name,' and the 'Power' is in the Person of Christ. This recognizes Him

totally as the Head of the Church.)

"*To deliver such an one* (the one committing the sin of incest) *unto Satan for the destruction of the flesh* (it refers to ceasing all prayer for such an individual, and can be done by the local Body, providing the church is correct in its position; God will no more honor wrong committed by the church than He will by an individual), *that the spirit may be saved in the Day of the Lord Jesus* (it is hoped that such action will cause the person to repent)" (I Cor. 5:1-5).

As Paul gave that admonition in his First Letter to the Corinthians, we have no idea as to the outcome; however, quite possibly the end of the matter is given us in his Second Letter to the Church at Corinth. Some say that this, which we are about to give had nothing to do with the situation addressed in the Fifth Chapter of I Corinthians. That may be true; however, the principle is the same irrespective! In his Second Letter to the Church at Corinth, the Apostle said:

FORGIVENESS

"*But if any have caused grief, he has not grieved me, but in part* (presents the Apostle dealing with the person who is probably the incestuous one of I Cor., Chpt. 5)*: that I may not overcharge you all.* (He didn't want everyone in the Church at Corinth to think he was putting all in the same category of wrong direction.)

"*Sufficient to such a man is this punishment* (means that turning him over to Satan had accomplished all that was desired [I Cor. 5:4-5])*, which was inflicted of many.* (Most of the Church obeyed Paul by turning the man over to Satan for the destruction of the flesh. Some few didn't, which means they didn't go along with what Paul had said.)

"*So that contrariwise you ought rather to forgive him, and comfort him* (show love toward the man who had sinned and now repented), *lest perhaps such a one should be swallowed up with overmuch sorrow* (sink into despair).

"*Wherefore I beseech you that you should confirm your love toward him* (do more than just say you love him, but rather show your love to him).

NOTES

"*For to this end also did I write, that I might know the proof of you, whether you be obedient in all things.* (In I Cor., Chpt. 5, the man was on trial, now the Church is on trial.)

"*To whom you forgive anything* (forgive the man), *I forgive also* (I forgive you for taking the wrong direction at the beginning)*: for if I forgave anything, to whom I forgave it, for your sakes forgave I it in the Person of Christ* (forgiveness is a great part of the Christian Faith, and is demanded by Christ [Mat. 6:14-15]);

"*Lest Satan should get an advantage of us* (if we obey the Word, Satan will have no advantage)*: for we are not ignorant of his devices.* (His ways, which take advantage of the Christian's wrong direction)" (II Cor. 2:5-11).

Once again we make mention of the fact that some say what Paul is addressing in the Second Chapter of II Corinthians has nothing to do with what he addressed in the Fifth Chapter of I Corinthians. Again, we also reiterate, that may very well be the case; however, it really doesn't matter, because the principle is the same whoever it was.

The man had committed a grievous sin. It was called to Paul's attention and, in essence, he says that the man must repent or be disfellowshipped. And, of course, to repent meant that he would have to cease living with his stepmother, in essence, committing the terrible sin of incest.

If, in fact, the situation addressed in Paul's Second Letter to the Church at Corinth, was the same situation, then it seems that the man truly repented. Paul is telling the Church, due to this fact, to welcome him back into the fellowship. So, in essence, even as we stated, whereas in his First Letter, the man was on trial, now the Church is on trial. Every evidence is that they heeded Paul's admonition, and forgave the man, and welcomed him back.

In such a situation as that, which was bad to say the least, the person had to repent or be disfellowshipped. And if he properly repented, which means he ceased doing what he had been doing, which was wrong, and such was obvious to all, he was to be forgiven and welcomed back. That was the Word of the Lord, and that is the Word of the Lord.

While something like that most definitely

has to be dealt with, it is to be done the Biblical way.

Some Bible Scholars actually think that this man committing this terrible sin was one of the leaders in the Church, i.e., one of the pastors. It really doesn't matter, because the situation is the same irrespective. However, the point I wish to make is, the same rules that applied to others in the Church, and I speak of the laity, also applied to the preacher, that is if he really was one of the preachers.

As it regards forgiveness of sin, the Lord does not have one type of Repentance for one and another type for another. It is all the same.

It's sad, in the Bible Repentance guarantees Restoration, fellowship and ministry, while in the modern church, Repentance represents destruction. However, that is a sure portrayal of self-righteousness. It is the Believer joining hands and mouth with Satan, seeking to *"steal, kill, and destroy."* Jesus does the opposite, He gives *"more abundant life"* (Jn. 10:10).

SIN AND CALVARY

Sin can only be addressed at Calvary and, in fact, can be addressed in no other way. This is the problem with the world, it tries to address sin by changing its name, or by proposing every scheme of which one could think. Everything is to no avail, as everything in such a case has to be of no avail. The sad thing is, the church is adopting the ways of the world as it regards dealing with this monster. This is a tragedy, because it will cause spiritual wreckage, and perhaps the wreckage in every capacity, of anyone who follows such a course.

When Jesus died on Calvary, the sacrifice of Himself, which God accepted, atoned for all sin, past, present, and future, at least for all who will Believe (Jn. 3:16).

One of the major sins of the church, is trying to add something to the Grace of God. When a Believer repents of their sin, whomever they might be, and whatever sin it is that has been committed, such a person is promised instant forgiveness and cleansing (I Jn. 1:9). And please understand, the Lord never partially forgives, but always forgives totally and completely. In other words, there is no such thing as a partial justification. One is either Justified wholly, or not justified at all!

All too often, the church is not satisfied to accept that which the Lord has provided, but rather attempts to introduce something else along with Repentance. The Catholic Church calls it *"penance."* The Protestant Church doesn't refer to such as *"penance,"* but that's exactly what it is.

If a person is told they have to repent before the Lord and, as well, perform some type of work before their Repentance is recognized, to be sure, such an effort, whatever it might be, nullifies the Repentance. It makes a mockery of Christ and what Christ did at the Cross.

While sin is a bitter business, in fact, the most destructive on the face of the Earth; still, and because it is so terrible, the Cross is the only answer for this thing.

In the Assemblies of God Denomination, if a preacher does something wrong, he is not allowed to preach for two years. At least that's what it was some time ago. It may possibly be changed by now.

But to clarify what I said, he can preach in old folk's homes, or on the street corner, or at jails, but not in a church.

Does that make sense?

Of course, the answer to that is an obvious *"no."* Preaching is preaching, and if it's wrong to preach in the church, then it's wrong to preach anywhere else.

Such is penance, whatever other name it might be given, and is a mockery in the sight of God.

When the Denomination previously mentioned was first formed, if a preacher did something wrong, he was to never be allowed to preach again. That was later shortened to five years, and then to two. As stated, I don't know what it is at present.

The answer to that is, if what was being done originally was Scriptural, how could it be changed? The truth is, none of it was Scriptural, as none of it is Scriptural.

Furthermore, if one submits to such error, one is joining in such a sin, thereby, as well, making a mockery of Christ and what He did at the Cross, which the Lord can never accept.

THE ATONEMENT

The Atonement of Christ, that is, what He did for us at the Cross, is very, very special. In fact, it is the single-most important thing in the annals of human history. To tamper with it in any way, is to make a mockery of the great price that Jesus has paid for us.

These religious leaders, whomever they might have been, and whomever they might be, are simply engaging in punishment. They desire to punish the individual for what he has done. Do they not stop to realize, that Christ has already been punished for us? And if we engage in punishment, thinking somehow it atones for sin, we are, in effect, saying that what Christ did at the Cross was not sufficient, in other words, He didn't suffer enough, and we have to add our suffering to His. I think it should go without saying, and be overly obvious, that such is an insult to Christ!

For any individual to even insinuate that Christ did not suffer enough on the Cross is an insult to Him of the highest order. When men make rules that aren't Scriptural, those rules always have negative repercussions. If it is unscriptural, in getting back to the original thought, those who demand such have become *"an accuser of the Brethren,"* which is Satanic!

This is exactly what the *"three friends"* and Elihu were doing. They were accusing Job, and to be sure, the Lord did not take kindly to such an action.

(26) "BEHOLD, GOD IS GREAT, AND WE KNOW HIM NOT, NEITHER CAN THE NUMBER OF HIS YEARS BE SEARCHED OUT.

(27) "FOR HE MAKES SMALL THE DROPS OF WATER: THEY POUR DOWN RAIN ACCORDING TO THE VAPOUR THEREOF:

(28) "WHICH THE CLOUDS DO DROP AND DISTIL UPON MAN ABUNDANTLY.

(29) "ALSO CAN ANY UNDERSTAND THE SPREADINGS OF THE CLOUDS, OR THE NOISE OF HIS TABERNACLE?

(30) "BEHOLD, HE SPREADS HIS LIGHT UPON IT, AND COVERS THE BOTTOM OF THE SEA.

(31) "FOR BY THEM JUDGES HE THE PEOPLE; HE GIVES MEAT IN ABUNDANCE.

(32) "WITH CLOUDS HE COVERS THE LIGHT; AND COMMANDS IT NOT TO SHINE BY THE CLOUD THAT COMES BETWIXT.

(33) "THE NOISE THEREOF SHOWS CONCERNING IT, THE CATTLE ALSO CONCERNING THE VAPOUR."

The pattern is:

1. (Vs. 27) All of this stated by Elihu is from intellectualism.

It shows not at all any relationship with the Lord; and regrettably, it is the state of many modern professing Believers as well!

2. While Elihu utters many words, still, in reality, he is saying nothing.

INTELLECTUALISM

Intellectualism is the power of knowing as distinguished from the power to feel and to will. It has to do with the capacity for knowledge and, thereby, rational or intelligent thought. Intellectualism concerns what a person has learned, or rather think they have learned. It has nothing to do with God, Who deals with mankind in the realm of Revelation. While the Lord most definitely places no premium whatsoever on ignorance, as ought to be obvious, still, men cannot reach God by the means of intellectualism. In fact, man cannot reach God at all by his own ingenuity.

As stated, God has to reveal Himself to the individual, and He does such through many avenues, i.e., *"the Word, the preaching and teaching of the Word, the Word in a song, with the Holy Spirit acting upon that Word relative to the person in question, whomever they might be."*

It is quickly obvious that Elihu is lifted up in himself because of his intellectualism. He has evidently studied much and, thereby, knows some things about God. But, as we have previously stated, while he knew some things about the Lord, the truth is, he did not really know the Lord.

As well, when a person truly knows the Lord, meaning they have been Born-Again and, thereby, has a relationship with the Lord, they will then really begin to learn Who the Lord is, what the Lord is, and how the Lord is. The Born-Again experience literally makes us a Child of God, and as Paul put it, an heir of God, and a joint-heir with Jesus Christ. Concerning this, Paul said:

"*For as many as are led by the Spirit of God* (the Spirit will always lead us to the Cross), *they are the Sons of God* (we live as Sons of God, which refers to total Victory within every aspect of our lives; if the sin nature is dominating a person, he certainly isn't living as a Son of God).

"*For you have not received the spirit of bondage* (to try to live after a system of works and laws will only succeed in placing one in '*bondage*') *again to fear* (such living creates a perpetual climate of fear in the heart of such a Believer); *but you have received the Spirit of Adoption* (the Holy Spirit has adopted us into the Family of God), *whereby we cry, Abba Father* (the Holy Spirit enables the Child of God to call God '*Father*,' which is done so because of Jesus Christ).

"*The Spirit itself* (Himself) *bears witness with our spirit* (means that He is constantly speaking and witnessing certain things to us), *that we are the Children of God* (meaning that we are such now, and should enjoy all the privileges of such; we can do so if we will understand that all these privileges come to us from God, by the means of the Cross):

"*And if children* (Children of God), *then heirs* (a privilege); *heirs of God* (the highest enrichment of all), *and joint-heirs with Christ* (everything that belongs to Christ belongs to us through the Cross, which was done for us); *if so be that we suffer with Him* (doesn't pertain to mere suffering, but rather suffering '*with Him*,' referring to His Suffering at the Cross which brought us total Victory), *that we may be also glorified together* (He has been glorified, and we shall be glorified; all made possible by the Cross)" (Rom. 8:14-17).

Millions have tried to learn about God without becoming a Child of God first, and such pursuits only lead to great confusion.

For all his pontificating, Elihu did not know the Lord!

"*I was sinking deep in sin,*
"*Far from the peaceful shore,*
"*Very deeply stained within,*
"*Sinking to rise no more;*
"*But the Master of the sea,*

NOTES

"*Heard my despairing cry,*
"*From the waters lifted me,*
"*Now safe am I.*"

"*All my heart to Him I give,*
"*Ever to Him I'll cling,*
"*In His blessed Presence live,*
"*Ever His Praises sing.*
"*Love so mighty and so true,*
"*Merits my soul's best songs;*
"*Faithful, loving service too,*
"*To Him belongs.*"

"*Souls in danger, look above,*
"*Jesus completely saves;*
"*He will lift you by His Love,*
"*Out of the angry waves.*
"*He's the Master of the sea,*
"*Billows His Will obey;*
"*He your Saviour wants to be,*
"*Be Saved today.*"

"*Love lifted me!*
"*Love lifted me!*
"*When nothing else could help,*
"*Love lifted me.*
"*Love lifted me!*
"*Love lifted me!*
"*When nothing else could help,*
"*Love lifted me.*"

CHAPTER 37

(1) "AT THIS ALSO MY HEART TREMBLES, AND IS MOVED OUT OF HIS PLACE.

(2) "HEAR ATTENTIVELY THE NOISE OF HIS VOICE, AND THE SOUND THAT GOES OUT OF HIS MOUTH.

(3) "HE DIRECTS IT UNDER THE WHOLE HEAVEN, AND HIS LIGHTNING UNTO THE ENDS OF THE EARTH.

(4) "AFTER IT A VOICE ROARS: HE THUNDERS WITH THE VOICE OF HIS EXCELLENCY; AND HE WILL NOT STAY THEM WHEN HIS VOICE IS HEARD.

(5) "GOD THUNDERS MARVELLOUSLY WITH HIS VOICE; GREAT THINGS DOES HE, WHICH WE CANNOT COMPREHEND.

(6) "FOR HE SAYS TO THE SNOW, BE YOU ON THE EARTH; LIKEWISE TO THE SMALL RAIN, AND TO THE GREAT RAIN

OF HIS STRENGTH.

(7) "HE SEALS UP THE HAND OF EVERY MAN; THAT ALL MEN MAY KNOW HIS WORK.

(8) "THEN THE BEASTS GO INTO DENS, AND REMAIN IN THEIR PLACES.

(9) "OUT OF THE SOUTH COMES THE WHIRLWIND: AND COLD OUT OF THE NORTH.

(10) "BY THE BREATH OF GOD FROST IS GIVEN: AND THE BREADTH OF THE WATERS IS STRAITENED.

(11) "ALSO BY WATERING HE WEARIES THE THICK CLOUD: HE SCATTERS THE BRIGHT CLOUD:

(12) "AND IT IS TURNED ROUND ABOUT BY HIS COUNSELS: THAT THEY MAY DO WHATSOEVER HE COMMANDS THEM UPON THE FACE OF THE WORLD IN THE EARTH.

(13) "HE CAUSES IT TO COME, WHETHER FOR CORRECTION, OR FOR HIS LAND, OR FOR MERCY."

The construction is:

1. (Vs. 1) It seems that Elihu's fear of God was somewhat misplaced. He seems to be far more concerned about God's *"acts"* than of God Himself.

2. As it regards Verse 2, the facts were that Job had heard; neither Elihu nor the three friends had. They were judging from outward appearance, as all judging is done. That's the reason we are told not to judge (Mat. 7:1-2).

3. (Vs. 5) If it is to be noticed, all of these things said by Elihu are that which every Believer already knows.

4. (Vs. 10) Please remember, Inspiration guarantees that what is said was actually said, and by the person to whom it is attributed. However, that doesn't mean that it is true; in fact, much of what the *"three friends"* and Elihu said was completely untrue.

THAT WHICH THE LORD ALLOWS IS NOT ALTOGETHER THAT WHICH HE CAUSES

The terminology used by Elihu as it regards the Lord is from the basis, as stated, of intellectualism rather than relationship. His *"fear"* was more of what God could do than Who God was. Even though God would ignore Elihu, seemingly considering that due to his youthfulness that his statements were not worthy of response, still, had he known that God would register great anger at Job's *"three friends"* for basically similar statements, perhaps his fear would have been directed differently.

He claims to fear God, but thinks nothing of judging Job very harshly. And why not? Job is obviously under the judging Hand of God because of his great iniquity, or so he thinks! He is bereft of all his possessions and his health. He is sitting at the very edge of death; consequently, it is very easy for the *"three friends"* and for *"Elihu"* to render their judgments and rather loudly at that. There was not one single person who contradicted what they said; all agreed; consequently, they felt very safe. Little did they realize the following:

• That God was testing them as well as Job. Job would pass the test; they would fail.

• Public opinion has no bearing whatsoever on God.

• All of their judgment and, in fact, the judging of the entirety of the world of that day was wrong.

• God had already said of Job, *"There is none like him in all the Earth."*

• Because of their statements about God, they would come very close to eternal damnation. They did not realize that when they were making their accusations against Job, they were, in effect, making their accusations against God.

The Lord allowed all of this to happen, although He most definitely did not cause it. While He did cause the situation that took place with Job, in no way was He responsible for the action of the individuals who judged Job, and most severely.

THE FREE WILL OF MAN

God gave man the capacity for free will. In that free will he has the capacity also to *"reason,"* which sets man apart, and greatly so, from the animal kingdom. Let it be known first of all, man is not an animal. He is a human being, in effect, a *"living soul"* (Gen. 2:7).

The Scripture tells us that God made animals before He made man. It says:

"And God said, Let the Earth bring forth the living creature after his kind, cattle, and creeping thing, and beasts of the Earth after his kind: and it was so (proclaims the fact that God leaves nothing empty that He has made, but furnishes all with His store and riches).

"And God made the beasts of the Earth after his kind, and cattle after their kind, and everything that creeps upon the Earth after his kind: and God saw that it was good (tells us unequivocally that God designed each species of the animal kingdom in such a way that it cannot be crossed).

"And God said, Let Us make man in Our Image, after Our Likeness (the creation of man was preceded by a Divine consultation; as well, the pronouns *'Us'* and *'Our'* proclaim the consultation held by the Three Persons of the Divine Trinity, Who were One in the creative work; *'image'* and *'likeness'* enable us to have fellowship with God; however, it does not mean we are gods, or can become gods; *'in Our Image, after Our Likeness'* actually refers to true Righteousness and Holiness [Eph. 4:24])*: and let them have dominion over the fish of the sea, and over the fowl of the air, and over the cattle, and over all the Earth, and over every creeping thing that creeps upon the Earth* (this dominion was given by God to man, and is always subject to God; the relationship of man to the balance of creation is now defined to be one of rule and supremacy; this sphere of His lordship is from the lowest of the highest of the subjects placed beneath his sway).

"So God created man in His Own Image (the word *'man'* should have the definite article and should read *'the man,'* that is, Adam — the same man Adam spoken of in 2:7; these are not, therefore, two accounts of the creation of man, but one Divine statement)*, in the Image of God created He them* (the Image of God was lost at the Fall; however, the restoration of the Image was carried out at the Cross, but the completion of that restoration will not take place until the First Resurrection)*; male and female created He them* (represents, at least as far as we know, the first time that God has created the female gender, at least as it regards

NOTES

intelligent beings; there is no record of any female Angels).

"And God blessed them (again, speaks of the ability to reproduce), *and God said unto them, Be fruitful, and multiply, and replenish the Earth* (the word *'replenish'* carries the idea of a former creation on the Earth before Adam and Eve; according to Isa., Chpt. 14 and Ezek., Chpt. 28, Lucifer ruled this world for an undetermined period of time, and did so in Righteousness and Holiness as a beautiful Angel created by God; if, in fact, he did rule the world at that time, it would stand to reason that there had to be some type of creation on the Earth for him to rule; the word *'replenish'* refers to that creation), *and subdue it* (and that man has done; however, he would have done it much sooner, but for the Fall)*: and have dominion over the fish of the sea, and over the fowl of the air, and over every living thing that moves upon the Earth"* (Gen. 1:24-28).

HIGHER THAN THE ANGELS

The Bible teaches that man was originally made higher than the Angels, in fact, higher than any other creation of God.

David said:

"O LORD, our LORD, how excellent is Your Name in all the Earth! Who has set Your Glory above the heavens (this Psalm pictures the happiness that is to fill the Earth when, after the destruction of the Antichrist and his followers, the Messiah will establish His Kingdom of Righteousness and Peace, and His right to ascend the Throne).

"Out of the mouth of babes and sucklings have You ordained strength because of Your enemies, that You might still the enemy and the avenger (the word *'babes'* is figurative and portrays the redeemed; the redeemed will praise Him because He has *'stilled the enemy and the avenger'* — namely Satan).

"When I consider Your heavens, the work of Your Fingers, the moon and the stars, which You have ordained (the argument of Verses 3-8 is the amazing Love of Christ in coming forth from the Highest Glory to redeem a being so insignificant as man)*;*

"What is man, that You are mindful of him? And the son of man, that You visit him? (God became man and went to Calvary

in order to redeem fallen humanity. The price that was paid for that Redemption proclaims to us the worth of man, which, in fact, is God's highest Creation.)

"*For You have made him a little lower than the Angels, and have crowned him with glory and honor* (the Hebrew word '*Elohim*' here translated '*Angels*' should have been translated '*God*,' or '*Godhead*,' for that's what the word actually means; there is no place in the Old Testament where '*Elohim*' means '*Angels*'; this means that man was originally created higher than the Angels, and through Christ will be restored to that lofty position [Rom. 8:14-17]).

"*You made him to have dominion over the works of Your Hands; You have put all things under His Feet* (in their fullness, these words given here are only true of the God-Man, Jesus Christ [Mat. 28:18]; Christ has been exalted to a place higher than Angels or any other being except the Father; redeemed man is to be raised up to that exalted position with Him [Eph. 2:6-7])*:*

"*All sheep and oxen, yes, and the beasts of the field;*

"*The fowl of the air, and the fish of the sea, and whatsoever passes through the paths of the seas* (man was made to have dominion over all this).

"*O LORD, our LORD, how excellent is Your Name in all the Earth!* (Christ is the Head of the Church, which is His Body; ultimately, that which is given by Promise will, upon the Resurrection of Life, be carried to its ultimate victorious conclusion)" (Ps. 8:1-9).

So, the great Eighth Psalm, written by David, proclaims to us who and what man actually is, and how He was created.

Due to the Fall, we only see a shell of what God originally created. In fact, if one wants to know what man was originally like, and will be again in the coming Resurrection of Life, one need only look at Christ, Who was the perfect Man, the Man Christ Jesus.

The will of man is sacrosanct as far as God is concerned, meaning that God, despite having the power to do so, will never violate the free will of man. He will speak to man, deal with man, move upon man, try to persuade man, but He will never force man's will.

He says:

THE MANNER OF GOD

"*Come now, let us reason together, says the LORD: though your sins be as scarlet, they shall be as white as snow; though they be red like crimson, they shall be as wool*" (Isa. 1:18).

And then: "*And the Spirit and the Bride say, Come.* (This presents the cry of the Holy Spirit to a hurting, lost, and dying world. What the Holy Spirit says should also be said by all Believers.) *And let him who hears say, Come.* (It means if one can '*hear*,' then one can '*come*.') *And let him who is athirst come* (speaks of spiritual thirst, the cry for God in the soul of man). *And whosoever will, let him take the Water of Life freely* (opens the door to every single individual in the world; Jesus died for all and, therefore, all can be Saved, if they will only come)" (Rev. 22:17).

(14) "HEARKEN UNTO THIS, O JOB: STAND STILL, AND CONSIDER THE WONDROUS WORKS OF GOD.

(15) "DO YOU KNOW WHEN GOD DISPOSED THEM, AND CAUSED THE LIGHT OF HIS CLOUD TO SHINE?

(16) "DO YOU KNOW THE BALANCING OF THE CLOUDS, THE WONDROUS WORKS OF HIM WHO IS PERFECT IN KNOWLEDGE?

(17) "HOW YOUR GARMENTS ARE WARM, WHEN HE QUIETS THE EARTH BY THE SOUTH WIND?

(18) "HAVE YOU WITH HIM SPREAD OUT THE SKY, WHICH IS STRONG, AND AS A MOLTEN LOOKING GLASS?

(19) "TEACH US WHAT WE SHALL SAY UNTO HIM, FOR WE CANNOT ORDER OUR SPEECH BY REASON OF DARKNESS.

(20) "SHALL IT BE TOLD HIM THAT I SPEAK? IF A MAN SPEAK, SURELY HE SHALL BE SWALLOWED UP.

(21) "AND NOW MEN SEE NOT THE BRIGHT LIGHT WHICH IS IN THE CLOUDS: BUT THE WIND PASSES, AND CLEANSES THEM.

(22) "FAIR WEATHER COMES OUT OF THE NORTH: WITH GOD IS TERRIBLE MAJESTY.

(23) "TOUCHING THE ALMIGHTY, WE CANNOT FIND HIM OUT: HE IS

EXCELLENT IN POWER, AND IN JUDGMENT, AND IN PLENTY OF JUSTICE: HE WILL NOT AFFLICT.

(24) "MEN DO THEREFORE FEAR HIM: HE RESPECTS NOT ANY WHO ARE WISE OF HEART."

The synopsis is:

1. (Vs. 14) Elihu felt perfectly comfortable in admonishing Job. There was a time that the mightiest of men held their tongues when in Job's presence. Now, even this youthful Elihu harshly commands Job to *"listen."*

2. Elihu should have heeded carefully his own statement uttered in Verse 20; God, being God, would certainly hear his prattling, but would totally ignore him.

3. (Vs. 24) Elihu closes his statement by saying *"He respects not any who are wise of heart."* So, by his own words, Elihu is ruled out!

SAYING MUCH BUT SAYING NOTHING

If it is to be noticed, none of these prattlings by Elihu addressed Job's situation, at least not in a personal way. Anything and everything said by this young man has no bearing on Job whatsoever. It doesn't encourage him, it doesn't give him hope, and it doesn't let him know anything about the Lord. In fact, to use some modern vernacular, Job has forgotten more about the Lord than Elihu has learned. And to be sure, before the whole world, and for all time, these *"three friends,"* and *"Elihu,"* will be shown up for what they really are, in the sight of God as it regards their knowledge of Him, nothing!

How much does this fit so many in the modern world!

> *"I cannot tell why He, Whom Angels worship,*
> *"Should set His Love upon the sons of men,*
> *"Or why, as Shepherd, He should seek the wanderers,*
> *"To bring them back, they know not how or when.*
> *"But this I know, that He was born of Mary,*
> *"When Bethlehem's manger was His only Home,*
> *"And that He lived at Nazareth and labored,*
> *"And so the Saviour, Saviour of the world, is come."*

> *"I cannot tell how silently He suffered,*
> *"As with His Peace He graced this place of tears,*
> *"Or how His Heart upon the Cross was broken,*
> *"The crown of pain to three and thirty years.*
> *"But this I know, He heals the brokenhearted,*
> *"And stays our sin, and calms our lurking fear,*
> *"And lifts the burden from the heavy laden,*
> *"For yet the Saviour, Saviour of the world is here."*

> *"I cannot tell how He will win the nations,*
> *"How He will claim His earthly Heritage,*
> *"How satisfy the needs and aspirations,*
> *"Of east and west, of sinner and of sage.*
> *"But this I know, all flesh shall see His Glory,*
> *"And He, shall reap the harvest He has sown,*
> *"And some glad day His sun shall shine in splendor,*
> *"When He, the Saviour, Saviour of the world, is known."*

> *"I cannot tell how all the lands shall worship,*
> *"When, at His bidding, every storm is stilled,*
> *"Or who can say how great the jubilation,*
> *"When all the hearts of men with love are filled.*
> *"But this I know, the skies will thrill with rapture,*
> *"And myriad human voices sing,*
> *"And Earth to Heaven, and Heaven to Earth, will answer:*
> *"At last the Saviour, Saviour of the world, is King."*

CHAPTER 38

(1) "THEN THE LORD ANSWERED JOB OUT OF THE WHIRLWIND, AND SAID,

(2) "WHO IS THIS WHO DARKENS COUNSEL BY WORDS WITHOUT KNOWLEDGE?

(3) "GIRD UP NOW YOUR LOINS LIKE A MAN; FOR I WILL DEMAND OF YOU, AND ANSWER YOU ME.

(4) "WHERE WERE YOU WHEN I LAID THE FOUNDATIONS OF THE EARTH? DECLARE, IF YOU HAVE UNDERSTANDING.

(5) "WHO HAS LAID THE MEASURES THEREOF, IF YOU KNOW? OR WHO HAS STRETCHED THE LINE UPON IT?

(6) "WHEREUPON ARE THE FOUNDATIONS THEREOF FASTENED? OR WHO LAID THE CORNER STONE THEREOF;

(7) "WHEN THE MORNING STARS SANG TOGETHER, AND ALL THE SONS OF GOD SHOUTED FOR JOY?"

The exposition is:

1. (Vs. 1) The Lord, it seems, appeared suddenly and without warning. He did so with some type of atmospheric disturbance. His appearing would have been cataclysmic, startling, and absolutely overwhelming.

2. In Verse 2, the Lord is not speaking of Job, but rather these *"three friends"* and Elihu. The Lord said of Job that he had *"spoken of Me the thing which is right"* (42:7).

3. (Vs. 3) Even though Job has been reduced to the most humiliating position, still, God will demand that he stand while being spoken to. In fact, this Command of God is the beginning of Job's Restoration. God picks men up; He does not put men down, unless He has no choice but to do so.

4. (Vs. 4) The Truth that God made all things is obvious according to the Creation. A creation must have a Creator; therefore, the alleged theory of evolution is a farce. Evolution, in fact, cannot even be honestly called a *"theory,"* because a theory has to have at least some rudiments of facts to buttress its claims. Evolution has no facts whatsoever.

5. The idea of Verse 5 is that God has planned and created the universe, down to the finest detail.

6. As it regards Verse 6, the facts are, the worlds are held up by the Word of God, and the Word of God alone (Heb. 11:3).

7. As it regards Verse 7, the Lord is speaking here of the completion of the Earth and the universe, and of the celebration that followed by the Angels of Heaven.

Lucifer, before his Fall, was called the *"son of the morning,"* corresponding somewhat with the phrase *"morning stars"* (Isa. 14:12).

There is a possibility that these *"morning stars"* who *"sang together"* were led in their worship and celebration by Lucifer, the *"son of the morning."*

GOD THE CREATOR

Moses wrote as it regards God and His Creation. He said:

"In the beginning (refers to the beginning of Creation, or at least the creation as it refers to this universe; God, unformed, unmade, uncreated, had no beginning; He always was, always is, and always shall be) *God* (the phrase, *'In the beginning God,'* explains the first cause of all things as it regards creation) *created the heaven and the Earth* (could be translated *'the heavens and the Earth'* because God created the entirety of the universe).

"And the Earth was without form, and void; and darkness was upon the face of the deep (God did not originally create the Earth without form and void; it became this way after a cataclysmic happening; this happening was the revolt of Lucifer against God, which took place some time in the dateless past). *And the Spirit of God* (Holy Spirit) *moved upon the face of the waters* (the Moving of the Holy Spirit signified and signifies the beginning of life).

"And God said (presents the manner in which creation or re-creation was carried out; some ten times this phrase is used, and in the exact manner, with the exception of the last time, where it says, *'And the LORD God said'* [Gen. 2:18]), *Let there be light: and there was light* (God is the essence of light [Jn. 1:4-9]; God's Word is of such magnitude that light continues to expand in the universe at the rate of 186,000 miles a second).

"And God saw the light, that it was good

(it did what it was designed to do): *and God divided the light from the darkness* (simply refers to the fact that there were now periods of light and darkness; darkness is simply the absence of light).

"And God called the light Day (a character description), *and the darkness He called Night* (has to do with the revolution of the Earth). *And the evening and the morning were the first day* (literal 24-hour days)" (Gen. 1:1-5).

DID JOB ACTUALLY SEE GOD?

We know that the Lord approached Job as the Scripture says, *"Out of the whirlwind,"* however, Job did say, *"I have heard of You by the hearing of the ear: but now my eye sees You"* (42:5). From this we must believe that God made a visible appearance to Job, and that he was able to see His bodily shape. As well, we must conclude that God is a literal Person with a Spirit Body.

The Lord approaches Job from His Position as Creator of all things, which, in fact, is beyond the comprehension of man; however, the order of events were as follows:

• The question, *"Who is this who darkens counsel by words without knowledge?"* pertains, as stated, to the *"three friends"* and *"Elihu."* So, first of all, they are reprimanded. He will have more to say to them later.

• He then tells Job, that irrespective of his physical condition, he is to stand up like a man, which means, that he is to quit wallowing in the dust of defeat. Job belonged to God. In fact, one might say that Job was God's General on Earth. We do know that the Lord had said of him, *"There is none like him in the Earth, a perfect and an upright man, one who fears God, and hates evil"* (1:8).

Irrespective as to his physical condition, irrespective that he had lost all of his material gain, irrespective that he had been laughed at and lampooned by all around him at this time, and insulted as few men have been insulted, still, he was God's General! And now the Lord is telling him, *"Gird up now your loins like a man; for I will demand of you, and answer you Me"* (Job 38:3).

One wants to shout, *"Hallelujah!"* Things are about to change, because God the Creator of the Ages, is now on the scene. I sense the Presence of God, and greatly, even as I dictate these notes.

The very thing that the Lord said to the Patriarch so long ago, He is, as well, saying to every single one of His Children. You are special! You have been bought with a price, that price being the precious, shed Blood of the Lord Jesus Christ. You belong to God, and you should conduct yourself accordingly!

• The Lord now portrays His creative Power.

Why?

In essence, He is telling Job, *"If I can do all of this, don't you think I can take care of your little problem?"*

• When the Lord created the universe, the Scripture says *"The morning stars sang together, and all the sons of God shouted for joy."* Lucifer was then one of those *"sons of God."* In fact, he was possibly the most beautiful Angel ever created by God, and maybe even the wisest. The Scripture says of him, *"Thus says the Lord GOD; You seal up the sum, full of wisdom, and perfect in beauty"* (Ezek. 28:12). There is even a great possibility that he was in charge of *"praise and worship"* one might say. So, one might say, as well, that he was in the inner circle, that is if there is such a thing in the Portals of Glory. What caused his Fall, the Scriptures do not actually say. But, what Jesus did at Calvary, addressed that problem, as well as the Salvation of mankind, with the full force of that Victory yet to come. Thank God we now have the *"firstfruits,"* and to be sure, the balance will ultimately be forthcoming at the Second Coming, and above all, when the Lord transfers His Headquarters from Heaven to Earth, which is described in the last two Chapters of Revelation.

(8) "OR WHO SHUT UP THE SEA WITH DOORS, WHEN IT BROKE FORTH, AS IF IT HAD ISSUED OUT OF THE WOMB?

(9) "WHEN I MADE THE CLOUD THE GARMENT THEREOF, AND THICK DARKNESS A SWADDLINGBAND FOR IT,

(10) "AND BROKE UP FOR IT MY DECREED PLACE, AND SET BARS AND DOORS,

(11) "AND SAID, HITHERTO SHALL YOU COME, BUT NO FURTHER: AND

HERE SHALL YOUR PROUD WAVES BE STAYED?

(12) "HAVE YOU COMMANDED THE MORNING SINCE YOUR DAYS; AND CAUSED THE DAYSPRING TO KNOW HIS PLACE;

(13) "THAT IT MIGHT TAKE HOLD OF THE ENDS OF THE EARTH, THAT THE WICKED MIGHT BE SHAKEN OUT OF IT?

(14) "IT IS TURNED AS CLAY TO THE SEAL; AND THEY STAND AS A GARMENT.

(15) "AND FROM THE WICKED THEIR LIGHT IS WITHHELD, AND THE HIGH ARM SHALL BE BROKEN.

(16) "HAVE YOU ENTERED INTO THE SPRINGS OF THE SEA? OR HAVE YOU WALKED IN THE SEARCH OF THE DEPTH?

(17) "HAVE THE GATES OF DEATH BEEN OPENED UNTO YOU? OR HAVE YOU SEEN THE DOORS OF THE SHADOW OF DEATH?"

The overview is:

1. In these Passages, the Lord gives us an elementary insight as to the manner of His Creation.

2. According to Verse 8, the Lord put boundaries on the mighty oceans. So the idea of global warming, etc., will not noticeably alter those boundaries.

3. Verse 11 plainly states again, and graphically so, that the oceans have boundaries, and boundaries set by the Lord Himself.

4. Verse 12 proclaims the fact that all days and nights are fixed by the Lord, and are ruled by the sun, moon, and stars (Gen. 1:14-19; 8:22).

5. Verse 13 proclaims the fact that the *"wicked"* cannot do anything about God's Order.

6. Verse 14, in effect, tells us that everything is obvious as to its function, but not so obvious as to exactly how it functions.

7. Verse 15 proclaims the fact that the Lord will allow the *"wicked"* to go only so far, before He steps in and breaks their arms, which He has done many times in the past, and will yet do in the future.

8. Verse 16, in effect, asks the question as to the capability of man to go to the bottom of anything, explore its secrets, and explain its cause and origin. It cannot be done by man.

NOTES

9. Verse 17 reveals openings and doors to Hell and Death (Rev. 1:18).

THE WAYS AND MEANS OF CREATION

Williams says, *"Modern Science defines light to be the result of rapid vibrations in the ether. Verse 19 in Chapter 38 asks: 'Where is the way where light dwells?' Not, 'Where is the place?' As light involves motion it can only dwell in a 'way' — traveling, according to science, at the rate of 186,000 miles a second."*[1]

Concerning Creation, John the Beloved wrote in his Book:

"In the beginning (does not infer that Christ as God had a beginning, because as God He had no beginning, but rather refers to the time of Creation [Gen. 1:1]) *was the Word* (the Holy Spirit through John describes Jesus as *'the Eternal Logos'*), *and the Word was with God* (*'was in relationship with God,'* and expresses the idea of the Trinity), *and the Word was God* (meaning that He did not cease to be God during the Incarnation; He *'was'* and *'is'* God from eternity past to eternity future).

"The same was in the beginning with God (this very Person was in eternity with God; there's only One God, but manifested in three Persons — God the Father, God the Son, and God the Holy Spirit).

"All things were made by Him (all things came into being through Him; it refers to every item of Creation one by one, rather than all things regarded in totality)*; and without Him was not anything made that was made* (nothing, not even one single thing, was made independently of His cooperation and volition).

"In Him was Life (presents Jesus, the Eternal Logos, as the first cause)*; and the Life was the Light of men* (He Alone is the Life Source of Light; if one doesn't know Christ, one is in darkness)*"* (Jn. 1:1-4).

SUSTAINING THE UNIVERSE

Paul said, and concerning Creation: *"God, Who at sundry times and in divers manners* (refers to the many and varied ways) *spoke in time past unto the fathers by the Prophets* (refers to Old Testament Times),

"Has in these last days (the Dispensation

of Grace, which is the Church Age) *spoken unto us by His Son* (speaks of the Incarnation), *Whom He has appointed Heir of all things* (through the means of the Cross), *by Whom also He made the worlds* (proclaims His Deity, as the previous phrase of Him being the *'Heir of all things'* proclaims His humanity);

"*Who being the brightness of His Glory* (the radiance of God's Glory), *and the express Image of His Person* (the exact reproduction), *and upholding all things by the Word of His Power* (carries the meaning of Jesus not only sustaining the weight of the universe, but also maintaining its coherence and carrying on its development), *when He had by Himself purged our sins* (which He did at the Cross, dealing with sin regarding its cause, its power, and its guilt), *sat down on the Right Hand of the Majesty on High* (speaks of the Finished Work of Christ, and that the Sacrifice was accepted by the Father)" (Heb. 1:1-3).

THE CREATION OF THE WORLDS

Paul also stated: "*Now Faith is the substance* (the title deed) *of things hoped for* (a declaration of the action of Faith), *the evidence of things not seen.* (Faith is not based upon the senses, which yield uncertainty, but rather on the Word of God.)

"*For by it* (by Faith, and as we shall see, it is Faith in the Cross) *the Elders obtained a good report* (the approval of the Lord).

"*Through Faith we understand that the worlds were framed by the Word of God* (refers to Creation, along with everything that goes with Creation), *so that things which are seen were not made of things which do appear.* (God began with nothing, thereby speaking into existence the things needed to create the universe)" (Heb. 11:1-3).

THE CREATIVE WORK OF THE LORD

The Apostle continues: "*In Whom we have Redemption through His Blood* (proclaims the price that was paid for our Salvation), *even the forgiveness of sins* (at the Cross, the Lord broke the power of sin, and took away its guilt [Rom. 6:6]):

"*Who is the Image of the invisible God* (the Son is the exact reproduction of the Father; a derived Image), *the Firstborn of every creature* (actually means Jesus is the Creator of all things):

"*For by Him were all things created* (presents the Justification of the title given Christ in the preceding Verse), *that are in Heaven, that are in the earth, visible and invisible* (things seen and not seen), *whether they be thrones, or dominions, or principalities, or powers* (refers to both Holy and fallen Angels): *all things were created by Him and for Him* (Christ is the Creator of all [Jn. 1:3]):

"*And He is before all things* (preexistence), *and by Him all things consist.* (All things come to pass within this sphere of His Personality, and are dependent upon it)" (Col. 1:14-17).

(18) "HAVE YOU PERCEIVED THE BREADTH OF THE EARTH? DECLARE IF YOU KNOW IT ALL.

(19) "WHERE IS THE WAY WHERE LIGHT DWELLS? AND AS FOR DARKNESS, WHERE IS THE PLACE THEREOF,

(20) "THAT YOU SHOULD TAKE IT TO THE BOUND THEREOF, AND THAT YOU SHOULD KNOW THE PATHS TO THE HOUSE THEREOF?

(21) "DO YOU KNOW IT, BECAUSE YOU WERE THEN BORN? OR BECAUSE THE NUMBER OF YOUR DAYS IS GREAT?

(22) "HAVE YOU ENTERED INTO THE TREASURES OF THE SNOW? OR HAVE YOU SEEN THE TREASURES OF THE HAIL,

(23) "WHICH I HAVE RESERVED AGAINST THE TIME OF TROUBLE, AGAINST THE DAY OF BATTLE AND WAR?

(24) "BY WHAT WAY IS THE LIGHT PARTED, WHICH SCATTERS THE EAST WIND UPON THE EARTH?

(25) "WHO HAS DIVIDED A WATERCOURSE FOR THE OVERFLOWING OF WATERS, OR A WAY FOR THE LIGHTNING OF THUNDER;

(26) "TO CAUSE IT TO RAIN ON THE EARTH, WHERE NO MAN IS; ON THE WILDERNESS, WHEREIN THERE IS NO MAN;

(27) "TO SATISFY THE DESOLATE AND WASTE GROUND; AND TO CAUSE THE BUD OF THE TENDER HERB TO SPRING FORTH?

(28) "HAS THE RAIN A FATHER? OR

WHO HAS BEGOTTEN THE DROPS OF DEW?

(29) "OUT OF WHOSE WOMB CAME THE ICE? AND THE HOARY FROST OF HEAVEN, WHO HAS GENDERED IT?

(30) "THE WATERS ARE HID AS WITH A STONE, AND THE FACE OF THE DEEP IS FROZEN."

The composition is:

1. (Vs. 18) As we read these things said by the Almighty, we wonder how they relate to Job's condition?

The reason for the Lord giving this information is many fold; however, in essence, the Lord is saying to Job, *"If I can do all of this, don't you realize how easy it is for Me to change your situation?"*

2. We know from Verse 19, and Genesis 1:3, 16, that *"light"* is a thing quite distinct from the Sun.

3. As it regards Verse 22, no two flakes of snow or two pieces of hail are alike.

4. As it respects Verse 23, many times the Lord has used the elements against His enemies (Ex. 9:22-26; Josh. 10:11; Ps. 18:12-13). In the future, hail will fall again as a part of Judgment (Rev. 8:7; 11:19; 16:21).

THE ALMIGHTY

In these Verses we see Who God is and what He is, at least as far as a poor human can grasp such; and, as well, we see who and what man is. The Lord in these Passages, presents Himself as the Creator. Actually, He goes into detail to a far greater extent than anywhere else in the Word of God.

Why would the Lord do such at this time?

Why would He give all this information, especially considering Job's condition?

Of course, everything the Lord does is right. It's not right merely because He does it, but He does it because, in fact, it is right. Actually, that's what the word *"Righteousness"* means. It is that which is right, but yet, right by God's Standards, and not man's.

The Lord knew and intended for all of this to be placed in the Sacred Text, i.e., *"the Word of God."* The lesson, I think, as far as Job was concerned, pertained to the following:

Until the Lord appeared, Job was totally in the dark as it regards what had happened and what was happening to him. He was totally nonplussed.

I have no doubt that thoughts crossed his mind as to the Might and Power of God! In other words, was he wrong about God? Was God Almighty? And if He was, why would He allow Job to be placed in this position?

I have no doubt that these thoughts, and a thousand more, crossed the mind of the Patriarch. Of course, the Lord knew everything that Job was thinking.

THE APPEARANCE OF THE LORD

So, when He appears to Job, and every evidence is that He appeared to the *"three friends"* as well, He would lay to rest every question that Job had. He didn't seem too concerned about the questions the *"three friends"* or Elihu had, but Job was different. He would answer every question the Patriarch had. First of all, He would lay to rest the idea of Him lacking in capabilities. He would proclaim the wonder of His Creation, and His Power as Creator. And in all of this, and as previously stated, this would tell Job, and glaringly so, that if the Lord could do this, if He could create everything in this world, and could literally uphold the worlds by His Word, well then Job's problem was of little consequence. In other words, the Lord was able to change the situation, whatever it may be, and to change it in a manner and way that no one would think possible.

As well, the appearance of the Lord to Job and the others, was not only for their benefit, but for every other Believer as well. As the Lord conveyed to Job the messages that needed conveying, the questions that needed answering, the power that needed to be revealed, He has said the same thing to every Believer who has ever lived, and is saying the same now to every Believer presently living. If God can do all these things, then He can easily address our problems, whatever those problems might be.

As well, and in all of this, the Lord tells Job and us, as well, that Satan is not running free doing whatever he bids. He is on a leash so to speak, and can only do what the Lord allows him to do.

All of this tells us that the Child of God need have no fear of the Evil One. We are an heir of God, the same One Who spoke to Job, and a joint-heir with Jesus Christ, which guarantees the help of the Holy Spirit at all times.

GOD AND MODERN MAN

The problem in the modern church is that we have made man too big and God too little! There are certain things we must never forget. They are:

• No matter what man does, man cannot save himself. He can only be Saved, irrespective as to what he does, or who he is, by effecting Faith in Christ and what Christ has done for us at the Cross. Salvation is all of the Lord, and none of us. In other words, man cannot contribute anything at all toward his Salvation except Faith, and that Faith must be registered absolutely in Christ.

• After Salvation, believing man cannot sanctify himself, no matter how good he tries to be, no matter how much religious ritual he performs, he cannot sanctify himself. One of the great lessons taught in this great Book of Job is that God took the most perfect man on the face of the Earth to use as an illustration of this great Truth. In other words, even though Job tried his very best to be what he ought to be in the Lord, so much that the Lord said that there was none like him in all the Earth, still, that which needed to be done, which was a purification of the heart, which would result in the purification of the walk before God, only Christ could carry out. It is very hard for believing man to come to the place that he understands this. He keeps thinking that his religious works translate into religious merit. It doesn't! While the works are something that every good Christian will do, and gladly so, still, it is our Faith in Christ and what He did for us at the Cross, and that alone, that sanctifies our walk before God. Jesus addressed that in one of His Parables. He said:

THE FAITHFUL SERVANT

"But which of you, having a servant plowing or feeding cattle, will say unto him by and by (immediately), *when he is come from the field, Go and sit down to meat?*

"And will not rather say unto him, Make ready wherewith I may sup, and gird yourself, and serve me, until I have eaten and drank; and afterward you shall eat and drink? (A faithful servant will attend to his duties first, and himself second.)

"Does he thank that servant because he did the things that were commanded him? I trow not (I think not!).

"So likewise, when you shall have done all those things which are commanded you, say, We are unprofitable servants: we have done that which was our duty to do (the Lord, in essence, says that having fulfilled all these conditions, which were their duty to do, they would be no better than unprofitable servants; this is a fatal blow to the doctrine of Salvation by works; the Disciple is to say, *'I am an unprofitable servant'*; the Master will then say, *'Well done, good and faithful servant'* [Mat. 25:21])" (Lk. 17:7-10).

The idea of *"the faithful servant"* is that all these things we do, which we think merits us something, in reality, is what we should do and, as such, it merits us nothing. But, as also stated, it's very hard for us to see that.

The idea is, and what the Lord is teaching us, in the doing of all these religious works, which we should do, still, it effects nothing toward our Sanctification. That great Work being performed by the Holy Spirit Alone.

HOW IS THE WORK OF SANCTIFICATION PERFORMED BY THE HOLY SPIRIT?

How He performs it is not really our affair. The following is what we must do:

• The Believer must come to the place that we understand that no matter what we do within ourselves, we cannot effect Sanctification within our lives, which refers to a oneness with the Lord (Rom. 8:8).

• We must understand that it is the Holy Spirit Alone Who can perform this Work within our lives (Rom. 8:1-2, 11).

• The only obligation of the Believer is that of Faith; however, without exception, it must be Faith in Christ and the Cross (Lk. 9:23-24; Rom. 6:1-14; Gal. 2:20-21). The Cross of Christ provided the legal means by which the Holy Spirit works; consequently, it is the Cross, referring to what Christ did there, which makes all things possible to us, hence, the Cross of Christ must ever be the Object of our Faith (I Cor. 1:17-18, 23; 2:2).

(31) "CAN YOU BIND THE SWEET

INFLUENCES OF PLEIADES, OR LOOSE THE BANDS OF ORION?

(32) "CAN YOU BRING FORTH MAZZAROTH IN HIS SEASON? OR CAN YOU GUIDE ARCTURUS WITH HIS SONS?

(33) "DO YOU NOT KNOW THE ORDINANCES OF HEAVEN? CAN YOU SET THE DOMINION THEREOF IN THE EARTH?

(34) "CAN YOU LIFT UP YOUR VOICE TO THE CLOUDS, THAT ABUNDANCE OF WATERS MAY COVER YOU?

(35) "CAN YOU SEND LIGHTNINGS, THAT THEY MAY GO AND SAY UNTO YOU, HERE WE ARE?

(36) "WHO HAS PUT WISDOM IN THE INWARD PARTS? OR WHO HAS GIVEN UNDERSTANDING TO THE HEART?

(37) "WHO CAN NUMBER THE CLOUDS IN WISDOM? OR WHO CAN STAY THE BOTTLES OF HEAVEN,

(38) "WHEN THE DUST GROWS INTO HARDNESS, AND THE CLODS CLEAVE FAST TOGETHER?

(39) "WILL YOU HUNT THE PREY FOR THE LION? OR FILL THE APPETITE OF THE YOUNG LIONS,

(40) "WHEN THEY COUCH IN THEIR DENS, AND ABIDE IN THE COVERT TO LIE IN WAIT?

(41) "WHO PROVIDES FOR THE RAVEN HIS FOOD? WHEN HIS YOUNG ONES CRY UNTO GOD, THEY WANDER FOR LACK OF MEAT."

The pattern is:

1. The Thirty-seventh Verse tells us that all the clouds, coming and going, are numbered by the Lord.

2. Verse 41 proclaims the fact that God provides for all, even the lowliest of Creation. If He does this for them, how much more would He care for us, *"O you of little Faith"* (Mat. 6:30).

3. When one looks at all of this, and I speak of the Creation and its provision, all made possible by the Lord, one cannot help but say, *"What a mighty God we serve!"*

THE ORDINANCES OF HEAVEN

The Thirty-first Verse mentions the *"Pleiades."* This is a conspicuous loose cluster of stars in the constellation Tarsus that includes six stars visible to the average eye.

The Lord, in speaking to Job, used the phrase *"the sweet influences of the Pleiades,"* which seemed to be a matter of common knowledge at that time. In fact, modern astronomers do not know very much about them even at present.

The ancient Greeks called them the *"Seven Stars"* and named them the *"Pleiades,"* because their appearance indicated a favorable time for sea voyages. The Chaldaic name means a *"pivot,"* and astronomers some time ago claimed to have discovered that the largest of these stars form a pivot around which the Solar System revolves.

When it is remembered that the sun is more than 3,000 billion miles away from the Pleiades, some idea is arrived at of the amazing *"influence"* of these seven stars in swinging this vast universe — the Earth included — at the rate of more than 150 million miles a year in an orbit so vast that one revolution occupies thousands of years to make, and yet, does so with unvarying regularity and smoothness.

Thus, this remote Verse in what is generally accepted to be the oldest Book in the world speaks of the influences of these stars as a matter of everyday knowledge, and it is remarkable that the expression *"sweet"* is employed — the very word, which engineers use in describing the smooth working of complex machinery.

"Orion," another name mentioned by the Lord, is the constellation commonly known as *"the Giant."* The space in the sword of the Giant alone is estimated to be two trillion two hundred billion (2,200,000,000,000) times larger than the Sun.

The Lord also used the name *"Mazzaroth,"* which refers to the twelve signs of the Zodiac; it is only mentioned here in Scripture.

THE CREATION

In this Chapter, as stated, the Lord will little address Himself to Job's problem, but, instead, will extol the greatness of His Creation. Actually, He will ask some thirty-six questions about the inanimate Creation — questions that at least give us some idea as to the greatness of God, because of the greatness of His Creation. And, again we state, considering the greatness of that Creation, and considering that God is the Heavenly Father to all who have accepted Christ, it should stand to reason that our little problem can be easily handled as well!

How insignificant we are, and how great He is, yet, He loves us with an undying love. In fact, He loves us so much, that He gave His only Begotten Son, meaning that He gave Him as a Sacrifice which paid the debt we owed, but could not pay. This is a love that is beyond our comprehension. We must never forget that!

The truth is, we have failed Him many, many times, but He has never failed us. And furthermore, He will never fail us.

"Marvelous Grace of our Loving Lord,
"Grace that exceeds our sin and our guilt,
"Yonder on Calvary's mount outpoured,
"There where the Blood of the Lamb was shed."

"Sin and despair like the sea waves cold,
"Threaten the soul with infinite loss;
"Grace that is greater, yes, Grace untold,
"Points to the Refuge, the mighty Cross."

"Dark is the stain that we cannot hide,
"What can avail to wash it away?
"Look! There is flowing a crimson tide;
"Whiter than snow you may be today."

"Marvelous, infinite, matchless Grace,
"Freely bestowed on all who believe;
"You that are longing to see His Face,
"Will you this moment His Grace receive?"

CHAPTER 39

(1) "DO YOU KNOW THE TIME WHEN THE WILD GOATS OF THE ROCK BRING FORTH? OR CAN YOU MARK WHEN THE HINDS DO CALVE?

(2) "CAN YOU NUMBER THE MONTHS THAT THEY FULFILL? OR KNOW YOU THE TIME WHEN THEY BRING FORTH?

(3) "THEY BOW THEMSELVES, THEY BRING FORTH THEIR YOUNG ONES, THEY CAST OUT THEIR SORROWS.

(4) "THEIR YOUNG ONES ARE IN GOOD LIKING, THEY GROW UP WITH CORN; THEY GO FORTH, AND RETURN NOT UNTO THEM.

(5) "WHO HAS SENT OUT THE WILD ASS FREE? OR WHO HAS LOOSED THE BANDS OF THE WILD ASS?

(6) "WHOSE HOUSE I HAVE MADE THE WILDERNESS, AND THE BARREN LAND HIS DWELLINGS.

(7) "HE SCORNS THE MULTITUDE OF THE CITY, NEITHER REGARDS HE THE CRYING OF THE DRIVER.

(8) "THE RANGE OF THE MOUNTAINS IS HIS PASTURE, AND HE SEARCHES AFTER EVERY GREEN THING.

(9) "WILL THE UNICORN BE WILLING TO SERVE YOU, OR ABIDE BY YOUR CRIB?

(10) "CAN YOU BIND THE UNICORN BY HIS BAND IN THE FURROW? OR WILL HE HARROW THE VALLEYS AFTER YOU?

(11) "WILL YOU TRUST HIM, BECAUSE HIS STRENGTH IS GREAT? OR WILL YOU LEAVE YOUR LABOUR TO HIM?

(12) "WILL YOU BELIEVE HIM, THAT HE WILL BRING HOME YOUR SEED, AND GATHER IT INTO YOUR BARN?"

The pattern is:

1. The word *"unicorn"* in Verse 9 is an unfortunate translation, since there is no word correspondent to *"unicorn"* in the original. It actually pertains to the wild bull.

2. (Vs. 10) In fact, the type of wild bull here mentioned cannot be harnessed, meaning that it cannot be domesticated.

3. In this Chapter we will find ten illustrations chosen by the Lord. They are: lions, ravens, wild goats, deer, the wild ass, the wild bull, the ostrich, the war-horse, the hawk, and the eagle. The lion, the king of beasts, opens this dialogue, with the eagle, the king of birds, closing the list.

THE ANIMATE CREATION

Actually, the insertion of the Chapter division probably would have been better placed after the Thirty-eighth Verse of the last Chapter instead of going on to Verse Forty-one.

The reason for a better break at that time is because the Lord dealt with the inanimate creation in the entirety of the last Chapter, with the exception of the last three Verses. In other words, He begins His discourse on the animate creation in the Thirty-ninth Verse of the last Chapter.

The first three words of this Chapter, *"Do you know,"* pretty well tell the story. The fact is that man does not know. Man is able to study each animal and to understand its basic instincts, as well as its habits, strength, or peculiarities; nevertheless, man is totally unable to even begin to understand the manner in which God created the animal kingdom. This we do know:

The Bible declares that, after its own kind (some ten times in Gen., Chpt. 1), everything created by God was given power to reproduce *"its own kind."* No one thing could break this law and produce any other kind (Gen. 1:20-28). Now, after more than 6,000 years of recorded history, the law of reproduction is still unbroken, and the fact is that it will forever remain that way. The sponge is still a sponge and has not become an oyster, octopus, a turtle, frog, fish, or crab. None of these have ever reproduced anything except *"their own kind."*

No lowly earthworm has ever turned into a spider, tarantula, scorpion, lizard, tortoise, snake, or crocodile.

No bug, bird, or animal has ever changed from its own kind or reproduced another kind which was fertile and could produce a new kind. For instance, the crossing of an ass and a mare will produce a mule which cannot reproduce itself.

No monkey has ever produced a man, and the missing link is still missing and always will be.

THE SPECIES

All of this is quite remarkable in view of the fact that there are over 2,000,000 different species of plant and animal life. Each species proves the law of reproduction established by God — *"after his own kind."*

It is claimed that there are more than

NOTES

1,000,000 species of insects. Species of beetles number approximately 250,000; butterflies and moths, 110,000; shellfish, 80,000; snails, 80,000; arachnids, 60,000; flies, 40,000; barnacles, crabs, lobsters, and shrimp, 25,000; fish, 20,000; bees, 10,000; wasps, 10,000; worms, 9,000; ants, 5,000; birds, 1,200; and, cockroaches, 1,000 (numbers have been rounded off).

Beside these, there are many species of larger animals and over 180,000 species of plants. Species of fungi number at 100,000; algae, 20,000; mosses, 20,000; coral, 5,000; and sponges, 3,000, beside many other species of living things.

THE CLAIMS OF EVOLUTION

Evolution claims a progression; however, all species exist in great variety, and the so-called proofs of evolutionists are merely *"variations"* or *"minor changes"* within the same species. Out of billions of organisms and fossils, there is no evidence of the slightest tendency to evolve out of the original kind to which each belongs. There is only evidence of development and normal growth, but these are not evolution. Likewise, the improvement of a species and new varieties within the species are not evolution.

The fabrication of evolution teaches transmutations, a change in nature, substance, form, and alteration of essence by a slow and gradual process of mutation from one species to another, and from the lower to the higher. This has never been done, nor can it be done.

In nature we find endless variety within each species or kind, but not change from one species to another. Without a change of species there can be no evolution. God has made life so that it interbreeds in closely related variations, and when interbreeding is attempted between different kinds of species, it is found that there is an impassable gulf which cannot be crossed.

Out of the billions of yearly reproductions of nature, not one monkey's tail has been produced by anything except a monkey. There is no proof of man in various stages from a molecule to a monkey, or from a monkey to a man!

There can be no evolution without the

power of reproduction in living things. Since reproduction is a prior condition to evolution, it cannot be a product of it. Hence, we face the logical necessity for the creation of life and its power of continued reproduction. The power of reproduction is not in the embryo, but only in the mature parent. An egg cannot produce an egg. It is also true that the egg is not improvable by itself. Improvement can come only in and through the mature form; therefore, the parent form of life must have been created in the beginning to have produced an egg from which offspring alone can come.

DEAD MATTER

Science has proved that dead matter cannot generate life, and that only life can come from preexisting life. When test tubes were filled with hay and other organic matter, when all cells were completely destroyed, when the tube was hermetically sealed to exclude outer air, and while it was absolutely free of living cells, not one vestige of life appeared. The attempt to get the living out of the dead completely failed. The theory of spontaneous generation has had to be given up. It is now recognized that life can only come from life. All life is dependent upon other life: the lower upon the higher, the simple upon the complex, the powerless upon the powerful, the impersonal upon the personal, the unintelligent upon the intelligent, the nonexisting upon the existing, the natural upon the spiritual, the temporary upon the eternal. Nothing can come from nothing nor be produced by nothing.

EMBRYOLOGY

The argument of evolution from embryology that embryos of different forms of life are somewhat alike so they must have come from a common ancestor has utterly failed, as have the theories of *"natural selection,"* and the *"survival of the fittest."*

The similarity of embryos and their fast development to full growth are contrary to the principles of the evolutionary hypothesis. The foundation of evolution is that of a slow and tedious process over millions and millions of years. What the evolution teachers have to face is the fact that no single example of evolution from one species to another can be cited. Human and other embryos pass through various stages of growth very rapidly. In the case of some, the progress of growth is so rapid that it is miraculous. Thus, evolutionists are forced to believe in miracles, which they deny in other fields but sustain in their own in the effort to prove their claims.

DIFFERENCES

It is now known that there are radical differences between the embryos of vertebrates (backboned animals) and invertebrates (animals without backbones) which we would not have if all things had a common ancestor. Some similarity among embryos of all forms of life should be expected since all start individually from a single cell or a combination of two.

If a botanist would be asked the difference between an oak, a palm tree, and a lichen, he would declare that they are separated from one another by the broadest line of classification. But if the cells of these plants were placed before him to choose one from the other, he could not do it. Under the most powerful microscope they would yield no clue. If analyzed by the chemist, they would still keep their secret. The same is true of the cells of various animals and man. No one can tell which is which. What makes the little speck grow into the millions of different kinds of creatures? What is there, which the eye cannot see that determines which of the many creatures it will be? Only a personal and infinite intelligent being could make such unfailing laws of reproduction — *"after his kind."*

THE MAN AND THE MONKEY

It is further argued that man and monkey are so similar that they must have come from a common ancestor. This is neither sound logic nor sound science. Resemblance proves nothing but resemblance. Similarity proves nothing but similarity. Resemblance and similarity run throughout all nature and things that have no connection with each other.

Resemblance or similarity on some points is to be expected even though we accept creation by God. This only magnifies the fact of an intelligent operator. This is true whether it is the Creator or a manufacturer as in every factory of man. The wheel, for example, is the same in the wagon, car, locomotive, and airplane. But such similarity does not prove that the wagon evolved into an automobile, then into a locomotive, and finally into an airplane.

All animals and men have the same kind of faculties to breath, eat food, and perform other bodily functions, but no such similarity proves close relationship. God made them so that all could exist alike in the same air and on similar foods.

The dissimilarities between man and lower animals, not only in body, but also in brain, spirit, and soul faculties prove that they are not vitally related. The differences between man and monkey are so wide that any single bodily part is sufficient in itself to prove whether it is a part of a man or a monkey.

Evolutionists themselves confirm this fact by their promptness in deciding whether a bone is from a monkey or a man. There are hundreds of differences between the bodies of men and apes, and thousands of differences between these two in mental, moral, spiritual, and habitual matters which prove evolution of man from apes or lower life an impossibility.

DEGENERATION

The similarities between man and lower animals could be used to prove a process of degeneration from man more than a process of evolution to man. The Bible teaches that God made man before He made land animals — on day six. Therefore, man came first, and then the monkey (Gen. 2:7, 19-25). Darwin's argument that plants and animals have within themselves tendencies to vary on their own accord in many and all directions to an unlimited degree has been disproved many times.

Mendel's experiments prove conclusively that plants and animals, even under man's selective skill in breeding, do not tend to vary in all directions and to an unlimited degree, but that the variations are within strict limits and work according to fixed laws producing unvarying results. The theory of natural selection and of inheritance of acquired characteristics have failed of proof. The forms of vegetables, plants, and animals that man succeeds in improving by human selection and cultivation revert rapidly to type as soon as man's directing skill is removed.

In all man's selection and cultivation, he can work only within the limits of the species. No change into new species has been produced either by natural or artificial selection.

The iron law of sterility stands guard at the far frontiers of the species, and everything continues to reproduce *"after his kind."*

FOSSIL REMAINS

Fossil remains have been referred to as one of the strongest proofs of evolution. But evolutionists themselves acknowledge that this proof is extremely fragmentary, limited, and obscure due to the fact that only a few fossils remain; hence, they are forced to guess without proof.

The *"missing links"* between man and monkey have never been found. The manufactured bones of prehistoric men are fakes. The *"Piltdown man,"* for example, was no man at all. The facts are the different parts of fragments were found at different times and in different places in different years. From these few scraps, so-called scientists constructed the *"Piltdown man"* and named it the *"Dawn-man"* of the dateless past.

From the same bones another later type was made by another team of so-called scientists. Finally, it was acknowledged that the jaw bone and tooth did not belong to the skull, but were those of a chimpanzee. The *"Java-man"* was built in Java from a skull bone, leg bone, two molars, and plaster of Paris; the *"Heidelberg-man"* was built in Germany from a jawbone which was unquestionably human; the *"Peking-man"* of China was made from human skull fragments found in a cave. The first *"Neanderthal-man"* was made from a skull cap in Germany which one great German pathologist declared to be the cranium of an idiot.

Pictures of these man-made specimens have been the so-called proof shown in school text books. Such are the hoaxes, which are being passed upon our innocent boys and girls by some educators in the name of science!

THE RESPONSIBILITY

If evolution is responsible for all the vast creations in space and the endless varieties of species of life on the innumerable planets, then why is the law not working today? Why do we not have actual and unquestionable examples of the various stages of evolution from the lowest to the highest forms of life?

If evolution ever worked, it should be working today so that every form or stage of development could be seen as proof that the lower forms of life will eventually be the higher in the ages to come.

Is it not strange that the process has been at a standstill for the period man has been on Earth to observe the law of evolution at work? Is it not strange that man has not produced one example of change from one species to another, not even the losing of the monkey tail and hair?

JUDGMENT AND RE-CREATION

There is evidence now that the whole world and all in it are degenerating and moving toward some climax or judgment and re-creation instead of evolving upward into higher and better forms. In *"chemistry,"* which is closest to the deeper facts and forces of inanimate matter and life, there is no evidence of a surge upward. Not only are the laws of chemical affinity static and unchangeable in their operations, but there is a disintegrating tendency downward instead of upward that seems to characterize all matter. The tendency of atoms of high atomic weight to break up into other atoms of lower weight seems to be the universal tendency of all matter. Scientists declare that this is also true in the vegetable and animal kingdoms.

ABSURD

The evolution theory is not only absurd, its so-called proofs are so contradictory that they cause increasing doubt regarding its guesses.

Tyndall says that the world began in a *"firemist"* that contracted as it became cold, but Spencer says that it was a *"cold-cloud"* that became heated and contracted.

The age of man is estimated all the way from 500,000,000 years to as little as 6,000,000 years. The age of the Earth is put by guessers at 10,000,000,000 years to the lowest estimate of 10,000,000 years.

All of this proves nothing but the unreliability of data, which are used in the effort to prove diverse conclusions.

(It is not known where the above information on evolution was derived; consequently, we are unable to give credit to the original author.)

(13) "DO YOU GIVE GOODLY WINGS UNTO THE PEACOCKS? OR WINGS AND FEATHERS UNTO THE OSTRICH?

(14) "WHICH LEAVES HER EGGS IN THE EARTH, AND WARMS THEM IN DUST,

(15) "AND FORGETS THAT THE FOOT MAY CRUSH THEM, OR THAT THE WILD BEAST MAY BREAK THEM.

(16) "SHE IS HARDENED AGAINST HER YOUNG ONES, AS THOUGH THEY WERE NOT HERS: HER LABOUR IS IN VAIN WITHOUT FEAR;

(17) "BECAUSE GOD HAS DEPRIVED HER OF WISDOM, NEITHER HAS HE IMPARTED TO HER UNDERSTANDING.

(18) "WHAT TIME SHE LIFTS UP HERSELF ON HIGH, SHE SCORNS THE HORSE AND HIS RIDER.

(19) "HAVE YOU GIVEN THE HORSE STRENGTH? HAVE YOU CLOTHED HIS NECK WITH THUNDER?

(20) "CAN YOU MAKE HIM AFRAID AS A GRASSHOPPER? THE GLORY OF HIS NOSTRILS IS TERRIBLE.

(21) "HE PAWS IN THE VALLEY, AND REJOICES IN HIS STRENGTH: HE GOES ON TO MEET THE ARMED MEN.

(22) "HE MOCKS AT FEAR, AND IS NOT AFRAID; NEITHER TURNS HE BACK FROM THE SWORD.

(23) "THE QUIVER RATTLES AGAINST HIM, THE GLITTERING SPEAR AND THE SHIELD.

(24) "HE SWALLOWS THE GROUND WITH FIERCENESS AND RAGE: NEITHER BELIEVES HE THAT IT IS THE SOUND OF THE TRUMPET.

(25) "HE SAYS AMONG THE TRUMPETS, HA, HA; AND HE SMELLS THE

BATTLE AFAR OFF, THE THUNDER OF THE CAPTAINS, AND THE SHOUTING.

(26) "DOES THE HAWK FLY BY YOUR WISDOM, AND STRETCH HER WINGS TOWARD THE SOUTH?

(27) "DOES THE EAGLE MOUNT UP AT YOUR COMMAND, AND MAKE HER NEST ON HIGH?

(28) "SHE DWELLS AND ABIDES ON THE ROCK, UPON THE CRAG OF THE ROCK, AND THE STRONG PLACE.

(29) "FROM THERE SHE SEEKS THE PREY, AND HER EYES BEHOLD AFAR OFF.

(30) "HER YOUNG ONES ALSO SUCK UP BLOOD: AND WHERE THE SLAIN ARE, THERE IS SHE."

The diagram is:

1. The Eighteenth Verse portrays the fact that at full pace, the fastest horse can little catch, if at all, the ostrich, at least when she starts to fly.

2. (Vs. 25) A description is given here of the war-horse, but, we know that the horse eats only grass or such like feed, and yet, is powerful and strong.

3. The idea of all of this is meant to portray the creative Power of God, which, in effect, defies all understanding.

THE POWER OF GOD

The Twenty-sixth Verse says, *"Does the hawk fly by your wisdom, and stretch her wings toward the south?"*

That same question could be asked of all of mankind. Can the earthly wisdom of even the most brilliant scientists create the hawk and teach it to fly?

By asking this series of questions, God proves His Glory and Power and man's weakness and inability.

There are nine questions asked by the Lord of Job in this Chapter. The questions and information given are clearly not designed to test the amount of accuracy of Job's information concerning natural history, but rather that this interrogation seems as little meant to affirm that everything connected with the pregnancy and activity of these creatures is all a mystery. Pulpit says, *"Its intention rather is to emphasize the fact that the whole process of conception and parturition is carried on with such admirable regularity, ease, and success, as to suggest the thought that it must be owing to the wise guidance and watchful care of some presiding mind."*[1] In effect, Jehovah asked of Job, *"Is it yours, or is it not rather Mine?"*

Of course, we know the answer to that question. Our Lord can best describe the creatures because He knows all about them, having made them. We should well learn from all of this, that every creature on the face of the Earth has its peculiar nature, instincts, habitat, all by Divine appointment. It's a beautiful thing, that wherever God assigns dwelling to a creature, there also he provides means of subsistence.

We might as well learn from this, that the study of zoology is somewhat fitted to convey important lessons concerning the power, wisdom, goodness, and sovereignty of God.

Once again let us venture the thought, that the Lord, at least up to this time, does not even mention Job's plight, but rather gives a long dissertation regarding His Creation.

He, no doubt, did this for many and varied reasons; however, I think the greatest point to be made is, the Lord portrays His Creation, at least a small part of it, with all of its mystery, in order to show Job and all of us as well, that up beside His Creation, our little problems are puny.

In all of this He tells us, that He has a watchful eye over everything, and above all upon Believers. This means that nothing can happen to us, and I mean nothing, but that the Lord allows it to happen, or causes it to happen. To be sure, He does not cause anyone to sin, as should be obvious; however, He does allow it, while at the same time telling us of the consequences of such.

We serve an all-wise God, Who knows all things, past, present, and future, and the moment we come to Christ, He sets about to bring us in line with His Word, which is not an easy task.

WHY IS IT A DIFFICULT TASK FOR US TO BE BROUGHT IN LINE WITH GOD'S WORD?

The difficulty lies not at all on His Part, but altogether on ours.

Do you realize that virtually the entirety

of the Bible is given over to tell mankind how to live for God? By comparison, there are only a few Passages in the Word that portrays Salvation to the sinner, in other words, how to be saved. All the balance is given over to this all-encompassing subject at hand, our Sanctification. For the Holy Spirit to devote such time and attention to this problem, and it is a problem, tells us how important that it is, and how difficult that it is.

The reason?

In essence, the Holy Spirit through Paul gave us the answer to that question. He said:

"For what the Law could not do, in that it was weak through the flesh (those under Law had only their willpower, which is woefully insufficient; so despite how hard they tried, they were unable to keep the Law then, and the same inability persists presently; any person who tries to live for God by a system of laws is doomed to failure, because the Holy Spirit will not function in that capacity), *God sending His Own Son* (refers to man's helpless condition, unable to save himself and unable to keep even a simple Law, and, therefore, in dire need of a Saviour) *in the likeness of sinful flesh* (this means that Christ was really human, conformed in appearance to flesh which is characterized by sin, yet sinless), *and for sin* (to atone for sin, to destroy its power, and to save and sanctify its victims), *condemned sin in the flesh* (destroyed the power of sin by giving His Perfect Body as a Sacrifice for sin, which made it possible for sin to be defeated in our flesh; it was all through the Cross)" (Rom. 8:3).

WHY IS THE FLESH WEAK?

The Holy Spirit through Paul answered that as well. He said:

"And if Christ be in you (He is in you through the Power and Person of the Spirit [Gal. 2:20]), *the body is dead because of sin* (means that the physical body has been rendered helpless because of the Fall; consequently, the Believer trying to overcome by willpower presents a fruitless task); *but the Spirit is Life because of Righteousness* (only the Holy Spirit can make us what we ought to be, which means we cannot do it ourselves; once again, He performs all that He does within the confines of the Finished Work of Christ).

"But if the Spirit (Holy Spirit) *of Him* (from God) *Who raised up Jesus from the dead dwell in you* (and He definitely does), *He Who raised up Christ from the dead shall also quicken your mortal bodies* (give us power in our mortal bodies that we might live a victorious life) *by His Spirit Who dwells in you* (we have the same Power in us, through the Spirit that raised Christ from the dead, and is available to us only on the premise of the Cross and our Faith in that Sacrifice)" (Rom. 8:10-11).

MAN IS CREATED SPIRIT, SOUL, AND BODY

While every part of man was affected at the Fall, and we speak of the spirit, soul, and body, it seems from the Sacred Text, that the physical body was affected more than anything else. In other words, it was greatly weakened. The following should be noted:

- The spirit of man is that which reaches out to God, i.e., the spirit world.
- The *"soul"* deals with the individual, i.e., *"with self."*
- The *"material body"* deals with the world.

When the Bible uses the word *"heart"* as it regards the human being, it is not speaking of the physical organ, but rather the whole of the person, but more specifically, the soul and the spirit.

- The spirit of man is that which knows, which pertains to the intellect and the mind. Paul said:

"For what man knows the things of a man, save the spirit of man which is in him?" (I Cor. 2:11).

The soul of man is that which feels, and which pertains to the passions. Peter said:

"Dearly beloved, I beseech you as strangers and pilgrims, abstain from fleshly lusts, which war against the soul" (I Pet. 2:11).

Man is a soul, and has a spirit, both which reside in a physical body, referred to by Paul as a *"tent"* or *"tabernacle"* (II Cor. 5:1). The soul and the spirit are immortal, while the physical body is mortal. To describe man, the Holy Spirit uses the term, *"spirit and* soul and body" (I Thess. 5:23).

When the Lord saves a soul, the person is Saved *"spirit, soul, and body."* However, the physical body, although Saved, one might say, is not yet redeemed (Rom. 8:23).

The *"redemption of the body,"* which refers to the physical body as Paul uses the term, pertains to the coming Resurrection when this physical body will be changed and, thereby, *"glorified"* (I Cor. 15:51-54).

As well, the spirit of the Christian can become polluted. Paul also said:

"Having therefore these Promises, dearly beloved, let us cleanse ourselves from all filthiness of the flesh and spirit, perfecting holiness in the fear of God" (II Cor. 7:1).

The idea is, when a person comes to Christ, they are Saved, *"spirit, soul, and body."* Likewise, we are to be sanctified, *"spirit, soul, and body"* (I Thess. 5:23).

The idea that our spirit is Saved, with our soul being Saved, as some teach, is not taught in the Word of God. When the person comes to Christ, the whole man is Saved. As well, when a Christian sins, it's the whole man that sins; spirit, soul, and body. As stated, as it regards the Sanctification process, it is the spirit, soul, and body, which are sanctified, and not just the body, etc. There is no such thing as one part being affected without the other parts being affected. Even though man is a trilogy so to speak, he is at the same time *"one."*

When a person dies, if the person is Saved, their soul and their spirit instantly go to be with the Lord Jesus Christ (Phil. 1:23).

If the person is unsaved, their soul and spirit instantly go to Hell (Lk. 16:19-31).

The body goes back to dust, there awaiting the Resurrection, and as it regards the Saved, it is the Resurrection of Life, in which the physical body will be changed and, thereby, given a Glorified Body (I Cor. 15:52-54).

If the person is unsaved, they too will be given an indestructible body, which will take place at the resurrection of damnation, which will be approximately 1,000 years after the Resurrection of Life. The unsaved with the indestructible bodies will then be put in the Lake of Fire, where they will be *"tormented day and night forever and ever"* (Rev. 20:10-15).

NOTES

Incidentally, there is no such thing as *"soul sleep"* taught in the Bible. This teaching claims that the spirit and the soul at death will sleep until the Resurrection. One only has to read the Sixteenth Chapter of Luke to disprove that.

As well, Paul said, *"For I am in a strait betwixt two, having a desire to depart, and to be with Christ; which is far better"* (Phil. 1:23).

Of the triune being of man, the physical body is the weakest part. It is through the physical body that the soul and the spirit operate. Paul told us in the Sixth Chapter of Romans how to bring the physical body in line, that it not be used as an instrument of uncleanness. Please understand, the physical body is neutral. Within itself, it's not holy or unholy. To be sure, it can be made unholy, and quick, but within itself, it is not good or evil.

GOD'S PRESCRIBED ORDER OF VICTORY

Understanding that the Fall made the physical body ineffective, at least as far as overcoming the world, the flesh, and the Devil, the Lord has provided a way of Victory. That way is the Cross of Christ.

When Jesus came to this world, He came for the express purpose of going to the Cross, where there He would serve as a Perfect Sacrifice, thereby, paying the sin debt to God, which man owed and could not pay.

The Believer is to anchor his Faith exclusively in Christ and the Cross. The Scripture says:

"Know you not, that so many of us as were baptized into Jesus Christ (plainly says that this Baptism is into Christ and not water [I Cor. 1:17; 12:13; Gal. 3:27; Eph. 4:5; Col. 2:11-13]) *were baptized into His Death?* (When Christ died on the Cross, in the Mind of God, we died with Him; in other words, He became our Substitute, and our identification with Him in His Death gives us all the benefits for which He died; the idea is that He did it all for us!)

"Therefore we are buried with Him by baptism into death (not only did we die with Him, but we were buried with Him as well, which means that all the sin and transgression

of the past were buried; when they put Him in the tomb, they put all of our sins into that tomb as well): *that like as Christ was raised up from the dead by the Glory of the Father, even so we also should walk in newness of life* (we died with Him, we were buried with Him, and His Resurrection was our Resurrection to a *'Newness of Life'*).

"For if we have been planted together (with Christ) *in the likeness of His Death* (Paul proclaims the Cross as the instrument through which all Blessings come; consequently, the Cross must ever be the Object of our Faith, which gives the Holy Spirit latitude to work within our lives), *we shall be also in the likeness of His Resurrection* (we can have the *'likeness of His Resurrection,'* i.e., *'live this Resurrection Life,'* only as long as we understand the *'likeness of His Death,'* which refers to the Cross as the means by which all of this is done):

"Knowing this, that our old man is crucified with Him (all that we were before conversion), *that the body of sin might be destroyed* (the power of sin broken — made ineffective), *that henceforth we should not serve sin* (the guilt of sin is removed at conversion, because the sin nature no longer rules within our hearts and lives).

"For he who is dead (He was our Substitute, and in the Mind of God, we died with Him upon Believing Faith) *is freed from sin* (set free from the bondage of the sin nature).

"Now if we be dead with Christ (once again pertains to the Cross, and our being Baptized into His Death), *we believe that we shall also live with Him* (have Resurrection Life, which is more Abundant Life)" (Rom. 6:3-8).

That in brief, is God's Prescribed Order of Victory. We must ever understand the following:

The Lord Jesus Christ is the Source of all things that we receive from God, while the Cross is the Means by which those things are received, with the Holy Spirit ever being the Superintendent of all that is done.

It all comes down to the fact that whatever needs to be done, man within himself is incapable of doing it, whether Salvation for the sinner, or Sanctification for the Saint. It is the Holy Spirit Alone Who can perform the Work within our lives, and He does such totally by and through the Finished Work of Christ, which demands our Faith, and exclusively, in that Finished Work, i.e., *"the Cross of Christ."*

"Under the burdens of guilt and care,
"Many a spirit is grieving,
"Who in the joy of the Lord might share,
"Life everlasting receiving."

"Burdened one, why will you longer bear,
"Sorrows from which He releases?
"Open your heart, and rejoicing share,
"Life more abundant in Jesus."

"Leaving the mountain, the streamlet grows,
"Flooding the vale with a river;
"So, from the hill of the Cross there flows,
"Life more abundant forever."

"Oh, for the floods on the thirsty land!
"Oh, for a mighty revival!
"Oh, for a sanctified, fearless band,
"Ready to hail its arrival!"

CHAPTER 40

(1) "MOREOVER THE LORD ANSWERED JOB, AND SAID,

(2) "SHALL HE WHO CONTENDS WITH THE ALMIGHTY INSTRUCT HIM? HE WHO REPROVES GOD, LET HIM ANSWER IT.

(3) "THEN JOB ANSWERED THE LORD, AND SAID,

(4) "BEHOLD, I AM VILE; WHAT SHALL I ANSWER YOU? I WILL LAY MY HAND UPON MY MOUTH.

(5) "ONCE HAVE I SPOKEN; BUT I WILL NOT ANSWER: YES, TWICE; BUT I WILL PROCEED NO FURTHER."

The construction is:

1. (Vs. 2) The basic sin of the human race is *"contending with the Almighty."* Men have a tendency to blame God for the terrible problems of mankind.

2. (Vs. 4) Job, convicted of his ignorance, his impotence, and his sinfulness, at last learns the lesson that it seems none of us

can learn without at least some such trial.

As a son of Adam, Job was a total moral wreck and, consequently, he loathed himself, though he had done all he could to live right. This shows that within ourselves, we cannot be what we ought to be in Christ. This is a Work that only the Holy Spirit can perform.

Job did not learn this humiliating lesson so long as he confronted the church, i.e., his *"three friends,"* but he learned it directly when he entered into the sinless Light of the Presence of God. That Light showed his comeliness to actually be corruption, and his righteousness to be as filthy rags.

3. (Vs. 5) Job now realizes the futility, and even the foolishness of his arguments.

CONTENDING WITH THE ALMIGHTY

The basic sin of the human race is *"contending with the Almighty."* Men have a tendency to blame God for the terrible problems of mankind, or to claim that the Lord isn't treating them right, etc.

Bertrand Russell, a philosopher of the 1940's and 50's, asked this question:

"If there is a God, does He consider the creation of an Adolph Hitler, or a Joseph Stalin to be adequate compensation for His creation?"

Men pose such foolish questions simply because they do not believe the Bible. God is not the creator of a Hitler or a Stalin or such like. Sin and Satan are the authors of such.

Many Believers have cried to God from the very beginning, *"Your will be done in Earth as it is in Heaven."* That prayer has not yet been answered. It will be shortly. John writes in the Book of Revelation, *"When He shall begin to sound, the Mystery of God should be finished, as He has declared to His servants the Prophets"* (Rev. 10:7). The *"mystery of God"* is the fact that God has allowed Satan to continue since the Garden of Eden episode. It is a *"mystery"* to man why the Lord has allowed such. Yet this we do know: God does all things perfectly. The Prophet Isaiah said the following:

"For thus says the LORD Who created the heavens; God Himself Who formed the Earth and made it; He has established it, He created it not in vain, He formed it to be inhabited: I am the LORD; and there is none else. I have not spoken in secret, in a dark place of the Earth: I said not unto the seed of Jacob, Seek you Me in vain: I the LORD speak Righteousness, I declare things that are right" (Isa. 45:18-19).

So, whatever God has done is *"right,"* and soon this *"mystery of God"* will be finished. Satan will be locked away, then pain, suffering, sorrow, sickness, and death will be eternally finished.

Men contend with God because they do not want to take responsibility themselves; consequently, in their contending with Him, they at the same time from their ignorance endeavor to *"instruct Him."*

The humanistic world of psychology even advises its clientele to *"forgive God."* This is blasphemy pure and simple. God has never done anything bad to anyone for anyone to have to forgive Him.

THE VILENESS OF THE HUMAN HEART

Concerning the human heart, the great Prophet Jeremiah said: *"The heart is deceitful above all things, and desperately wicked: who can know it?"* (Jer. 17:9).

God knows the hopeless corruption of the natural heart, and so He said to Nicodemus that no one, however cultured and moral, can either see or enter into the Kingdom of God without the New Birth.

The Lord went on to say: *"I the LORD search the heart, I try the reins, even to give every man according to his ways, and according to the fruit of his doings* (Jer. 17:10).

"I the LORD search the heart," refers to the fact that only God knows the heart. *"I try the reins,"* refers to the Lord allowing certain particulars to take place, according to the disposition of the individual involved, in order to bring out what is actually there. The Lord through Omniscience already knows all things, in other words, what is in the heart of man, even before man knows it. But in order that man not be able to say that he is unjustly judged, the Lord allows events to transpire, uncaused or caused by Him, which always reveal exactly what is in the heart, whether good or bad. This is done in order that the Judgment Day will be fair and impartial, and that the record of

such actions can be shown in black and white to the individual, who, at that time, will be without argument. Therefore, his judgment will be *"according to his ways, and according to the fruit of his doings."*

THE INTERCESSION OF CHRIST

All Believers, even the godliest among us, whomever that might be, still have to have the constant intercession of Christ. As someone said, *"without that intercession we wouldn't last a day."* Concerning this, the Apostle Paul wrote:

"Wherefore He is able also to save them to the uttermost who come unto God by Him, seeing He ever lives to make intercession for them" (Heb. 7:25).

All of this means that any Believer who claims sinless perfection, simply does not know his own heart, does not know what sin is, and does not know Who God is.

Job thought pretty highly of himself until he saw the Lord. When he sensed the Presence of the Lord, and that was when the Lord appeared to him, his answer was, *"I am vile."*

Comparing ourselves to others is one thing, but comparing ourselves to Christ is something else altogether. To be sure, the answer of any honest person would be, in such a situation, the same as that of Job, *"I am vile."*

THE RIGHTEOUSNESS OF GOD

Man has ever contended with God from the position of *"Righteousness."* Man tries to produce Righteousness, and demands that God accept it, when the truth is, God cannot accept any Righteousness whatsoever, that does not come solely from Him. The Righteousness that He freely imputes to man, at least upon the Faith of the individual, is that which was purchased by Christ at the Cross of Calvary. Upon Faith in Christ, the Lord will instantly impute a perfect, stainless, spotless Righteousness to the believing sinner. That and that alone is the only Righteousness that God will accept; however, that doesn't keep man from continuing to offer up to God that which the Lord can never accept.

The simple meaning of Righteousness is, *"that which is right;"* however, it's that in the Eyes of God, which is right, and not in the eyes of man. In other words, it's God Who sets the Standard, and not man. God's Standard for this Righteousness to be imputed to anyone, is Faith in Christ and what Christ did for us at the Cross.

Oswald Chambers wrote the following article concerning this subject.

IT IS FINISHED

"I have finished the work which You gave Me to do (Jn. 17:4)."

"The Death of Jesus Christ is the performance in history of the very Mind of God. There is no room for looking on Jesus Christ as a martyr; His death was not something that happened to Him which might have been prevented: His death was the very reason why He came."

Chambers went on to say, *"Never build your preaching of forgiveness on the fact that God is our Father and He will forgive us because He loves us. It is untrue to Jesus Christ's revelation of God; it makes the Cross unnecessary, and the Redemption 'much ado about nothing.' If God does forgive sin, it is because of the Death of Christ, and the Death of Christ alone! God could forgive men in no other way than by the death of His Son, and Jesus is exalted to be Saviour because of His death. 'We see Jesus because of the suffering of death, crowned with glory and honour.' The greatest note of triumph that ever sounded in the ears of a startled universe was that sounded on the Cross of Christ — 'It is finished.' That is the last word in the Redemption of man."*

And then: *"Anything that belittles or obliterates the Holiness of God by a false view of the Love of God, is untrue to the Revelation of God given by Jesus Christ. Never allow the thought that Jesus Christ stands with us against God out of pity and compassion; that He became a curse for us out of sympathy with us. Jesus Christ became a curse for us by the Divine Decree. Our portion of realizing the terrific meaning of the curse is conviction of sin, the gift of shame and penitence is given us — this is the great mercy of God. Jesus Christ hates the wrong in man, and Calvary is the estimate of His hatred."*[1]

(6) "THEN ANSWERED THE LORD UNTO JOB OUT OF THE WHIRLWIND, AND SAID,

(7) "GIRD UP YOUR LOINS NOW LIKE A MAN: I WILL DEMAND OF YOU, AND YOU DECLARE UNTO ME.

(8) "WILL YOU ALSO DISANNUL MY JUDGMENT? WILL YOU CONDEMN ME, THAT YOU MAY BE RIGHTEOUS?

(9) "HAVE YOU AN ARM LIKE GOD? OR CAN YOU THUNDER WITH A VOICE LIKE HIM?

(10) "DECK YOURSELF NOW WITH MAJESTY AND EXCELLENCY; AND ARRAY YOURSELF WITH GLORY AND BEAUTY.

(11) "CAST ABROAD THE RAGE OF YOUR WRATH: AND BEHOLD EVERY ONE WHO IS PROUD, AND ABASE HIM.

(12) "LOOK ON EVERYONE WHO IS PROUD, AND BRING HIM LOW; AND TREAD DOWN THE WICKED IN THEIR PLACE.

(13) "HIDE THEM IN THE DUST TOGETHER; AND BIND THEIR FACES IN SECRET.

(14) "THEN WILL I ALSO CONFESS UNTO YOU THAT YOUR OWN RIGHT HAND CAN SAVE YOU."

The diagram is:

1. (Vs. 7) Job is given every opportunity of making good his pleas before God. If he has anything to say that he really wishes to urge, God is ready, even anxious, to hear him.

2. (Vs. 8) Men have been trying to disannul the Judgment of God from the very beginning. God's Judgment is His Word.

3. As it regards Verse 10, Job could not *"array himself with glory and beauty;"* however, even though Job could not do such, the Lord could and, in fact, ultimately did!

4. According to Verse 14, man's problem has ever been that he thinks that he can save himself. There's only one answer for man, and that is *"Jesus Christ and Him Crucified"* (I Cor. 1:23).

STAND UP LIKE A MAN

I'm sure the Command by the Lord was instantly obeyed; however, Job must have been a pitiful sight.

No doubt, he had lost much weight, down to the proverbial skin and bones and, as well, his body filled with sore boils, with him sitting in ashes. He had been reduced to a most humiliating position. And the Lord had allowed it so!

And now as the Lord speaks to him, which very well could have been in the presence of his *"three friends,"* and even others, He demands that Job, despite his forlorn appearance, stand up like a man. This within itself was a sign that the Lord was about to turn the thing around, which He most definitely did. With the Lord on the scene, it didn't really matter what others thought, as should be obvious. The Lord had the Power to do whatever it is He so desired. As He speaks to the Patriarch, He demands that he comport himself with dignity, even though the truth is, he has no dignity left.

The Lord doesn't push people down, He lifts them up, and Job is an excellent example of what I say. Satan is the one who steals, kills, and destroys. The Lord is the One Who gives *"more abundant life"* (Jn. 10:10).

CAN MAN'S OWN RIGHT HAND SAVE HIM?

This is the great question, and hits at the very heart of the Gospel of Jesus Christ.

Emphatically no! Man cannot save himself, irrespective as to what he might do, or might not do. Not only can man not save himself, neither can Believers sanctify themselves. And yet, we seem to keep on trying.

If one were to ask what the real problem in the modern church is and, in fact I suppose in every church, it would be the answer to this question. It's somewhat ironical! The church, at least those who claim to believe the Bible, tell the unconverted, that their good works will not save them and, in fact, there's nothing they can do to save themselves, except place their Faith and trust exclusively in the Lord Jesus Christ and what He did for us at the Cross. And then Believers, after relaying that correct information to the world, turn right around, and try to sanctify ourselves, in effect, doing the very thing that we're telling the world that they cannot do. It's the biggest problem in the church and, in fact, has always been the biggest problem in the church.

There is absolutely nothing the Believer can do within himself, within his own ability and strength, within his own sincerity and efforts, that can perfect holiness, righteousness, the Fruit of the Spirit, etc. Paul said that if we could do these things, then Christ died in vain (Gal. 2:21). But we keep trying!

The very reason that God became man, which is the Incarnation, and came for the express purpose of going to the Cross, is because what we need to do, and what we need to have, which we cannot accomplish. So, He did it all for us.

IT'S ALL IN THE CROSS

While the Conception of Christ was of vast significance, and while His virgin Birth was again of vast significance and all absolutely necessary, while His Miracles and Healings were of vast significance, and His Perfect Life of vast significance, again, all absolutely necessary, still, had it stopped there, man would have been left out in the cold. While all these other things were of vast significance, and were something that had to be, it was the Cross where Jesus paid the price, satisfied the ransom owed by man to God, and, thereby, did so by atoning for all sin. As we say it again and again, Christ is the Source of all things we receive from God, while the Cross is the Means by which these things come to us, all superintended by the Holy Spirit. Jesus said:

"In the last day, that great day of the feast, Jesus stood and cried, saying, If any man thirst, let him come unto Me, and drink.

"He who believes on Me, as the Scripture has said, out of his belly shall flow rivers of Living Water.

"But this spoke He of the Spirit, which they who believed on Him should receive..." (Jn. 7:37-39).

When I learned that the victory was not in me but rather in Christ, then I found Victory! When I learned that the overcoming Grace was not in me, but solely in Christ, then I became an overcomer, and did so instantly.

We keep trying to find victory by doing certain things, or not doing certain things. We keep trying to be an overcomer by not doing certain things, or doing certain things. We always fail, as fail we must.

EVERYTHING CHRIST DID WAS FOR YOU AND ME

This is the first lesson that we as Believers must learn. He did nothing for Himself, did nothing for the Father in Heaven per se, did nothing for Angels, and because nothing was needed in that capacity. He came to this world for us! He lived a Perfect Life for us! He went to the Cross for us! As stated, it was all for us. We must get that in our mind and our spirit.

Now, if He had to do all of these things, live a Perfect Life, not sin even one time in word, thought, or deed, and then go to the Cross in order that our sin debt may be paid, from all of that we should realize that the grasp of those things is completely out of our reach. He did it for us, because we could not do it for ourselves.

We often hear preachers say, *"Jesus took our place on the Cross."*

That's not exactly correct!

It would not have done anybody or anything any good whatsoever for us to have hung on a thousand crosses. If we had died on Crosses, suffering exactly as He suffered, it would have Saved no one, not even ourselves. We would have been looked at by God as a polluted sacrifice, which we most definitely were.

He took our place only in the capacity, of becoming Man, and doing for us what we could not do. In fact, what He did for us was not something that was merely difficult or hard, it was completely out of our reach in totality. In other words, had Christ not gone to the Cross, we could not have been Saved, meaning that we would have burned in Hell forever and forever. That's how important that He is, and what He did!

PREACHING THE CROSS

That's the reason that it's absolutely imperative that the preacher preach the Cross (I Cor. 1:23), sing the Cross, proclaim the Cross, and look to the Cross. That's the reason that Jesus said that if we did not do this, *"you cannot be My Disciple"* (Lk. 14:27).

The only way a person can be Saved, the

only way a Believer can be baptized with the Holy Spirit, and live a victorious life, is by the means of what Jesus did at the Cross. It can come no other way. So, when these preachers get over television, or anywhere else, and claim that we can save ourselves, that we can sanctify ourselves, and do so by merely changing our habits, etc. they are preaching a worthless gospel.

THE MORALITY GOSPEL

Everyone wants to better themselves. I read the other day, that self-improvement is now America's pastime. It used to be baseball, but it has been replaced by the self-help efforts.

It sounds good to the carnal ear, because everyone needs improvement. So, when the preacher talks about changing bad habits into good habits, which speaks of morals, we all applaud such statements; however, all must learn and understand that there is no such thing as *"moral evolution."*

WHAT DO WE MEAN BY MORAL EVOLUTION?

This addresses the idea, that man can be what he ought to be, by his own efforts and ability, in other words, his own right hand can save him! This type of preaching will be grandly applauded, but it is totally and completely a wasted effort. Let us say it again:

"There is no such thing as moral evolution."

That's the reason that man must be *"born again,"* and until he is Born-Again, he cannot know or see any change in his morals. Even when he is Born-Again, he will find that still there are some things in his life, that aren't right, which he struggles with. In other words, every single Believer has to pass somewhat through the Seventh Chapter of Romans. But the trouble is, most Believers do not pass through the Seventh Chapter of Romans, they remain in the Seventh Chapter of Romans all of their life and living.

THE CHILDREN OF ISRAEL

The wilderness experience of the Children of Israel after being delivered from Egyptian bondage is a perfect example of the Seventh Chapter of Romans. The Lord could have taken them to the Promised Land in any number of ways. But he chose the wilderness, where there was no food, no water, no visible means of support. They had to go through this trackless, waterless desert, in order to know that God could set a table in the wilderness. In other words, they were to learn trust and obedience. That sojourn in the Mind of God, was intended to last approximately two years. They stayed there forty years, because of unbelief, which was not the Will of God.

As stated, every Believer has to pass through this Seventh Chapter of Romans, but we are only meant to be there a short while, only long enough to learn and understand that there is no profit in the flesh, and that what we need can only be done by the Holy Spirit, Who Works exclusively within the parameters of the Finished Work of Christ. Like the Children of Israel of old, most Christians come to the Seventh Chapter of Romans, and remain there all of their days. To be sure, as the wilderness was not a very happy place, neither is the Seventh Chapter of Romans.

The Lord intends for us to go on the Eighth Chapter of Romans, where we can say with Paul:

"There is therefore now no condemnation (guilt) *to them which are in Christ Jesus* (refers back to Rom. 6:3-5 and our being baptized into His Death, which speaks of the Crucifixion), *who walk not after the flesh* (depending on one's personal strength and ability or great religious efforts in order to overcome sin), *but after the Spirit* (the Holy Spirit works exclusively within the legal confines of the Finished Work of Christ; our Faith in that Finished Work, i.e., *'the Cross,'* guarantees the help of the Holy Spirit, which guarantees Victory)" (Rom. 8:1).

WHY DO BELIEVERS HAVE TO GO THROUGH THE SEVENTH CHAPTER OF ROMANS AT ALL?

If it is to be noticed, the three great Chapters of the Bible, at least as it regards victorious living, are Romans, Chapters 6, 7, and 8. If it is to be noticed, the Seventh Chapter is sandwiched between the Sixth and the Eighth.

The Sixth Chapter of Romans tells us how to have Victory, so that being the case, why is the Seventh Chapter necessary at all?

It is necessary, because the mere fact of theoretically learning something is not enough. We have to experience it. Theoretically we learn the Victory walk in Romans 6. It is referred to as the mechanics of the Holy Spirit, which tells us how He works. But then when we start to put it to the test, we find that old nemesis the flesh rearing its ugly head. We do not recognize it at first as the flesh, because the flesh can imitate the Holy Spirit almost to perfection. Despite knowing what the Sixth Chapter says, the flesh fools us, which means we think that we are following after the Spirit, when in reality we are following after the flesh. To come to know the difference in the two is not done quickly or easily. We find that failure comes our way and even repeated failure. Unfortunately, it seems like we cannot learn what we ought to learn without the failure. While it's definitely not God's Will for such to be, still, He uses these failures, whatever they might be, to teach us many valuable lessons.

But none of this comes quickly or easily. To come from the place of *"O wretched man that I am . . ."* to *"There is therefore now no condemnation . . ."* presents itself as a difficult process.

Someone has said that lack of knowledge is when you don't know. But ignorance is when you don't know that you don't know. Unfortunately, most of the modern church falls into the latter category.

To come from Chapter 7 of Romans to Chapter 8, is not only a matter of knowing and understanding the price that Christ has paid for us at the Cross, but, as well, that we have learned to apply it to our hearts and lives, even on a daily basis (Lk. 9:23).

IT'S ALL A MATTER OF FAITH

Yet, the Faith, of which we speak, has to have the Cross of Christ as its Object. Anything else is spurious. In other words, every single Christian in the world has faith, but for the majority it's not in the correct Object. It's in themselves, their religious denominations, their good works, etc., but it's not really in Christ and the Cross, even though Christ is constantly mentioned.

At the same time, our Faith is never quite what we think it is. In other words, it's not as strong as we think it is, and on the other hand, it's not as weak as we think it is. But this one thing we do know, if one's Faith is exclusively in Christ and what He did at the Cross, that person is on the right track. There will be some ups and downs, some good days and bad days, but if one is on the right road, one will eventually arrive at the correct destination. The problem with the modern church is it's altogether on the wrong road, and irrespective as to what happens, the situation can't get better, but rather worse. If it's not the Cross of Christ then it's not proper Faith. Once again allow us to enumerate this little formula:

FOCUS: The Lord Jesus Christ (Jn. 14:6).

OBJECT OF FAITH: The Cross of Christ (Rom. 6:3-5).

POWER SOURCE: The Holy Spirit (Rom. 8:1-2, 11).

RESULTS: Victory (Rom. 6:15).

(15) "BEHOLD NOW BEHEMOTH, WHICH I MADE WITH YOU; HE EATS GRASS AS AN OX.

(16) "LO NOW, HIS STRENGTH IS IN HIS LOINS, AND HIS FORCE IS IN THE NAVEL OF HIS BELLY.

(17) "HE MOVES HIS TAIL LIKE A CEDAR: THE SINEWS OF HIS STONES ARE WRAPPED TOGETHER.

(18) "HIS BONES ARE AS STRONG PIECES OF BRASS; HIS BONES ARE LIKE BARS OF IRON.

(19) "HE IS THE CHIEF OF THE WAYS OF GOD: HE WHO MADE HIM CAN MAKE HIS SWORD TO APPROACH UNTO HIM.

(20) "SURELY THE MOUNTAINS BRING HIM FORTH FOOD, WHERE ALL THE BEASTS OF THE FIELD PLAY.

(21) "HE LIES UNDER THE SHADY TREES, IN THE COVERT OF THE REED, AND FENS.

(22) "THE SHADY TREES COVER HIM WITH THEIR SHADOW; THE WILLOWS OF THE BROOK COMPASS HIM ABOUT.

(23) "BEHOLD, HE DRINKS UP A RIVER, AND HASTES NOT: HE TRUSTS THAT HE CAN DRAW UP JORDAN INTO

HIS MOUTH.

(24) "HE TAKES IT WITH HIS EYES: HIS NOSE PIERCES THROUGH SNARES."

The pattern is:

1. (Vs. 15) The *"behemoth"* is probably the hippo. This particular animal eats grass.

2. Verse 21, as well, lends more credence to the idea that this is exactly descriptive of the hippopotamus, and far less so of the elephant, or any other such like animal.

3. (Vs. 24) Once again, why would the Lord address these things which seem to have no bearing whatsoever on Job's situation? The idea is, this great contest, with Job caught in the middle between God and Satan, is being played out before the entire spirit world. Among other things, the Lord desires to show the futility of man, or even Satan and fallen Angels, contending with Him. It cannot successfully be done, as should be obvious!

THE BEHEMOTH

In the Fifteenth Verse we are told that the Lord made the *"behemoth"* at the same time He created man. Actually, Genesis tells us that both man and the animal kingdom were created on the Sixth Day, with the man it seems, created first (Gen. 1:24-31).

Some claim that the *"behemoth"* is the Lord's description of the dinosaur; however, even though these things existed, there is no evidence in the Bible of when they existed.

THE DINOSAURS

These huge beasts, none of which are on the Earth at present, came in varied shapes and sizes. But yet the Bible doesn't mention them at all.

Why?

Some have claimed that these beasts existed before the flood, with that deluge destroying them; however, once again, there is no proof of such. While such is possible, it cannot be proven by Scripture.

It is my personal belief, that these prehistoric monsters, as they are sometime called, existed on the pre-Adamic Earth.

There is some Scriptural evidence, that Lucifer, the mighty Archangel ruled this Planet under God in the dateless past (Gen. 1:28; Isa., Chpt. 14; Ezek., Chpt. 28).

NOTES

At a point in time, Lucifer rebelled against God, with approximately one third of the angelic creation throwing in their lot with him. It is my belief that dinosaurs and such creatures existed on the Earth at that time, which is after the rebellion of Lucifer, and before the Planet became *"without form and void"* (Gen. 1:2). How long it remained in this state is anyone's guess. It could have been several thousands of years. At any rate, it is my personal belief that these beasts existed at that time, with some of their bones being unearthed even at present. And yet, all of this is speculative at best. But, to place the dinosaurs as having existed on Earth before the flood, has no Scriptural verification. Yet, we know these things existed, and because the evidence is irrefutable.

THE ORIGINAL CREATION

As it regards the present animal kingdom, we know that during the coming Kingdom Age, that those which are carnivorous (meat eaters), at that time, will revert back to their original creation. The Scriptures says:

"The wolf also shall dwell with the lamb, and the leopard shall lie down with the kid; and the calf and the young lion and the fatling together; and a little child shall lead them. (The character and nature of the Planet, including its occupants and even the animal creation, will revert to their posture as before the Fall.)

"And the cow and the bear shall feed (feed together)*; their young ones shall lie down together: and the lion shall eat straw like the ox.* (This Passage plainly tells us that the carnivorous nature of the animal kingdom will be totally and eternally changed.)

"And the sucking child shall play on the hole of the asp, and the weaned child shall put his hand on the cockatrice' den. (Even though some of the curse will remain on the serpent in the Millennium, in that he continues to writhe in the dust, still, the deadly part will be removed [Gen. 3:14])" (Isa. 11:6-8).

We know that the Fall had an affect on some of the animal kingdom, as is here described.

And then the Scriptures describe *"locusts"*

that will be loosed out of the bottomless pit in the coming Great Tribulation, and the Scripture describes them thusly: *"And the shapes of the locusts were like unto horses prepared unto battle; and on their heads were as it were crowns like gold, and their faces were as the faces of men.* (These are demon spirits, but will be invisible. If they could be seen, this is what they would look like. We aren't told their origin in the Bible. We know they were not originally created in this manner, but evidently became this way in the revolution instigated by Lucifer against God.)"

The description goes on: *"And they had hair as the hair of women, and their teeth were as the teeth of lions.* (They were, no doubt, originally created by God to perform a particular function of praise and worship, even as the *'Living Creatures,'* but they have suffered this fate due to rebellion against God.)

"And they had breastplates, as it were breastplates of iron; and the sound of their wings was as the sound of chariots of many horses running to battle. (We are given a glimpse here into the spirit world. This is the reason such foolish efforts as humanistic psychology are helpless against such foes. The only answer is Christ and the Cross.)

"And they had tails like unto scorpions, and there were stings in their tails: and their power was to hurt men five months. (This judgment is limited to five months, which tells us Satan can only do what God allows him to do.)

"And they had a king over them, which is the Angel of the bottomless pit (gives us further insight into the spirit world of darkness), *whose name in the Hebrew tongue is Abaddon, but in the Greek tongue has his name Apollyon.* (This is a powerful fallen Angel, who evidently threw in his lot with Lucifer in the great rebellion against God. Only four Angels are named in Scripture, *'Gabriel, Michael, Lucifer, and Apollyon,'* the first two being Righteous)" (Rev. 9:3-11).

DEMON SPIRITS

The question has often been asked, where did demon spirits come from? We know that God did not originally create them in this fashion, inasmuch as He has never created anything of such like. They are not fallen Angels as some claim, but rather disembodied spirits, which seek to inhabit a man or a woman, or even a child, or even an animal.

The only answer to this question is that they must have been connected with Lucifer when he originally ruled this Earth under God, which was before Adam and Eve. They evidently served God in righteousness and holiness along with their leader Lucifer, for a period of time. But at the Fall, evidently the creation that was here then, whatever it was, threw in their lot with the Evil One, and then degenerated into spirits of darkness.

We are given very little information concerning all of this, because the Bible is not the account of the fall of Lucifer and those with him, but rather the Fall of man, and man's Redemption, which is by the Lord Jesus Christ.

"There is life for the look at the Crucified One,
"There is life at this moment for thee;
"Then look, sinner, look unto Him and be Saved,
"Unto Him Who was nailed to the tree."

"Oh, why was He there as the bearer of sin,
"If on Jesus your guilt was not laid?
"Oh, why from His Side flowed the sin-cleansing Blood,
"If His dying your debt has not paid?"

"It is not your tears of repentance or prayers,
"But the Blood, that atones for the soul;
"On Him, then, Who shed it, you may at once,
"Your weight of iniquities roll."

"Then doubt not your welcome, since God has declared,
"There remains no more to be done;
"That once in the end of the world He appeared,

"And completed the Work He begun."

"Then take with rejoicing from Jesus at once,
"The life everlasting He gives;
"And know with assurance, you never can die,
"Since Jesus, your Righteousness lives."

CHAPTER 41

(1) "CAN YOU DRAW OUT LEVIATHAN WITH AN HOOK? OR HIS TONGUE WITH A CORD WHICH YOU LET DOWN?

(2) "CAN YOU PUT AN HOOK INTO HIS NOSE? OR BORE HIS JAW THROUGH WITH A THORN?

(3) "WILL HE MAKE MANY SUPPLICATIONS UNTO YOU? WILL HE SPEAK SOFT WORDS UNTO YOU?

(4) "WILL HE MAKE A COVENANT WITH YOU? WILL YOU TAKE HIM FOR A SERVANT FOR EVER?

(5) "WILL YOU PLAY WITH HIM AS WITH A BIRD? OR WILL YOU BIND HIM FOR YOUR MAIDENS?

(6) "SHALL THE COMPANIONS MAKE A BANQUET OF HIM? SHALL THEY PART HIM AMONG THE MERCHANTS?

(7) "CAN YOU FILL HIS SKIN WITH BARBED IRONS? OR HIS HEAD WITH FISH SPEARS?

(8) "LAY YOUR HAND UPON HIM, REMEMBER THE BATTLE, DO NO MORE.

(9) "BEHOLD, THE HOPE OF HIM IS IN VAIN: SHALL NOT ONE BE CAST DOWN EVEN AT THE SIGHT OF HIM?

(10) "NONE IS SO FIERCE WHO DARE STIR HIM UP: WHO THEN IS ABLE TO STAND BEFORE ME?

(11) "WHO HAS PREVENTED ME, THAT I SHOULD REPAY HIM? WHATSOEVER IS UNDER THE WHOLE HEAVEN IS MINE.

(12) "I WILL NOT CONCEAL HIS PARTS, NOR HIS POWER, NOR HIS COMELY PROPORTION.

(13) "WHO CAN DISCOVER THE FACE OF HIS GARMENT? OR WHO CAN COME TO HIM WITH HIS DOUBLE BRIDLE?

(14) "WHO CAN OPEN THE DOORS OF HIS FACE? HIS TEETH ARE TERRIBLE ROUND ABOUT.

(15) "HIS SCALES ARE HIS PRIDE, SHUT UP TOGETHER AS WITH A CLOSE SEAL.

(16) "ONE IS SO NEAR TO ANOTHER, THAT NO AIR CAN COME BETWEEN THEM.

(17) "THEY ARE JOINED ONE TO ANOTHER, THEY STICK TOGETHER, THAT THEY CANNOT BE SUNDERED."

The synopsis is:

1. (Vs. 1) This Chapter is, no doubt, one of the most misunderstood in the entirety of the Word of God. Many have ascertained the description as to refer to some type of huge animal; however, there are certain things said that make us understand that God was not speaking of some such creature, but rather this is a description given of Satan. He is portrayed as a great dragon who is the enemy of both God and man.

2. Regarding Verse 2, the Lord is telling man here that, within himself, he cannot seduce Satan. The battle is not physical, mental, or financial; the battle is Spiritual.

3. According to Verse 3, Satan plies the heart of man continually, seeking to deceive him and, thereby, to lead him astray. Deception is his greatest weapon. He uses *"soft words"* to carry it through to its successful conclusion.

4. According to Verse 4, Satan strongly desires to make a covenant with man. He will promise riches, power, influence, fame, etc. Inasmuch as he is a liar and the father of it, he will make any covenant that man likes, knowing that he will not keep his side of the bargain.

5. Unfortunately, untold millions attempt to do that which is stated in Verse 5; however, they soon find out that Satan and sin are not playthings.

6. (Vs. 6) How many hundreds of millions through the centuries have thought that they were man or woman enough to defeat Satan in their own strength? They found out the hard way that they couldn't!

7. Regarding Verse 8, in effect, the Lord is saying, *"When man attempts to do battle*

with Satan, he should remember that he has lost all of these conflicts in the past. Consequently, he should desire to 'do no more' in this capacity." The Lord Jesus Christ has defeated Satan; He did so at Calvary's Cross.

8. (Vs. 9) No one can bargain with Satan. Every effort is in vain. The one who attempts to do business with him will be *"cast down."*

9. The last phrase of Verse 10 refers to the Lord Himself. Man cannot defeat Satan, but God can and, in effect, has, by the Death, Burial, and Resurrection of the Lord Jesus Christ, which atoned for all sin, thereby completely defeating the Evil One.

10. Verse 11 proclaims the fact that all things belong to God; one day, the Lord will make an end of Satan; the Bible tells us so (Rev. 20:1-3).

11. Verse 12 proclaims the fact that God created the one now called Satan, but not as a fallen Angel, but rather the beautiful Angel, Lucifer. In fact, he served the Lord in righteousness and holiness for an undetermined period of time (Ezek. 28:11-19).

12. (Vs. 14) Satan is very successful in making that which is ugly seem beautiful; that which is wicked seem righteous; that which is evil seem not evil; but behind *"his face"* is terrible destruction.

13. (Vs. 16) The idea of this Chapter, among other things, is that man is unable within himself to oppose Satan, as he would other creatures.

SATAN

This Chapter is, as stated, one of the most misunderstood in the entirety of the Word of God. Many have ascertained the description to refer to any number of things; the Loch Ness monster, or some type of sea dragon of which we now have no knowledge; however, there are certain things said that make us understand that God is not speaking of some undersea animal or any such creature.

The description given by the Lord is a symbol of Satan.

The Fifteenth Verse speaks of his pride.

The word *"pride"* is not used of beasts in all the Book of Job, nor anywhere else in the Bible. In Verse 34, he is called the *"king over all the children of pride."* Thus, Leviathan could be none other than Satan, *". . . the spirit that now works in all sons of disobedience and pride"* (Eph. 2:1-3).

There are some things that are said by the Lord in these Passages that give us an idea as to how Satan works. Why the Lord would have chosen this manner in which to describe Satan is not known; nevertheless, if man will take the trouble to look deep into that which God has said, asking the Holy Spirit to give Guidance and Direction, the truth of the Text will become more obvious.

Most of mankind doesn't even believe there is a creature called *"Satan."* Irrespective, he exists, and heads up the world of spiritual darkness.

PLAYING WITH SATAN

The Fifth Verse proclaims the Lord asking, *"Will you play with him as with a bird? Or will you bind him with your maiden?"*

Strangely enough, most of the world plays with Satan every day. Every time you turn on your television set and see the telephone numbers of *"psychics,"* urging the unwary viewer to seek such services, this is men *"playing with Satan."* The reading of every horoscope is men *"playing with Satan."* Likewise, every person who views an obscene movie, or looks at an obscene magazine, or engages in obscene joke-telling is, in effect, *"playing with Satan."* Most of the music industry is inspired by the powers of darkness; consequently, when these records or tapes are bought and played, one is literally *"playing with Satan;"* however, the end results cease to be *"play"* and become *"death."*

As well, there is no way that one can *"bind him for your maidens."* How many teenage girls each year become pregnant without the benefit of a husband? When the tryst began, they may have been innocent, but Satan soon stripped them of their innocence. How many lovely young ladies have popped pills into their mouths or put a needle into their veins thinking they could beat the odds? But they find that Satan cannot be *"bound."* The end results are death.

TRYING TO DEFEAT SATAN

As stated, most of the world doesn't even

believe there is such a being as Lucifer, i.e., "*Satan.*" And if they have any thought of him at all, it's mostly in a lackadaisical way. In their thinking they do not need the Word of God. Anyway, according to the modern pundits, the Bible is outdated, old-fashioned, and useless. As well, they do not need the Lord Jesus Christ and His Saving Grace. Many have tried this route, and it should be understood, all have failed.

Furthermore, Satan is big business. In fact, one of the biggest businesses in the world is the elicit drug business; likewise, alcohol; as well, most of what Hollywood produces, which covers all of the entertainment business. In fact, Satan is big business! Truly, they have *"parted him among the merchants"* — but at what price?

Men have ever tried to conquer Satan by their *"good conduct,"* *"New Year's resolutions,"* *"good intentions,"* and even *"religiosity."* Men deceive themselves. Satan does not respond to all the efforts made, be they ever so intelligent, to subdue evil.

According to the Eighth Verse our Lord said, *"Lay your hand upon him, remember the battle, do no more."* In effect, he is saying, *"When man attempts to do battle with Satan, he should remember that he has lost all these conflicts in the past; consequently, he should desire to 'do no more' in this capacity."* In fact, the Lord Jesus Christ has defeated Satan; He was the only One Who could do so; consequently, we do not have to defeat him and, in fact, could not if we tried.

HOW DID JESUS DEFEAT SATAN AT CALVARY?

When we speak of our Lord defeating Satan, exactly what do we mean by that?

As I'm certain is understood, this was not a physical conflict. As it regards power, our Lord is the Creator of all things, meaning that He is all-powerful. Satan is a created being, which means in one way or the other, he must answer to the Lord. In effect, he is no match for the Creator in any capacity.

The manner in which he was defeated was in that which Jesus did in atoning for all sin. Sin is that which gave Satan the legal right to hold man captive. In fact, inasmuch as God makes all the Laws, this is a Law that God made. Of course, Satan took full advantage of it. The Word of God says, *"The wages of sin is death"* (Rom. 6:23). So, it is sin that gave and gives the Evil One the legal right to do the things that he does. And yet, our Lord atoned for all sin, past, present, and future at Calvary's Cross. That being the case, and it most definitely is, how is it that Satan can hold anyone in bondage at the present?

As it regards those who do not know the Lord, they are held captive, simply because they will not avail themselves of that which our Lord has done, namely the Redemption afforded at Calvary. So Satan has the legal right to continue to hold them in bondage. That bondage includes alcoholism, drug addiction, gambling, hate, murder, nicotine, in fact, every vice that one can mention, coupled with fear, doubt, unbelief, etc.

That having been said, it still leaves in question the millions of Christians, who are truly Saved, many of them baptized with the Holy Spirit, but are yet in bondage. How is this?

CHRISTIANS HELD CAPTIVE BY SATAN

In fact, most Christians are in bondage in some way. I realize that is quite a statement, and upon reading this, many may ask as to how I could know that? Please read the next two paragraphs and I will tell you.

The Cross of Christ is the only answer for the Child of God as it regards living a godly life. In other words, even as we have said over and over again in this Volume, the Believer must make the Cross of Christ the Object of his Faith, and that in totality. Then and only then will the Holy Spirit exert His almighty Power on behalf of the Child of God. It is the Cross which gives the Holy Spirit the legal means to do all that He does. Calvary was a legal Work, which makes possible Justification by Faith. And what Jesus did there, which means to atone for all sin, which means that the sin debt was lifted from everyone who has placed their Faith in Christ, this gave liberty to the Holy Spirit to come into the heart and life of the Believer and there to abide forever (Jn. 14:16).

But the trouble is, even though the Holy Spirit most definitely abides in the heart and life of every Believer, still, He is greatly limited as to what He can do on our behalf according to the object of our faith. And the reason I know that most Believers are in bondage in some way, is because the object of their faith is anything and everything except the Cross of Christ. And how do I know that? I know it simply because the Cross is not being preached in most Churches.

THE CROSS OF CHRIST AND SANCTIFICATION

While all true Believers have at least a modicum of knowledge as it regards the Cross of Christ and Salvation, heralded by the words, *"Jesus died for me,"* still, that is about their limit of knowledge as it regards the Cross. Most Christians don't have the foggiest idea of what we are talking about when we speak of the Cross of Christ and our Sanctification, in other words, as to how the Believer is to live for God.

Please read the next paragraph very carefully.

Virtually the entirety of the Bible, which means all but a small part, is given over to telling us how to live for God. Now think about that for a moment!

Only a small part of the Word of God is devoted to telling people how to be Saved. The reason for that is obvious, the unsaved do not understand the Bible anyway (I Cor. 2:14). This means that the Word of God was given to Believers. And considering that almost all of it is given over to telling people how to live for God, tells us just how important this really is.

A person can be Saved in a moment's time, which is the greatest thing that could ever happen to anyone; however, living for God, at least living victoriously is something else altogether. One can do so only on the premise of functioning according to God's Prescribed Order of Victory.

GOD'S PRESCRIBED ORDER OF VICTORY

The Believer is to understand that everything that we receive from God, and I mean everything, comes from Christ as the Source;

NOTES

however, the Believer must also understand, that it is the Cross which has made it all possible. The Cross made possible the Born-Again experience, made possible the Baptism with the Holy Spirit, made possible Divine Healing, made possible the Fruit of the Spirit being developed within our lives, made possible Righteousness and Holiness, made possible the Grace of God, in fact, the Cross has made possible all things that we receive from the Lord. We must never forget that. But this is where the problem comes in.

Most Christians simply do not believe that which I've just stated. They do not believe the Cross of Christ is the means by which we receive everything. It is because they are taught the very opposite from behind the pulpit.

Every type of scheme, effort, work, and devotion that one can think of is trotted out for Believers, telling them that this thing, whatever it might be, is the key to all victory. One year it is manifestations, the next year it is memorizing three Scriptures, the next year it's the family curse, the next year it's falling out under the power, the next year it's *"The Purpose Driven Life,"* the next year it's whatever preachers can think up. And please believe me, the more outrageous the claim, it seems the more it is accepted.

The Scriptural Truth is, it is impossible for the Believer to live a victorious life, outside of the Cross of Christ. While that individual can continue to be Saved, they cannot live a life of victory outside of the Cross. Paul said:

"For if Righteousness come by the Law, then Christ is dead in vain" (Gal. 2:21).

Satan was defeated at Calvary, and defeated in totality. As a Believer, I do not have to fight those battles all over again.

IF MY FAITH IS RIGHT DOES THAT MAKE IT EASY TO LIVE FOR GOD?

No it doesn't!

I'll be as honest with you as I know how, living for the Lord is the most difficult thing that an individual can ever do. To be sure, the rewards are so astronomical as to defy all description, and I suppose that's the reason that Satan contests every Believer, and does so with all of his power and strength.

Listen to Paul:

"*. . . In labours more abundant, in stripes above measure, in prisons more frequent, in deaths oft* (means that he was exposed to death often).

"Of the Jews five times received I forty stripes save one.

"Thrice was I beaten with rods (different from the beatings listed in the previous Verse), *once was I stoned, thrice I suffered shipwreck, a night and a day I have been in the deep* (probably refers to a particular time when the Apostle was adrift on the open sea for a night and a day, and was in constant danger of drowning);

"In journeyings often, in perils of waters, in perils of robbers, in perils by my own countrymen, in perils by the heathen, in perils in the city, in perils in the wilderness, in perils in the sea, in perils among false brethren (this probably represents the crowning danger);

"In weariness and painfulness, in watchings often, in hunger and thirst, in fastings often, in cold and nakedness" (II Cor. 11:23-27).

But the following is that which we must remember:

This life is merely a dress rehearsal for eternity. We must never forget, eternity is a long, long time. It is forever! So, Paul also said: *"For I reckon that the sufferings of this present time* (speaks of the world and its condition because of the Fall) *are not worthy to be compared with the glory* (the glory of the coming future time will bear no relation to the misery of this present time) *which shall be revealed in us* (our Glory will be a reflected Glory, coming from Christ)" (Rom. 8:18).

The Lord's Way is the Cross of Christ. It was there that every Victory was won, and this great Salvation experience was completed. When Jesus said, *"It is finished,"* it meant exactly what was said.

All of this means that the sinner can be Saved only because of what Jesus did at the Cross. It also means that the Christian can live a sanctified life, which means to be separated totally and completely unto the Lord, only by the means of the Cross.

NOTES

WAS IT WHO HE WAS OR WHAT HE DID?

It was both!

Most of the time when this question is asked, the individual doing the asking is denigrating the Cross. The truth of the Scripture concerning this is:

First of all, there is no one that could have carried out the great Plan of Redemption but Christ. That's the reason that God became Man, i.e., *"the Incarnation."* He had to be virgin born, as He was, and had to live a perfect life, never failing not even one time in word, thought, or deed. In other words, He had to keep the Law perfectly, which He did! But had it stopped there, Salvation could never have been effected.

Not only did He have to keep the Law perfectly, but, as well, He had to address the broken Law, which was incumbent upon every individual, which He did at Calvary. Let's look at it another way.

Jesus Christ has always been God. In fact, He was very God at the same time that He was very Man. He never ceased to be God and, in fact, will always be God. When He became Man, He laid aside the expression of His Deity, He never for a moment lost the possession of His Deity. As stated, He was very God and very Man. This doesn't mean half God and half man, but totally God and totally Man.

But, as God, which He always was, that did not within itself save anyone. Now think about that for a while. If it was only Who He was, well then He would not have had to go to the Cross. He could have just Saved man by decree, because He was and is Deity. But, that wasn't done, because to have done such would have been in opposition to the Nature and the Character of God. While God has the Power to do anything, He will never violate His Nature, His Being, His Character, or His Righteousness. So, to pay the terrible debt of sin, He would have to become man, which was the very reason that He became man, and go to the Cross.

God cannot die, so in order for the Sacrifice to be complete, He would have to become Man, which He did. He did it in order to die on the Cross.

The Cross was perfected in the Mind of the Godhead from before the foundation of the world.

THE CROSS OF CHRIST IS THE FOUNDATION OF REDEMPTION

Peter said:

"Forasmuch as you know that you were not redeemed with corruptible things, as silver and gold (presents the fact that the most precious commodities [silver and gold] could not redeem fallen man), *from your vain conversation* (vain lifestyle) *received by tradition from your fathers* (speaks of original sin that is passed on from father to child at conception);

"But with the Precious Blood of Christ (presents the payment, which proclaims the poured out Life of Christ on behalf of sinners), *as of a Lamb without blemish and without spot* (speaks of the lambs offered as substitutes in the old Jewish economy; the Death of Christ was not an execution or assassination, but rather a Sacrifice; the Offering of Himself presented a Perfect Sacrifice, for He was Perfect in every respect [Ex. 12:5]):

"Who verily was foreordained before the foundation of the world (refers to the fact that God, in His Omniscience, knew He would create man, man would Fall, and man would be redeemed by Christ going to the Cross; this was all done before the universe was created; this means the Cross of Christ is the Foundation Doctrine of all Doctrine, referring to the fact that all Doctrine must be built upon that Foundation, or else it is specious), *but was manifest in these last times for you* (refers to the invisible God Who, in the Person of the Son was made visible to human eyesight by assuming a human body and human limitations),

"Who by Him do believe in God (it is only by Christ and what He did for us at the Cross that we are able to 'Believe in God'), *Who raised Him* (Christ) *up from the dead* (His Resurrection was guaranteed insomuch as He atoned for all sin [Rom. 6:23]), *and gave Him Glory* (refers to the exaltation of Christ); *that your Faith and Hope might be in God.* (This speaks of a heart Faith in God, Who saves sinners in answer to our Faith in the Resurrected Lord Jesus Who died for us)" (I Pet. 1:18-21).

Let us say it again:

The Cross of Christ was ordained by the Godhead even before the foundation of the world. This means that every single Doctrine in the Bible must be built exclusively on the Foundation of the Cross of Christ, or else it will be specious in some way. In fact, that's the reason for all false doctrine. It is a false interpretation of the Cross, a wrong interpretation of the Cross, i.e., *"sincere but wrong,"* or it is a denial of the Cross. Let us say it again:

Our Lord is the Source of all things that we receive from God, and I mean all things, with these things being given to us exclusively by the Means of the Cross, all superintended exclusively by the Holy Spirit (Jn. 3:16; Rom. 6:1-14; 8:1-2, 11; I Cor. 1:17-18, 21, 23; 2:2; Gal., Chpt. 5; 6:14; Eph. 2:13-18; Col. 2:14-15).

(18) "BY HIS NEESINGS A LIGHT DOES SHINE, AND HIS EYES ARE LIKE THE EYELIDS OF THE MORNING.

(19) "OUT OF HIS MOUTH GO BURNING LAMPS, AND SPARKS OF FIRE LEAP OUT.

(20) "OUT OF HIS NOSTRILS GOES SMOKE, AS OUT OF A SEETHING POT OR CALDRON.

(21) "HIS BREATH KINDLES COALS, AND A FLAME GOES OUT OF HIS MOUTH.

(22) "IN HIS NECK REMAINS STRENGTH, AND SORROW IS TURNED INTO JOY BEFORE HIM.

(23) "THE FLAKES OF HIS FLESH ARE JOINED TOGETHER: THEY ARE FIRM IN THEMSELVES; THEY CANNOT BE MOVED.

(24) "HIS HEART IS AS FIRM AS A STONE; YES, AS HARD AS A PIECE OF THE NETHER MILLSTONE.

(25) "WHEN HE RAISES UP HIMSELF, THE MIGHTY ARE AFRAID: BY REASON OF BREAKINGS THEY PURIFY THEMSELVES.

(26) "THE SWORD OF HIM WHO LAYS AT HIM CANNOT HOLD: THE SPEAR, THE DART, NOR THE HABERGEON.

(27) "HE ESTEEMS IRON AS STRAW, AND BRASS AS ROTTEN WOOD.

(28) "THE ARROW CANNOT MAKE HIM FLEE: SLINGSTONES ARE TURNED WITH HIM INTO STUBBLE.

(29) "DARTS ARE COUNTED AS STUBBLE: HE LAUGHS AT THE SHAKING OF A SPEAR.

(30) "SHARP STONES ARE UNDER HIM: HE SPREADS SHARP POINTED THINGS UPON THE MIRE.

(31) "HE MAKES THE DEEP TO BOIL LIKE A POT: HE MAKES THE SEA LIKE A POT OF OINTMENT.

(32) "HE MAKES A PATH TO SHINE AFTER HIM; ONE WOULD THINK THE DEEP TO BE HOARY.

(33) "UPON EARTH THERE IS NOT HIS LIKE, WHO IS MADE WITHOUT FEAR.

(34) "HE BEHOLDS ALL HIGH THINGS: HE IS A KING OVER ALL THE CHILDREN OF PRIDE."

The composition is:

1. Verse 25 lends some credence to the idea that Lucifer could have been the most powerful of all the Angels ever created by God.

2. The Twenty-sixth Verse proclaims the fact that no natural weapon will suffice against Satan.

3. (Vs. 34) Pride is the crowning sin that besets the human race. It is the foundation sin of all sin; it is the *"good side"* of the *"Tree of the Knowledge of Good and Evil."* Behind every sin, one ultimately will find pride. It is that which God cannot abide. It is the sin that caused the downfall of Lucifer (Ezek. 28:17). Pride is the sin that caused the Fall of Adam and Eve in the Garden of Eden (Gen. 3:5-7). Pride is the sin that God hates more than any sin, *"a proud look"* (Prov. 6:16-17).

PRIDE

The Scripture says concerning pride, *"These six things does the LORD hate: yes, seven are an abomination unto Him* (the phrase, 'six things . . . yes, seven . . .' is a figure of speech arresting attention and signifying that the list is not exhausted):

"A proud look (pride leads the list), *a lying tongue* (such always follows 'a proud look'), *and hands that shed innocent blood* (this pertains to murderers; however, it also pertains to those who murder someone's character),

"And an heart that devises wicked imaginations (the 'heart' of the 'proud' devises 'wicked imaginations' because the heart has not been changed), *feet that be swift in running to mischief* (as pride is deceptive, this sin is, therefore, cloaked; it actually believes it is doing right),

"A false witness that speaks lies (the difference in the 'lying tongue' of Verse 17 and the 'false witness' of Verse 19 is that the 'lying tongue' will only tell the truth if it suits his advantage; otherwise, he will lie; the 'false witness' premeditates lies; he concocts schemes that are made up of lies, in order to carry out a perfidious evil design), *and he who sows discord among brethren* (individuals who 'sow discord' do so for the purpose of carrying out schemes)" (Prov. 6:16-19).

As stated, *"A proud look,"* i.e., *"pride,"* leads the list.

Solomon also wrote: *"He who is of a proud heart stirs up strife: but he who puts his trust in the LORD shall be made fat.* (The 'proud heart' is the bane of all people, but especially the Christian. Such pertains to a greedy disposition. It will always 'stir up strife,' because it is never satisfied with the path that God has laid out, but rather seeks its own direction)" (Prov. 28:25).

The Beatitudes begin with, *"Blessed are the poor in spirit: for theirs is the Kingdom of Heaven"* (Mat. 5:3).

The *"poor in spirit"* are those who are *"conscious of their moral poverty."* It is the opposite of pride.

This is the reason it is so difficult for most people to accept Christ. They refuse to admit what they are, morally bankrupt, and Who He is, the Son of the Living God!

THE CROSS OF CHRIST

Pride, no doubt, is the biggest reason that many Christians will not accept the Cross as it regards their Sanctification. They refuse to admit that what God demands of them as Believers, they cannot supply. No matter how hard they try, no matter how sincere they might be, there is no way that we, at least of ourselves, can attain to that which is demanded of us. It is impossible!

But to admit that, which means to admit that we are helpless as it regards our passions, and the desires of the flesh, is very hard for many to do. And as a result, many, if not most, continue to go their own way, which means they are rejecting God's Way, which is the Cross of Christ, which direction, and without a doubt, will guarantee defeat and even wreckage.

I remember at a particular time mentioning the Cross to a preacher. I will not forget his answer. He said:

"That's good for some people, but it's not needed for all."

How utterly ridiculous!

Sadly and regrettably, that preacher completely lost his way, and as far as I know, is not presently even making an attempt to live for God.

No, there are no exceptions to this. Pride is the culprit, and Satan is the chief of pride.

The Scripture says: *"For all those things have My Hand made, and all those things have been, says the LORD: but to this man will I look, even to him who is poor and of a contrite spirit, and trembles at My Word.* (The Great Temple fashioned by Jehovah's Hand, i.e., the heavens and the Earth, is contrasted in Verse 2, and the statement is made that God's true Temple is the heart that trembles at His Word.

"The 'contrite man' is one with a broken, crushed, contrite spirit. The only One Who actually fits this description is Christ; therefore, for the Lord to properly look at us, one must be properly in Christ, which can only be by the means of the Cross [Rom. 6:3-5])" (Isa. 66:2).

All of this means that the Cross of Christ is the only answer for pride. In fact, there is no other! If men refuse the Cross, and whomever they might be, they are left with no solution.

"Look to the Saviour on Calvary's tree,
"See how He suffered for you and me;
"Hark, while He lovingly calls to thee,
"Look, and you shall live!"

"Have you a sin-burdened soul to save?
"Life everlasting would you have?
"Jesus Himself a ransom gave:
"Look, and you shall live!"

"Look to the Saviour Who rose from the tomb,
"Come now to Him, while there yet is room;
"His saving Grace will dispel your gloom,
"Look, and you shall live!"

"Jesus on high lives to intercede,
"He knows the weary sinner's need;
"Surely your footsteps He will lead,
"Look, and you shall live!"

NOTES

CHAPTER 42

(1) "THEN JOB ANSWERED THE LORD, AND SAID,

(2) "I KNOW THAT YOU CAN DO EVERYTHING, AND THAT NO THOUGHT CAN BE WITHHELD FROM YOU.

(3) "WHO IS HE WHO HIDES COUNSEL WITHOUT KNOWLEDGE? THEREFORE HAVE I UTTERED THAT I UNDERSTOOD NOT; THINGS TOO WONDERFUL FOR ME, WHICH I KNEW NOT.

(4) "HEAR, I BESEECH YOU, AND I WILL SPEAK: I WILL DEMAND OF YOU, AND DECLARE THOU UNTO ME.

(5) "I HAVE HEARD OF YOU BY THE HEARING OF THE EAR: BUT NOW MY EYE SEES YOU.

(6) "WHEREFORE I ABHOR MYSELF, AND REPENT IN DUST AND ASHES."

The diagram is:

1. (Vs. 2) From the Lord's questions to Job, he knows that God is Omnipotent (all-powerful) as well as Omniscient (all-knowing).

2. As it regards Verse 3, even though it seems that God did not directly accuse Job of such, still, after Job saw and heard the Lord, he realized how woeful that his knowledge of God actually was.

3. (Vs. 4) Many times in the last few months, Job had longed for this opportunity to speak to God; now the opportunity presents itself. What he will say after seeing the Lord will not be nearly what he thought he would say. He had spoken of how he would

demand of God, but now he falls silent, and rightly so.

4. From Verse 5, we must believe that God made a visible appearance to Job, and that he was able to see His bodily Shape. As well, we must conclude that God is a literal Person with a Spirit Body.

5. (Vs. 6) Job had previously reported that he had not abhorred himself, but, on the contrary, thought well of himself and had held fast to his moral excellency. The discovery of the deep corruption of the heart is the most painful and humbling that a man can make.

So the Patriarch had to crucify all his goodness as truly as all his badness, and sit in wood ashes as a public confession that he merited death because of his sin-defiled nature.

This moral principle governs the Salvation of the sinner as well as the Sanctification of the Saint.

KNOWLEDGE OF GOD

Correct knowledge of God is found in the Word of God, and only in the Word of God. But yet, to properly understand the Word, one must properly understand the Cross. And that is the problem in this present age in which we live. The Cross is a nonentity, which means that the Word of God is taking second place, if any place at all, hence, the reason that false doctrine is rampant.

The Apostle Paul referred to the Judaisers as *"dogs"* (the word *"dogs"* was used by the Jews for homosexuals.) So, Paul was saying that the Judaisers were to the True Gospel of Jesus Christ, what homosexuals are to the human race. He could not have insulted them more, and above all, it was put in writing and, thereby, done publicly.

What would Paul think of that which passes for the Gospel presently?

From studying him as much as I have, I personally think that he would be just as adamantly opposed to much of that which presently makes the rounds, as he was then, if not more!

Incidentally, Judaisers were Jews from Jerusalem, even probably from the mother Church, who claimed Christ, but at the same time claimed that Believers must also keep the Law, that is if they were to be Saved.

Concerning them, the Scripture says: *"And certain men which came down from Judea taught the Brethren* (presents the greatest crisis of the Early Church), *and said, Except you be circumcised after the manner of Moses, you cannot be Saved* (they were attempting to refute Paul's Message of Grace through Faith; in other words, they were attempting to circumvent the Cross, trying to add the Law of Moses to the Gospel of Grace)" (Acts 15:1).

In fact, this was the reason for the first General Counsel conducted in Jerusalem, and with a favorable decision, we might quickly add, handed down by James the Lord's Brother, who was the senior Pastor of the Church in Jerusalem. In other words, he stated that Gentiles did not have to keep the Law of Moses (Acts 15:19-21).

At the particular time of Job, the Patriarch probably had as great a knowledge of God as anyone in the world at that particular time; however, Job's knowledge would have been woefully lacking by comparison to the privilege and opportunity we have presently. Job had no Bible, except the account passed down from father to son, as it regarded particular experiences. While these were graphic and extremely real, still, it left much to be desired.

Now, and because of the Cross, we look back on a finished Plan of Redemption, where then it was only in the Promise stage. But the question should be asked, as to how many modern Believers truly study the Word of God as they should, thereby, being led of the Spirit to master its contents. A few do, most don't!

Job himself admitted, that when he finally saw the Lord, and was given the opportunity to speak with Him, that he had uttered things of which he had little understanding, *"things too wonderful for me, which I knew not."*

A CORRECT EVALUATION OF SELF

Up until seeing the Lord, Job had thought quite highly of himself. And one can understand such thinking. Job was sincere in his consecration and dedication. He loved the Lord very much. In fact, even though Job did not know such at the time, the conversation in Heaven, at least when the Lord was addressing Satan, was about Job, and his consecration and dedication. In fact, the Lord had said of him, *"there is none like him in the Earth, a perfect and an upright man, one who fears God, and hates evil."* And this was said of Job after he had suffered the onslaught of Satan, with the Evil One taking all of his wealth away, as well as the death of all of Job's children. The Lord said of him, *"He holds fast his integrity, although you move Me against him, to destroy him without cause"* (2:3).

None of this means that Job was remiss. The idea is this:

The Lord was showing the great Patriarch that no matter how sincere he was, no matter how consecrated, no matter how dedicated, that within his own ability he did not have the wherewithal, and neither does anyone else, to be what one ought to be in the sight of God. He fell woefully short, despite his consecration, and so do we. This is, no doubt, the hardest lesson for man to learn, and especially believing man, and especially those who are deeply consecrated.

The Lord appeared to Job, and for several reasons. Now, we have the Word of God, which tells us what we are, and what we ought to be, and how that we can be that which we ought to be only by making the Cross of Christ the Object of our Faith, which then gives the Holy Spirit liberty to work in our lives Who Alone can make us what we should be (Rom. 6:1-14; 8:1-2, 11; I Cor. 1:17-18, 23; 2:2; Eph. 2:13-18; Gal. 6:14; Col. 2:14-15).

THE SANCTIFICATION OF THE SAINT

What we're talking about is the *"Sanctification of the Saint."* Believing man has ever tried to accomplish this task by making more and more rules. Such only succeeds in bringing about self-righteousness, which is the bane of the church and, in fact, always has been. It was self-righteousness which nailed our Lord to the Tree. It continues to do the same presently!

This was not only the hardest lesson for Job to learn, and the main lesson which the Lord was teaching the great Patriarch, but it was the hardest lesson for me personally to learn as well! Until I learned that the Victory was all in Christ, and none at all in me, did I find Victory. Until I learned that overcoming Grace was all in Christ, and none at all in me, did I become an overcomer. It's a hard lesson, however, to learn. Paul didn't learn it until he came to the place that he would cry, *"O wretched man that I am! Who shall deliver me from the body of this death?"* (Rom. 7:24).

Please believe me, the hardest leap of all is to come from Romans 7:24 to Romans 8:1-2.

"There is therefore now no condemnation to them which are in Christ Jesus, who walk not after the flesh, but after the Spirit.

"For the Law of the Spirit of Life in Christ Jesus has made me free from the Law of Sin and Death" (Rom. 8:1-2).

And yet, at the same time, the journey of which I speak is so simple. It merely consists of the Believer saying, and meaning with all of his heart, *"I cannot do that which is required, but Christ has already done it for me. I will place my Faith exclusively in Christ and the Cross, and then the Holy Spirit will make me, as I yield to Him, what I ought to be."*

In effect, when Job said, *"Wherefore I abhor myself, and repent in dust and ashes,"* he was saying the same thing that Paul said, *"O wretched man that I am...."*

(7) "AND IT WAS SO, THAT AFTER THE LORD HAD SPOKEN THESE WORDS UNTO JOB, THE LORD SAID TO ELIPHAZ THE TEMANITE, MY WRATH IS KINDLED AGAINST YOU, AND AGAINST YOUR TWO FRIENDS: FOR YOU HAVE NOT SPOKEN OF ME THE THING THAT IS RIGHT, AS MY SERVANT JOB HAS.

(8) "THEREFORE TAKE UNTO YOU NOW SEVEN BULLOCKS AND SEVEN RAMS, AND GO TO MY SERVANT JOB, AND OFFER UP FOR YOURSELVES BURNT OFFERINGS; AND MY SERVANT JOB SHALL PRAY FOR YOU: FOR HIM WILL I ACCEPT: LEST I DEAL WITH YOU AFTER YOUR FOLLY, IN THAT YOU HAVE NOT SPOKEN OF ME THE THING WHICH IS RIGHT, LIKE MY SERVANT JOB.

(9) "SO ELIPHAZ THE TEMANITE AND BILDAD THE SHUHITE AND

ZOPHAR THE NAAMATHITE WENT, AND DID ACCORDING AS THE LORD COMMANDED THEM: THE LORD ALSO ACCEPTED JOB."

The structure is:

1. (Vs. 7) We find in this account that the Lord completely ignored Elihu.

We will find in this narrative that even though the Lord has spoken well of Job, still, everyone had to change except God! This is a crowning Truth that all must understand and believe. It is not God Who needs to change; we do.

2. (Vs. 8) The answer to Job's *"three friends"* was Calvary, as Calvary is the answer to all. The number *"seven"* speaks of the Perfect Offering of the Lord Jesus Christ at Calvary by the offering of Himself.

3. (Vs. 9) The Lord accepted the intercession of Job on behalf of his *"three friends."* Job is thus a Type of Christ, not merely in his sufferings, but also in his mediatorial character.

THE WRATH OF GOD

We learn from the Seventh Verse, that the Wrath of the Lord is kindled against those who do not *"speak of the Lord the thing that is right,"* which is according to the Word of God.

If one would read carefully the Chapters which proclaim the sayings of Eliphaz, Zophar, and Bildad, we would find that there would not be a derogatory remark about the Lord. So what is the Lord speaking of?

Their statements proclaim the fact that while they knew some things about God, the truth is, they really did not know God. As a result, they were trying to explain something of which they knew precious little.

But the main idea, as presented here as it regards the Wrath of God against these individuals is, they were speaking harshly against Job, and they made God a part of their lie. This is what aroused His Anger. He had said of Job, *"there is none like him in the Earth, a perfect and an upright man, one who fears God, and hates evil"* (1:8). They had said the very opposite of Job.

All of this tells us that the Lord does not take lightly the following:

• He does not enjoy at all lies told about His Children.

• It angers Him greatly, to have His Name made a part of such self-righteousness.

When the modern preacher says over television, or wherever, *"If you will give $1,000, the Lord has told me that all of your bills will be paid by the end of the year,"* such must anger God greatly. In the first place, He hasn't said anything to such a preacher. As well, for His Name to be brought into this evil, and evil it is, makes Him a part of the lie. One should certainly understand how this would anger Him. Such as I see, it is far worse than what Job's *"three friends"* did. And if the Lord had His Wrath stirred up by what they said, what must be His Attitude toward this modern evil!

While it's perfectly proper to say, *"The Lord told me,"* if, in fact, He did; however, we had better be certain that the Lord has spoken to us before we make such a statement.

THE BURNT OFFERING

The answer for the sin of these *"three friends,"* was the Cross of Calvary, typified by the *"seven bullocks and seven rams."* As we stated previously, the number *"seven,"* is God's Perfect Number, and in this case, typifying the perfect Redemption that would be afforded by the Cross of Calvary, at least when that great Work would be brought about. Let the reader understand, there is no other answer for sin except the Cross. In fact, the Cross of Christ is the answer and the only answer for anything and everything that pertains to God and His Dealings with man. In other words, every experience that man has ever had with God has been because of Calvary. Before the Cross, it was typified by the animal sacrifices, as here recorded. But even then, one had to have faith in what those sacrifices represented, which was, namely, the coming Redeemer, the Lord Jesus Christ. The animal sacrifices within themselves contained no Redemption, no forgiveness of any nature. It was what they represented that made the difference. We speak of the Cross.

These *"three friends"* were to take these animals to Job, where they were to be offered in sacrifice. They were to humble themselves before the man whom they had striven to abase and bring low.

As the sacrifice was to be offered, Job was to intercede on their behalf, which the Lord told these *"three friends"* that the Patriarch would do, which he did.

Plainly and clearly the Lord said of this incident as it regards their situation and Job praying for them, *"For him will I accept."* In other words, He is saying that He would not accept their petition. They could not act as their own priest, Job having to function in this capacity.

There was a double reason in this:
• They were to humble themselves before the Patriarch, which they did.
• Job was to humble himself, and despite what they had said about him, to intercede before the Lord on their behalf!

As we have stated over and over, everything that God does with us, is a test. How will we act? How will we react?

So, it was a test not only for these *"three friends"* but for Job as well. Thankfully, all passed this test of the sacrifices.

One can well imagine the fear that filled the hearts of these men when the Lord appeared to Job, and it seems to them as well, when He said, *"My wrath is kindled against you* (speaking to Eliphaz), *and against your two friends: for you have not spoken of Me the thing that is right, as My servant Job has"* (Job 42:7).

First of all, the august Glory of the Lord must have overwhelmed them, and Job as well. But now knowing that the Lord was severely displeased with their attitude and actions, they hardly knew what to expect. The Cross was offered to them, and wisely accepted. It is being offered presently to all the inhabitants of the world, but regrettably, only a few accept.

(10) "AND THE LORD TURNED THE CAPTIVITY OF JOB, WHEN HE PRAYED FOR HIS FRIENDS: ALSO THE LORD GAVE JOB TWICE AS MUCH AS HE HAD BEFORE.

(11) "THEN CAME THERE UNTO HIM ALL HIS BRETHREN, AND ALL HIS SISTERS, AND ALL THEY WHO HAD BEEN OF HIS ACQUAINTANCE BEFORE, AND DID EAT BREAD WITH HIM IN HIS HOUSE: AND THEY BEMOANED HIM, AND COMFORTED HIM OVER ALL THE EVIL THAT THE LORD HAD BROUGHT UPON HIM: EVERY MAN ALSO GAVE HIM A PIECE OF MONEY, AND EVERYONE AN EARRING OF GOLD.

(12) "SO THE LORD BLESSED THE LATTER END OF JOB MORE THAN HIS BEGINNING: FOR HE HAD FOURTEEN THOUSAND SHEEP, AND SIX THOUSAND CAMELS, AND A THOUSAND YOKE OF OXEN, AND A THOUSAND SHE ASSES.

(13) "HE HAD ALSO SEVEN SONS AND THREE DAUGHTERS.

(14) "AND HE CALLED THE NAME OF THE FIRST, JEMIMA; AND THE NAME OF THE SECOND, KEZIA; AND THE NAME OF THE THIRD, KEREN-HAPPUCH.

(15) "AND IN ALL THE LAND WERE NO WOMEN FOUND SO FAIR AS THE DAUGHTERS OF JOB: AND THEIR FATHER GAVE THEM INHERITANCE AMONG THEIR BRETHREN.

(16) "AFTER THIS LIVED JOB AN HUNDRED AND FORTY YEARS, AND SAW HIS SONS, AND HIS SONS' SONS, EVEN FOUR GENERATIONS.

(17) "SO JOB DIED, BEING OLD AND FULL OF DAYS."

The pattern is:

1. (Vs. 10) Job had to humble himself and pray for God to bless these three chieftains who had so despitefully used him and persecuted him. And the three princes themselves had to confess themselves worthy of death and seek forgiveness from God through the Precious Blood of Christ, as foreshadowed in Verse 8, and acceptance before God in the Person of Christ, as typified in Verse 9.

The Book sets off the action of God in leading His Children into a higher Christian experience. The subject of this Book is not how God justifies a sinner so much as it is how God sanctifies a Saint. Hence, none but a good man such as Job could have been chosen for the process or profited by it.

2. (Vs. 11) All of those who had previously spoken so harshly of Job would change their minds now that God has appeared. Public opinion is fickle and always according to appearances and circumstances. Now they would attempt to atone for their judgmental attitudes by giving Job an offering.

3. (Vs. 12) We learn from this narrative, that all goodness and beauty, which men recognize in themselves and in others must be nailed in death to the Cross, and the only Man Who is to live must be the risen Man, Christ Jesus.

True self-abhorrence comes not from self-examination, but in looking away from self to Jesus, the Perfecter, as well as the Author of Faith. Job was very much satisfied with himself until he saw God. *"Self"* is very enticing to man, especially religious self, and self-examination is an interesting occupation and, accordingly, it is found very difficult to learn the lesson to crucify it, and to find that victory is enjoyed when self is ignored and Christ adored — Williams.

4. (Vs. 16) It has been concluded from Verse 16, combined with that at the close of Verse 10, that Job was exactly seventy years of age when his calamities fell upon him. That being the case, Job would have lived to the age of 210.

5. (Vs. 17) In effect, the Book of Job reveals the death of self, the risen life, the school of God, the emptiness of the world, the ugliness of self-righteousness and, above all, the fullness of Christ.

THE DOUBLE PORTION

We learn from Verse 10, that *"The LORD turned the captivity of Job, when he prayed for his friends."*

Quite possibly this wasn't an easy thing for the Patriarch to do. These men, and before all concerned, had ridiculed Job in every capacity, even giving him the worst slur of all, which was to refer to him as a hypocrite. But Job had to forget that, and to pray for those who had despitefully used him, which he did! And when he did that, which means that he held no grudges, forgot the past and what had happened, and wept and cried for them, exactly as he, no doubt, had done the same for himself, then, *"The LORD turned the captivity of Job."*

Then, as well, *"when he prayed for his friends, also the LORD gave him twice as much as he had before."*

All of this is said matter of factly, but we're seeing here an astounding Miracle.

It must be remembered that before this great trial took place that Job *"was the greatest of all the men of the east."* This spoke of his place and position and, as well, of his riches. But now, the Lord will give him twice as much as he *"had before."* It pays to serve God! It pays to live for God! It pays to obey God!

Thus, we have the story of one of the greatest men of God who ever lived, Job. His lesson was not only for himself, but for all of us as well. May God give us the Grace to learn the lesson here taught, in fact, the many lessons here taught. For all of this was meant not only for Job, but for us as well!

CONCLUSION

It is October 9, 2008, as I conclude our efforts as it regards this great Book of Job. I have found that it is one of the greatest studies in the entirety of the Word of God. I would pray that you, the reader, and who I must conclude to be an avid Bible student, has received as much from studying this effort, as I have received from endeavoring to put it together.

I love the Word of God. I do not have the proper vocabulary to express the feelings of my heart as it regards the Sacred Scriptures. To know that what I am studying is in actuality the Word of God, puts it in a category all to itself, as should be obvious. As we have said over and over again, the Bible is the road map for life, and the blueprint for eternity. He who makes every effort to master its contents can be concluded as none other than wise, very wise!

Thank you so very much for being a part of our efforts.

Even though it has only been a short time as it regards the beginning of our efforts concerning this Commentary, still, the effort contains a lifetime of experience, work, and labor. The song says:

"I can see far down the mountain,
"Where I have wandered many years,
"Often hindered on my journey,
"By the ghosts of doubts and fears,
"Broken vows and disappointments,
"Thickly strewn along the way,
"But the Spirit has led unerring,
"To the land I hold today."

BIBLIOGRAPHY

INTRODUCTION

George Williams, *The Students Commentary on the Holy Scriptures,* Grand Rapids, Kregel Publications, 1949, pg. 274.

CHAPTER 2

George Williams, *The Student's Commentary On The Holy Scriptures,* Grand Rapids, Kregel Publications, 1949, pg. 274.

CHAPTER 8

J.W. Meiklejohn, M.B.E., M.A., *New Bible Dictionary: Second Edition,* Wheaton, Tyndale House Publishers, Inc., 1982, pgs. 1211-1212.

CHAPTER 16

H.D.M Spence, *The Pulpit Commentary: Vol. 7,* Grand Rapids, Eerdmans Publishing Company, 1978, pg. 281.

CHAPTER 19

George Williams, *The Student's Commentary On The Holy Scriptures,* Grand Rapids, Kregel Publications, 1949, pgs. 21-22.

CHAPTER 23

Edward R. Pinckney & Cathey Pinckney, *The Fallacy Of Freud And Psychoanalysis,* Englewood Cliffs, New Jersey, Prentice Hall, 1965, pg. 56.

CHAPTER 25

Rick Warren, *The Purpose Driven Life,* Grand Rapids, Zondervan, 2002, pg. 134.
Rick Warren, *The Purpose Driven Church,* Grand Rapids, Zondervan, 1995, pg. 340.
Ibid., pg. 334.

CHAPTER 30

George Williams, *The Student's Commentary On The Holy Scriptures,* Grand Rapids, Kregel Publications, 1949, pg. 290.

CHAPTER 38

George Williams, *The Student's Commentary On The Holy Scriptures,* Grand Rapids, Kregel Publications, 1949, pg. 295.

CHAPTER 39

H.D.M Spence, *The Pulpit Commentary: Vol. 7,* Grand Rapids, Eerdmans Publishing Company, 1978, pg. 634.

CHAPTER 40

Oswald J. Chambers, *The Complete Works Of Oswald Chambers,* Grand Rapids, Discovery House Publishers, 2000, pg. 847.

REFERENCE BOOKS

Atlas Of The Bible — Rogerson
Notes On Exodus — C.H. Mackintosh
Strong's Exhaustive Concordance Of The Bible
The Complete Word Study Dictionary
The Interlinear Greek — English New Testament — George Ricker Berry
The International Standard Bible Encyclopedia
The New Bible Dictionary — Tyndale
The Pulpit Commentary — H.D.M Spence
The Student's Commentary On The Holy Scriptures — George Williams
The Zondervan Pictorial Encyclopedia Of The Bible
Vine's Expository Dictionary Of New Testament Words
Webster's New Collegiate Dictionary
Word Studies In The Greek New Testament, Volume I — Kenneth S. Wuest
Young's Literal Translation Of The Holy Bible

INDEX

The index is listed according to subjects. The treatment may include a complete dissertation or no more than a paragraph. But hopefully it will provide some help.

As well, even though extended treatment of a subject may not be carried in this Commentary, one of the other Commentaries may well include the desired material.

25,000 THOUSAND 108
ABRAHAM AND ISHMAEL 140
ABSURD 271
ACCOUNT OF JOB 28
ACCUSATION THAT SATAN MADE AGAINST GOD AND AGAINST JOB 10
ACCUSATIONS 248
AGAIN 14
AGAINST MERE PROFESSION 126
ALL TRUE CHRISTIANS ARE SAINTS 111
ALMIGHTY 264
ALMIGHTY WILL ANSWER 228
ANCIENT MANUSCRIPTS 173
ANGRY RELIGIOUS LEADERS 199
ANIMATE CREATION 267
ANOTHER EXAMPLE 139
APOSTLE PAUL 130
APOSTOLIC TESTIMONY 55
APPEARANCE OF THE LORD 264
ARROGANCE 241
ARROGANCE, IGNORANCE, AND SELF-RIGHTEOUSNESS 237
ASAPH'S REPENTANCE 155
ATONEMENT 73, 254
AUTHOR OF THE BOOK OF JOB 1
BAPTISM WITH THE HOLY SPIRIT 237
BARBS DIRECTED AT JOB 147
BEFORE THE CROSS 78
BEHEMOTH 282
BELIEVERS AND OUR WORK FOR GOD 51
BITING ACCUSATION 84
BLAMING GOD! 25
BODY IS DEAD BECAUSE OF SIN 132
BONDAGE BROKEN 223

BOOK OF JOB 142
BURNT OFFERING 294
BYWORD 217
CAN A HOMOSEXUAL BE SAVED? 222
CAN MAN'S OWN RIGHT HAND SAVE HIM? 278
CAN THE BELIEVER EVER REACH A STATE OF PERFECTION? 4
CATHOLIC CHARISMATICS 118
CAUSE 66
CHILDREN OF ISRAEL 280
CHRISTIAN PSYCHOLOGY? 167
CHRISTIAN TRADITION 55
CHRISTIANS HELD CAPTIVE BY SATAN 286
CLAIMS OF EVOLUTION 268
COMING OF THE SON OF MAN 210
CONCLUSION 296
CONDITION OF THE WORLD 67
CONTENDING WITH THE ALMIGHTY 276
CONVERSATION WITH SATAN ABOUT JOB 10
CORRECT EVALUATION OF SELF 292
CORRECT OBJECT OF FAITH 99
COUNSELING 168
COVENANT 181
COVERING 123
CREATION 266
CREATION OF THE WORLDS 263
CREATIVE WORK OF THE LORD 263
CROSS OF CALVARY 182
CROSS OF CHRIST 37, 88, 145, 169, 180, 222, 290
CROSS OF CHRIST AND SANCTIFICATION 287
CROSS OF CHRIST AND THE HOLY SPIRIT 121
CROSS OF CHRIST AS A SYNONYM 152
CROSS OF CHRIST IS THE FOUNDATION OF REDEMPTION 289

CROSS OF CHRIST, THE HOLY SPIRIT, AND THE BELIEVER 23
CROSS OF CHRIST, THE OBJECT OF OUR FAITH 104
CROSS OF CHRIST, THE ONLY ANSWER FOR MAN 235
CROSS OF CHRIST, THE ONLY ANSWER TO SELF-RIGHTEOUSNESS? 162
CROSS OF CHRIST, THE ONLY WAY TO VICTORY 40
CROSS OF CHRIST WAS AND IS A LEGAL WORK 35
CRUSADE IN BATON ROUGE 2
DAYSMAN 70
DEAD MATTER 269
DEATH 76
DEFEAT OF SATAN 192
DEGENERATION 270
DELIVERED TO THE UNGODLY 117
DEMON SPIRIT 195, 283
DESTINY OF THE WICKED 157
DID JOB ACTUALLY SEE GOD? 261
DIFFERENCES 269
DINOSAURS 282
DISEASE? 168
DOES ECONOMIC PROSPERITY ALWAYS FOLLOW THE FAITHFUL? 87
DOES GOD HAVE A BODY? 83
DOMINION 185
DOUBLE PORTION 296
DREAM 243
EARLY MORNING PRAYER MEETING 2
EARTHLY GOLD AND SPIRITUAL GOLD 206
EDIFICATION OF THE BELIEVER 36
EMBRYOLOGY 269
ENEMIES OF THE CROSS 201
ENVYING THE WICKED 154
ERRONEOUS DOCTRINE OF ELIPHAZ 28
EVERYTHING CHRIST DID WAS FOR YOU AND ME 279
EXAMPLE! 94
EXAMPLE OF CORINTH 251
FAITHFUL SERVANT 265
FALL OF MAN 97
FALSE PROPHETS 126
FAMILY CURSE 32
FEAR? 26
FEELINGS OF JOB! 174
FEW DAYS AND FULL OF TROUBLE 97
FIERY TRIAL 139
FINAL DOOM OF SATAN 68
FIRST PROMISE OF REDEMPTION 181
FORGIVENESS 252
FOSSIL REMAINS 270

FREE WILL OF MAN 256
FRUITLESS WISDOM OF THE WORLD 129
GIANTS 191
GOD AND MODERN MAN 265
GOD DOES NOT ADDRESS BELIEVERS FROM THE VIEWPOINT OF GOOD AND EVIL 40
GOD IS MY REFUGE 122
GOD THE CREATOR 260
GOD'S PLAN OF SALVATION 101
GOD'S PRESCRIBED ORDER OF VICTORY 92, 99, 194, 274, 287
GOD'S WAYS AND THE WORLD'S WAYS DON'T MIX 170
GOOD MAN AND THE BAD MAN 227
GRACE AND FAITH IS THE ONLY WAY TO HAVE VICTORY OVER SIN 114
GRACE OF GOD? 186
GREAT DOCTRINES 143
GREAT PROBLEM 108
GREAT STRUGGLE 132, 188
GREAT WHITE THRONE JUDGMENT 159
HEARKEN TO ALL MY WORDS? 234
HEDGE 10
HIGHER THAN THE ANGELS 257
HOLY SPIRIT 89, 184, 204
HOMOSEXUALITY 222
HOPE 127
HOPE OF A TREE 104
HOUSE 194
HOW CAN A MAN BE JUSTIFIED WITH GOD? 181
HOW CAN A RIGHTEOUS GOD HONESTLY JUSTIFY AN OBVIOUSLY UNRIGHTEOUS SINNER, AND RETAIN HIS INTEGRITY? 62
HOW CAN THE BELIEVER FIND THIS PATH AND STAY ON THIS PATH? 207
HOW DID JESUS DEFEAT SATAN AT CALVARY? 286
HOW DO WE TAP INTO THIS LIVING WATER? 148
HOW DOES THE BREAKING COME ABOUT? 139
HOW DOES THE HOLY SPIRIT ACCOMPLISH THAT TASK? 104
HOW DOES THE HOLY SPIRIT QUICKEN OUR MORTAL BODY? 134
HOW IS IT THAT THE CROSS OF CHRIST IS THE ANSWER? 6
HOW IS THE CROSS OF CHRIST THE ANSWER FOR SIN? 59
HOW IS THE CROSS OF CHRIST THE ANSWER TO OUR DIFFICULTIES? 34
HOW IS THE CROSS THE POWER OF GOD? 225
HOW IS THE WORK OF SANCTIFICATION PERFORMED BY THE HOLY SPIRIT? 265
HOW MANY CHRISTIANS ARE DOING THE WORK

OF SATAN? 251
HUMAN TRADITION 54, 180
HUMANISTIC PSYCHOLOGY 166, 233
HYPOCRISY 116
HYPOCRISY AND THE TRUE BELIEVER 116
HYPOCRITE 57, 203, 245
I SHALL COME FORTH AS GOLD 171
I'M AS GOOD AS YOU ARE! 227
IF A BELIEVER DOESN'T UNDERSTAND GOD'S PRESCRIBED ORDER OF VICTORY, SATAN CAN FORCE THAT BELIEVER TO DO SOMETHING AGAINST THEIR WILL 59
IF A MAN DIE, SHALL HE LIVE AGAIN? 105
IF MY FAITH IS RIGHT DOES THAT MAKE IT EASY TO LIVE FOR GOD? 287
IMMORALITY 221
IMPERTINENCE OF ELIHU 231
IN CHRIST JESUS 204
IN CLOSING 112
IN THE NAME OF JESUS 195
INSPIRATION 177
INTELLECTUALISM 254
INTERCESSION OF CHRIST 277
INTRODUCTION 1
IS AN ACT OF SIN SIMPLY A MATTER OF SAYING *"YES"* OR *"NO"*? 58
IS FAITH THE GROUND OF JUSTIFICATION? 64
IS IT POSSIBLE FOR SANCTIFYING RIGHTEOUSNESS TO BE BROUGHT UP TO THE LEVEL OF JUSTIFYING RIGHTEOUSNESS? 200
IS IT POSSIBLE TO MERGE BIBLICAL AND CLINICAL COUNSELING? 169
IS IT THAT EASY? 204
IS THERE ENOUGH STRENGTH IN THE HUMAN BEING? 42
IS THERE PLEASURE IN SIN? 158
IS THERE SUCH A THING AS A FAMILY CURSE? 33
ISRAEL AND SELF-RIGHTEOUSNESS 248
IT IS FINISHED 277
IT MATTERS WHAT WE SAY 52
IT'S ALL A MATTER OF FAITH 281
IT'S ALL IN THE CROSS 279
JEWISH TRADITION 55
JOB AND THE HOLY SPIRIT 23
JOB ASKS FOR DEATH 24
JOB DID NOT SIN WITH HIS LIPS 18
JOB KNEW WHAT WAS HAPPENING BUT HE DID NOT KNOW WHAT WAS GOING ON 22
JOB MAKES STATEMENTS CONCERNING GOD 117
JOB PLEADS WITH THE LORD 95
JOB THINKS HE IS DYING 51
JOB'S CONTENTION WITH GOD 72
JOB'S POSITION BEFORE HIS CALAMITY 216
JOB'S REPLY TO ELIPHAZ 39
JOB'S THREE FRIENDS 20
JOB'S THREE FRIENDS AND THE PHARISEES OF JESUS' DAY 144
JOB'S WEALTH 6
JUDGING ONE WHO IS USED OF GOD 20
JUDGMENT AND RE-CREATION 271
JUST UPRIGHT MAN 86
JUSTIFICATION BY FAITH 61, 218
JUSTIFICATION BY FAITH AND SANCTIFICATION BY FAITH 188
JUSTIFYING RIGHTEOUSNESS AND SANCTIFYING RIGHTEOUSNESS 200
KNOWLEDGE OF GOD 292
KNOWLEDGE, WISDOM, AND JOB 246
LAMB OF GOD 69
LAUGHING AT THE CALAMITY OF THE WICKED 161
LEGALISM 187
"LEST THE CROSS OF CHRIST BE OF NONE EFFECT" 90
LET HIM BE ACCURSED 102
LET US HELP OUR BROTHER ON THE JOURNEY OF LIFE 46
LIFE AND LIVING 74
LIMITS OF THE HUMAN SPIRIT 39
LORD GIVES AND THE LORD TAKES AWAY 12
MAJORITY AREN'T ALWAYS RIGHT 141
MAN AND THE MONKEY 269
MAN CANNOT REDEEM MAN 100
MAN IN THE LAND OF UZ WHOSE NAME WAS JOB 4
MAN IS CREATED SPIRIT, SOUL, AND BODY 273
MANNER IN WHICH THE LORD DEALS WITH US 17
MANNER OF GOD 258
MANNER OF REDEMPTION 101
MAN'S APPOINTED TIME ON EARTH 50
MAN'S WISDOM 232
MEANING OF THE NEW COVENANT 163
MEDIATOR 123
METHOD OF VALID TRADITION 55
MILLENNIAL REIGN 210
MISERABLE COMFORTERS 117
MODERN CHURCH 165
MODERN PREACHERS 166
MORALITY GOSPEL 280
MOST CHRISTIANS DON'T KNOW HOW TO LIVE FOR THE LORD 193
MOVING OF THE HOLY SPIRIT 1
NEW COVENANT 226
NEW HEAVEN AND THE NEW EARTH 68
NEW JERUSALEM 69

NEW TESTAMENT EXAMPLE 138
NICODEMUS 175
NO SUCH THING AS MORAL EVOLUTION 214
NOT THE HINT OF SUCH IN SCRIPTURE OR IN THE EARLY CHURCH 109
NUMBER OF MAN'S DAYS 103
ONE WAY 184
OPINIONS 232
ORDINANCES OF HEAVEN 266
ORIGINAL CREATION 282
OUR MINISTRY AT THAT TIME 118
OUR ONLY REFUGE IS THE LORD 166
PARABLE OF THE FIG TREE 210
PARABLE OF THE TALENTS 50
PEACE THAT GOD ALONE CAN GIVE 156
PENANCE 86
PERFECT IN KNOWLEDGE 250
PERFECTION OF CHRIST 41
PERFECTION OF JOB 6
PERMISSION OF THE LORD 11
PERSECUTION 142
PERSONAL 81
PERSONAL EXAMPLE 207, 221, 223
PERSONAL EXPERIENCE 19, 64, 86, 91, 104, 117, 188, 198, 203, 243
PERSONAL ILLUSTRATION 44, 206
PERSONAL RELATIONSHIP 242
PERSONAL RIGHTEOUSNESS OF JOB 197
PERSONAL SALVATION 7
PHYSICIANS OF NO VALUE 90
PIOUS SELF-RIGHTEOUSNESS 162
PLACE AND POSITION OF JOB 214
PLACE CALLED HELL 178
PLAYING WITH SATAN 285
PLIGHT OF THE MODERN CHURCH 113
POLICY OF THE PENTECOSTAL AND CHARISMATIC WORLDS 119
POSITION OF HUMAN MERIT 79
POSSIBLE EXPANSION 78
POWER 224
POWER OF GOD 196, 272
PREACHING OF THE CROSS 131
PREACHING THE CROSS 279
PRESENCE OF THE LORD 243
PRIDE 290
PROBLEM OF SIN IN THE LIFE OF CHRISTIANS 58
PROMISE 182
PROPHECY 195
PUNISHMENT? 47
QUESTIONING GOD! 64
REASON FOR THE BOOK 1
REASONING OF THE HOLY SPIRIT 136

REGION OF HELL 177
REMOVAL OF HOSTILITY BETWEEN GOD AND MAN 63
RENEWED STRENGTH, GREATER THAN EVER 195
RESPONSIBILITY 271
RESURRECTION OF LIFE 105
REVELATION 88
RIGHTEOUSNESS 197
RIGHTEOUSNESS AFTER THE CROSS 199
RIGHTEOUSNESS AND THE BELIEVER 200
RIGHTEOUSNESS OF CHRIST 231
RIGHTEOUSNESS OF GOD 277
SAINTS 31
SANCTIFICATION 138, 183
SANCTIFICATION AND THE CROSS 5
SANCTIFICATION BY WORKS TRANSLATES INTO SELF-RIGHTEOUSNESS 114
SANCTIFICATION OF THE SAINT 75, 293
SARCASM 86
SATAN 8, 14, 285
SATAN CAN DO ONLY WHAT THE LORD ALLOWS HIM TO DO 9
SATAN DECEIVES PEOPLE 111
SATAN'S ATTACK AGAINST THE BIBLE 172
SAVE HIS LIFE 17
SAYING MUCH BUT SAYING NOTHING 259
SECOND RESURRECTION OF DAMNATION 106
SECOND SPEECH OF ELIPHAZ 113
SECULAR HUMANISM 168
SELF 213
SELF-RIGHTEOUSNESS 46, 80
SELF-RIGHTEOUSNESS AND THE CROSS 5
SELF-RIGHTEOUSNESS IN ACTION 164
SELF-RIGHTEOUSNESS IS A WICKED SIN 113
SIGMUND FREUD 167
SIMON PETER 176
SIN 53
SIN AND CALVARY 253
SIN NATURE 88
SIN SHALL NOT HAVE DOMINION OVER YOU 184
SO WHAT IS THE SOLUTION TO OUR PROBLEMS? 34
SOCIOLOGY 167
SOUND OF A RUSHING MIGHTY WIND 195
SPEAKING WICKEDLY FOR GOD 91
SPECIES 268
SPIRIT OF GOD 133
SPIRITUAL GROWTH 121
STAND UP LIKE A MAN 278
STANDPOINT OF HUMAN EXPERIENCE 160
SUBJECT OF WILLPOWER 135
SUBSTITUTE A CHRISTIAN-SOUNDING NAME 108

SUFFERING 131
SUSTAINING THE UNIVERSE 262
TEACHING OF THE ROMAN CATHOLIC CHURCH TODAY 108
TERRIBLE CALAMITIES OF JOB 12
TERRIBLE PROBLEM OF SIN 43
TEST OF FAITH 175
THAT I MAY KNOW HIM 201
THAT WHICH THE LORD ALLOWS IS NOT ALTOGETHER THAT WHICH HE CAUSES 256
THAT WHICH THE LORD GAVE TO PAUL 63
THERE IS A PATH, WHICH NO FOWL KNOWS 206
THIS TRIAL WOULD PROVE HE HEARTS OF ALL 18
THOUGH HE SLAY ME, YET WILL I TRUST HIM 93
THRESHINGFLOOR 119
TONGUE 48
TOTAL DEPRAVITY 214
TROUBLE 98
TRUTH SHALL SET YOU FREE 151
TRYING TO DEFEAT SATAN 285
ULTIMATE END OF SATAN 15
UNDERSTANDING THE CROSS 145
UNLESS YOU BECOME AS A LITTLE CHILD 81
URGENT NEED OF BEING BAPTIZED WITH THE SPIRIT 237
USE OF IMAGES CONDEMNED BY MANY 110
VICARIOUS ASPECT OF THE ATONEMENT 74
VILENESS OF THE HUMAN HEART 276
VISION 29, 118
VISION WAS FOR ME PERSONALLY 120
VOICE OF THE ELDERS IN THE EARLY CHURCH 109
WAS IT WHO HE WAS OR WHAT HE DID? 288
WAYS AND MEANS OF CREATION 262
WAYS OF THE LORD 247
WEAPONS OF OUR WARFARE 194
WHAT ABOUT THE GREAT PREACHERS OF THE PAST WHO WERE NOT BAPTIZED WITH THE SPIRIT? 238
WHAT ABOUT THE MIRACLES AND THE SHRINES? 111
WHAT DID JESUS MEAN BY *"DAILY"*? 149
WHAT DO WE MEAN BY MORAL EVOLUTION? 280
WHAT DO WE MEAN BY THE WORTHLESSNESS OF SELF? 41
WHAT DO WE MEAN *"COHABITING WITH THE LAW"*? 185
WHAT DOES IT MEAN TO BE UNDER GRACE AND NOT LAW? 224
WHAT DOES IT MEAN TO EMBRACE THE CROSS? 92
WHAT DOES IT MEAN TO FRUSTRATE THE GRACE OF GOD? 186, 224
WHAT DOES IT MEAN TO PREACH THE CROSS RELATIVE TO SANCTIFICATION? 235
WHAT DOES IT SHOW US? 94
WHAT DOES THE BIBLE SAY? 110
WHAT DOES THE CROSS ACTUALLY MEAN? 132
WHAT EXACTLY HAPPENED TO MAN AT THE FALL? 98
WHAT EXACTLY IS JUSTIFICATION BY FAITH? 62
WHAT HAPPENS TO THE BELIEVER WHO DOES NOT COME TO THE TRUTH OF THE CROSS, AND FOR WHATEVER REASON? 230
WHAT HAPPENS WHEN A CHRISTIAN SINS? 229
WHAT HELP CAN WE PROVIDE A FELLOW BELIEVER? 125
WHAT IS GOD LIKE? 72, 82
WHAT IS GOD'S PRESCRIBED ORDER OF VICTORY? 59
WHAT IS MAN? 53
WHAT IS RIGHTEOUSNESS? 164
WHAT IS SELF-RIGHTEOUSNESS? 145
WHAT IS THE ALMIGHTY, THAT WE SHOULD SERVE HIM? 158
WHAT IS THE DIVINE NATURE? 215
WHAT IS THE FLESH? 120
WHAT IS THE GOSPEL? 102
WHAT IS THE KEY TO LIFE AND LIVING? 148
WHAT IS THE LAW OF THE SPIRIT OF LIFE IN CHRIST JESUS? 203
WHAT IS THE SIN NATURE? 99, 133
WHAT IS THE TRUTH? 34
WHAT IS TRUTH? 43
WHAT WAS THE REASON FOR ALL OF THIS? 93
WHAT WILL MY ANSWER BE? 226
WHAT WORDS WILL CHANGE PEOPLE'S LIVES? 235
WHEN I LOOKED FOR GOOD, EVIL CAME! 219
WHEN I WAITED FOR LIGHT, THERE CAME DARKNESS 220
WHEN THE LORD VISITS, WHAT SHALL I ANSWER HIM? 225
WHERE DID THE CATHOLIC WORSHIP OF SAINTS AND IMAGES ORIGINATE? 108
WHERE SHALL WISDOM BE FOUND? 207
WHY? 25
WHY DO BELIEVERS HAVE TO GO THROUGH THE SEVENTH CHAPTER OF ROMANS AT ALL? 280
WHY DO THE WICKED OFTENTIMES PROSPER? 153
WHY DOES GOD AT TIMES DELAY JUDGMENT? 174
WHY HAS THE LORD ALLOWED SATAN TO CONTINUE? 9
WHY HAS THE LORD DONE THIS? 137

WHY IS IT A DIFFICULT TASK FOR US TO BE BROUGHT IN LINE WITH GOD'S WORD? 272
WHY IS IT SO HARD TO TRUST EXCLUSIVELY IN THE CROSS OF CHRIST? 186
WHY IS THE FLESH WEAK? 273
WHY THE CROSS OF CHRIST IS IGNORED 91
WILL WE SEE ALL THREE MEMBERS OF THE GODHEAD IN HEAVEN? 82
WISDOM AND KNOWLEDGE 209
WISDOM OF MAN AND THE WISDOM OF GOD 56
WISE MAN AND THE FOOLISH MAN 126
WITHOUT CAUSE 16
WORD OF GOD 86, 211
WORD OF GOD IS TO BE THE CRITERIA 29
WORDS AND WOUNDS 127
WORDS OF HIS MOUTH ARE MORE VALUABLE THAN MY NECESSARY FOOD 172
WORDS OF THE HOLY ONE 42
WORSHIP 12
WORSHIP OF SAINTS AND IMAGES 107
WORTHLESSNESS OF HUMAN REASONING 190
WORTHLESSNESS OF SELF AND THE WORTHFULNESS OF CHRIST 40
WRATH OF GOD 294
WRONG METHODS 150
YET TROUBLE CAME! 27
ZOPHAR CLAIMS TO HAVE ALL THE ANSWERS 144

For all information concerning the *Jimmy Swaggart Bible Commentary*, please request a Gift Catalog.

You may inquire by using Books of the Bible.

- » Genesis [639 PAGES 11-201]
- » Exodus [639 PAGES 11-202]
- » Leviticus [435 PAGES 11-203]
- » Numbers
  Deuteronomy [493 PAGES 11-204]
- » Joshua
  Judges
  Ruth [329 PAGES 11-205]
- » I Samuel
  II Samuel [528 PAGES 11-206]
- » I Kings
  II Kings [560 PAGES 11-207]
- » I Chronicles
  II Chronicles [505 PAGES 11-226]
- » Ezra
  Nehemiah
  Esther [288 PAGES 11-208]
- » Job [320 PAGES 11-225]
- » Psalms [688 PAGES 11-216]
- » Proverbs [320 PAGES 11-227]
- » Ecclesiastes
  Song Of Solomon [245 PAGES 11-228]
- » Isaiah [688 PAGES 11-220]
- » Jeremiah
  Lamentations [688 PAGES 11-070]
- » Ezekiel [520 PAGES 11-223]
- » Daniel [403 PAGES 11-224]
- » Hosea
  Joel
  Amos [496 PAGES 11-229]
- » Obadiah
  Jonah
  Micah

- Nahum
  Habakkuk
  Zephaniah [530 PAGES 11-230]
- » Haggai
  Zechariah
  Malachi [448 PAGES 11-231]
- » Matthew [625 PAGES 11-073]
- » Mark [606 PAGES 11-074]
- » Luke [626 PAGES 11-075]
- » John [717 PAGES 11-076]
- » Acts [832 PAGES 11-077]
- » Romans [536 PAGES 11-078]
- » I Corinthians [632 PAGES 11-079]
- » II Corinthians [589 PAGES 11-080]
- » Galatians [478 PAGES 11-081]
- » Ephesians [550 PAGES 11-082]
- » Philippians [476 PAGES 11-083]
- » Colossians [374 PAGES 11-084]
- » I Thessalonians
  II Thessalonians [498 PAGES 11-085]
- » I Timothy
  II Timothy
  Titus
  Philemon [687 PAGES 11-086]
- » Hebrews [831 PAGES 11-087]
- » James
  I Peter
  II Peter [730 PAGES 11-088]
- » I John
  II John
  III John
  Jude [377 PAGES 11-089]
- » Revelation [602 PAGES 11-090]

For telephone orders you may call 1-800-288-8350 with bankcard information.
All Baton Rouge residents please use (225) 768-7000. For mail orders send to:

Jimmy Swaggart Ministries
P.O. Box 262550
Baton Rouge, LA 70826-2550

Visit our website: www.jsm.org

NOTES

NOTES

NOTES

NOTES

NOTES

NOTES

NOTES

NOTES

NOTES